Archaeology

Theories, Methods, and Practice

THAMES AND HUDSON

Archae

with over 500 illustrations

COLIN RENFREW   PAUL BAHN

Archaeology

Theories
Methods
and
Practice

CONTENTS

PART II
Discovering the Variety of Human Experience

page 149

8
How Did They Make and Use Tools? Technology

page 271

9
What Contact Did They Have? Trade and Exchange

page 307

10
What Did They Think? Cognitive Archaeology, Art, and Religion

page 339

Introduction: The Nature and Aims of Archaeology

Archaeology is partly the discovery of the treasures of the past, partly the meticulous work of the scientific analyst, partly the exercise of the creative imagination. It is toiling in the sun on an excavation in the deserts of Iraq, it is working with living Eskimos in the snows of Alaska. It is diving down to Spanish wrecks off the coast of Florida, and it is investigating the sewers of Roman York. But it is also the painstaking task of interpretation so that we come to understand what these things mean for the human story.

Archaeology, then, is both a physical activity out in the field, and an intellectual pursuit in the study or laboratory. That is part of its great attraction. The rich mixture of danger and detective work has also made it the perfect vehicle for fiction writers and film-makers, from Agatha Christie with *Murder in Mesopotamia* to Steven Spielberg with Indiana Jones. However far from reality such portrayals may be, they capture the essential truth that archaeology is an exciting quest – the quest for knowledge about ourselves and our human past.

But how does archaeology relate to disciplines such as anthropology and history that are also concerned with the human story? And is archaeology itself a science?

Archaeology as Anthropology

Anthropology at its broadest is the study of humanity – our physical characteristics as animals, and our unique non-biological characteristics that we call *culture*. Culture in this general sense includes what the early anthropologist Edward Tylor usefully summarized in 1871 as "knowledge, belief, art, morals, law, custom and any other capabilities and habits acquired by man as a member of society." Anthropologists also use the term culture in a more restricted sense when they refer to the culture of a particular society, meaning the non-

biological characteristics unique to that society and which distinguish it from other societies. (An "archaeological culture" has a specific and somewhat different meaning, as will be explained in Chapter 3.)

Clearly, therefore, anthropology is a broad discipline – so broad in fact that it is broken down into three smaller disciplines: physical anthropology, cultural or social anthropology, and archaeology.

Physical anthropology, also called biological anthropology, concerns the study of human biological or physical characteristics and how they evolved.

Cultural anthropology – or social anthropology as it is called in Europe and elsewhere – analyzes human culture and society. Two important branches of cultural anthropology are *ethnography* (the study at first hand of individual living cultures), and *ethnology* (which attempts to compare cultures using ethnographic evidence with a view to deriving general principles about human society).

Archaeology is the "past tense of cultural anthropology." Whereas cultural anthropologists will often base their conclusions on the experience of actually living within contemporary communities, archaeologists study past societies primarily through their material remains – the buildings, tools, and other artifacts that constitute what is known as the *material culture* left over from former societies.

Nevertheless, one of the most challenging tasks for the archaeologist today is to know how to interpret material culture in human terms. How were those pots used? Why are some dwellings round and others square? Here the methods of archaeology and ethnography overlap. Archaeologists in recent decades have developed *ethnoarchaeology*, where like ethnographers they live among contemporary communities, but with the specific purpose of understanding how such societies use material culture – how they make their tools and weapons, why they build their settlements where they do, and so on.

Archaeology as History

If, then, archaeology deals with the past, in what way does it differ from history? In the broadest sense, just as archaeology is an aspect of anthropology, so too is it a part of history – where we mean the whole history of humankind from its beginnings over 3 million years ago. Indeed for more than 99 percent of that huge span of time archaeology – the study of past material culture – is the only significant source of information, if one sets aside physical anthropology, which focuses on our biological rather than cultural progress. Conventional historical sources begin only with the introduction of written records around 3000 BC in western Asia, and considerably later in most other parts of the world (not until AD 1788 in Australia, for example). A commonly drawn distinction, therefore, is that between *prehistory* – the period before written records – and history in the narrow sense, meaning the study of the past using written evidence. As will become abundantly clear in this book, however, archaeology can contribute a great deal to the understanding even of those periods and places where documents, inscriptions, and other literary evidence exist. Quite often, it is the archaeologist who unearths such evidence in the first place.

Archaeology as a Science

Since the aim of archaeology is the understanding of humankind, it is a humanistic discipline, a humane study. And since it deals with the human past it is a historical discipline. But it differs from the study of written history – although it uses written history – in a fundamental way. The material the archaeologist finds does not tell us directly what to think. Historical records make statements, offer opinions, pass judgments (even if those statements and judgments themselves need to be interpreted). The objects that archaeologists discover, on the other hand, tell us nothing directly in themselves. It is *we* today who have to make sense of these things. In this respect the practice of archaeology is rather like that of the scientist. The scientist collects data (evidence), conducts experiments, formulates a hypothesis (a proposition to account for the data), tests the hypothesis against more data, and then in conclusion devises a model (a description that seems best to summarize the pattern observed in the data). Archaeology is in many ways very like that. The archaeologist has to develop a picture of the past, just as the scientist has to develop a coherent view of the natural world. It is not found ready made.

Archaeology, in short, is a science as well as a humanity. That is one of its fascinations as a discipline: it reflects the ingenuity of the modern scientist as well as the modern historian. The technical methods of archaeological science are the most obvious, from radiocarbon dating to studies of food residues in pots. Equally important are scientific methods of analysis, of inference. Some writers have spoken of the need to define a separate "Middle Range Theory," referring to a distinct body of ideas to bridge the gap between raw archaeological evidence and the general observations and conclusions to be derived from it. That is one way of looking at the matter. But we see no need to make a sharp distinction between theory and method. Our aim is to describe clearly the methods and techniques used by archaeologists in investigating the past. The analytical concepts of the archaeologist are as much a part of that battery of approaches as are the instruments in the laboratory.

The vast timespan of prehistory compared with the relatively short period for which written records are available (conventional "history"). Before c.3000 BC, material remains are our only source of evidence.

The Variety and Scope of Archaeology

Today archaeology is a broad church, encompassing a number of different "archaeologies" which are nevertheless united by the common methods and approaches outlined in this book. We have already drawn attention to the distinction between the archaeology of the long prehistoric period and that of historic times. Often this chronological division is accentuated by further subdivisions so that archaeologists specialize in, say, the earliest periods (the Old Stone Age or Paleolithic, before 10,000 years ago) or the later ones (the great civilizations of the Americas and China; Egyptology; the Classical archaeology of ancient Greece and Rome). One of the major developments of the last two or three decades has been the realization that archaeology has much to contribute not just to an understanding of prehistory and ancient history, but to the more recent historic periods as well. In North America and Australia historical archaeology – the archaeological study of colonial and postcolonial settlement in those continents – has expanded greatly, as has the analogous medieval and postmedieval archaeology in Europe. So that whether we are speaking of colonial Jamestown in the United States, or medieval London, Paris, and Hamburg in Europe, archaeology is a prime source of evidence.

Cutting across these chronological subdivisions are specializations that can contribute to many different archaeological periods. Environmental archaeology is one such field, where archaeologists and specialists from other sciences study the human use of plants and animals, and how past societies adapted to the ever-changing environment. Underwater archaeology is another such field, demanding great courage as well as skill. In the last 30 years it has become a highly scientific exercise, yielding time capsules from the past in the form of shipwrecks that shed new light on ancient life on land as well as at sea.

Ethnoarchaeology, too, as we discussed briefly above, is a major specialization in modern archaeology. We now realize that we can only understand the archaeological record – that is to say, what we find – if we understand in much greater detail how it came about, how it was formed. Formation processes are now a focus of intensive study. It is here that ethnoarchaeology has come into its own: the study of living peoples and of their material culture undertaken with the aim of improving our understanding of the archaeological record. For instance, the study of butchery practices among living hunter-gatherers, undertaken by Lewis Binford among the Nunamiut

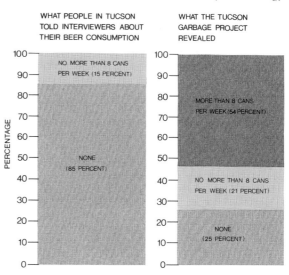

WHAT PEOPLE IN TUCSON TOLD INTERVIEWERS ABOUT THEIR BEER CONSUMPTION

WHAT THE TUCSON GARBAGE PROJECT REVEALED

The Garbage Project, Tucson, Arizona. An ethnoarchaeological survey among Tucson's modern inhabitants showed a marked discrepancy between people's accounts of their behavior and what excavation of their trash cans actually revealed.

Eskimo of Alaska, has given him many new ideas about the way the archaeological record may have been formed, allowing him to re-evaluate the bone remains of animals eaten by very early humans elsewhere in the world. Nor are these studies confined to simpler communities or small groups. In Tucson, Arizona, the Garbage Project, set up by William L. Rathje, involves the collection of garbage from the trash cans of a sector of the city, and the careful sorting in the laboratory of all that they contain. This rather unsavory task has given some valuable and unexpected insights into the pattern of consumption of the modern urban population – and the methods employed are purely archaeological.

Aims and Questions

If our aim is to learn about the human past, there remains the major issue of what we hope to learn. Traditional approaches tended to regard the objective of archaeology mainly as reconstruction: piecing together the jigsaw. But today it is not enough simply to re-create the material culture of remote periods, or to complete the picture for more recent ones.

A further objective has been termed "the reconstruction of the lifeways of the people responsible for the archaeological remains." We are certainly interested in having a clear picture of how people lived, and how

The diversity of modern archaeology. **Top row** *(Near right) An archaeologist at Sutton Hoo, eastern England (box, Chapter 3), records the outlines of a human body. The work resulted (second right) in a computer-generated image. (Third right) Two archaeologists at the site of Batán Grande in Peru trace frescoes in position, evidence for a major pre-Inca civilization. (Far right) A triumph of salvage archaeology: the rescuing of pharaoh Ramesses II's temples at Abu Simbel, Egypt, in advance of the rising waters of the Aswan Dam.* **Bottom row** *(Below left) Urban archaeology: excavation of a Roman site in the heart of London, with St Paul's Cathedral in the background. (Below center) An ethnoarchaeologist in the field in Alaska, sharing and studying the lives of modern Eskimo as they hunt caribou. (Below center right) An underwater archaeologist records finds from a Byzantine wreck off the coast of Turkey. (Below far right) Conservation of a mosaic at London's Institute of Archaeology.*

they exploited their environment. But we also seek to understand *why* they lived that way: why they had those patterns of behavior, and how their lifeways and material culture came to take the form they did. We are interested, in short, in *explaining* change. This interest in the processes of cultural change has come to define what is known as *processual archaeology*. Processual archaeology moves forward by asking a series of questions, just as any scientific study proceeds by defining aims of study – formulating questions – and then proceeding to answer them.

There are many big questions that preoccupy us today. We want to understand the circumstances in which our human ancestors first emerged. Was this in Africa and only in Africa, as currently seems the case? Were these early humans proper hunters or merely scavengers? What were the circumstances in which our own subspecies *Homo sapiens sapiens* evolved? How do we explain the emergence of Paleolithic art? Why was it apparently so limited in its distribution? How did the shift from hunting and gathering to farming come about in western Asia, in Mesoamerica, and in other parts of the world? Why did this happen in the course of just a few millennia? How do we explain the rise of cities, apparently quite independently in different parts of the world? The list of questions goes on, and after these general questions there are more specific ones. We wish to know why a particular culture took the form it did: how its particularities emerged, and how they influenced developments.

This book does not set out to review the provisional answers to all these questions – although many of the impressive results of recent archaeology will emerge in the following pages. In this book we examine rather the *methods* by which such questions can be answered.

Plan of the Book

The methods of archaeology could be surveyed in many different ways. We have chosen to think in terms of the many kinds of *questions* to which we wish to have answers. Indeed the form of the question is often crucial. It could be argued that the whole philosophy of archaeology is implied in the questions we ask and the form in which we frame them.

Part I reviews the whole field of archaeology, looking first at the history of the subject, and then asking three specific questions: how are materials preserved, how are they found, and how are they dated?

Part II sets out the further and more searching questions we need to ask – about social organization, about environment, and about subsistence; about technology and trade, and about the way people thought and communicated. We then ask what they were like physically. And then the interesting question is posed as to *why* things changed.

Part III follows this review of methods with a review of archaeology in practice, showing how the different ideas and techniques can be brought together in individual field projects. Three such projects are chosen as case studies: one from the eastern Mediterranean, the second from southern Mexico, and the third from northern Australia. Finally there is a chapter on public archaeology, which discusses the uses and abuses of archaeology in the modern world and the obligations these things have placed on the archaeologist.

In this way we plan that the book should give a good overview of the whole range of methods and ideas of archaeological investigation.

Further Reading

The following books give an indication of the rich variety of archaeology today. Most of them are enhanced by good illustrations:

Bass, G.F. (ed.). 1988. *Ships and Shipwrecks of the Americas: A History Based on Underwater Archaeology.* Thames & Hudson: London & New York.

Binford, L.R. 1983. *In Pursuit of the Past.* Thames & Hudson: London & New York.

Daniel, G. and Renfrew, C. 1988. *The Idea of Prehistory.* Edinburgh University Press: Edinburgh; Columbia University Press: New York.

Deetz, J. 1977. *In Small Things Forgotten* Anchor/Doubleday: New York.

Fagan, B.M. 1987. *New Treasures of the Past.* Windward: Leicester; Barron: Hauppage, NY.

Gowlett, J. 1984. *Ascent to Civilization: The Archaeology of Early Man.* Collins: London; Knopf: New York.

Kemp, B.J. 1989. *Ancient Egypt: Anatomy of a Civilization.* Routledge: London & New York.

Scarre, C. (ed.). 1988. *Past Worlds: The Times Atlas of Archaeology.* Times Books: London; Hammond: Maplewood, NJ.

Sherratt, A. (ed.). 1980. *The Cambridge Encyclopedia of Archaeology.* Crown/Cambridge University Press: New York; CUP: Cambridge.

Throckmorton, P. (ed.). 1987. *The Sea Remembers: Shipwrecks and Archaeology.* Weidenfeld: New York (in Britain published as *History from the Sea.* Mitchell Beazley: London).

PART I

The Framework of Archaeology

Part I: Introduction

Archaeology is concerned with the full range of past human experience – how people organized themselves into social groups and exploited their surroundings; what they ate, made, and believed; how they communicated and why their societies changed. These are the engrossing questions we address later in the book. First, however, we need a framework in space and time. It is little use beginning our pursuit of ideas and methods concerning the past without knowing what materials archaeologists study, or where these might be found and how dated. Indeed, we also want to know how far previous generations of archaeologists have traveled and along which roads before setting off on our own journey of discovery.

Part I therefore focuses on the fundamental framework of archaeology. The first chapter looks at the history of the discipline, showing in particular how successive workers have redefined and enlarged the questions we ask about the past. Then we pose the first question: "What?" – what is preserved, and what is the range of archaeological materials that have come down to us? The second question, "Where?," addresses methods for finding and surveying sites, and principles of excavation and preliminary analysis. Our third question, "When?," considers the human experience of time and its measurement, and assesses the huge battery of techniques now available to help the archaeologist date the past. On this basis we are able to set out a chronology summarizing the human story, as a conclusion to Part I and a prelude to Part II.

1
The Searchers
The History of
Archaeology

The history of archaeology is commonly seen as the history of great discoveries: the tomb of Tutankhamun in Egypt, the lost Maya cities of Mexico, the painted caves of the Old Stone Age, such as Lascaux in France, or the remains of our human ancestors buried deep in the Olduvai Gorge in Tanzania. But even more than that it is the story of how we have come to look with fresh eyes at the material evidence for the human past, and with new methods to aid us in our task.

It is important to remember that just a century and a half ago, most well-read people believed that the world had been created only a few thousand years earlier (in the year 4004 BC according to the then-standard interpretation of the Bible), and that all that could be known of the remote past had to be gleaned from the surviving pages of the earliest historians, notably those of the ancient Near East, Egypt, and Greece. There was no awareness that any kind of coherent history of the periods before the development of writing was possible at all. In the words of the Danish scholar Rasmus Nyerup (1759–1829):

> Everything which has come down to us from heathendom is wrapped in a thick fog; it belongs to a space of time which we cannot measure. We know that it is older than Christendom, but whether by a couple of years or a couple of centuries, or even by more than a millennium, we can do no more than guess.

Today we can indeed penetrate that "thick fog" of the remote past. This is not simply because new discoveries are being made all the time. It is because we have learnt to ask some of the *right questions*, and have developed some of the *right methods* for answering them. The material evidence of the archaeological record has been lying around for a long time. What is new is our awareness that the methods of archaeology can give us information about the past, even the prehistoric past (before the invention of writing). The

history of archaeology is therefore in the first instance a history of *ideas*, of theory, of ways of looking at the past. Next it is a history of developing research methods, employing those ideas and investigating those questions. And only thirdly is it a history of actual discoveries.

We can illustrate the relationship between these aspects of our knowledge of the past with a simple diagram:

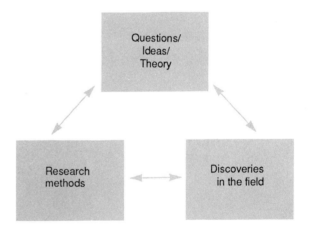

In this chapter and in this book it is the development of the questions and ideas that we shall emphasize, and the application of new research methods. The main thing to remember is that every view of the past is a product of its own time: ideas and theories are constantly evolving, and so are methods. When we describe the archaeological research methods of today we are simply speaking of one point on a trajectory of evolution. In a few decades or even a few years time these methods will certainly look old-fashioned and out of date. That is the dynamic nature of archaeology as a discipline.

THE SPECULATIVE PHASE

Humans have always speculated about their past, and most cultures have their own foundation myths to explain why society is how it is. The Greek writer Hesiod, for instance, who lived around 800 BC, in his epic poem *Works and Days* envisaged the human past as falling into five stages: the Age of Gold and the Immortals, who "dwelt in ease and peace upon their lands with many good things;" the Age of Silver, when humans were less noble; the Age of Bronze; the Age of Epic Heroes; and lastly his own time, the Age of Iron and Dread Sorrow, when "men never rest from labor and sorrow by day and from perishing by night."

Most cultures, too, have been fascinated by the societies that preceded them. The Aztecs exaggerated their Toltec ancestry, and were so interested in Teotihuacan, the huge Mexican city abandoned hundreds of years earlier which they mistakenly linked with the Toltecs, that they incorporated ceremonial stone masks from that site in the foundation deposits of their own Great Temple (see box, Chapter 14). A rather more detached curiosity about the relics of bygone ages developed in several early civilizations, where scholars and even rulers collected and studied objects from the past. Nabonidus, last native king of Babylon (reigned 555–539 BC), took a keen interest in antiquities. In one important temple he dug down and discovered the foundation stone which had been laid some 2200 years before. He housed many of his finds in a kind of museum at Babylon.

During the revival of learning in Europe known as the Renaissance (14th to 17th centuries), princes and people of refinement began to form "cabinets of curiosities" in which curios and ancient artifacts were displayed somewhat haphazardly alongside exotic minerals and all manner of specimens illustrative of what was called "natural history." During the Renaissance also scholars began to study and collect the relics of Classical antiquity. And they began too in more northern lands, far from the civilized centers of ancient Greece and Rome, to study the local relics of their own remote past. At this time these were mainly the field monuments – those conspicuous sites, often made of stone, which immediately attracted attention, such as the great stone tombs of northwestern Europe, and such impressive sites (which we should now call prehistoric) as Stonehenge, or Carnac in Brittany.

Stonehenge in the 18th century: one of the many fine engravings by the English antiquary, William Stukeley.

Careful scholars, such as the Englishman William Stukeley (1687–1765), made systematic studies of some of these monuments, with accurate plans which are still useful today.

The First Excavations

And then in the 18th century more adventurous researchers initiated excavation of some of the most prominent sites. Pompeii in Italy was one of the first of these, with its striking Roman finds, although proper excavation did not begin there until the 19th century (see box). But the credit for conducting what has been called "the first scientific excavation in the history of archaeology" goes to Thomas Jefferson (1743–1826), later in his career third President of the United States, who in 1784 dug a trench or section across a burial mound on his property in Virginia. His work marks the beginning of the end of the Speculative Phase. In Jefferson's time people were speculating that the hundreds of unexplained mounds known east of the Mississippi river had been built not by the indigenous American Indians, but by a mythical and vanished race of Moundbuilders. Jefferson adopted what today we should call a scientific approach, that is, he tested ideas about the mounds against hard evidence – by excavating one of them. His methods were careful enough to allow him to recognize different layers in his trench, and to see that the many human bones present were less well preserved in the lower layers. From this he deduced that the mound had been reused as a place of burial on many separate occasions. Although Jefferson admitted, rightly, that more evidence was needed to resolve the Moundbuilder question, he saw no reason why ancestors of the Indians themselves could not have raised the mounds.

Jefferson was ahead of his time. His sound approach – logical deduction from carefully excavated evidence, in many ways the basis of modern archaeology – was not taken up by any of his immediate successors in North America. In Europe, meanwhile, extensive excavations were being conducted, for instance by the Englishman Richard Colt Hoare (1758–1838), who dug into hundreds of burial mounds in southern Britain during the first decade of the 19th century. None of these excavations, however, did much to advance the cause of knowledge about the distant past, since their interpretation was still within the Biblical framework of ideas, which insisted on a short time-span for human existence.

Early excavations: Colt Hoare and William Cunnington direct a dig north of Stonehenge in 1805.

POMPEII: ARCHAEOLOGY PAST AND PRESENT

In the history of archaeology, the sites of Pompeii and Herculaneum, lying at the foot of Mount Vesuvius in the Bay of Naples, Italy, hold a very special place. Even today, when so many major sites have been systematically excavated, it is a moving experience to visit these wonderfully preserved Roman cities.

Pompeii's fate was sealed on the momentous day in August AD 79 when Vesuvius erupted, a cataclysmic event described by the Roman writer, the younger Pliny. The city was buried under several meters of volcanic ash, many of the inhabitants being asphyxiated in their houses. Herculaneum nearby was engulfed in volcanic mud. There the complete cities lay, known only from occasional chance discoveries, until the advent of antiquarian curiosity in the early 18th century.

In 1710 the Prince of Elboeuf, learning of the discovery of worked marble in the vicinity, proceeded to investigate by shafts and tunnels what we now know to be the site of Herculaneum. He had the good luck to discover the ancient theater – the first complete Roman example ever found – but he was mainly interested in works of art for his collection. These he removed without any kind of record of their location.

Following Elboeuf, clearance resumed in a slightly more systematic way in 1738 at Herculaneum, and in 1748 Pompeii was discovered. Work proceeded under the patronage of the King and Queen of Naples, but they did little more than quarry ancient masterpieces to embellish their royal palace. Shortly afterwards, on the outskirts of Herculaneum, the remains of a splendid villa were revealed, with statues and an entire library of carbonized papyri that have given the complex its name: the Villa of the Papyri. The villa's dimensions were closely followed by J. Paul Getty in the construction of his museum at Malibu, California.

The first catalog of the royal collection was published in 1755. Seven years later the German scholar Johann Joachim Winckelmann, often regarded as the father of Classical archaeology, published his first Letter on the discoveries at Herculaneum. From that time onward the finds from both cities attracted enormous international attention, influencing styles of furniture and interior decoration, and inspiring several pieces of romantic fiction.

Not until 1860, however, when Giuseppe Fiorelli was put in charge of the work at Pompeii, did well-recorded excavations begin. Buildings were consolidated and where necessary roofed, and wall paintings for the first time left in place. In 1864 Fiorelli devised a brilliant way of dealing with the cavities in the ash within which skeletons were found: he simply filled

T = TEMPLE

500 ft / 100 m

to Herculaneum
Herculaneum Gate
to Vesuvius
Gate
Gate
Gate
UNEXCAVATED
Gate
UNEXCAVATED
T. of Fortuna Augusta
Central Baths
Forum Baths
Bakery of Modestus
Amphitheater
T. of Jupiter
Provision Market
T. of Apollo
T. of Lares
T. of Vespasian
Insula of the Menander
Large palaestra
Building of Eumachia
Basilica
T. of Isis
T. of Jupiter Milichius
Gate
Gate
T. of Venus
Small theater
Large theater
Town Council
Triangular Forum
Gate
Gladiatorial barracks
Tombs

Sketch plan of Pompeii, showing the excavated areas.

1 Pumice and ash bury a victim in AD 79.

2 The body gradually decays, leaving a hollow.

3 Archaeologists find the hollow, and pour in wet plaster.

4 The plaster hardens, allowing the pumice and ash to be chipped away.

How a body shape is retrieved.

them with plaster of Paris. The ash around the cavity acted as a mold, and the plaster took the accurate shape of the decayed body. (In a recent technique, the excavators pour in transparent glass fiber. This allows bones and artifacts to be visible.)

During the present century, Amedeo Maiuri excavated at Pompeii between 1924 and 1961, revealing extensive remains of earlier phases of the town beneath the AD 79 ground level. In recent years his work has been supplemented by limited excavations carried out by Paul Arthur. Another recent project under the direction of Roger Ling has focused on the detailed analysis of one insula, or city block, the Insula of the Menander. The project has revealed changes in the property boundaries and uses of different parts of the insula that have thrown much new light on the social and economic development of Roman Pompeii.

Pompeii remains the most complete urban excavation ever undertaken. The town plan is clear in its essentials, and most of the public buildings have been investigated, along with innumerable shops and private houses. Yet the potential for further study and interpretation is enormous.

Today it is not difficult for the visitor to Pompeii to echo the words of Shelley in his Ode to Naples, written more than a century and a half ago:
"I stood within the city disinterred; / And heard the autumn leaves like light footfalls/Of spirits passing through the streets; and heard/The mountain's slumberous voice at intervals/Thrill through those roofless halls."

Crude excavations at Herculaneum (top left), an engraving of 1782. In the wall painting from the House of the Vettii, Pompeii (center left), gazelles draw the god of love, Cupid, in a cart. A plaster cast (left) recreates the shape of a Pompeian struck down in flight. Conditions of preservation at Pompeii are remarkable: for example, many carbonized loaves of bread have survived (right).

THE BEGINNINGS OF MODERN ARCHAEOLOGY

It was not until the middle of the 19th century that the discipline of archaeology became truly established. Already in the background there were the significant achievements of the newly developed science of geology. The Scottish geologist James Hutton (1726–1797), in his *Theory of the Earth* (1785), had studied the stratification of rocks (their arrangement in superimposed layers or strata), establishing principles which were to be the basis of archaeological excavation, as foreshadowed by Jefferson. Hutton showed that the stratification of rocks was due to processes which were still going on in seas, rivers, and lakes. This was the principle of "uniformitarianism." It was argued again by Charles Lyell (1797–1875) in his *Principles of Geology* (1833): that geologically ancient conditions were in essence similar to, or "uniform with," those of our own time. This idea could be applied to the human past also, and it marks one of the fundamental notions of modern archaeology: that in many ways the past was much like the present.

The Antiquity of Humankind

These ideas did much to lay the groundwork for what was one of the significant events in the intellectual history of the 19th century (and an indispensable one for the discipline of archaeology): the establishment of the antiquity of humankind. It was a French customs inspector, Jacques Boucher de Perthes (1788–1868), working in the gravel quarries of the Somme river, who in 1841 published convincing evidence for the association there of human artifacts (of chipped stone, what we would today call "hand-axes") and the bones of extinct animals. Boucher de Perthes argued that this indicated human existence for a long time before the biblical Flood. His view did not at first win wide acceptance, but in 1859 two leading British scholars, John Evans and Joseph Prestwich, visited him in France and returned persuaded of the validity of his findings. It was now widely agreed that human origins extended far back into a remote past, so that the biblical notion of the creation of the world and all its contents just a few thousand years before our own time could no longer be accepted. The possibility of a prehistory of humankind, indeed the *need* for one, was established (the term "prehistory" itself came into general use after the publication of John Lubbock's book *Prehistoric Times* in 1865, which went on to become a bestseller).

The Concept of Evolution

These ideas harmonized well with the findings of another great scholar of the 19th century, Charles Darwin (1809–1882), whose fundamental work, *On the Origin of Species*, published in 1859, established the concept of evolution as the best explanation for the origin and development of all plants and animals. The idea of evolution itself was not new – earlier scholars had suggested that living things must have changed or evolved through the ages. What Darwin demonstrated was *how* this change occurred. The key mechanism was, in Darwin's words, "natural selection, or the survival of the fittest." In the struggle for existence, environmentally better-adapted individuals of a particular species would survive (or be "naturally selected") whereas less well-adapted ones would die. The surviving individuals would pass on their advantageous traits by heredity to their offspring and gradually the characteristics of a species would change to such an extent that a new species emerged. This was the process of evolution. Darwin's other great work, *The*

The title page of Darwin's book, whose ideas about evolution proved highly influential, not least in archaeology.

Descent of Man, was not published until 1871, but already the implications were clear: that the human species had emerged as part of this same process. The search for human origins in the material record, by the techniques of archaeology, could begin.

The Three Age System

As we have noted, some of these techniques, notably in the field of excavation, were already being developed. So too was another conceptual device which proved very useful for the progress of European prehistory: the Three Age System. In 1836 the Danish scholar C.J. Thomsen (1788–1865) published his guidebook to the National Museum of Copenhagen which appeared in English in 1848 with the title, *A Guide to Northern Antiquities*. In it he proposed that the collections could be divided into those coming from a Stone Age, a Bronze Age, and an Iron Age, and this classification was soon found useful by scholars throughout Europe. Later a division in the Stone Age was established between the Paleolithic or Old Stone Age and the Neolithic or New Stone Age. These terms were less applicable to Africa, where bronze was not used south

of the Sahara, or to the Americas, where bronze was less important and iron was not in use before the European conquest. But it was conceptually significant. It established the principle that by studying and classifying prehistoric artifacts one could produce a chronological ordering, and say something of the periods in question. Archaeology was moving beyond mere speculation about the past, and becoming instead a discipline involving careful excavation and the systematic study of the artifacts unearthed.

These three great conceptual advances – the *antiquity of humankind*, Darwin's *principle of evolution* and the *Three Age System* – at last offered a framework for studying the past, and for asking intelligent questions about it. Darwin's ideas were influential also in another way. They suggested that human cultures might have evolved in a manner analogous to plant and animal species. Soon after 1859, British scholars such as General Pitt-Rivers (whom we shall meet again below) and John Evans were devising schemes for the evolution of artifact forms which gave rise to the whole method of "typology" – the arrangement of artifacts in chronological or developmental sequence – later greatly elaborated by the Swedish scholar Oscar Montelius (1843–1921).

C.J. Thomsen shows visitors an antiquity at the Danish National Museum, arranged according to his Three Age System.

The influence of Darwin is evident in these early typologies. (Left) John Evans sought to derive the Celtic British coinage, bottom, from the gold stater of Philip of Macedon, top. (Right) Montelius' arrangement of Iron Age fibulae (cloak pins), showing their evolution.

THE IMPACT OF EVOLUTIONARY THOUGHT

The idea of evolution has been of central significance in the development of archaeological thinking. In the first place it is associated with the name of Charles Darwin, whose *On the Origin of Species* (1859) effectively explained the problem of the origin and development of the plant and animal species, including humankind. It did so by insisting that within a species there is variation (one individual differs from another), that the transmission of physical traits is by heredity alone, and that natural selection determines survival. Darwin certainly had precursors, among whom Thomas Malthus was influential with his notion of competition through population pressure, and the geologist Charles Lyell with his insistence upon gradual change.

Darwin's work had an immediate impact on archaeologists such as Pitt-Rivers, John Evans, and Oscar Montelius, laying the foundations for the study of the typology of artifacts. His influence on social thinkers and anthropologists was even more significant: among them was Karl Marx (Marx was also influenced by the American anthropologist, Lewis Henry Morgan – see main text).

The application of the principles of evolution to social organization does not always follow the detailed mechanisms of hereditary transmission which apply to the biologically defined species. For culture can be *learned*, and passed on between generations more widely than between parents and their children. Often, indeed, the term "evolutionary" applied to an argument or an explanation simply means "generalizing." Here it is important to be aware of the great swing in anthropology at the end of the 19th century away from the broad generalizations of L.H. Morgan and E.B.Tylor in favor of a much more detailed, descriptive approach, often termed "historical particularism," and associated with the name of the anthropologist Franz Boas. In the

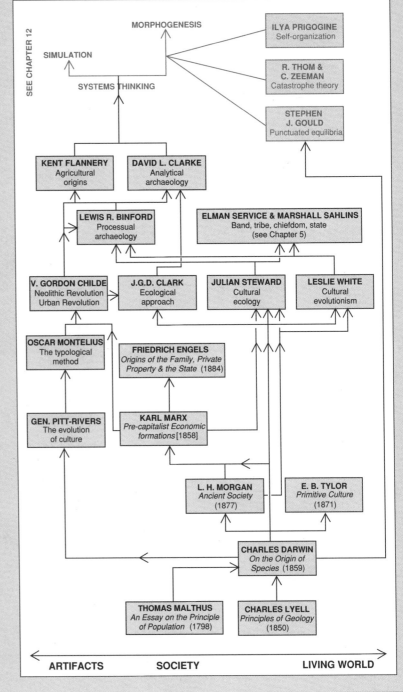

SEE CHAPTER 12

MORPHOGENESIS

SIMULATION

SYSTEMS THINKING

ILYA PRIGOGINE
Self-organization

R. THOM & C. ZEEMAN
Catastrophe theory

STEPHEN J. GOULD
Punctuated equilibria

KENT FLANNERY
Agricultural origins

DAVID L. CLARKE
Analytical archaeology

LEWIS R. BINFORD
Processual archaeology

ELMAN SERVICE & MARSHALL SAHLINS
Band, tribe, chiefdom, state
(see Chapter 5)

V. GORDON CHILDE
Neolithic Revolution
Urban Revolution

J.G.D. CLARK
Ecological approach

JULIAN STEWARD
Cultural ecology

LESLIE WHITE
Cultural evolutionism

OSCAR MONTELIUS
The typological method

FRIEDRICH ENGELS
Origins of the Family, Private Property & the State (1884)

GEN. PITT-RIVERS
The evolution of culture

KARL MARX
Pre-capitalist Economic formations [1858]

L. H. MORGAN
Ancient Society
(1877)

E. B. TYLOR
Primitive Culture
(1871)

CHARLES DARWIN
On the Origin of Species (1859)

THOMAS MALTHUS
An Essay on the Principle of Population (1798)

CHARLES LYELL
Principles of Geology
(1850)

ARTIFACTS   SOCIETY   LIVING WORLD

Ethnography and Archaeology

Another important strand in the thought of the time was the realization that the study by ethnographers of living communities in different parts of the world could be a useful starting point for archaeologists seeking to understand something of the lifestyles of their own early native inhabitants who clearly had comparably simple tools and crafts. Scholars such as Daniel Wilson and John Lubbock made systematic use of such an ethnographic approach.

And at the same time ethnographers and anthropologists were themselves producing schemes of human progress. Strongly influenced by Darwin's ideas about evolution, the British anthropologist Edward Tylor (1832–1917), and his American counterpart Lewis Henry Morgan (1818–1881), both published important works in the 1870s arguing that human societies had evolved from a state of *savagery* (primitive hunting) through *barbarism* (simple farming) to *civilization* (the highest form of society). Morgan's book, *Ancient Society* (1877), was partly based on his great knowledge of living North American Indians. His ideas – particularly the notion that people had once lived in a state of primitive communism, sharing resources equally – strongly influenced Karl Marx and Friedrich Engels, who drew on them in their writings about pre-capitalist societies, thus influencing many later Marxist archaeologists.

Discovering the Early Civilizations

By the 1880s, then, many of the ideas underlying modern archaeology had been developed. But these ideas themselves took shape against a background of major 19th-century discoveries of ancient civilizations in the Old World and the New.

The splendors of ancient Egyptian civilization had already been brought to the attention of an avid public after Napoleon's military expedition there of 1798–1800. It was the discovery by one of his soldiers of the Rosetta Stone that eventually provided the key to understanding Egyptian hieroglyphic writing. Inscribed on the stone were identical texts written in both Egyptian and Greek scripts. The Frenchman Jean-François Champollion (1790–1832) used this bilingual inscription finally to decipher the hieroglyphs in 1822, after 14 years' work. A similar piece of brilliant scholarly detection helped unlock the secrets of cuneiform writing, the script used for many languages in ancient Mesopotamia. In the 1840s the French and British, under Paul Emile Botta (1802–1870) and

Charles Darwin as a "venerable Orang-utang," a caricature published in 1871.

years before and after World War II American anthropologists like Leslie White and Julian Steward were therefore innovators in rejecting Boas and seeking to generalize, to find explanations for long-term change. White was for many years the only protagonist of what may be termed cultural evolutionism, with books such as *The Evolution of Culture* (1959). White and Steward strongly influenced the New Archaeologists of the 1960s and 1970s, in particular Lewis Binford, Kent Flannery, and D.L. Clarke.

It should be noted that in the past 15 years three lines of thinking from the sciences have been influential in reminding us that evolutionary change need not always be gradual: these concepts of punctuated equilibrium, catastrophe theory, and self-organizing systems are discussed further in Chapter 12.

19th-CENTURY PIONEERS OF NORTH AMERICAN ARCHAEOLOGY

Squier   Haven   Powell   Thomas   Putnam   Holmes

Two themes dominate the study of North American archaeology in the 19th century: the enduring belief in a vanished race of Moundbuilders; and the search for "glacial man" – the idea, sparked off by Boucher de Perthes' Somme river discoveries in mid-century, that human fossils and Stone Age tools would be found in the Americas in association with extinct animals, as they had been in Europe. One way to gain insight into these issues is to view them through the work of some of the main protagonists.

Caleb Atwater (1778–1867)
The newly formed American Antiquarian Society's first Transactions, *Archaeologia Americana*

Plan of Serpent Mound, Ohio, as prepared by Squier and Davis in 1846.

(1820), contained a paper by Atwater, a local postmaster, on burial mounds and earthworks around Circleville, Ohio. His survey work is valuable since the mounds he studied were already disappearing fast, and are now gone. But he took little interest in their contents, and his interpretations were idiosyncratic. Atwater divided the mounds into three periods – modern European, modern American Indian, and those built by the original Moundbuilder people whom he believed to have been Hindus from India who later moved on to Mexico.

Ephraim Squier (1821–1888)
Squier was an Ohio newspaperman who later became a diplomat. He is best known for his work on the prehistoric mounds with Edwin Davis, an Ohio physician. Between 1845 and 1847 they excavated over 200 mounds, and accurately surveyed many other earthworks. Their landmark volume of 1848, *Ancient Monuments of the Mississippi Valley*, was the first publication of the newly founded Smithsonian Institution, and is still useful. It recorded hundreds of mounds, including many being destroyed as settlers moved westwards, gave cross-sections and plans, and adopted a simple classification system which inferred function in a general way (burial places, building platforms, effigies, fortifications/defence, etc.).

Like most of their contemporaries,

Squier and Davis considered the mounds to be beyond the capabilities of any Indians, who were "hunters averse to labor," and so they maintained the myth of the intrusive race of Moundbuilders.

Samuel Haven (1806–1881)
As Librarian of the American Antiquarian Society, Haven built up an encyclopedic knowledge of publications on American archaeology. From this wealth of reading he produced a remarkable synthesis in 1856, *The Archaeology of the United States*, published by the Smithsonian Institution, which is considered a foundation stone of modern American archaeology. In it, Haven argued persuasively that the native Americans were of great antiquity, and, through cranial and other physical characteristics, he pointed to their probable links with Asiatic races. Disagreeing strongly with Atwater and Squier, he concluded that the mysterious mounds had been built by the ancestors of living American Indians. The controversy continued to rage, but Haven's rigorous approach paved the way for the resolution of the issue by John Wesley Powell and Cyrus Thomas.

John Wesley Powell (1834–1902)
Raised in the Midwest, Powell spent much of his youth digging into mounds and learning geology. He became famous for canoeing down

A 348-ft long painting used by lecturer Munro Dickeson in the 19th century to illustrate his mound excavations.

the Colorado and shooting the rapids.

Eventually Powell was appointed director of the U.S. Geographical and Geological Survey of the Rocky Mountain region. He published a wide range of information on the rapidly dwindling Indian cultures. Moving to Washington, this energetic scholar headed not only the Geological Survey but also his own brainchild, the Bureau of American Ethnology, an agency set up to study the North American Indians. A fearless campaigner for Indian rights, he recommended the setting up of reservations, and also began the recording of tribal oral histories.

In 1881 Powell recruited Cyrus Thomas to head the Bureau's archaeology program, and to settle the Moundbuilder question once and for all. After 7 years of fieldwork and the investigation of thousands of mounds, Thomas proved that the Moundbuilder race had never existed: the monuments had been erected by the ancestors of modern Indians.

But that was not the only controversial issue confronting Powell's Bureau. In 1876, a New Jersey physician named Charles Abbott showed his collection of flaked stone tools to Harvard archaeologist Frederick Putnam, who thought they must be Paleolithic specimens, resembling as they did Stone Age tools found in France. The issue of the "paleoliths" was brought to a head in 1887 when another archaeologist, Thomas Wilson, fresh from a period in France, embarked on a campaign to prove there had been Stone Age occupation of North America. Powell for his part hired William Henry Holmes to look into the question.

William Henry Holmes (1846–1933)

Holmes began his career as a geological illustrator, a training that stood him in good stead when he later turned to archaeology. At Powell's request he spent 5 years studying the "paleolith" question. He collected innumerable specimens and proved that they were not Stone Age tools at all but simply "the refuse of Indian implement making" from recent times. He even manufactured identical "paleoliths" himself. Abbott, Putnam, and Wilson had been deceived into making false comparisons with the French stone tools by superficial similarities.

Holmes' systematic methods also helped him to produce brilliant survey classifications of aboriginal pottery of the eastern United States, and studies of ruins in the Southwest and Mexico. He eventually succeeded Powell as head of the Bureau of American Ethnology. But his obsession with facts rather than theories made it difficult for him to accept the possibility that humans had after all reached North America in the Old Stone Age, as new discoveries at the end of his career in the 1920s began to suggest.

Putnam mistakenly compared prehistoric stone axes from France (left) with Charles Abbott's "paleoliths" (right), which Holmes subsequently proved to be of recent date.

"Lowering the Bull," the frontispiece from Layard's bestseller, Nineveh and Its Remains, *published in 1867.*

Austen Henry Layard (1817–1894) respectively, had vied with one another using crude "excavations" to see which side could obtain from the Mesopotamian ruins the "largest number of works of art with the least possible outlay of time and money." Layard wrote bestselling books and became famous for his discoveries, which included huge Assyrian sculptures of winged bulls, and a great library of cuneiform tablets from the site of Küyünjik. But it was only the final decipherment of cuneiform by Henry Rawlinson (1810–1895) in the 1850s, building on the work of others, that proved that Küyünjik was biblical Nineveh. Rawlinson spent 20 years copying and studying a 6th-century BC trilingual inscription located on an inaccessible cliff-face between Baghdad and Tehran before cracking the code of cuneiform.

Egypt and the Near East also held a fascination for the American lawyer and diplomat John Lloyd Stephens (1805–1852), but it was in the New World that he was to make his name. His travels in Yucatán, Mexico, with the English artist Frederick Catherwood, and the superbly illustrated books they produced together in the early 1840s, revealed for the first time to an enthusiastic public the ruined cities of the ancient Maya. Unlike contemporary researchers in North America, who continued to argue for a vanished white race of Moundbuilders as the architects of the earthworks there (see box, previous two pages) Stephens rightly believed that the Maya monuments were, in his own words, "the creation of the same races who inhabited the country at the time of the Spanish conquest." Stephens also noted that there were similar

hieroglyphic inscriptions at the different sites, which led him to argue for Maya cultural unity – but no Champollion or Rawlinson was to emerge to decipher the glyphs until the 1960s (Chapter 10).

If the Bible was one of the main inspirations behind the search for lost civilizations in Egypt and the Near East, it was Homer's account of the Trojan Wars in his narrative poem the *Iliad* that fired the imagination of the German banker Heinrich Schliemann (1822–1890), and sent him on a quest for the city of Troy. With remarkable luck and good judgment he successfully identified it in a series of field campaigns at Hissarlik, western Turkey, in the 1870s and 1880s. Not content with that achievement he also dug at Mycenae in Greece and revealed – as he had at Troy – a hitherto unknown prehistoric civilization. Schliemann's methods of excavation have been criticized as crude and cavalier, but few were very rigorous in his day, and he demonstrated how interpretation of the stratigraphy of a mound site could be used to reconstruct the remote past. Nevertheless it fell to the next generation of archaeologists, led by General Pitt-Rivers and Flinders Petrie, to establish the true basis of modern field techniques (see box).

Part of Schliemann's excavations at Troy, from his Ilios: City and Country of the Trojans *(1840).*

THE DEVELOPMENT OF FIELD TECHNIQUES

It was only in the late 19th century that a sound methodology of scientific excavation began to be generally adopted. From that time, and during the current century, major figures stand out who in their various ways have helped create the modern field methods we use today.

General Augustus Lane-Fox Pitt-Rivers (1827 – 1900)
For much of his life a professional soldier, Pitt-Rivers brought long experience of military methods, survey, and precision to impeccably organized excavations on his estates in southern England. Plans, sections, and even models were made, and the exact position of every object was recorded. He was not concerned with retrieving beautiful treasures, but with recovering all objects, no matter how mundane. He was a pioneer in his insistence on total recording, and his four privately printed volumes, describing his excavations on Cranborne Chase from 1887 to 1898, represent the highest standards of archaeological publication.

General Pitt-Rivers, excavator of Cranborne Chase, and pioneer in recording techniques.

Excavation (above) in progress at Wor Barrow, Cranborne Chase. The barrow was eventually removed.

A view (below) of the Wor Barrow ditch during Pitt-River's excavation at the site in the mid 1890s.

An example (below) of Pitt-Rivers' meticulous records: his plan of Barrow 27 at Cranborne Chase.

Sir William Flinders Petrie (1853 – 1942)

A younger contemporary of Pitt-Rivers, Petrie was likewise noted for his meticulous excavations and his insistence on the collection and description of everything found, not just the fine objects, as well as on full publication. He employed these methods in his exemplary excavations in Egypt, and later in Palestine, from the 1880s until his death. Petrie also devised his own technique of seriation or "sequence dating," which he used to bring chronological order to the 2200 pit graves of the Naqada cemetery in Upper Egypt (see Chapter 4).

Sir Mortimer Wheeler (1890 – 1976)

Wheeler fought in the British army in both world wars and, like Pitt-Rivers, brought military precision to his excavations, notably through techniques such as the grid-square method (Chapter 3). He is particularly well known for his work at British hillforts, notably Maiden Castle. Equally outstanding, however, was his achievement from 1944 to 1948 as Director-General of Archaeology in India, where he held training schools in modern field methods, and excavated at the important sites of Harappa, Taxila, and Arikamedu.

Petrie *(above) at the Egyptian site of Abydos in 1922.*

Petrie's *card (right) for grave no. 1848 at Naqada, showing grave goods in position*

Sir Mortimer Wheeler *(above), and one of his most famous excavations (left): Arikamedu, India, in 1945.*

Max Uhle (1856 – 1944)

Scientific archaeology in South America owes much to the work of Uhle, a German scholar who trained as a philologist and then turned to archaeology and ethnography. His excavation of Pachacamac, a coastal site just south of Lima, in the 1890s became the first important step in establishing an area-wide chronology for Peru. Uhle's concentration on graves and the careful recording of grave-good associations recall Petrie's early work in Egypt.

Alfred Kidder (1885–1963)

Kidder was the leading Americanist of his time. As well as being a major figure in Maya archaeology, he was largely responsible for putting the Southwest on the archaeological map with his excavations at Pecos Ruin, a large pueblo in northern New Mexico, from 1915 to 1929. His survey of the region, *An Introduction to the Study of Southwestern Archaeology* (1924) has become a classic.

Kidder was one of the first archaeologists to use a team of specialists to help analyze artifacts and human remains. He is also important for his "blueprint" for a regional strategy: (1) reconnaissance; (2) selection of criteria for ranking the remains of sites chronologically; (3) seriation into a probable sequence; (4) stratigraphic excavation to elucidate specific problems; followed by (5) more detailed regional survey and dating.

Fieldwork after 1960

Since 1960, archaeological fieldwork has developed in several new directions. One of these is underwater archaeology, which began as a serious method of research in 1960 with the work of George Bass at the Bronze Age Gelidonya shipwreck off the south coast of Turkey. This was the first ancient vessel ever excavated in its entirety on the sea bed. Bass and his team invented or developed many now standard underwater techniques (see boxes, Underwater Archaeology, Chapter 3; The Kas Wreck, Chapter 9).

Max Uhle's drawing of the stratigraphy from his excavations at Pachacamac, Peru.

Alfred Kidder (above) and his cross-sectional drawing of the stratigraphy at the Pecos pueblo site.

On dry land, the economic boom of the 1960s led to construction of new roads and buildings, which threatened and destroyed many archaeological sites and led to a new emphasis on managing the cultural heritage (Culture Resource Management, or CRM), either by preservation, or by recording and excavation prior to destruction (see box, The Practice of CRM in the United States, Chapter 14). In Europe, the redevelopment of historic city centers led to highly complex excavations spanning many periods and demanding new techniques of analysis. Finally, in recent years, the application of computerization in fieldwork has offered powerful new tools to help us recover and understand the remains left by past societies.

CLASSIFICATION AND CONSOLIDATION

Thus, well before the end of the 19th century, many of the principal features of modern archaeology had been established and many of the early civilizations had been discovered. There now ensued a period, which lasted until about 1960, which Gordon Willey and Jeremy Sabloff in their *A History of American Archaeology* have described as the "classificatory-historical period." Its central concern, as they rightly characterize it, was chronology. Much effort went into the establishment of regional chronological systems, and the description of the development of culture in each area.

In regions where the early civilizations had flourished new research and discoveries filled out the chronological sequences. Alfred Maudslay (1850–1931) laid the real scientific foundations of Maya archaeology, while the German scholar Max Uhle (1856–1944) began to establish a sound chronology for Peruvian civilization with his excavation in the 1890s at the coastal site of Pachacamac, Peru. The meticulous work of Flinders Petrie (1853–1942) in Egypt was followed up by the spectacular discovery in the 1920s of Tutankhamun's tomb by Howard Carter (1873–1939) (see box, Chapter 2). In the Aegean area, Arthur Evans (1851–1941) revealed a previously unknown civilization that he called Minoan on the island of Crete; the Minoans proved to be even earlier than Schliemann's Mycenaeans. And in Mesopotamia Leonard Woolley (1880–1960) excavated at Ur, the biblical city of Abraham's birth, and put the Sumerians on the map of the ancient world.

It was, however, scholars studying primarily the prehistoric societies of Europe and North America who made some of the most significant contributions during the first half of the 20th century. Gordon Childe (1892–1957), a brilliant Australian based in Britain, was the leading thinker and writer about European prehistory and Old World history in general. In the United States there was a close link between anthropologists and archaeologists studying the American Indians. The anthropologist Franz Boas (1858–1942) reacted against the broad evolutionary schemes of his predecessors Morgan and Tylor and demanded much greater attention to the collection and classification of information in the field. Huge inventories of cultural traits, such as pot and basket designs or types of moccasins, were built up. This tied in with the so-called "direct historical approach" of the archaeologists, who attempted to trace modern Indian pottery and other styles "directly" back into the distant past. The work of Cyrus Thomas and later W.H. Holmes (see box

pp. 26, 27) in the east was complemented by that of A.V. Kidder (1885–1963), whose excavations at Pecos Pueblo in the Southwest from 1915 to 1929 established a chronological framework for that region (box p. 31). James A. Ford later developed the first major framework for the Southeast. By the 1930s the number of separate regional sequences was so great that a group of scholars led by W.C. McKern devised what became known as the "Midwestern Taxonomic System," which correlated sequences in the Midwest by identifying similarities between artifact collections. This was applied to other areas.

Gordon Childe meanwhile had almost single-handedly been making comparisons of this sort between prehistoric sequences in Europe. Both his methods and the Midwestern Taxonomic System were designed to order the material: to answer the question, To what period do these artifacts date? and also, With which other materials do they belong? This latter question usually carried with it an assumption which Gordon Childe made explicit: that a constantly recurring collection or "assemblage" of artifacts (a "culture" in his terminology, or an "aspect" in that of McKern) could be taken as the material equipment of a particular group of people. This approach thus offered the hope of answering, in a very general sense, the question, Who did these artifacts belong to? The answer would be in terms of a named people, even if the name for a prehistoric people would be a modern one, not the original name. (There are now seen to be dangers in this approach, as we shall discuss in Chapter 12.)

But in his great works of synthesis, such as *The Dawn of European Civilization* (1925) and *The Danube in Prehistory* (1929), Childe went beyond merely describing and correlating the culture sequences and attempted to account for their origin. In the late 19th century scholars such as Montelius had looked at the richness of the early civilizations then being uncovered in the Near East, and argued that all the attributes of civilization, from stone architecture to metal weapons, had spread or "diffused" to Europe from the Near East by trade or migration of people. With the much greater range of evidence available to him, Childe modified this extreme diffusionist approach and argued that Europe had undergone some indigenous development – but he nevertheless attributed the major cultural changes to Near Eastern influences.

In his later books, such as *Man Makes Himself* (1936), Childe went on to try and answer the much more difficult question: why had civilization arisen in the Near East? Himself influenced by Marxist ideas and the relatively recent Marxist revolution in Russia, he proposed that there had been a Neolithic Revolution which gave rise to the development of farming, and later an Urban Revolution which led to the first towns and cities. Childe was one of the few archaeologists of his generation bold enough to address this whole broad issue of why things happened or changed in the past. Most of his contemporaries were more concerned with establishing chronologies and cultural sequences. But after World War II scholars with new ideas began to challenge conventional approaches.

The Ecological Approach

One of the most influential new thinkers in North America was the anthropologist Julian Steward (1902–1972). Like Childe he was interested in explaining cultural change, but he brought to the question an anthropologist's understanding of how living cultures work. Moreover he highlighted the fact that cultures do not interact simply with one another but with the environment as well. The study of ways in which adaptation to the environment could cause cultural change Steward christened "cultural ecology." Perhaps the most direct archaeological impact of these ideas can be seen in the work of Gordon Willey, one of Steward's graduate associates, who carried out a pioneering investigation in the Virú Valley, Peru, in the late 1940s. This study of 1500 years of pre-Columbian occupation involved a combination of observations from detailed maps and aerial photographs (see box, Chapter 3), survey at ground level, and excavation and surface potsherd collection to establish dates for the hundreds of prehistoric sites identified. Willey then plotted the geographical distribution of these sites in the valley at different periods – one of the first settlement pattern studies in archaeology (see Chapters 3 and 5) – and set them against the changing local environment.

Quite independently of Steward, however, the British archaeologist Grahame Clark developed an ecological approach with even more direct relevance for archaeological fieldwork. Breaking away from the artifact-dominated culture-historical approach of his contemporaries, he argued that by studying how human populations adapted to their environments we can understand many aspects of ancient society. Collaboration with new kinds of specialists was essential: specialists who could identify animal bones or plant remains in the archaeological record to help build up a picture not only of what prehistoric environments were like, but what foods prehistoric peoples ate. Clark's landmark excavation at Star Carr in northeast Britain in the early 1950s demonstrated just how much information could be gleaned from what appeared to be an unpromising site without stone structures and dating to just after the end of the Ice Age. Careful environmental analysis and recovery of organic remains showed that this had been a camp on the edge of a lake, where people had hunted red deer and eaten a wide variety of wild plant foods. Nor need the insights from an ecological approach be confined to individual sites or groups of sites: in a remarkable work of synthesis, *Prehistoric Europe: the Economic Basis* (1952), Clark provided a panoramic view of the varying human adaptations to the European landscape over thousands of years.

Out of this early ecological research has grown the whole field of environmental and dietary reconstruction discussed in Chapters 6 and 7.

The Rise of Archaeological Science

The other striking development of the period immediately after World War II was the rapid development of scientific aids for archaeology. We have already seen how pioneers of the ecological approach forged an alliance with specialists from the environmental sciences. Even more important, however, was the application to archaeology of the physical and chemical sciences.

The greatest breakthrough came in the field of dating. In 1949 the American chemist Willard Libby (1908–1980) announced his invention of radiocarbon

Willard Libby in his laboratory at UCLA.

(C14) dating. It was not until well over a decade later that the full impact of this momentous technical achievement began to be felt (see below), but the implications were clear: here at last archaeologists might have a means of directly determining the age of undated sites and finds anywhere in the world without recourse to complicated cross-cultural comparisons with areas already dated by historical methods (usually written records). Thus, traditionally, prehistoric Europe had been dated by virtue of supposed contacts with early Greece and hence (indirectly) with ancient Egypt, which could itself be dated historically. The radiocarbon method held the prospect of providing a completely independent chronology for ancient Europe. Chapter 4 discusses dating methods in general, and radiocarbon in particular.

The growth in archaeological applications for scientific techniques was such that by 1963 a volume entitled *Science in Archaeology*, edited by Don Broth-well and Eric Higgs, could be published which ran to nearly 600 pages, with contributions from 55 experts, not merely on dating techniques and plant and animal studies, but methods for analyzing human remains (see Chapter 11) and artifacts (Chapters 8 and 9). Artifact studies, for instance, could contribute to an understanding of early trade: it proved possible to identify the raw materials of certain artifacts and the sources from which they had come through the technique of trace-element analysis (the measurement of elements present in the material only in very small amounts). As with many of the new methods, research stretched back to the 1930s, when the Austrian archaeologist Richard Pittioni had begun to apply trace-element analysis to early copper and bronze artifacts. Nevertheless it was not until the postwar years that this and a number of other newly developed scientific techniques really began to make an impact on archaeology.

A TURNING POINT IN ARCHAEOLOGY

The 1960s mark a turning point in the development of archaeology. By this time various dissatisfactions were being expressed with the way research in the subject was being conducted. These dissatisfactions were not so much with excavation techniques, or with the newly developed scientific aids in archaeology, but with the way conclusions were drawn from them. The first and most obvious point concerned the role of dating in archaeology. The second went beyond this: it focused on the way archaeologists explain things, on the procedures used in archaeological reasoning.

With the advent of the radiocarbon method, dates could in many cases be assigned very rapidly, and without the long and laborious framework of cross-cultural comparisons which had been needed previously. To establish a date was no longer one of the main end products of research. It was still important, but it could now be done much more efficiently, allowing the archaeologist to go on to ask more challenging questions than merely chronological ones.

The second, and perhaps more fundamental cause for dissatisfaction with the traditional archaeology was that it never seemed to explain anything, other than in terms of migrations of peoples and supposed "influences." Already in 1948 the American archaeologist Walter W. Taylor had in his *A Study of Archaeology* formulated some of these dissatisfactions. He had argued for a "conjunctive" approach, in which the full range of a culture system would be taken into consideration. And in 1958, Gordon Willey and Philip Phillips in their *Method and Theory in American Archaeology* had argued for a greater emphasis on the social aspect, for a broader "processual interpretation" or study of the general processes at work in culture history. They also spoke of "an eventual synthesis in a common search for sociocultural causality and law."

That was all very well, but what would it mean in practice?

The Birth of the New Archaeology

In the United States the answer was provided, at least in part, by a group of younger archaeologists, led by Lewis Binford, who set out to offer a new approach to the problems of archaeological interpretation, which was soon dubbed by its critics and then by its supporters "the New Archaeology." In a series of articles, and later in an edited volume, *New Perspectives in Archaeology* (1968), Binford and his colleagues argued against the approach which tried to use archaeological data to write a kind of "counterfeit history."

They argued that the potential of the archaeological evidence was much greater than had been realized for the investigation of social and economic aspects of past societies. Their view of archaeology was more optimistic than that of many of their predecessors.

They argued that archaeological reasoning should be made explicit. Conclusions should be based not simply on the personal authority of the scholar making the interpretation, but on an explicit framework of logical argument. In this they relied on current ideas within the philosophy of science where conclusions, if to be considered valid, must be open to testing.

Within the spirit of processual archaeology advocated by Willey and Phillips, they sought to *explain* rather than simply to describe, and to do so, as in all sciences, by seeking to make valid generalizations.

In doing this they sought to avoid the rather vague talk of the "influences" of one culture upon another, but rather to analyze a culture as a system which could be broken down into subsystems. This led them to study subsistence in its own right, and technology, and the social subsystem, and the ideological subsystem, and trade and demography and so forth, with much less emphasis on artifact typology and classification. In this way they had been partly anticipated by the ecological approach of the 1950s, which was already studying what one might call "the subsistence subsystem" in very much these terms.

In order to fulfill these aims, the New Archaeologists to a large extent turned away from the approaches of history towards those of the sciences. Very similar developments were under way in Britain at the same time, well exemplified by the work of David L. Clarke (1937–1976), particularly in his book *Analytical Archaeology* (1968), which reflected the great willingness of the New Archaeologists to employ more sophisticated quantitative techniques, where possible computer-aided, and to draw on ideas from other disciplines, notably geography. In a preliminary study published in another influential book which he edited, *Models in Archaeology* (1972), Clarke showed how the new ideas could be applied even to an old excavation, in this case the Iron Age lake village of Glastonbury in southwest Britain (box overleaf). New concepts derived from architecture were applied at the household level, new concepts from geography and ecological studies at the level of the site and region – and all were integrated to give a wholly archaeological and new perspective.

It must be admitted that in their enthusiasm to seize on and utilize a battery of new techniques, the New Archaeologists drew also on a range of previously unfamiliar vocabularies (drawn from systems theory, cybernetics etc.), which their critics tended to dismiss as jargon. Indeed in recent years, several critics have reacted against some of those aspirations to be scientific, which they have categorized as "scientistic" or "functionalist." Many of these points are considered in

THE NEW ARCHAEOLOGY: KEY CONCEPTS

In the early days of the New Archaeology, its principal exponents were very conscious of the limitations of the older, traditional archaeology. The following contrasts were among those which they often emphasized:

THE NATURE OF ARCHAEOLOGY:
Explanatory *vs* Descriptive
Archaeology's role was now to *explain* past change, not simply to reconstruct the past and how people had lived. This involved the use of *explicit theory*.

EXPLANATION: Culture process *vs* Culture history
Traditional archaeology was seen to rely on historical explanation: the New Archaeology, drawing on the *philosophy of science*, would think in terms of *culture process*, of how changes in economic and social systems take place. This implies *generalization*.

REASONING: Deductive *vs* Inductive
Traditional archaeologists saw archaeology as resembling a jigsaw puzzle: the task was one of "piecing together the past." Instead, the appropriate procedure was now seen as formulating *hypotheses*, constructing *models*, and deducing their consequences.

VALIDATION: Testing *vs* Authority
Hypotheses were to be tested, and conclusions should not be accepted on the basis of the authority or standing of the research worker.

RESEARCH FOCUS:
Project design *vs* Data accumulation
Research should be designed to answer specific *questions* economically, not simply to generate more information which might not be relevant.

CHOICE OF APPROACH:
Quantitative *vs* Simply qualitative
The benefits were seen of quantitative data, allowing computerized statistical treatment, with the possibility of *sampling* and *significance testing*. This was often preferred to the purely verbal traditional approach.

SCOPE: Optimism *vs* Pessimism
Traditional archaeologists often stressed that archaeological data were not well suited to the reconstruction of *social organization* or *cognitive systems*. The New Archaeologists were more positive and argued that one would never know how hard these problems were until one had tried to solve them.

GLASTONBURY: CHANGING IDEAS AND APPROACHES

ENGLAND

• Glastonbury

The history of research at the 2000-year-old lake village of Glastonbury, southwest England, well illustrates the changing nature of archaeology.

During the 19th century, wooden artifacts were often recovered in the wet and often waterlogged Somerset Levels, the general area of flatlands surrounding Glastonbury. In 1893, a local scholar and doctor, Arthur Bulleid, began working at the Glastonbury site. He had been inspired by Ferdinand Keller's pioneering book of 1878, *The Lake Dwellings of Switzerland*, in which wet-site excavations were first reported. Bulleid's Glastonbury excavations showed the site to be a village settlement, preserving the waterlogged foundation timbers and floors of some round huts and smaller structures, and plentiful remains of pottery, bones, and a variety of artifacts.

Bulleid and his colleague H. St George Gray continued work at Glastonbury and the nearby site of Meare for more than half a century. Their work was outstanding in at least three ways. First, they chose a seemingly unglamorous waterlogged site, where organic remains were well preserved and a wider range of artifacts could be recovered than is possible on drier sites. Secondly, they recorded finds with care, plotting findspots on site plans, so that they and future archaeologists could analyze the material. And thirdly, they published most of their work – unlike so many excavations where fieldwork loses its value through the failure to publish.

Clarke's Reinterpretation

The great value of Bulleid and Gray's work was emphasized in 1972 by David L. Clarke's innovative study, "A Provisional Model of an Iron Age Society and its Settlement System." He assembled a detailed plan for the complete site (which Bulleid and Gray had published as a series of sheets) and proceeded to interpret groups of structures in the settlement as residential or "modular" units, on the basis of where certain artifacts and types of structure were located on the plan. For example, in phase III he envisaged that there were 7 modular units, consisting of a total of 21 houses plus subsidiary buildings, giving a population of about 105 individuals. Clarke also sought to identify male and female activity areas within the modular units.

Finally he looked at how the village related economically and socially to other settlements in the region and to the surrounding landscape.

In their book *Sweet Track to Glastonbury* (1986), Bryony and John Coles have cast doubt on the accuracy of many of Clarke's interpretations, based on their own study of Bulleid's work. But, as they write, Clarke has "provoked many new thoughts" about the site. His analysis shows how well-recorded evidence can be interpreted and reinterpreted in the light of changing archaeological theories and methods.

Over the past two decades Bryony and John Coles have themselves obtained major new evidence from the Somerset Levels. Among other research, they have made a systematic study of the various trackways (one nearly 6000 years old) that were used to cross marshy areas between the settlements. Thus, the farsighted work of Bulleid and Gray at a single site has now expanded into much wider environmental and landscape archaeology, where the individual settlement is seen as just one component in the broader pattern of human activity.

Glastonbury excavations at the turn of the century. Note the well-preserved waterlogged timbers.

Plan of *Glastonbury Lake Village* (above), redrawn after Bulleid.

Clarke's reinterpretation of Bulleid's plan (above), and the modular unit (below), Clarke's hypothetical Glastonbury residential unit.

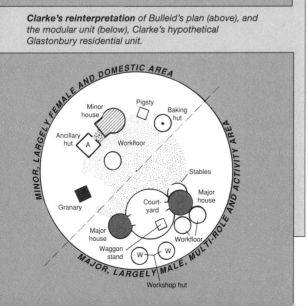

Chapter 12. But there can be no doubt that archaeology will never be the same again. Most workers today, even the critics of the early New Archaeology, implicitly recognize its influence when they agree that it is indeed the goal of archaeology to explain what happened in the past as well as to describe it. Most of them agree too that in order to do good archaeology it is necessary to make explicit, and then to examine, our underlying assumptions. That was what David Clarke meant when he wrote in a 1973 article of "the loss of innocence" in archaeology.

WORLD ARCHAEOLOGY

The questioning approach of the New Archaeology and the demand for explicit and quantitative procedures led to new developments in field research, many of which built on or coincided with the programs of fieldwork already being conducted by archaeologists who would not necessarily have thought of themselves as followers of the new school of thought.

In the first place, there was a much greater emphasis on field projects with well-defined research objectives – projects which set out to answer specific questions about the past. In the second place, the new insights yielded by the ecological approach made it clear that satisfactory answers to many major questions would only be forthcoming if whole regions and their environments were looked at, rather than single sites in isolation. And the third development, very much linked to the first and second, was the realization that in order to carry out these objectives effectively, new techniques needed to be introduced of intensive field survey and selective excavation, coupled with statistically based sampling procedures and improved recovery methods, including screening (sieving) of excavated material. These are the key elements of modern field research, discussed in detail in Chapter 3. Here we should observe that their widespread application has begun to create for the first time a true world discipline: an archaeology that reaches geographically right round the globe, and an archaeology that reaches back in time to the beginnings of human existence and right up to the modern period.

The Search for Origins

Among the pioneers of well-focused project design was Robert J. Braidwood, of the University of Chicago, whose multi-disciplinary team in the 1940s and 1950s systematically sought out sites in the Iraqi Kurdistan

Human origins: Louis Leakey (above) and his wife Mary Leakey spent almost three decades working in Olduvai Gorge, East Africa, before making the first of many crucial finds there of fossil bones belonging to our earliest ancestors.

whole history of archaeology should perhaps go to Louis Leakey (1903–1972) and his wife Mary Leakey, who between them pushed back the known dates for our immediate ancestors by several million years. As long ago as 1931 they began their search in the Olduvai Gorge, East Africa, for fossil human bones, but it was not until 1959 that their extraordinary perseverance was rewarded and Mary Leakey made the first of many fossil hominid (early human) finds in the Gorge. Africa has now become the great focus of study for the early phases of humankind, and has seen crucial theoretical debate between Lewis Binford, C.K. Brain, Glynn Isaac, and others over the likely hunting and scavenging behavior of our ancestors (Chapters 2, 7).

The Archaeology of Continents

Research in Africa exemplifies the pushing back of archaeology's frontiers in both time and space. The quest for human origins has been one success story, but so too has been the rediscovery through archaeology of the achievements and history of the Iron Age peoples of Africa, including the building of Great Zimbabwe (box, Chapter 12). By 1970 archaeological knowledge of the whole continent was sufficiently advanced for J. Desmond Clark, one of the leading researchers, to produce the first synthesis, *The Prehistory of Africa*. Meanwhile, in another equally little-studied continent, Australia, John Mulvaney's excavations in the early 1960s at Kenniff Cave, South Queensland, produced radiocarbon dates proving occupation there during the last phase of the Ice Age – thus establishing Australasia as one of the most fruitful regions for new archaeological research in the world.

Work in Australia highlights two further important trends in modern archaeology: the rise of ethnoarchaeology or "living archaeology;" and the increasing worldwide discussion about who should control or "own" monuments and ideas about the past.

The Living Past

From its beginnings the New Archaeology placed great emphasis on explanation – in particular explaining how the archaeological record was formed, and what excavated structures and artifacts might mean in terms of human behavior. It came to be realized that one of the most effective ways of addressing such questions would be to study the material culture and behavior of

region that would provide evidence for the origins of agriculture in the Near East (see Chapter 7). Another American project, headed by Richard MacNeish, did the same for the New World: their research in the 1960s in the Tehuacán Valley of Mexico moved our understanding of the long-drawn-out development of maize farming an immense step forward.

If the origins of farming have been the subject of much well-targeted research in recent decades, the rise of complex societies, including civilizations, has been another. In particular, two American field projects have been outstandingly successful: one in Mesopotamia led by Robert Adams (with much use of aerial photography as well as field survey), and the other in the Valley of Oaxaca, Mexico, led by Kent Flannery (see Chapter 13).

However the credit for the most determined pursuit of a project with a clear archaeological objective in the

Revealing Australia's past: archaeologist John Mulvaney at the Shelter 2 site, Fromm's Landing, South Australia. In 1956, during his first season of fieldwork here, Mulvaney excavated some 5000 years of occupation deposit.

living societies. Ethnographic observation itself was nothing new – anthropologists had studied the American Indians and Australian Aborigines since the 19th century. What was new was the archaeological focus: the new name, ethnoarchaeology, emphasized this. The work of Richard Gould among the Australian Aborigines, Richard Lee among the !Kung San of southern Africa, and Lewis Binford among the Nunamiut Eskimo has established ethnoarchaeology – discussed in more detail in Chapter 5 – as one of the most significant recent developments in the whole discipline.

However, the increasing involvement of archaeologists with living societies, and the simultaneous rise among such societies of an awareness of their own heritage and their own claims to it, have brought to the fore the question: Who should have access to, or ownership of, the past? It is clear, for example, that the

only inhabitants of Australia before European settlement were the Aborigines. Should it therefore be the Aborigines themselves who control archaeological work on their forebears, even those dating back 20,000 years or more? This important issue is explored further in Chapter 14.

Archaeologists such as John Mulvaney have stood shoulder to shoulder with the Aborigines in the fight to prevent destruction by developers of parts of Australia's precious ancient heritage, for instance in Tasmania. Inevitably, though, as the pace of worldwide economic development has quickened in the last 30 years, archaeologists everywhere have had to adapt and learn to salvage what they can about the past in advance of the bulldozer or plow. Indeed the massive upsurge of this salvage or rescue archaeology, much of it government-funded, has given a new impetus to the archaeology of our towns and cities – to what in Europe is known as medieval or postmedieval archaeology, and what in the United States is called historical archaeology.

Who are the Searchers?

The growth of salvage work also leads us to ask: Who today actually are the searchers in archaeology? A century ago they were often wealthy individuals, who had the leisure to speculate about the past, and to undertake excavations. Or in other cases, they were travelers who had reason to be in remote places, and used the opportunity to undertake researches in what was effectively their spare time. Thirty years ago the searchers in the field of archaeology tended to be university scholars, or the representatives of national museums seeking to enlarge their collections, or the employees of learned societies and academic institutions (like the Egypt Exploration Society), nearly all of them based in the more prosperous capitals of Europe and the United States.

Today most countries in the world have their own government archaeological or historical services. The scope of current public archaeology is reviewed in Chapter 14. But it is worth noting here that today a "searcher" (i.e. a professional archaeologist) is more likely to be an employee, often directly or indirectly a government employee, on a salvage or rescue project than a more independent research worker. How this shift in the center of gravity of archaeological activity will affect the questions asked, and hence the future growth of the discipline of archaeology, remains to be seen.

SUMMARY

The history of archaeology, then, is a history of new ideas, methods, and discoveries. Modern archaeology took root in the 19th century with the acceptance of three key concepts: the great antiquity of humanity, Darwin's principle of evolution, and the Three Age System for ordering material culture. Many of the early civilizations, especially in the Old World, had been discovered by the 1880s, and some of their ancient scripts deciphered. This was followed by a long phase of consolidation – of improvement in methods of fieldwork and excavation and the establishment of regional chronologies.

After World War II the pace of change in the discipline quickened. New ecological approaches sought to help us understand human adaptation to the environment. New scientific techniques introduced among other things reliable means of dating the prehistoric past. Spurred on by these developments, the New Archaeology of the 1960s and 1970s turned to questions not just of what happened when, but why they happened, in an attempt to explain processes of change. Meanwhile, pioneer fieldworkers studying whole regions opened up a truly world archaeology in time and space – in time back from the present to the earliest toolmakers, and in space across all the world's continents.

Precisely how archaeologists today are continuing to push back the frontiers of knowledge about our planet's human past forms the subject of the remainder of this book.

Further Reading

Good introductions to the history of archaeology include:

Ceram, C.W. 1967. *Gods, Graves and Scholars.* (2nd ed.) Knopf: New York; Gollancz: London 1971.

Daniel, G. 1967. *The Origins and Growth of Archaeology.* Penguin Books: Harmondsworth and Baltimore. (Quotations from the writings of early archaeologists.)

Daniel, G. 1975. *150 Years of Archaeology.* Duckworth: London.

Daniel, G. & Renfrew, C. 1988. *The Idea of Prehistory.* Edinburgh University Press: Edinburgh; Columbia University Press: New York.

Fagan, B.M. 1985. *The Adventure of Archaeology.* National Geographic Society: Washington, D.C.

Trigger, B.G. 1989. *A History of Archaeological Thought.* Cambridge University Press: Cambridge & New York.

Willey, G.R. and Sabloff, J.A. 1980. *A History of American Archaeology.* (2nd ed.) Freeman: San Francisco.

2
What Is Left?
The Variety of
the Evidence

The relics of past human activity are all around us. Some of them were deliberate constructions, built to last, like the pyramids of Egypt, the Great Wall of China, or the temples of Mesoamerica and India. Others, like the remains of the Maya irrigation systems of Mexico and Belize, are the visible relics of activities whose aim was not primarily to impress the observer, but which still command respect today for the scale of the enterprise they document.

Most of the remains of archaeology are far more modest, however. They are the discarded refuse from the daily activities of human existence: the food remains, the bits of broken pottery, the fractured stone tools, the debris that everywhere is formed as people go about their daily lives.

In this chapter we define the basic archaeological terms, briefly survey the scope of the surviving evidence and look at the great variety of ways in which it has been preserved for us. From the frozen soil of the Russian steppes, for instance, have come the wonderful finds of Pazyryk, those great chieftains' burials where wood and textiles and skins are splendidly preserved. From the dry caves of Peru and other arid environments have come remarkable textiles, baskets, and other remains that often perish completely. And by contrast, from wetlands, whether the swamps of Florida or the lake villages of Switzerland, further organic remains are being recovered, this time preserved not by the absence of moisture, but by its abundant presence to the exclusion of air.

Extremes of temperature and of humidity have preserved much. So too have natural disasters. The volcanic eruption that destroyed Pompeii and Herculaneum (box, Chapter 1) is the most famous of them, but there have been others, such as the eruption of the Ilopango volcano in El Salvador in the 3rd century AD, which buried land surfaces and settlement remains in a large part of the southern Maya area.

Our knowledge of the early human past is dependent in this way on the human activities and natural processes that have formed the archaeological record, and on those further processes that determine, over long periods of time, what is left and what is gone for ever. Today we can hope to recover much of what is left, and to learn from it by asking the right questions in the right way.

BASIC CATEGORIES OF ARCHAEOLOGICAL EVIDENCE

Undoubtedly one of the main concerns of the archaeologist is the study of *artifacts* – objects used, modified, or made by people. But, as the work of Grahame Clark and other pioneers of the ecological approach has demonstrated (Chapter 1), there is a whole category of nonartifactual *organic and environmental remains* – sometimes called "ecofacts" – that can be equally revealing about many aspects of past human activity. Much archaeological research has to do with the analysis of artifacts and these organic and environmental remains found together on *sites*, them-selves most productively studied with surrounding landscapes and grouped together in *regions*.

Artifacts are humanly made or modified portable objects, such as stone tools, pottery, and metal weapons. In Chapter 8 we look at methods for analyzing human technological prowess in the mastery of materials for artifacts. But artifacts provide crucial evidence to help us answer all the key questions – not just technological ones – addressed in this book. A single clay vessel or pot, for example, can be the subject of several lines of inquiry. The clay may be tested to produce a date for the vessel and therefore perhaps a date for the location where it was found (Chapter 4), and tested as well to find the source of the clay and thus give evidence for the range and contacts of the human group that made the vessel (Chapters 5 and 9). Pictorial decoration on the pot's surface may be used in a typological sequence of pots (Chapter 3), and may reveal something about ancient beliefs, particularly if it shows gods or other figures (Chapter 10). And analysis of the vessel's shape and any food or other residues found in it can yield information about the pot's use, perhaps in cooking, as well as about ancient diet (Chapter 7).

Some researchers broaden the meaning of the term "artifact" to include all humanly modified components of a site or landscape, such as hearths, postholes, and storage pits – but these are more usefully described as *features*, defined in essence as nonportable artifacts. Simple features such as postholes may themselves, or in combination with remains of hearths, floors, ditches, etc., give evidence for complex features or *structures*, defined as buildings of all kinds, from houses and granaries to palaces and temples.

Nonartifactual organic and environmental remains or ecofacts include animal bones and plant remains, but also soils and sediments – all of which may shed light on past human activities. They are important because they can indicate, for example, what people ate or the environmental conditions under which they lived (Chapters 6 and 7).

Archaeological sites may be thought of as places where artifacts, features, structures, and organic and environmental remains are found together. For working purposes one can simplify this still further and define sites as places where significant traces of human activity are identified. Thus a village or town is a site, and so too is an isolated monument like Serpent

Mound in Ohio or Stonehenge in England. Equally, a surface scatter of stone tools or potsherds may represent a site occupied for no more than a few hours, whereas a Near Eastern *tell* or mound is a site indicating human occupation over perhaps thousands of years. In Chapter 5 we consider the great variety of sites in more detail and look at the ways in which archaeologists classify them and study them regionally – as part of the investigation of settlement patterns. Here, however, we are more concerned with the nature of individual sites and how they are formed.

The Importance of Context

In order to reconstruct past human activity at a site it is crucially important to understand the *context* of a find, whether artifact, feature, structure, or organic remain. A find's context consists of its immediate *matrix* (the material surrounding it, usually some sort of sediment such as gravel, sand, or clay), its *provenience* (horizontal and vertical position within the matrix), and its *association* with other finds (occurrence together with other archaeological remains, usually in the same matrix). In the 19th century the demonstration that stone tools were associated with the bones of extinct animals in sealed deposits or matrices helped establish the idea of humanity's high antiquity (Chapter 1). Increasingly since then archaeologists have recognized the importance of identifying and accurately recording associations between remains on sites. This is why it is such a tragedy when looters dig up sites indiscriminately in the search for rich finds, without recording matrix, provenience, or associations. All the contextual information is lost. A looted vase may be an attractive object for a collector, but far more could have been learnt about the society that produced it had

SMALL REGION

Areas with soils suitable for first farmers (loess soils)

Rhine R.

Sites

1:400,000

GROUP OF SITES
in association with river

Merzbach R.

1:40,000

INDIVIDUAL SITE (SMALL VILLAGE)

Early phase house (*structure*)

Refuse pit (*feature*) containing organic remains (*ecofacts*)

Path (*feature*)

Silo (*small structure*)

Later phase house (*structure*)

1:4000

Different scales and terminology used in archaeology, from the continental region (opposite page, top left) to the individual structure (right). In this representation of the pattern of settlement of Europe's first farmers (5th millennium BC), the archaeologist might study – at the broader scale – the interesting association between sites and light, easily worked soils near rivers (see Chapter 7). At the smaller scale, the association – established by excavation (Chapter 3) – of houses with other houses and with structures such as silos for grain storage raises questions, for example, about social organization and permanence of occupation at this period.

INDIVIDUAL STRUCTURE (HOUSE)

Scatter of *artifacts*

Posthole (*feature*)

1:400

Artifacts and features are found *in association* with the structure archaeologists been able to record where it was found (in a tomb or ditch or house?) and in association with what other artifacts or organic remains (with weapons or tools or animal bones?). Much precious information about the Mimbres people of the American Southwest has been lost forever because looters bulldozed their sites, hunting for the superbly painted – and highly sought after – bowls made by the Mimbres 1000 years ago (box, Chapter 14).

When modern (or ancient) looters disturb a site, perhaps shifting aside material they are not interested in, they destroy that material's *primary context*. If archaeologists subsequently excavate that shifted material, they need to be able to recognize that it is in a secondary context. This may be straightforward for, say, a Mimbres site, looted quite recently, but it is much more difficult for a site disturbed in antiquity. Nor is disturbance confined to human activity: archaeologists dealing with the tens of thousands of years of the Old Stone Age or Paleolithic period know well that the forces of nature – encroaching seas or ice sheets, wind and water action – invariably destroy primary context. A great many of the Stone Age tools found in European river gravels are in a secondary context, transported by water action far from their original, primary context.

FORMATION PROCESSES

In recent years archaeologists have become increasingly aware that a whole series of *formation processes* may have affected both the way in which finds came to be buried and what happened to them after they were buried.

The American archaeologist Michael Schiffer has made the useful distinction between *cultural formation processes* (C-transforms) and noncultural or *natural formation processes* (N-transforms). C-transforms involve the deliberate or accidental activities of human beings as they make or use artifacts, build or abandon buildings, plow their fields and so on. N-transforms are natural events that govern both the burial and the survival of the archaeological record. The sudden fall of volcanic ash that covered Pompeii (Chapter 1) is an exceptional N-transform; a more common one would be the gradual burial of artifacts or features by wind-borne sand or soil. Likewise the transporting of stone tools by river action, referred to above, is an example of an N-transform. But the activities of animals on a

Early humans as mighty hunters (left) or mere scavengers (right)? Our understanding of formation processes governs the way in which we interpret associations of human tools with animal bones from the fossil record in Africa.

EXPERIMENTAL ARCHAEOLOGY

One effective way to study formation processes is through long-term experimental archaeology. An excellent example is the experimental earthwork constructed on Overton Down, southern England, in 1960.

The earthwork consists of a substantial chalk and turf bank, 21 m (69 ft) long, 7 m (25 ft) wide, and 2 m (6 ft 7 in) high, with a ditch cut parallel to it. The aim of the experiment has been to assess not only how the bank and ditch alter through time, but also what happens to materials such as pottery, leather, and textiles that were buried in the earthwork in 1960. Sections (trenches) have been – or will be – cut across the bank and ditch at intervals of 2, 4, 8, 16, 32, 64 and 128 years (in real time, 1962, 1964, 1968, 1976, 1992, 2024, and 2088): a considerable commitment for all concerned.

On this timescale, the project is still at an early stage. But preliminary

The bank and ditch as cut in 1960, together with the changes revealed by sections cut across the earthwork in 1962 and 1976.

- 1960
- 1962
- 1976

results are interesting. In the 1960s the bank dropped some 25 cm (10 in) in height and the ditch silted up quite rapidly. Since the mid-1970s, however, the structure has stabilized. As for the buried materials, tests after 4 years showed that pottery was unchanged and leather little affected, but textiles were already becoming weakened and discolored.

---

site – burrowing into them or chewing bones and pieces of wood – are also N-transforms.

At first sight these distinctions may seem of little interest to the archaeologist. In fact they are vital to the accurate reconstruction of past human activities. It may be important, for instance, to know whether certain archaeological evidence is the product of human or non-human activity (the result of C-transforms or N-transforms). If you are trying to reconstruct human woodworking activities by studying cutmarks on timber, then you should learn to recognize certain kinds of marks made by beavers using their teeth and to distinguish these from cutmarks made by humans using stone or metal tools (Chapter 8).

Let us take an even more significant example. For the earliest phases of human existence in Africa, at the beginning of the Old Stone Age or Paleolithic period, great theoretical schemes about our primitive hunting ability have been based on the association between stone tools and animal bones found at archaeological sites. The bones were assumed to be those of animals hunted and slaughtered by early humans who made the tools. But studies in recent years of animal

behavior and cutmarks on animal bones by C.K. Brain, Lewis Binford, and others suggest that in many cases the excavated bones are the remains of animals hunted by other predator animals and largely eaten by these. The humans with their stone tools would have come upon the scene as mere scavengers, at the end of a pecking order of different animal species. By no means everyone agrees with this scavenging hypothesis. The point to emphasize here is that the issue can best be resolved by improving our techniques for distinguishing between cultural and natural formation processes – between human and non-human activity. Many studies are now focusing on the need to clarify how one differentiates cutmarks on bones made by stone tools from those made by the teeth of animal predators (Chapter 7). Modern experiments using replica stone tools to cut meat off bones are one helpful approach. Other kinds of experimental archaeology can be most instructive about some of the formation processes that affect physical preservation of archaeological material (see box).

The remainder of this chapter is devoted to a more detailed discussion of the different cultural and natural formation processes.

CULTURAL FORMATION PROCESSES – HOW PEOPLE HAVE AFFECTED WHAT SURVIVES IN THE ARCHAEOLOGICAL RECORD

One may separate these processes rather crudely into two kinds: those that reflect the original human behavior and activity before a find or site became buried; and those (such as plowing or looting) that came after burial. Now of course most major archaeological sites are formed as the result of a complex sequence of use, burial, and reuse repeated many times over, so that a simple two-fold division of cultural formation processes may not be so simple to apply in practice. Nevertheless, since one of our main aims is to reconstruct original human behavior and activity, we must make the attempt.

Original human behavior is often reflected archaeologically in at least four major activities: in the case of a tool, for example, there may be

1   acquisition of the raw material;
2   manufacture;
3   use; and finally
4   disposal or discard when the tool is worn out or broken. (The tool may of course be reworked and *recycled*, i.e. repeating stages 2 and 3.)

Similarly a food crop such as wheat will be acquired (harvested), manufactured (processed), used (eaten), and discarded (digested and the waste products excreted) – here one might add a common intermediate stage of storage before use. From the archaeologist's point of view the critical factor is that remains can enter the archaeological record at any one of these stages – a tool may be lost or thrown out as inferior quality during manufacture, a crop may be accidentally burnt and thus preserved during processing. In order accurately to reconstruct the original activity it is therefore crucial to try to understand which of the stages one is looking at. It may be quite easy to identify, say, the first stage for stone tools, because stone quarries can often be recognized by deep holes in the ground with piles of associated waste flakes and

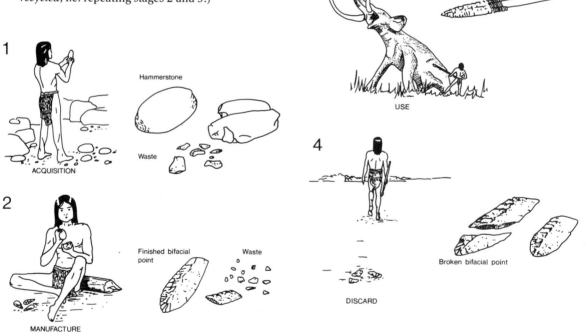

1   ACQUISITION — Hammerstone — Waste
2   MANUFACTURE — Finished bifacial point — Waste
3   USE — Bifacial point in haft
4   DISCARD — Broken bifacial point

An artifact may have entered the archaeological record at any one of these four stages in its life cycle. The archaeologist's task is to determine which stage is represented by the find in question.

blanks which survive well. But it is much more difficult to know beyond reasonable doubt whether a sample of charred plant remains comes from, say, a threshing floor or an occupation floor – and this may also make it difficult to reconstruct the true plant diet, since certain activities may favor the preservation of certain species of plant. This whole controversial issue is discussed further in Chapter 7.

Deliberate burial of valuables or the dead is another major aspect of original human behavior that has left its mark on the archaeological record. In times of conflict or war people often deposit prized possessions in the ground, intending to reclaim them at a later date but sometimes for one reason or another failing to do so. These *hoards* are a prime source of evidence for certain periods, such as the European Bronze Age, for which hoards of metal goods are common, or later Roman Britain, which has yielded buried treasures of silver and other precious metals. The archaeologist, however, may not find it easy to distinguish between hoards originally intended to be reclaimed and valuables buried perhaps to placate supernatural powers (placed for example at a particularly dangerous part of a crossing over a bog) with no reclamation intended.

How archaeologists set about trying to demonstrate belief in supernatural powers and an afterlife is the subject of Chapter 10. Here we may note that, in addition to hoards, the major source of evidence comes from *burial of the dead*, whether in simple graves, elaborate burial mounds, or giant pyramids, usually with grave-goods such as ceramic vessels or weapons, and sometimes with painted tomb-chamber walls, as in ancient Mexico or Egypt. The Egyptians indeed went so far as to mummify their dead (see below) – to preserve them, they hoped, for eternity – as did the Incas of Peru, whose kings were kept in the Temple of the Sun at Cuzco and brought outside for special ceremonies.

Human destruction of the archaeological record might be caused by burials of the kind just described being dug into earlier deposits. But people in the past deliberately or accidentally obliterated traces of their predecessors in innumerable other ways. Rulers, for instance, often destroyed monuments or erased inscriptions belonging to previous chiefs or monarchs. A classic example of this occurred in ancient Egypt, where the heretic pharaoh Akhenaten, who tried to introduce a new religion in the 14th century BC, was reviled by his successors and his major buildings were torn down for reuse in other monuments. A Canadian team led by Donald Redford has spent many years recording some of these reused stone blocks at Thebes and has successfully matched them with the help of a computerized database in order to reconstruct (on paper), like a giant jigsaw, part of one of Akhenaten's temples.

Some human destruction meant to obliterate has inadvertently preserved material for the archaeologist to find. Burning, for example, may not always destroy. It can often improve the chances of survival of a variety of remains such as of plants: the conversion into carbon greatly increases the powers of resistance to the ravages of time. Clay daubing and adobe usually decay, but if a structure has been fired, the mud is baked to the consistency of a brick. In the same way thousands of clay writing tablets from the Near East have been baked accidentally or deliberately in fires and thus preserved. Timbers too may char and survive in structures, or at least leave a clear impression in the hardened mud.

Today human destruction of the archaeological record continues at a frightening pace, through land drainage, plowing, building work, looting, etc. In Chapter 14 we discuss how this affects archaeology generally and what the potential implications are for the future.

NATURAL FORMATION PROCESSES – HOW NATURE AFFECTS WHAT SURVIVES IN THE ARCHAEOLOGICAL RECORD

We saw above how natural formation processes such as river action can disturb or destroy the primary context of archaeological material. Here we will focus on that material itself, and the natural processes that cause decay or lead to preservation.

Practically any archaeological material can survive in exceptional circumstances. Usually, however, inorganic materials survive far better than organic ones.

Inorganic materials

The most common inorganic materials to survive archaeologically are stone, clay, and metals.

Stone tools survive extraordinarily well – some are over 2 million years old. Not surprisingly they have always been our main source of evidence for human activities during the Old Stone Age, even though

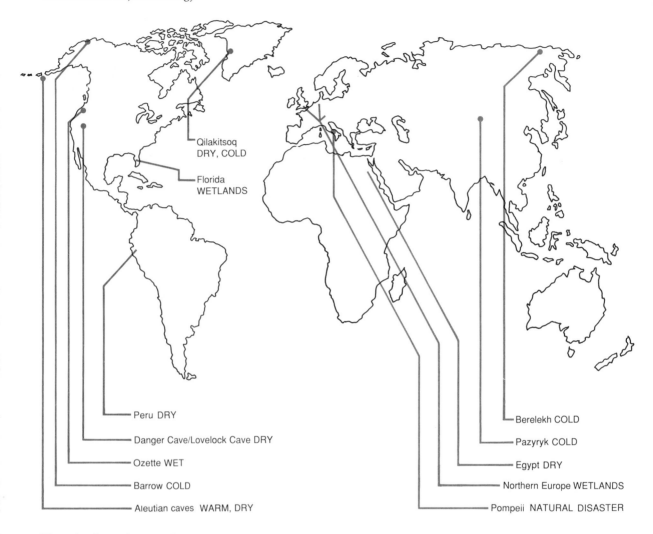

Qilakitsoq
DRY, COLD

Florida
WETLANDS

Peru DRY

Danger Cave/Lovelock Cave DRY

Ozette WET

Barrow COLD

Aleutian caves WARM, DRY

Berelekh COLD

Pazyryk COLD

Egypt DRY

Northern Europe WETLANDS

Pompeii NATURAL DISASTER

The major sites and regions discussed in this chapter where natural formation processes – from wet to very dry or cold conditions – have led to exceptionally good preservation of archaeological remains.

wooden and bone tools (which are less likely to be preserved) may originally have equalled stone ones in their importance. Stone tools sometimes come down to us so little damaged or altered from their primary state that archaeologists can examine microscopic patterns of wear on their cutting edges and learn, for example, whether the tools were used to cut wood or animal hides. This is now a major branch of archaeological inquiry (Chapter 8).

Fired clay, such as pottery and baked mud brick or adobe, is virtually indestructible if well fired. It is therefore again not surprising that for the periods after the introduction of pottery making (some 12,000 years

ago in the Old World, 5000 years ago in the New World) ceramics have traditionally been the archaeologist's main source of evidence. As we saw at the beginning of this chapter, pots can be studied for their shape, surface decoration, mineral content, and even the food or other residues left inside them. Acid soils can damage the surface of fired clay, and porous or badly-fired clay vessels or mud brick can become fragile in humid conditions. However, even disintegrated mud brick can help to assess rebuilding phases in Peruvian villages or Near Eastern tells.

Metals such as gold, silver, and lead survive well. Copper, and bronze with a low-quality alloy, are

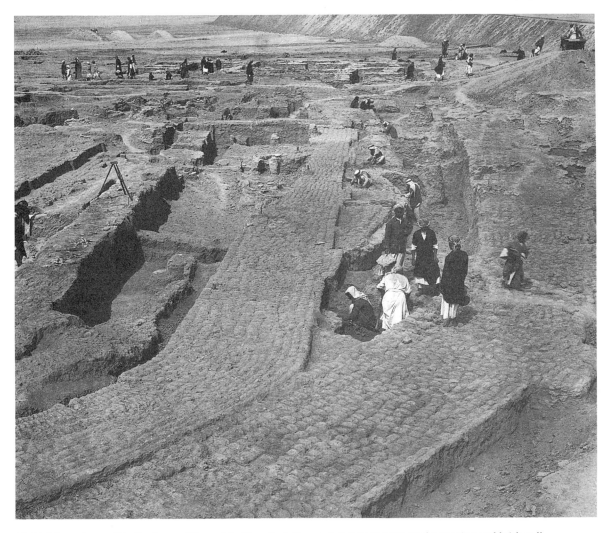

Mud brick survives well in the dry conditions of the Near East. Here archaeologists excavate the massive mud-brick wall foundations of the Oval Temple at Khafaje, Iraq, dating from 2650–2350 BC.

attacked by acid soils, and can become so oxidized that only a green deposit or stain is left. Oxidation is also a rapid and powerful agent of destruction of iron, which rusts and may likewise leave only a discoloration in the soil. However, as will be seen in Chapter 8, it is sometimes possible to retrieve vanished iron objects by making a cast of the hollow they have left within the soil or within a mass of corrosion.

The sea is potentially very destructive, with underwater remains being broken and scattered by currents, waves, or tidal action. It can on the other hand cause metals to be coated with a thick, hard casing of metallic salts (such as chlorides, sulphides, and car-

bonates) from the objects themselves; this helps to preserve the artifacts within. If the remains are simply taken out of the water and not treated, the salts react with air, and give off acid which destroys the remaining metal. But the use of electrolysis – placing the object in a chemical solution and passing a weak current between it and a surrounding metal grill – causes the destructive salts to move slowly from the cathode (object) to the anode (grill), leaving the metal artifact clean and safe. This is a standard procedure in underwater archaeology and is used on all types of objects from cannons (see illus. overleaf) to the finds recently recovered from the *Titanic*.

Metal artifacts from a 1554 shipwreck in the Caribbean, before and after conservation. Use of electrolysis (see p.49) has revealed a unique group of 16th-century armaments, anchors, and navigational instruments.

Organic Materials

Survival of organic materials is determined largely by the matrix (the surrounding material) and by climate (local and regional) – with the occasional influence of natural disasters such as volcanic eruptions, which are often far from disastrous for archaeologists.

The *matrix*, as we saw earlier, is usually some kind of sediment or soil. These vary in their effects on organic material; chalk, for example, preserves human and animal bone well (in addition to inorganic metals). Acid soils destroy bones and wood within a few years, but will leave telltale discolorations where postholes or hut foundations once stood. Similar brown or black marks survive in sandy soils, as do dark silhouettes which used to be skeletons (see Sutton Hoo box, Chapter 3, and also Chapter 11).

But the immediate matrix may in exceptional circumstances have an additional component such as metal ore, salt, or oil. Copper can favor the preservation of organic remains, perhaps by preventing the activity of destructive micro-organisms. The prehistoric copper mines of central and southeast Europe have many remains of wood, leather, and textiles. Organic packing material found between copper ingots on the 14th-century BC Kaş shipwreck, off the coast of Turkey (box, Chapter 9), survived for the same reason.

Salt mines such as those of Iron Age Hallstatt, Austria, have helped preserve organic finds. Even more remarkably, a combination of salt and oil ensured the preservation of a woolly rhinoceros at Starunia, Poland, with skin and hair intact, and the leaves and fruits of tundra vegetation around it. The animal had been carried by a strong current into a pool saturated with crude oil and salt from a natural oil seep, which prevented decomposition: bacteria could not operate in these conditions, while salt had permeated the skin and preserved it. Similarly, the asphalt pits of La Brea, Los Angeles, are world famous for the fine condition of the skeletons of a wide range of prehistoric animals and birds recovered from them.

Climate plays an important role too in the preservation of organic remains. Occasionally one can speak of the "local climate" of an environment such as a cave. Caves are natural "conservatories" because their interiors are protected from outside climatic effects, and (in the case of limestone caves) their alkaline conditions permit excellent preservation. If undisturbed by floods or the trampling feet of animals and people, they can preserve bones and such fragile remains as footprints, and sometimes even plant fibers such as the short length of rope found in the Upper Paleolithic decorated cave of Lascaux, France.

More usually, however, it is the regional climate that is important. *Tropical climates* are the most destructive, with their combination of heavy rains, acid soils, warm temperatures, high humidity, erosion, and wealth of vegetation and insect life. Tropical rainforests can overwhelm a site remarkably quickly, with roots that dislodge masonry and tear buildings apart, while torrential downpours gradually destroy paint and plasterwork, and woodwork rots away completely. Archaeologists in southern Mexico, for example, constantly have to battle to keep back the jungle. From one field season to the next, primary growth of more than 2 m (6 ft 7 in) in height may appear in areas that had been totally cleared the year before. On the other hand, one can also look on jungle conditions as benign, in that they hinder looters from easily reaching even more sites than they do already.

Temperate climates, as in much of Europe and North America, are not beneficial, as a rule, to organic materials; their relatively warm but variable temperatures and fluctuating precipitation combine to accelerate the processes of decay. In some circumstances, however, local conditions can counteract these processes. At the Roman fort of Vindolanda, near Hadrian's Wall in northern England, over 1000 letters, written in ink on wafer-thin sheets of birch and alderwood, have been found by the archaeologist Robin Birley. The fragments, dating to about AD 100, have survived because of the soil's unusual chemical condition: clay compacted between layers in the site created oxygen-free pockets (the exclusion of oxygen is vital to the preservation of organic materials), while chemicals produced by bracken, bone, and other remains effectively made the land sterile in that locality, thus preventing disturbance by vegetation and other forms of life.

A different example of freak preservation in temperate conditions occurred at Potterne, a Late Bronze Age refuse heap in southern England dating to about 1000 BC. Whereas bones normally become mineralized through the percolation of groundwater, in this site bones – as well as unburned seeds, and even pottery – have been preserved because a mineral called glauconite (a mica) has translocated from the greensand bedrock and entered into a stable compound with the organic materials.

Natural disasters sometimes preserve sites, including organic remains, for the archaeologist. The most common are violent storms, such as that which covered the coastal Neolithic village of Skara Brae, Orkney Islands, with sand, the mudslide that engulfed the prehistoric village of Ozette on America's Northwest Coast (box overleaf), or volcanic eruptions such

WET PRESERVATION: THE OZETTE SITE

Ozette
UNITED STATES

A special kind of waterlogging occurred at the Ozette site, Washington, on the U.S. Northwest Coast. About AD 1750, a huge mudslide created by a seasonally swollen underground stream completely buried part of a whale-hunting settlement. The village lay protected for two centuries – but not forgotten, for the descendants of the village kept the memory of their ancestors' home alive. Then the sea began to strip away the mud, and it seemed as if the site would fall prey to looters. Local people called on the government to excavate the site and to protect the remains. Richard Daugherty was appointed to organize the excavation of the site.

As the archaeologists cleared away the mud with high-pressure hoses, a wealth of organic material came to view. Daugherty and his team found several cedarwood long houses, up to 21 m (68 ft 3 in) in length and 14 m (45 ft 6 in) wide, with adzed and carved panels (painted with black designs including wolves and thunderbirds), roof-support posts, and low partition walls. These houses contained hearths, cooking platforms, sleeping benches, and mats.

Over 50,000 artifacts were recovered in a fine state of preservation – almost half in wood or other plant material. The most spectacular find was a huge block of red cedar, a meter high, carved in the form of a whale's dorsal fin, and inlaid with over 700 sea-otter teeth arranged in the shape of a thunderbird holding a serpent in its claws. Even ferns and cedar leaves had survived together with an abundance of whale bones.

PERISHABLE ARTIFACTS FROM OZETTE

Woven material 1330 baskets • 1466 mats • 142 hats • 37 cradles • 96 tump lines • 49 harpoon sheaths
Weaving equipment 14 loom uprights • 14 roller bars • 10 swords • 23 spindle whorls • 6 spools
Hunting equipment 115 wooden bows and fragments • 1534 arrow shafts • 5189 wooden arrow points • 124 harpoon shafts • 22 harpoon finger rests • 161 plugs from seal-skin floats
Fishing equipment 131 bent wood halibut hooks • 607 curved halibut hook shanks • 117 blanks for making hooks • 7 herring rakes • 57 single-barbed hooks • 15 double-barbed hooks
Containers 1001 wooden boxes and fragments • 120 wooden bowls and fragments • 37 wooden trays
Watercraft 361 canoe paddles and fragments • 14 canoe bailers • 14 canoe fragments
Miscellaneous 40 game paddles • 45 carved miniature items (canoes, figurines, etc) • 52 carved wooden clubs • 1 carved effigy of a whale fin inlaid with sea-otter teeth

General view from the south of the area around the Ozette site. Vancouver Island lies on the horizon.

A Makah Indian crew member (above) cleans a basket found on the site. (Above right) Another crew member measures a piece of wood in one of the Ozette houses.

Richard Daugherty (below) with the carved cedar representation of the dorsal fin of a whale.

Wooden clubs from the site. (Above, left to right) Head of a seal club; an owl head on a shaman's club; a face on the handle end of a seal club.

53

DRY PRESERVATION: THE TOMB OF TUTANKHAMUN

The arid conditions that prevail in Egypt have helped preserve a wide range of ancient materials, ranging from numerous written documents on papyrus (made of the pith of a Nile water plant) to two full-size wooden boats buried beside the Great Pyramid at Giza. But the best known and most spectacular array of objects was that discovered in 1922 by Howard Carter and Lord Carnarvon in the tomb at Thebes of the pharaoh Tutankhamun, dating to the 14th century BC.

Tutankhamun had a short reign and was relatively insignificant in Egyptian history, a fact reflected in his burial, a poor one by pharaonic standards. But within the small tomb, originally built for someone else, was a wealth of treasure. For Tutankhamun was buried with everything he might need in the next life. The entrance corridor and the four chambers were crammed with thousands of individual grave goods. They include objects of precious metal, like the jewelry and famous gold mask, and food and clothing. But wooden objects, such as statues, chests, shrines, and two of the three coffins, make up a large part of the tomb's contents. The human remains – the mummies of the king and his two stillborn children – have been the subject of scientific analysis more than once. A lock of hair found separately among the grave goods has been analyzed and is thought to come from a mummy in another tomb believed to be Tiye, the young king's grandmother.

The grave furniture was not all originally intended for Tutankhamun. Some of it had been made for other members of his family, and then hastily adopted when the young king died unexpectedly. There were also touching items, such as a chair the king had used as a child, and a simple reed stick mounted in gold labeled as "A reed which His Majesty cut with his own hand." Even wreaths and funerary bouquets had survived in the dry conditions, left on the second and third coffins by mourners.

A cutaway view of the tomb and its treasures, as found in 1922.

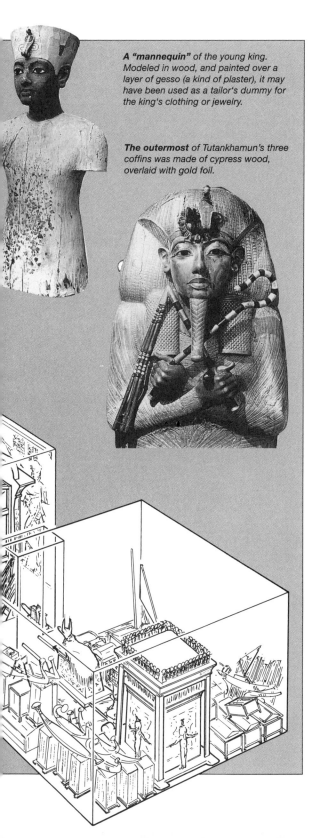

A "mannequin" of the young king. Modeled in wood, and painted over a layer of gesso (a kind of plaster), it may have been used as a tailor's dummy for the king's clothing or jewelry.

The outermost of Tutankhamun's three coffins was made of cypress wood, overlaid with gold foil.

as that of Vesuvius which buried and preserved Roman Pompeii under a blanket of ash (box, Chapter 1). Volcanic eruptions in El Salvador in about AD 260 deposited a thick and widespread layer of ash over a densely populated area of Maya settlement, where work by Payson Sheets and his associates has uncovered a variety of remains in the Zapotitán Valley, including preserved agricultural furrows. As will be seen in Chapter 6, volcanic ash has even preserved part of a prehistoric forest at Miesenheim in Germany.

Apart from these special circumstances, the survival of organic materials is limited to cases involving extremes of moisture: that is, arid, frozen, or waterlogged conditions.

Preservation of Organic Materials: Extreme Conditions

Dry Environments. Great aridity or dryness prevents decay through the shortage of water, which ensures that many destructive micro-organisms are unable to flourish. Archaeologists first became aware of the phenomenon in Egypt (see Tutankhamun box), where much of the Nile Valley has such a dry atmosphere that bodies of the predynastic period (before 3000 BC) have survived intact, with skin, hair, and nails, without any artificial mummification or coffins – the corpses were simply placed in shallow graves in the sand. Rapid drying out or desiccation, plus the draining qualities of the sand, produced such spectacular preservative effects that they probably suggested the practice of mummification to the later Egyptians of the dynastic period.

The pueblo dwellers of the American Southwest (*c.* AD 700–1400) buried their dead in dry caves and rockshelters where, as in Egypt, natural desiccation took place: these are not therefore true, humanly created mummies, although they are often referred to as such. The bodies survive, sometimes wrapped in fur blankets or tanned skins, and in such good condition that it has been possible to study hair styles. Clothing (from fiber sandals to string aprons) also remains, together with a wide range of goods such as basketry, feathered ornaments, and leather. Some far earlier sites in the same region also contain organic remains: Danger Cave, Utah (occupied from 9000 BC onward) yielded wooden arrows, trap springs, knife handles, and other wooden tools; Lovelock Cave, Nevada, had nets; while caves near Durango, Colorado, had preserved maize cobs, squashes, and sunflower and mustard seeds. Plant finds of this type have been crucial in helping archaeologists to reconstruct ancient diet (Chapter 7).

The coastal dwellers of central and southern Peru lived – and died – in a similarly dry environment, so that it is possible today still to see the tattoos on their desiccated bodies, and admire the huge and dazzlingly colorful textiles from cemeteries at Ica and Nazca, as well as basketry and featherwork, and also maize cobs and other items of food.

Finally, a slightly different phenomenon occurred in the Aleutian Islands, off the west coast of Alaska, where the dead were kept and naturally preserved in volcanically warmed caves that were extremely dry. Here the islanders seem to have enhanced the natural desiccation by periodically drying the bodies by wiping or suspension over a fire; in some cases they removed the internal organs and placed dry grass in the cavity.

Cold Environments. Natural refrigeration can hold the processes of decay in check for thousands of years. Perhaps the first frozen finds to be discovered were the numerous remains of mammoths encountered in the permafrost (permanently frozen soil) of Siberia, many with their flesh, hair, and stomach contents intact. The unlucky creatures probably fell into crevices in snow, and were buried by silt in what became a giant deep-freeze. The best known are those of Beresovka and Berelekh, the latter location revealing more than 140 mammoths. Preservation can be so good that dogs find the meat quite palatable and have to be kept well away from the carcasses.

The most famous frozen archaeological remains are undoubtedly those from the burial mounds of steppe nomads at Pazyryk in the Altai, southern Siberia, dating to the Iron Age, about 400 BC. They comprise pits dug deep into the ground, lined with logs, and covered with a low cairn of stones. They could only have been dug in the warm season, before the ground froze solid. Any warm air in the graves rose and deposited its moisture on the stones of the cairn; moisture also gradually infiltrated down into the burial chambers, and froze so hard there during the harsh winter that it never thawed during subsequent summers, since the cairns were poor conductors of heat and shielded the pits from the warming and drying effects of wind and sun. Consequently, even the most fragile materials have survived intact – despite the boiling water that had to be used by the Soviet excavator, Sergei Rudenko, to recover them.

The Pazyryk bodies had been placed inside log coffins, with wooden pillows, and survived so well that their spectacular tattoos can be seen. Clothing included linen shirts, decorated caftans, aprons, stockings, and headdresses of felt and leather. There were also rugs, wall-coverings, tables laden with food, and horse carcasses complete with elaborate bridles, saddles, and other trappings.

Similar standards of preservation have also been encountered in other circumpolar regions such as Greenland and Alaska. The Barrow site is a good case in point (see box). Another Alaskan example comes from St Lawrence Island, where the permafrost has yielded the body of an Eskimo woman with tattooed arms dating to the early centuries AD. More southerly regions can produce the same effect at high altitude, such as the Inca-period tomb at Cerra El Plomo in the

Frozen conditions of southern Siberia helped to preserve the remarkable finds from burial mounds of steppe nomads at Pazyryk dating from about 400 BC. (Left) Tattoo pattern on the torso and arms of a chieftain. (Right) Drawing of part of a Pazyryk wall-hanging in appliquéd felt, showing a horseman approaching an enthroned figure.

COLD PRESERVATION: THE BARROW SITE

Barrow
ALASKA

Many former living sites of Eskimo, such as those of the Thule culture north of Hudson Bay, have fragile materials in a good state of preservation: wood, bone, ivory, feathers, hair, and eggshell. In the early 1980s, a driftwood-and-sod house was excavated by Albert Dekin and his colleagues at Utqiagvik, modern Barrow, on Alaska's north coast. Built by Inupiat Eskimo about 500 years ago, the house had been destroyed one winter's night by a storm which brought a mass of ice crashing down on its sleeping occupants. Like the Pazyryk tombs (see main text), the ruined house had been infiltrated by summer meltwater, which then froze permanently. Inside the solid earth, the excavators found the intact bodies of two women, while the bones of three youngsters lay nearer the surface (and thus had not been permanently frozen). Dekin and his colleagues also found clothing of caribou and sealskin; implements in a wide range of materials, including a wooden bucket; and tools and weapons arranged in kits according to function and season. Winter hunting equipment, for example – including snow goggles, ice picks, and harpoons – was stored in skin bags.

An autopsy on the two women – carried out with the permission of the modern community, to which all the bodies were later returned for reburial – showed that they had been adequately nourished in life, but had suffered from anthracosis (black lungs, from breathing smoke and oil-lamp fumes during the long winters) and also atherosclerosis (a narrowing of the arteries caused by deposits of cholesterol and fat, the result of a diet rich in whale and seal blubber). The older woman had recovered from pneumonia, but may also have suffered from trichinosis, a painful parasite infection of the muscles, perhaps caused by eating raw polar-bear meat.

One of the two female bodies (above; below) found on the house floor. KEY: a, wood snow goggles; b, skin-wrapped arrowpoints; c, skin bag with weights; d, hide fragment; e, whalebone ice pick; f, polar-bear-hide mitten; g, ivory comb; h, baleen comb; i, wood shaft; j, wood buckets; k, wood ladel; l, hide blanket; m, skin bag used as pillow; n, boots; o, gut bag; p, antler arrowpoint; q, baleen container; r, skin bag with sewing kit; s, bird-skin bag; t, slate blade; u, wood slat; v, walrus hide; w, ceramic pot.

50 cm
20 in

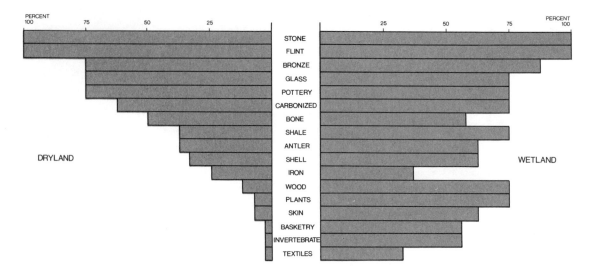

Survival rates for different materials in wet and ordinary dryland sites. Organic remains survive best in wetlands.

Andes, which contained the naturally freeze-dried corpse of a boy wearing a camelid-wool poncho.

In Greenland, the Eskimo bodies of Qilakitsoq, dating to the 15th century AD, had also undergone natural freeze-drying in their rock-overhang graves protected from the elements; their tissue had shrunk and become discolored, but tattoos were still visible (see Chapter 11), and their clothes were in particularly fine condition.

A more modern example of natural refrigeration can be found in the Arctic graves of three British sailors who died in 1846. The bodies were perfectly preserved in the ice of northern Canada's Beechey Island. In 1984 a team led by the Canadian anthropologist Owen Beattie simply removed samples of bone and tissue for an autopsy, before reburying the corpses.

Waterlogged Environments. A useful distinction in land archaeology (as opposed to archaeology beneath the sea) can be drawn between dryland and wetland sites. The great majority of sites are "dry" in the sense that moisture content is low and preservation of organic remains is poor. Wetland sites include all those found in lakes, swamps, marshes, fens, and peat bogs. Here organic materials are effectively sealed in a wet and airless (anaerobic) environment which favors their preservation, as long as the waterlogging is more or less permanent up to the time of excavation. (If a wet site dries out, even only seasonally, decomposition of the organic materials can occur.) One of the pioneers of wetland archaeology in Britain, John Coles, estimates that on a wet site often 75–90 percent,

sometimes 100 percent, of the finds are organic. Little or none of this material, such as wood, leather, textiles, basketry, and plant remains of all kinds, would survive on most dryland sites. It is for this reason that archaeologists are turning their attention more and more to the rich sources of evidence about past human activities to be found on wet sites. Growing threats from drainage and peatcutting in the wetlands, which form only about 6 percent of the world's total land area, give this work an added urgency.

Wetlands vary a great deal in their preservative qualities. Acidic peat bogs are kind to wood and plant remains, but may destroy bone, iron, and even pottery. The famous lake sites of the Alpine regions of Switzerland, Italy, France, and southern Germany on the other hand preserve most materials well.

Peat bogs, nearly all of which occur in northern latitudes, are some of the most important environments for wetland archaeology. The Somerset Levels in southern England, for example, have been the scene not only of excavations earlier this century to recover the well-preserved Iron Age lake villages of Glastonbury and Meare (box, Chapter 1), but of a much wider campaign in the last two decades that has unearthed numerous wooden trackways (including the world's "oldest road," a 6000-year-old 1.6-km (1-mile) stretch of track), and many details about early woodworking skills (Chapter 8), and the ancient environment (Chapter 6). On the continent of Europe, and in Ireland, peat bogs have likewise preserved many trackways – sometimes with evidence for the wooden carts that ran along them – and other fragile remains.

Wet site archaeology began in 19th-century Switzerland with the discovery of wooden piles when lake levels were low.

Other types of European wetlands, such as coastal marshes, have yielded dugout logboats, paddles, even fish-nets and fish-weirs.

Bog bodies, however, are undoubtedly the best-known finds from the peat bogs of northwest Europe. Most of them date from the Iron Age. The degree of preservation varies widely, and depends on the particular conditions in which the corpses were deposited. Most individuals met a violent death and were probably either executed as criminals or killed as a sacrifice before being thrown into the bog. The best-preserved examples, such as Denmark's Tollund man, were in a truly remarkable state, with only the staining caused by bogwater and tannic acid as an indication that they were ancient rather than modern. Within the skin, the bones have often disappeared, as have most of the internal organs, although the stomach and its contents may survive (Chapter 7). In Florida, prehistoric human brains have even been recovered (Chapter 11).

Occasionally, waterlogged conditions can occur inside burial mounds – a temperate-climate version of the Siberian phenomenon. The oak-coffin burials of Bronze Age northern Europe, and most notably those of Denmark dating to about 1000 BC, had an inner core of stones packed round the tree-trunk coffin, with a round barrow built above. Water infiltrated the inside of the mound and by combining with tannin exuding from the tree trunks, set up acidic conditions which destroyed the skeleton but preserved the skin (discolored like the bog bodies), hair, and ligaments of the bodies inside the coffins, as well as their clothing and objects such as birch-bark pails.

A somewhat similar phenomenon occurred with the ships that the Vikings used as coffins. The Oseberg ship in Norway, for example, held the body of a Viking queen of about AD 800, and was buried in clay, covered by a packing of stones and a layer of peat that sealed it in and ensured its preservation.

Lake-dwellings have rivaled bog bodies in popular interest ever since the first discovery of wooden piles or house supports in the Swiss lakes well over a century ago. The romantic notion of whole villages built on stilts over the water has, thanks to detailed research since the 1940s, given way to the idea of predominantly lake-edge settlements. The range of preserved material is astonishing, not simply wooden structures and artifacts, and textiles but, at Neolithic Charavines in France for example, nuts, berries, and other fruits.

Perhaps the greatest contribution to archaeology lake-dwellings and also other European wetland sites have made in recent years, however, is to provide abundant well-preserved timber for the study of tree rings, the annual growth rings in trees. In Chapter 4 we explore the breakthrough this has brought about in the establishment of an accurate tree-ring chronology for parts of northern Europe stretching back thousands of years.

One might add that another rich source of waterlogged and preserved timbers in land archaeology can be found in the old waterfronts of towns and cities. Archaeologists have been particularly successful in uncovering parts of London's Roman and medieval waterfront, but such discoveries are not restricted to Europe. In the early 1980s New York City archaeolog-

Reconstruction of Okeechobee burial platform, Florida.

ists excavated a well-preserved 18th-century ship that had been sunk to support the East River waterfront there. Underwater archaeology itself, in rivers and lakes and especially beneath the sea, is not surprisingly the richest source of all for waterlogged finds (box, Chapter 3).

The major archaeological problem with waterlogged finds, and particularly wood, is that they deteriorate rapidly when they are uncovered, beginning to dry and crack almost at once. They therefore need to be kept wet until they can be treated or freeze-dried at a laboratory. Conservation measures of this kind help to explain the enormous cost of wetland and underwater archaeology. It has been estimated that "wet archaeology" costs four times as much as "dry." But the rewards, as we have seen, are enormous.

The rewards in the future, too, will be very great. Florida, for example, has about 1.2 million hectares (3 million acres) of peat deposits, and on present evidence these probably contain more organic artifacts than anywhere else in the world. So far the wetlands here have yielded the largest number of prehistoric watercraft from any one region, together with totems, masks, and figurines dating as far back as 5000 BC. In the Okeechobee Basin, for instance, a 1st-millennium BC burial platform has been found, decorated with a series of large carved wooden totem posts, representing an array of animals and birds. After a fire, the platform had collapsed into its pond. Yet it is only recently that wet finds in Florida have come to us from careful excavation rather than through the drainage that is destroying large areas of peat deposit and, with them, untold quantities of the richest kinds of archaeological evidence.

SUMMARY

The archaeological evidence available to us depends on a number of important factors: first, what people, past and present, have done to it (cultural formation processes); second, what natural conditions such as soil and climate have preserved or destroyed (natural formation processes); and third, our ability to find, recognize, recover, and conserve it. We can do nothing about the first two factors, being at the mercy of the elements and previous human behavior. But the third factor, which is the subject of this book, is constantly improving, as we understand better the processes of decay and destruction, and design research strategies and technical aids to make the most of what archaeological evidence actually survives.

Further Reading

Good introductions to the problems of differential preservation of archaeological materials can be found in:

Binford, L.R. 1983. *In Pursuit of the Past: Decoding the Archaeological Record.* Thames & Hudson: London & New York.

Clark, J.G.D. 1960. *Archaeology and Society.* (3rd ed.) Methuen: London; Barnes & Noble: New York. (Chapter 3.)

Coles, B. & J. 1989. *People of the Wetlands: Bogs, Bodies and Lake-Dwellers.* Thames & Hudson: London & New York.

Dimbleby, G. 1978. *Plants and Archaeology.* Paladin: London. (Chapter 7.)

Nash, D.T. and Petraglia, M.D. (eds.). 1987. *Natural Formation Processes and the Archaeological Record.* British Arch. Reports, Int. Series 352: Oxford.

Schiffer, M.B. 1976. *Behavioral Archaeology.* Academic Press: New York & London.

Schiffer, M.B. 1987. *Formation Processes of the Archaeological Record.* University of New Mexico Press: Albuquerque.

3
Where?
Survey and Excavation
of Sites and Features

It has been said that the person with a clear objective and a plan of campaign is more likely to succeed than the person with neither, and this is certainly true of archaeology. The military overtones of the words "objective" and "campaign" are entirely appropriate for archaeology, which often requires the recruitment, funding, and coordination of large numbers of people in complex field projects. It is no accident that two pioneers of field techniques – Pitt-Rivers and Mortimer Wheeler – were old soldiers (box, Chapter 1). Today, thanks to the impact of such practitioners, and the major influence of the New Archaeology with its desire for scientific rigor, archaeologists try to make explicit at the outset of research what their objectives are and what their plan of campaign will be. This procedure is commonly called devising a *research design*, which broadly has four stages:

1 the *formulation* of a research strategy to resolve a particular question or test a hypothesis or idea;
2 the *collecting and recording of evidence* against which to test that idea, usually by the organization of a team of specialists and the conducting of fieldwork;
3 the *processing and analysis* of that evidence and its *interpretation* in the light of the original idea to be tested;
4 the *publication* of the results in journal articles, books etc.

There is seldom if ever a straightforward progression from stage 1 to stage 4. In real life the research strategy will constantly be refined as evidence is collected and analyzed. All too often, and inexcusably, publication may be neglected (Chapter 14). But in the best planned research the overall objective – the broad question or questions to be answered – will stand even if the strategy for achieving it alters.

In Part II (Chapters 5–12) we shall study some of the research strategies archaeologists adopt in order to answer important questions about how societies were organized, what the ancient environment was like, the kinds of foods people ate, the tools they made, their trading contacts and beliefs, and indeed *why* societies evolved and changed over thousands of years. Chapter 13 then examines a small number of projects in detail, to show how research is carried out in practice, from start to finish.

In this chapter, however, we will focus on stage 2 of the research process – on the methods and techniques archaeologists use to obtain evidence against which to test their ideas. It should not be forgotten that suitable evidence can often come just as well from old as from new fieldwork: David Clarke's reanalysis of the Glastonbury Iron Age village excavations (box, Chapter 1) demonstrates this point. Much potentially rich and rewarding material also lies locked away in museum and institution vaults, waiting to be analyzed by imaginative modern techniques. It is only recently, for example, that the plant remains discovered in Tutankhamun's tomb in the 1920s (box, Chapter 2) have received thorough analysis. Yet it remains true that the great majority of archaeological research is still dependent on the collection of new material by fresh fieldwork.

Traditionally, fieldwork used to be seen almost exclusively in terms of the discovery and excavation of individual sites. Today, however, while sites and their excavation remain of paramount importance, the focus has broadened to take in whole landscapes, and surface survey at sites in addition to – or instead of – excavation. Archaeologists have become aware that there is a great range of "off-site" or "non-site" evidence, from scatters of artifacts to features such as plowmarks and field boundaries, that provides important information about human exploitation of the environment. The study of entire landscapes by regional survey is thus now a major part of archaeological fieldwork. Archaeologists have also become increasingly aware of the high cost and destructiveness of excavation. Site surface survey and subsurface detection using non-destructive remote sensing devices have therefore likewise taken on a new importance.

We may usefully distinguish between *methods used in the discovery* of archaeological sites and non-site features or artifact scatters, and those employed *once those sites and features have been discovered*, which include detailed survey and selective excavation at individual sites.

DISCOVERING ARCHAEOLOGICAL SITES AND FEATURES

One major task of the archaeologist is to locate and record the whereabouts of sites and features. In this section we will be reviewing some of the principal techniques of site discovery. But we should not forget that many monuments have never been lost to posterity: the massive pyramids of Egypt, or of Teotihuacan near modern Mexico City, have always been known to succeeding generations, as have the Great Wall of China or many of the buildings in the Forum in Rome. Their exact function or purpose may indeed have aroused controversy down the centuries, but their presence, the fact of their existence, was never in doubt. Nor can one credit archaeologists with the discovery of all those sites that were once lost. No one has ever made a precise count but a significant number of sites known today were found by accident, from the decorated cave of Lascaux in southwest France, revealed by schoolboys in World War II, to the terracotta army of China's first emperor, unearthed in 1974 by farmers digging for a well, or the countless underwater wrecks first spotted by fishermen, sponge-gatherers, and sport-divers. Construction workers building new roads, subways, dams, and office blocks have made their fair share of discoveries too – for example, the *Templo Mayor* or Great Temple of the Aztecs in Mexico City (box, Chapter 14).

Nevertheless it is archaeologists who have systematically attempted to record these sites, and it is archaeologists who seek out the full range of sites and features, large or small, that make up the great diversity of past landscapes. How do they achieve this?

A practical distinction can be drawn between site discovery conducted at ground level (*ground reconnaissance*) and discovery from the air or from space (*aerial reconnaissance*), although any one field project will usually employ both types of reconnaissance.

Partially buried but never lost: buildings in the Forum of ancient Rome, as depicted in an 18th-century etching by the Italian artist, Piranesi.

The Great Wall of China, over 2000 km (1250 miles) long, was begun in the 3rd century BC. Like the Forum, it has never been lost to posterity.

Ground Reconnaissance

Methods for identifying individual sites include consultation of documentary sources and place-name evidence, but primarily actual fieldwork, whether the monitoring of building developers' progress in salvage archaeology, or reconnaissance survey in circumstances where the archaeologist is more of a free agent.

Documentary Sources. In Chapter 1 we saw how Schliemann's firm belief in the historical accuracy of Homer's writings led directly to the discovery of ancient Troy. A more recent success story of the same kind was the location and excavation by Helge and Anne Stine Ingstad of the Viking settlement of L'Anse aux Meadows in Newfoundland, thanks in large part to clues contained in the medieval Viking sagas. Much of modern biblical archaeology concerns itself with the search all over the Near East for hard evidence of the places – as well as the people and events – described in the Old and New Testaments. Treated objectively as one possible source of information about Near Eastern sites, the Bible can indeed be a rich source of documentary material, but there is certainly the danger that belief in the absolute religious truth of the texts can cloud an impartial assessment of their archaeological validity.

Much research in biblical archaeology involves attempting to link named biblical sites with archaeologically known ones – an effort spurred on in the 1970s by the discovery at Tell Mardikh (ancient Ebla), Syria, by an Italian team of Bronze Age writing tablets that refer to biblical cities. Place-name evidence, however, can also lead to actual discoveries of new archaeological sites. In southwest Europe, for example, many prehistoric stone tombs have been found thanks to old names printed on maps that incorporate local words for "stone" or "tomb."

Early maps and old street names are even more important in helping archaeologists work out the former plans of historic towns. In England, for example, it is possible in the better documented medieval towns to map many of the streets, houses, churches, and castles back to the 12th century AD, or even earlier, using this kind of evidence. These maps then form a reliable basis on which to decide where it would be most profitable to carry out survey work and excavation.

Salvage Archaeology. In this specialized work – discussed more fully in Chapter 14 – the role of the archaeologist is to locate and record as many sites as possible before they are destroyed by new roads,

Salvage archaeology: the Aztec temple of Ehecatl-Quetzalcoatl, discovered during the excavation of the Piño Suarez subway station, Mexico City.

buildings, or dams, or by peatcutting and drainage in wetland environments. Proper liaison with the developer should allow archaeological survey to take place in advance along the projected line of road or in the path of development. Important sites thus discovered may require excavation, and in some cases can even cause construction plans to be altered. Certain archaeological remains unearthed during the digging of subways in Rome and Mexico City were incorporated into the final station architecture.

Reconnaissance Survey. How does the archaeologist set about locating sites, other than through documentary sources and salvage work? A conventional and still valid method is to look for the most prominent remains in a landscape, particularly surviving remnants of walled buildings, and burial mounds such as those in eastern North America or Wessex in southern Britain. But many sites are visible on the surface only as a scatter of artifacts and thus require more thorough survey – what we may call reconnaissance survey – to be detected. Furthermore in recent years, as archaeologists have become more interested in reconstructing the full human use of the landscape, they have begun to realize that there are very faint scatters of artifacts that might not qualify as sites, but which nevertheless represent significant human activity. Scholars such as Robert Dunnell and William Dancey have therefore suggested that these "off-site" or "non-site" areas (that is, areas with a low density of artifacts) should be located and recorded, which can only be done by systematic survey work involving careful sampling procedures (see below). This approach is particularly useful in areas where people leading a mobile way of life have left only a sparse archaeological record, as in much of Africa: see further discussion in Chapter 5.

Reconnaissance survey has become important for another major reason: the growth of regional studies. Thanks to the pioneering researches of scholars such as Gordon Willey in the Virú Valley, Peru, and William T. Sanders in the Basin of Mexico, archaeologists increasingly seek to study settlement patterns – the distribution of sites across the landscape within a given region. The significance of this work for the under-standing of past societies is discussed further in Chapter 5. Here we may note its impact on archaeolo-gical fieldwork: it is rarely enough now simply to locate an individual site and then to survey it and/or excavate it in isolation from other sites. Whole regions need to be explored. This necessarily involves a program of survey.

In the last few decades, survey has developed from being simply a preliminary stage in fieldwork (looking for appropriate sites to excavate) to a more or less independent kind of inquiry, an area of research in its own right which can produce information quite diffe-rent from that achieved by digging. In some cases excavation may not take place at all, perhaps because permission to dig was not forthcoming, or because of a lack of time or funds – modern excavation is slow and costly, whereas survey is cheap, quick, relatively non-destructive, and requires only maps, compasses, and tapes. Usually, however, archaeologists deliberately choose a surface approach as a source of regional data in order to investigate specific questions that interest them and that excavation could not answer.

Reconnaissance survey encompasses a broad range of techniques: no longer just the identification of sites and the recording or collection of surface artifacts, but sometimes also the sampling of natural and mineral resources such as stone and clay. Much survey today is aimed at studying the spatial distribution of human activities, variations between regions, changes in population through time, and relationships between people, land, and resources (see Melos box).

Reconnaissance Survey in Practice. For questions formulated in regional terms, it is necessary to collect data on a corresponding scale, but in a way which provides a maximum of information for a minimum of cost and effort. First, the region to be surveyed needs to be defined: its boundaries may be either natural (such as a valley or island), cultural (the extent of an artifact style) or purely arbitrary, though natural boundaries are the easiest to establish.

The area's history of development needs to be examined, not only to familiarize oneself with pre-vious archaeological work and with the local materials but also to assess the extent to which surface material may have been covered or removed by geomorphologi-cal processes. There is little point, for example, in searching for prehistoric material in sediments only recently laid down by river action. Other factors may have affected surface evidence as well. In much of Africa, for example, great animal herds or burrowing animals will often have disturbed surface material, so that the archaeologist may be able to examine only very broad distribution patterns. Geologists and en-vironmental specialists can generally provide useful advice in these matters.

This background information will help determine the intensity of surface coverage of the survey. Other factors to take into consideration are the time and resources available, and how easy it is actually to reach and record an area. Arid (dry) and semi-arid environ-ments with little vegetation are among the best for this type of work, whereas in equatorial rainforest survey may be limited to soil exposures along river banks, unless time and labor permit the cutting of trails to form a survey grid. Many regions, of course, contain a variety of landscapes, and a single survey strategy is often inadequate to cover them. Flexibility of approach is required, with the area "stratified" into zones of differing visibility, and an appropriate technique de-vised for each. Moreover, it must be remembered that some archaeological phases (with diagnostic artifacts or pottery styles) are more "visible" than others, and that mobile hunter-gatherer or pastoral communities leave a very different – and generally sparser – imprint on the landscape than do agricultural or urban communities (see Chapter 5). All these factors must be taken into account when planning the search patterns and recovery techniques.

Another point to consider is whether material should be collected or merely examined for its associa-tions and context (where context is disturbed, as in parts of Africa, mentioned above, collection is often the most sensible option). And should collection be total or partial? Usually, a sampling method is employed (see box, pp. 66, 67).

There are two basic kinds of surface survey: the *unsystematic* and the *systematic*. The former is the simplest, involving walking across each part of the area (for example, each plowed field), scanning the strip of ground along one's path, collecting or examin-ing artifacts on the surface, and recording their location together with that of any surface features. It is generally felt, however, that the results may be biased and misleading. Walkers have an inherent desire to find material, and will therefore tend to concentrate on

REGIONAL SURVEY ON MELOS

In 1976 and 1977 a team led by John Cherry undertook a survey on the Greek island of Melos in the eastern Mediterranean. The island's relatively small size (151 sq. km or 94 sq. miles) made it an ideal unit for investigation. The survey aimed to study several questions, including how the number, size, and location of sites have changed through time. The investigation was linked to Colin Renfrew's excavations on the island at the Bronze Age site of Phylakopi (see Chapter 13), and a major aim was to ascertain whether this was the only settlement site on Melos during most of the 2nd millennium BC.

It was decided to undertake an intensive survey of all parts of the island, but severe constraints on time, funds, and personnel meant that only a 20 percent sample could be examined. The survey design was a systematic random sample (see box overleaf) made up of transects, the first chosen at random, the rest at intervals of 5 km (3.1 miles) from it. These transects comprised kilometer-wide strips running north-south across the island. Some areas took up to 3 hours to reach, being inaccessible to vehicles. Each transect was examined by groups of 10 to 12 people, in 1 or 2 teams, walking in parallel lines spaced 15 m to 25 m (49–82 ft) apart. In this way an average of 1.5 to 2 sq. km (0.6–0.8 sq. miles) per day was covered.

The location of sites was plotted on detailed maps prepared from air photographs, and their approximate extent and any noteworthy features were also recorded. Further mapping was undertaken using photographs

***The random sample** transects selected for intensive study.*

taken by radio-controlled cameras attached to low-level tethered balloons. Little material was collected in order to minimize disturbance of the spatial patterning on the surface (for example, diagnostic potsherds were identified and photographed but left in the field), and most of the sites were revisited in order to expand the data recorded about them.

As a result of the survey, the total number of sites known on Melos increased from 47 to 130 (of all periods), and the island's overall site density proved to be at least six times greater than had been thought, in part through the recognition and recording of small, low-density scatters of material. No other sites of the same date as Phylakopi were found.

Changes in the number and size of sites through time gave evidence of repeated cycles of aggregation and dispersal of settlement, with notable population peaks in the Late Bronze Age and the late Roman period. Throughout the project, close collaboration was maintained with experts in geology, geomorphology, and historical geography.

SAMPLING STRATEGIES

Archaeologists cannot usually afford the time and money necessary to investigate fully the whole of a large site or all sites in a given region. Some sort of sample is required. But of what kind?

If the objective is to be able to draw reliable general conclusions about the whole site or region from the small areas sampled, one should try to make use of statistical methods. These employ probability theory, hence the term **probabilistic sampling**. Through mathematical means, they attempt to improve the probability that generalizations from the sample will be correct. This is the

technique employed by public opinion polls, which may sample fewer than 2000 people yet will extrapolate from the results to generalize about the opinions of millions. Quite often the polls are proved wrong, yet surprisingly often they are more or less right. As with opinion polls, in archaeological work the larger and better designed the sample, the more likely the results are to be valid.

The alternative is to adopt a non-statistical approach: **non-probabilistic sampling**. Some sites in a given region may be more accessible than others, or more prominent in the landscape, which

may prompt a less formally scientific research design. Long years of experience in the field will also give some archaeologists an intuitive "feel" for the right places to undertake work. But in order to judge in any quantitative manner how representative the sample is of a site or region, some form of probabilistic sampling needs to be used.

Types of Probabilistic Sampling
The simplest form is a **simple random sample**, where the areas to be sampled are chosen using a table of random numbers. Research at the small Formative-period hamlet of Tierras Largas in the Oaxaca highlands, Mexico, can serve as an example. Marcus Winter set out to trace this 3000-year-old site's overall layout and house plans in what was simply a plowed field. First he defined the *sample universe* (the site boundaries) from the area of sherd scatter. Next he chose his *sampling units* (the size of the squares, also called quadrats, in his grid). An initial small test excavation suggested that squares 2 m on a side would be large enough to reveal intelligible features beneath the surface. Finally, Winter needed to determine how large a *sample fraction* would be sufficient (how many squares to investigate). The greater the number of squares, the more precise the predictions. In this case, Winter estimated from the average size of known Formative houses that they would occupy less than 5 percent of the site's area. With an expected rate of occurrence of less than 5 percent in the 5000 squares of his site grid, he calculated from statistical tables that a sample size of 197 squares would suffice. The squares were chosen with a table of random numbers. From this sample he was able to estimate the number of houses, pits, burials, and other features which would be found if

Area
A

Area of dirt road

Mound
1

Other
mounds

N

100ft
30m

Simple random sample of squares chosen for excavation at Tierras Largas, Mexico.

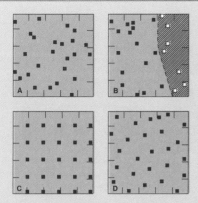

Types of sampling: (A) simple random; (B) stratified random; (C) systematic; (D) stratified systematic.

Stratified systematic sample of squares, 5 m on a side, chosen for investigation at Girik-i-Haciyan, Turkey.

the entire site were to be exposed.

There are drawbacks to this method. First, it entails defining the site's boundaries beforehand, and these are not always known with certainty. Second, the nature of random numbers results in some areas being allotted clusters of squares, while others remain untouched – the sample is, therefore, inherently biased.

One answer is the **stratified random sample**, where the region or site is divided into its natural zones (strata, hence the technique's name), such as cultivated land and forest, and squares are then chosen by the same random-number procedure, except that each zone has the number of squares proportional to its area. Thus, if forest comprises 85 percent of the area, it must be allotted 85 percent of the squares.

Another solution, **systematic sampling**, entails the selection of a grid of equally spaced locations – e.g. choosing every other square (for an adaptation, see the box, Regional Survey on Melos, above). By adopting such a regular spacing one runs the risk of missing (or hitting) every single example in an equally regular pattern of distribution – this is another source of potential bias.

A more satisfactory method is to use a **stratified systematic sample**, which combines the main elements

from all three techniques just described. In collecting artifacts from the surface of a large tell or mound site at Girik-i-Haciyan in Turkey, Charles Redman and Patty Jo Watson used a grid of 5 m squares, but oriented it along the site's main N-S/E-W axes, and the samples were selected with reference to these axes. The strata chosen were blocks of 9 squares (3x3), and one square in each block was picked for excavation by selecting its N-S/E-W coordinates from a table of random numbers. Not only does this method ensure an unbiased set of samples, more evenly distributed over the whole site, but it also makes it unnecessary to define the boundaries, since the grid can be extended in any direction.

In large-scale surveys, *transects* (linear paths) are sometimes preferable to squares (see box, Regional Survey on Melos, above). This is particularly true in areas of dense vegetation such as tropical rainforest. It is far easier to walk along a series of paths than to locate accurately and investigate a large number of randomly distributed squares. In addition, transects can easily be segmented into units, whereas it may be difficult to locate or describe a specific part of a square; and transects are useful not merely for finding sites but also for recording

artifact densities across the landscape. On the other hand, squares have the advantage of exposing more area to the survey, thus increasing the probability of intersecting sites. A combination of the two methods is often best: using transects to cover long distances, but squares when larger concentrations of material are encountered.

The four probabilistic sampling methods described above have been tested by Stephen Plog on distribution maps from the Valley of Oaxaca, Mexico, in an attempt to assess their comparative efficiency at predicting the total number of sites from a 10 percent sample. He concluded that systematic and stratified systematic sampling were slightly more efficient than the simple or stratified random sampling techniques – but the differences were not statistically significant and therefore archaeologists could in most circumstances use the simpler methods.

Some allowance needs also to be made for the danger that probabilistic sampling, used on its own in regional survey, might easily fail to reveal a major site – a site that may at one time have dominated the whole region. Where there is likely to be a hierarchy of sites, some larger and more dominant than others, it is therefore only prudent to combine probabilistic sampling with conventional survey to discover prominent sites. For further discussion of this point, see Chapter 5.

those areas that seem richer, rather than obtaining a sample representative of the whole area that would enable the archaeologist to assess the varying distribution of material of different periods or types.

Hence, most modern survey is done in a systematic way, employing either a grid system or a series of equally spaced traverses. The area to be searched is divided into sectors, and these (or a sample of them, see Melos box) are walked systematically. In this way, no part of the area is either under- or over-represented in the survey. This method also makes it easier to plot the location of finds since one's exact position is always known. Even greater accuracy can be attained by subdividing the traverses into units of fixed length.

Results tend to be more reliable from long-term projects that cover the region repeatedly, since the visibility of sites and artifacts can vary widely from year to year or even with the seasons, thanks to vegetation and changing land-use. In addition, members of field crews inevitably differ in the accuracy of their observations, and in their ability to recognize and describe sites (the more carefully one looks, and the more experience one has, the more one sees); this factor can never be totally eliminated, but repeated coverage can help to counter its effects. The use of standardized recording forms makes it easy to put the data into a computer at a later stage.

Finally, it may be necessary or desirable to carry out small excavations to supplement or check the surface data (particularly for questions of chronology, contemporaneity, or site function), or to test hypotheses which have arisen from the survey. The two types of investigation are complementary, not mutually exclusive. Their major difference can be summarized as follows: excavation tells us a lot about a little of a site, and can only be done once, whereas survey tells us a little about a lot of sites, and can be repeated.

Extensive and Intensive Survey. Surveys can be made more extensive by combining results from a series of individual projects in neighboring regions to produce very large-scale views of change in landscape, land-use, and settlement through time – though, as with individual members of a field crew, the accuracy and quality of different survey projects may vary widely. Outstanding syntheses of regional survey have been produced in parts of Mesoamerica (see Chapter 13) and Mesopotamia, areas which already have a long tradition of this type of work.

In Mesopotamia, for example, the pioneering work by Robert Adams and others, combining surface and aerial survey, has produced a picture of changing settlement size and spacing through time leading to the first cities: scattered agricultural villages became

Surface survey: an archaeological team uses an EDM (electronic distance measurer) to map features at the Maya site of Sayil, in the Mexican rainforest. An infrared beam directed at the survey rod (center) records spot heights.

more clustered as population increased, and eventually by the Early Dynastic Period (3rd millennium BC) major centers of distribution had arisen, interconnected by routes of communication. The work has also revealed former watercourses and canals, and even probable zones of cultivation.

Alternatively survey can be made more intensive by aiming at total coverage of a single large site or site-cluster – what one might call micro-regional survey. It is a paradox that some of the world's greatest and most famous archaeological sites have never, or only recently, been studied in this way, since attention has traditionally focused on the grandiose monuments themselves rather than on any attempt to place them within even a local context. At Teotihuacan, near Mexico City, the major mapping project initiated in the 1960s has added hugely to our knowledge of the area around the great pyramid-temples (box, pp. 76, 77).

Surface survey has a vital place in archaeological work, and one that continues to grow in importance. In modern projects, however, it is usually supplemented (and often preceded) by reconnaissance from the air, one of the most important advances made by archaeology this century. In fact, the availability of air photographs can be an important factor in selecting and delineating an area for surface survey.

Aerial Reconnaissance

It must be stressed that aerial reconnaissance, particularly aerial photography, is not merely or even predominantly used for the discovery of sites, being more crucial to their recording and interpretation, and to monitoring changes in them through time. Nevertheless, air photography – together with remote sensing from space (see below) – has been responsible for a large number of discoveries, and continues to find more sites every year.

Aerial Photography. The first major archaeological applications of this technique occurred at the start of the century with photographs of the Roman town of Ostia taken from a balloon, and in 1913 when Sir Henry Wellcome took vertical pictures of his excavations in the Sudan by means of a box kite. World War I gave the technique a great impetus when archaeologists such as O.G.S. Crawford in England realized that air photographs taken from aircraft and balloons could for the first time provide a plan view of prehistoric monuments.

In Syria, from 1925 onward Father Antoine Poidebard began tracing ancient caravan routes leading to Roman frontier defences in the desert; using observation from the air, he discovered many new forts and

Two early examples of aerial photography. (Left) Bronze Age pile structures visible in Lake Neuchâtel, Switzerland, in 1927. (Right) Cropmarks reveal massive earthworks at Poverty Point, Louisiana, dating from 1500–700 BC.

SITE DISCOVERY BY AERIAL PHOTOGRAPHY

Oblique photographs, taken from planes or balloons at low altitude, are the principal means of site discovery from the air, since they provide perspective and a better pictorial effect than vertical photographs.

Shadow sites are usually the most visible archaeological features on the landscape. Where there are walls or earthworks, the raking light of the low sun, early or late in the day, accentuates the highlights, and the whole shape can spring into life. Slopes facing the sun are very bright, and cast long shadows, while depressions are also in deep shade.

Crop sites or **cropmark sites** are the other common archaeological feature visible from the air. Here variations in the height, vigor, and type of crops and other vegetation can help indicate that a feature lies buried beneath the surface. Where the soil is rich in moisture and phosphates – as, for example, over a buried ditch or pit where the earth has been disturbed in the past – the vegetation will tend to be taller, lusher, and more dense (*positive cropmarks*). Over a buried wall, however, the soil will be thinner, drier, and poorer, and the vegetation will be sparser, or somewhat stunted in growth (*negative cropmarks*). The richer, denser growth appears darker from the air. Wheat, barley, potatoes, and maize are all good producers of this phenomenon. Some other crops ripen more quickly over walls due to lack of available moisture, and produce visible color differences; their stunted growth over these features may also produce shadow marks. Visibility of cropmarks varies with the time of day, the season, and because of many other factors. In dry years, the lusher growth will be greener than the rest. Grass has to be really parched before it reveals any buried features but, because it is so widespread, it has proved immensely valuable in drought years in pinpointing new sites. In the dry summer in Britain of 1984, over 500 previously unknown sites were photographed from the air in one county (Devon) alone, a total exceeding all discoveries there in the preceding 40 years.

Soilmarks are also visible from the air. These consist of traces of differently colored or textured soil. Plowed-out burial mounds, for example, may show up clearly, thanks to the different soil textures of mounds and ditches.

Differences in moisture can also be revealing. *Damp sites* are caused after rain when worked soil keeps its moisture longer over walls or embankments than it does over silted-up pits or ditches: the phenomenon is short-lived but clear. Similarly, snow or frost can show up subsurface features by melting more quickly over buried ditches, or by lingering longer in cooler depressions.

Shadow sites. *The vertical air photograph of Stonehenge, southern England (above), throws the main features into high relief, and is suitable for accurate site planning. The oblique view of Stonehenge (left) sets the site in its broader archaeological landscape, revealing for example the avenue leading to the monument (left to right in the photograph).*

The outlines of a Gallo-Roman villa in France are made brilliantly clear by frost in the soil.

How cropmarks are formed: crops grow taller and more thickly over sunken features such as ditches (1), and show stunted growth over buried walls (2). Such variations may not be obvious at ground level, but are often visible from the air, when ditches appear darker and walls lighter than the surrounding vegetation.

Cropmarks clearly reveal the double line of a so-called "cursus" monument (function unknown) in Dorset, southern England, together with other prehistoric features.

SOIL

roads. He also showed that underwater sites could be detected from the air, revealing for the first time the ancient harbor beneath the sea at Tyre, Lebanon – a study which was combined with survey by divers and partial excavation. Similarly, in 1927, military planes photographed Late Bronze Age oak pile structures through the waters of Lake Neuchâtel, Switzerland. In the New World, Alfred Kidder flew in 1929 with pioneer aviator Charles Lindbergh over central and eastern Yucatán, in Mexico, and discovered half-a-dozen new sites. They also made flights over Arizona and New Mexico looking for ancient villages.

From these beginnings aerial photography has developed into one of the archaeologist's most valued aids.

How Are Aerial Photographs Used? Photographs taken from the air are merely tools; they are means to an end. Photographs do not themselves reveal sites – it is the photographer and the interpreter who do so, by examination of the terrain and the pictures. This is a specialized skill. Long experience and a keen eye are needed to differentiate archaeological traces from other features such as vehicle tracks, and old river beds, and canals. Indeed, most military intelligence units during the final years of World War II had archaeologists on their staff as interpreters of air photographs. Glyn Daniel's expertise, for example, proved invaluable to British military photo-intelligence, and he ended the war running a large unit in India.

Aerial photographs are of two types: the *oblique* and the *vertical*. Each has its advantages and drawbacks, but broadly one can say that oblique photographs – those taken at an angle to reveal contours and provide perspective – are best for discovering sites and vertical photographs for mapping them. Methods of site discovery from the air are discussed in the box. Accurate plans and maps of the layout of sites can be made quite easily from vertical photographs so long as there is one feature of known dimensions in the picture. Overlapping photographs can also be used to create a stereoscopic effect, so that sites and landscapes are seen in three dimensions. Stereoscopic pictures taken of the ancient city of Mohenjodaro in Pakistan from a tethered balloon, for example, have enabled photogrammetric – accurately contoured – plans to be made of its surviving structures. Similarly, large areas can be surveyed with overlapping photographs, which are then processed into a very accurate photogrammetric base map of all the archaeological evidence identified from the air. Analytical ground survey can then proceed on a much surer basis.

Oblique photographs are harder to transform into maps because of the way they distort perspective. However, features in these pictures can now be mapped quite accurately and rapidly using relatively simple computer programs, providing at least four points in a given picture have known positions on the ground. Tests run to check reliability of the method have demonstrated reasonable accuracy, to within a few meters, particularly in lowland areas of flat relief.

(Above) Aerial photographs are of two types: oblique and vertical. Each has different merits. Oblique views reveal contours and provide a better sense of perspective. Vertical views are best for drawing up plans and maps.

(Right) Map of landscape features around Danebury, an Iron Age hillfort in southern Britain (6th–2nd centuries BC), created from aerial survey. Details of the ancient fields, trackways, and enclosures are all visible.

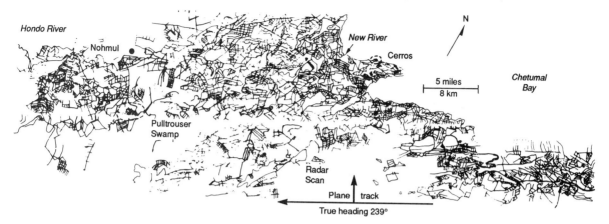

Remote sensing from high altitude: a plot produced by SLAR (sideways-looking airborne radar–see p. 74) of features around Pulltrouser Swamp, Belize. Preliminary checking on the ground suggested these might be ancient Maya canals.

Individual plans can thus be made quickly from oblique photographs, at selected scales; these can be compared, used as a source of measurements, and combined into maps of an area. For example, Roger Palmer has used thousands of individual photographs of a 453-sq. km (175-sq. mile) territory around the British Iron Age hillfort of Danebury to produce accurate maps and plans which show that the site lay within a populous and very complex agricultural landscape. Crop- and soil-marks (see box, pp. 70, 71) revealed the presence of at least 8 other hillforts, 120 ditched farming enclosures, hundreds of acres of small fields, regularly arranged, and 240 km (150 miles) of linear ditches and boundary works, many of which were probably roughly contemporaneous with Danebury to judge by their forms and/or surface finds.

Recent Developments in Aerial Photography. New technology is also having an impact on aerial photography in other ways. Computer enhancement of pictures improves their sharpness and contrast. Digital imagery has also been introduced: photographs are quantified in digital form, and the image can then be manipulated so that, for example, features of particular interest are highlighted.

Although black-and-white panchromatic film is still generally used in air photography – because of its cheapness and high resolution – it is worth employing infrared film as well. This detects reflected radiation from the sun and shows up differences in color, particularly in cereal crops. Innovations now appearing include false-color and photomicrography color film, acoustic holography, and the study of negatives by optic-filtering by laser. Thermal prospection (*thermography*), using thermal or heat sensors in aircraft, is a non-photographic technique that records the temperature of the soil surface by means of a scanner, with warmer zones appearing white on the image. Variations in soil temperature are caused in part by buried structures and by differential water content, so thermography has been used successfully to detect archaeological features such as subsurface ditches. But at present conventional air photography continues to be the commonest and most cost-effective technique of aerial reconnaissance for most archaeological purposes.

Remote Sensing from High Altitude. Photographs taken from satellites have a limited application to archaeology, since their scale is often huge, but images from the LANDSAT (Earth Resources Technology) Satellites have proved useful. Scanners record the intensity of reflected light and the infrared radiation from the earth's surface, and convert these electronically into photographic images. LANDSAT images have been used to trace large-scale features such as ancient levee systems in Mesopotamia.

The most remarkable archaeological application so far, however, has been in Mesoamerica. Using false-color LANDSAT imagery, in which natural colors are converted into more sharply contrasting hues, NASA scientists working with archaeologists in 1983 found an extensive network of Maya farmed fields and settlements in the Yucatán peninsula of Mexico. In this expensive experiment, costing $250,000, Maya ruins showed up in false color as tiny dots of blue, pink and light red – blue for ancient reservoirs cut out of the limestone surface, pink and light red for vegetation on and adjacent to the sites. By looking for examples of blue dots next to pink and light red ones, archaeologists were able to pinpoint 112 sites. They visited 20 by helicopter in order to verify their conclusions.

The project also found an unknown city with twin pyramids, dating to the Classic Maya phase of AD 600–900; and relocated the major city of Oxpemul which had been discovered in the early 1930s but then lost again in the thick jungle. However, the most important result was the detection of a large network (covering an area 65 km (40 miles) long and 4.8 km (3 miles) wide) of walled fields and house-mounds near Flores Magón, which effectively destroys the already discredited theory that Maya civilization was based on a shifting type of agriculture, without regularly maintained fields.

Another remote sensing technique, *sideways-looking airborne radar* (SLAR), has also yielded evidence suggesting that Maya agriculture was more intensive than previously imagined. The technique involves recording in radar images the return of pulses of electromagnetic radiation sent out from a flying aircraft. Since radar will penetrate cloud cover and to some extent dense rainforest, Richard Adams and his colleagues were able to use SLAR from a high-flying NASA aircraft to scan 80,000 sq. km (31,200 sq. miles) of the Maya lowlands. The SLAR images revealed not only ancient cities and field systems, but an enormous lattice of grey lines some of which may have been canals, to judge by subsequent inspections by canoe. If field testing – which has scarcely begun – shows that the canals are ancient, it will show that the Maya had an elaborate irrigation and water transport system.

High altitude radar mapping has also helped reveal a hitherto undocumented people in Costa Rica. In 1984–85, Thomas Sever of NASA flew over the area around the volcano of Mt Arenal, which was of interest to archaeologists because local people had found potsherds and tools when roads were cut through the terrain of ash. Sever scanned the area using radar, infrared photographic film, and a device called lidar (light detection apparatus). The resulting images showed roadways radiating from a central graveyard. Subsequent excavation of 62 sites by Payson Sheets

revealed that a wandering people had lived in the volcano's shadow since about 10,000 BC, and had settled permanently on the shore of Lake Arenal in 2000 BC. Their campsites, graves, and houses had been buried and protected by a volcanic eruption.

The application of these exciting new techniques to archaeology is only just beginning. So long as they remain expensive, conventional air photography will continue to dominate aerial reconnaissance. But advanced airborne remote sensing techniques will no doubt become cheaper and more widespread in the future.

Recording Sites in Reconnaissance Survey

As we have already seen in the discussion of air photography, the pinpointing of sites and features on regional maps is an essential next step in reconnaissance survey. To have discovered a site is one thing, but only when adequately recorded does it become part of the sum total of knowledge about the archaeology of a region.

In addition to plotting a site on a map – including its exact latitude, longitude, and map grid reference – proper recording entails giving the site some kind of locational designation and entering this on a site record form, along with information about who owns the site, its condition, and other details. Locational designations vary in different parts of the world. In the United States they usually consist of a two-digit number for the state, a pair of letters for the county, and a number indicating that this is the 59th (or whatever) site discovered in that county. Thus site 36WH297 designates the 297th site discovered in Washington County, in the state of Pennsylvania (36). This is the locational designation for the famous Paleo-Indian site of Meadowcroft Rockshelter. One of the great values of designating sites using these alpha-numerical systems is that they can be entered easily on computer files, for quick data retrieval e.g. in salvage archaeology or settlement pattern studies.

ASSESSING THE LAYOUT OF SITES AND FEATURES

Finding and recording sites and features is the first stage in fieldwork, but the next stage is to make some assessment of site size, type, and layout. These are crucial factors for archaeologists, not only for those trying to decide whether, where, and how to excavate, but also for those whose main focus may be the study

of settlement patterns, site systems, and landscape archaeology without recourse to excavation. We have already seen how aerial photographs may be used to plot the layout of sites as well as helping to locate them in the first place. What are the other main methods for investigating sites without excavating them?

Two ways of presenting survey results, as exemplified by the Maya site of Nohmul, Belize. (Left) A topographic map relating the site to its landscape. (Right) A planimetric map showing the individual features of the site.

Site Surface Survey

The simplest way to gain some idea of a site's extent and layout is through a site surface survey – that is, by studying the distribution of surviving features, and recording and possibly collecting artifacts from the surface. In the study of Teotihuacan described in the box overleaf, we see how careful survey of this kind was used to produce detailed maps of the city.

The Teotihuacan example highlights the important point that site surface survey is only as good as the methods used to record it. Mapping is the key to the accurate recording of most such survey data. For surface features such as buildings and roads, both topographic and planimetric maps are used. Topographic maps represent differences in elevation or height by means of contour lines and help relate ancient structures to the surrounding landscape. Planimetric maps exclude contour lines and topographic information, concentrating instead on the broad outlines of features, thus making it easier, for example, to understand the relationship of different buildings to each other. On some site maps the two techniques are combined, with natural relief depicted topographically and archaeological features planimetrically.

For artifacts and other objects collected or observed during surface survey, it may not be worth mapping their individual locations if they appear to come from badly disturbed secondary contexts. Or there may simply be too many artifacts realistically to record all their individual provenances. In this latter instance the archaeologist will probably use sampling procedures for the selective recording of surface finds (see box on sampling strategies, above). However, where time and funds are sufficient and the site is small enough, collection and recording of artifacts from the total site

area may prove possible. For example, Frank Hole and his colleagues picked up everything from the entire surface of a 1.5 ha (3.7 acres) open-air prehistoric site in the Valley of Oaxaca, Mexico, plotting locations using a grid of 5 m squares. They then transformed the results into maps with contour lines indicating not differences in elevation, but relative densities of various types of materials and artifacts. As a result it became clear that, although some objects such as projectile points were evidently in a secondary context displaced down slopes, others seemed to lie in primary context and revealed distinct areas for flintworking, seed-grinding, and butchering. These areas then served as guides for subsequent excavation.

Reliability of Surface Finds. Archaeologists have always used limited surface collection of artifacts as one way of trying to assess the date and layout of a site prior to excavation. However, now that surface survey has become not merely a preliminary to excavation but in some instances a substitute for it – for cost and other reasons, as outlined earlier in this chapter – a vigorous debate is taking place in archaeology about how far surface traces do in fact reflect distributions below ground.

One would logically expect single-period or shallow sites to show the most reliable surface evidence of what lies beneath – an assumption that seems to be borne out by the shallow site of Teotihuacan, or Frank Hole's Oaxaca site mentioned above. Equally one might predict that multi-period, deep sites such as Near Eastern tells or village mounds would show few if any traces on the surface of the earliest and deepest levels. Proponents of the validity of surface survey, while agreeing that there is bound to be a quantitative bias in favor of the most recent periods on the surface,

TEOTIHUACAN MAPPING PROJECT

In 1962 the University of Rochester initiated a project, directed by René Millon, to map the pre-Columbian city of Teotihuacan. Located 40 km (25 miles) northeast of Mexico City, the site had been the largest and most powerful urban center in Mesoamerica in its heyday from AD 200 to 650. But no detailed plan had ever been attempted because of the city's daunting size. Attention had been focused on the grandiose pyramid-temples, plazas, and giant market of the city center.

Fortunately, the structural remains lay buried just beneath the surface, so that Millon and his team were able to undertake the mapping from a combination of aerial and surface survey, with only small-scale excavation.

The survey began with low-altitude aerial photography and preliminary ground reconnaissance to establish a survey grid made up of 147 squares, each 500 m on a side and each with its own map data sheet to be filled in. Using the grid, the city's irregular boundary, enclosing about 20 sq.km (*c.* 8 sq. miles), was defined by walking the perimeter. The city area itself was then intensively surveyed and mapped, and surface collections made. Individual structures were plotted for each 500-m square, and surface data recorded on special forms. Millions of potsherds were collected, and over 5000 structures and activity areas recorded. Small-scale excavations were also conducted to test the survey results. Eventually Millon and his colleagues combined the architectural interpretation of all this information on to the base map of the whole site, which they then published in conjunction with an explanatory text.

The mapping project yielded many new insights. Teotihuacan had been laid out on a regular plan, with four quadrants oriented on the great north-south "Street of the Dead" and another major avenue running east-west across it. Construction had occurred over several centuries, but always following the master plan. The northern quadrant was the oldest residential area, with certain neighborhoods (*barrios*) here and elsewhere in the city apparently reserved for particular craft specialists, as shown by concentrations of obsidian, pottery, feathers, and other goods.

Since 1980, a new multi-disciplinary team directed by Ruben Cabrera Castro has been broadening the picture so successfully established by the Teotihuacan Mapping Project.

Archaeological and topographic map of Teotihuacan produced by René Millon and his team. The survey grid system of 500-m squares is oriented to the north-south axis of the city, in particular the central "Street of the Dead" (dividing W1 and E1 on the map).

LEGEND

EXCAVATED ROOM COMPLEX OR OTHER STRUCTURE
UNEXCAVATED ROOM COMPLEX
POSSIBLE ROOM COMPLEX
RM. CMPL.- SOME LIMITS UNCLEAR
TEMPLE PLATFORM
SINGLE STAGE PLATFORM
INSUBSTANTIAL STRUCTURES
MAJOR WALL
WATER COURSE
PROBABLE OLD WATER COURSE
METERS ABOVE MEAN SEA LEVEL —2275—
MAPPING PROJECT EXCAVATION

TEOTIHUACAN IS 40 KILOMETERS (25 MILES)
NORTHEAST OF MEXICO CITY

TEOTIHUACAN

CENTRAL PLATEAU

OF MEXICO

ARCHAEOLOGICAL AND

TOPOGRAPHIC MAP

SEPTEMBER 1970
COPYRIGHT 1972 BY RENÉ MILLON

K E Y

PYRAMID OF THE MOON ___ 1	PLAZA ONE ___ 14
PYRAMID OF THE SUN ___ 2	HOUSE OF THE EAGLES ___ 15
CIUDADELA ___ 3	"OLD CITY" ___ 16
TEMPLE OF QUETZALCOATL ___ 4	OAXACA BARRIO ___ 17
"STREET OF THE DEAD" ___ 5	ATETELCO ___ 18
GREAT COMPOUND ___ 6	LA VENTILLA A ___ 19
WEST AVENUE ___ 7	LA VENTILLA B ___ 20
EAST AVENUE ___ 8	LA VENTILLA C ___ 21
"MERCHANTS' BARRIO" ___ 9	TEOPANCAXCO ___ 22
TLAMIMILOLPA ___ 10	RIO SAN LORENZO ___ 23
XOLALPAN ___ 11	RIO SAN JUAN ___ 24
TEPANTITLA ___ 12	RESERVOIRS ___ 25, 26, 27, 51
MAGUEY PRIEST MURALS ___ 13	ACUMULCO ___ 52

GRID IS ORIENTED
CA. 15°25' EAST OF
ASTRONOMIC NORTH.

SUN PYRAMID
19°41'30" N. LAT.
98°50'30" W. LONG.

MAP SHOWS EXTENT OF ANCIENT CITY CA. 600 A.D.; CA. 20 SQ. KMS. OR 8 SQ. MI.
SHOWN ARE (1) PARTIALLY OR COMPLETELY EXCAVATED STRUCTURES, PRIMARILY
ALONG THE "STREET OF THE DEAD" (NORTH-SOUTH AXIS), AND (2) RECONSTRUCTIONS
BASED ON TEOTIHUACAN MAPPING PROJECT SURVEY OF SURFACE REMAINS OF UNEX-
CAVATED AND PARTIALLY EXCAVATED STRUCTURES. AN UNDETERMINED NUMBER OF
STRUCTURES IN VARIOUS PARTS OF THE CITY HAVE BEEN BURIED UNDER SILT
OR LEVELLED FOR AGRICULTURE IN MODERN TIMES. NOTE CANALIZATION OF
MOST WATER COURSES WITHIN THE ANCIENT CITY.

CONTOUR INTERVAL FIVE METERS

MILES

KILOMETERS

TEOTIHUACAN MAPPING PROJECT
RENÉ MILLON, DIRECTOR
DEPARTMENT OF ANTHROPOLOGY   AIDED BY GRANTS FROM THE
UNIVERSITY OF ROCHESTER   NATIONAL SCIENCE FOUNDATION
ROCHESTER, NEW YORK   CHIEF DRAFTSMAN J. ARMANDO CERDA
PRINCIPAL ASSOCIATES, BRUCE DREWITT AND GEORGE COWGILL

nevertheless point out that one of the surprises for most survey archaeologists is how many of their sites, if collected with care, are truly multi-period, reflecting many phases of a site's use, not just the latest one. The reasons for this are not yet entirely clear, but they certainly have something to do with the kind of formation processes discussed in Chapter 2 – from erosion and animal disturbance to human activity such as plowing.

The relationship between surface and subsurface evidence is undoubtedly complex and varies from site to site. It is therefore wise wherever possible to try to determine what really does lie beneath the ground, perhaps by digging test pits (usually meter squares) to assess a site's horizontal extent, ultimately by more thorough excavation (see below). There are, however, a whole battery of subsurface detection devices that can be brought into play before – or indeed sometimes instead of – excavation, which of course is destructive as well as expensive.

Subsurface Detection

Probes. The most traditional technique is that of probing the soil with rods or borers, and noting the positions where they strike solids or hollows. Metal rods with a T-shaped handle are the most common, but augers – large corkscrews with a similar handle – are also used, and have the advantage of bringing samples of soil to the surface, clinging to the screw. Probing of this type is still employed routinely by some archaeologists – for example, to gauge the depth of the midden at the Ozette site in Washington State (Chapter 2) or by Chinese archaeologists to plot the 300 pits remaining to be investigated near the first emperor's buried terracotta army. In the mid-1980s, the American archaeologist David Hurst Thomas and his team used over 600 systematically spaced test probes with a gasoline-powered auger in their successful search for a lost 16th-century Spanish mission on St Catherine's Island off the coast of Georgia. Augers are also used by geomorphologists studying site sediments. However, there is always a risk of damaging fragile artifacts or features.

One notable advance in this technique was developed by Carlo Lerici in Italy in the 1950s for Etruscan tombs of the 6th century BC. Having detected the precise location of a tomb through aerial photography and soil resistivity (see below), he would bore down into it a hole 8 cm (3 in) in diameter, and insert a long tube with a periscope head and a light, and also a tiny camera attached if needed. Lerici examined some 3500 Etruscan tombs in this way, and found that almost all

SURFACE INVESTIGATION AT ABU SALABIKH

An effective and simple site investigation strategy has been adopted at Abu Salabikh, Iraq, by Nicholas Postgate. He wanted to study the large-scale layout of an early Mesopotamian city – a considerable challenge, since many of the relevant archaeological deposits lie buried deep within multi-period mounds. However, at Abu Salabikh Postgate found a series of low mounds where occupation layers of a suitably early date lay conveniently just beneath the surface. The site was of a size to daunt most archaeologists (50 ha or 124 acres), but Postgate and his team found that they could obtain good results over wide areas simply by scraping away the shallow topsoil. Exposed immediately beneath were quite clear wall lines which could then be mapped almost as accurately as after actual excavation, and far more quickly. Scraping was combined with collection of surface potsherds in order to date the walls and selective excavation to test the results.

It also proved possible to distinguish earlier and later phases using the scraping method. Surface deposits of a mound on the western side of the site belonged to about 2900 BC, and displayed large, thick-walled, self-contained compounds, each containing separate rectangular houses with courtyards, storerooms, and drainage, as well as fire installations. The main mound, however, revealed houses of c.2500 BC packed tightly side by side, separated by an occasional narrow street. Although only part of the site has been uncovered in this way, it nevertheless represents the largest area of housing known from any 3rd millennium site in southern Iraq.

Scraping away the shallow topsoil to uncover wall outlines of the early Mesopotamian city.

Plan of part of the main mound in 1986, showing walls revealed by scraping and selective excavation. Contours are at 50 cm intervals.

City wall
Excavated walls
Streets and open spaces
Walls defined at surface
N.W. Building
4J89 House
5J91 House
S. Building

65ft
20m

N

were completely empty, thus saving future excavators a great deal of wasted effort. He also discovered over 20 with painted walls, thus doubling the known heritage of Etruscan painted tombs at a stroke.

Probing the Pyramids. Modern technology has taken this kind of work even further, with the development of the endoscope (see Chapter 11) and miniature TV cameras. In a project reminiscent of Lerici, a probe was carried out in 1987 of a boat pit beside the Great Pyramid of Cheops, in Egypt. This lies adjacent to another pit, excavated in 1954, that contained the perfectly preserved and disassembled parts of a 43-m (141-ft) long royal cedarwood boat of the 3rd millennium BC. The $250,000 probe revealed that the unopened pit does indeed contain all the dismantled timbers of a second boat but that the pit was not airtight – thus dashing hopes of analyzing the "ancient" air to see whether carbon dioxide in the atmosphere had increased over the millennia, and which component of the air preserves antiquities so efficiently.

Projects of this kind are beyond the resources of most archaeologists. Nevertheless in the future, funds permitting, probes of this type could equally well be applied to other Egyptian sites, to cavities in Maya structures, or to the many unexcavated tombs in China.

The Great Pyramid itself has recently been the subject of probes by French and Japanese teams who believe it may contain as yet undiscovered chambers or corridors. Using ultrasensitive microgravimetric equipment – which is normally employed to search for deficiencies in dam walls, and can tell if a stone has a hollow behind it – they detected what they think is a cavity some 3 m (10 ft) beyond one of the passage walls. However test drilling to support this claim has not been completed and all tests are under review by the Egyptian authorities until their potential contribution to Egyptology has been established.

Remote Sensing beneath the Surface

Probing techniques are useful, but inevitably involve some disturbance of the site. There are, however, a wide range of non-destructive techniques ideal for the archaeologist seeking to learn more about a site before – or without – excavation. These are geophysical remote sensing devices which involve either passing energy of various kinds through the soil in order to "read" what lies below the surface from the anomalies encountered by the energy, or measuring the intensity of the earth's magnetic field.

Seismic and Acoustic Methods. The simplest way to pass energy through the ground is to strike it. In *bosing* (or *bowsing*) the earth is struck with a heavy wooden mallet or a lead-filled container on a long handle. Recording the resulting sound helps to locate underground features, since a dull sound indicates undisturbed ground, while buried ditches or pits produce a more resonant effect. This crude technique has now been made virtually obsolete through technological advances.

A more refined method, developed by the U.S. Army, has recently been applied to archaeological projects in Japan by Yasushi Nishimura. This *standing wave technique* employs a device which produces and amplifies so-called Rayleigh waves by striking the ground softly and repeatedly. A striker weighing 20 kg (44 lb) can reach depths of 10 m (33 ft), but bigger machines can reach 70 m or even 100 m (230–330 ft). The speed of the waves can be calculated by having two pick-up points a fixed distance apart. Since the waves move fast in hard materials, more slowly in clay or soft materials, features such as buried land surfaces can be detected. The sections produced by the machine can then be transformed into a contour map of the subsurface features.

Other types of echo-sounding, such as sonar, have been employed elsewhere. For example, Kent Weeks and his team from the University of California have been systematically mapping tombs in the Valley of the Kings at Thebes in Egypt. Using sonar devices in 1987 they successfully located a major tomb, only 15 m (49 ft) from that of the pharaoh Ramesses II, which is thought to have belonged to some of Ramesses' many sons.

Detection of gravitational anomalies, as mentioned in the section on probing the pyramids, can find cavities such as caves. And seismic methods normally used by oil prospectors have helped to trace details of the foundations of St Peter's Basilica in the Vatican in Rome.

One of the most important archaeological applications of echo-sounding techniques, however, is in underwater projects (see box). For example, after a bronze statue of an African boy was brought up in a sponger's net off the Turkish coast, George Bass and his colleagues were able to make a successful search for the Roman ship from which it came by means of echo-location systems.

Radio Waves and Electrical Impulses. A basically similar method, which employs not sonic but radio pulses, is *soil-sounding radar*, developed a few years ago. The emitter, in the form of a small trolley

UNDERWATER ARCHAEOLOGY

Underwater archaeology is generally considered to have been given its first major impetus during the winter of 1853–54, when a particularly low water level in the Swiss lakes laid bare enormous quantities of wooden posts, pottery, and other artifacts. From the earliest investigations, using crude diving-bells, it has developed into a valuable complement to work on land. It encompasses a wide variety of sites, including wells, sink holes, and springs (e.g. the great sacrificial well at Chichén Itzá, Mexico); submerged lakeside settlements (e.g. those of the Alpine region); and marine sites ranging from shipwrecks to sunken harbors (e.g. Caesarea, Israel) and drowned cities (e.g. Port Royal, Jamaica).

The invention in recent times of miniature submarines, other submersible craft, and above all of scuba diving gear has been of enormous value, enabling divers to stay underwater for much longer, and to reach sites at previously impossible depths. As a result, the pace and scale of discovery have greatly increased over the last few decades. For example, in the Mediterranean and Black Sea about 1000 shipwrecks are now known for the Classical and medieval periods.

Underwater Reconnaissance

Geophysical methods are as useful for finding sites underwater as they are for locating land sites (see diagram). For example, in 1979 it was magnetometry combined with side-scan sonar that discovered the *Hamilton* and the *Scourge*, two armed schooners sunk during the War of 1812 at a depth of 90 m (295 ft) in Lake Ontario, Canada. Nevertheless, in regions such as the Mediterranean the majority of finds have resulted from methods as simple as talking to local sponge divers, who collectively have spent thousands of hours on the seabed.

Underwater Excavation

Excavation underwater is complex and expensive (not to mention the highly demanding post-excavation conservation and analytical work that is also required). Once underway, the excavation may involve shifting vast quantities of sediment, and recording and removing bulky objects as diverse as storage jars (amphorae), metal ingots, and cannons. George Bass, founder of the Institute of Nautical Archaeology in Texas, and others have developed many helpful devices, such as baskets attached to balloons to raise objects, and air lifts (suction hoses) to remove sediment (see diagram). If the vessel's hull survives at all, detailed drawings must be made so that specialists can later reconstruct the overall form and lines, either on paper or in three dimensions as a model or full-size replica (see box, The Red Bay Wreck, below). In some rare cases, like that of England's Mary Rose (16th century AD), preservation is sufficiently good for the remains of the hull to be raised – funds permitting.

Nautical archaeologists have now excavated more than 100 sunken vessels, revealing not only how they were constructed but also many insights into shipboard life, cargoes, trade routes, early metallurgy, and glassmaking. We look in more detail at two projects: the Red Bay Wreck, Canada (overleaf) and the Kaş Wreck, Turkey (box, Chapter 9).

Three methods (near right) of geophysical underwater survey. (1) The proton magnetometer is towed well behind the survey boat, detecting iron and steel objects (e.g. cannons, steel hulls) that distort the earth's magnetic field. (2) Side-scan sonar transmits sound waves in a fan-shaped beam to produce a graphic image of surface (but not sub-surface) features on the seafloor. (3) The sub-bottom profiler emits sound pulses that bounce back from features and objects buried beneath the seafloor.

Underwater excavation techniques (far right): at left, the lift bag for raising objects; center, measuring and recording finds in situ; right, the air lift for removing sediment.

THE RED BAY WRECK: DISCOVERY AND EXCAVATION

Underwater archaeology, in conjunction with archival research and land archaeology, is beginning to yield a detailed picture of whaling undertaken by Basque fishermen at Red Bay, Labrador, in the 16th century AD. The Basques were the largest suppliers to Europe at this time of whale oil – an important commodity used for lighting and in products such as soap.

In 1977, prompted by the discovery in Spanish archives that Red Bay had been an important whaling center, the Canadian archaeologist James A. Tuck began an excavation on the island closing Red Bay harbor. Here he found remains of structures for rendering blubber into whale oil. The next year, the nautical archaeologist Robert Grenier led a Parks Canada team in search of the Basque galleon *San Juan*, which the archives said had sunk in the harbor in 1565.

Structural plan of the wreck on the harbor bottom (2 m grid squares).

Model, at a scale of 1:10, to show how the galleon's surviving timbers may have fitted together.

Project director Robert Grenier (top) examines the remains of an astrolabe (navigational instrument) from Red Bay

Discovery and Excavation

A wreck believed to be that of the *San Juan* was located at a depth of 10 m (33 ft) in 1978, by a diver towed behind a small boat. A feasibility study carried out the following year confirmed the site's potential, and from 1980 to 1984 Parks Canada undertook a survey and excavation project that employed up to 15 marine archaeologists, backed up by 15–25 support staff, including conservators, drafts persons, and photographers. Two more galleons were discovered in the harbor, but only the supposed *San Juan* was excavated.

The dig was controlled from a specially equipped barge, anchored above the site, that contained a workshop, storage baths for artifacts, a crane for lifting timbers, and a compressor able to run 12 air lifts for removing silt. Salt water was heated on board and pumped down through hoses direct to the divers' suits to maintain body warmth in the near-freezing conditions.

An important technique devised during the project was the use of latex rubber to mold large sections of the ship's timbers in position underwater, thereby reproducing accurately the hull shape and details such as toolmarks and wood grain. The remains of the vessel were also raised in pieces to the surface for precise recording, but the latex molds eliminated the need for costly conservation of the original timbers, which were reburied on-site.

Analysis and Interpretation

On the evidence of the meticulous drawings and molds made during the excavation, a 1:10 scale model was constructed as a research tool to help reveal how the vessel had been built, and what she had looked like. Many fascinating details emerged, for instance that the 14.7-m (48-ft) long keel and bottom row of planks (garboard strakes) had – most unusually for this size of ship – been carved from a single beech tree. Nearly all the rest of the vessel was of oak. In overview, the research model

revealed a whaling ship with fine lines, far removed from the round, tubby shape commonly thought typical of 16th-century merchant vessels.

As the accompanying table indicates, a wealth of artifacts from the wreck shed light on the cargo, navigational equipment, weaponry,

and life on board the unlucky galleon. Thanks to the integrated research design of this Parks Canada project – the largest ever conducted in Canadian waters – many new perspectives are emerging on 16th-century Basque seafaring, whaling, and shipbuilding traditions.

CULTURAL MATERIAL RECOVERED AT RED BAY

THE VESSELS
Whaling ship believed to be the San Juan: Hull timbers (more than 3000) • Fittings: capstan, rudder, bow sprit • Rigging: heart blocks, running blocks, shrouds, other cordage • Anchor • Iron nail fragments
Two other whaling ships
Four small boats, some used for whaling
RECOVERED ARTIFACTS
Cargo-Related: Wooden casks (more than 10,000 individual pieces) • Wooden stowage articles: billets, chocks, wedges • Ballast stones (more than 13 tons)
Navigational Instruments: Binnacle • Compass • Sand glass • Log reel and chip • Astrolabe
Food Storage, Preparation, and Serving: Ceramics: coarse earthenware,

majolica • Glass fragments • Pewter fragments • Treen: bowls and platters • Basketry • Copper-alloy spigot key
Food-Related: Cod bones • Mammal bones: polar bear, seal, cow, pig • Bird bones: ducks, gulls, auk • Walnut shells, hazelnut shells, plum pits, bakeapple seeds
Clothing-Related: Leather shoes • Leather fragments • Textile fragments
Personal Items: Coins • Gaming piece • Comb
Weaponry-Related: Verso • Lead shot • Cannonballs • Possible wooden arrow
Tool-Related: Wooden tool handles • Brushes • Grindstone
Building Material: ceramic roof tile fragments
Whaling-Related: Whale bones

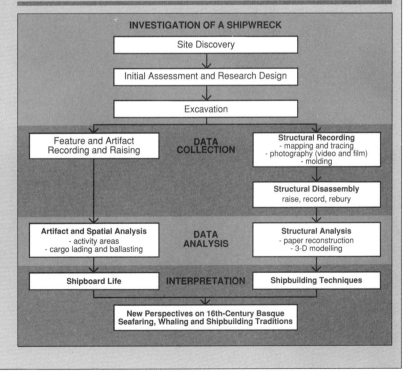

INVESTIGATION OF A SHIPWRECK

Site Discovery

Initial Assessment and Research Design

Excavation

Feature and Artifact Recording and Raising | **DATA COLLECTION** | **Structural Recording** - mapping and tracing - photography (video and film) - molding

Structural Disassembly raise, record, rebury

Artifact and Spatial Analysis - activity areas - cargo lading and ballasting | **DATA ANALYSIS** | **Structural Analysis** - paper reconstruction - 3-D modelling

Shipboard Life | INTERPRETATION | **Shipbuilding Techniques**

New Perspectives on 16th-Century Basque Seafaring, Whaling and Shipbuilding Traditions

(nicknamed the "moon-buggy"), sends short pulses through the soil, and the echoes reflect back any change in soil conditions encountered, such as filled ditches, graves, walls, etc. The buggy moves 10 cm (4 in) for each reading, along parallel tracks 1 m (3 ft 4 in) wide, and its pulses can reach depths of 3 m. Readings are fed into a computer which produces a series of radiographic slices; when integrated, these constitute a 3-D image of what lies beneath the soil. The technique works best in dry, well-drained sandy soil, conditions that exist at Sutton Hoo, England,

where the buggy has detected a large anomaly in one mound which may represent a burial chamber (see box below).

This ground-penetrating radar device is somewhat slow, and is still being tested archaeologically but holds great promise for the future. A variation on this method, *georadar*, was also developed recently by U.S. and Swedish technicians. It comprises a much larger antenna mounted on a boom, attached to a full-sized radar truck. It transmits electromagnetic energy into the ground, and part of this is reflected if it encounters an interface between two different materials of different electrical properties, such as bedrock and soil, or soil and an object. Measurement of the time between the transmitted and reflected signals helps to locate the position of the different layers and any objects present. The device has been found capable of reaching depths of 4 m (13 ft) in terrain such as peat and has, for example, traced the course of a Bronze Age oak trackway half a meter below the surface of a Danish peat bog.

A commonly used method that has been employed on archaeological sites for several decades, particularly in Europe, is *electrical resistivity*. The technique derives from the principle that the damper the soil the more easily it will conduct electricity, i.e. the less resistance it will show to an electric current. A resistivity meter attached to electrodes in the ground can thus measure varying degrees of subsurface resistance to a current passed between the electrodes. Silted up ditches or filled-in pits retain more moisture than stone walls or roads and will therefore display lower resistivity than stone structures.

The technique works particularly well for ditches and pits in chalk and gravel, and masonry in clay. Although slow, because it involves placing a line of four electrodes in the ground for each reading, it is an effective complement to other remote sensing survey methods. Indeed it often replaces magnetic methods (see below) since, unlike some of these, it can be used in urban areas, close to power lines, and in the vicinity of metal. Most things detectable by magnetism can also be found through resistivity; and in some field projects it has proved the most successful device for locating features (see Sutton Hoo box). Nevertheless, techniques based on magnetism are of great importance to archaeologists.

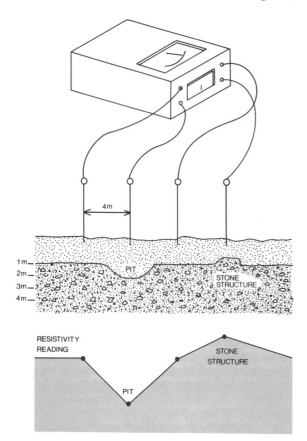

Electrical resistivity: this technique involves placing a line of four electrodes in the ground for each reading. Current is passed into the ground through the outer pair, and the resistivity is calculated from the measured resistance between the inner pair and their distance apart. Stone structures have a high resistivity compared with that of soil, while ditches and pits give low readings. This contrast depends on the moisture in the ground, which varies with the weather and the seasons. In temperate climates, the summer is the best season in which to use the technique.

Magnetic Survey Methods. These are among the most widely used methods of survey, being particularly helpful in locating fired clay structures such as hearths and pottery kilns; iron objects; and pits and ditches. Such buried features all produce slight but measurable

MEASURING MAGNETISM

The main instruments for tracing buried features using magnetic methods are magnetometers and gradiometers, and metal detectors.

The **proton precession magnetometer** consists of a sensor (a bottle of water) encircled by an electrical coil, mounted on a staff and connected by a cable to a small portable box of electronics. The device can detect small but sharp differences in magnetic field intensity caused by buried objects and features.

Proton magnetometers are usually employed using a grid divided into squares 1 m to 3 m on a side. Their chief virtue is that they take measurements rapidly and easily. Their drawbacks include the fact that the operator cannot wear any iron: all buckles, watches, bootnails, metal pens, etc. must be kept several meters away; there must be no wire fences or corrugated sheeting in the vicinity; and overhead cables also interfere with the equipment. In a small, crowded country such as Japan, where one is never far from electrified rail lines or other direct current power lines, two magnetometers have to be used simultaneously in order to overcome the "noise" that causes fluctuations in the magnetic field.

Fluxgate magnetometers do not have this problem, and nor do gradiometers, which work on the same principle.

The **differential fluxgate magnetometer** has the added advantage of giving a continuous reading, but it is more complex to set up and operate – it is a directional instrument, and all measurements must be made with the sensor pointing in precisely the same direction (usually by hanging it vertically).

The **fluxgate gradiometer** is a light, self-contained instrument which produces a continuous output, and records differences in magnetic

intensities on a meter. This can be combined with automatic trace recording and computer processing – consequently, it can do fast, accurate surveys of large areas. It has been used to survey the future paths of highways, at a rate of 1.6 to 2.4 km (0.9 – 1.5 miles) per day. For example, along one stretch of the future M3 highway in England, it found 8 sites in 10 km (6.2 miles).

Metal detectors employ both magnetism and conductivity – they respond to the high electrical conductivity of all metals and to the high magnetic susceptibility of ferrous metals. There are two main instruments. The **soil conductivity meter** comprises a radio transmitter and receiver in continuous operation, and detects subsurface features by measuring the distortion of the transmitted field caused by changes in the conductivity or susceptibility of the soil. Metals, for example, produce strong anomalies, while pits produce weak ones. The **pulsed induction meter** can find metal objects and magnetic soil anomalies such as pits by applying pulses of magnetic field to the ground from a transmitter coil – the larger the coil, the deeper the penetration.

Similar devices are also employed in underwater archaeology (see box, above).

Results of a fluxgate gradiometer survey, carried out while testing possible routes for a new road in Wiltshire, southwest England. The strip shown is 30 m (100 ft) wide and runs through a Romano-British settlement. In the dot density plot (near right), the darkest areas indicate maximum magnetic disturbance created by features beneath the ground. The contour trace of the same area (far right) produces contour lines of like magnetic values, highlighting the subsoil features to give a more three-dimensional effect.

distortions in the earth's magnetic field. The reasons for this vary according to the type of feature, but are based on the presence of iron, even if only in minute amounts. For example, grains of iron oxide in clay, their magnetism randomly orientated if the clay is unbaked, will line up and become permanently fixed on the direction of the earth's magnetic field when heated to about 700°C (1292°F) or more. The baked clay thus becomes a weak permanent magnet, creating an anomaly in the surrounding magnetic field. (This phenomenon of thermoremanent magnetism also forms the basis for magnetic dating – see Chapter 4.) Anomalies caused by pits and ditches, on the other hand, occur because the so-called magnetic susceptibility of their contents is greater than that of the surrounding subsoil.

The most commonly employed piece of equipment that will measure these magnetic anomalies is the proton magnetometer. However, this suffers from background interference from electric trains and power lines, a problem that does not arise with other instruments that can be used such as gradiometers (see box, previous page).

All the magnetic instruments can produce informative site plans which help to delimit archaeological potential. Two common means of presentation are contour maps and dot density maps, both also used to display resistivity survey results. In the case of magnetic survey, the contour map has contour lines that join all points of the same value of the magnetic field intensity – this quite successfully reveals separate anomalies, such as tombs in a cemetery. In dot-density mapping, individual magnetometer readings are plotted as dots on a plan, with shading dependent on the magnetic intensity, and the blacker areas therefore

representing the highest anomalies in the local magnetic field. This makes it easier for the eye to pick up regular features, even where changes may be slight.

An alternative, simpler mapping method has been devised which presents the data as a series of stacked profiles. Each traverse with the equipment is plotted as a curved profile. These are then placed in order, parallel to each other but aligned on an oblique plan, so that one obtains a kind of 3-D image of the site's magnetic variations.

Metal Detectors. These electromagnetic devices are also helpful in detecting buried remains – and not just metal ones. An alternating magnetic field is generated by passing an electrical current through a transmitter coil. Buried metal objects distort this field and are detected as a result of an electrical signal picked up by a receiver coil. Features such as pits, ditches, walls, and kilns can also sometimes be recorded with these instruments because of their different magnetic susceptibilities as compared to the surrounding soil or subsoil (see magnetism box for types of equipment).

Metal detectors can be of great value to archaeologists, particularly in giving quick general results and locating modern metal objects that may lie near the surface (see Sutton Hoo box). They are also widely used by non-archaeologists, most of whom are responsible enthusiasts, but some of whom vandalize sites mindlessly and often illegally digging holes without recording or reporting the finds they make.

Other Techniques. There are a few other prospection methods which are not often used but which may become more widely adopted in the future, particularly geochemical analysis, discussed below.

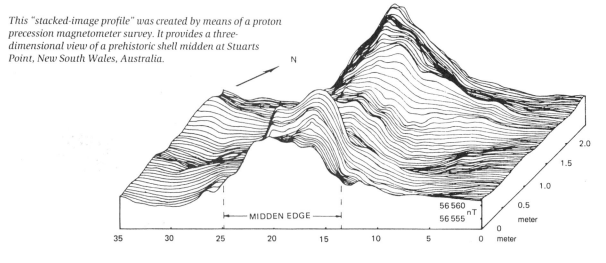

This "stacked-image profile" was created by means of a proton precession magnetometer survey. It provides a three-dimensional view of a prehistoric shell midden at Stuarts Point, New South Wales, Australia.

Both *radioactivity* and *neutron scattering* have been tried out in remote sensing tests, but it was found that both work only if the soil cover is very thin. Most soils and rocks have some radioactive content, and, as with resistivity and magnetic surveying, in the radioactivity technique readings measure discontinuity between buried ditches or pits and the surrounding earth. In the neutron method, a probe that is both a source of fast neutrons and a detector of slow ones is inserted into the soil: measurement of their rate of slowing and scattering through the ground is taken. Stone produces a lower count rate than soil, so buried features can sometimes be detected.

Thermal prospection, already mentioned in the section on aerial photography, is based on weak variations in temperature (tenths of a degree) which can be found above buried structures whose thermal properties are different from those of their surroundings. It is an expensive technique and needs to be done from an airplane, but it is possible to scan one square meter of a site at a time. So far, the method has been used primarily on long or massive structures such as prehistoric enclosures or Roman buildings.

The mapping and study of the *vegetation* at a site can be very informative about previous work – certain species will grow where soil has been disturbed, and at Sutton Hoo, for example, an expert on grasses was able to pinpoint many holes that had been dug into this mound site in recent years (see box overleaf).

Geochemical analysis involves taking samples of soil at intervals (such as every meter) from the surface of a site and its surroundings, and measuring their phosphate (phosphorus) content. It was fieldwork in Sweden in the 1920s and 1930s that first revealed the close correlation between ancient settlement and high concentrations of phosphorus in the soil. The organic components of occupation debris may disappear, while the inorganic remain: of these, magnesium or calcium can be analyzed, but it is the phosphates that are the most diagnostic and easily identified. Subsequently, the method was used to locate sites in North America and northwest Europe: Ralph Solecki, for example, detected burials in West Virginia by these means.

Recent phosphate tests on sites in England, examining samples taken at 20 cm (8 in) intervals from the surface downwards, have confirmed that undisturbed archaeological features in the subsoil are accurately reflected in the topsoil. In the past, topsoil was considered to be unstratified and hence devoid of archaeological information; it was often removed mechanically and quickly without investigation. Now, however, it is becoming clear that even a site that appears totally plowed-out can yield important chemical information about precisely where its occupation was located. The phosphate method is also invaluable for sites with no apparent internal architectural features. In some cases it may help clarify the function of different parts of an excavated site as well. For example, in a Romano-British farmstead at Cefn Graeanog, North Wales, J.S. Conway took soil samples at 1 m (3 ft 4 in) intervals from the floors of excavated huts and from neighboring fields, and mapped their phosphorus content as contour lines. In one building a high level of phosphorus across the middle implied the existence of two animal stalls with a drain for urine running between them. In another, the position of two hearths was marked by high readings.

Investigations of this type are slow, because one has to lay down a grid, collect, weigh, and analyze the samples. But they are becoming increasingly common in archaeological projects, because they can reveal features not detected by other techniques. Like magnetic and resistivity methods (to which they are complementary), they help to construct a detailed picture of features of special archaeological interest within larger areas already identified by other means such as aerial photography or surface survey.

In concluding this section on subsurface detection, we may refer in passing to a controversial technique that has a few followers. *Dowsing* – the location of subsurface features by holding out a twig, copper rod, coathanger, pendulum or some such instrument and waiting for it to move – has been applied to archaeological problems for at least 50 years, but without being taken seriously by most archaeologists. In the mid-1980s, however, it was used in a project to trace medieval church foundations in Northumberland, England, and the skeptical archaeologists involved became convinced of the technique's validity. While keeping an open mind, most archaeologists remain extremely doubtful. Only excavation can test the predictions made, and in the church project digging confirmed some of the dowser's predictions, but not all of them; this is hardly surprising, since a dowser often has a good chance of being right – either the feature is there or it is not. Tests by the physicist Martin Aitken to find a correlation between dowsing responses and magnetic disturbance in a Romano-British pottery kiln proved entirely negative.

For the moment, therefore, until overwhelming proof of the validity of dowsing and other unconventional methods is forthcoming, archaeologists should continue to put their faith in the ever-growing number of tried-and-trusted scientific techniques for obtaining data about site layout without excavation.

SURVEY AT SUTTON HOO

One of this century's most famous excavations took place during 1938/39 in an Anglo-Saxon cemetery at Sutton Hoo, in eastern England. Magnificent treasures were retrieved from a royal grave in one of the burial mounds, and the excavators displayed considerable archaeological expertise in uncovering the imprint left in sand by the decayed wooden ship used for that burial.

As in most archaeological projects of the time, attention was focused on the burial mounds and their contents, on establishing their date (the 6th-7th centuries AD) and the identity of their occupants (the great ship burial is thought to be that of Raedwald, a local king). Further work at the site in the 1960s largely continued this traditional approach.

However, in the 1980s a new campaign of research, directed by Martin Carver, shifted the focus toward setting the site in its local and regional context. An area of 14 ha (35 acres) was surveyed around the site, with the site's "edges" defined by detailed plotting of surface finds. A grid was laid out, and surface measurements from 11,000 points entered onto a computer file in order to produce contour maps. Visible damage to the area (by burrows, or by the tanks used during army training here during World War II) was recorded. And an expert on grasses examined the distribution of different species and pinpointed some 200 holes dug into the mound site in recent years, probably only a few of them by archaeologists. A phosphate survey of the plowed area east of the mounds showed zones of concentration that

Profile *of ship burial excavation, 1939.*

15 ft
5 m

TBM 33.42m A.O.D

TBM 31.79m A.O.D

TBM 32.63m A.O.D

TBM 31.73m A.O.D

Reconstructed helmet from Mound 1

12

2 · Chamber grave 1938/1985

Cremations 1968

5 · Graves 1968

14

6

7

Ship burial 1939

13

Tray Cremation 1938

3

Bronze vessel cremation 1938

4

8

10

15

9

11

Graves 1984

TRIAL AREA FOR REMOTE SENSING

Track

Modern track

N

100 ft
50 m

○ Mound

Phosphate survey

Surface survey (fieldwalking)

Contour and vegetation mapping, metal detection, and radar

Trial area for remote sensing (proton magnetometer, fluxgate gradiometer, resistivity)

corresponded with the results from surface survey.

Before undertaking any excavation, the team wished to learn as much as possible about what lay beneath the surface, and a whole range of techniques were employed with varying results. Metal detectors were used in the main mound area to map modern garbage such as farm debris, bullets, and bottle tops. Magnetometry and resistivity were tested on a small area to the east of the mounds which was later excavated. The proton magnetometer proved not to be particularly informative; slightly better results were obtained with a fluxgate gradiometer. The best results, however, came from soil resistivity which, in addition to a large ditch already identified by the other methods, revealed a modern anti-glider ditch and a double palisade, as well as other anomalies. Even so,

excavation subsequently uncovered smaller features such as graves that had been missed by all the remote sensing devices.

Resistivity is now being applied to help survey the main area around the mounds. The mounds themselves are being surveyed using soil-sounding radar, because resistivity does not penetrate deep enough.

At Sutton Hoo, geophysical survey is seen not simply as prospection, but as an additional method of acquiring information complementary to excavation. The tests, together with subsequent excavation, have shown that the mounds are not isolated, but stand in a sea of other features, including Anglo-Saxon flat graves and, most notably, a Late Neolithic/Early Bronze Age settlement.

Resistivity meter being used in survey work at Sutton Hoo.

Proton magnetometer

Fluxgate gradiometer

Resistivity

Survey at Sutton Hoo *included a contour survey (far left), using an electronic distance measurer (EDM), with contours computer-plotted at 10-cm vertical intervals. The topography of the site was thus recorded before the new campaign began. The general plan (left) indicates the variety of survey techniques used in different parts of the site, including the trial area for remote sensing. Tests in this trial area (above and right) showed that while resistivity was the most sensitive device on this sandy soil, excavation revealed features that all the remote sensing techniques missed.*

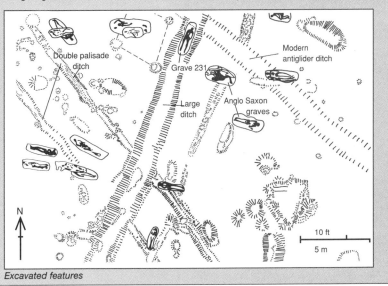

Double palisade ditch

Grave 231

Large ditch

Modern antiglider ditch

Anglo Saxon graves

N

10 ft

5 m

Excavated features

EXCAVATION

So far, we have discovered sites and mapped as many of their surface and subsurface features as possible. But, despite the growing importance of survey, the only way to check the reliability of surface data, confirm the accuracy of the remote sensing techniques, and actually see what remains of these sites is to excavate them.

Purposes of Excavation

Excavation retains its central role in fieldwork because it yields the most reliable evidence for the two main kinds of information archaeologists are interested in: (1) human activities at a particular period in the past; and (2) changes in those activities from period to period. Very broadly we can say that contemporary activities take place *horizontally in space*, whereas changes in those activities occur *vertically through time*. It is this distinction between horizontal "slices of time" and vertical sequences through time that forms the basis of most excavation methodology.

In the horizontal dimension archaeologists demonstrate contemporaneity – that activities did indeed occur at the same time – by proving to their satisfaction through excavation that artifacts and features are found in association in an undisturbed context. Of course, as we saw in Chapter 2, there are many formation processes that may disturb this primary context. One of the main purposes of the survey and remote sensing procedures outlined in the earlier sections is to select for excavation sites, or areas within sites, that are reasonably undisturbed. On a single-period site such as an East African early human camp site this is vital if human behavior at the camp is to be reconstructed at all accurately. But on a multi-period site, such as a longlived European town or Near Eastern tell, finding large areas of undisturbed deposits will be virtually impossible. Here archaeologists have to try to reconstruct during and after excavation just what disturbance there has been and then decide how to interpret it. Quite clearly, adequate records must be made as excavation progresses if the task of interpretation is to be undertaken with any chance of success (see below). In the vertical dimension archaeologists analyze changes through time by the study of stratigraphy.

Stratigraphy. As we saw in Chapter 1, one of the first steps in comprehending the great antiquity of humankind was the recognition by geologists of the process of stratification – that layers or strata are laid down, one on top of the other, according to processes that still continue. Archaeological strata (the layers of cultural or natural debris visible in the side of any excavation) accumulate over much shorter periods of time than geological ones, but nevertheless conform to the same *law of superposition*. Put simply, this states that where one layer overlies another, the lower layer was deposited first. Hence, an excavated vertical profile showing a series of layers constitutes a sequence that has accumulated through time. Chapter 4 explores the significance of this for dating purposes. Here we should note that the law of superposition refers only to the sequence of deposition, *not* to the age of the material in the different strata. The contents of lower layers are indeed usually older than those of upper layers, but the archaeologist must not simply assume this. Pits dug down from a higher layer or burrowing animals (even earthworms) may introduce later materials into lower levels. Moreover, occasionally strata can become inverted, as when they are eroded all the way from the top of a bank to the bottom of a ditch.

In recent years, archaeologists have developed an ingenious and effective method of checking that artifacts – so far mostly of stone or bone – discovered in a particular deposit are contemporaneous and not intrusive. They have found that in a surprising number of cases flakes of stone or bone can be fitted back together again, reassembled in the shape of the original stone block or pieces of bone from which they came. At the British Mesolithic (Middle Stone Age) site of Hengistbury Head, for example, reanalysis of an old excavation showed that two groups of flint flakes, found in two different layers, could be refitted. This cast doubt on the stratigraphic separation of the two layers, and demolished the original excavator's argument that the flints had been made by two different groups of people. As well as clarifying questions of stratification, these refitting or conjoining exercises are transforming archaeological studies of early technology (Chapter 8).

Stratigraphy, then, is the study and validating of stratification – the analysis in the vertical, time dimension of a series of layers in the horizontal, space dimension (although in practice few layers are precisely horizontal).

What are the best excavation methods for retrieving this information?

MODERN DISTURBANCE

PRESENT GROUND
SURFACE

CELLAR

DRAIN

NATURAL
SOIL LEVEL

WALL FOUNDATIONS

INTACT STRATIFICATION

PRESERVED ORGANIC MATERIAL

WATER TABLE

The complexity of stratification varies with the type of site. This hypothetical section through an urban deposit indicates the kind of complicated stratigraphy, in both vertical and horizontal dimensions, that the archaeologist can encounter. There may be few undisturbed stratified layers. The chances of finding preserved organic material increase as one approaches the water table, near which deposits may be waterlogged.

Methods of Excavation

Excavation is both costly and destructive, and therefore never to be undertaken lightly. Wherever possible the non-destructive approaches outlined earlier should be used to meet research objectives in preference to excavation. But assuming excavation is to proceed, and the necessary funding and permission to dig have been obtained, what are the best methods to adopt?

This book is not an excavation manual, and the reader is referred for detailed information to the texts listed at the end of this chapter and in the bibliography. In fact, a few days or weeks spent on a well-run dig are worth far more than reading any book on the subject. Nevertheless some brief guidance as to the main methods can be given here.

It goes without saying that all excavation methods need to be adapted to the research question in hand and the nature of the site. It is no good digging a deeply stratified urban site, with hundreds of complex structures, thousands of intercutting pits, and tens of thousands of artifacts, as if it were the same as a shallow Paleolithic open site, where only one or two structures and a few hundred artifacts may survive. On the Paleolithic site, for example, one has some hope of uncovering all the structures and recording the exact position, vertically and horizontally – i.e. the *provenience* – of each and every artifact. On the urban site one has no chance of doing this, given time and funding constraints. Instead, one has to adopt a sampling strategy (see box above) and only key artifacts such as coins (important for dating purposes: see Chapter 4) will have their provenience recorded with three-dimensional precision, the remainder being allocated simply to the layer and perhaps the grid-square in which they were found.

One should note, however, that we have already reintroduced the idea of the vertical and horizontal dimensions. These are as crucial to the methods of excavation as they are to the principles behind excavation. Broadly speaking one can divide excavation techniques into:

1   those that emphasize the vertical dimension, by cutting into deep deposits to reveal stratification;
2   those that emphasize the horizontal dimension, by opening up large areas of a particular layer to reveal the spatial relationships between artifacts and features in that layer.

Most excavators employ a combination of both strategies, but there are different ways of achieving this. All presuppose that the site has first been surveyed and a grid of squares laid down over it to aid in accurate recording.

The *Wheeler box-grid* – developed, as we saw in Chapter 1, from the work of General Pitt-Rivers – seeks to satisfy both vertical and horizontal requirements by retaining intact baulks of earth between the squares of the grid so that different layers can be traced and correlated across the site in the vertical profiles. Once the general extent and layout of the site have been ascertained, some of the baulks can be removed and the squares joined into an open excavation to expose any features (such as a mosaic floor) that are of special interest.

Advocates of *open-area excavation*, such as the English excavator Philip Barker, criticize the Wheeler method, arguing that the baulks are invariably in the wrong place or wrongly orientated to illustrate the relationships required from sections, and that they

Open-area excavation at Sutton Hoo, eastern England (see box above). A large area, 32 x 64 m, was uncovered to establish the perimeters of two burial mounds (nos. 2 and 5 on the site plan: see box). Detailed stratigraphy was then studied in smaller squares. Immediately below the topsoil lay early medieval features, recorded using overhead color photographs to emphasize soil variations, and plotted on site plans at scales of 1:10 and 1:100.

prevent the distinguishing of spatial patterning over large areas. It is far better, these critics say, not to have such permanent or semi-permanent baulks, but to open up large areas and only to cut vertical sections (at whatever angle is necessary to the main site grid) where they are needed to elucidate particularly complex stratigraphic relationships. Apart from these "running sections," the vertical dimension is recorded by accurate three-dimensional measurements as the dig proceeds and reconstructed on paper after the end of the excavation. The introduction since Wheeler's day of more advanced recording methods, including field computers, makes this more demanding open-area method feasible, and it has become the norm, for instance, in much of British archaeology. The open-area method is particularly effective where single-period deposits lie near the surface as for instance with remains of American Indian or European Neolithic long houses. Here the time dimension may be repre-

sented by lateral movement (a settlement may have been rebuilt adjacent to, not on top of, an earlier one) and it is essential to expose large horizontal areas in order to understand this complex pattern of rebuilding.

Sometimes, if time and money are short, and structures lie sufficiently close to the surface, the topsoil can simply be scraped away over large areas, as has been done to good effect at Tell Abu Salabikh (box, above, pp. 78, 79).

No single method, however, is ever going to be universally applicable. The rigid box-grid, for instance, has rarely been employed to excavate very deep sites, such as Near Eastern tells, because the trench squares rapidly become uncomfortable and dangerous as the dig proceeds downwards. One solution commonly adopted is *step-trenching*, with a large area opened at the top which gradually narrows as the dig descends in a series of large steps. This technique was used effectively at the Koster site, Illinois.

Step-trench excavation at the American Indian site of Koster, Illinois. Large horizontal areas were uncovered in order to locate living floors and activity zones. However, so that the vertical dimension could be analyzed at this deep site, vertical sections were cut as steps as the dig descended. Here archaeologists study a stratigraphic profile representing 14 occupation levels stretching from c.7500 BC to AD 1200.

Excavation methods. (Left) Sectioning a burial mound at Moundville, Alabama (see box, Chapter 5). (Above) Six stages of the quadrant method for excavating burial mounds. The objective is to expose subsurface features while retaining four transverse sections for stratigraphic analysis. (Below) Excavation of 70,000 years of deposits at Boomplaas Cave, South Africa (see Chapter 6), demanded meticulous recording controls, using grid lines attached to the cave roof.

Excavation using a cofferdam: the wreck – visible as air bubbles – of the merchant brig designated YO 88 at Yorktown, Virginia, scuttled during the War of Independence.

Another solution to the problem of dangerously deep excavations, successfully adopted on the salvage excavations at Coppergate, York (box, Chapter 14) and Billingsgate, London, is to build a *cofferdam* of sheet piling around the area to be dug. Cofferdams have also been used in shipwreck excavations, either simply to control the flow of water – as on a War of Independence wreck at Yorktown, Virginia – or to pump out the water altogether. Cofferdams are expensive, of course, and require the dig to be well funded.

Whatever the method of excavation – and the accompanying illustrations show other techniques e.g. for the excavation of burial mounds and cave sites – a dig is only as good as its methods of recovery and recording. Since excavation involves destruction of much of the evidence, it is an unrepeatable exercise. Well thought out recovery methods are therefore essential, and careful records must be kept of every stage of the dig.

Recovery and Recording of the Evidence

As we saw above, different sites have different requirements. One should aim to recover and plot the three-dimensional provenience of every artifact from a shallow single-period Paleolithic or Neolithic site, an objective that is simply not feasible for the urban archaeologist. On both types of site, a decision may be made to save time by using heavy mechanical diggers to remove topsoil, but thereafter the Paleolithic or Neolithic specialist will usually want to screen or sieve as much excavated soil as possible in order to recover tiny artifacts, animal bones, and in the case of wet

sieving (see Chapter 6), plant remains. The urban archaeologist on the other hand will only be able to adopt sieving much more selectively, as part of a sampling strategy, for instance where plant remains can be expected to survive, as in a latrine or refuse pit.

Once an artifact has been recovered, and its provenience recorded, it must be given a number which is entered in a catalog book or field computer and on the bag in which it is to be stored. Day-to-day progress of the dig is recorded in site notebooks, or on data sheets preprinted with specific questions to be answered (which helps produce uniform data suitable for later analysis by computer).

Unlike artifacts, which can be removed for later analysis, features and structures usually have to be left where they were found (*in situ*), or destroyed as the excavation proceeds to another layer. It is thus imperative to record them, not simply by written description in site notebooks, but by accurately scaled drawings and photography. The same applies to vertical profiles (sections), and for each horizontally exposed layer good overhead photographs taken from a stand or tethered balloon are also essential.

Screening: archaeologists at the Maya site of Cozumel, Mexico, screen excavated dirt through a mesh to recover tiny artifacts, animal bones, and other remains.

The ultimate value of an excavation lies in the records produced during actual fieldwork. Good organization is essential. Here we show the step-by-step methods adopted by the Museum of London. (Right) A flow diagram of procedures for the excavator to follow once a context (deposit) has been identified during the dig. (Below) Recording sheets must be meticulously completed as work proceeds. Most features are excavated and thus destroyed, so post-excavation analysis and layer-by-layer reconstructions of the site depend entirely on accurate field notes. (Opposite) The Roman baths at Huggin Hill in London. A Museum of London archaeologist uses a theodolite to measure the accurate position of a column base on which another archaeologist holds a survey rod (range pole). Their measurements will later form the basis for a detailed plan.

CONTEXT RECORDING SHEET

| Grid Square(s) | 110 — 115/210 | Area/Section | B | Context type | DEPOSIT | Site Code | XYZ | 89 | Context | 138 |

DEPOSIT
1. Compaction
2. Colour
3. Composition / Particle size (over 10%)
4. Inclusions (under 10%) occa / mod / freq
5. Thickness & extent
6. Other comments
7. Method & conditions

1) VARIES FROM LOOSE TO COMPACT
2) DARK GREYISH BROWN
3) SAND (40%)   SILT (60%)
4) FREQUENT LARGE FRAGMENTS OF POTTERY AND TILE; FREQUENT MEDIUM AND SMALL FRAGMENTS OF BONE, OCCASIONAL MEDIUM AND SMALL FRAGMENTS OF LEATHER, SMALL FRAGMENTS METAL, AND WHOLE OYSTER SHELLS (ALL INCLUSIONS WELL SORTED)
5) THICKEST AT NORTH (25mm) SLOPING DOWN TO THE SOUTH / EAST (10mm) THE LOWER BOUNDARY TO THE NEXT HORIZON IS IRREGULAR.
6) OCCASIONAL LENSES OF ORGANIC MATERIAL
7) WEATHER DRY, EXCAVATED WITH MATTOCK.

CUT
1. Shape in plan
2. Corners
3. Dimensions/Depth
4. Break of slope- top
5. Sides
6. Break of slope- base
7. Base
8. Orientation
9. Inclination of axis
10. Truncated (if known)
11. Fill nos
12. Other comments
Draw profile overleaf

PTO

Stratigraphic matrix

| 121 | 135 | | | | | | |

This context is | 138 |

| 154 | 157 | 148 | | | | | |

Your interpretation : Internal (External) Structural Other (specify)

A DUMPED DEPOSIT, (PROBABLY REFUSE)

Your discussion :
LARGE QUANTITY OF POTTERY AND BONE PLUS OTHER MATERIAL, AND WELL SORTED NATURE SUGGEST IT IS A DUMP OF REFUSE MATERIAL.
(MIGHT BE ASSOCIATED WITH STRUCTURE [95])?

Context same as : PTO

Plan nos : P 138 (X 2)	Site book refs :	Initials & date NH 24/8/89
Other drawings : S/E	Matrix location : C3	Checked by & date BP 2/9/89
Photographs : ☐ Card nos :		

Levels on reverse
Tick when reduced and transferred to plans : ☑
Highest :   Lowest :

Finds (tick)
None Pot Bone Glass Metal CBM BM Wood Other Leather
☐ ☑ ☑ ☐ ☑ ☑ ☐ ☐ ☐ ☑

Environmental samples
Sample nos & type (23) BULK SAMPLE FOR SIEVING — FISH BONES etc.

Other finds (specify) : 1 WHOLE CERAMIC VESSEL
Finds sample (BM) nos :

Checked Interpretation :

PTO

| Provisional period | Group | Initials & date |

MUSEUM OF LONDON

CLEAN AREA

IDENTIFY LIMITS OF CONTEXT

CHECK WITH SUPERVISOR AS TO NEED OF PHOTOGRAPH

IDENTIFY NUMBER OF GRID SQUARES IN WHICH FEATURE LIES

TAKE SHEET(S) OF PERMATRACE FROM FILE IN SITE OFFICE

DRAW A PLAN OF FEATURE AT A SCALE OF 1:20 UNLESS ADVISED OTHERWISE

TAKE RELEVANT TYPE OF CONTEXT SHEET FROM FILE IN SITE OFFICE

TAKE CONTEXT NUMBERS FROM SITE CONTEXT REGISTER

RECORD CONTEXT NUMBER ON PLAN(S)

TAKE LEVELS; MARK SPOT HEIGHTS ON PLAN, RECORD BACKSIGHT AND FORESIGHTS ON REVERSE OF CONTEXT SHEET

REDUCE LEVELS TO O.D. AND TRANSFER TO PLAN

DESCRIBE CONTEXT

OBTAIN FINDS BAG AND LABEL, AND ENTER SITE CODE AND CONTEXT NUMBER ON LABEL

CHECK WITH SUPERVISOR AS TO SUITABLE METHOD OF EXCAVATION, NEED FOR SAMPLING AND METHOD OF FINDS COLLECTION

EXCAVATE CONTEXT, AMENDING AND ADJUSTING DESCRIPTION AS NECESSARY

TAKE FINDS TO APPROPRIATE PLACE

DETERMINE RELATIONSHIPS OF NEWLY-RECORDED CONTEXT TO PREVIOUSLY EXCAVATED STRATIGRAPHY BY OVERLAYING PLANS

CROSS-REFERENCE RELATIONSHIPS ON CONTEXT SHEET AND FILL IN MATRIX

ENTER DATE AND INITIALS ON CONTEXT SHEET

PLACE PLAN AND CONTEXT SHEET IN RELEVANT 'TO BE CHECKED' FILES

[ALL PLANS, CONTEXT SHEETS AND RELATIONSHIPS SHOULD BE CHECKED BEFORE LEAVING SITE]

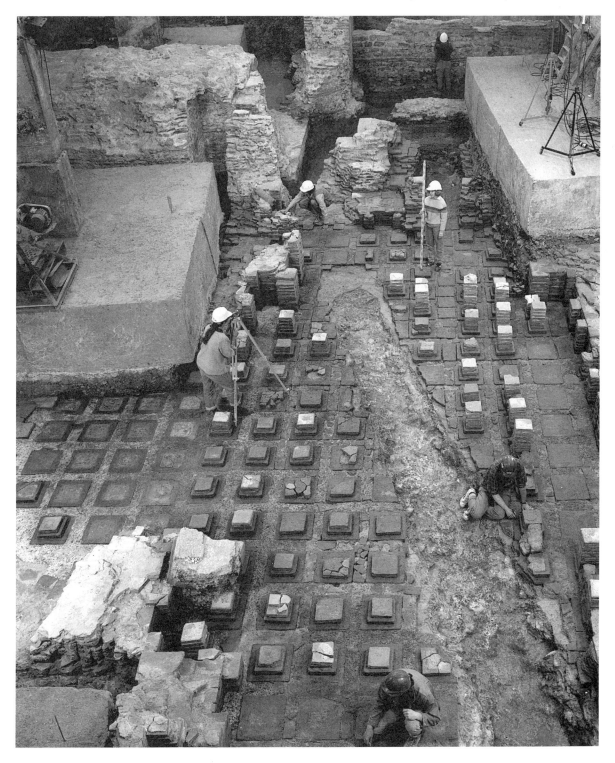

It is the site notebooks, scaled drawings, photographs and computer disks – in addition to the recovered artifacts, animal bones, and plant remains – that form the total record of the excavation, on the basis of which all interpretations of the site will be made. This post-excavation analysis will take many months, perhaps years, and often much longer than the excavation itself. However, some of the preliminary analysis, particularly sorting and classification of the artifacts, will be made in the field during the course of the excavation.

Processing and Classification

Like excavation itself, the processing of excavated materials in the field laboratory is a specialized activity that demands careful planning and organization. For example, no archaeologist should undertake the excavation of a wet site without having on hand team members expert in the conservation of waterlogged wood, and facilities for coping with such material. The reader is referred for further guidance to the many manuals now available that deal with conservation problems confronting archaeologists.

There are, however, two aspects of field laboratory procedure that should be discussed briefly here. The first concerns the cleaning of artifacts; the second, artifact classification. In both cases we would stress the need for the archaeologist always to consider in advance what kinds of questions the newly excavated material might be able to answer. Thorough cleaning of artifacts, for example, is a traditional part of excavations worldwide. But many of the new scientific techniques discussed in Part II make it quite evident that artifacts should *not* necessarily be cleaned thoroughly before a specialist has had a chance to study them. For instance, we now know that food residues are often preserved in pots and blood residues on stone tools (Chapter 7). The chances of such preservation need to be assessed before evidence is destroyed.

Nevertheless most artifacts eventually have to be cleaned to some degree if they are to be sorted and classified. Initial sorting is into broad categories such as stone tools, pottery, and metal objects. These categories are then subdivided or classified, so as to create more manageable groups that can later be analyzed. Classification is commonly done on the basis of three kinds of characteristics or *attributes:*

1 surface attributes (including decoration and color);
2 shape attributes (dimensions as well as shape itself);
3 technological attributes (primarily raw material).

Artifacts found to share similar attributes are grouped together into artifact types – hence the term *typology*, which simply refers to the creation of such types.

Typology dominated archaeological thinking until the 1950s, and still plays an important role in the discipline. The reason for this is straightforward. Artifacts make up a large part of the archaeological record, and typology helps archaeologists create order in this mass of evidence. As we saw in Chapter 1, Thomsen and Worsaae demonstrated early on that artifacts could be ordered in a three-age system or sequence of stone, bronze, and iron. This discovery underlies the continuing use of typology as a method of dating – of measuring the passage of time (Chapter 4). Typology has also been used as a means of defining archaeological entities at a particular moment in time. Groups of artifact (and building) types at a particular time and place are termed *assemblages*, and groups of assemblages have been taken to define *archaeological cultures*. As we shall see in Part II, the difficulty comes when one tries to translate this terminology into human terms and to relate an archaeological culture with an actual group of people in the past.

This brings us back to the purpose of classification. Types, assemblages, and cultures are all artificial constructs designed to put order into disordered evidence. The trap that former generations of scholars fell into was to allow these constructs to determine the way they thought about the past, rather than using them merely as one means of giving shape to the evidence. We now recognize more clearly that different classifications are needed for the different kinds of questions we want to ask. A student of ceramic technology would base a classification on variations in raw material and methods of manufacture, whereas a scholar studying the various functions of pottery for storage, cooking etc. might classify the vessels according to shape and size. Our ability to construct and make good use of new classifications has been immeasurably enhanced by computers, which allow archaeologists to compare the association of different attributes on hundreds of objects at once.

In a recent salvage project – involving the survey, testing, and excavation of some 500 sites along the 2250-km (1400-mile) route of a pipeline from California to Texas – Fred Plog, David L. Carlson, and their associates developed a computerized system using a video camera for automatic recording of different attributes of artifacts. Four to six people could process 1000–2000 artifacts a day, some 10 times quicker than normal methods. The standardization of recording methods allows rapid and highly accurate comparisons to be made between different artifact types.

INDIVIDUALS ATTRIBUTES ARTIFACTS

Attribute patterning reflects individual behavior patterns

GROUPS ARTIFACTS SUBASSEMBLAGES

Artifact patterning reflects group behavior patterns

COMMUNITIES SUBASSEMBLAGES ASSEMBLAGES

Sub - assemblage patterning reflects community behavior patterns

SOCIETIES ASSEMBLAGES ARCHAEOLOGICAL CULTURES

Assemblage patterning reflects societal behavior patterns

Terms used in archaeological classification, from individual attributes (shape, decoration) of a pot to the complete archaeological culture: a diagram developed by the American archaeologist James Deetz. The columns at left and right give the inferred human meaning of the terms. The extent to which one can draw behavioral inferences from such classification is discussed in Chapter 12.

In conclusion, it cannot be stressed too strongly that all the effort put into survey, excavation, and post-excavation analysis will have been largely wasted unless the results are published, initially as interim reports and subsequently in a full-scale monograph (see Chapter 14).

SUMMARY

Until the present century, individual sites were the main focus of archaeological attention, and the only remote sensing devices used were a pair of eyes and a stick. The development of aerial photography and reconnaissance techniques have shown archaeologists that the entire landscape is of interest, while geophysical and geochemical methods have revolutionized our ability to detect what lies beneath the soil.

Today archaeologists study whole regions, often employing sampling techniques to bring ground reconnaissance (surface survey) within the scope of individual research teams. Having located sites within those regions, and mapped them with the aid of aerial reconnaissance techniques, archaeologists can then turn to a whole battery of remote sensing site survey devices able to detect buried features without excavation. The geophysical methods almost all involve either passing energy into the ground and locating buried features from their effect on that energy, or measuring the intensity of the earth's magnetic field. In either case, they depend on some contrast between the buried features and their surroundings. Many of the techniques are costly in both equipment and time, but they are often cheaper and certainly less destructive than random test-pits or trial trenches. They allow archaeologists to be more selective in deciding which parts of a site, if any, should be fully excavated.

Excavation itself relies on methods designed to elucidate the horizontal extent of a site in space, and the vertical stratification representing changes through time (though time can be represented by a horizontal movement of the site as well). Good recording methods are essential, as are a well-equipped field laboratory for processing and classifying the finds. Classification based on selected attributes (decoration, shape, material) of each artifact is the fundamental means of organizing the excavated material, usually into types – hence typology. But classification is only a means to an end, and different schemes are needed for different questions archaeologists want to address.

However, little of the material retrieved during survey and excavation will be of much use unless it can be dated in some way. In the next chapter we turn to this crucial aspect of archaeology.

Further Reading

Useful introductions to methods of locating and surveying archaeological sites can be found in the following:

Clark, J.D.G. 1960. *Archaeology and Society*. (3rd ed.) Methuen: London; Barnes and Noble: New York. (Chapter 2.)

Colwell, R.N. (ed.). 1983. *Manual of Remote Sensing*. (2nd ed.) Society of Photogrammetry: Falls Church, Virginia.

Flannery, K.V. (ed.). 1976. *The Early Mesoamerican Village*. Academic Press: New York. (Helpful examples of surface survey.)

Lyons, T.R. & Avery, T.E. 1977. *Remote Sensing: A Handbook for Archaeologists and Cultural Resource Managers*. U.S. Dept of the Interior: Washington, D.C.

Tite, M.S. 1972. *Methods of Physical Examination in Archaeology*. Seminar Press: London & New York.

Among the most widely used field manuals are:

Barker, P. 1983. *Techniques of Archaeological Excavation*. (2nd ed.) Batsford: London; Humanities Press: New York. (British methods.)

Connah, G. (ed.). 1983. *Australian Field Archaeology. A Guide to Techniques*. Australian Institute of Aboriginal Studies: Canberra. (Australian methods.)

Hester, T.N., Shafer, H.J., & Heizer, R.F. 1987. *Field Methods in Archaeology*. (7th ed.) Mayfield: Palo Alto, Calif. (American methods.)

Joukowsky, M. 1980. *A Complete Manual of Field Archaeology*. Prentice-Hall: Englewood Cliffs, N.J. (American methods.)

Spence, C. (ed.). 1990. *Archaeological Site Manual*. (2nd ed.) Museum of London. (British methods.)

Also useful for beginners, and extremely well illustrated:

McIntosh, J. 1986. *The Practical Archaeologist*. Facts on File: New York (published in Britain as *The Archaeologist's Handbook*. Bell and Hyman: London.)

4
When?
Dating Methods
and Chronology

All human beings experience time. An individual experiences a lifetime of perhaps 70 years or so. That person, through the memories of his or her parents and grandparents, may also indirectly experience earlier periods of time, back over one or two generations. The study of history gives one access – even less directly but often no less vividly – to hundreds of years of recorded time. But it is only archaeology, in particular prehistoric archaeology, that opens up the almost unimaginable vistas of thousands and even a few millions of years of past human existence.

In order to study the past it is not, rather surprisingly, always essential to know precisely how long ago in years a particular period or event occurred. As we saw in Chapter 1, Thomsen and Worsaae's great achievement in the 19th century was to establish a three-part organization of tools for the Old World into those of stone, bronze, and iron which stratigraphic excavation confirmed was a chronological sequence: stone artifacts came before bronze ones, and iron ones came after. Archaeologists could use this sequence to study, say, changes in tool technology from one stage of the sequence to the next, even without knowing how long each stage lasted or how many years ago such developments took place. This idea that something is older (or younger) relative to something else is the basis of *relative dating*. The initial steps in most archaeological research today still depend crucially on relative dating, on the ordering of artifacts, deposits, societies, and events into sequences, earlier before later.

Ultimately, however, we want to know the full or absolute age in years before the present of the different parts of the sequence – we need methods of *absolute dating* (sometimes called chronometric dating). Absolute dates help us find out how quickly changes such as the introduction of agriculture occurred, and whether they occurred simultaneously or at different times in different regions of the world. Before World

War II for much of archaeology virtually the only reliable absolute dates were historical ones – Tutankhamun reigned in the 14th century BC, Caesar invaded Britain in 55 BC. Only in the last 40 years have independent means of absolute dating become available, transforming archaeology in the process.

Measuring Time

How do we detect the passage of time? In our own lives, we observe its passing through the alternating darkness and light of nights and days, and then through the annual cycle of the seasons. In fact, until the development of modern astronomy and nuclear physics, these were the only ways of observing time, other than by the human lifespan. As we shall see, some dating methods still rely on the annual passage of the seasons. Increasingly, however, dating methods in archaeology have come to rely on other physical processes, many of them not observable to the human eye. The most significant of these is the use of radioactive clocks.

Whatever the dating method, we need an agreed measure of time in order to construct a chronology. Most human measuring systems reckon on the basis of years. Thus even age measurements such as radioactive clocks that are independent of annual cycles need for our purposes to be converted into years. Often when there are dating errors it is the conversion into years rather than the dating method itself that is at fault.

Our timescale in years must date from or to a fixed point in time. In the Christian world, this is by convention taken as the birth of Christ, supposedly in the year AD 1 (there is no year 0), with years counted back before Christ (BC) and forwards after Christ (AD or *Anno Domini*, Latin for "In the Year of Our Lord"). In the Greek world, the notional starting point was the holding of the first Olympic Games (reckoned at 776 BC in the Christian calendar), whereas for Muslims the basic fixed point is the date of the Prophet's departure from Mecca, the Hegira (reckoned at AD 622 in the Christian calendar). The starting point in the Maya calendar is equivalent to 3114 BC in the Christian calendar.

Scientists who derive dates from radioactive methods, wanting a neutral international system without allegiance to any of the above calendars, have chosen to count years back from the present (BP). But since scientists too require a firm fixed point, they take BP to mean "before 1950" (the approximate year of Libby's establishment of the first radioactive method, radiocarbon). This may be convenient for scientists, but can be confusing for everyone else (a date of 400 BP is not 400 years ago but AD 1550, currently about 440 years ago). It is therefore clearest to convert any BP date for the last few thousand years into the BC/AD system. For the Paleolithic period, however (stretching back two or three million years before 10,000 BC), archaeologists use the terms "BP" and "years ago" interchangeably, since a difference of 40 years or so

between them is irrelevant. For this remote epoch one is dating sites or events at best only to within several thousand years of their "true" date.

Discussion of the Paleolithic makes it evident that our whole conception and interpretation of time and its measurement needs to be adapted to the period being studied. If even the most precise dates for the Paleolithic give us glimpses of that epoch only at intervals of several thousand years, clearly archaeologists can never hope to reconstruct Paleolithic events in the manner of conventional history, peopled with individuals as, for instance, in ancient Egypt during the era of the pharaohs. On the other hand, Paleolithic archaeologists can gain insights into some of the broad long-term changes that shaped the way modern humans evolved – insights that are denied archaeologists working with shorter periods of time, where in any case there may be too much "detail" for the broader pattern to be easily discernible.

The way in which archaeologists carry out their research is therefore very much dependent on the precision of dating – the sharpness of focus – obtainable for the period of time in question.

RELATIVE DATING

The first, and in some ways the most important, step in much archaeological research involves ordering things into sequences. The things to be put into sequence can be archaeological deposits in a stratigraphic excavation. Or they can be artifacts as in a typological

sequence. Changes in the earth's climate also give rise to local, regional, and global environmental sequences – the most notable being the sequence of global fluctuations during the Ice Age. All these sequences can be used for relative dating.

STRATIGRAPHY

Stratigraphy, as we saw in Chapter 3, is the study of stratification – the laying down or depositing of strata or layers (also called deposits) one above the other. From the point of view of relative dating, the important principle is that the underlying layer was deposited first and therefore earlier than the overlying layer. Thus a succession of layers should provide a relative chronological sequence, from earliest (bottom) to latest (top).

Good stratigraphic excavation at an archaeological site is designed to obtain such a sequence. Part of this work involves detecting whether there has been any human or natural disturbance of the layers since they were originally deposited. In Chapter 2 we discussed some of these cultural and natural formation processes – such as rubbish pits dug down by later occupants of a

site into earlier layers, animals burrowing holes, and floods washing layers away and redepositing them elsewhere in secondary context. Armed with carefully observed stratigraphic information, the archaeologist can hope to construct a reliable relative chronological sequence for the deposition of the different layers.

But of course what we mostly want to date are not so much the layers or deposits themselves as the humanly generated materials within them – artifacts, structures, organic remains – which ultimately (when systematically studied) reveal past human activities at the site. Here the idea of *association*, touched on in Chapter 2, is important. When we say that two objects were found in association within the same archaeological deposit, we generally mean that they became buried at the same time. Provided that deposit is a sealed one,

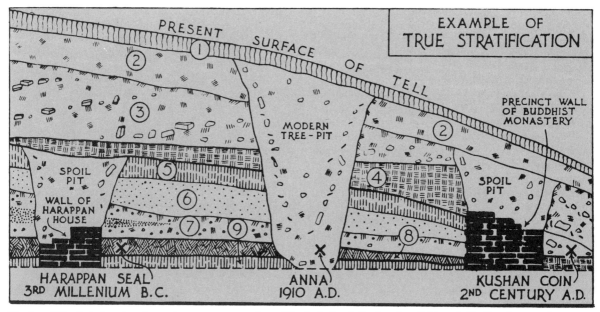

PRESENT SURFACE OF TELL

EXAMPLE OF
TRUE STRATIFICATION

PRECINCT WALL
OF BUDDHIST
MONASTERY

MODERN
TREE-PIT

SPOIL
PIT

WALL OF
HARAPPAN
HOUSE

SPOIL
PIT

HARAPPAN SEAL
3RD MILLENIUM B.C.

ANNA
1910 A.D.

KUSHAN COIN
2ND CENTURY A.D.

Mortimer Wheeler's drawing of a section across a mound or tell in the Indus Valley (modern Pakistan). Pit disturbance makes dating difficult, but the Harappan seal, for example (age known from similar seals found elsewhere), lies in an undisturbed context in layer 8, and can therefore help date that layer and the wall against which the layer abuts.

without stratigraphic intrusions from another deposit, the associated objects can be said to be no later (no more recent) than the deposit itself. A sequence of sealed deposits thus gives a sequence – and relative chronology – for the time of burial of the objects found associated in those deposits.

This is a crucial concept to grasp, because if one of those objects can later be given an absolute date – say a piece of charcoal that can be dated by radiocarbon in the laboratory – then it is possible to assign that absolute date not only to the charcoal but to the sealed deposit and the other objects associated with it as well. A series of such dates from different deposits will give an absolute chronology for the whole sequence. It is this interconnecting of stratigraphic sequences with absolute dating methods that provides the most reliable basis for dating archaeological sites and their contents. The section on radiocarbon dating below illustrates this for the site of Gatecliff Shelter, Nevada.

But there is another important point to consider. So far we have dated, relatively and with luck absolutely, the time of burial of the deposits and their associated material. As we have observed, however, what we want ultimately to reconstruct and date are the past human activities and behavior that those deposits and materials represent. If one of those deposits is a rubbish pit with pottery in it, the deposit itself is of

interest as an example of human activity, and the date for it will be the date of human use of the pit. This will also be the date of final burial of the pottery – but it will *not* be the date of human use of that pottery, which could have been in circulation tens or hundreds of years earlier, before being discarded, perhaps buried in another deposit and then dug up inadvertently with other rubbish to be thrown into the pit.

It is necessary therefore always to be clear about which activity one is trying to date, or can reliably date in the circumstances. The cultural formation processes discussed in Chapter 2 all have to be taken into account in any assessment of this question.

Bone Age

A useful method of assessing whether several bones found in association in the same stratigraphic deposit are in fact of the same relative age is chemical dating by studying nitrogen, fluorine, and uranium content.

In the deposit the bone's protein (mainly collagen) content is very gradually reduced by the processes of chemical decay. The most useful index for the amount of protein present is the bone's nitrogen content, which, for modern bone, is around 4 percent. The rate at which the level of nitrogen declines depends on the temperature and the water, chemical, and bacteriological content of the environment in which the bone is buried.

At the same time, percolating ground water has significant effects on the composition of bone. Two elements present in solution in the ground water – fluorine and uranium – are absorbed gradually by the bone. Thus, the content of fluorine and uranium in buried bone gradually increases, and can be measured in the laboratory. Like the rate of decrease in nitrogen, the rates of increase in fluorine and uranium depend strongly on local factors. All these rates of change are thus too variable to form the basis of an absolute dating method, nor can one compare relative ages so derived at one site with those at another site. But on an individual site chemical dating can distinguish bones of different age found in apparent stratigraphic association.

The most famous application of the method was in the case of the Piltdown forgery. In the early 1900s, pieces of human skull, an ape-like jawbone, and some teeth were found in a Lower Paleolithic gravel pit in Sussex, southern England. The discoveries led to claims that the "missing link" between apes and humans had been found. Piltdown man (*Eoanthropus dawsoni*) had an important place in textbooks until 1953, when it was exposed as a complete hoax. Fluorine, uranium, and nitrogen dating at the British Museum (Natural History) showed that the skull was human but of relatively recent age (it was subsequently dated at about 620 years old); the jawbone

Piltdown Man: a reconstruction made shortly before the remains were discovered to be a hoax. Fluorine, uranium, and nitrogen dating of the skull, jawbone, and teeth proved that they were of different relative ages, and not associated.

came from an orang-utan and was a modern "plant." Both the skull and the jawbone had been treated with pigment (potassium dichromate) to make them look old and associated.

TYPOLOGICAL SEQUENCES

When we look at the artifacts, buildings, and indeed any of the human creations around us, most of us can mentally arrange some of them into a rough chronological sequence. One kind of aircraft looks older than another, one set of clothes looks more "old-fashioned" than the next. How do archaeologists exploit this ability for relative dating?

As we saw in Chapter 3, the form of an artifact such as a pot can be defined by its specific attributes of material, shape, and decoration. Several pots with the same attributes constitute a pot type, and typology groups artifacts into such types. Underlying the notion of relative dating through typology are two further ideas.

The first is that the products of a given period and place have a recognizable style: through their distinctive shape and decoration they are in some sense characteristic of the society that produced them. This point is further discussed in Chapters 5 and 10. The archaeologist or anthropologist can often recognize and classify individual artifacts by their style, and hence assign them to a particular place in a typological sequence.

The second idea is that the change in style (shape and decoration) of artifacts is often quite gradual, or evolutionary. Indeed, this idea came from the Darwinian theory of the evolution of species, and was embraced by 19th-century archaeologists, who realized that here was a very convenient rule, that "like goes with like." In other words, particular artifacts (e.g. bronze daggers) produced at about the same time are often alike, whereas those produced several centuries apart will be different as a result of centuries of change. It follows, then, that when one is faced with a

The arrangement of artifact types in a sequence is based on two simple ideas: first, that products of a given period and place have a distinctive style or design; and second, that changes in each style are gradual, or evolutionary. Gradual changes in design are evident in the history of the automobile (top) and of the prehistoric European axe (above: (1) stone, (2-5) bronze). However, the rate of change (a century for the automobile, millennia for the axe) has to be deduced from absolute dating methods.

series of daggers of unknown date, it is logical first to arrange them in a sequence in such a way that the most closely similar are located beside each other. This is then likely to be the true chronological sequence, because it best reflects the principle that "like goes with like."

Such arguments were developed by many archaeologists, who found that relative chronologies could be established for different classes of artifacts from different regions. The great master of the "typological method" was the 19th-century Swedish scholar Oscar Montelius, who formulated local relative chronologies for many of the regions of Bronze Age Europe, drawing upon a whole series of bronze tool and weapon forms. These regional sequences could in many cases be confirmed in their outlines by stratigraphic excavations where it was indeed found that the simpler forms were the earliest.

Montelius went on to use the same arguments also in spatial terms to show how the artifact types in one region influenced those in adjacent areas. In this way, making certain assumptions about the direction of influence, he established a relative chronology of tool and weapon forms for the whole of Europe in the Bronze Age. (The assumption about the direction of influence – the famous principle that progress origin-

ated in the Near East and spread out from there – has been challenged and in part overthrown by more recent work. But in other respects the Montelius system for the European Bronze Age, as refined by the German prehistorian Paul Reinecke and others, is effectively still in use.)

For many purposes, it remains true that the best way to assign a relative date to an artifact is to match it with an artifact already recognized within a well-established typological system. In Europe, this is true for Bronze Age artifacts, but it applies very much more widely, at a world level. In the Paleolithic period, the first approximate (relative) dating of a layer will often come from an examination of the stone tools found within it: hand-axes imply Lower (or to a lesser extent Middle) Paleolithic, blades Upper Paleolithic. In later periods, pottery typologies usually form the backbone of the chronological system. Good examples are the detailed studies on the pottery of Greece in the Mycenaean period by the Swedish archaeologist Arne Furumark and his successors, and the ceramic sequence established for the Pueblo Indians of the American Southwest. But nearly every area has its own well-established ceramic succession. If this is tied into a stratigraphic sequence of deposits that can be dated by radiocarbon or other absolute means, then the artifacts

PHASE	DECORATION	SHAPE
SACATON AD 1000-1175		
SANTA CRUZ AD 875-1000		
GILA BUTTE AD 800-875		
SNAKETOWN AD 750-800		
SWEETWATER AD 700-750		
ESTRELLA AD 650-700		

Pottery typology, as exemplified by this 500-year sequence of changing Hohokam bowl styles from the American Southwest.

in the typological sequence can themselves be assigned absolute dates in years.

It is also worth noting that different types of artifact change in style (decoration and shape) at different rates, and therefore vary in the chronological distinctions that they indicate. For example, the changes in decoration of the painted Mycenaean pottery mentioned above may have occurred at intervals of 20 years or so, whereas other types of decorated pottery often lasted more than a century. Undecorated pottery could keep much the same shape for several centuries. By and large, with pottery, surface decoration changes more rapidly than shape and is therefore the most chronologically sensitive attribute to use for a typological sequence. Shape of a vessel or container may in any case be most strongly influenced by a practical requirement such as water storage which need not alter for hundreds of years.

Other artifacts, such as metal weapons or tools, can change in style quite rapidly, and so may be useful chronological indicators. By contrast stone tools, such as hand-axes, are often notoriously slow to change in form and therefore rarely make sensitive indicators of the passage of time.

Seriation

The insights of the principle that "like goes with like" have been developed further to deal with associations of finds (assemblages), rather than with the forms of single objects taken in isolation. This technique of seriation allows assemblages of artifacts to be arranged in a succession, or serial order, which is then taken to indicate their ordering in time: it is thus an exercise in relative chronology.

Two versions of the technique have been applied: *contextual seriation* and *frequency seriation*.

Contextual Seriation. Here it is the duration of different artifact styles (shape and decoration) that governs the seriation. The pioneer of the method was Flinders Petrie. Working at Diospolis Parva in Upper Egypt at the very end of the 19th century, he excavated several predynastic graves that could be neither stratigraphically linked to each other nor tied into the historical king-lists of the subsequent dynastic period. Petrie wanted to put the graves into chronological order, so he began by making an inventory of their contents. Each grave was allocated a separate slip of paper listing its artifact types. Petrie then placed the separate slips parallel to each other, one above the other in a column, and kept re-arranging their position

= 10% of the stones in a ten year period

Contextual seriation: Flinders Petrie's own serial ordering of predynastic Egyptian pottery from the site of Diospolis Parva. Starting at the top, seven successive stages are identified, each linked to the one before and after by at least one similar shape. At the left of the five lower rows are the "wavy-handled" pots, arranged by Petrie in a sequence of "degradation" – his clue to the order of the whole series. Subsequent research in Egypt has largely supported Petrie's relative chronological sequence.

Frequency seriation: changes in the popularity (or frequency) of three tombstone designs in central Connecticut cemeteries, from 1700 to 1860. Rises and falls in popularity have produced the characteristic battleship-shaped curve for the fluctuating fortunes of each design. As elsewhere in New England, the Death's head design (peak popularity 1710-1739) was gradually replaced by the Cherub (peak 1760-1789) which in turn was replaced by the urn and willow tree (peak 1840-1859).

up or down the column. He believed that the best arrangement would be the one where the greatest number of individual types had the shortest duration across the various slips. In this way he arrived at a sequence of assemblages – and thus of graves – arranged in what he thought was relative chronological order.

Subsequent work in Egypt has largely vindicated Petrie and shown that his serial ordering of the graves does in fact generally reflect their true chronological sequence.

Frequency Seriation. A similar problem – the lack of any external chronological information – was faced by American archaeologists working at Maya sites in the Yucatán in the 1940s. Their material consisted of ceramic collections which had been recovered without stratigraphic context. There was a need to place the ceramic assemblages in serial order so as to construct a relative chronology of the buildings and monuments with which they were associated.

The solution was frequency seriation, which relies principally on measuring changes in the proportional abundance, or frequency, of a ceramic style. The two basic assumptions behind the method were set out in a classic paper by W.S. Robinson and another by G.W. Brainerd, both published in *American Antiquity* in 1951. First, they assumed that pottery styles gradually become more popular, reach a peak popularity and then fade away (a phenomenon that diagrammatically produces a shape like a battleship as viewed from above – hence the common term for them, *battleship curves*). Secondly, they argued that at a given time period, a pot style popular at one site would similarly

Bowl type 13	Bowl type 1	Bowl type 14	Bases, bowl type 14	Bowl type 12	Low-necked jars

Frequency seriation: Frank Hole's ordering of bowl types representing Susiana Black-on-Buff pottery from sites in the Deh Luran Plain, Iran. The battleship curves are again evident, indicating rises and falls in popularity. Stratigraphic excavation confirmed the validity of these sequences.

be popular at another. Thus if the style in question represented 18 percent of the total pottery found at site A at a particular period, the pottery from site B for the same period would have a similar proportion or frequency of that style.

Using these two assumptions, Robinson and Brainerd were able to put the assemblages into a sequence so that those with the most similar percentage of certain pot styles were always together. The chronological validity of the method has since been demonstrated by American archaeologists such as James A. Ford working in the American Southeast and Frank Hole in Iran. Both Ford and Hole studied ceramic assemblages mainly derived from stratigraphic excavations. They were able to compare the sequences obtained from frequency seriation with the true stratigraphic sequences in the excavations. There were no serious contradictions.

Nevertheless it should be borne in mind that seriation by itself does not tell us which end of a given sequence is first and which last – the true chronology has to be determined by other means, as by links with the stratigraphic sequences just mentioned.

LINGUISTIC DATING

For completeness, it is appropriate to mention an interesting approach to questions of chronology, in this case applied not to artifacts but to *language* change, as studied by comparisons in the vocabularies of related languages. Earlier claims suggested that here might be some sort of absolute dating method; these have been widely (and rightly) rejected. However, the method remains of real interest from the standpoint of relative chronology.

The basic principle is straightforward. If you take two groups of people, speaking the same language, and separate them without further contact between them, both groups will no doubt continue to speak the same tongue. But in each population, over the years, changes will occur; new words will be invented and introduced whereas others fall out of use. So, after a few centuries, the two independent groups will no longer be speaking quite the same language; after a few thousand years, the language of one group will be quite unintelligible to the other.

The field of *lexicostatistics* sets out to study such changes of vocabulary. A popular method has been to choose a list of either 100 or 200 common vocabulary terms and to see how many of these, in the two

languages being compared, share a common root-word. The positive score, out of 100 or 200, gives some measure of how far the two languages have diverged since the time when they were one.

The rather suspect discipline of *glottochronology* would claim to go further, and use a formula to pronounce, from this measure of similarity, how long in years it is since the two languages diverged. The American scholar, Morris Swadesh, the principal exponent of the method, concluded that two related languages would retain a common vocabulary of 86 percent of the original after a period of separation of 1000 years. In reality, however, there is no basis for assuming a constant rate of change in this way: many factors influence linguistic change (the existence of literacy among them). And the method is complicated by various other factors, such as the existence of loan-words (borrowed from elsewhere, and not part of the common heritage) in both of the languages under study. But the underlying idea that two languages with a very high score for the common vocabulary are more recently related than those with a low score is itself reasonable, and the approach cannot be excluded from a discussion of methods of relative dating.

CLIMATE AND CHRONOLOGY

So far we have been discussing sequences that can be established stratigraphically for individual sites, or typologically for artifacts. In addition, there is a major class of sequences, based on changes in the earth's climate, that have proved useful for relative dating on a local, regional, and even global scale. Some of these environmental sequences can also be dated by various absolute methods. (The impact of climatic and environmental fluctuations on human life is discussed in detail in Chapter 6.)

Pleistocene Chronology

The idea of a great Ice Age (the Pleistocene epoch), that occurred in the distant past, has been with us since the 19th century. As world temperatures fell, ice sheets – or glaciers – expanded, mantling large parts of the earth's surface and lowering world sea levels (the lost water being quite literally locked up in the ice). Early geologists and paleoclimatologists, studying the clear traces in geological deposits, soon realized that the Ice Age was not one long unbroken spell of colder climate. Instead it had witnessed what they identified as four major *glacials*, or periods of glacial advance (labeled, from earliest to latest, Günz, Mindel, Riss, and Würm in continental Europe; in North America different names were chosen – Wisconsin, for example, being the equivalent of Würm). Punctuating these cold periods were warmer interludes known as *interglacials*. More minor fluctuations within these major phases were called *stadials* and *interstadials*. Until the arrival after World War II of absolute dating methods such as those based on radioactive clocks, archaeologists depended very largely for their dating of the long Paleolithic peroid on attempts to correlate archaeological sites with this glacial sequence. Far away from the

YEARS AGO	CLIMATE cool warm	GEOLOGICAL PERIODS	GEOLOGICAL EPOCHS	GLACIALS (EUROPE)	GLACIALS (N. AMERICA)	ARCHAEOLOGICAL STAGES
10,000			HOLOCENE			
				Würm (Weichsel)	Wisconsin	UPPER PALEOLITHIC
100,000			UPPER PLEISTOCENE			MIDDLE PALEOLITHIC
				Riss (Saale)	Illinoian	
		QUA-TERNARY	MIDDLE PLEISTOCENE	Mindel (Elster)	Kansan	
700,000				Günz (Menapian)	Nebraskan	LOWER PALEOLITHIC
	(uncertain)		LOWER PLEISTOCENE			
1,600,000						
		TERTIARY				

Table summarizing the main climatic changes, glacial terminology, and archaeological stages of the Pleistocene epoch.

ice sheets, in regions such as Africa, strenuous efforts were made to link sites with fluctuations in rainfall (*pluvials* and *interpluvials*); the hope was that the fluctuations might somehow themselves be tied in with the glacial sequence.

In recent decades, however, scientists have come to recognize that fluctuations in climate during the Ice Age were much more complex than originally supposed. From the beginning of the Pleistocene, more than 1.6 million years ago, down to 700,000 years ago (the end of the so-called Lower Pleistocene), there were perhaps ten cold periods separated by warmer interludes. Another eight or nine distinct periods of cold climate may have characterized the Middle and Upper Pleistocene, from 700,000 to 10,000 years ago. (The period of warmer climate known as the Holocene covers the last 10,000 years.) Archaeologists no longer rely on complex glacial advances and retreats as the basis for dating the Paleolithic. However, fluctuations in Pleistocene and Holocene climate as recorded in deep-sea cores, ice cores, and sediments containing pollen have proved to be of considerable value for dating purposes.

Deep-Sea Cores and Ice Cores

As indicated in Chapter 6, the most coherent record of climatic changes on a worldwide scale is now provided by deep-sea cores, drilled from the ocean bed. These cores contain shells of microscopic marine organisms known as foraminifera, laid down on the ocean floor through the slow continuous progress of sedimentation. Variations in the ratio of two oxygen isotopes in the calcium carbonate of these shells give a sensitive indicator of sea temperature at the time the organisms were alive. We now have an accurate temperature sequence stretching back 2.3 million years which reflects climate change on a global scale. Thus the cold episodes in the deep-sea cores relate to glacial periods of ice advance, and the warm episodes to interglacial or interstadial periods of ice retreat. The deep-sea core oxygen isotope record in this way provides a relative chronology for the Pleistocene.

This chronology is invaluable for reconstructing a record of past environmental change, as will be discussed in Chapter 6. Radiocarbon and uranium-series dating (see below) can also be applied to the foraminiferan shells to provide absolute dates for the sequence. In addition, the phenomenon of geomagnetic reversals (reversals in the earth's magnetic field), discussed in a later section, can be used to link the sequence to Paleolithic sites in the East African Rift Valley. Such reversals are recorded in both the cores

and the rock strata at the archaeological sites (see box below, Dating Our African Ancestors).

Ice Cores. As with deep-sea cores, cores extracted from the polar ice of the Arctic and Antarctic have been made to yield impressive sequences revealing climatic oscillations. Here again these are most useful for reconstructing ancient environments (Chapter 6), but they have relevance for dating as well.

The layers of compacted ice form annual deposits for the last 2000–3000 years that can be counted – thus giving an absolute chronology for this part of the sequence. As we shall see in the box on Dating the Thera Eruption (below), this has proved useful as one possible means of cross-checking the date of that volcanic explosion, which some scholars believe severely disrupted the Minoan civilization of Crete. For earlier time periods, however – at greater depths – the annual stratification is no longer visible, and dating of the ice cores is much less certain. The Vostok core in Antarctica reached a depth of about 2200 m (7200 ft), and spans a time-range which has been estimated at 160,000 years. Good correlations have been made with climatic oscillations deduced from the study of the deep-sea cores.

Pollen Dating

All flowering plants produce the almost indestructible grains called pollen, and their preservation in bogs and lake sediments has allowed pollen experts (palynologists) to construct detailed sequences of past vegetation and climate. These sequences are an immense help in understanding ancient environments, as we shall discuss in Chapter 6. But they have also been – and to a limited extent still are – important as a method of relative dating.

The best-known pollen sequences are those developed for the Holocene (postglacial) of northern Europe, where an elaborate succession of so-called *pollen zones* covers the last 10,000 years. By studying pollen samples from a particular site, that site can often be fitted into a broader pollen zone sequence and thus assigned a relative date. Isolated artifacts and finds such as bog-bodies discovered in contexts where pollen is preserved can also very usefully be dated in the same way. However, it is important to remember that the pollen zones are not uniform across large areas. In any one local region, such as the Somerset Levels of southern England, it is best to work with a specialist who can build up a sequence of pollen zones for that region. The sites and finds in the vicinity can then be linked to it. If tree-ring or radiocarbon dates

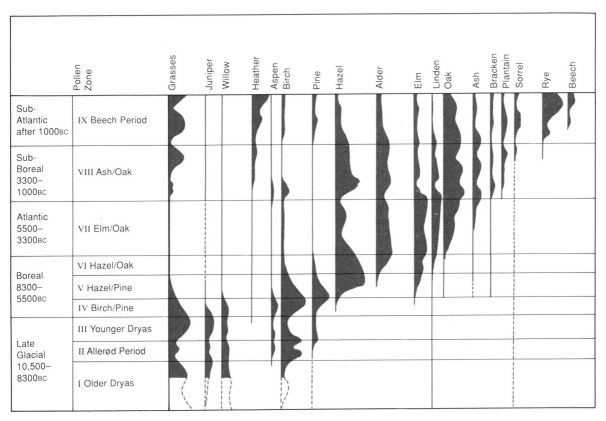

Idealized diagram illustrating the Holocene (postglacial) pollen zone sequence in Jutland, Denmark. Each pollen zone is characterized by rises and falls in pollen of certain plant species, e.g. birch and pine in zone IV, beech in zone IX. Dates are given in uncalibrated radiocarbon years BC (see p. 124).

can then be determined for all or at least part of the sequence, one has the makings of an absolute chronology for the region.

Thanks to the durability of pollen grains, they can yield environmental evidence even as far back as 3 million years ago for sites in East Africa (Chapter 6). Different interglacial periods in areas such as northern Europe have also been shown to have characteristic pollen sequences, which means that the pollen evidence at an individual site in the area can sometimes be matched to a particular interglacial – a useful dating mechanism given that radiocarbon does not operate at these early time periods.

Faunal Dating

There is a further method of relative dating relevant for the Pleistocene epoch, though one not based on the sedimentary processes that lie behind the methods already discussed. This is the old-established technique of faunal dating, which relies on the fact that many mammal species have evolved considerably over the last few million years, new forms emerging and old ones dying out. The changes in each species have been charted to create a rough sequence, for instance of elephants or pigs. In theory, if a similar sequence of pig species is found at two different sites, those sites can be assigned the same relative age. In practice the method is very imprecise for many reasons, including the fact that species extinct in one area may have continued much longer in another.

Nevertheless its imprecision does not rule out faunal dating altogether as a useful method for the Pleistocene, where even an accuracy only to within the nearest quarter million years can be of value. Faunal dating has proved particularly important in the correlation of the early human sites that have been discovered in East and South Africa.

ABSOLUTE DATING

Despite the great utility of methods of relative dating, archaeologists ultimately want to know how old sequences, sites, and artifacts are in calendar years. To achieve this they need to use the methods of absolute dating described in the following sections – from traditional historical methods to those which are based on the great variety of modern scientific techniques now available.

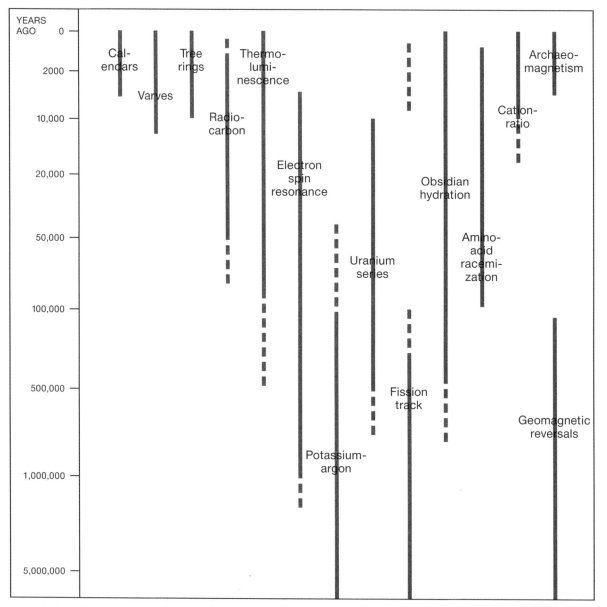

Chronological table summarizing the spans of time for which different absolute dating methods are applicable.

CALENDARS AND HISTORICAL CHRONOLOGIES

Until the development of the first scientific dating techniques around the beginning of this century, dating in archaeology depended almost entirely on historical methods. That is to say, it relied on archaeological connections with chronologies and calendars that people in ancient times had themselves established. Such dating methods are still of immense value today.

In the ancient world, literate societies recorded their own history in written documents. The Romans recorded events in terms of the year of rule of their consuls and emperors, although they sometimes referred events back to the foundation of the city of Rome itself. The Greeks reckoned from the date of the first Olympic Games, today usually set in the year 776 BC. In Egypt, the Near East, and ancient China history was recorded in terms of the successive kings, who were organized in groups of "dynasties." As we shall see, there were also very precise calendrical systems in Mesoamerica.

Archaeologists have to bear in mind three main points when working with early historical chronologies. First, the chronological system requires careful reconstruction, and any list of rulers or kings needs to be reasonably complete. Secondly, the king list, although it may reliably record the number of years in each reign, has still to be linked with our own calendar if it is not to remain merely a "floating chronology." Thirdly, the artifacts, features, or structures to be dated at a particular site have somehow to be related to the historical chronology, perhaps by their association with an inscription referring to the ruler of the time.

These points can be well illustrated by the Egyptian and Maya chronologies. Egyptian history is arranged in terms of 31 dynasties, themselves organized into the Old, Middle, and New Kingdoms. The modern view is a synthesis based on several documents including the so-called Turin Royal Canon. This synthesis gives an estimate of the number of years in each reign, right down to the conquest of Egypt by Alexander the Great, which can be set firmly, using information from Greek historians, in the year 332 BC. So the Egyptian dynasties can be dated by working backwards from there, although the exact length of every reign is not known. This system can be confirmed and refined using astronomy. Egyptian historical records describe observations of certain astronomical events that can be dated, quite independently, using current astronomical knowledge and knowledge of where in Egypt the ancient observations were carried out.

Egyptian dates are generally considered to be very reliable after 664 BC. For the New Kingdom (*c.* 1550–1070 BC), the margin of error may be one or two decades, and by the time one goes back to the beginning of the First Dynasty, around 3000 BC, the accumulated errors might amount to some 200 years or so.

Of the calendrical systems of Mesoamerica, the Maya calendar was the most elaborate (see box overleaf). It does not depend, as do those of Europe and the Near East, on a record of dynasties and rulers. Other areas of Mesoamerica had their own calendrical systems which operated on similar principles.

EGYPTIAN CHRONOLOGY
EARLY DYNASTIC (Archaic) (3000–2575 BC)   Dynasties 1–3
OLD KINGDOM (2575–2134)   Dynasties 4–8
FIRST INTERMEDIATE PERIOD (2134–2040)   Dynasties 9–11
MIDDLE KINGDOM (2040–1640)   Dynasties 11–14
SECOND INTERMEDIATE PERIOD (1640–1532)   Dynasties 15–17
NEW KINGDOM (1550–1070)   Dynasties 18–20
THIRD INTERMEDIATE PERIOD (1070–712)   Dynasties 21–25
LATE PERIOD (712–332 BC)   Dynasties 25–31

A historical chronology for ancient Egypt. The broad terminology is generally agreed by Egyptologists, but the precise dating of the earlier periods is disputed. Overlapping dates between dynasties/kingdoms (e.g. First Intermediate period and Middle Kingdom) indicate that separate rulers were accepted in different parts of the country.

THE MAYA CALENDAR

The Maya calendar was one of great precision, used for recording dates in inscriptions on stone columns or stelae erected at Maya cities during the Classic period (AD 300–900). The elucidation of the calendar, and the more recent decipherment of the Maya glyphs, mean that a well-dated Maya history is now emerging in a way which seemed impossible a few decades ago.

To understand the Maya calendar it is necessary to comprehend the Maya numerical system, and to recognize the various glyphs or signs by which the various days (each of which had a name, like our Monday, Tuesday, etc.) were distinguished. In addition, it is

necessary to follow how the calendar itself was constructed.

The Maya numerals are relatively straightforward. A stylized shell meant zero, a dot "one," and a horizontal bar "five."

The Maya used two calendrical systems: the Calendar Round and the Long Count.

The **Calendar Round** was used for most everyday purposes. It involved two methods of counting. The first is the Sacred Round of 260 days, which is still used in some parts of the Maya highlands. We should imagine two interlocking cog wheels, one with numbers from 1 to 13, the other with 20 named days. Day 1 (to use our terminology) will be 1 Imix, day 2 is 2 Ik, day 3 is 3 Akbal, and so on until day 13, which is 13 Ben. But then day 14 is 1 Ix, and so the system continues. The sequence coincides again after 260 days and the new Sacred Round begins with 1 Imix once more.

In conjunction with this, the solar year was recorded, consisting of 18 named

months, each of 20 days, plus a terminal period of 5 days. The Maya New Year began with 1 Pop (Pop being the name of the month); the next day was 2 Pop, and so on.

These two cycles proceeded simultaneously, so that any day could be designated in both (e.g. 1 Pop 1 Kan). A specific combination of that kind could occur only once in every 52 years. This calendar was therefore sufficient for most daily purposes, and the 52-year cycle had symbolic significance for the Maya.

The **Long Count** was used for historical dates. Like any unique calendrical system, it needed to have a starting or zero date, and for the Maya this was 13 August 3114 BC (according to a commonly agreed correlation with the Christian calendar). A Long Count date takes the form of five numbers (e.g. in our own numerical notation 8.16.5.12.7). The first figure records the number elapsed of the largest unit, the *baktun* (of 144,000 days or about 400 years). The second is the *katun* (7200 days or

The Calendar Round (left) can be visualized as a set of interlocking cog wheels. The 260-day cycle is created by the interlocking of the two wheels shown above. Meshing with this is the 365-day cycle (part of which is shown below). The specific conjoining of day names given here (1 Kan 1 Pop) cannot return until 52 years (18,980 days) have passed.

The Long Count (right) was used to record historical dates. Here, in Burial 48 at the city of Tikal, the date given – reading from top to bottom – is 9.1.1.10.10 4 Oc, or 9 baktuns, 1 katun, 1 tun, 10 uinals, and 10 kins, with the day name 4 Oc at the bottom. In modern terms this is 19 March AD 457.

Using a Historical Chronology

It is relatively easy for the archaeologist to use a historical chronology when abundant artifacts are found that can be related closely to it. Thus, at major Maya sites such as Tikal or Copán there are numerous stelae with calendrical inscriptions that can often be used to date the buildings with which they are associated. The artifacts associated with the buildings can in turn be dated: for instance, if a pottery typology has been worked out, the finding of known types of pottery in such historically dated contexts allows the pottery typology itself to be dated. Contexts and buildings on other sites lacking inscriptions can be dated approximately through the occurrence of similar pot types.

Sometimes artifacts themselves carry dates, or the names of rulers that can be dated. This is the case with many Classic Maya ceramics that bear hieroglyphic inscriptions. For the Roman and medieval periods of Europe, coins offer a similar opportunity, as they normally carry the name of the issuing ruler, and inscriptions or records elsewhere usually allow the ruler to be dated. To date a coin or an artifact is not the same thing as to date the context in which it is found. The date of the coin indicates the year in which it was made. Its inclusion within a sealed archaeological deposit establishes simply a *terminus post quem* ("date after which"): in other words, the deposit can be no earlier than the date on the coin – but it could be later than that date.

A well-established historical chronology in one country may be used to date events in neighboring and more far-flung lands that lack their own historical records but are mentioned in the histories of the literate homeland. Similarly, archaeologists can use exports and imports of objects to extend chronological linkages by means of *cross-dating.* For instance, Flinders Petrie, in his excavations in 1891–92 at Tell el Amarna, capital of the heretic pharaoh Akhenaten (now dated in the Egyptian historical chronology to about 1353–1335 BC), discovered pottery that he recognized to be of Aegean origin: Mycenaean pottery in fact. Within the typological system of Mycenaean pottery later established by the Swedish scholar Arne Furumark it can be termed Late Helladic IIIA2 (one of the divisions in a relative chronology). Its presence in a well-dated Egyptian context establishes a *terminus ante quem* ("date before which") for the manufacture in Greece of that pottery: it cannot be more recent than the Amarna context. Likewise, actual Egyptian objects, some with inscriptions allowing them to be accurately dated in Egyptian terms, occur at various Aegean sites,

---

20 years), the third a *tun* of 360 days, the fourth a *uinal* of 20 days, and finally the *kin*, the single day.

A positional notation was used, starting at the top with the number of *baktuns*, and proceeding downwards through the lower units. Usually, each number was followed by the glyph for the unit in question (e.g. 8 *baktuns*) so that dates on the stelae can be readily recognized.

The earliest date yet noted on a stela in the Maya area proper is on Stela 29 at Tikal, and reads 8.12.14.8.15. In other words:

8 *baktuns*	1,152,000 days
12 *katuns*	86,400 days
14 *tuns*	5,040 days
8 *uinals*	160 days
15 *kins*	15 days
	or 1,243,615 days

since the zero date in 3114 BC. This is the equivalent of 6 July AD 292. According to the Maya, the end of the present world will come about on 24 December 2011.

European chronology. Until the 1960s, prehistoric Europe was largely dated by supposed typological links between neighboring lands that rested ultimately on the historical chronology of ancient Egypt. Calibrated radiocarbon dates (p.124) have shown many of these links to be false ones. Egypt and the Aegean can still be cross-dated by direct exports and imports, but the "fault line" indicates how links have been severed with regions to the north and west, where dates have been pushed back by several centuries.

thereby helping to date the contexts in which they are found. It is this linkage from A to B (Aegean to Egypt), and conversely from B to A, that has given rise to the term cross-dating.

Until 20 or 30 years ago, much of European prehistory was based on this method of dating, with successive links established between neighboring lands. Even the remotest parts of Europe were dated in absolute years BC using a system that rested ultimately on the Egyptian chronology. But the calibration of radiocarbon dates (see below) has brought about the collapse of this precarious chronological edifice. It is now clear that although the links between Egypt and the Aegean were valid, being based on actual imports and exports, those between the Aegean and the rest of Europe were not. The entire chronology of prehistoric Europe was constructed on false assumptions whose

rectification produced (so far as Europe is concerned) what has come to be called the Second Radiocarbon Revolution (see map).

Dating by historical methods remains the most important procedure for the archaeologist in countries with a reliable calendar supported by a significant degree of literacy. Where there are serious uncertainties over the calendar, or over its correlation with the modern calendrical system, the correlations can often be checked, at least in outline, by the other absolute dating methods to be described below.

Outside the historic and literate lands, however, cross-dating and broad typological comparisons have been almost entirely superseded by scientifically based dating methods. Now, all the world's cultures can be assigned absolute dates.

ANNUAL CYCLES: VARVES AND TREE-RINGS

Before the advent of radioactive methods after World War II, the counting of varves and tree-rings provided the most accurate means of absolute dating – but only in two regions of the world, Scandinavia for varves and the American Southwest for tree-rings. Today, while varves remain of restricted use, tree-rings have come to rival radiocarbon as the main method of dating for the last few thousand years in many parts of Europe, North America, and Japan, thanks to painstaking scientific work.

Any absolute dating method depends on the existence of a regular, time-dependent process. The most obvious of these is the system by which we order our modern calendar: the rotation of the earth around the sun once each year. Because this yearly cycle produces regular annual fluctuations in climate, it has an impact on features of the environment which can in certain cases be measured to create a chronology (as well as a record of environmental change: see Chapter 6).

Evidence of these annual fluctuations is widespread. For example, the changes in temperature in polar regions result in annual variations in the thickness of polar ice, which scientists can study from cores drilled through the ice (see section above, Climate and Chronology). Similarly, in lands bordering the polar regions, the melting of the ice sheets each year when temperatures rise leads to the formation of annual deposits of sediment, called *varves*, which can be counted. The growth of most species of plant varies annually, which makes possible the principle of *tree-ring dating* (dendrochronology). And growth in many animal species also varies during the year, so that annual variations in tissue deposits can sometimes be detected in skeletons or in shells of, for instance, marine molluscs (Chapter 6).

As with a historical king-list, for absolute dating purposes the sequence needs to be a long one (with no gaps), linked somehow to the present day, and capable of being related to the structures or artifacts one actually wants to date. Annual growth rings on molluscs found at a site can provide good evidence for season of occupation, for example (Chapter 7), but the ring sequence is much too short to form an absolute chronology. Varves and tree-rings, on the other hand, can be counted to produce unbroken sequences stretching back many thousands of years.

Varves

In 1878, the Swedish geologist Baron Gerard de Geer noticed that certain deposits of clay were layered in a regular way. He realized that these layers ("varves" in Swedish) had been deposited in lakes around the edges of Scandinavian glaciers by the annual melting of the ice sheets, which had been steadily retreating since the end of the Pleistocene epoch, or last Ice Age. The layers varied in thickness from year to year, a thick layer resulting from a warm year with increased glacial melting, a thin layer indicating colder conditions. By measuring the successive thicknesses of a whole sequence, and comparing the pattern with varves in nearby areas, it proved possible to link long sequences together.

This was the first geochronological method to be developed. Considerable deposits were found, representing thousands of years, stretching (when linked

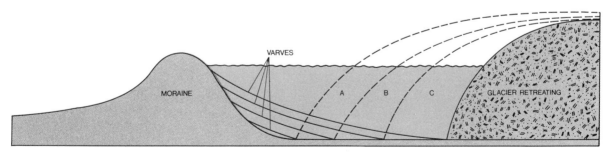

Varves are sediment layers that were deposited in lakes by melting glaciers. When the ice retreated to position A, the sediments contained in the melted waters settled to form the lowermost varve. In successive years (B, C, etc.), more sediments were deposited, each varve extending horizontally to the point where that winter halted the glacier's thaw and representing in thickness the amount of glacial discharge. When varves from several glacial lakes have been recorded they can be correlated, to create a master sequence for an area. Such sequences have been established in Scandinavia and North America.

together) from the present back to the beginning of the retreat of the glacial ice sheets in Scandinavia some 12,000 years ago. The method allowed, for the first time, a fairly reliable estimate for the date of the end of the last Ice Age, and hence made a contribution to archaeological chronology not only in Scandinavia but in many other parts of the world as well.

Comparable studies have been undertaken in North America, for instance in Wisconsin. But there are problems in correlating the North American and North European (Finnish and Swedish) data. For direct archaeological applications, radiocarbon dating and tree-ring work are in general much more useful.

Tree-Ring Dating

The modern technique of tree-ring dating (dendrochronology) was developed by an American astronomer, A.E. Douglass, in the early decades of this century – although many of the principles had been understood long before that. Working on well-preserved timbers in the arid American Southwest, by 1930 Douglass could assign absolute dates to many of the major sites there, such as Mesa Verde and Pueblo Bonito. But it was not until the end of the 1930s that the technique was introduced to Europe, and only in the 1960s that the use of statistical procedures and

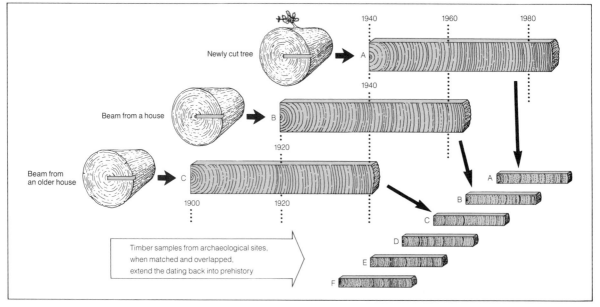

Tree-ring dating. (Top) Section across an Irish oak, the varying thickness of the annual growth rings clearly visible. The inner rings here date to the AD 1550s. (Above) Diagram to show how the annual growth rings can be counted, matched, and overlapped, to build up a master sequence for a particular region.

computers laid the foundations for the establishment of the long tree-ring chronologies now so fundamental to modern archaeology. Today dendrochronology has two distinct archaeological uses: (1) as a successful means of calibrating or correcting radiocarbon dates (see below); and (2) as an independent method of absolute dating in its own right.

Basis of Method. Most trees produce a ring of new wood each year and these circles of growth can easily be seen in a cross-section of the trunk of a felled tree. These rings are not of uniform thickness. In an individual tree, they will vary for two reasons. First, the rings become narrower with the increasing age of the tree. Second, the amount a tree grows each year is affected by fluctuations in climate. In arid regions, rainfall above the average one year will produce a particularly thick annual ring. In more temperate regions, sunlight and temperature may be more critical than rainfall in affecting a tree's growth. Here, a sharp cold spell in spring may produce a narrow growth ring.

Dendrochronologists measure and plot these rings and produce a diagram indicating the thickness of successive rings in an individual tree. Trees of the same species growing in the same area will generally show the same pattern of rings so that the growth sequence can be matched between successively older timbers to build up a chronology for an area. (It is not necessary to fell trees in order to study the ring sequence: a usable sample can be extracted by boring without harming the tree.) By matching sequences of rings from living trees of different ages as well as from old timber, dendrochronologists can produce a long, continuous sequence extending back hundreds, even thousands, of years from the present. Thus, when an ancient timber of the same species (e.g. Douglas fir in the American Southwest or oak in Europe) is found, it should be possible to match its tree-ring sequence of, say, 100 years with the appropriate 100-year length of the master sequence or chronology. In this way, the felling date for that piece of timber can usually be dated to within a year.

Applications: (1) The Long Master Sequences and Radiocarbon. Perhaps the greatest contribution so far of dendrochronology to archaeological dating has been the development of long tree-ring sequences, against which it has proved possible to check and calibrate radiocarbon dates. The pioneering research was done in Arizona on a remarkable species, the California bristlecone pine (*Pinus aristata*), some of which are up to 4900 years old – the oldest living things on earth. By matching samples from these living trees with rings

from dead pines preserved in the region's arid environment, the scientists – led by E. Schulman and later C. Wesley Ferguson – built up an unbroken sequence back from the present as far as 6700 BC. Just how this sequence has been used for calibration work will be discussed in the section on radiocarbon below.

The research in the American Southwest has now been complemented by studies in Europe of tree-rings of oak, often well preserved in waterlogged deposits. Two separate oak sequences in Northern Ireland and western Germany both now stretch back unbroken into the distant past, as far as c. 5300 BC in the Irish case and c. 7500 BC in the German. The scientists who did the work – Michael Baillie in Belfast, Bernhard Becker in Stuttgart, and their colleagues – have also succeeded in matching the two separate sequences, thus creating a reliable central and west European absolute chronology against which to calibrate radiocarbon dates, as well as to use in direct tree-ring dating.

Applications: (2) Direct Tree-Ring Dating. Where people in the past made use of timber from a species, such as oak, that today forms one of the dendrochronological sequences, one can obtain an archaeologically useful absolute date by matching the preserved timber with part of the master sequence. This is now feasible in many parts of the world outside the tropics.

Results are particularly impressive in the *American Southwest*, where the technique is longest established and wood is well preserved. Here Pueblo Indians built their dwellings from trees such as the Douglas fir and piñon pine that have yielded excellent ring sequences. Dendrochronology has become the principal dating method for the Pueblo villages, the earliest dates for which belong to the 1st century BC, although the main period of building came a millennium later.

One brief example from the Southwest will serve to highlight the precision and implications of the method. In his pioneer work, A.E. Douglass had established that Betatakin, a cliff dwelling in northwest Arizona, dated from around AD 1270. Returning to the site in the 1960s, Jeffrey Dean collected 292 tree-ring samples and used them to document not just the founding of the settlement in AD 1267, but its expansion room by room, year by year until it reached a peak in the mid-1280s, before being abandoned shortly thereafter. Estimates of numbers of occupants per room also made it possible to calculate the rate of expansion of Betatakin's population to a maximum of about 125 people. Dendrochronology can thus lead on to wider considerations beyond simple questions of dating.

In *central and western Europe*, the oak master sequences now allow the equally precise dating of the

1 1010 - 1009 BC
2 1008 - 1007 BC
3 1005 - 1001 BC 5 992 - 989 BC
4   996 - 993 BC 6 985 BC

50ft

15m

Tree-ring dating of the late Bronze Age settlement of Cortaillod-Est, Switzerland, is remarkably precise. Founded in 1010 BC with a nucleus of four houses (phase 1), the village was enlarged four times, and a fence added in 985 BC.

development of Neolithic and Bronze Age lake villages, such as Cortaillod in Switzerland. Sometimes local chronologies remain "floating" – their short-term sequences have not been tied into the main master sequences.

In many parts of the world master sequences are gradually being extended and floating chronologies fitted into them. In the Aegean area, for example, a master sequence is now available back to early medieval times (the Byzantine period), with an earlier floating sequence stretching over several centuries for the Classical period. In due course, the link between them will no doubt be found.

Limiting Factors. Unlike radiocarbon, dendrochronology is not a worldwide dating method because of two basic limitations:

1 it applies only to trees in regions outside the tropics where pronounced differences between the seasons produce clearly defined annual rings;

2 for a direct tree-ring date it is restricted to wood from those species that (a) have yielded a master sequence back from the present and (b) people actually used in the past.

In addition, there are important questions of interpretation to consider. A tree-ring date refers to the date of felling of the tree. This is determined by matching the outermost rings (the sapwood) to a regional sequence. Where most or all of the sapwood is missing, the felling date cannot be identified. But even with an accurate felling date, the archaeologist has to make a judgment – based on context and formation processes – about how soon after felling the timber entered the archaeological deposit. Timbers may be older or younger than the structures into which they were finally incorporated, depending on whether they were reused from somewhere else, or used to make a repair in a long-established structure. As always, the best solution is to take multiple samples, and to check the evidence carefully on-site.

Despite these qualifications, dendrochronology looks set to become the major dating technique alongside radiocarbon for the last 8000 years in temperate and arid lands.

RADIOACTIVE CLOCKS

Many of the most important developments in absolute dating since World War II have come from the use of what one might call "radioactive clocks," based on that widespread and regular feature in the natural world, radioactive decay (see box). The best known of these methods is radiocarbon, today the main dating tool for the last 50,000 years or so. Thermoluminescence (TL), a dating technique that relies indirectly on radioactive decay, overlaps with radiocarbon in the time period for which it is useful, but also has the potential for dating earlier epochs – as does electron spin resonance, a new technique related to TL. However the main radioactive methods for periods before the timespan of radiocarbon are potassium-argon, uranium-series dating, and fission-track dating. In the following sections we will discuss each method in turn.

Radiocarbon Dating

Radiocarbon is the single most useful method of dating for the archaeologist. As we shall see, it has its limitations, both in terms of accuracy, and for the time range where it is useful. Archaeologists themselves are also the cause of major errors, thanks to poor sampling

THE PRINCIPLES OF RADIOACTIVE DECAY

Carbon-12 atom

Carbon-14 atom

 Neutron

 Proton

Like most other elements, carbon exists in more than one form. It has three isotopes: the first is the common form, with six protons and six neutrons in the nucleus, and hence atomic weight 12 (^{12}C); the second has seven neutrons in the nucleus, and hence atomic weight 13 (^{13}C); the third isotope has eight neutrons, and hence atomic weight of 14 (^{14}C). Of the three isotopes, ^{14}C or radiocarbon is the only unstable one; it disintegrates in the environment to produce ^{14}N (nitrogen with atomic weight 14) giving off weak beta radiation as it does so. This radioactive decay proceeds in a regular way. In fact, all radioactive decay processes, although they may be faster or slower than the decay of radiocarbon, show a similar exponential pattern.

The time taken for half of the atoms of a radioactive isotope to decay is called its half-life. In other words, after one half-life, there will be half of the atoms left; after two half-lives, one-quarter of the original quantity of isotope remains, and so on. In the case of ^{14}C, the half-life is now agreed to be 5730 years. For ^{238}U (uranium with atomic weight 238), it is 4,500 million years. For certain other isotopes, the half-life is a minute fraction of a second. But in every case, there is a regular pattern to the decay.

Radioactive isotope decay curve.

procedures and careless interpretation. Nevertheless, radiocarbon has transformed our understanding of the past, helping archaeologists to establish for the first time a reliable chronology of world cultures.

History and Basis of Method. In 1949, the American chemist Willard Libby published the first radiocarbon dates. During World War II he had been one of several scientists studying cosmic radiation, the sub-atomic particles that constantly bombard the earth, producing high-energy neutrons. These neutrons react with nitrogen atoms in the atmosphere to produce atoms of carbon–14 (^{14}C), or radiocarbon, which are unstable because they have eight neutrons in the nucleus instead of the usual six as for ordinary carbon (^{12}C) (see box above). This instability leads to radioactive decay of ^{14}C at a regular rate. Libby estimated that it took 5568 years for half the ^{14}C in any sample to decay – its half-life – although modern research indicates that the more accurate figure is 5730 years (for consistency laboratories still use 5568 years for the half-life; the difference no longer matters now that we have a calibrated radiocarbon timescale: see below).

Libby realized that the decay of radiocarbon at a constant rate should be balanced by its constant production through cosmic radiation, and that therefore the proportion of ^{14}C in the atmosphere should remain the same throughout time. Furthermore, this steady atmospheric concentration of radiocarbon is passed on uniformly to all living things through

carbon dioxide. Plants take up carbon dioxide during photosynthesis, they are eaten by herbivorous animals, which in turn are eaten by carnivores. Only when a plant or animal dies does the uptake of ^{14}C cease, and the steady concentration of ^{14}C begin to decline through radioactive decay. Thus, knowing the decay rate or half-life of ^{14}C, Libby recognized that the age of dead plant or animal tissue could be calculated by measuring the amount of radiocarbon left in a sample.

Libby's great practical achievement was to devise an accurate means of measurement. (The traces of ^{14}C are minute to start with, and are reduced by half after 5730 years. After 23,000 years, therefore, only one sixteenth of the original tiny concentration of ^{14}C is available to be measured in the sample.) Libby discovered that each atom of ^{14}C decays by releasing beta particles, and he succeeded in counting these emissions using a Geiger counter. This is the basis of the conventional method still employed by many radiocarbon laboratories today. Samples usually consist of organic materials found on archaeological sites, such as charcoal, wood, seeds, and other plant remains, and human or animal bone. The accurate measurement of the ^{14}C activity of a sample is affected by counting errors, background cosmic radiation, and other factors that contribute an element of uncertainty to the measurements. This means that radiocarbon dates are invariably accompanied by an estimate of the probable error: the plus/minus term (standard deviation) attached to every radiocarbon date (see box).

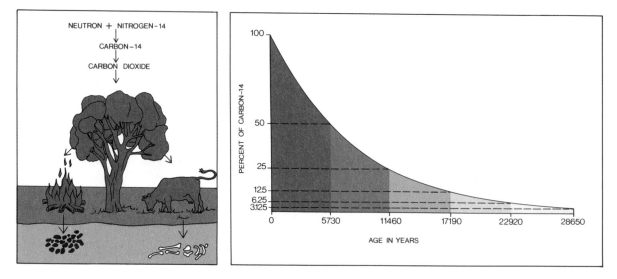

(Left) Radiocarbon (carbon-14) is produced in the atmosphere and absorbed by plants through carbon dioxide, and by animals through feeding off plants or other animals. Uptake of ^{14}C ceases when the plant or animal dies. (Right) After death, the amount of ^{14}C decays at a known rate (50 percent after 5730 years, etc.). Measurement of the amount left in a sample gives the date.

THE PUBLICATION OF RADIOCARBON DATES

Radiocarbon laboratories provide an estimate of age based on their measurement of the amount of radiocarbon activity in a sample. The level of activity is converted to an age expressed in number of years between the death of an organism and the present. To avoid confusion caused by the fact that the "present" advances each year, radiocarbon laboratories have adopted AD 1950 as their "present" and all radiocarbon dates are quoted in years BP or years "before the present," meaning before 1950. Thus, in scientific publications, radiocarbon dates are given in the form:

3700 ± 100 BP (P 685)

The first figure is the year BP (i.e. before AD 1950). Next is the associated probable error known as the standard deviation (see below). Finally, in parentheses is the laboratory analysis number. Each laboratory has its own letter code (e.g. P for Philadelphia and Q for Cambridge, England).

As we have seen, various factors prevent the precise measurement of radiocarbon activity in a sample and, consequently, there is a statistical error or standard deviation (which may not have been realistically calculated: see main text) associated with all radiocarbon dates. Thus, when a radiocarbon date is quoted as 3700 ± 100 BP this means that there should be a 68 percent probability – two chances in three – that the correct estimate of age in radiocarbon years lies between 3800 and 3600 BP. Since there is also a one-in-three chance that the correct age does *not* fall within this range, archaeologists are advised to convert the date range to two standard deviations, i.e. to double the size of the standard deviation, so that there should be a 95 percent chance that the age estimate will be bracketed. For example, for an age estimate of 3700 ± 100 BP there is a 95 percent

chance that the radiocarbon age of the sample will lie between 3900 (3700 + 200) and 3500 (3700 - 200) BP. Obviously, the larger the standard deviation, the less precise (and for those dealing with later prehistory or historical times, the less useful) the date. For example, the 95 percent probability range of a date of 3700 ± 150 BP brackets the time period 4000 to 3400 BP, which is 200 years more than a date quoted at ± 100 years.

The forms of the dates given above are laboratory determinations. They represent the uncalibrated age estimate of the sample and are based on the assumption, now known to be erroneous, that the levels of radiocarbon produced in the atmosphere have been constant through time. Thus, whenever possible the radiocarbon age should be calibrated to actual calendar years. To make clear whether or not a date has been calibrated, archaeologists often follow one of two conventions in their publications:

	Uncali- brated date	Cali- brated date
"Scientific"	BP	Cal BC/AD
"Historical"	bc/ad	BC/AD

The "scientific" convention (used and promoted by the radiocarbon laboratories) has the merit of being very clear, but has the inconvenience of not providing for the discussion of an uncalibrated date in years BC or AD. The "historical" convention is less cumbersome and is for this reason preferred by many archaeologists. However, the style for distinguishing dates by simply using lower case letters (bc/ad) and upper case ones (BC/AD) is vulnerable to editorial inconsistency and to printing errors. Moreover, it is important (and difficult) to remember that an uncalibrated date of say 3500 bc is not linked to any system of reckoning in calendar

years, nor is it a century older than a date of 3400 bc. Where the archaeologist is discussing absolute chronology generally – perhaps using radiocarbon alongside other methods of dating, including historical ones – it seems logical to employ the simple BC/AD system, provided an attempt has been made to calibrate any radiocarbon dates incorporated in the chronology, and that this is stated clearly at the outset.

Tiny samples can be dated by the AMS method: charred seeds, piece of linen, small bone (metacarpal), charcoal.

A significant advance on the conventional method came with the introduction in some laboratories in the late 1970s and early 1980s of special gas counters capable of taking measurements from very small samples. In the conventional method one needs some 5 g of pure carbon after purification, which means an original sample of some 10–20 g of wood or charcoal, or 100–200 g of bone. The special equipment requires only a few hundred milligrams (mg) of charcoal.

Several laboratories have now adopted an even more radical method, accelerator mass spectrometry (AMS), which requires smaller samples still. AMS counts the atoms of ^{14}C directly, disregarding their radioactivity altogether. The minimum sample size is reduced, at any rate in principle, to as little as 5–10 mg – thus enabling precious organic materials, such as the Turin Shroud (see below), to be sampled and directly dated. Moreover, the datable timespan for radiocarbon using AMS can theoretically be pushed back from 50,000 to 80,000 years, although this is proving difficult to achieve, in part because of sample contamination.

Calibration of Radiocarbon Dates. One of the basic assumptions of the radiocarbon method has turned out to be not quite correct. Libby assumed that the concentration of ^{14}C in the atmosphere has been constant through time; but we now know that it has varied, largely due to changes in the earth's magnetic field. The method that demonstrated the inaccuracy – tree-ring dating – has also provided the means of correcting or calibrating radiocarbon dates.

Radiocarbon dates obtained from tree-rings show that before about 1000 BC dates expressed in radiocarbon years are increasingly too young in relation to true calendar years. In other words, before 1000 BC trees (and all other living things) were exposed to greater concentrations of atmospheric ^{14}C than they are today.

By obtaining radiocarbon dates systematically from the long tree-ring master sequences of bristlecone pine and oak (see above), scientists have been able to plot radiocarbon ages against tree-ring ages (in calendar years) to produce calibration curves back to around 7000 BC. The journal *Radiocarbon* publishes the most up-to-date curves. The curves then in principle allow archaeologists to calibrate a radiocarbon date by reading it off against a calendar date. Very broadly, radiocarbon ages diverge increasingly from true ages before 1000 BC, so that by 5000 BC in calendar years the radiocarbon age is 900 years too young. Thus an age estimate in radiocarbon years of 4100 BC might well in fact when calibrated be somewhere near 5000 BC. It is this pushing back of many dates that has brought about the Second Radiocarbon Revolution (see above).

Calibration is not a straightforward matter. Back to *c*.2500 BC the internationally recognized curve is that of Stuiver and Pearson (1986), but before that period a curve is only now being agreed, extending no further back than 4000–5000 BC. Moreover, there are short-term wiggles in the curve and, occasionally, sections of the curve that run so flat that two samples with the same age in radiocarbon years might in reality be 400 years apart in calendar years, a problem that is particularly irksome for the period 800–400 BC in calendar years. To be accurate one needs to calibrate not merely the central radiocarbon date (e.g. 2200 BP) but its error estimate as well (2200±100 BP), which will produce an *age range* in calendar years (see box). Some of the ranges will be narrower and more precise

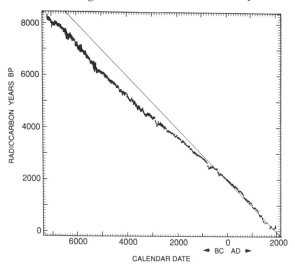

Stuiver and Pearson's calibrated radiocarbon timescale based on Irish oak. The straight line indicates the ideal 1:1 radiocarbon/calendar age timescale.

HOW TO CALIBRATE RADIOCARBON DATES

Although radiocarbon laboratories will generally supply calibrated dates of their samples, archaeologists must frequently calibrate raw radiocarbon dates themselves, generally from a calibration graph. The tree-ring calibration curve shown in the diagram illustrates the relationship between radiocarbon years (BP) and tree-ring samples dated in actual calendar years (Cal BC/AD). The central line of the curve defines the mean estimate of age while the other two lines indicate the band width of the probable error at one standard deviation. In order to find the appropriate calibrated age range of a radiocarbon sample dated 2200 ± 100 BP, we should do the following:

1 We should first convert the radiocarbon age estimate into a time range defined at two standard deviations in order to insure that there will be 95 percent probability that our calibrated date range will include the age of the sample. Thus 2200±100 BP at two standard deviations would bracket the age estimates between 2400 and 2000 BP.

2 We should then read, or draw, lines (A1 and A2) from the BP axis horizontally across the graph to the appropriate central point on the curve.

3 We then drop lines B1 and B2 vertically from these two points to establish the range of calibrated dates. Thus there is approximately a 95 percent chance that the date of our sample falls between c.405 Cal BC and 5 Cal BC.

This is the easiest and quickest way to work with the graphs for routine radiocarbon dates. There are also desktop computer programs available for somewhat (though not significantly) more precise conversions.

It will be immediately apparent that a calibrated age range of 405 Cal BC to 5 Cal BC is too broad to be useful for most archaeological purposes. Fortunately there are two ways of narrowing the

age range: high-precision dates and multiple dates. High precision dates, obtainable so far from only a handful of the world's radiocarbon laboratories, can offer dates quoted with a realistic error of ±20 years, which, after calibration, generally allows the sample to be dated within a century or less at

the 95 percent probability level. Otherwise one can resort to multiple dates of the same sample to produce mean dates with a smaller standard deviation – hoping that the standard deviations of the routine dates have been realistically measured by the laboratory.

A section of the calibration curve from Stuiver and Pearson (1986).

than others, depending on where on the curve the radiocarbon date with its error estimate falls.

The crucial point is that in any publication it should be indicated whether or not the radiocarbon determination has been calibrated, and if it has been, by which particular system or curve.

Contamination and Interpretation of Radiocarbon Samples. Although radiocarbon dates have certain inescapable levels of error associated with them, erroneous results are as likely to derive from poor sampling and incorrect interpretation by the archaeologist as from inadequate laboratory procedures.

The major sources of error in the field are as follows:

1   *Contamination before sampling.* Problems of contamination of the sample within the ground can be serious. For instance, groundwater on waterlogged sites can dissolve organic materials and also deposit them, thus changing the isotopic composition; the formation of mineral concretions around organic matter can also bring calcium carbonate entirely lacking in radiocarbon, and thus fallaciously increase the apparent radiocarbon age of a specimen by effectively "diluting" the ^{14}C present. These matters can be tackled in the laboratory.

2   *Contamination during or after sampling.* All radiocarbon samples should be sealed within a clean container such as a plastic bag at the time of recovery. They should be labeled in detail at once on the outside of the container; cardboard labels inside can be a major source of contamination. The

container should be placed inside another: one plastic bag, well sealed, inside another bag separately sealed can be a sound procedure for most materials. But wood or carbon samples that may preserve some tree-ring structure should be more carefully housed in a rigid container. Wherever possible exclude any modern carbon, such as paper, which can be disastrous. However, modern roots and earth cannot always be avoided: in such cases, it is better to include them, together with a note for the laboratory, where the problem can be tackled.

Application of any organic material later – such as glue or carbowax – is likewise disastrous (although the laboratory may be able to remedy the disaster). So is continuing photosynthesis within the sample: for this reason, the relevant containers should be stored in the dark. A green mold is not uncommon in sample bags on some projects. It automatically indicates contamination of the sample.

3   *Context of deposition.* Most errors in radiocarbon dating arise because the excavator has not fully understood the formation processes of the context in question. Unless it is appreciated how the organic material found its way to the position where it was found, and how and when (in terms of the site) it came to be buried, then precise interpretation is impossible. The first rule of radiocarbon dating must be that the excavator should not submit a sample for dating unless he or she is sure of its archaeological context.

Samples for radiocarbon dating should be obtained, wherever possible, from the kind of contexts shown here – where the material to be dated has been sealed in an immobilizing matrix. The stratigraphic context of the sample must be clearly established by the excavator before the material is submitted to the laboratory for dating.

Master profile for Gatecliff Shelter, Nevada, produced by David Hurst Thomas, showing how dates derived from radiocarbon determinations are consistent with the stratigraphic succession.

Natural Strata

A.D. 1300

A.D. 700

1250 B.C.

1300 B.C.

1400 B.C.

2100-1450 B.C.

2300-2150 B.C.

3050-2300 B.C.
3150-3050 B.C.

3300-3150 B.C.

3400-3300 B.C.
3550-3400 B.C.

4 *Date of context.* Too often, it is assumed that a radiocarbon determination, e.g. on charcoal, will give a straightforward estimate for the date of the charcoal's burial context. However, if that charcoal derives from roof timbers that might themselves have been several centuries old when destroyed by fire, then one is dating some early construction, not the context of destruction. There are numerous examples of such difficulties, one of the most conspicuous being the re-use of such timbers or even of fossil wood (e.g. "bog oak") whose radiocarbon date could be centuries earlier than the context in question. For this reason, samples with a short life are often preferred, such as twigs of brushwood, or charred cereal grains that are not likely to be old at the time of burial.

A strategy for sampling will recall the wise dictum that "one date is no date:" several are needed. The best dating procedure is to work towards an internal

relative sequence – for instance, in the stratigraphic succession on a well-stratified site such as the Gatecliff Shelter, Monitor Valley, Nevada, excavated by David Hurst Thomas and his associates. If the samples can be arranged in relative sequence in this way with the lowest unit having the earliest date and so on, then there is an internal check on the coherence of the laboratory determinations and on the quality of field sampling. Some of the dates from such a sequence may come out older than expected. This is quite reasonable

– as explained above, some of the material may have been "old" at the time of burial. But if they come out younger (i.e. more recent) than expected, then there is something wrong. Either some contamination has affected the samples, or the laboratory has made a serious error, or – as not infrequently happens – the stratigraphic interpretation is wrong.

Although many problems with radiocarbon dates may be attributed to the submitter, recent evidence suggests that radiocarbon laboratories themselves may be overestimating the precision of their own dates. In one comparative study, over 30 radiocarbon laboratories dated the same sample. While some estimated their errors within reasonable accuracy others did not, and one laboratory produced systematic errors of 200 years. In general, it was seen that although radiocarbon laboratories might quote levels of precision of ±50 years, in fact it was safer to assume that their actual errors were ±80 years or more. As the interlaboratory study comprised an anonymous sample of the world's radiocarbon laboratories, the archaeological community has no way of knowing how widespread the underestimation of errors is or how systematically biased in their radiocarbon dates some laboratories are. Archaeologists would be best advised to treat radiocarbon laboratories like purveyors of any other service and request evidence that they deliver both the accuracy and the precision they purport to offer. Many laboratories are aware of their past biases and could be approached to quote new and more realistic errors for their earlier dates.

Applications: The Impact of Radiocarbon Dating. If we seek to answer the question "When?" in archaeology, radiocarbon has undoubtedly offered the most generally useful way of finding an answer. The greatest advantage is that the method can be used anywhere, whatever the climate, as long as there is material of organic (i.e. living) origin. The method works as well in South America or Polynesia as it does in Egypt or Mesopotamia. And it can take us back 50,000 years, and potentially even to 80,000 years using the accelerator mass spectrometry (AMS) technique – although at the other end of the timescale, it is too imprecise to be of much use for the 400 years of the most recent past.

The use of the method on a single site has been illustrated above by reference to the Gatecliff Shelter in Nevada. On a wider scale radiocarbon has been even more important in establishing for the first time broad chronologies for the world's cultures that previously lacked timescales (such as calendars) of their own. Calibration of radiocarbon has heightened, not diminished, this success. As we saw in the section above on

Calendars and Historical Chronologies, calibration has helped assert the validity of an independent radiocarbon chronology for prehistoric Europe, free from false links with the Egyptian historical chronology.

Now radiocarbon dating by the AMS technique is opening up new possibilities. Precious objects and works of art can be dated for the first time because minute samples are all that is required. In 1988 AMS dating resolved the longstanding controversy over the age of the Turin Shroud, a piece of cloth with the image of a man's body on it that many genuinely believed to be the actual imprint of the body of Christ. Laboratories at Tucson, Oxford, and Zurich all placed it in the 14th century AD, not from the time of Christ at all. Likewise it is now possible to date a single grain of wheat or a fruit pip. An AMS reading on a grape pip from Hambledon Hill, southern Britain, shows that grapes – and probably vines as well – had reached this part of the world by 3500 BC in calendar years, over 3000 years earlier than had previously been supposed.

Part of the Turin Shroud, bearing the image of a man's head. Radiocarbon AMS dating has given a calibrated age range for the cloth of AD 1260–1390.

Radiocarbon looks set to maintain its position as the main dating tool back to 50,000–80,000 years ago for organic materials. For inorganic materials, however, thermoluminescence is developing into a useful new technique.

Thermoluminescence Dating

Thermoluminescence (TL) has two advantages over radiocarbon: it can date pottery, the most abundant inorganic material on archaeological sites of the last 10,000 years; and it can in principle date inorganic materials (such as burnt flint) before 50,000–80,000 years ago, the limit of radiocarbon. But TL is less precise than radiocarbon in the accuracy of its dates.

Basis of Method. Materials with a crystalline structure such as ceramics (pottery and terracotta) contain small amounts of radioactive elements, notably uranium, thorium, and radioactive potassium. These decay at a known and steady rate, emitting alpha, beta, and gamma radiation that bombards the crystalline structure and displaces electrons, which then become trapped at points of imperfection in the crystal lattice. More and more electrons are trapped as time elapses. Only when the material is heated rapidly to 500°C (932°F) or above can the trapped electrons escape, resetting the clock to zero, and as they do so they emit light known as thermoluminescence.

In the case of pottery, the TL clock will have been reset to zero when it was fired. By measuring the amount of TL emitted when a sample is heated in the laboratory to 500°C or more one can calculate the age of the piece since the original firing. To arrive at the date, the radioactive content of the sample should already have been measured. In addition, that sample's inherent susceptibility to the accumulation of trapped electrons has to be assessed by subjecting it in the laboratory to a known radiation dose, reheating it to 500°C or more, and then measuring the TL emitted.

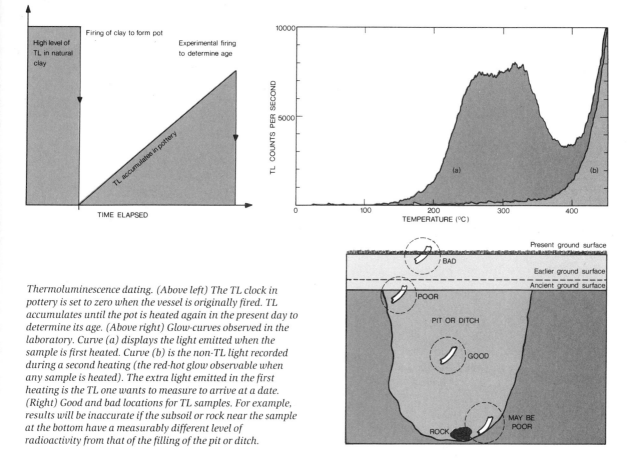

Thermoluminescence dating. (Above left) The TL clock in pottery is set to zero when the vessel is originally fired. TL accumulates until the pot is heated again in the present day to determine its age. (Above right) Glow-curves observed in the laboratory. Curve (a) displays the light emitted when the sample is first heated. Curve (b) is the non-TL light recorded during a second heating (the red-hot glow observable when any sample is heated). The extra light emitted in the first heating is the TL one wants to measure to arrive at a date. (Right) Good and bad locations for TL samples. For example, results will be inaccurate if the subsoil or rock near the sample at the bottom have a measurably different level of radioactivity from that of the filling of the pit or ditch.

It is vital that the radioactivity from impurities *within* the sample, which is the basis for the TL date, is distinguished from sources of radiation such as those in the soil *surrounding* the sample. Under ideal circumstances the radioactivity of the soil is measured on site by the burial of a small capsule containing a radiation-sensitive material, which is left for about a year. Where this is not possible, a more rapid determination using a radiation counter can be used, or samples of the soil collected in plastic bags and dispatched to the laboratory along with the object to be dated. Where the radioactivity of the burial context cannot be determined, e.g. for an object not in situ, the TL date is much less accurate.

Applications. A good example of the archaeological application of TL is the dating of the terracotta known as the Jemaa head, from the alluvium of a tin mine near the Jos Plateau of Nigeria. The head and similar examples belong to the Nok culture, but such sculptures could not be dated reliably at the site of Nok itself

Terracotta head from Jemaa, Nigeria, belonging to the Nok culture. A TL reading for the age of the sculpture has provided the first reliable date for this and other terracottas from the Nok region. Height 23 cm.

because of the lack of any plausible radiocarbon dates. A TL reading on the head gave an age of 1520±260 years BC, allowing this and similar terracotta heads from the Nok region to be given a firm chronological position for the first time.

Of even greater potential is the development of the TL method for dating artifacts made before 50,000 years ago (beyond the basic limit of radiocarbon). Pottery itself is not found at this early time, nor are baked clay artifacts. But the method can be applied to stone (lithic) materials with a crystalline structure, always provided that they were heated at the time of their production as artifacts, or at the time of their use, to a temperature of around 500°C. In this way, geological TL in the stone would be emitted and the TL clock effectively set at zero. Therefore, the measurement of their TL age genuinely dates their archaeological use. In practice, burnt flint has proved a very informative material. For example, the method has been used in France to date flint tools of so-called Mousterian type found at sites occupied by Neanderthal people (*Homo sapiens neanderthalensis*) in the Middle Paleolithic period. Most of the dates fall between 70,000 and 40,000 years ago. Despite their limited precision, the dates establish a very useful pattern for the tools that has advanced the understanding of the French Middle Paleolithic.

Hélène Valladas and her colleagues have also employed the TL method to date flint tools used at different times by both Neanderthals and the first people of modern appearance (*Homo sapiens sapiens*). Their research at caves in Israel suggests controversially and somewhat surprisingly that Neanderthals came to the area tens of thousands of years after the first anatomically modern humans. This, and related work, implies that Neanderthals were not our direct ancestors.

In addition to lithic material heated in antiquity, TL dates can be obtained from sediments and from calcium carbonate deposits in caves (e.g. stalagmites and travertines) with which artifacts are associated. For sediments, the TL clock is set to zero by bleaching with light at the time at which the sediment is deposited. For calcium carbonate, TL starts to accumulate from the time the carbonate crystallizes from the solution to form the deposit. TL dating has shown, for instance, that the stalagmitic floor of the Lower Paleolithic cave site of Caune de l'Arago in southern France formed around 350,000 years ago.

There is also a special application of TL dating, in the identification of fake pottery and terracotta objects. TL can easily distinguish between a genuine antiquity and a fake made within the last 100 years.

Limiting Factors. Various complications remain with thermoluminescence, and TL dates rarely have an accuracy of better than ±10 percent. In general, therefore, the TL method is most useful in circumstances where radiocarbon dating cannot be used, either because no suitable organic samples are available or because the site lies beyond the range of radiocarbon.

Electron Spin Resonance

In recent years a new method, electron spin resonance (ESR), has become available which enables the trapped electrons within bone or shell to be measured without the heating that the thermoluminescence technique requires. As with TL, the number of trapped electrons indicates the age of the specimen. In the new method, the object to be dated is placed within a strong magnetic field. The energy absorbed by the object as the strength of the field is varied provides a spectrum from which the trapped electron population can be measured. The method has the advantage over TL that it is non-destructive. It also requires only very small samples of less than 1 g. On the other hand it is less sensitive than TL and not as widely available.

ESR has already proved useful in helping to resolve the controversy surrounding the date of a skull found as long ago as 1959 at Petralona Cave, northern Greece. The calcite on the bone gave a date of 198,000±40,000 years and the bone itself a date of 127,000±35,000 years. The low date of the bone is regarded as erroneous due to recrystallization since burial, and a date of around 200,000 years old appears to be established for this contentious specimen. Though still in the early stages of development, ESR is likely to prove a powerful dating tool in the future, especially for bone and tooth samples which lie beyond the range of radiocarbon dating.

Potassium-Argon Dating

The potassium-argon (K-Ar) method is used by geologists to date rocks hundreds or even thousands of millions of years old. It is also one of the most appropriate techniques for dating early human (hominid) sites in Africa, which can be up to 5 million years old. It is restricted to volcanic rock no more recent than around 100,000 years.

Basis of Method. Potassium-argon dating, like radiocarbon dating, is based on the principle of radioactive decay: in this case, the steady but very slow decay of the radioactive isotope potassium−40 (^{40}K) to the inert gas argon−40 (^{40}Ar) in volcanic rock.

Knowing the decay rate of ^{40}K – its half-life is around 1.3 billion years – a measure of the quantity of ^{40}Ar trapped within a 10 g rock sample gives an estimate of the date of the rock's formation. As with all radioactive methods, it is important to be clear about what sets the radioactive clock to zero. In this case, it is the formation of the rock through volcanic activity, which drives off any argon formerly present.

The dates obtained in the laboratory are in effect geological dates for rock samples. Happily, some of the most important areas for the study of the Lower Paleolithic, notably the Rift Valley in East Africa, are areas of high volcanic activity. This means that archaeological remains often lie on geological strata formed by volcanic action, and hence suitable for K-Ar dating. In addition, they are often overlain by comparable volcanic rock, so that dates for these two geological strata provide a chronological sandwich, between the upper and lower slices of which the archaeological deposits are set.

Applications: Early Human Sites in East Africa. Olduvai Gorge in Tanzania is one of the most crucial sites for the study of hominid evolution, as it has yielded fossil remains of *Australopithecus (Paranthropus) boisei*, *Homo habilis*, and *Homo erectus* (see pp.142, 143) as well as large numbers of stone artifacts and bones. Being in the Rift Valley, Olduvai is a volcanic area, and its 2-million-year chronology has been well established by K-Ar dating of the relevant deposits of hardened volcanic ash (tuff) and other materials between which the archaeological remains are found (see box below, Dating Our African Ancestors). The K-Ar method has also been immensely important in dating other early East African sites, such as Hadar in Ethiopia.

Limiting Factors. The results of K-Ar dating are generally accompanied by an error estimate, as in the case of other radioactivity-based methods. For example, the date of Tuff IB at Olduvai has been measured as 1.79±0.03 million years. An error estimate of 30,000 years at first seems a large one, but it is in fact only of the order of 2 percent of the total age. (Note that here, as in other cases, the estimate of error relates to the counting process in the laboratory, and does not seek to estimate also other sources of error arising from varying chemical conditions of deposition, or indeed from uncertainties of archaeological interpretation.)

The principal limitations of the technique are that it can only be used to date sites buried by volcanic rock, and that it is rarely possible to achieve an accuracy of better than ±10 percent. Potassium-argon dating has nevertheless proved a key tool in areas where suitable volcanic materials are present.

Uranium-Series Dating

This is a dating method based on the radioactive decay of isotopes of uranium. It has proved particularly useful for the period 500,000–50,000 years ago, which lies outside the time range of radiocarbon dating. In Europe, where there are few volcanic rocks suitable for dating by the potassium-argon technique, uranium-series (U-series) dating may be the method of first choice for clarifying when a site was occupied by early humans.

Basis of Method. Two radioactive isotopes of the element uranium (^{238}U and ^{235}U) decay in a series of stages into daughter elements. Two of these daughter elements, thorium (^{230}Th, also called "ionium") and protactinium (^{231}Pa), themselves also decay with half-

lives useful for dating. The essential point is that the parent uranium isotopes are soluble in water, whereas the daughter products are not. This means, for instance, that only the uranium isotopes are present in waters that seep into limestone caves. However, once those waters are precipitated to form calcium carbonate on cave walls and floors (this material is often called travertine), the radioactive clock is set going, because now the daughter products are trapped in the travertine along with the parent isotopes. The greater the amount of the daughter products present in relation to that of the parent uranium isotopes, the greater the age of the travertine. Roughly 100 g of calcium carbonate are needed for a satisfactory date.

Applications and Limiting Factors. The method is used to date rocks rich in calcium carbonate, often those deposited by the action of surface or ground waters around lime-rich springs or by seepage into limestone caves. Stalagmites form on cave floors in this way. As early humans used caves and overhanging rocks for shelter, artifacts and bones often became embedded in a layer of calcium carbonate or in another type of sediment between two layers of the calcareous deposit.

The difficulty of determining the correct order of deposition in a cave is one reason why the U-series method is prone to give ambiguous results. For this and other reasons, several layers of deposit in a cave need to be sampled and the geology meticulously examined. The method has nevertheless proved very useful. At the Pontnewydd Cave in North Wales, the lower breccia which contained the bulk of the archaeological finds there was shown by U-series dating to be at least 220,000 years old. The important site of Bilzingsleben in eastern Germany was also dated by this method, the travertine layer which enclosed the artifacts and human skeletal remains giving an age of around 414,000 years, though some uncertainty remains, as with many U-series determinations.

In favourable circumstances, the method leads to dates with an associated uncertainty (standard error) of ±12,000 years for a sample with an age of 150,000 years, and of about ±25,000 years for a sample of age 400,000 years. In practice, the inaccuracy may be greater than these figures suggest. Wherever possible, alternative methods (e.g. thermoluminescence) should be used to check the results.

Fission-Track Dating

Fission-track dating is another method based on the operation of a radioactive clock. This time, it is the spontaneous fission of an isotope of uranium (^{238}U) present in a wide range of rocks and minerals, in obsidian and other volcanic glasses, in glassy meteorites (tektites), in manufactured glasses, and in mineral inclusions in pottery. As in the case of potassium-argon dating – with whose time range it overlaps – the method produces useful dates from suitable rocks that

Uranium-series dating and Pontnewydd Cave, North Wales (left, deep section; above, measurements being taken in the cave). The lower breccia contained the bulk of the archaeological finds at this important Paleolithic site, including hominid remains such as a tooth of Neanderthal type. A stalagmite on the lower breccia was found by the U-series method to be more than 220,000 years old. This result was confirmed by a TL determination on the same stalagmite, and by another TL reading on a burnt flint core – from a layer immediately underlying the lower breccia – which gave a statistically consistent age of 200,000 ± 25,000 years.

Examples of fission tracks, after etching.

contain or are adjacent to those containing archaeological evidence.

Basis of Method. As well as decaying naturally to a stable lead isotope, ^{238}U occasionally also divides in half. During this process of spontaneous fission the halves move apart at high speed, coming to a halt only after causing much damage to structures in their path. In materials containing ^{238}U, such as natural glasses, this damage is recorded in the form of pathways called *fission tracks*. The tracks are counted under an optical microscope after the polished surface of the glass has been etched with acid to improve visibility. The quantity of uranium present in the sample is then determined by counting a second set of tracks created by artificially inducing fission in atoms of ^{235}U. (The ratio of ^{235}U to ^{238}U is known, so that the second count indirectly measures the amount of ^{238}U present.) Knowing the rate of fission of ^{238}U, one arrives at a date – the age since the setting of the clock to zero – by comparing the number of spontaneously induced tracks with the quantity of ^{238}U in the sample.

The radioactive clock is set at zero by the formation of the mineral or glass, either in nature (as with obsidian and tektites) or at the time of manufacture (as with manufactured glass).

Applications and Limiting Factors. The fission-track technique is most useful for early Paleolithic sites, especially where the potassium-argon method cannot be applied. Even where it can be, fission-track provides independent confirmation of dating results. For example, the date of 2.03±0.28 million years obtained by fission-track analysis for Tuff IB at Olduvai Gorge, Tanzania, falls within the age determination by potassium-argon and other methods of 2.1–1.7 million years for this important early hominid site (see box). Fission-track also helped to settle the controversy over the date of the KBS Tuff and associated hominid remains and artifacts at the East Turkana sites, Kenya.

DATING OUR AFRICAN ANCESTORS

In the 19th century, Charles Darwin firmly believed that human origins lay in Africa, and the 20th century has proved him right. Our earliest ancestors have been discovered at several sites in East Africa and southern Africa (see p. 142). One of the greatest triumphs of scientific chronology in the postwar years has been the successful dating and correlating of these sites – particularly those in East Africa – derived from three main methods: potassium-argon (K-Ar), fission-track, and geomagnetic dating. In addition, the relative method of faunal dating has been used to check these results.

Olduvai Gorge
Thanks to the discoveries of early hominid fossils in the gorge by Louis and Mary Leakey, Olduvai is one of the most crucial sites for the study of human evolution. It has proved possible to establish a chronology for the site, particularly on the basis of K-Ar dating of deposits of hardened volcanic ash (tuff), between which the fossil remains lie. For example, the

Principal early hominid sites in East Africa.

age of the important Tuff IB in Bed I was estimated as 1.79±0.03 my (million years).

As with all archaeological dating, for a reliable result one should cross-check age estimates derived from one method with those from another. In the case of Tuff IB, a fission-track reading gave a date of 2.03±0.28 my, which is within the statistically acceptable confidence limits for the K-Ar estimate.

Another means of checking the K-Ar sequence proved to be geomagnetic dating. As explained on p. 139, there have been periodic reversals in the direction of the earth's magnetic field (the North Pole becoming the South Pole and vice versa). Magnetically charged particles in rocks preserve a record of the sequence of these reversals (from "normal" to "reversed" and back again). It transpired that Beds I-III and part of IV at Olduvai lay within the so-called Matuyama epoch of reversed polarity, with a significant period of normal polarity 1.87–1.67 million years ago first demonstrated at the site and now known, appropriately, as the "Olduvai event." The discovery of the same sequence of reversals at other East African sites (e.g. East Turkana and Omo) has helped correlate their deposits with those at Olduvai.

A further check on the validity of these sequences is the relative method of faunal dating (biostratigraphy), explained on p. 111. The evolutionary tree for the pig family has proved among the most useful, helping to confirm the correlations among East African sites, including Olduvai, derived from other dating methods.

The KBS Tuff Controversy

Nowhere has the need for extreme care in dating fossil human remains been more evident than in the case of the *Homo habilis* skull, "1470," unearthed by Richard Leakey at East Turkana, Kenya, in 1972. Preliminary K-Ar results from a British laboratory on the so-called KBS tuff above the skull deposit gave a date of *c.*2.6 my, at least 0.8 my earlier than *H. habilis* finds elsewhere. Could the K-Ar date be right? At first cross-checking by geomagnetic reversals and fission-track seemed to support it. But there was the worrying fact that pig fossil correlations with other sites implied a date no earlier than 2 my. And in 1974 an American laboratory produced K-Ar readings of *c.*1.8 my for the tuff.

The controversy dragged on for several years. Eventually one of the scientists who had originally published fission-track dates supporting the older K-Ar readings re-ran fission-track tests and confirmed the younger estimate of *c.*1.8 my. Finally, to resolve the issue, Leakey commissioned an Australian laboratory to obtain new K-Ar dates. The result was a now generally accepted age for the KBS tuff of 1.88±0.02 my.

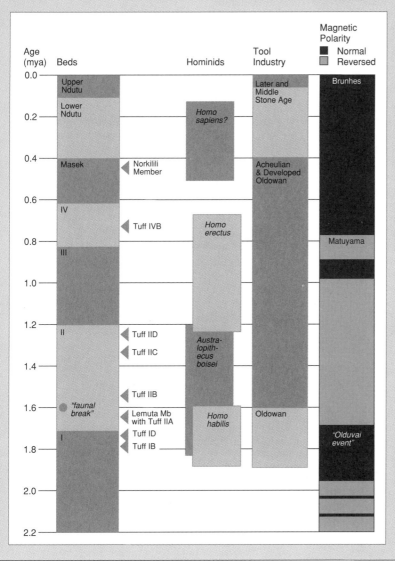

Olduvai Gorge schematic stratigraphy, together with hominids and tool industries from the site, and magnetic reversals.

The fission-track technique is most easily applied to naturally occurring materials such as pumice and obsidian, but minerals within rock formations (e.g. zircon and apatite which contain high amounts of uranium) can also be dated in this way. The potential time range is considerable: micas from Zimbabwe in Africa have been dated back to more than 2,500 million (or 2.5 billion) years ago. Generally, the method is used for geological samples no younger than about 300,000 years old. For more recent material, the method is too time-consuming to operate; here thermoluminescence dating or some other method is generally better. There are a few exceptions. For

example, artificial glass and pottery glazes less than 2000 years old have been dated by the fission-track method. A rather different application is to obsidian artifacts that have been exposed to fire during manufacture, or during or after use. The heat has the effect of setting the radioactive clock to zero and the tracks left after the fission of ^{238}U can be counted as if this were an artificial glass.

In favorable circumstances, the error associated with the method is of the order of ±10 percent (one standard deviation), assuming that at least 100 tracks are counted.

CALIBRATED RELATIVE METHODS

Radioactive decay is the only completely regular time-dependent process known; it is uninfluenced by temperature or other environmental conditions. There are however other natural processes which, while not completely regular, are sufficiently steady over the course of time to be of use to the archaeologist. We have already seen how natural annual cycles produce varves and tree-rings, which of course are immensely useful because they give dates calibrated in years. Other processes that form the basis of the first three techniques described below are not naturally calibrated in years, but in principle they can be made to yield absolute dates if the rate of change inherent in the process can be independently calibrated by one of the absolute methods already discussed. In practice, as we shall see, the calibration for each technique often

has to be done afresh for each site or area because of environmental factors that influence the rate of change. This makes these techniques difficult to use as reliable absolute dating methods. They can, however, still prove enormously helpful simply as means of ordering samples in a relative sequence, in which older is distinguished from younger.

Obsidian Hydration

Basis of Method and Limiting Factors. This technique was first developed by the American geologists Irving Friedman and Robert L. Smith. It is based on the principle that when obsidian (the volcanic glass often used rather like flint to make tools, see Chapter 8) is fractured, it starts absorbing water from its surroundings to form a hydration layer that can be measured in the laboratory. In a section through an obsidian blade or flake viewed under the optical microscope, the layer appears as a distinct zone at the surface. It increases in thickness through time.

If the layer increases in thickness in a linear way, then assuming we know the rate of growth and the present thickness, we ought to be able to calculate the length of time elapsed since growth began. The zero moment, when the hydration zone started forming, is the moment when the flake tool was freshly made by removing it from the original obsidian block, or by trimming it. Unfortunately, there is no universally valid rate of growth or hydration rate. For one thing, the rate is dependent on temperature, and exposure to direct sunlight over long periods increases hydration. Moreover, obsidians from different quarries have different chemical compositions, and this can affect the picture. It is necessary, therefore, to establish separately the hydration rate for the different kinds of

Obsidian hydration dating: a hydration layer visible in an obsidian artifact. The layer increases in thickness as time passes, but there is no universally valid rate of growth.

obsidian found in a given area, and to keep in mind the temperature factor, which can be allowed for.

To use the method for absolute dating, it has to be calibrated against an established chronological sequence (taking into account the chemical and temperature factors) for the region in question. Samples for dating need to come from one or more well-defined contexts that can be dated securely by other means. A single obsidian artifact cannot be expected to give a reliable date. It is thus safer to use an assemblage of about 10 pieces, so that the date of each one can be separately calculated. In addition to providing direct chronological information, the method can be useful in assessing the relative ages of different strata within a site or region where obsidian is abundant.

Though principally relevant to sites and artifacts of the last 10,000 years (the postglacial period), obsidian hydration has given acceptable dates of around 120,000 years for Middle Paleolithic material from East Africa.

Applications. One of the boldest applications of the method so far has been by one of the pioneers of obsidian dating, Joseph Michels, in his study of the rural hinterland around the important ancient center of Kaminaljuyu in Guatemala. The sites were difficult to date from the pottery found on the surface, which was much abraded, so an attempt was made to date them by measuring the hydration layer on at least four obsidian artifacts from each site. If at least two of the obsidian dates fell within one of the already established chronological phases (ranging from Early Formative *c.* 2500 BC to Late Postclassic *c.*AD 1500), the site was assigned to that phase. In the principal survey area some 70 rural settlements were dated in this way, on the evidence of a total of 288 obsidian samples. The results indicated an increase in the density of rural settlement up to the Early Late Classic period (AD 600–800), then a gradual fall as Kaminaljuyu went into decline.

Amino-Acid Racemization

This method, first applied in the early 1970s and still at an experimental stage, is used to date bone, whether human or animal (only 10 g are required). Its special significance is that it can be applied to material up to about 100,000 years old, i.e. beyond the time range of radiocarbon dating.

Basis of Method. The technique is based on the fact that amino acids, which make up proteins present in all living things, can exist in two mirror-image forms, termed enantiomers. These differ in their chemical structure, which shows in their effect on polarized light. Those that rotate polarized light to the left are *laevo*-enantiomers or L-amino acids; those that rotate the light to the right are *dextro*-enantiomers or D-amino acids.

The amino acids present in the proteins of living organisms contain only L-enantiomers. After death, these change at a steady rate (they racemize) to D-enantiomers. The rate of racemization is temperature-dependent, and therefore likely to vary from site to site. But by radiocarbon-dating suitable bone samples at a particular site, and measuring the relative proportions (ratio) of the L and D forms in them, one should be able to work out what the local racemization rate is. This calibration is then used to date bone samples from earlier levels at the site beyond the time range of radiocarbon.

Applications and Limiting Factors. Aspartic acid has the fastest racemization rate of the stable amino acids and is the acid usually chosen for dating bone samples. For instance, at the Nelson Bay Cave in Cape Province, South Africa, samples with a D / L aspartic acid ratio of 0.167 gave radiocarbon ages of roughly 18,000 years. This allowed a conversion rate to be calculated, calibrating the racemization rate for that site. Measurements of the ratio were then made on fossil bone samples from the important site of Klasies River Mouth in the same area, giving for the lower levels (18 and 19) D / L aspartic acid ratios of 0.474 and 0.548. From these values, ages of about 90,000 and 110,000 years respectively were estimated. In this case, the "calibration" sample was derived from a different site than the one from which the samples to be dated came. This is less than ideal, because the racemization rates for the different sites, even though geographically the sites are not far apart, could differ to some extent.

As a means of absolute dating the method is of course entirely dependent on the accuracy of its calibration (as are other relative methods). This has led to controversy, particularly as regards the date of fossil human remains from California. Early radiocarbon determinations from skulls found near Los Angeles were used to calibrate aspartic acid racemization rates, which then yielded ages as high as 48,000 years for other remains near San Diego – suggesting human colonization of the Americas much earlier than had been supposed (Chapter 11). More recent radiocarbon dates on the Los Angeles bones by the AMS method have altered the calibration, lowering the oldest age-estimates for the California remains to no earlier than 8000 years.

Cation-Ratio Dating

In recent years an interesting new technique has been developed which for the first time allows the direct dating of rock carvings and engravings; it is also potentially applicable to Paleolithic artifacts that have a strong patina which will have been caused by exposure to desert dust.

Basis of Method. In desert conditions, a varnish forms on rock surfaces exposed to desert dust. The varnish is composed of clay minerals, oxides, and hydroxides of manganese and iron, minor and trace elements, and a very small amount of organic matter. The dating method depends on the principle that the cations of certain elements (i.e. charged atoms of those elements which combine with oxide and hydroxide ions of opposite charge to form stable compounds) are more soluble than those of certain other elements. They leach out of rock varnish more rapidly than the less-soluble elements and their concentration thus decreases in time. The method simply requires the measurement of the ratio of these mobile cations, usually of potassium (K) and calcium (Ca), to the more stable cations of titanium (Ti). The ratio is assumed to decrease exponentially with time (giving a decay curve similar in shape to the decay curves of radioactive isotopes discussed above). However, the pioneers of the technique, Ronald Dorn and his associates, do not claim that there is an absolute decay rate (as there is for radioactive decay processes); the method has to be calibrated for the area in question using other dating methods.

Applications. An example of cation-ratio dating is offered by rock carvings (petroglyphs) in the Western Great Basin (from the Coso Range of Inyo County, California). The varnish on them was analyzed by Ronald Dorn and David Whitley. The samples used for calibrating the varnish were (a) certain soils from sites in the area, to establish the modern K+Ca:Ti ratio; (b) varnish from the high shoreline of the nearby Searles Lake (independently dated by geological means at 10,500 years); and (c) rock varnish on volcanic outcrops in the area that formed between 3 million and 39,000 years ago, according to potassium-argon dating. These various datings were used to establish a calibration curve for the cation-ratio change, and allowed the varnish on the petroglyphs to be assigned an age of 6400 years (within a one standard deviation error range from 5600 to 8600). A date of around 6400 years ago is about twice as old as that previously assigned to these features.

Limiting Factors. This method has not yet been widely applied, and it is not clear in what climatic conditions the varnish may be damaged or destroyed, nor indeed whether variations in climate might affect the process of cation-ratio reduction. Nevertheless, the technique holds some promise for the dating of surface finds in arid areas.

Archaeomagnetic Dating

Archaeomagnetic (or Paleomagnetic) dating has so far been of only limited usefulness to archaeology, in part because not enough work has been done in different regions.

Basis of Method. The earth's magnetic field is constantly changing in both direction and intensity. Historical records from London, Paris, and Rome have allowed scientists to plot changes in the direction of magnetic north observed there from compass readings over the last 400 years. Scientists have also been able to trace these changes farther back in time in Europe and elsewhere by studying the magnetization at earlier periods of baked clay structures (ovens, kilns, hearths) that have been independently dated, for instance by radiocarbon. (Provided clay is baked to 650–700°C (1202–1292°F) and not reheated, the iron particles in it permanently take up the earth's magnetic direction and intensity at the time of firing. This principle is called thermoremanent magnetism (TRM).) Plots can thus be built up of the variation through time in magnetic *direction* which can be used to date other baked clay structures of unknown age, whose TRM is measured and then matched to a particular point (date) on the master sequence. Different master sequences have to be built up for variations in magnetic *intensity*, which varies independently of magnetic direction.

Applications and Limiting Factors. Regional variations within the global magnetic field mean that a separate master sequence is needed for each region. For magnetic direction these have been created in a few parts of the world such as Britain and the American Southwest back over the last 2000 years. A baked clay kiln or oven from this time period, measured in situ at a site in one of these regions, can be dated quite accurately by the magnetic direction method. Once the structure is moved, however, its ancient magnetic direction can no longer be compared with that of the present day.

Magnetic intensity can be measured when the baked clay is out of context, and so can be applied to pottery

Magnetic direction dating. The changing positions of magnetic north, as plotted here for Britain (left) and the American Southwest (right), can be used to date baked clay structures such as kilns which preserve a record of the direction of magnetic north at the time they were fired.

unlike the directional method. A recent application to pottery from different provinces of China has yielded a master sequence for the last 4000 years, promising to make it possible to date Chinese pottery of unknown age. But so far the intensity method has proved inherently much less accurate than the directional method.

Geomagnetic Reversals. Another aspect of archaeomagnetism, relevant for the dating of the Lower Paleolithic, is the phenomenon of complete reversals in the earth's magnetic field (magnetic north becomes magnetic south, and vice versa). The most recent reversal occurred about 700,000 years ago, and a sequence of such reversals stretching back several million years has been built up with the aid of potassium-argon and other dating techniques. The finding of part of this sequence of reversals in the rock strata of African early hominid sites has proved a helpful check on the other dating methods that have been used at those sites (see box above, Dating Our African Ancestors).

CHRONOLOGICAL CORRELATIONS

One of the most promising avenues for future work in chronology is the correlation of different dating methods. The use of one absolute method in support of another can often bring very powerful results. An excellent example is the way that tree-ring dating has been used to support and indeed calibrate radiocarbon, as a result of which the latter has gained greatly in accuracy and reliability. The same observation is true of the relationship between relative and absolute dating. Although actual dates in years are provided by absolute methods, much of the reliability and internal consistency of those dates (and therefore the possibility of recognizing and weeding out inaccurate absolute

age determinations) comes from the framework provided by the relative dating method.

Links between chronological sequences that are geographically remote from each other – "teleconnections" – can present considerable difficulties. The most common of these are those that depend on the comparison of sequences – for instance, the comparison of sequences of tree-ring widths. This is certainly valid for adjacent trees or for trees within a small area; over a wide region such "teleconnections" must be treated with caution. In the same way, the correlation of varve sequences in Scandinavia and in North America has proved contentious. With such methods

DATING THE THERA ERUPTION

More than 3500 years ago the volcanic island of Thera (also known as Santorini) in the Aegean Sea erupted, burying the prehistoric settlement of Akrotiri on its southern shore. Akrotiri – excavated since the 1960s by the Greek archaeologists Spyridon Marinatos and more recently Christos Doumas – has proved to be a prehistoric Pompeii, with well-preserved streets and houses, some with remarkable wall paintings, all buried beneath many meters of volcanic ash. The eruption itself offers interesting problems and opportunities in dating.

As long ago as 1939, Marinatos suggested that the Thera eruption was responsible for the destruction of the Minoan palaces of Crete (110 km or 69 miles to the south), many of which were abandoned during the Late Bronze Age. This idea sparked off a debate that still continues.

In the first place, the problem can be approached in terms of the **relative chronology** offered by the evolution of pottery styles. There is a well-established stylistic sequence for Minoan pottery, and it was found that the most recent pottery style in the relevant Minoan palaces was Late Minoan IB. This was assigned an absolute date in years by cross-dating between the Minoan sequence and the well-established Egyptian historical chronology. On this basis, the date of the end of Late Minoan IB (and hence of the destruction of the Minoan palaces) was set around 1450 BC.

This date however made any link with the destruction of Akrotiri on Thera problematic, because Akrotiri has no late Minoan IB pottery but abundant material of the Late Minoan IA style. Some scholars thus concluded that the Thera eruption had nothing to do with the destruction of the Minoan palaces, which might well have been a later event. They were therefore happy to date the Thera eruption within the Late Minoan IA period, perhaps (again using the Egyptian-based chronology for Minoan Crete) around 1500 BC.

Other scholars, however, believed that the effects of the Thera eruption would have been widely felt. Here, they were certainly aided by the application of **tephra studies**. Deep-sea coring on the bed of the Mediterranean gave evidence for the Thera ash fall (and the ash was shown by laboratory analysis to be from the appropriate eruption of this particular volcano). Subsequently, traces of ash from the Thera eruption were identified (using refractive index studies) in samples from sites on Minoan Crete, and also from the site of Phylakopi on the Aegean island of Melos. However, this ash has not yet been documented in strata at archaeological sites where there is a clear distinction between the use of Late Minoan IA and Late Minoan IB pottery, so it is premature to speak here of tephrachronology. Nevertheless a major ash layer has been recognized at the archaeological site of Trianda on Rhodes, so the method should offer an answer in due course.

The problem is one that **radiocarbon dating** should theoretically help resolve, but the distinction between 1500 BC and 1450 BC is a relatively narrow one. However, samples have been analyzed, including short-lived samples (carbonized grain, etc.), that could not have been old at the time of the eruption. The mean date obtained from such short-lived samples is 1615 BC (after calibration). The date range for a single standard deviation, which implies 65 percent probability, is 1630 to 1530 BC. (The range is not symmetrical about the mean date because of irregularities in the calibration curve at this time.) The radiocarbon data thus favor the earlier of the two dates in question.

The matter does not rest there. It has been shown for more recent times that major volcanic eruptions have global effects (since the dust thrown into the atmosphere reduces solar radiation reaching the earth). These can show up as anomalously narrow

The Thera volcano is still sporadically active, the focus of the eruptions being on this small island in the center of the semi-submerged volcano.

rings for a year or two in **tree-ring sequences**. Such effects have been sought in the tree-ring record of the California bristlecone pine during the middle of the 2nd millennium BC. One such, firmly dated 1628–1626 BC, has been proposed for the Thera eruption. A comparable ring has been reported for the tree-ring sequence for Irish oak.

It has been similarly shown that **ice cores** reveal a short peak of high acidity for recently observed major eruptions, when these are on a scale large enough to have global effects. An ice core from Greenland shows such a peak for 1390 BC, and this has been claimed as a possible date for the Thera eruption. More recent work at the Dye 3 site in Greenland has, however, suggested that an acidity maximum in 1645 BC would be more appropriate.

The problem here is that there is absolutely nothing in the tree-rings or indeed in the ice cores that allows one major volcanic eruption in one part of the world to be distinguished from another, other than its date in years. So a connection has to be assumed before the event in question can be dated. In due course, however, it is to be expected that a correlation between the Thera eruption and the tree-ring and ice-core sequences will be found.

Fresco from Akrotiri called the "Fisherman."

Map indicating isopachs (contours of equal thickness) for tephra fallout from the eruption of Thera, as determined from deep-sea cores. The figures in brackets give an estimate of the corresponding depth of tephra falling on land.

there is always the risk of arriving at a "correlation" between sequences which, while initially plausible, is incorrect.

Global Events

One of the most powerful ways of establishing a correlation between sequences is by seeing within them the occurrence of the same significant event, one with wide repercussions geographically, even on a global scale.

Such events are naturally very rare, and are generally catastrophic in their nature. The impact on earth of large meteorites would fall in this category. Much more common are large-scale volcanic eruptions. Close to the volcano these events have striking effects, with mud and lava flows and thick falls of ash, often with devastating consequences for human occupation. At intermediate distances, up to a few hundred kilometers, they can still have a marked effect, with tsunamis ("tidal waves," although they are not in fact tidal) and falls of tephra (volcanic ash). Scientists have sought to correlate earthquake damage at intermediate distances with volcanic eruptions, but the two events are often not connected. Major volcanic eruptions also project significant quantities of tephra into the earth's upper atmosphere, with global effects. Such ash or dust increases the acidity of the snow falling in polar areas, and thus leaves its trace in ice cores. Its effect on tree-rings has also been noted: by reducing the amount of solar radiation reaching the earth (and thus also reducing the temperature) the volcanic dust reduces the growth rate of trees for a short but significant time.

The developing field of tephrachronology is proving useful. Its aim is to distinguish unequivocally, and hence date, the tephra from different volcanic eruptions that may be present in terrestrial deposits, or in deep-sea cores. The products of each eruption are often significantly different, so that measurements of refractive index may be sufficient to distinguish one ash from another. In other cases, analysis of trace elements will separate the two.

When all the sites and objects in an area are buried under a layer of volcanic ash at the same instant – a "freeze-frame" effect – one has a very precise dating method that can be used to correlate the age of all those archaeological materials. Examples include the great eruption of Mount Vesuvius in AD 79 that covered Pompeii, Herculaneum, and other Roman settlements (box, Chapter 1); and the eruption of the Ilopango volcano in El Salvador in about AD 260 that buried Early Classic settlements there under 0.5–1 m (1.6–3.3 ft) of volcanic ash. The Ilopango eruption must have disrupted agriculture for several years and interrupted pyramid construction at the site of Chalchuapa, where the break in work can clearly be seen.

Another good example of tephrachronology comes from New Guinea, where various sites have been related chronologically by the presence of up to a dozen identifiable ash falls within them. Australian archaeologists Edward Harris and Philip Hughes were able to relate the horticultural system at Mugumamp Ridge in the Western Highland Province of Papua New Guinea with another at Kuk Swamp, some kilometers to the south, by the characteristics of the volcanic ash overlying both horticultural systems. The ash is thought to derive from the volcanic Mount Hagen some 40 km (25 miles) to the west. A combination of tephrachronology and radiocarbon suggests that horticulture in this area may have begun as early as 7000 BC (see box on Kuk Swamp, Chapter 6).

The most intensively studied question in the field of tephrachronology, however, is the date of the major eruption of the volcanic island of Thera in the Aegean sometime around the late 17th century BC (see box, pp.140–141). The eruption buried the Late Bronze Age town of Akrotiri on the island. There were also marked effects on islands nearby.

An important general moral arises from the long dispute over the date of the Thera eruption. It is indeed all too common, when dating evidence is being discussed, to assume long-distance connections without being able to document them. For instance, several writers have tried to link the volcanic eruption of Thera with the Plagues of Egypt reported in the Book of Exodus in the Bible. This is intriguing, and worth investigating. But when it is actually used to date the eruption, as it has been by some, this is no more than a supposed equivalence, a supposition masquerading as a dating.

At the same time, however, there is an important future for the use of several methods in combination to date the eruption. For instance, it is perfectly appropriate to date the eruption approximately using radiocarbon on samples from Thera and then to seek a more precise date, indeed a date in calendar years, from indications in ice cores or tree-rings. The assumptions underlying the correlation – that these different kinds of evidence are telling us about the same event – should not, of course, be forgotten. It would be much more satisfactory if traces of tephra could be found in the ice cores, and if these could be shown by analysis to derive from the eruption in question. Were this to be done, it would be the Greenland or Antarctic ice cores that would, in effect, become responsible for the very precise dating of one important event in the Aegean Late Bronze Age, and hence for a calibration of Aegean Late Bronze Age dating in general. It might even lead to modifications in the Egyptian historical chronology.

WORLD CHRONOLOGY

As a result of the application of the various dating techniques discussed above, it is possible to summarize the world archaeological chronology.

The human story as at present understood begins in East Africa, with the emergence there of the earliest hominids of the genus *Australopithecus* around 4 or 5 million years ago. By around 2 million years ago, there is clear fossil evidence for the first known representative of our own genus, *Homo habilis*, from such sites as Koobi Fora (Kenya) and Olduvai Gorge (Tanzania). The earliest stone tools (from Hadar, Ethiopia) date from about 2.5 million years ago, but it is not known which hominid made them because *Homo habilis* fossils of this age have not yet been found. It is possible that australopithecines also had a tool culture before or during *Homo habilis*'s time. The early toolkits, which comprise flake and pebble tools, are collectively called the Oldowan industry, after Olduvai Gorge where they are particularly well represented.

By around 1.6 million years ago, the next stage in human evolution, *Homo erectus* had emerged in East Africa. These hominids had larger brains than *Homo habilis*, their probable ancestor, and were makers of the characteristic teardrop-shaped stone tools flaked on both sides called Acheulean hand-axes. These artifacts are the dominant tool form of the Lower Paleolithic. By the time *Homo erectus* became extinct (400,000–200,000 years ago), the species had colonized the rest of Africa, southern, eastern, and western Asia, and central and western Europe.

The Middle Paleolithic period – from about 200,000 to 40,000 years ago – saw the emergence of *Homo sapiens*. Neanderthals, who are generally classed as a subspecies of *Homo sapiens* (*Homo sapiens neanderthalensis*), lived in Europe, and western and central Asia from about 130,000 to 30,000 years ago. Their role in later human evolution is unclear, some specialists believing Neanderthals ultimately evolved into fully modern humans, others that they were an evolutionary dead end. The latter theory is gaining ground now that we have increasing evidence for fully modern people – our own subspecies, *Homo sapiens*

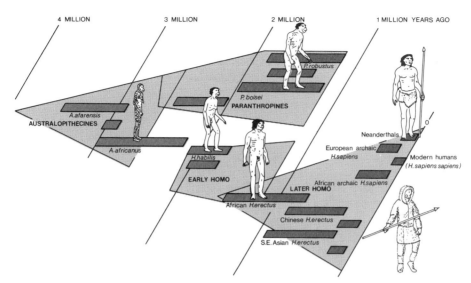

4 MILLION   3 MILLION   2 MILLION   1 MILLION YEARS AGO

P.robustus

P. boisei
PARANTHROPINES

A.afarensis
AUSTRALOPITHECINES

A.africanus

H.habilis

EARLY HOMO

Neanderthals

European archaic
H. sapiens

Modern humans
(*H. sapiens sapiens*)

African archaic *H.sapiens*

LATER HOMO

African *H.erectus*

Chinese *H.erectus*

S.E.Asian *H.erectus*

Paleoanthropologists hold strongly differing views on how the fossil remains for human evolution should be interpreted. This family tree presents the evidence as four adaptive radiations: the australopithecines, paranthropines, early Homo, and later Homo (including modern humans).

sapiens – in Africa by at least 100,000 years ago. They seem to have reached the eastern Mediterranean 100,000–90,000 years ago, and Europe and Asia by at least 40,000 years ago. Australia was colonized by humans some 40,000 or 50,000 years ago. It is uncertain when humans first crossed from northeastern Asia into North America across the Bering Strait, and south to Central and South America. The earliest secure dates for early Americans are around 14,000 years ago, but there is controversial evidence that the continent was populated before then. The Brazilian rockshelter site of Pedra Furada has recently, for instance, produced disputed evidence for human occupation some 30,000 years ago.

By 10,000 BC, most of the land areas of the world, except the deserts and Antarctica, were populated. The most conspicuous exception is the Pacific, where Western Polynesia does not seem to have been colonized until the first millennium BC, and Eastern Polynesia progressively from c.AD 300. By AD 1000 the colonization of Oceania was complete.

Nearly all the societies so far mentioned may be regarded as hunter-gatherer societies, made up of relatively small groups of people, often termed hunter-gatherer *bands* (see Chapter 5).

When surveying world history or prehistory at a global level, one of the most significant occurrences is the development of food production, based on domesticated plant species and also (although in some areas to a lesser extent) of domesticated animal species as well.

One of the most striking facts of world prehistory is that the transition from hunting and gathering to food production seems to have occurred independently in several areas, in each case after the end of the Ice Age, i.e. after c.10,000 years ago.

In the Near East, we can recognize the origins of this transition even before this time, for the process may have been gradual, the consequence (as well as the cause) of restructuring of the social organization of human societies. At any rate, well-established farming, dependent on wheat and barley as well as sheep and goats (and later cattle), was under way there by about 8000 BC. Farming had spread to Europe by 6500 BC, and is documented in South Asia at Mehrgarh in Baluchistan at about the same time.

A separate development, based at first on the cultivation of millet, seems to have taken place in China, in the valley of the Huang Ho by 5000 BC, and a separate focus on southeast Asia, with the exploitation of rice, began at about the same time. The position in Africa south of the Sahara is more complicated due to the diversity of environments, but millet and sorghum wheat were cultivated by the 3rd millennium BC. The Western Pacific (Melanesian) complex of root and tree crops had certainly developed by that time: indeed, there are indications of field drainage for root crops very much earlier.

In the Americas, a different crop spectrum was available. Cultivation of beans, squash, peppers and some grasses may have begun before 8000 BC in Peru,

First colonization of the world by modern humans, with very approximate dates (years BP), and ice sheets/low sea levels of c.18,000 BP. Many scholars believe the Americas were settled as early as 30,000–15,000 BP.

and was certainly under way both there and in Mesoamerica by the 7th millennium BC. Other South American species, including manioc and potato, were soon added to this list, but the plant with the greatest impact on American agriculture was maize, first brought into cultivation in Mexico around 5000 BC.

These agricultural innovations were rapidly adopted in some areas (e.g. in Europe), but in others, such as North America, their impact was less immediate. Certainly, by the time of Christ, hunter-gatherer economies were very much in the minority.

It is not easy to generalize about the very varied

societies of the first farmers in different parts of the world. But in general they may, in the early days at least, be described as *segmentary societies* (see Chapter 5): small, independent sedentary communities without any strongly centralized organization. They seem in the main to have been relatively egalitarian communi-

ties. In some cases they were related to their neighbors by tribal ties, whereas in others there was no larger tribal unit.

In each area, following the development of farming, there is much diversity. In many cases, the farming economy underwent a process of intensification,

Potato	Cotton	Guinea pig	Goat	Sorghum
Maize	Amaranth	Dog	Cattle	Yam
Gourd	Sunflower	Cat	Chicken	Oil palm
Squash	Llama	Pig	Wheat & Rye	Millet
Beans	Alpaca	Sheep	Barley	Rice

YEARS AD/BC	NEAR EAST	EGYPT & AFRICA	MEDI-TERRANEAN	NORTH EUROPE	INDIA	E. ASIA & PACIFIC	MESO-AMERICA	SOUTH AMERICA	NORTH AMERICA
1500		Great Zimbabwe					AZTEC	INCA	
1000			BYZANTINE EMPIRE	Medieval states		New Zealand settled	TOLTEC	CHIMU	Cahokia Chaco
500	ISLAM	Towns (Africa) AXUM	ROMAN EMPIRE	ROMAN EMPIRE		States (Japan)	MAYA TEOTI-HUACAN	MOCHE	HOPEWELL PUEBLOS
AD / BC						Great Wall (China)			
500	PERSIA BABYLON	LATE PERIOD	CLASSICAL GREECE	IRON AGE	MAURYAN	Cast iron (China)			
1000	ASSYRIA	NEW KINGDOM	Iron		Iron	Lapita (Polynesia)	OLMEC	CHAVIN	Maize (Southwest)
1500	HITTITES Iron	MIDDLE KINGDOM	MYCENAE	BRONZE Stonehenge AGE		SHANG (China)			
2000		OLD (pyramids) KINGDOM	MINOAN						
2500					INDUS	Walled villages (China)		Temple-mounds	
3000	SUMER Writing	EARLY DYNASTIC							
3500	Cities	Towns (Egypt)						Maize, llama, cotton	
4000	Wheeled vehicles								
4500			Copper (Balkans)	Megaliths					
5000				Farming, pottery			Maize		
5500	Irrigation					Rice Millet (China)		Manioc	
6000									
6500	Copper	Cattle (N. Africa)	Farming, pottery				Beans, squash peppers	Beans, squash peppers	
7000	Pottery				Farming	Gardens (New Guinea)			
7500		Pottery (Sudan)						Pottery (Amazonia)	
8000	Wheat, rye etc								
8500									
9000	Sheep								
9,500									
10,000						Pottery (Japan)			

The rise of farming and civilization. (Opposite page, above) Locations where major food species were first domesticated. (Opposite page, below) Locations of some of the earliest monumental architecture in various regions of the world. (Above) Chronological chart summarizing worldwide cultural development, including first domestication of certain plants and animals.

where more productive farming methods were accompanied by an increase in population. In such cases, there was usually increased contact between different areas, associated with developing exchange. Often, too, the social units became less egalitarian, displaying differences in personal status and importance sometimes summarized by anthropologists by the term *ranked societies*. Occasionally, it is appropriate to use the term *chiefdom* (Chapter 5).

These terms are usually restricted, however, to non-urban societies. The urban revolution, the next major transformation that we recognize widely, is not simply a change in settlement type: it reflects profound social changes. Foremost among these is the development of *state societies* displaying more clearly differentiated institutions of government than do chiefdoms. Many state societies had writing. We see the first state societies in the Near East by about 3500 BC, in Egypt only a little later, and in the Indus Valley by 2500 BC. In the Near East, the period of the early Mesopotamian city-states was marked by the rise of famous sites such as Ur, Uruk and later Babylon, and was followed in the 1st millennium BC by an age of great empires, notably those of Assyria and Achaemenid Persia. In Egypt, it is possible to trace the continuous development of cultural and political traditions over more than 2000 years, through the pyramid age of the Old Kingdom and the imperial power of New Kingdom Egypt. On the western edge of the Near East, further civilizations developed: Minoans and Mycenaeans in Greece and the Aegean during the 2nd millennium BC, Etruscans and Romans in the 1st millennium BC. At the opposite end of Asia, state societies with urban centers appear in China before 1500 BC, marking the beginnings of the Shang civilization. At about the same time, Mesoamerica saw the rise of the Olmec, the first in a long sequence of central American civilizations including Maya, Zapotec, Toltec, and Aztec. On the Pacific coast of South America, the Chavín (from 900 BC), Moche, and Chimu civilizations laid the foundations for the rise of the vast and powerful Inca empire that flourished in the 15th century AD.

The further pattern is the more familiar one of literate history, with the rise of the Classical world of Greece and Rome as well as of China, and then of the world of Islam, the Renaissance of Europe and the development of the colonial powers. From the 18th century to the present there followed the independence of the former colonies, first in the Americas, then in Asia and in Africa. We are talking now not simply of state societies but of nation states and, especially in colonial times, of empires.

SUMMARY

The answer to the question "When?" in archaeology has two main components. Relative dating methods allow us to determine that something is *relatively* older or younger than something else. Absolute methods make it possible to give a date in years. Archaeological dating is at its most reliable when the two methods are used together, e.g. when the relative order assigned to layers in an excavation can be confirmed by absolute dates for each layer. Wherever possible, results from one absolute method should be cross-checked by those from another, e.g. radiocarbon by tree-ring dating, or uranium-series by TL.

Ultimately the precision of dating attainable for each period helps determine the kinds of questions we ask about the past—for the Paleolithic, questions about long-term change; for later periods, questions more usually concerned with the shorter-term variations in worldwide human development.

Further Reading

The following provide a good introduction to the principal dating techniques used by archaeologists:

Aitken, M. J. 1990. *Science-based Dating in Archaeology.* Longman: London & New York.

Bowman, S.G.E. 1990. *Radiocarbon Dating.* British Museum Publications: London.

Brothwell, D.R. & Higgs, E.S. (eds.). 1969. *Science in Archaeology.* (2nd ed.) Thames and Hudson: London; Praeger: New York. (Chapters 1–8.)

Fleming, S. 1976. *Dating in Archaeology: A Guide to Scientific Techniques.* Dent: London; St Martin's Press: New York.

Michael, H.N. & Ralph, E.K. (eds.). 1971. *Dating Techniques for the Archaeologist.* MIT Press: Cambridge, Mass.

Michels, J.W. 1973. *Dating Methods in Archaeology.* Seminar Press: New York.

Parkes, P.A. 1986. *Current Scientific Techniques in Archaeology.* Croom Helm: London & Sydney.

Tite, M.S. 1972. *Methods of Physical Examination in Archaeology.* Seminar Press: London & New York. (Chapters 3–6.)

PART II

Discovering the Variety of Human Experience

Part II:
Introduction

In Part I certain basic problems were tackled. The methods were set out by which the space-time framework of the past can be established. We need to know *where* things happened, and *when* they happened. That has always been one of the basic objectives of archaeology, and it remains so.

For traditional archaeology, it was indeed the main task. It seemed sufficient to classify the various finds into different assemblages, which themselves could be grouped to form archaeological cultures, as we saw in Chapter 3. It seemed plausible to Gordon Childe, and to most of those who followed him, that these cultures were the material remains of distinct groups of people, of what we would today call ethnic groups – not in the racial sense, but groups of people with their own distinctive lifestyle and identity. As Childe put it, writing in 1929:

> We find certain types of remains – pots, implements, ornaments, burial sites, house forms – constantly recurring together. Such a complex of regularly associated traits we shall term a "cultural group" or just a "culture." We assume that such a complex is the material expression of what today would be called a "people."

Since the 1960s, however, it has been realized that this conventional way of treating the past is a limiting one. The concept of the archaeological culture is merely a classificatory device that does not necessarily relate to any reality in the archaeological record. And certainly to equate such notional "cultures" with "peoples" is now seen to be extremely hazardous. These issues will be looked at again in Chapter 12.

What archaeologists eventually recognized is that progress comes from asking a different set of questions. These form the basis for the organization of Part II. They have to do with the nature of a society or culture, and how such societies change over time.

At its simplest, a society may be viewed as having several interconnecting parts, as indicated in the accompanying diagram. The British archaeologist Christopher Hawkes, writing in 1954, argued that it is easiest in archaeology to find out about technology and diet, and most difficult to discover social organization or what people believed and thought. Archaeologists should therefore start by analyzing aspects of society like technology and diet. This is not an argument we accept. As will be shown in Chapter 5, it is

Model of the interrelated parts of a social system, which forms the basis for the organization of Part II.

essential first to have some idea about the social organization of the society being studied in order to be able to go on to ask the right questions about other aspects of that society. For example, groups organized as so-called band societies, subsisting by hunting and gathering food, and constantly on the move, are never in one place long enough to build towns or cities – nor is their population sufficient or their social and economic organization complex enough to support such communities. It would be pointless therefore to expect to find towns or cities among such societies. But equally one must study what band societies *do* build in the way of structures, and learn what traces these may leave in the archaeological record. Modern observers commonly underestimate the capabilities of simpler societies, believing, for instance – as most archaeologists once did – that the famous monument of Stonehenge in southern England could only have been built by more advanced visitors from the civilization of Mycenae in Greece. (It is explained in Chapter 5 what type of society is now thought to have been responsible for erecting Stonehenge.)

We thus start, in Chapter 5, with the question, "How were societies organized?," and go on in subsequent chapters to consider environment and diet before turning to tools and technology, contact and exchange between societies, the way people thought, and the way people evolved and colonized the world – biological anthropology and population. In Chapter 12 we ask, "Why were things as they were?" and "Why did they change?," and in some ways these are the most interesting questions of all. In their *History of American Archaeology*, Gordon Willey and Jeremy Sabloff have argued that, in the 1960s, archaeology moved on from a period preoccupied with classification, description, and the function of things, and entered an Explanatory Period. Certainly explanation has come to be seen by many as a central goal of archaeological research.

5
How Were Societies Organized? Social Archaeology

Some of the most interesting questions we can ask about early societies are social. They are about people and about relations between people, about the exercise of power and about the nature and scale of organization.

As is generally the case in archaeology, the data do not speak for themselves: we have to ask the right questions, and devise the means of answering them. There is a contrast here with cultural or social anthropology, where the observer can visit the living society and rapidly form conclusions about its social and power structures before moving on to other matters, such as the details of the kinship system or the minutiae of ritual behavior. The social archaeologist has to work systematically to gain even basic details, but the prize is a rich one: an understanding of the social organization not just of societies in the present or very recent past (like cultural anthropology) but of societies at many different points in time, with all the scope that that offers for studying change. Only the archaeologist can obtain that perspective, and hence seek some understanding of the processes of long-term change.

The first question to address is the size or *scale* of the society. The archaeologist will often be excavating a single site. But was that an independent political unit, like a Maya or Greek city state, or a simpler unit, like the base camp of a hunter-gatherer group? Or was it, on the other hand, a small cog in a very big wheel, a subordinate settlement in some far-flung empire, like that of the Incas of Peru? Any site we consider will have its own hinterland, its own catchment area for the feeding of its population. But one of our interests is to go beyond that local area, and to understand how that site articulates with others. From the standpoint of the individual site – which is often a convenient perspective to adopt – that raises questions of *dominance*. Was the site politically independent, autonomous? Or, if it was part of a larger social system, did it take a

dominant part (like the capital city of a kingdom) or a subordinate one?

If the scale of the society is a natural first question, the next is certainly its internal organization. What kind of society was it? Were the people forming it on a more-or-less equal social footing? Or were there instead prominent differences in status, rank, and prestige within the society – perhaps different social classes? And what of the professions: were there craft specialists? And if there were, were they controlled within some centralized system, as in some of the palace economies of the Near East and Egypt? Or was this a freer economy, with a flourishing free exchange, where merchants could operate at will in their own interest?

These are just some of the questions we may ask. Provided we ask the right questions, the issues touched on above, and many more besides, can usually find some sort of answer from the archaeological record.

Different kinds of society need different kinds of question. For example, if we are dealing with a mobile group of hunter-gatherers, there is unlikely to be a complex centralized organization. And the techniques of investigation will need to vary radically with the nature of the evidence. One cannot tackle an early hunter-gatherer camp in Australia in the same way as the capital city of a province in China during the Shang Dynasty. Thus, the questions we put, and the methods for answering them, must be tailored to the sort of community we are dealing with. So it is all the more necessary to be clear at the outset about the general nature of that community, which is why the basic social questions are the first ones to ask.

Precisely because the scale of a society is crucial in determining the way many aspects of its social organization work in practice, this chapter deals first with smaller, simpler societies, building towards larger, more complex ones. Certain questions, such as settlement archaeology or the study of burials, are therefore discussed in the context of each type of society. This involves some repetition between sections but it allows us to deal more coherently with the different social aspects of societies organized on approximately the same scale.

ESTABLISHING THE NATURE AND SCALE OF THE SOCIETY

The first step in social archaeology is so obvious that it is often overlooked. It is to ask, what was the scale of the largest social unit, and what kind of society, in a very broad sense, was it?

The obvious is not always easy, and it is neccessary to ask rather carefully what we mean by the "largest social unit," which we shall term the *polity*. This term does not in itself imply any particular scale or complexity of organization. It can apply as well to a city state, a hunter-gatherer band, a farming village, or a great empire. A polity is a politically independent or autonomous social unit, which may in the case of a complex society, such as a state society, comprise many lesser components. Thus, in the modern world, the autonomous nation state may be subdivided into districts or counties, each one of which may contain many towns and villages. The state as a whole is the polity. At the other end of the scale, a small group of hunter-gatherers may make its own decisions and recognize no higher authority: that group also constitutes a polity. Sometimes communities may join together to form some kind of federation, and we have to ask whether those communities are still autonomous polities, or whether the federation as a whole is now the effective decision-making organization. These points are not yet archaeological ones: however, they illustrate how important it is to be clear about what we wish to know about the past.

In terms of research in the field, the question is often best answered from a study of settlement: both in terms of the scale and nature of *individual sites* and in relationships between them, through the analysis of *settlement pattern*. But we should not forget that *written records*, where a society is literate and uses writing, *oral tradition*, and *ethnoarchaeology* – the study from an archaeological point of view of present-day societies – can be equally valuable in assessing the nature and scale of the society under review.

First, however, we need a frame of reference, a hypothetical classification of societies against which to test our ideas.

Classification of Societies

The American anthropologist Elman Service developed a four-fold classification of societies that many archaeologists have found useful. Associated with these societies are particular kinds of site and settlement pattern.

Bands. These are small-scale societies of hunters and gatherers, generally of less than 100 people, who move seasonally to exploit wild (undomesticated) food resources. Most surviving hunter-gatherer groups today are of this kind, such as the Hadza of Tanzania or the San of southern Africa. Band members are generally kinsfolk, related by descent or marriage. Bands lack formal leaders, so that there are no marked economic differences or disparities in status among their members.

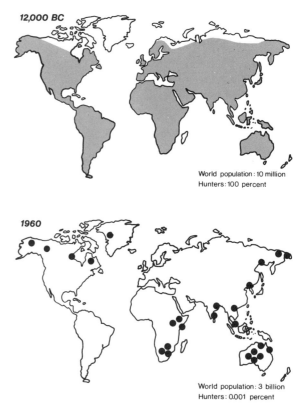

12,000 BC

World population: 10 million
Hunters: 100 percent

1960

World population: 3 billion
Hunters: 0.001 percent

(Above) Before the advent of farming, all human societies were hunter-gatherer bands. Today bands scarcely exist. (Right) Classification of societies.

	BAND	SEGMENTARY SOCIETY	CHIEFDOM	STATE
	San hunters, South Africa	Man plowing, Valcamonica, N. Italy	Horseman, Gundestrup caldron	Terracotta army, tomb of first emperor of China
TOTAL NUMBERS	Less than 100	Up to few 1,000	5,000–20,000+	Generally 20,000+
SOCIAL ORGANIZATION	Egalitarian Informal leadership	Segmentary society Pan-tribal associations Raids by small groups	Kinship-based ranking under hereditary leader High-ranking warriors	Class-based hierarchy under king or emperor Armies
ECONOMIC ORGANIZATION	Mobile hunter-gatherers	Settled farmers Pastoralist herders	Central accumulation and redistribution Some craft specialization	Centralized bureaucracy Tribute-based Taxation Laws
SETTLEMENT PATTERN	Temporary camps	Permanent villages	Fortified centers Ritual centers	Urban: cities, towns Frontier defences Roads
RELIGIOUS ORGANIZATION	Shamans	Religious elders Calendrical rituals	Hereditary chief with religious duties	Priestly class Pantheistic or monotheistic religion
ARCHITECTURE	Temporary shelters	Permanent huts Burial mounds Shrines	Large-scale monuments	Palaces, temples, and other public buildings
	Paleolithic skin tents, Siberia	Neolithic shrine, Çatal Hüyük, Turkey	Stonehenge, England – final form	Pyramids at Giza Castillo, Chichén Itzá, Mexico
ARCHAEOLOGICAL EXAMPLES	All Paleolithic societies, including Paleo-Indians	All early farmers (Neolithic/ Archaic)	Many early metalworking and Formative societies Mississippian, USA Smaller African kingdoms	All ancient civilizations e.g. in Mesoamerica, Peru Near East, India and China; Greece and Rome
MODERN EXAMPLES	Eskimo Kalahari Bushmen Australian Aborigines	Pueblos, Southwest USA New Guinea Highlanders Nuer & Dinka in E. Africa	Northwest Coast Indians, USA 18th-century Polynesian chiefdoms in Tonga, Tahiti, Hawaii	All modern states

Because bands are composed of mobile groups of hunter-gatherers, their sites consist mainly of seasonally occupied camps, and other smaller and more specialized sites. Among the latter are kill or butchery sites – locations where large mammals are killed and sometimes butchered – and work sites, where tools are made or other specific activities carried out. The base camp of such a group may give evidence of rather insubstantial dwellings or temporary shelters, along with the debris of residential occupation.

During the Paleolithic period (before 12,000 years ago) most archaeological sites seem to conform to one or other of these categories – camp sites, kill sites, work sites – and archaeologists usually operate on the assumption that most Paleolithic societies were organized into bands.

Ethnoarchaeology (see below) has devoted much attention to the study of living bands of hunter-gatherers, yielding many insights relevant to the more remote past.

Tribes. These are generally larger than bands, but rarely number more than a few thousand, and their diet or subsistence is based largely on cultivated plants and domesticated animals. Typically, they are settled farmers, but they may be nomad pastoralists with a very different, mobile economy based on the intensive exploitation of livestock. These are generally multi-community societies, with the individual communities integrated into the larger society through kinship ties. Although some tribes have officials and even a "capital" or seat of government, such officials lack the economic base necessary for effective use of power.

The typical settlement pattern for tribes is one of settled agricultural homesteads or villages. Characteristically, no one settlement dominates any of the others in the region. Instead, the archaeologist finds evidence for isolated, permanently occupied houses (a *dispersed* settlement pattern) or for permanent villages (a *nucleated* pattern). Such villages may be made up of a collection of free-standing houses, like those of the first farmers of the Danube valley in Europe, *c.*4500 BC. Or they may be clusters of buildings grouped together – so-called *agglomerate* structures, for example, the pueblos of the American Southwest, and the early farming village or small town of Çatal Hüyük, *c.*7000 BC, in what is now Turkey.

Chiefdoms. These operate on the principle of ranking – differences in social status between people. Different lineages (a lineage is a group claiming descent from a common ancestor) are graded on a scale of prestige, and the senior lineage, and hence the society as a whole, is governed by a chief. Prestige and rank are determined by how closely related one is to the chief, and there is no true stratification into classes. The role of the chief is crucial.

Often, there is local specialization in craft products, and surpluses of these and of foodstuffs are periodically paid as obligations to the chief. He uses these to maintain his retainers, and may use them for redistribution to his subjects. The chiefdom generally has a center of power, often with temples, residences of the chief and his retainers, and craft specialists. Chiefdoms vary greatly in size, but the range is generally between about 5000 and 20,000 persons.

One of the characteristic features of the chiefdom is the existence of a permanent ritual and ceremonial center that acts as a central focus for the entire polity. This is not a permanent urban center (such as a city) with an established bureaucracy, as one finds in state societies. But chiefdoms do give indications that some sites were more important than others (site hierarchy), as discussed later in this chapter. Examples are Moundville in Alabama, USA, which flourished *c.* AD 1000–1500, and the late Neolithic monuments of Wessex in southern Britain, including the famous ceremonial center of Stonehenge (see boxes below).

The personal ranking characteristic of chiefdom societies is visible in other ways than in settlement patterning: for instance, in the very rich grave-goods that often accompany the burials of deceased chiefs.

Early States. These preserve many of the features of chiefdoms, but the ruler (perhaps a king or sometimes a queen) has explicit authority to establish laws and to enforce them by the use of a standing army. The society no longer depends totally on kin relationships: it is now stratified into different classes. Agricultural workers or serfs and the poorer urban dwellers form the lowest classes, with the craft specialists above, and the priests and kinsfolk of the ruler higher still. The functions of the ruler are often separated from those of the priest: palace is distinguished from temple. The society is viewed as a territory owned by the ruling lineage and populated by tenants who have the obligation of paying taxes. The central capital houses a bureaucratic administration of officials; one of their principal purposes is to collect revenue (often in the form of taxes and tolls) and distribute it to government, army, and craft specialists. Many early states developed complex redistributive systems to support these essential services.

Early state societies generally show a characteristic urban settlement pattern in which *cities* play a prominent part. The city is typically a large population center (often of more than 5000 inhabitants) with major public buildings, including temples and work places for the administrative bureaucracy. Often, there is a pronounced settlement hierarchy, with the capital city as the major center, and with subsidiary or regional centers as well as local villages.

This rather simple social typology, set out by Elman Service and elaborated by William Sanders and Joseph Marino, can be criticized, and it should not be used unthinkingly. Some scholars find the concept of the tribe a rather vague one, and prefer to speak of "segmentary societies." The term "tribe," implying a larger grouping of smaller units, carries with it the assumption that these communities share a common ethnic identity and self-awareness, which is now known not generally to be the case. The term "segmentary society" refers to a relatively small and autonomous group, usually of agriculturalists, who regulate their own affairs: in some cases, they may join together with other comparable segmentary societies to form a larger ethnic unit or "tribe;" in other cases, they do not. For the remainder of this chapter, we shall therefore refer to *segmentary societies* in preference to the term "tribe."

Certainly, it would be wrong to overemphasize the importance of the four types of society given above, or to spend too long agonizing as to whether a specific group should be classed in one category rather than another. It would also be wrong to assume that somehow societies inevitably evolve from bands to segmentary societies, or from chiefdoms to states. One of the challenges of archaeology is to attempt to explain why some societies become more complex and others do not, and we shall return to the fundamental issue of explanation in Chapter 12.

Nevertheless, if we are seeking to talk about early societies, we must use words and hence concepts to do so. Service's categories provide a good framework to help organize our thoughts. They should not, however, deflect us from focusing on what we are really looking for: changes over time in the different institutions of a society – whether in the social sphere, the organization of the food quest, technology, contact and exchange, or spiritual life. For archaeology has the unique advantage of being able to study processes of change over thousands of years, and it is these processes we are seeking to isolate. Happily there are sufficiently marked differences between simple and more complex societies for us to find ways of doing this. As we saw above in the description of Service's four types of society, complex societies show in particular an increased specialization in, or separation between, different aspects of their culture. In complex societies people no longer combine, say, the tasks of obtaining food, making tools, or performing religious rites but become specialists at one or other of these tasks, either as full-time farmers, craftspeople, or priests. As technology develops, for example, groups of individuals may acquire particular expertise in pottery-making or metallurgy, and will become full-time *craft specialists*, occupying distinct areas of a town or city and thus leaving distinct traces for the archaeologist to discover. Likewise, as farming develops and population grows, more food will be obtained from a given piece of land (food production will *intensify*) through the introduction of the plow or irrigation. As this specialization and intensification take place, so too does the tendency for some people to become wealthier and wield more authority than others – differences in social status and *ranking* develop.

It is methods for looking at these processes of increasing specialization, intensification, and social ranking that help us identify the presence of more complex societies in the archaeological record – societies here termed for convenience chiefdoms or states. For simpler band or segmentary societies, other methods are needed if we are to identify them archaeologically, as will become apparent in a later section.

Scale of the Society

With this general background in mind one can develop a strategy for answering the first, basic question: what is the scale of the society? One answer may come from an understanding of the settlement pattern, and this can only come from survey (see below).

For a first approximation, however, an elaborate field project may be unnecessary. If, for instance, we are dealing with archaeological remains dating to before about 12,000 years ago, then we are dealing with a society from the Paleolithic period. On present evidence, nearly all the societies known from that enormously long period of time – spanning hundreds of thousands of years – consisted of mobile hunter-gatherers, occupying camps on a seasonal and temporary basis. On the other hand, where we find indications of permanent settlement this will suggest a segmentary society of agricultural villages or something more complex.

At the other end of the scale, if there are major urban centers the society should probably rank as a state. More modest centers, or ceremonial centers without urban settlement, may be indicative of a chiefdom. To use these classificatory terms is a worthwhile first step in social analysis, provided we bear in mind again that these are only very broad categories designed to help us formulate appropriate methods for studying the societies in question.

If it is clear that we are dealing with communities with a mobile economy (i.e. hunter-gatherers, or possibly nomads), highly intensive techniques of survey will have to be used, because the traces left by mobile communities are generally very scanty. If, on the other hand, these were sedentary communities, a straightforward field survey is now called for. It will have as its first objective the establishment of *settlement hierarchy*.

The Survey

The techniques of field survey were discussed in Chapter 3. Surveys can have different purposes: in this case, our aim is to discover the hierarchy of settlement. We are particularly interested in locating the major centers (because our concern is with organization) and in establishing the nature of the more modest sites. This implies a dual sampling strategy. At the intensive level of survey, systematic surface survey of carefully selected transects should be sufficient, although the ideal would be a total survey of the entire area. A random stratified sampling strategy – as outlined in Chapter 3 – taking into account the different environmental areas within the region, should offer adequate data about the smaller sites. However, random sampling of this kind could, in isolation, be highly misleading and subject to what Kent Flannery has called "the Teotihuacan effect." Teotihuacan is the huge urban site in the Valley of Mexico that flourished in the 1st millennium AD (see box, Chapter 3). Random stratified sampling alone could easily miss such a center, and to do so would ruin any effective social analysis.

The other aim of the strategy must be, therefore, to go for the center. Means must be devised of finding the remains of the largest center in the region, and as many lesser centers as can be located. Fortunately, if it was an urban site, or had monumental public buildings, such a center should become obvious during even a non-intensive survey, so long as a good overview of the area as a whole is obtained. In most cases the existence of such a prominent site will already be well known to the local population, or indeed recorded in the available archaeological or antiquarian literature. All such sources, including the writings of early travelers in the region, should be scrutinized in order to maximize the chances of finding major centers.

The main centers usually have the most impressive monuments, and contain the finest artifacts. So it is imperative to visit all the major monuments of the period, and to follow up the circumstances of any particularly rich finds in the region. Where appropriate, there is plenty of scope too for remote sensing methods such as were described in Chapter 3.

Settlement Patterning

Any survey will result in a map of the areas intensively surveyed and a catalog of the sites discovered, together with details of each site including size, chronological range (as may be determined from surface remains such as pottery), and architectural features. The aim is then to reach some classification of the sites on the basis of this information. Possible site categories include Regional Center, Local Center, Nucleated Village, Dispersed Village, and Hamlet.

The first use we will make of settlement pattern information is to identify the social and political territories around centers, in order to establish the political organization of the landscape. Many archaeological approaches here give prominence to Central Place Theory (see below), which we feel has some limitations. It assumes that the sites in a given region will fall neatly into a series of categories according to variations in site size. All the primary centers should be in one size category, all the secondary centers in the next, etc. This technique cannot cope with the true situation which is that secondary centers in one area are sometimes larger than primary centers in another. More recent work has found a way of overcoming this difficulty (the XTENT technique), but we will deal here with the earlier methods first.

Site Number Ch-LT-41

Natural Setting: 2450 meters, in the Smooth Lower Piedmont. Situated on gently sloping ground. Shallow to medium soil cover. Moderate erosion.
Modern Utilization: Rainfall cultivation.
Archaeological Remains: Light surface pottery over an area of 0.8 hectare. No structural remains. Mixed with heavier Aztec material (Ch-Az-102). Traces of Terminal Formative pottery also occur.
Classification: Small hamlet, 5–10 people.

An example of a formal site description from the catalog of sites produced for the Basin of Mexico survey by Jeffrey Parsons and his colleagues.

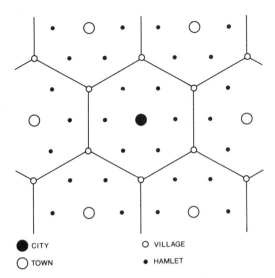

CITY

TOWN

VILLAGE

HAMLET

Central Place Theory: in a flat landscape, with no rivers or variations in resources, a central place (town or city) will dominate a hexagonal territory, with secondary centers (villages or hamlets) spaced at regular intervals around it.

Central Place Theory. This theory was developed by the German geographer Walter Christaller in the 1930s to explain the spacing and functions of cities and towns in modern-day southern Germany. He argued that in a uniform landscape – without mountains or rivers or variations in the distribution of soils and resources – the spatial patterning of settlements would be perfectly regular. Central places or settlements (towns or cities) of the same size and nature would be situated equidistant from each other, surrounded by a constellation of secondary centers with their own, smaller satellites. Under these perfect conditions, the territories "controlled" by each center would be hexagonal in shape, and the different levels of center would together give rise to an intricate settlement lattice.

Such perfect conditions do not occur in nature, of course, but it is still quite possible to detect the workings of Central Place Theory in the distributions of modern or ancient cities and towns. The basic feature is that each major center will be some distance from its neighbors and will be surrounded by a ring of smaller settlements in a hierarchically nested pattern. In political and economic terms the major center will supply certain goods and services to its surrounding area and will exact certain goods and services in return. Even in an area so far from uniform as Mesopotamia (modern Iraq), Central Place Theory has its uses (see box overleaf).

Site Hierarchy. Despite the reservations we have expressed about Central Place Theory, the analysis of site sizes is a useful basic approach. In archaeological studies, the sites are usually listed in rank order by size (i.e. in a site hierarchy), and then displayed as a histogram. There are normally many more small villages and hamlets in a settlement system than large towns or cities. Histograms allow comparisons to be made between the site hierarchies of different regions, different periods, and different types of society. In band societies, for example, there will usually be only a narrow range of variation in site size and all the sites will be relatively small. State societies, on the other hand, will have both hamlets and farmsteads and large towns and cities. The degree to which a single site is dominant within a settlement system will also be evident from this type of analysis, and the organization of the settlement system will often be a direct reflection of the organization of the society which created it. In a general way, the more hierarchical the settlement pattern, the more hierarchical the society.

Thiessen Polygons. Another relatively simple method that can be used in the study of settlement patterns is the construction of Thiessen polygons. These are simple geometrical shapes that divide an area into a number of separate territories, each focused on a single site. The polygons are created by drawing straight lines between each pair of neighboring sites, then at the mid-point along each of these lines a second series of lines, at right angles to the first. Linking up the second series of lines creates the Thiessen polygons, and in this way the whole of an area can be apportioned among the sites it contains. It should be noted, however, that this procedure takes no account of differences in size or importance of sites; a small site will have as big a polygon as a large site. Thus it is important to use only sites of the same rank in the settlement hierarchy when this technique is being applied. A further question, more difficult to resolve, is contemporaneity, since clearly it would be meaningless to draw Thiessen polygons between sites which were not in occupation at the same time.

XTENT Modeling. One of the shortcomings of Central Place Theory and other approaches is that sites occupying the same level in a settlement hierarchy might not be of the same size. Thus the capital city of a state on the periphery of a distribution could be smaller than a secondary city in the center. We are now able to cope with this using the technique of XTENT modeling. This has the aim of assigning territories to centers according to their scale. To do this, it assumes that a large center will dominate a small one if they are close together. In such a case, of so-called *dominance*, the territory of the smaller site is simply absorbed in the study into that of the larger one: in political terms the smaller site has no independent or autonomous existence. This approach overcomes the limitation of the Thiessen polygon method,

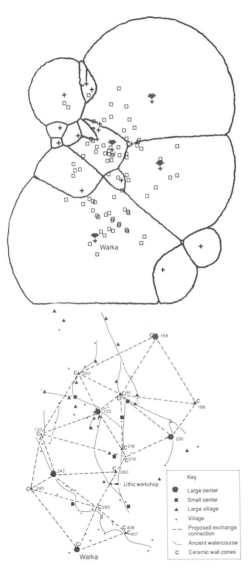

(Top) XTENT model territories, Late Uruk period, Warka area, Mesopotamia. Arrows indicate four centers that emerge as autonomous. Compare Greg Johnson's hierarchy (above) for the same region. Note how four of the five "large centers" correspond with the autonomous centers in the XTENT model.

SETTLEMENT PATTERNS IN MESOPOTAMIA

Gregory Johnson's work in the Diyala region of Mesopotamia, to the east of Baghdad in modern Iraq, provides a good illustration of the way in which Central Place Theory can be applied to archaeological survey results. Thirty-nine settlements of the Early Dynastic

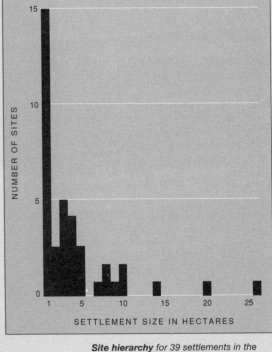

Site hierarchy for 39 settlements in the Diyala region, expressed as a histogram. As is usually the case with such hierarchies, there is a decline in the number of sites as site size increases. There are normally many more small villages and hamlets in a settlement system than large towns or cities. Any analysis of this kind has to make certain assumptions – for instance, that evidence for sites in each category has been uniformly preserved, which may not always be the case.

period (c.2800 BC) are known from this area. They range in size from 25 hectares (60 acres) to just over one-tenth of a hectare (0.25 acre), and on this basis Johnson divided them into five categories: large towns, towns, large villages, small villages, and hamlets.

The distribution of sites suggested that there were four lattice cells, each lattice cell being the network of settlements grouped around a first order center or central place. In theory, each cell should have had a large town at the center, towns at each of the four corners, and large villages at the mid-points between the towns and at the mid-points between the towns and the large towns. Small villages and hamlets completed the pattern to create a model settlement lattice which could be compared with the real pattern as revealed by the Diyala survey. Discrepancies could then be identified and explained.

It is precisely the discrepancies from the expected pattern that are of interest. Johnson found that maximization of usable land (which would have been implied had there been even spacing of settlements) was less significant in determining settlement location than were water transport networks. Settlements of successively smaller size were located along watercourses – lines of communication – between the larger settlements.

Nevertheless, it was only after considerable modification that the lattice model could be made to fit the Diyala evidence. Several of the predicted primary and secondary centers were lacking, while others were smaller than they were expected to be. Thus, though the exercise was certainly valuable, it highlighted the difficulties of applying Central Place Theory to a real archaeological case.

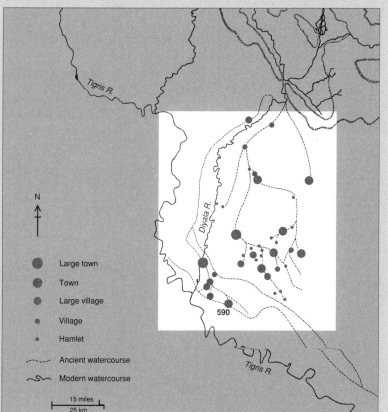

N

- ● Large town
- ● Town
- ● Large village
- ● Village
- • Hamlet
- ---- Ancient watercourse
- ～ Modern watercourse

15 miles
25 km

590

Tigris R.

Diyala R.

Tigris R.

Early Dynastic *settlement pattern in the Diyala region of Iraq, based on survey work originally carried out by Robert Adams.*

590

Derivation *of the proposed settlement lattice for the Diyala region, from the idealized, regular four lattice cells (top) to the final pattern (above) that seemed best to fit the actual settlement locations on the ground.*

where territories are assigned irrespective of the size of the center, and where there are no dominant or subordinate centers.

In XTENT modeling, the size of each center is assumed to be directly proportional to its area of influence. The influence of each center is thought of as analogous to a bell or bell-tent in shape: the greater the size of the center the higher the tent. Centers are considered to be subordinate if their associated bell tents fall entirely within that of a larger center. If they protrude beyond, they will have their own autonomous existence as centers of political units.

Although the XTENT model can never offer more than a simple approximation of the political reality, it does allow a hypothetical political map to be constructed from appropriate survey data (see illustration on p.160).

By methods such as these, information derived from settlement surveys can be used to produce what is in effect a political and administrative map, even though such maps will always rely on certain basic assumptions that cannot easily be proved. And while the examples given in the box above have been drawn from studies of state societies, it is possible to apply similar techniques to the settlement patterns of less complex societies, such as the Neolithic of southern Britain (see box, Early Wessex, below). In the Iron Age of southern Britain, more hierarchically organized societies developed, with prominent hillforts dominating the tribal territories. A pioneering analysis by David Clarke interpreted the social position of the Iron Age site of Glastonbury (see box, Chapter 1) in these terms, as belonging within a territory dominated by such a fortified center.

FURTHER SOURCES OF INFORMATION FOR SOCIAL ORGANIZATION

If the first approach by archaeologists to the study of social organization must be through the investigation of settlement and settlement pattern, this should not exclude other possible avenues of approach, including the use of written records, oral tradition, and ethnoarchaeology.

Here it is appropriate to mention the argument of Lewis Binford, that if we are to bridge the gap between the archaeological remains and the societies those remains represent we need to develop a systematic body of what he terms *Middle Range Theory*. For the moment, however, we believe it is difficult to justify the division of archaeological theory into high, middle, and low. We choose not to use the term Middle Range Theory.

Some scholars also lay great emphasis on the concept of *analogy*. Arguments by analogy are based on the belief that where certain processes or materials resemble each other in some respects, they may resemble each other in other ways also. Thus it may be possible to use details from one body of information to fill the gaps in another body of information from which those details are missing. Some have considered an analogy a fundamental aspect of archaeological reasoning. In our view this emphasis is misplaced. It is true that archaeologists use information from the study of one society (whether living or dead) to help understand other societies they may be interested in, but these are usually in the nature of general observations and comparisons, rather than specific detailed analogies.

Written Records

For literate societies – those that use writing, for instance all the great civilizations in Mesoamerica, China, Egypt, and the Near East – historical records can answer many of the social questions set out at the beginning of this chapter. A prime goal of the archaeologist dealing with these societies is therefore to find appropriate texts. Many of the early excavations of the great sites of the Near East had the recovery of archives of clay writing tablets as their main goal. Major finds of this kind are still made today – for example, at the ancient city of Ebla (Tell Mardikh) in Syria in the 1970s, where an archive of 15,000 clay tablets has yielded evidence of a previously unknown language and state of the 3rd millennium BC.

In each early literate society, writing had its own functions and purposes. For instance, the clay tablets of Mycenaean Greece, dating from *c.*1200 BC, are almost without exception records of commercial transactions (goods coming in or going out) at the Mycenaean palaces. This gives us an impression of many aspects of the Mycenaean economy, and a glimpse into craft organization (through the names for the different kinds of craftspeople), as well as introducing the names of the offices of state. But here, as in other cases, accidents of preservation may be important. It could be that the Mycenaeans wrote on clay only for their commercial records, and used other, perishable materials for literary or historical texts now lost to us. It is certainly true that for the Classical Greek and Roman civilizations, it is mainly official decrees inscribed on marble that have survived. Fragile rolls of papyrus – the predecessor of modern paper – with precious literary texts on them, have usually only remained intact in the dry air of Egypt, or buried in the volcanic ash covering Pompeii (see box, Chapter 1).

An important written source that should not be overlooked is coinage. The findspots of coins give interesting economic evidence about trade (Chapter 9). But the inscriptions themselves are informative about the issuing authority – whether city state (as in ancient Greece) or sole ruler (as in Imperial Rome, or the kings of medieval Europe).

The decipherment of an ancient language transforms our knowledge of the society that used it. The brilliant work of Champollion in the 19th century in cracking the code of Egyptian hieroglyphs was mentioned in Chapter 1. In recent years, one of the most significant advances in Mesoamerican archaeology has come from the reading of many of the inscribed symbols (glyphs) on the stone stelae at the largest ceremonial centers. It had been widely assumed that the Maya inscriptions were exclusively of a calendrical nature, or that they dealt with purely religious matters, notably the deeds of deities. But the inscriptions can now in many cases be interpreted as relating to real historical events, mainly the deeds of the Maya kings (see boxes, Chapters 4 and 10). We can also now begin to deduce the likely territories belonging to individual Maya centers (see box below). Maya history has thus taken on a new dimension.

As a more detailed example of the value of written sources for reconstructing social archaeology, it is useful to take Mesopotamia, where a huge number of the records of ancient Sumer and Babylon (*c.*3000–1600 BC), mainly in the form of clay tablets, have been preserved. The uses of writing in Mesopotamia may be summarized as follows:

Recording information for future use	Administrative purposes
	Codification of law
	Formulation of a sacred tradition
	Annals
	Scholarly purposes
Communicating current information	Letters
	Royal edicts
	Public announcements
	Texts for training scribes
Communicating with the gods	Sacred texts, amulets, etc.

The Sumerian king list provides an excellent example of annals recording information for future use. It is extremely useful to the modern scholar for dating purposes, but it also offers social insights into the way the Sumerians conceived of the exercise of power – for example, the terminology of rank that they used. Similarly, inscriptions on royal statues (such as those of Gudea, ruler of Lagash) help us perceive how the Sumerians viewed the relationship between their rulers and the immortals. This important kind of information concerning how societies thought about themselves and the world – *cognitive* information – is discussed in more detail in Chapter 10.

Of even greater significance for an understanding of the structure of Sumerian society are the tablets associated with the working or organizing centers, which in Sumerian society were often temples. For instance, the 1600 tablets from the temple of Bau at Tello give a close insight into the dealings of the shrine, listing fields and the crops harvested in them, craftspeople, and receipts or issues of goods such as grain and livestock.

Perhaps most evocative of all are the law codes, of which the most impressive example is the law code of Hammurabi of Babylon, written in the Akkadian language (and in cuneiform script) around 1750 BC. The ruler is seen (illus. p.165) at the top of the stone, standing before Shamash, the god of justice. The laws were promulgated, as Hammurabi states, "so that the strong may not oppress the weak, and to protect the rights of the orphan and widow." These laws cover many aspects of life – agriculture, business transactions, family law, inheritance, terms of employment for different craftspeople, and penalties for crimes such as adultery and homicide.

Impressive and informative as it is, Hammurabi's law code is not straightforward to interpret, and emphasizes the need for the archaeologist to reconstruct the full social context that led to the drafting of a text. As the British scholar Nicholas Postgate has pointed out, the code is by no means complete, and seems to cover only those areas of the law that had proved troublesome. Moreover, Hammurabi had recently conquered several rival city states, and the law code was therefore probably designed to help integrate the new territories within his empire.

Written records thus undoubtedly contribute greatly to our knowledge of the society in question. But one should not accept them uncritically at face value. Nor should one forget the bias introduced by the accident of preservation and the particular uses of literacy in a society. The great risk with historical records is that they can impose their own perspective, so that they begin to supply not only the answers to our questions, but subtly to determine the nature of those questions,

The variety of historical evidence. (Left and above) Scribes were accorded high status in ancient civilizations. Among the Maya, a rabbit god (left) is shown as a scribe on an 8th-century AD painted vase. A scribe from Classical Greek times (above left) is depicted on a 5th-century BC bowl. Egyptian military scribes (above center) record on papyrus rolls the submission of Egypt's New Kingdom foes – a relief carving from Saqqara. The Inca (above right) had no writing system as such, but kept records of accounts and other transactions using knotted ropes called quipu.

Clay tablets and coins. (Left) Some of the 15,000 clay tablets discovered in the royal palace at Ebla (Tell Mardikh in modern Syria), dating from the late 3rd millennium BC. The tablets formed part of the state archives, recording over 140 years of Ebla's history. Originally they were stored on wooden shelving, which collapsed when the palace was sacked. (Below) Hoard of Arabic coins found in Gotland, Sweden, belonging to the Viking period (8th/9th centuries AD). Inscriptions on coins can be informative not only about dating (Chapter 4) and trade (Chapter 9), but also about the issuing authority.

Seals and seal impressions. (Above) Rollout impression from a cylinder seal of c.500 BC which depicts the Persian king Darius in his chariot hunting lions. The inscription is written in the cuneiform script, like Hammurabi's law code (left). The scene is intended to convey the authority, strength, and dominant status of the king. Such seals were used to mark ownership or authenticity. Many thousands have been recovered from Mesopotamian sites.

Oral tradition. (Below) Scenes from the Hindu epic, the Ramayana, on a late 18th-century AD temple-hanging, Mathura, India. The story describes the exploits of a great ruler (Rama) in his attempt to rescue his consort, carried off to Sri Lanka by a demon king. The legend may have its origins in southward movements of Hindu peoples after 800 BC but – as always with oral tradition – the difficulty comes in disentangling history from myth.

Inscriptions. (Above) The famous law code of the Babylonian king Hammurabi, c.1750 BC. The laws are carved in 49 vertical columns on a black basalt stela, 2.25 m (7 ft 4 in) high. In this detail the king is seen confronting the seated figure of Shamash, god of justice. See also main text p.163.

Early medieval documents. (Below) An Anglo-Saxon king and his council depicted in an 11th-century AD manuscript. Historical documents require careful interpretation just as much as archaeological evidence.

and even our concepts and terminology. A good example is the question of kingship in Anglo-Saxon England. Most anthropologists and historians tend to think of a "king" as the leader of a state society. So when the earliest records for Anglo-Saxon England, *The Anglo-Saxon Chronicle*, which took final shape in about AD 1155, refer to kings around AD 500, it is easy for the historian to think of kings and states at that period. But the archaeology strongly suggests that a full state society did not emerge until the time of King Offa of Mercia in around AD 780, or perhaps King Alfred of Wessex in AD 871. It is fairly clear that the earlier "kings" were generally less significant figures than some of the rulers in Africa or Polynesia in recent times, whom anthropologists would term "chiefs."

Thus, if the archaeologist is to use historical records in conjunction with the material remains, it is essential at the outset that the questions are carefully formulated and the vocabulary is well defined.

Oral Tradition

In non-literate societies, valuable information about the past, even the remote past, is often enshrined in oral tradition – poems or hymns or sayings handed on from generation to generation by word of mouth. This can be of quite remarkable antiquity. A good example is offered by the hymns of the *Rigveda*, the earliest Indian religious texts, in an archaic form of the language, which were preserved orally for hundreds of years, before being set down by literate priests in the mid-1st millennium AD. Similarly, the epics about the Trojan War written down by Homer in about the 8th century BC may have been preserved orally for several centuries before that time, and are thought by many scholars to preserve a picture of the Mycenaean world of the 12th or 13th century BC.

Epics such as Homer's *Iliad* and *Odyssey* certainly offer remarkable insights into social organization. But, as with so much oral tradition, the problem is actually to demonstrate to which period they refer – to judge how much is ancient and how much reflects a much more recent world. Nevertheless, in Polynesia, in Africa, and in other areas that have only recently become literate, the natural first step in investigating the social organization of earlier centuries is to examine the oral traditions.

Ethnoarchaeology

Another fundamental method of approach for the social archaeologist is ethnoarchaeology. It involves the study of both the present-day use and significance of artifacts, buildings, and structures within the living societies in question, and the way these material things become incorporated into the archaeological record – what happens to them when they are thrown away or (in the case of buildings and structures) torn down or abandoned. It is therefore an *indirect* approach to the understanding of any past society.

There is nothing new in the idea of looking at living societies to help interpret the past. In the 19th and early 20th centuries European archaeologists often turned for inspiration to researches done by ethnographers among societies in Africa or Australia. But the so-called "ethnographic parallels" that resulted – where archaeologists often simply and crudely likened past societies to present ones – tended to stifle new thought rather than promote it. In the United States archaeologists were confronted from the beginning with the living reality of complex American Indian societies, which taught them to think rather more deeply about how ethnography might be used to aid archaeological interpretation. Nevertheless, fully-fledged ethnoarchaeology is a development really of only the last 20 or 25 years. The key difference is that now it is archaeologists themselves, rather than ethnographers or anthropologists, who carry out the research among living societies.

A good example is the work of Lewis Binford among the Nunamiut Eskimo, a hunter-gatherer group of Alaska. In the 1960s Binford was attempting to interpret archaeological sites of the Middle Paleolithic of France (the Mousterian period, 100,000–40,000 years ago). He came to realize that only by studying how *modern* hunter-gatherers used and discarded bones and tools, or moved from site to site, could he begin to understand the mechanisms that had created the Mousterian archaeological record – itself almost certainly the product of a mobile hunter-gatherer economy. Between 1969 and 1973 he lived intermittently among the Nunamiut and observed their behavior. For instance, he studied the way bone debris was produced and discarded by men at a seasonal hunting camp (the Mask site, Anaktuvuk Pass, Alaska). He saw that, when sitting round a hearth and processing bone for marrow, there was a "drop zone" where small fragments of bone fell as they were broken. The larger pieces, which were thrown away by the men, formed a "toss zone," both in front and behind them.

Such seemingly trivial observations are the very stuff of ethnoarchaeology. The Nunamiut might not provide an exact "ethnographic parallel" for Mousterian societies, but Binford recognized that there are certain actions or *functions* likely to be common to all hunter-

Ethnoarchaeology: the work of Lewis Binford. (Right) From observations among living Nunamiut Eskimo in Alaska, Binford derived this model of bone processing around an outside hearth. Small bone fragments fall in a "drop zone" around the men, while larger pieces are thrown both in front and behind them in two "toss zones." (Below center) At the Paleolithic site of Pincevent, France, dating from about 15,000 years ago, the excavator Leroi-Gourhan interpreted three hearths as being evidence for a complex skin tent (reconstruction, center right). (Below) Binford applied his "outside hearth model" to the three Pincevent hearths, and deduced from the distribution of bones that his model fitted the evidence better than that of Leroi-Gourhan: i.e. that the hearths lay outside, and not within a tent. (Below right) Classic semi-circular arrangement around an outside hearth as demonstrated by Nharo Bushmen at Ganzi, Botswana, c.1969.

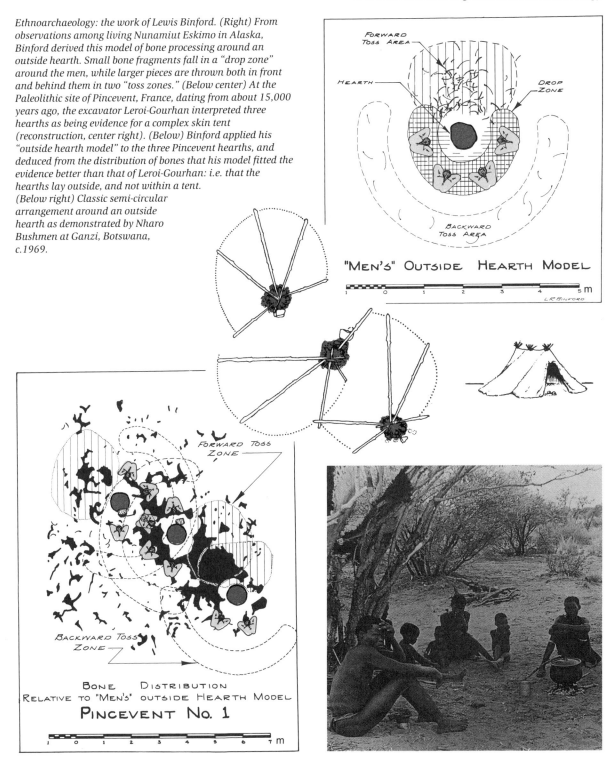

"MEN'S" OUTSIDE HEARTH MODEL

FORWARD TOSS AREA
HEARTH
DROP ZONE
BACKWARD TOSS AREA
L.R.BINFORD

FORWARD TOSS ZONE

BACKWARD TOSS ZONE

BONE DISTRIBUTION
RELATIVE TO "MEN'S" OUTSIDE HEARTH MODEL
PINCEVENT No. 1

gatherers because – as in the case of the processing of bone – the actions are dictated by the most convenient procedure when seated round a camp fire. The discarded fragments of bone then leave a characteristic pattern round the hearth for the archaeologist to find and interpret. From such analysis, it has proved possible to go on to infer roughly how many people were in the group, and over what period of time the camp site was used. These are questions very relevant to our understanding of the social organization (including the size) of hunter-gatherer groups.

With the benefit of his observations at the Mask site, Binford was able to reinterpret the plan of the French Paleolithic site of Pincevent, occupied during the last Ice Age about 15,000 years ago. The excavator, André Leroi-Gourhan, interpreted the remains as indicating a complex skin tent covering three hearths. Binford at the Mask site had noted how when wind direction had changed, people seated outside next to a hearth would swivel round and make up a new hearth downwind so as to remain out of the smoke. The distribution of debris around the Pincevent hearths suggested to Binford that two of them were the result of just such an event, one succeeding the other as wind direction changed and a seated worker rotated his position. He further argued that this kind of behavior is found only with outside hearths, and that therefore the excavator's reconstruction of a covering tent is unlikely.

Ethnoarchaeology is not restricted to observations at the local scale. The British archaeologist Ian Hodder, in his study of the female ear decorations used by different tribes in the Lake Baringo area of Kenya, undertook a regional study to investigate the extent to which material culture (in this case personal decoration) was being used to express differences between the tribes. Partly as a result of such work, archaeologists no longer assume that it is an easy task to take archaeological assemblages and group them into regional "cultures," and then to assume that each "culture" so formed represents a social unit (see Chapter 12). Such a procedure might, in fact, work quite well for the ear decorations Hodder studied, because the people in question chose to use this feature to assert their tribal distinctiveness. But, as Hodder showed, if we were to take other features of the material culture, such as pots or tools, the same pattern would not necessarily be followed. His example documents the important lesson that material culture cannot be used by the archaeologist in a simple or unthinking manner in the reconstruction of supposed ethnic groups.

Ethnoarchaeology: the work of Ian Hodder. In the Lake Baringo area of Kenya, East Africa, Hodder studied the female ear decorations worn by the Tugen (right), Njemps, and Pokot tribes, and showed on a map (left) how these ornaments were used to assert tribal distinctiveness. Other features of the material culture (e.g. pots or tools), would reveal a different spatial patterning.

Ethnicity (i.e. the existence of ethnic groups, including tribal groups) is difficult to recognize from the archaeological record. For example, the view that Mousterian tool assemblages represented different social groups, as suggested by François Bordes, has been criticized (see discussion in Chapter 10); and the notion that such features as pottery decoration are automatically a sign of ethnic affiliation has been questioned. This is a field where ethnoarchaeology is only now beginning to make some headway.

One field of information, however, once overused by archaeologists, has in recent years been much neglected: the study of languages. For there is no doubt that ethnic groups often correlate with language areas, and that ethnic and linguistic boundaries are often the same. But it should also be remembered that human societies can exist quite well without tribal or ethnic affiliations: there is no real need to divide the social world up into named and discrete groups of people.

Ethnicity should not be confused with race, which insofar as it exists (Chapter 11) is a physical attribute, not a social one. The *ethnos*, the ethnic group, may be defined as "a firm aggregate of people, historically established on a given territory, possessing in common relatively stable peculiarities of language and culture, and also recognizing their unity and difference from other similar formations (self-awareness) and expressing this in a self-appointed name (ethnonym)" (Dragadze 1980, 162).

The languages of the world can be divided into different linguistic groupings. It is generally agreed that the different languages within a given group (e.g. Hebrew and Arabic within the Semitic group) are genetically related: they have a common origin, at least to some extent. The supposed

LANGUAGE AND ETHNICITY

common origin is not always easy to explain in social terms. For instance, the so-called Indo-European languages present a longstanding puzzle. Nearly all the languages of Europe (and now of the former colonies of Europe, including most of the inhabitants of the Americas, Australia, and New Zealand) are related to each other, as well as to the languages of Iran and northern India and Pakistan. However, the historical background is much disputed.

It seems likely that in some cases the scale of the area in which a language came to be spoken was influential in determining the scale of the ethnic group that later came to be formed. For instance, in Greece in the 7th and 6th centuries BC the political reality was one of small, independent city states (and some larger tribal areas). But in the wider area where Greek was spoken there was already an awareness that the inhabitants were together Hellenes (i.e. Greeks). Only Greeks were allowed to compete in the great Panhellenic Games held every 4 years in honor of Zeus at Olympia. It was not until later, with the expansion of Athens in the 5th century BC and then the conquests of Philip of Macedon and his son Alexander the Great in the next century, that the whole territory occupied by the Greeks became united into a single nation. Language is an important component of ethnicity.

In Mesoamerica, Joyce Marcus has drawn on linguistic evidence in analyzing the development of the Zapotec and Mixtec cultures. She notes that their languages belong to the Otomanguean family, and follows

the assumption that this relationship implies a common origin. Marcus and Kent Flannery, in their remarkable book *The Cloud People* (1983), seek to trace through time "the divergent evolution of the Zapotec and Mixtec from a common ancestral culture and their general evolution through successive levels of sociopolitical evolution" (Flannery and Marcus 1983, 9). They see in certain shared elements of the two cultures the common ancestry suggested by the linguistic arguments.

Using glottochronology (Chapter 4) Marcus suggests a date of 3700 BC for the beginning of the divergence between the Zapotec and Mixtec; she then seeks to correlate this with archaeological findings. It is questionable whether glottochronology can be used in this over-precise way. But this criticism in no way undermines the relevance of her introduction of the Zapotec and Mixtec languages into the discussion of the social evolution of the two cultures.

At this point it is appropriate to move on to consider how one actually sets about systematically searching for evidence of social organization in archaeological remains, using the techniques and sources of information just outlined. Here we will find it useful to look first at bands, then segmentary societies, and finally at chiefdoms and states.

TECHNIQUES OF STUDY FOR BAND SOCIETIES

In band societies economic organization and to a large extent political organization are exclusively at a local level – there are no permanent administrative centers. The nature of such societies can be investigated in several ways.

Investigating Activities within a Site

Having identified various sites by employing the methods outlined in Chapter 3, the first approach is to concentrate on the individual site, with an investigation of the variability *within* it. (Off-site archaeology is discussed in the next section.) The aim is to understand the nature of the activities that took place there, and of the social group that used it.

The best approach depends on the nature of the site. In Chapter 3 a site was defined as a place of human activity, generally indicated by a concentration of artifacts and discarded materials. Here we need to be aware that, on sites of sedentary communities (generally, food-producers living in permanent structures), the remains are different in character from the temporary camp sites of mobile communities, whether hunter-gatherers or nomad herders. Sedentary communities are considered in a later section. Our focus in this section is on mobile communities, particularly hunter-gatherers of the Paleolithic period. Here the timescale is so great that the effects of geological processes on sites must be taken into account.

Among mobile communities a distinction can be drawn between *cave sites* and *open sites*. In cave sites, the physical extent of human occupation is largely defined by debris scattered within the cave itself and immediately outside it. Occupation deposits tend to be deep, usually indicating intermittent human activity over thousands or tens of thousands of years. For this reason it is vital to excavate and interpret accurately the stratigraphy of the site – the superimposed layers. Meticulous controls are needed, including the recording in three dimensions of the position of each object (artifact or bone), and the sieving or screening of all soil to recover smaller fragments. Similar observations apply to open sites, except that here one needs to allow for the fact that occupation deposits – without the protection provided by a cave – may have suffered greater erosion.

If it proves possible to distinguish single, short phases of human occupation at a site, one can then look at the distribution of artifacts and bone fragments within and around features and structures (hut found-ations, remains of hearths) to see whether any coherent patterns emerge. For the way such debris was discarded can shed light on the behavior of the small group of people who occupied the site at that time. This is where ethnoarchaeology has proved of great value. Lewis Binford's research among the Nunamiut Eskimo, described above, has shown for example that hunter-gatherers discard bone in a characteristic pattern around a hearth. The human behavior documented among the living Nunamiut therefore helps us understand the likely behavior that gave rise to similar scatters of bone around hearths on Paleolithic sites.

Often, it is not possible to distinguish single, short phases of occupation, and the archaeologist recovers instead evidence resulting from repeated activities at the same site over a long period. There may also be initial doubt as to whether the distribution observed is the result of human activity on the spot (*in situ*), or whether the materials have been transported by flowing water and redeposited. In some cases, too, the distribution observed, especially of bone debris, may be the result of the action of predatory animals, not of humans. These are questions to do with formation processes, as discussed in Chapter 2.

The study of such questions requires sophisticated sampling strategies and very thorough analysis. The work of Glynn Isaac's team at the Early Paleolithic sites of Koobi Fora on the eastern shore of Lake Turkana, Kenya, gives an indication of the recovery and analytical techniques involved. The first essential was a highly controlled excavation procedure with, within the areas chosen for detailed sampling, the careful recording of the coordinates of every piece of bone or stone recovered. Plotting the densities of finds was a first step in the analysis. One important question was to decide whether the assemblage was a primary one, *in situ*, or whether it was a secondary accumulation, the result of movement by water in a river or lake. The study of the orientation of the long limb bones proved helpful at Koobi Fora: if the bones had been deposited or disturbed by flowing water, they are likely to show the same orientation. In this case the remains were found to be essentially *in situ*, with only a small degree of post-depositional disturbance.

Isaac's team was also able to fit some fragments of bone back together again. The network of joins could be interpreted as demarcating areas where hominids broke open bones to extract marrow – so-called *activity areas*. (Different techniques had to be applied to try to determine that it was indeed humans

BONES

STONES

CONJOINING BONES

CONJOINING STONES

Glynn Isaac's research at the Early Paleolithic site of Koobi Fora, Kenya, East Africa. (Top row) Location of bones and stone artifacts plotted at site FxJj 50. (Second row) Lines joining bones and stones that could be fitted back together, perhaps indicating activity areas where bones were broken open to extract marrow, and stone tools were knapped.

and not predatory animals that had broken open the bone. This specialized and important field of study – called taphonomy – is discussed in detail in Chapter 6.)

A comparable analysis of joins among stone artifacts proved rewarding. Webs of conjoining lines were interpreted as indicating activity areas where stones were knapped. In these ways, the site was made to yield important information about specific human activities.

Broader interpretive questions arise from the consideration of individual camp sites of modern hunter-gatherer communities. One issue is the estimation of population size from camp area. Various models have been proposed, and these have been compared with ethnographic examples among the !Kung San hunter-

gatherers of the Kalahari Desert. Another question is the relationship between people (in kinship terms) and space in hunter-gatherer camps: recent studies have shown a strong correlation between kin distance and the distance between huts. Both questions are discussed in the accompanying box.

These are speculative areas at present, but they are now being systematically researched. Such inferences are bound to become part of the stock-in-trade of the Paleolithic archaeologist.

Investigating Territories in Mobile Societies

The detailed study of an individual site cannot, for a mobile group, reveal more than one aspect of social behavior. For a wider perspective, it is necessary to consider the entire territory in which the group or band operated, and the relationship between sites.

Once again, ethnoarchaeology has helped to establish a framework of analysis, so that one may think in terms of an annual home range (i.e. the whole territory covered by the group in the course of a year) and specific types of site within it, such as a home base camp (for a particular season), transitory camps, hunting blinds, butchery or kill sites, storage caches, and so on. Such concerns are basic to hunter-gatherer archaeology, and a regional perspective is essential if insight is to be gained into the annual life cycle of the group and its behavior. In archaeological terms this means that, in addition to conventional sites (with a high concentration of artifacts), one needs to look for very sparse scatters of artifacts, consisting of perhaps just one or two objects in every 10-m survey square (this is often referred to as off-site or non-site archaeo-

logy – see Chapter 3). One must also study the whole regional environment (Chapter 6) and the likely human use of it by hunter-gatherers.

A good example of off-site archaeology is provided by the work of the British anthropologist Robert Foley in the Amboseli region of southern Kenya. He collected and recorded some 8531 stone tools from 257 sample locations within a study area of 600 sq. km (270 sq. miles). From this evidence he was able to calculate the rate of discard of stone tools within different environmental and vegetation zones, and interpret the distribution patterns in terms of the strategies and movements of hunter-gatherer groups. In a later study, he developed a general model of stone tool distribution based on a number of studies of hunter-gatherer bands in different parts of the world. One conclusion was that a single band of some 25 people might be expected to discard as many as 163,000 artifacts within their annual territory in the course of a single year. These

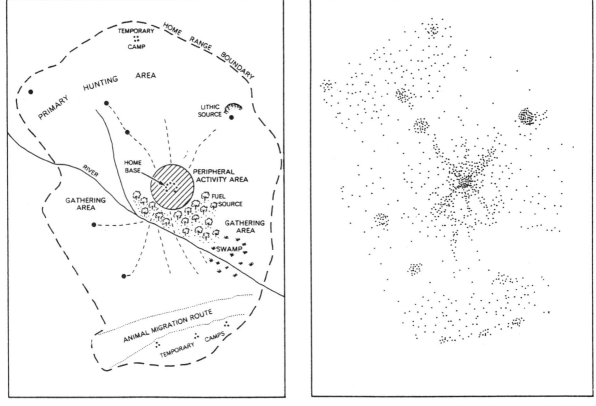

Robert Foley's model (left) of activities within the annual home range of a hunter-gatherer band, and the artifact scatters (right) resulting from such activities. Notice how artifacts appear between the home base/temporary camp sites as well as within them. The home range might be 30 km (19 miles) north-south in tropical environments, but considerably more in higher latitudes.

SPACE AND DENSITY IN HUNTER-GATHERER CAMPS

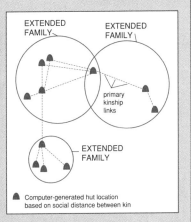

An important question to ask of any settlement site is the size of the population. The interpretation of ethnographic work undertaken by John Yellen among the !Kung San hunter-gatherers of the Kalahari Desert in southern Africa shows how this problem can fruitfully be tackled.

In the dry season, Yellen had noted that large aggregate camps are established for the entire band, ranging from 35 to 60 individuals. In the rainy season, when the band splits up, camps are occupied for just a few days by a single nuclear family, or by several families linked by marriage. Yellen noted that !Kung camp sites are formed of a circle of huts, each of which is a private activity space for a single person, with a shelter, hearth, and hearthside activity area, oriented inwards around a central area. Yellen indicated that there is a strong relationship between the area of the camp (established by drawing a line around the perimeter of the hut circle) and its population.

More recently, the Cambridge archaeologist Todd Whitelaw has stressed that this general relationship between camp area and population does not take account of all the relevant factors, including the spacing between huts and the differences between the dry and rainy season camps. He took note of the observation that huts and fires belonging to members of the same extended families are close to each other, and he plotted to what extent social distance between kin matched physical distance between huts (measured around the circumference of the camp circle).

Using the data for the two years (1968-69) in which Yellen had observed dry-season camp structure, he obtained a good correlation between closeness of kin and proximity of the huts.

He then went an interesting step further. Using the information about kinship distance gathered for two

specific camp sites of the San, but not at this stage utilizing any prior information about where the huts were actually located, he constructed a model layout using a non-metric multi-dimensional scaling (MDSCAL) computer routine. This method – described in more detail in a separate box in this chapter, below – can be used to construct a spatial structure using only information about relative distance between units.

The hut locations produced by the computer utilizing the model for one dry season camp are seen in the diagram top right. For comparison, the actual locations of the huts are shown in the diagram, right. The arrows run from the computer locations to the actual locations. The impressive feature is that in most cases the arrows are quite short; that is, the model produced a good approximation to the actual camp plan, although it was utilizing only data about kinship distance.

This is a good example of the way ethnographic work can enrich one's general understanding of a problem, in this case the structure of hunter-gatherer settlement sites. Of course, not all hunter-gatherer settlements are the same. But Whitelaw's study brings out some of the relevant factors, and allows one to look at the archaeological plans of hunter-gatherer camp sites with a fresh eye.

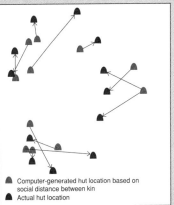

Hut locations in a San dry-season camp. *(Top) Todd Whitelaw's model of what the locations might be if one analyzes only the evidence for social relationships using a MDSCAL computer program. (Above) The MDSCAL locations compared with the actual ones.*

San hunter-gatherer camp, photographed in about 1927.

artifacts would be scattered across the territory, but with significant concentrations at home base camps and temporary camps. According to this model, however, only a very small proportion of the total annual artifact assemblage would be found by archaeologists working at a single site, and it is vitally important that individual site assemblages are interpreted as parts of a broader pattern.

TECHNIQUES OF STUDY FOR SEGMENTARY SOCIETIES

Segmentary societies operate on a larger scale than bands. They usually consist of farmers based in villages – permanent sedentary communities. The settlement is therefore the most appropriate aspect of such societies to investigate first. As we shall see, however, the cemeteries, public monuments, and craft specialization evident in these societies also form useful areas of study.

Investigating Settlements in Sedentary Societies

Although a completely excavated settlement from just one period is the ideal case for analysis, it is not often attainable. But much information can be obtained from intensive survey of surface features and from sample excavation. The initial aim is to investigate the structure of the site, and the functions of the different areas recognized. A permanent settlement incorporates a greater range of functions than a temporary hunter-gatherer camp. But the site should not be considered in isolation. As in the hunter-gatherer examples, it is necessary to consider exploitation of the territory as a whole. One means of achieving this is by so-called site catchment analysis, discussed in Chapter 6.

An intensive surface survey of the site can give good indications of the variation in deposits beneath. This was the technique used by Lewis Binford in 1963 at Hatchery West, a Late Woodland occupation site (*c.* AD 250–800) in Illinois. After a local farmer had plowed the topmost surface of the site, and after the summer rains had washed the surface to expose the artifacts, the surface materials were collected from each 6-m square. The resulting distribution maps gave useful indications of the structure of the site below. There were deposits of discarded debris (middens) where there was a high density of potsherds and, between them, houses in areas with a low density of sherds. The patterns indicated by the distribution maps were tested by excavation.

This was a favorable case, where there was a shallow depth of soil, and a close relationship between surface scatter and underlying structures. Remote-sensing techniques can also be helpful in revealing site structure, especially aerial photography (Chapter 3). Remote sensing can be a useful preliminary to excavation. At the Late Neolithic site of Divostin in Yugoslavia, Alan McPherron was able to use the proton magnetometer to locate the burnt clay floors of the houses in the village, and thus draw an approximate plan before excavation began. Often, however, the conditions are unsuitable for such methods. Furthermore, the site in question may be much larger than Hatchery West (which was less than 2 ha or 4.9 acres) and surface materials, especially pottery, may be abundant. For such sites a survey sampling method, such as random stratified sampling (Chapter 3) may be necessary. On a large site, sampling will also be required in the excavation. There are disadvantages in using small sampling units: they allow one to excavate a wider variety of different parts of the site, but fail to reveal much of the structures (houses, etc.) in question. In other words, there is no substitute for good, wide excavation areas.

For effective analysis of the community as a whole, some structures need to be excavated completely, and the remainder sampled intensively enough to obtain an idea of the variety of different structures (are they repeated household units, or are they more specialized buildings?).

In general, the settlement will be either agglomerate or dispersed. An agglomerate settlement consists of either one or several large units (clusters) of many rooms. A dispersed settlement plan has separate and free-standing house units, usually of smaller size. In the case of agglomerate structures there is the initial problem of detecting repeated social units (e.g. families or households) within them, and the functions of the rooms.

In a now-famous analysis published in 1970 of the agglomerate settlement of Broken K Pueblo, Arizona, in the American Southwest, James Hill undertook a detailed study of the functions of this 13th-century AD site. First he plotted the association of different types of artifact with different rooms. Then, in an ethnographic study of living Pueblo Indians, he identified for the modern period three different types of room – domestic (cooking, eating, sleeping etc.), storage, and ceremonial – and distinctions between rooms used by males

■	domestic room
■	storage room
■	ceremonial room
□	unexcavated room
●	firepit
■	corn grinder

30 ft
10 m

Broken K Pueblo, Arizona: research linked rooms containing firepits and corn grinders with domestic activities; smaller rooms with storage; and two rooms where floors were sunk below ground with ceremonial.

and by females. From this ethnographic evidence he derived 16 implications to test against his archaeological evidence, in order to discover whether or not the three room types and male/female distinctions could be identified at Broken K Pueblo itself. His testing suggested that the artifact patterning did indeed indicate the existence of similar distinctions at Broken K.

In recent years there have been criticisms of Hill's conclusions. New work implies that Pueblo architecture, not the artifacts found in them, may be a better guide to room function in prehistoric times. And the analogy between modern and prehistoric male/female distinctions is not satisfactorily demonstrated here. Cemetery analysis (see below) can provide a better correlation between sex and specific artifact types. But Hill's approach was a pioneering and interesting one in social archaeology, and his methods were commendably explicit, and therefore open to critical appraisal by other scholars (Chapter 12 considers this issue in more detail). William Longacre undertook similar research at a similar time at the nearby Carter Ranch site in Arizona, with results that have also recently been criticized. To some extent these problems of method – in particular, how to correlate ethnographic with archaeological data – are being solved by the kind of detailed ethnoarchaeological research, for instance by Ian Hodder, described in a previous section.

Another informative example of settlement study is offered by Todd Whitelaw's reinterpretation of the

Early Minoan site (*c.*2300 BC) of Myrtos in southern Crete. The excavator, Peter Warren, had suggested that this was a centralized community with a measure of craft specialization (see below). His published report was so commendably thorough as to allow Whitelaw to make a different suggestion – that there was a domestic (household) organization of production rather than craft specialization. By careful study of the function of the rooms (from the remains and features found in them), and their spatial arrangement, he was able to show that the settlement consisted of 5 or 6 household clusters, each probably with 4–6 individuals. Each cluster had cooking, storage, working, and general domestic areas – there was no evidence of centralization or specialized manufacturing.

The study of sedentary communities is made much easier when separate houses can be identified at the outset. In the 1930s, Gordon Childe excavated the extraordinarily well-preserved Neolithic village of Skara Brae in the Orkney Islands, north of Scotland. He found a settlement, now dated to around 3000 BC, where the internal installations (e.g. beds and cupboards) were still preserved, being made of stone. In such cases, the analysis of the community and the estimation of population size become much easier.

The Study of Ranking from Individual Burials

In archaeology, the individual is seen all too rarely. One of the most informative insights into the individual and his or her social status is offered by the discovery of human physical remains – the skeleton or the ashes – accompanied by artifacts deposited in the grave. Examination of the skeletal remains by a physical anthropologist (Chapter 11) will often reveal the sex and age at death of each individual, and possibly any dietary deficiency or other pathological condition. Communal or collective burials (burials of more than one individual) may be difficult to interpret, because it will not always be clear which grave-goods go with which deceased person. It is, therefore, from single burials that one can hope to learn most.

In segmentary societies, and others with relatively limited differentiation in terms of rank, a close analysis of grave-goods can reveal much about disparities in social status. One must take into account that what is buried with the deceased person is not simply the exact equivalent either of status or of material goods owned or used during life. Burials are made by living individuals, and are used by them to express and influence their relationships with others still alive as much as to symbolize or serve the dead. But there is nevertheless often a relationship between the role and rank of the deceased during life and the manner in which the remains are disposed of and accompanied by artifacts.

The analysis will seek to determine what differences are accorded to males and females in burial, and to assess whether these differences carry with them distinctions in terms of wealth or higher status. The other common factor involved with rank or status is age, and the possibility of age differences being systematically reflected in the treatment of the deceased is an obvious one. In relatively egalitarian societies, achieved status – that is, high status won through the individual's own achievements (e.g. in hunting) in his or her own lifetime – is something commonly encountered, and often reflected in funerary practice. But the archaeologist must ask, from the evidence available, whether the case in question is one of achieved status, or involves instead status ascribed through birth. To distinguish between the two is not easy. One useful criterion is to investigate whether children are in some cases given rich burial goods and other indications of preferential attention. If so, there may be a system of hereditary ranking, because at so early an age the child is not likely to have reached such a status through personal distinction.

Once the graves in the cemetery have been dated, the first step in most cases is simply to produce a frequency distribution (a histogram) of the number of different artifact types in each grave. For further analysis, however, it is more interesting to seek some better indication of wealth and status so that greater weight can be given to valuable objects, and less weight to commonplace ones. This at once raises the problem of the recognition of value (for we do not know in advance what value was given to objects at the time in question). This important subject is discussed in more detail in Chapters 9 and 10. From the point of view of social questions, the work of the British

archaeologist, Susan Shennan, is useful. In an innovative study of burials at the Copper Age cemetery at Branč in Czechoslovakia, she assigned points on a scale of "units of wealth," making the assumption that the valuable objects were those that took a long time to make, or were made of materials brought from a distance or difficult to obtain. This allowed her to produce a diagram of the wealth structure of the cemetery in relation to age and sex. Some individuals, particularly females, had much more elaborate sets of grave-goods than others. She concluded that there was a leading family or families, and status tended to be inherited through the male line, females possibly obtaining their rich artifacts only on marriage.

Sophisticated quantitative techniques can be used to analyze artifact patterning in a cemetery, including factor analysis and cluster analysis (see box).

Ranking is not expressed solely in the grave-goods, but in the entire manner of burial. Some workers, among them Joseph A. Tainter, have developed a more sophisticated approach, seeking to use a much wider range of variables. For instance, in Tainter's study of 512 Middle Woodland burials (*c.*150 BC–AD 400) from two mound groups in the lower Illinois river valley, he chose 18 variables that each burial might or might not show. He used cluster analysis to investigate relationships between the burials, and concluded from this that there were different social groups. The variables used are worth quoting, as they could be adapted to many different cases:

Checklist of Variables for Burials
1   Uncremated/cremated
2   Articulated/disarticulated
3   Extended/not extended
4   Earthwalls/log walls
5   Ramps/no ramps
6   Surface/sub-surface
7   Log-covered/not log-covered
8   Slab-covered/not slab-covered
9   Slabs in grave/no slabs
10   Interred in central location/not interred in central location
11   Supine/not supine
12   Single/multiple
13   Ocher/no ocher
14   Miscellaneous animal bones/none
15   Hematite/no hematite
16   Imported sociotechnic items (status indicators e.g. royal crown)
17   Locally produced sociotechnic items
18   Technomic items (utilitarian objects e.g. tools)

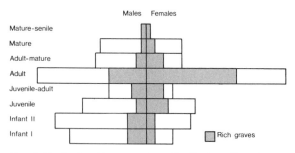

Branč, Czechoslovakia: age and sex distribution of burials.

FACTOR ANALYSIS AND CLUSTER ANALYSIS

Both of these techniques are multivariate statistical methods used to isolate patterning in archaeological data. They are alike in that both start with assemblages of artifacts, and these artifacts are listed in terms of types (sometimes referred to as variables). Factor analysis looks for variation among the artifact types within an assemblage. Cluster analysis identifies similarities and differences among complete assemblages, such as assemblages of burial goods from different graves in a cemetery.

Factor Analysis

The basic statistical data needed for a factor analysis is a matrix of correlation coefficients. (Correlation coefficients express, on a scale of from -1 to +1, the degree of correlation between two variables; they must be obtained for each pair of variables considered in the study.) The key concept is that of variance. Variance is of three kinds: common variance (which correlates with other variables), specific variance (which does not), and error variance (caused by errors in sampling, measurement, etc.).

The assumption is that a battery of intercorrelated variables has common factors running through it, and that the scores of any individual variable can be represented more economically in terms of these reference factors. The aim of factor analysis is to identify these factors.

Factor analysis was used by James Hill to study the co-occurrence of pottery types in the different rooms at Broken K Pueblo (see main text above), and by Lewis and Sally Binford to analyze stone tool types of the Middle Paleolithic in southwest France.

Cluster Analysis

Cluster analysis takes units or assemblages and arranges them in terms of the similarities between them, so that the most similar are grouped (i.e. clustered) together. The similarities are assessed in terms of the occurrence or non-occurrence of specific artifact types in the assemblages. If assemblages have the same types within them occurring in roughly the same quantities, they are obviously very similar and are clustered closely together.

The technique is frequently used in cemetery analysis to investigate the social structure in terms of the grave goods accompanying the dead. Here the grave goods listed for each grave represent the individual assemblages to be clustered. The different clusters can then be examined to see which artifacts are taking a predominant role in achieving the clustering. In particular, one may see whether the age and sex of the dead correlate closely with the clustering achieved by considering the grave goods alone. The occurrence of the graves of each cluster can also be plotted on a map of the cemetery to see whether the clusters as defined by the grave goods are reflected in the spatial arrangement of the cemetery.

Cluster analysis has been used successfully by John O'Shea for historic-period cemeteries of the Pawnee, Arikara, and Omaha Plains Indians, and by Christopher Peebles at Moundville in Alabama. The accompanying diagram shows the clustering achieved by Peebles. The box later in this chapter (Social Analysis at Moundville) goes on to consider how he deduced information about social organization from it.

Dendrogram produced by Peebles using a cluster analysis of 719 burials from Moundville, Alabama. Divisions were made successively according to the presence or absence of single attributes (- and + on the diagram). For example, the first major division depends on the presence or absence of attribute 2, "plain bowls." Division was terminated when 15 clusters had been defined (Roman numerals at far right). Each cluster box shows the number of burials assigned to it.

2 Plain bowls
3 Decorated water bottles
4 Plain water bottles
6 Plain pots or jars
24 Large fragments of pottery
36 Discoidals
99 Copper ear spools
109 Large bone awls
134 Shell beads

EARLY WESSEX

Prehistoric Wessex (the counties of Wiltshire, Dorset, Hampshire, and Berkshire in southern England) preserves a rich collection of major monuments from the early farming period, but few remains of settlements. Yet the analysis of the scale and the distribution of the monuments does allow the reconstruction of important aspects of social organization, and illustrates one approach to the study of early social relations.

In the **early phase** of monument construction (the earlier Neolithic, c. 4000–3000 BC), the most frequent monuments are long earthen burial mounds, termed long barrows, which are up to 70 m (230 ft) in length. They lie mainly on the chalklands of Wessex where the light soils were suitable for early farming. Excavations show that the monuments usually contained a wooden burial chamber: some of them have a chamber of stone. With each cluster of mounds is associated a larger, circular monument with concentric ditches termed a causewayed camp or enclosure.

Analysis of the spatial distribution and the size of the long barrows suggests a possible interpretation. Lines drawn between them divide the landscape into several possible territories, which are roughly equivalent in size. Each monument seems to have been the focal point for social activities and the burial place of the farming community inhabiting the local territory. A group of 20 people would have needed about 50 working days to construct a long barrow.

In the early phase of construction there is little suggestion of the ranking of sites or individuals: this was an egalitarian society. The causewayed enclosures may have served as a ritual focus and periodic meeting place for the larger group of people represented by one whole cluster of long barrows. (The 100,000 hours' labor required to construct one could be achieved in 40 working days by 250 people.) This would have been what anthropologists term a tribal or segmentary society.

In the **later phase** (the later Neolithic, c. 3000–2000 BC), the long barrows and causewayed camps went out of use. In place of the latter, major ritual enclosures are seen. These were large circular monuments delimited by a ditch with a bank usually outside it: they are termed henges. Each would

have required something of the order of 1 million hours of labor for its construction. The labor input suggests the mobilization of the resources of a whole territory. About 300 people working full time for at least a year would be needed: their food would have to be provided for them unless the process were spread over a very long period. This factor and the existence of the ritual centers themselves suggests that one may now speak of a chiefdom society. The central person controlling the central place would be an individual of high rank: the chief.

During this period (c. 2800 BC) the great earth mound at Silbury Hill was built. According to its excavator, it required 18 million hours of work, and was completed within 2 years. A few centuries later (c. 2100 BC) the great monument at Stonehenge took final shape, with its circle of stones, representing an even greater labor

In the early phase, clusters of burial mounds establish a social landscape (left), each cluster with its causewayed enclosure. Analysis indicates (above) that each mound was the territorial focus for a small group of farmers. This was a segmentary society, where no one group was dominant.

In the later phase, the causewayed enclosures were replaced by major henge monuments. Their scale indicates centralized organization, and hence probably a chiefdom society. At this time the two great monuments Stonehenge and Silbury Hill were built.

investment, if the transport of the stones is taken into account. This may imply the existence of a paramount chief capable of organizing a workforce drawn from the entire Wessex region.

Although burials with rich grave goods directly reflecting the wealth of prominent individuals are not found until the succeeding phase, the Early Bronze Age, the analysis of spatial organization among the monuments, and the consideration of the labor input contributed by their builders, does allow inferences to be drawn about the social organization of the time.

MAN HOURS REQUIRED FOR CONSTRUCTION	
Late Neolithic	
	STONEHENGE 30,000,000
	HENGE 1,000,000
Early Neolithic	
	CAUSEWAYED CAMP 100,000
	LONG BARROW 10,000

Analysis of the scale of the Wessex monuments in terms of labor hours needed for their construction suggests the emergence of a hierarchy in the later phase that may mirror a development in social relations and the emergence of a ranked society. Stonehenge, built at this time, is the greatest of the Wessex monuments. In the earlier Neolithic the scale of monuments is commensurate with an egalitarian, segmentary society.

This list of variables illustrates another important point: that what one is seeking to study is social structure as a whole, not just personal ranking. In life, and in some cases in death, the individual has a whole series of roles and statuses that we seek to detect and understand. To rank individuals in a simple linear order in terms of one variable or a combination of variables may be a considerable oversimplification.

Collective Works and Communal Action

Segmentary societies did not always bury individuals in cemeteries, so archaeologists cannot rely on this source of information being available. Similarly, settlement sites can be difficult to locate, and the remains scanty. The original ground surface may have been destroyed, either by plowing or erosion, so that house floors or structures are not preserved. For instance, all that remains for the early farming period of northern Europe in the way of houses and domestic evidence is often just a few postholes (where timber uprights for house frames were set in the ground) and the lower levels of rubbish pits. In all such cases, the archaeologist in search of social evidence needs to turn to another prime source: public monuments.

We all perhaps have a mental image of such major monuments as the temples of the Maya or the pyramids of Egypt, erected by centrally organized state societies. But a great many simpler societies, at the level of chiefdoms or tribes, have built substantial and conspicuous structures. One thinks of the great stone monuments of western Europe (the so-called "megaliths," see box, Chapter 12), or the giant stone statues of Easter Island in the Pacific Ocean. Indeed monuments like the Easter Island figures have in the past been interpreted, wrongly, as a sure sign of "civilization." When the indigenous society displays no other characteristics of "civilization," fantastic explanations have been put forward involving long-distance migrations, vanished continents, or even visitors from outer space. Such unsubstantiated notions are looked at again in Chapters 12 and 14. For present purposes we may turn instead to the techniques archaeologists apply when searching for social information from such monuments, particularly among segmentary societies. These involve questions about the size or scale of the monuments; their spatial distribution in the landscape; and clues about the status of individuals buried in certain monuments.

How Much Labor was Invested in the Monuments?
To begin with, the scale of the monument in terms of the number of hours it may have taken to build should

be investigated, using evidence not just from the structure itself but from experimental archaeology of the kind described in Chapters 2 and 8. As explained in the box (pp.178, 179), in the Wessex region of southern England the largest monuments (so-called causewayed enclosures) of the Early Neolithic period seem to have required some 100,000 hours of work to construct – within the capabilities of 250 people working together for perhaps 6 weeks. This does not suggest a very complex level of organization and might indicate a tribal, segmentary society. But by the Late Neolithic one of the biggest monuments, the great mound of Silbury Hill, demanded 18 million hours, which excavation of the site showed had been invested over a span of no more than 2 years. The workforce must have been of the order of 3000 individuals over this period of time, which suggests the kind of mobilization of resources indicative of a more centralized, chiefdom society.

How Are the Monuments Distributed in the Landscape? It is also useful to analyze spatial distribution of the monuments in question in relation to other monuments and to settlement and burial remains. For instance, the burial mounds (long barrows) of southern Britain around 3500–2800 BC each represented about 5000–10,000 hours of labor. Their distribution in well-defined regions can be examined by drawing Thiessen polygons around them (see above), and by considering land use, such as the relationship of long barrows to areas of lighter chalk soils most suitable for early agriculture. It has been suggested that each mound was the focal point of the territory of a group of people permanently established there – a symbolic center for the community.

The very act of creating a fixed area for the repeated disposal of the dead implies an element of permanence. The American archaeologist Arthur Saxe has suggested that in those groups where rights to the use of land are asserted by claiming descent from dead ancestors, there will be formal areas maintained exclusively for the disposal of the dead. In this perspective, collective burial in monumental tombs is not simply a reflection of religious beliefs: it has real social significance. Most of the megalithic tombs of western Europe might thus be regarded as the territorial markers of segmentary societies, because the spatial distribution does not suggest any higher level of organization. This and other ideas about the megaliths are more fully discussed in Chapter 12.

Quanterness, Orkney Islands: reconstruction of a chambered tomb dating to about 3300 BC. Burials found within it imply that this was the product of a segmentary society, not a hierarchical one, despite the sophistication of the architecture.

Which Individuals Are Associated with the Monuments? Finally it is necessary to investigate the relationship between individuals and monuments. When the monument is associated with a prominent individual, it might indicate that that person held high rank, and might therefore suggest a centralized society. This would not be the case for a monument associated with multiple burials of individuals of apparently similar status. For instance, in the chambered tomb at Quanterness in the Orkney Islands, off the north coast of Scotland, *c.* 3300 BC, remains of a large number of individuals were found, perhaps as many as 390. Males and females were about equally represented, and the age distribution could represent the pattern of deaths in the population at large; that is to say, that the age at death of the people buried in the tomb (46 percent below 20 years, 47 percent aged 20–30 years, and only 7 percent over the age of 30 years) could in proportional terms be the same as that of the whole population. The excavators concluded that this was a tomb equally available to most sectors of the community, and representative of a segmentary society rather than a hierarchical one, which the sophistication of its architecture might at first have suggested.

Similar observations apply to ritual monuments other than tombs, which similarly can give insights into social organization. So, too, can any other major corporate works, whether agricultural or defensive.

Relationships Between Segmentary Societies

Segmentary agricultural societies have a whole range of relationships with their neighbors – marriage ties, exchange partnerships, etc. The first step in investigating such relationships archaeologically is to look for the ritual centers that served for periodic meetings of several groups. A study can then be made of the sources of some of the artifacts found at these centers (the technique is explained in Chapter 9), to indicate the geographical extent of the network of contacts represented at each center.

Some of the major public monuments in southern Britain discussed in the previous section seem to have been just such ritual centers. In particular, the causewayed enclosures of the Early Neolithic have been interpreted as central meeting places – social and ritual centers for the tribal groups in whose territory they lay, and also for larger, periodic meetings with participants from a much greater area. Stone axes at these sites came from far-away sources, hinting at just how broadly based the social interconnections were at this early time.

Similarities and differences in the style and appearance of certain types of artifact – for instance, decorated pottery – can be an important clue to the interactions between societies. However, as we saw in an earlier section, Ian Hodder has shown that while various features of material culture are used to maintain tribal distinctions, others are not patterned in this way. At present archaeologists have not found a reliable way to distinguish in the archaeological record such symbols of ethnic differentiation and to "read" them correctly – for instance, to distinguish them from symbols of rank, or of some other specialization, or from mere examples of decorative fashion. Conventions of communication are considered further in Chapter 10.

Farming Methods and Craft Specialists

In segmentary societies the existence of settled villages, cemeteries, public monuments, and ritual centers all indicate greater social complexity than in band societies. One way to try to measure how societies begin to show still greater complexity is to look at farming methods and the growth of craft specialists. Here we shall be concerned with social implications: more detailed questions about how archaeologists look at dietary aspects of farming, and technological aspects of craft production, are considered in Chapters 7 and 8 respectively. The increasing need for communities to exchange goods as craft production developed is the subject of Chapter 9.

As the farming way of life took root in different parts of the world after 10,000 years ago, there is evidence in many areas for a gradual *intensification of food production*, manifested by the introduction of new farming methods such as plowing, terracing, and irrigation, the use of poorer quality land as better land grew scarce, and the exploitation for the first time of so-called "secondary products" such as milk and wool (the meat of domestic animals being the "primary product"). How archaeologists can identify such evidence is discussed in Chapters 6 and 7. What we should note here is that these are all developments requiring a greater expenditure of human effort – they are *labor-intensive* techniques – and new and varied kinds of expertise. For instance, plowing allows once unproductive poor-quality land to be cultivated but it takes more time and effort than cultivating better-quality land without the plow. Moreover, activities like terracing involve co-operative effort on the part of a whole community. These are all activities that can be looked at to measure the likely number of work hours and size of labor force required. As in the case of public monuments, a really significant increase in the effort expended (for instance, on the introduction of irrigation) would suggest some more centralized organization of the workforce, perhaps signaling the transition from a non-hierarchical, segmentary type of society to one that is much more centralized, such as a chiefdom.

If we turn now to *craft specialization* as a source of social information, there is a useful distinction to be drawn here between segmentary societies and centralized ones. In segmentary societies, craft production is mainly organized at the household level – what the American anthropologist Marshall Sahlins in his book *Stone Age Economics* (1972) has termed the Domestic Mode of Production. In more centralized societies such as chiefdoms and states, on the other hand, though the household unit may still play an important role, much of the production will often be organized at a higher, more centralized level. This distinction is useful at the practical level of survey and excavation. Even small

villages in segmentary societies will show signs of household craft production in the form of pottery kilns or perhaps slag from metalworking. But only in centralized societies does one find towns and cities with certain quarters given over almost entirely to specialized craft production. At the great 1st millennium AD metropolis of Teotihuacan, near modern Mexico City, for instance, specialized production of tools from the volcanic glass obsidian took place in designated areas of the city.

Quarries and mines to extract the raw materials for craft production developed with the crafts themselves, and provide another indicator of economic intensification and the transition to centralized social organization. For example, the flint quarries of the first farmers of Britain, around 4000 BC, required less specialized organization than the later flint mine at Grimes Graves in eastern Britain (*c.*2500 BC), with its 350 shafts up to 9 m (30 ft) deep and complicated network of underground galleries.

TECHNIQUES OF STUDY FOR CHIEFDOMS AND STATES

Most of the techniques of analysis appropriate to segmentary societies remain valid for the study of centralized chiefdoms and states, which incorporate within themselves most of the social forms and patterns of interaction seen in the simpler societies. The investigation of the household and degree of differentiation on the rural village site are just as relevant; so too is the assessment of the degree of intensification of farming. The additional techniques needed arise because of the centralization of society, the hierarchy of sites, and the organizational and communicational devices that characterize chiefdom and state societies. Once again, it is the nature of these devices that interests us, not simply the classification of society into one form or another.

Identifying Primary Centers

Techniques for the study of settlement patterning were discussed earlier in the chapter. As indicated there, the first step, given the results of the field survey, is to consider the size of the site, either in absolute terms, or in terms of the distances between major centers so as to determine which are dominant and which subordinate. This leads to the creation of a map identifying the principal independent centers and the approximate extent of the territories surrounding them.

The reliance on size alone, however, can be misleading, and it is necessary to seek other indications of

which are the primary centers. The best way is to try to find out how the society in question viewed itself and its territories. This might seem an impossible task until one remembers that, for most state societies at any rate, written records exist. Their immense value to the archaeologist has already been outlined. Here we need to stress their usefulness not so much in understanding what people thought and believed – that is the subject of Chapter 10 – but in giving us clues as to which were the major centers. Written sources may name various sites, identifying their place within the hierarchy. The archaeological task is then to find those named sites, usually by the discovery of an actual inscription including the name of the relevant site – one might for example hope to find such an inscription in any substantial town of the Roman Empire. In recent years, the decipherment of Maya hieroglyphs has opened up a whole new source of evidence of this sort (see box).

In some cases, however, the texts do not give direct and explicit indications of site hierarchy. But place-names within the archive can sometimes be used to construct a hypothetical map by means of multi-dimensional scaling – a computer technique for developing spatial structure from numerical data. The assumption is made that the names occurring together most frequently in the written record are those of sites closest to each other. The British archaeologist John Cherry has developed such a map for the lands of the

Late Bronze Age Greece: a map of territories derived from Homer's Iliad *(top) compares well with a territorial map (above) based solely on archaeological evidence.*

O PALACES
+ FORTIFIED SITES

50 miles
80 km

early Mycenaean state of Pylos in Greece (c.1200 BC) (see box overleaf).

Even myth and legend can sometimes be used in a systematic way to build up a coherent geographical picture. For instance, the so-called "Catalogue of Ships" in Homer's *Iliad*, which indicates how many ships each of the centers of Greece sent to the Trojan War, was used by Denys Page to draw up an approximate political map of the time. It is interesting to compare it with a map drawn using only the hard archaeological data for fortified sites and palace cen-

MAYA TERRITORIES

NORTH AMERICA

Copán

Tikal

Calakmul

Palenque

The lowland Classic Maya of the 1st millennium AD erected huge stone stelae at their principal centers to record, amongst other things, the events of their dynastic history. One such monument, Stela A at the city of Copán, dating to AD 731, displays so-called "emblem glyphs" that name four Maya cities: Copán, Tikal, Calakmul, and Palenque. These seem to have been the paramount centers of the time, each controlling a large region. This is demonstrated by the presence within each region of a fourfold hierarchy of sites. That is, the lowest or 4th-level sites display on their stelae the emblem glyph of the 3rd-level center to which they were subject, the 3rd-level centers mention 2nd-level ones, and the 2nd-level centers show the glyph of the paramount center. Joyce Marcus, an American scholar, has plotted the distribution of the different glyphs at these sites and produced a map suggesting contemporary political territories. In the years around AD 731 there were also two territorial units composed of secondary and lower-order centers: the Yaxchilán and Petexbatún regions. These later became regional states as well.

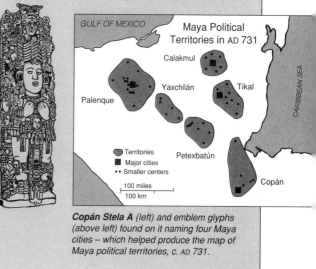

Maya Political Territories in AD 731

GULF OF MEXICO
CARIBBEAN SEA
Calakmul
Yaxchilán
Tikal
Palenque
Petexbatún
Copán

○ Territories
■ Major cities
•• Smaller centers

100 miles
100 km

Copán Stela A *(left) and emblem glyphs (above left) found on it naming four Maya cities – which helped produce the map of Maya political territories, c. AD 731.*

MULTI-DIMENSIONAL SCALING (MDSCAL)

Multi-dimensional scaling (MDSCAL) is a multivariate statistical technique, which, like factor analysis and cluster analysis, seeks to simplify complex information. The main aim is to develop spatial structure from numerical data. The starting point is a series of units, and some way of measuring or estimating the distances between them (often in terms of similarity and difference, where a larger difference is treated as much the same as a larger distance). The method allows one to reach the best arrangement (usually in two dimensions) of the various units in terms of similarities and differences.

One interesting feature of the method is that it does not need fully quantitative measures of similarity and difference: it is sufficient to know, for each unit, which the nearest unit is, and then the next and so on in rank order. For this reason, the method is sometimes called non-metric multi-dimensional scaling.

An ingenious use of the approach, which can serve as an example, was employed by the English archaeologist John Cherry. The problem was to try to reconstruct something of the geography of the Mycenaean kingdom of Pylos in Greece (c. 1200 BC). The information for the computer program came entirely from the palace archives recorded on clay tablets found at Pylos. The tablets, which mention many place names, give no direct geographical information whatever, although they contain sufficient hints about the approximate location of some places to have allowed speculative maps to be drawn. Cherry's rather different approach involved just one interesting assumption: that if two or more place names occurred on the same tablet, they were likely to be fairly close to each other in reality. So he studied the frequency with which certain place names were recorded on the tablets, and then compiled a table (or "incidence matrix") showing their co-occurrence on individual tablets. The computer then went to work using the MDSCAL program, and produced as its output a spatial configuration based entirely on these data. Bearing in mind that the MDSCAL map shows relationships rather than distances, Cherry was then able to compare his configuration with the positions of the same sites, suggested by other scholars, on a real geographic map of the area in question.

While the results remain hypothetical at this stage and have to be tested against further discoveries in the field, there are a number of intriguing similarities between the MDSCAL and geographic maps. For example, the computer was able to separate the towns of the kingdom's two provinces. It also confirmed much of the north-to-south order of the towns in the western province, if one ignores Pylos. Thus, on both MDSCAL and geographic maps, pi-*82 is the most northerly town, followed by me-ta-pa etc. Pylos appears unexpectedly at the top of the MDSCAL map probably because, as the "capital" of the kingdom, its interactions were different in kind from those amongst the satellite towns.

The essential point, however, is that Cherry used information about relationships between pairs of units (in this case places mentioned in the tablets) to produce an ordered spatial configuration of those units. That is the essence of non-metric multi-dimensional scaling.

	a-ke-re-wa	a-pu₂-we	e-ra-te-re-we	e-re-e	e-sa-re-wi-ja	ka-ra-do-ro	me-ta-pa	pa-ki-ja-pi	pe-to-no	pi-*82	pu-ro	ra-u-ra-ti-ja	ri-jo	ro-u-so	sa-ma-ra	ti-mi-to a-ke-e	za-ma-e-wi-ja
a-ke-re-wa		1	1	1	0	0	0	0	1	0	0	0	1	1	0	1	0
a-pu₂-we			0	0	0	1	0	1	0	0	0	0	0	0	0	0	0
e-ra-te-re-we				0	1	0	1	0	0	1	0	0	0	0	0	1	1
e-re-e					1	0	0	0	0	0	0	0	0	0	0	0	1
e-sa-re-wi-ja						0	0	0	0	0	0	1	0	0	1	1	1
ka-ra-do-ro							0	1	0	0	0	0	1	1	0	0	0
me-ta-pa								0	1	1	0	0	0	0	0	1	0
pa-ki-ja-pi									1	0	1	0	0	1	0	0	0
pe-to-no										0	0	0	0	0	0	0	0
pi-*82											1	0	0	0	0	0	0
pu-ro (=Pylos)												1	0	0	1	0	0
ra-u-ra-ti-ja													0	0	1	1	0
ri-jo														0	0	1	0
ro-u-so															0	0	0
sa-ma-ra																1	0
ti-mi-to a-ke-e																	0
za-ma-e-wi-ja																	

Table ("incidence matrix") showing 17 of the towns recorded on the tablets found at Pylos, and which of these names occur together on the same tablet (1 = link indicated; 0 = no link)

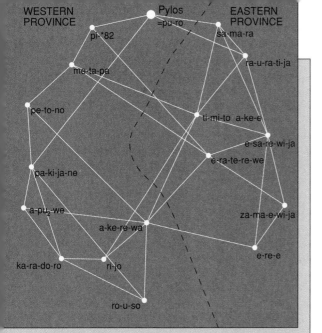

The MDSCAL output or map produced from the information in the incidence matrix, showing general relationships among the towns rather than distances. The computer has successfully reproduced the division of towns into two provinces, with a north- to-south ordering in the western province similar to that on the geographic map.

Geographic map of the Pylos area, with towns positioned approximately by John Chadwick using conventional archaeological and other evidence. The dashed line indicates the known division of the kingdom into two provinces.

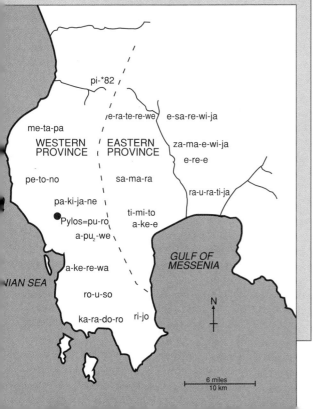

ters in Mycenaean Greece: the archaeological and the historical pictures correlate very well.

Usually, however, site hierarchy must be deduced by more directly archaeological means, without placing reliance on the written word. The presence of a "highest-order" center, such as the capital city of an independent state, can best be inferred from direct indications of central organization, on a scale not exceeded elsewhere, and comparable with that of other highest-order centers of equivalent states.

One such indication is the existence of an archive (even without understanding anything of what it says) or of other symbolic indications of centralized organization. For instance, many controlled economies used seals to impress in clay as indications of ownership, source, or destination. The finding of a quantity of such materials can indicate organizational activity. Indeed, the whole practice of literacy and of symbolic expression is so central to organization that such indications are of great relevance.

A further indication of central status is the presence of buildings of standardized form known to be associated with central functions of high order. In Minoan Crete, for instance, the "palace" plan around a central court is recognized in this way. Therefore, a relatively small palace site (e.g. Zakros) is accorded a status which a larger settlement lacking such buildings (e.g. Palaikastro) is not.

The same observation holds true for buildings of ritual function, because in most early societies the control of administration and control of religious practice were closely linked. Thus, a large ziggurat in Mesopotamia in Sumerian times, or a large plaza with temple-pyramids in the Maya lowlands, indicates a site of high status.

Failing these conspicuous indicators, the archaeologist must turn to artifacts suggestive of the function of a major center. This is particularly necessary for surface surveys, where building plans may not be clear. Thus, on site surveys in Iraq, workers studying the Early Dynastic period, such as Robert Adams and Gregory Johnson, have used terracotta wall cones as indicators of higher-than-expected status for the smaller sites where they are found. The cones, known to form part of the decoration of temples and other public buildings on larger sites in the region, suggest that such smaller sites may have been specialized administrative centers.

Among other archaeological criteria often used to indicate status are fortifications, and the existence of a mint in those lands where coinage was in use.

Clearly, when settlement hierarchy is under consideration, sites cannot be considered in isolation, but

185

only in relation to each other. The exercise is one of early political geography.

Functions of the Center

In a hierarchically organized society, it always makes sense to study closely the functions of the center, considering such possible factors as kingship, bureaucratic organization, redistribution and storage of goods, organization of ritual, craft specialization, and external trade. All of these offer insights into how the society worked.

Here, as before, the appropriate approach is that of the intensive site survey over the terrain occupied by the center and its immediate vicinity, together with excavation on as large a scale as is practicable. Again, this is a sampling problem, where the objective of comprehensiveness must be balanced against limited resources of time and finance. In the case of smaller centers, just a few hectares in extent, an intensive area survey will be perfectly appropriate. But for very large sites, a different approach is needed.

Abandoned Sites. Many of the most ambitious urban projects have been carried out at abandoned sites, or at sites where the present occupation is not of an urban character, and does not seriously impede the investigation. (The problems of continuously urban sites, i.e. ones that remain major centers today, are considered below.) The first requirement, which may present practical difficulties if the site is forested, is a good topographic map at something like a scale of 1:1000, although this may not be convenient for sites several kilometers in extent. This map will indicate the location of major structures visible on the surface, and some of these will be selected for more careful mapping. On sites where extensive excavations have already been conducted, their results can also be included.

Such topographic maps are among the most cost-effective undertakings of modern archaeology. One of the most interesting examples is Salvatore Garfie's survey of the site of Tell el Amarna, the capital city of the Egyptian pharaoh Akhenaten, as part of the British project of survey and excavation there. The site was occupied for only 13 years in the 14th century BC, and was then abandoned. The buildings were of mud brick and are not well preserved as surface features, so the map draws heavily on excavations over the course of a century. In the New World, there have been several projects of comparable scale, one of the most notable being the University of Pennsylvania's great mapping project at the Maya city of Tikal, and similar work is now under way at several Maya sites. Perhaps the most ambitious project of all, however, has been the survey at the greatest Mexican urban center, Teotihuacan (see Chapter 3).

The preparation of a topographic map is only the first stage. To interpret the evidence in social terms means that the function of any structures revealed has next to be established. This involves the study of the major ceremonial and public buildings – temples have a social as well as religious function – and other components of the city, such as areas for specialist craft manufacture, and residential structures. Differences in standards of housing will reveal inequalities between rich and poor and therefore an aspect of the social hierarchy. Quite often, however, the function of large and presumably public buildings is difficult to establish, and there is a temptation to ascribe purposes to them based on guesswork. For instance, the excavator of Knossos on Crete, Sir Arthur Evans, gave names such as "the Queen's Megaron" to some of the rooms there, without any good evidence for the term.

One way to begin studying the city in detail is the intensive sampling of materials from the surface. At Teotihuacan the topographic map (at a scale of 1:2000) was used as the basis for surface sampling on foot. Trained fieldworkers covered the whole site, walking a few meters apart, and collected all the rims, bases, handles, and other special sherds and objects visible to them. The data from Teotihuacan have been processed in an ambitious computer project by George Cowgill. In this way the spatial distribution of specific artifact types can be mapped, and inferences made about the patterns of occupation in different periods.

A stage beyond intensive surface sampling can be the kind of combined surface examination and selective excavation carried out at Tell Abu Salabikh, described in Chapter 3, which revealed the largest area of housing known from any 3rd-millennium BC site in southern Iraq.

Usually, however, excavation on a large scale will be needed for a major center such as a city. Some of the most famous and successful excavations earlier this century have been of this kind, from Mohenjodaro in the Indus Valley in what is now Pakistan to the biblical city of Ur in present-day Iraq.

With luck, the preservation conditions for the last period of occupation will be good. If the site is located in the vicinity of a volcano, this last period may very well be superbly preserved by volcanic ash and lava. Pompeii in southern Italy and Akrotiri on the Greek volcanic island of Thera (Santorini) have been mentioned in earlier chapters as examples of cities buried and preserved for posterity, but there are others: for example, Cuicuilco was the great rival to Teotihuacan in the Valley of Mexico until volcanic eruptions destroyed the city some 2000 years ago. In such extreme circumstances, however, preliminary topographic mapping of the kind just described may not be possible, since structures will be buried too deeply to show up on the surface.

Occupied Sites. The problems are similar, but much more difficult in practice, with continuously urban sites: early centers that remain urban centers to this day and have, therefore, not only a complex stratigraphic succession, but modern buildings on or around the site. For such sites, the approach has to be a longer-term one, taking every opportunity provided by the clearing of a site for new construction, and building up a pattern of finds that eventually take on a coherent shape. This has been very much the story of urban archaeology in Britain and Europe, where Roman and medieval towns are generally buried beneath the remains of modern ones. In a way, this is a kind of sampling, but one where the location from which the sample is taken is not the choice of the research worker but is determined by availability. The

work of the Winchester Research Unit in southern England between 1961 and 1971 is a good example. It was possible, by excavating beside the present cathedral, to trace the history of older structures. Evidence from previous archaeological work, together with the more recent excavations, have provided a good impression of the Roman, Saxon, and medieval towns underlying the present city of Winchester.

The whole issue of salvage or rescue archaeology on sites in cities and elsewhere threatened with destruction is discussed in Chapter 14.

Administration Beyond the Primary Center

Investigation of the mechanisms of organization need not be restricted to the primary, capital center. Outside the main center there may be many clues indicating a centrally organized administration. It is useful, for example, to search for *artifacts of administration*. Perhaps the most obvious of these are the clay sealings found at secondary centers where the redistributive system is administered. Equally useful are other imprints of central authority, such as the imperial seal

Occupied site: Winchester, southern England. (Left) Excavations in progress beside the cathedral. (Above) The complex development of the city up to AD 1400, based on a decade of excavation and many years of post-excavation analysis. Inhabited areas are shown in brown.

in any empire, or royal emblems such as the cartouche (royal name in a distinctive cigar-shaped frame) of an Egyptian pharaoh, or the display of a royal coat of arms. Nor need the existence of a central jurisdiction be indicated by only the actual emblems of power: a Roman milestone on a road, for instance, carries with it the message that it is part of a centrally administered system of imperial highways.

A second approach is to look at *standardization of weights and measures* (see the section on Measuring the World in Chapter 10). Such standardization is found within most centrally administered economic systems. In many cases, the standard units came to be utilized outside the boundaries of the particular state as well.

The existence of a good *road system* is important to the administration of any land-based empire, although less significant for the smaller nation states that could be crossed by an army on foot in the course of a couple of days. The road system within the Roman empire gives one of the clearest indications of central administration, and would do so even if written records were unavailable. (The Inca road network indicates central organization of a society without such records.)

Clear indications of the exercise of military power can give the most direct insight possible into the realities of administration: control of territory often depended heavily on military might. Defensive works on a major scale offer similar insights and mark decisive boundaries. The Great Wall of China, begun in the late 3rd century BC, is perhaps the best-known example.

Administration beyond the primary center: the elaborate road network of the Roman Empire (shown here in about AD 150) gives a clear indication of central administration.

Investigating Social Ranking

The essence of a centralized society and of centralized government are disparities between rich and poor in ownership, access to resources, facilities, and status. The study of social organization in complex societies is thus in large measure the study of social ranking.

Elite Residences. Residential structures can indicate marked differences in status. Large and grandiose buildings, or "palaces," are a feature of many complex societies, and may have housed members of the social elite. The difficulty comes in demonstrating that they actually did so. Among the Maya, for example, recent research has shown that the term "palace" is too general, covering a variety of structures that had different functions. Perhaps the best solution is to combine detailed study of the structure itself (architecture, location of different artifacts) with ethnoarchaeological or ethnohistoric research. David Freidel and Jeremy Sabloff did this successfully in their analysis of the island of Cozumel, off the east coast of Mexico's Yucatán peninsula. Using 16th-century Spanish descriptions of elite residences, they were able to identify architecturally similar structures in the pre-Columbian archaeological record dating to a couple of centuries earlier. Test excavations helped clarify the functions of the buildings.

Great Wealth. The very existence of great wealth, if it can be inferred to have been associated with particular individuals, is a clear indication of high status. For instance, the treasures of the Second City at Troy, unearthed (or so he claimed) by Heinrich Schliemann in 1873, must indicate considerable disparity in the ownership of wealth. The treasure included gold and silver jewelry as well as drinking vessels, and there can be little doubt that it was intended for personal use, perhaps on public occasions.

Depictions of the Elite. Perhaps even more impressive than wealth, however, are actual depictions of persons of high status, whether in sculpture, in relief, in mural decoration, or whatever. The iconography of power is further discussed in Chapter 10, but in many ways this is our most immediate approach to social questions. Although such depictions are not often found, it is not uncommon to find symbolic emblems of authority such as Egyptian cartouches, to which may be added artifacts such as royal scepters or swords.

Burials. Undoubtedly, the most abundant evidence of social ranking in centralized societies, just as in non-

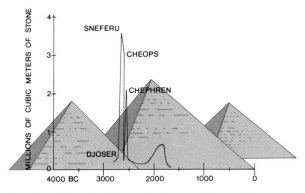

The colossal building effort required to erect the pyramids reflects the centralization of power in the hands of pharaohs such as Djoser, Sneferu, Cheops, and Chephren.

centralized ones, comes from burial, and from the accompanying grave-goods. As discussed in the section on segmentary societies, a profitable approach is to consider the labor input involved in constructing the burial monuments, and the social implications. The largest and most famous such monuments in the world are the pyramids of Egypt, over 80 of which still exist. At the most straightforward level of analysis they represent the conspicuous display of wealth and power of the highest ranking members of Egyptian society: the pharaohs. But fascinating new research by, amongst others, the British archaeologist Barry Kemp and the American archaeologist Mark Lehner is beginning to shed further light on the social and political implications of this colossal expenditure of effort – which involved in the case of the Great Pyramid at Giza the shifting of some 2.3 million limestone blocks each weighing 2.5–15 tons during pharaoh Cheops' 23-year reign (2589–2566 BC). As the accompanying diagram shows, there was a brief period of the most immense pyramid building activity in Egypt, dwarfing what had gone before and what followed. The peak period of this activity indicates the harnessing of huge resources by a highly centralized state. But what happened afterwards? Kemp has argued that the reduction in pyramid building coincides interestingly with a transfer of social and economic resources to the provinces, away from the main area of the pyramids.

The pyramids and other burial monuments are not the only source of information about social organization and ranking in ancient Egypt. Magnificent grave-goods have often been recovered, most spectacularly those belonging to the boy pharaoh Tutankhamun (box, Chapter 2). Nor of course were the ancient Egyptians alone in building monuments for their dead

rulers and burying the richest artifacts with them. In the New World one thinks, for instance, of the Temple of the Inscriptions at Palenque, which held deep within it the tomb of the Maya city's ruler, Lord Pacal, who died in AD 683 and was buried with his superb jade mosaic mask. Major excavations at Copán, Honduras, have likewise recently revealed a splendid Maya noble's tomb beneath the famous Hieroglyphic Stairway there.

In many early civilizations the ultimate power and rank of the dead ruler were emphasized by the ritual killing of royal retainers, who were interred with the monarch. Such funeral rites have been brought to light in the Sumerian Royal Graves at Ur, in modern Iraq, and among the burials of the Shang dynasty at Anyang in China. The huge army of terracotta warriors buried next to the tomb of the first Chinese emperor, Qin Shi Huangdi, represents a development of this practice, where the life-size terracotta figures take the place of members of the real imperial army.

There are many examples too of elite burials among smaller-scale state societies and chiefdoms. One of the most skillfully conducted excavations in western Germany in recent years has been that of a Celtic chieftain's grave at Hochdorf, dating to the 6th century BC, where Jorg Biel painstakingly recovered the col-

Cutaway view of the Temple of the Inscriptions, Palenque, Mexico, showing at the base the hidden burial chamber of Lord Pacal, ruler of this Maya city who died in AD 683, as we know from inscriptions at the site.

SOCIAL ANALYSIS AT MOUNDVILLE

During its heyday in the 14th and 15th centuries AD, Moundville was one of the greatest ceremonial centers of the Mississippian culture in North America. The site takes its name from an impressive group of 20 mounds constructed within a palisaded area, 150 ha (370 acres) in extent, on the banks of the Black Warrior river in west-central Alabama. Moundville was first dug into as long ago as 1840, but major excavations did not take place until this century, in particular by C.B. Moore in 1905 and 1906, and D.L. DeJarnette in the 1930s. More recently Christopher Peebles and his colleagues have combined systematic survey with limited excavation and reanalysis of the earlier work to produce a convincing social study of the site.

***Changing settlement patterns** in the Moundville region. In Phase I Moundville was simply a site with a single mound, like other similar sites in the area. By Phase II, however, it had grown larger, establishing itself as the major regional center. After its heyday in Phase III, Moundville disappeared as a significant site in Phase IV, when the region no longer had a dominant center.*

Peebles and his team first needed a reliable chronology. This was achieved through an analysis of the pottery by Vincas Steponaitis, using in the first instance a seriation study (see Chapter 4) of whole vessels from a sample of burials at the site. The

***Slate palette** from Moundville incised with a hand-and-eye motif within two entwined horned rattlesnakes. Diameter 32 cm.*

resultant relative chronology was then cross-checked with excavated ceramics from known stratigraphic contexts, whose radiocarbon dating helped convert the scheme into an absolute chronology.

Using this framework, it was now possible to study the development of the site through several phases. Preliminary survey of neighboring sites also established the regional settlement pattern for each phase.

Over 3000 burials have been excavated at Moundville, and Peebles

used the technique of cluster analysis (see box above) to group 2053 of them according to social rank. Peebles observed that the small number of people of highest rank (Segment A: classes IA, IB, and II in the pyramidal diagram) were buried in or near the mounds with artifacts exclusive to them, such as copper axes and earspools. Lower-ranking individuals of Segment B (Classes III, IV) had non-mound burials with some grave goods but no copper artifacts, while those of Segment C, buried on the periphery, had few or no grave goods.

Peebles found interesting differences according to age and sex. The 7 individuals in Class IA, the top of the social pyramid, were all adults, probably males. Those of Class IB were adult males and children, while Class II comprised individuals of all ages and both sexes. It seems clear that adult males had the highest status. The presence of children in Class IB suggests that their high status was inherited at birth.

There is much more to say about the work at Moundville. But it should be clear how the various dimensions of information already examined come together to suggest a regional organization with a well-marked hierarchy of sites, controlled by a highly ranked community at Moundville itself – what Peebles terms a chiefdom society.

Phase III at Moundville, AD 1400–1500, when the ceremonial center was at its height.

IA: Copper axes — **IA** — 7 burials in central mounds

IB: Copper earpools, bear teeth, stone discs — **IB** — 43 mound and non-mound burials — **A**

II: Shell beads, copper gorgets, galena — **II** — 67 mound and non-mound burials

III: Effigy vessels, animal bone, shell gorgets — **III** **IV** — Non-mound burials III: 221 IV: 50 — **B**
IV: Discoidals, bone awls, projectile points

V & VIII: Bowls **VI, VII & IX:** Water bottles — **V** **VI** **VII** **VIII** **IX** **X** — Non-mound burials V: 55 VI: 45 VII: 55 VIII:70 IX 46 X:70 — **C**

No grave goods — 1256 burials

Pyramid-shaped social hierarchy at Moundville, based on a cluster analysis of 2053 burials. Artifacts listed against each cluster (Classes I-X) are grave goods.

lapsed remains of a wagon, drinking vessels, and many other grave-goods, including the wheeled bronze couch on which the dead chief lay, covered with gold jewelry from head to foot. The Shaft Graves at Mycenae in Greece and the Anglo-Saxon ship burial at Sutton Hoo in England (box, Chapter 3) represent similar discoveries by earlier generations by archaeologists.

However, all these remarkable burials are of individuals uniquely powerful in their societies. To obtain a more comprehensive picture of a ranked society it is necessary to consider the burial customs of the society as a whole. In many cases, it has proved possible to discover something about the elites that existed at a level below that of the ruler. Research carried out over many years at Moundville, Alabama, is a good example (see box).

There is undoubtedly more scope for useful investigations of social structure through cemetery analysis in ranked societies. Up to now, most sophisticated cemetery studies have been devoted to less centralized societies, as reviewed in a previous section. Cemetery data of the early historic period in the Old World have conventionally been studied with a view to illustrating the existing historical texts, or refining typological schemes as an aid to chronology and the study of art history. Only now is the focus of attention shifting towards studies of disparities in social status.

Investigating Economic Specialization

Centralized societies differ from non-centralized ones in a number of important respects. In general, the more centralized structure allows greater economic specialization, and this in turn brings increased efficiency of production. Centralization is often associated with an increased intensification of farming, for not only do centralized societies normally have higher population densities, but they must also produce enough surplus to support full-time (as opposed to part-time) craft specialists. The greater degree of craft specialization is made possible only by the organizing abilities of a more centralized society, able to manage and promote an increase in agricultural productivity.

Intensified Farming. The initial development of new farming methods for more intensive food production was discussed above in the section on segmentary societies. In centralized societies the process is taken a stage further, with a still greater emphasis on labor-intensive techniques such as plowing. In addition, major public works such as irrigation canals are often undertaken for the first time, made possible by the coercive and organizing powers of a central authority.

Another indicator of growing intensification may be the reorganization of the rural landscape into smaller units, as population increases and the amount of land available for each farmstead diminishes.

Taxation, Storage, and Redistribution. An important indicator of centralized control of a society is the existence of permanent storage facilities for food and goods, which the central authority will draw on periodically to feed, reward, and thus indirectly control its warriors and the local population. It follows that taxes, for instance in the form of produce to replenish state storehouses, will also be found among centralized societies: without them the controlling authority would have no wealth to redistribute. In chiefdom societies "taxation" may take the form of offerings to the chief, but in more complex societies the obligation is generally formalized. Much of a state's bureaucracy will be devoted to the administration of taxation, and

direct indications of bureaucracy, such as recording and accounting systems, in general document it.

A good example of a research project that has helped clarify this interaction of taxation, storage, and redistribution in one part of the world is the work of the American archaeologist, Craig Morris, at the city of Huánuco Pampa, a provincial capital of the Inca empire high up in the Andes. This city, at one time inhabited by some 10,000–15,000 people, had been built from scratch by the Incas as an administrative center on the royal road to Cuzco, the imperial capital. We know from written accounts by early Spanish chroniclers that Inca rulers exacted taxation in the form of labor on state lands and state construction projects, including the building of Huánuco Pampa itself. Many of the goods thus produced were stored in state warehouses – but to what purpose? Close analysis by Morris of a sample of some 20 percent of the more than 500 warehouses at Huánuco, as well as other

Huánuco Pampa, Peru; a provincial capital of the Inca empire. Warehouses at the site (left, the Inca emperor checks warehouse accounts with an official) were used to store state goods that were later redistributed among the populace at public ceremonies held in the central plaza. Analysis of the site by Craig Morris also identified areas set apart for craft specialists, such as a compound where women made clothing and beer.

structures there, suggested that stored potatoes and maize were used primarily to supply the city at this high altitude, where food production was difficult. But the city itself functioned to accommodate highly organized ceremonies in its huge central plaza, during which feasting and ritual maize-beer drinking took place, thus redistributing much of the stored wealth to the local populace. As Morris says, this ceremonial aspect of administration seems to have been very important in early state societies. Sharing of food and drink reinforced the idea that participation in the empire was something more than working in state fields or fighting in a distant war.

Craft Specialists. The increased importance of craft specialists is another indicator of a centralized society that can be identified archaeologically. Full-time craft specialists leave well-defined traces, because each craft has its own particular technology and is generally practiced in a different location within the urban area. Huánuco Pampa again makes a helpful example. Although craft production here was much less developed than in many early cities elsewhere in the world, Morris successfully identified a compound of 50 buildings given over to the making of beer and clothing. Thousands of special ceramic jars and dozens of spindle whorls and weaving implements provided the archaeological clues; the ethnohistoric record linked these with beer and cloth production, more particularly with a special social class of Inca women known as *aklla*, who were kept segregated from the rest of the population. Morris was able to show that the distinctive architecture of the compound – enclosed by a surrounding wall with a single entrance – and the density of occupational refuse suggested the presence of permanently segregated *aklla* craft specialists.

Detailed archaeological research of this kind is being carried out in many parts of the world, particularly into the specialized production of pottery, metal, glass, and lithic materials such as obsidian (all of which are discussed more fully in Chapter 8). The work of the Italian archaeologist, Maurizio Tosi, at the site of Shahr-i-Sokhta in modern Iran is a case in point, providing as it does an impression of the scale of craft specialization and its relationship to the central administration on the Iranian plateau during the 3rd millennium BC. By studying the evidence of craft production in different parts of the site, Tosi showed that some activities (notably textiles and leather-working) were restricted to residential areas, while others (such as stone tool, lapis lazuli and chalcedony working) were strongly represented in specialist workshop areas.

Relationships Between Centralized Societies

External contacts between centralized societies cannot be understood simply in terms of the exchange of goods: they are also social relations. Traditionally, these have been examined, if at all, within the framework of dominance models, where the "influence" of a primary center on outlying secondary areas is considered, often in what has been called the "diffusion" of culture (see Chapter 12). Most interactions between societies, however, take place between neighbors of roughly equal scale and power. These have been termed interactions between peer polities. They need to be more carefully considered than has so far been the case in archaeology. One or two broad headings can be listed here.

The role of *warfare* in early societies needs further investigation. War need not be undertaken with the objective of permanently occupying the lands of the vanquished in a process of territorial expansion. The American archaeologist David Freidel made this point in his study of Maya warfare, based on the wall paintings at the site of Bonampak and deductions from early written sources. According to his somewhat controversial analysis, the function of Maya warfare was not to conquer new territory, and thus enlarge the frontiers of the state, but instead to give Maya rulers the opportunity of capturing kings and princes from neighboring states, many of whom were later offered as sacrifices to the gods. Warfare allowed rulers to re-affirm their royal status: it had a central role in upholding the system of government, but that role was not one of territorial expansion.

Competition is a frequent undertaking between societies, sometimes within a ritual framework. The study of places where games were played, or of certain ceremonial areas, may reveal that many interactions between societies took a competitive form. Such seems to be the case for the ball courts of Mesoamerica and was certainly so for the great Panhellenic games of ancient Greece, of which the Olympic Games were the most famous.

One of the most frequent features accompanying competition is *emulation*, where the customs, buildings, and artifacts employed in one society come to adopt the form of those used in neighboring ones. This proves to be so in almost every area, but these issues of style and symbolic form have scarcely been handled yet by archaeologists. In so far as they involve the use of symbols, and hence a consideration of what people think as much as what they do, they are discussed further in Chapter 10.

SUMMARY

This chapter has shown that a formidable battery of techniques is now available to archaeologists who wish to investigate the social organization of early societies. Only the salient themes have been touched on, but these will have made it clear that the potential for understanding the more complex and highly organized societies represented by states and chiefdoms is especially great. We can investigate these societies through their site hierarchies and, in the case of state societies, through their urban centers. It should be possible to identify the ruling center using archaeological methods alone, and the extent of the area over which it held jurisdiction. The study of the buildings and other evidence of administration at the center gives valuable information about the social, political, and economic organization of society, as well as a picture of the life of the ruling elite. We can identify and analyze their palaces and tombs, and the evidence left by craft specialists working under their direction. Road systems and lower-order administrative centers give further information about the social and political structure. The study of the differences in the treatment accorded to different individuals at death, in both the size and wealth of grave offerings, can reveal the complete range of status distinctions in a society.

As we have seen, similar approaches may be applied to segmentary societies: the study of individual settlements, the evidence for social ranking revealed by burials, and the existence of co-operative communal mechanisms for the construction of major monuments. The small-scale camps of band societies and the seasonal movement between different sites may also be studied using the methods outlined in this chapter, especially when the insights provided by ethnoarchaeological research on living societies are used in conjunction with direct study of the archaeological record.

Further Reading

The following works illustrate some of the ways in which archaeologists attempt to reconstruct social organization:

Binford, L.R. 1983. *In Pursuit of the Past*. Thames & Hudson: London & New York.

Hodder, I. 1982. *Symbols in Action*. Cambridge University Press: Cambridge & New York.

O'Shea, J. 1984. *Mortuary Variability. An Archaeological Investigation*. Academic Press: New York & London.

Renfrew, C. 1984. *Approaches to Social Archaeology*. Edinburgh University Press: Edinburgh.

Renfrew, C. & Cherry, J.F. (eds.). 1986. *Peer Polity Interaction and Sociopolitical Change*. Cambridge University Press: Cambridge & New York.

6
What was the Environment? Environmental Archaeology

Environmental archaeology is now a well-developed discipline in its own right. It views the human animal as part of the natural world, interacting with other species in the ecological system or *ecosystem*. The environment governs human life: latitude and altitude, landforms and climate determine the vegetation, which in turn determines animal life. And all these things taken together determine how and where humans have lived – or at least they did until very recently.

With a few exceptions, little attention was paid by archaeologists to nonartifactual (ecofactual) evidence until recent decades. Sites were studied more or less as self-contained packages of evidence, rather than in their context within the landscape. It is now regarded as important to see sites in their setting, and to consider the geomorphological and biological processes occurring in and around them. The environment is seen now as a variable, not as something which is constant or homogeneous through space and time.

The reconstruction of the environment first requires an answer to very coarse-grade questions of chronology and climate. We need to know when the human activities under study took place in terms of the broad world climatic succession. This then is partly a matter of chronology. A reliable date allows us, for instance, to determine whether the context belongs to a glacial or an interglacial phase, and what the temperature is likely to have been in that part of the globe. Sea-level and other questions will be related to this one.

Finer-grade questions will follow, and these are particularly relevant for all postglacial contexts, after about 10,000 years ago. The archaeologist usually turns then to the evidence of the vegetation at the time. Whether from pollen or from other plant remains, information is gained about the vegetation cover, which also contributes further data about the climate.

The logical next step is to turn to the fauna (animal remains), in the first place to the microfauna, including insects, snails, and rodents, all of which are very sensitive indicators of climatic change. Like some of the plant remains, they are indicators also of the microenvironment – of specific conditions at the site. Some of these conditions, of course, resulted from human activity when people erected structures and otherwise influenced the immediate surroundings to ensure survival and comfort.

Owing to the poor preservation of many forms of evidence, and to the distorted samples we recover, we can never arrive at the "true" facts for past environments. One simply has to aim for the best approximation available. No single method will give an adequate picture – all are distorted in one way or another – and so as many methods as data and funds will allow need to be applied to build up a composite image.

Despite these difficulties, the task of environmental reconstruction is a fundamental one. For if we are to understand how human individuals functioned, and the community of which they formed a part, we have to know first what their world was like.

INVESTIGATING ENVIRONMENTS ON A GLOBAL SCALE

The first step in assessing previous environmental conditions is to look at them globally. Local changes make little sense unless seen against this broader climatic background. Since water covers almost three-quarters of the earth, we should begin by examining evidence about past climates that can be obtained from this area. In the last few decades, thanks to developments in technology and scientific analysis, it has become possible not only to excavate shipwrecks and submerged sites, but also to extract data from the sea bed that are of great value in reconstructing past environments, particularly for earlier periods.

Evidence from the Oceans

The sediments of the ocean floor accumulate very slowly (a few centimeters every thousand years) and in some areas consist primarily of an ooze made up of microfossils such as the shells of planktonic foraminifera – tiny one-celled marine organisms that live in the surface water masses of the oceans and sink to the bottom when they die. As in an archaeological stratigraphy, one can trace changes in environmental conditions through time by studying cores extracted from the sea bed and fluctuations in the species represented and the morphology (physical form) of single species through the sequence (see box opposite).

Thousands of deep-sea cores have now been extracted and studied, and have produced consistent results that form an invaluable complement to data obtained from land (see below). For example, one 21 m (69 ft) core from the Pacific Ocean has given a climatic record of over 2 million years. In the eastern Mediterranean, analysis by Robert Thunell of foraminifera in sediment samples has enabled him to estimate sea-surface temperatures and salinities (salt levels) at different periods. He has established that about 18,000 years ago, at the height of the last Ice Age, the winter temperature was 6°C (43°F) cooler than now, and the summer temperature was 4°C (39°F) cooler. The Aegean Sea was also 5 percent less saline than at present, probably because cool, low-salinity water was being diverted into the Aegean from the large freshwater lakes that then existed over parts of eastern Europe and western Siberia.

In a new development, potentially important but still at an early stage, sea cores are also providing climatic information through the analysis of organic molecules in the sediment. Some of these molecules, and especially the so-called fatty lipids, can remain relatively intact, yielding climatic clues because cells adjust the fatty composition of their lipids according to temperature changes. In cold conditions the proportion of unsaturated lipids in marine organisms increases, with a corresponding rise in saturated lipids in warm conditions. Cores of deep-sea sediment have shown variations in the ratio of saturated to unsaturated fatty lipids through time which, according to the British chemist Simon Brassell and his German colleagues, seem to correlate well with changes in ocean temperature over the last half million years known from the oxygen isotope technique (explained in the sea cores box).

Using a similar technique, cores can also be obtained from stratified ice sheets, and here again the oxygen isotopic composition gives some guide to climatic oscillations. Results from cores in Greenland and the Antarctic (in particular the deep Vostok core covering the last 160,000 years) are consistent with those from deep-sea cores. Moreover, a recent study by Danish and Icelandic glaciologists has shown that the ice at the base of the Greenland ice sheet has not had time to warm up. Its colder temperature is a remnant from the climate during the last Ice Age – the ice sheet thus provides an accurate record of past climatic changes in the Arctic. Calculations based on differences between the expected temperature profile and the actual readings suggest that surface temperatures in the last Ice Age were 12°C (54°F) below those of the present day. By matching the core's temperature profile to computer simulations of different temperature and precipitation (rainfall or snowfall) patterns, the glaciologists concluded that the Ice Age was drier as well as colder than now, with snowfall about half that of the area today.

Ancient Winds. Isotopes can thus be used not merely for temperature studies but also for data on precipitation. And since it is the temperature differences between the equatorial and polar regions that largely determine the storminess of our weather, isotope studies can even tell us something about winds in different periods. As air moves from low latitudes to colder regions, the water it loses as rain or snow is enriched in the stable isotope oxygen 18 with respect to the remaining vapor which becomes correspondingly richer in the other stable isotope of oxygen, oxygen 16. Thus from the ratio between the two isotopes in precipitation at a particular place, one can calculate the temperature difference between that place and the equatorial region.

Using this technique, the changing ratios found over the last 100,000 years in ice cores from Greenland and the Antarctic have been studied. The results show that during glacial periods the temperature difference between equatorial and polar regions increased by 20–25 percent, and thus wind circulation must have been far more violent. Confirmation has come from a deep-sea core off the coast of West Africa, analysis of which led to estimates of wind strength over the last 700,000 years. Apparently wind "vigor" was greater by a factor of two during each glacial episode than at the present; and wind speeds were 50 percent greater during glacial than interglacial phases. In the future, analysis of the minute plant debris in these cores may also add to the history of wind patterns.

Why should archaeologists be interested in ancient winds? The answer is that winds can have a great impact on human activity. For example, it is thought

The stratigraphy of sediment on the ocean floor is obtained from cores taken out of the sea bed. Ships use a "piston-corer" to extract a thin column of sediment, usually about 10–30 m (33–98 ft) in length. The core can then be analyzed in the laboratory.

Dates for the different layers in the core are obtained by radiocarbon, paleomagnetism, or the uranium series method (Chapter 4). Changing environmental conditions in the past are then deduced by two kinds of tests on microscopic fossils of tiny one-

Microscopic fossils of the foraminiferan species Globorotalia truncatulinoides, which coils to the left during cold periods and to the right during warm ones.

celled organisms called foraminifera found in the sediment. First, scientists study the simple presence, absence, and fluctuations of different foraminiferan species. Second, they analyze, by mass spectrometer, fluctuations in the ratio of the stable oxygen isotopes 18 and 16 in the calcium carbonate of the foraminiferan shells. Variations discernible by these two tests reflect not simply changes in temperature, but also oscillations in the continental glaciers. For example, as the glaciers grew, water was drawn up into them, reducing sea levels and increasing the density and salinity of the oceans, and thus causing changes

RECONSTRUCTING CLIMATES FROM SEA AND ICE CORES

Three climate records compared. Left to right: proportions of different shell species in a deep sea core; ratio of oxygen 18 to oxygen 16 in shells from a deep sea core; and oxygen ratios from an ice core. The resemblance of the three records is good evidence that long-term climatic variation has been worldwide.

in the depths at which certain foraminiferan species lived. At the same time the proportion of oxygen 18 in seawater increased. When the glaciers melted during periods of warmer climate, the proportion of oxygen 18 decreased.

A similar technique can be used to extract cores from present-day ice sheets in Greenland and Antarctica. Here, too, variations in oxygen isotopic composition at different depths of the cores provide some indication of past changes in climate. These results coincide well with those from the deep-sea cores.

that increased storminess may have caused the Vikings to abandon their North Atlantic sea route at the onset of a cold period. Similarly, some of the great Polynesian migrations in the southwestern Pacific during the 12th and 13th centuries AD seem to have coincided with the onset of a short period of slightly warmer weather, when violent storms would have been rare. These migrations were brought to an end a few centuries later by the Little Ice Age, which may have caused a sharp increase in the frequency of storms. Had the Polynesians been able to continue, they would probably have gone on from New Zealand to colonize Tasmania and Australia.

Ancient Coastlines

Ancient life at sea is certainly of archaeological interest, but information on past climates is primarily of relevance to archaeology because of what it tells us about the effects on the land, and on the resources that people needed to survive. The most crucial effect of climate was on the sheer quantity of land available in each period, measurable by studying ancient coast-lines. These have changed constantly through time, even in relatively recent periods, as can be seen from the Neolithic stone circle of Er Lannic, Brittany, which now lies half submerged on an island (once an inland hill in the Neolithic), or medieval villages in east Yorkshire, England, that have tumbled into the sea in the last few centuries as the North Sea gnaws its way westward and erodes the cliffs. Conversely, silts deposited by rivers sometimes push the sea farther back, creating new land, as at Ephesus in western Turkey, a port on the coast in Roman times but today some 5 km (3 miles) inland.

Nevertheless, for archaeologists concerned with the long periods of time of the Paleolithic epoch there are variations in coastlines of much greater magnitude to consider. The expansion and contraction of the con-tinental glaciers, mentioned above, caused huge and uneven rises and falls in sea levels worldwide. When the ice sheets grew, sea level would drop as water became locked up in the glaciers; when the ice melted, sea level would rise again. Falls in sea level often exposed a number of important *land bridges*, such as those linking Alaska to northeast Asia, and Britain to northwest Europe, a phenomenon with far-reaching effects not only on human colonization of the globe, but also on the environment as a whole – the flora and fauna of isolated or insular areas were radically and often irreversibly affected. Between Alaska and Asia today there lies the Bering Strait, which is so shallow

that a fall in sea level of only 46 m (150 ft) would turn it into a land bridge. When the ice sheets were at their greatest extent some 18,000 years ago (the "glacial maximum"), it is thought that the fall here was about 120 m (395 ft), which therefore created not merely a bridge but a vast plain, 1000 km from north to south, which has been called Beringia. The existence of Beringia (and the extent to which it could have supported human life) is one of the crucial pieces of evidence in the continuing debate about the likely route and date of human colonization of the New World (see Chapter 11).

The assessment of past rises and falls in sea level requires study of submerged land surfaces off the coast and of raised or elevated beaches on land. Raised beaches are remnants of former coastlines at higher levels relative to the present shoreline and visible, for instance, along the California coast north of San Francisco. The height of a raised beach above the present shoreline, however, does not generally give a straightforward indication of the height of a former sea level. In the majority of cases, the beaches lie at a higher level because the land has literally been raised up through *isostatic uplift* or *tectonic movements*. Isostatic uplift of the land occurs when the weight of ice is removed as temperatures rise as at the end of an ice age; it has affected coastlines for example in Scandinavia, Scotland, Alaska, and Newfoundland during the postglacial. Tectonic movements involve displacements in the plates that make up the earth's

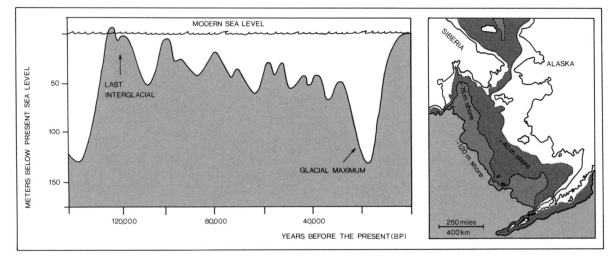

Sea levels and land bridges. (Left) Fluctuations in world sea levels over the last 140,000 years, based on evidence from uplifted coral reefs of the Huon Peninsula, New Guinea, correlated with the oxygen isotope record in deep-sea sediments (see p.200). (Right) Falls in sea level created a land bridge between Siberia and Alaska known as Beringia. At the coldest period of the last glaciation ("glacial maximum"), some 18,000 years ago, the fall was as much as 120 m.

Raised beaches along the California coast north of San Francisco. Such beaches usually lie at a higher level because of isostatic uplift of the land (see right).

crust; Middle and Late Pleistocene raised beaches in the Mediterranean are one instance of such movements. The interpretation of raised beaches in connection with past sea levels thus requires specialist expertise. For archaeologists they are equally if not more important as locations where early coastal sites may be readily accessible; coastal sites in more stable or subsiding areas will have been drowned by the rise in sea level.

In addition to the major importance of isostatic uplift and tectonic movements we may note in passing that volcanic eruptions can occasionally affect coastlines. It is thanks to the eruption of AD 79, for example, that the once coastal resorts of Pompeii and Herculaneum now lie some 1.5 km (0.9 miles) from the sea, their former shorelines buried under volcanic lava and mud.

Tracing Submerged Land Surfaces. The topography of submerged coastal plains can be traced offshore by echo-sounding or the closely related technique of seismic reflection profiling, which in water depths of over 100 m (330 ft) can achieve penetration of more than 10 m (33 ft) into the sea floor. Such acoustic devices are analogous to those used in locating sites (Chapter 3). Using these techniques in the bay in front of the important prehistoric site of Franchthi Cave, Greece, geomorphologists Tjeerd van Andel and Niko-laos Lianos found that the bay's central shelf is flat, with a series of small scarps (past shoreline positions) at various depths down to one at 118–120 m (387–394 ft) that marks the late glacial shoreline. From this survey it has been possible to reconstruct the coastline for the whole of the sequence represented by the cave's prehistoric occupation (23,000–5000 years ago). As will be seen later (Elands Bay Cave box), this kind of reconstruction also enables one to understand changes in the exploitation of marine resources, and to assess the marine molluscs that would have been available for food and ornamentation at different periods by

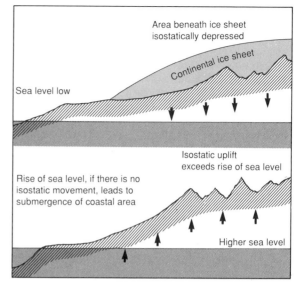

(Above) Principles of isostatic uplift. When sea levels are low and water is locked up in continental glaciers, land beneath the ice sheets is depressed by the weight of the ice. When the glaciers melt, sea level rises, but so too does the land in areas where once it was depressed.

(Below) Franchthi Cave, Greece. By plotting sea floor depths near Franchthi, and correlating these with known sea level fluctuations (see diagram, opposite page), van Andel and his colleagues produced this map of local changes in coastline.

seeing what is present in a range of environments in the Franchthi area today. The lack of seashells in the cave's deposits before 11,000 years ago reflects the distance to the shore at that time. Subsequently, the coast gradually approached the site, and shells accordingly become common in the occupation deposits. During the rise in sea level at the end of the Ice Age, almost half a kilometer of land would have been drowned every millennium, while after 8000 years ago this would have slowed to less than 100 m (330 ft) every millennium. At present, Franchthi is only a few meters from the sea.

Raised Beaches and Middens. Raised beaches often consist of areas of sand, pebbles, or dunes, sometimes containing seashells or middens comprising shells and bones of marine animals used by humans. Indeed, the location of middens can be an accurate indicator of earlier coastlines. In Tokyo Bay, for example, shell mounds of the Jomon period (dated by radiocarbon) mark the position of the shoreline at a time of maximum inundation by the sea (6500–5500 years ago), when, through tectonic movement, the sea was 3–5 m (10 ft–16 ft 5 in) higher in relation to the contemporary landmass of Japan than at present. Analysis of the shells themselves by Hiroko Koike confirms the changes in marine topography, for it is only during this "maximum phase" that subtropical species of mollusc are present, indicating a higher water temperature.

Occasionally, beaches may occur not in a vertical but in a horizontal stratigraphy. At Cape Krusenstern, Alaska, a series of 114 minor relic beach terraces, up to 13 km (8 miles) long, form a peninsula extending into the Chukchi Sea. In 1958, American archaeologist J. Louis Giddings began work here, and his excavations beneath the frozen sod that now covers these ridges revealed settlements and burials dating from prehistoric to historic times. He found that people had abandoned successive beaches as the changing ocean conditions caused a new one to be formed in front of the old. The modern shoreline is Beach 1, and the oldest dune ridge (no. 114) is now about 4.8 km (3 miles) inland. In this way, six millennia of local occupation are stratified horizontally, with 19th-century AD occupation on Beach 1, Western Thule material (c.AD 1000) about five beaches inland, Ipiutak material (2000–1500 years ago) around Beach 35, an Old Whaling Culture village (c. 3700 years ago) at Beach 53, and so on.

Coral Reefs. In tropical areas, fossil coral reefs provide evidence similar to that of raised beaches. Since coral grows in the upper part of the water, and extends more or less up to sea level, it indicates the position of previous shorelines, and its organisms give information on the local marine environment. For example, the Huon Peninsula, on the northeast coast of Papua New Guinea, has a spectacular shoreline sequence, comprising a stepped series of raised coral terraces produced by an upward tilting of the coast together with falling sea levels during cold glacial periods. The scientists J. M. A. Chappell, Arthur Bloom and others studied more than 20 reef complexes on the Huon Peninsula dating back over 250,000 years and calculated the sea level at different periods – for instance, 125,000 years ago it was 6 m (20 ft) higher than at present, 82,000 years ago it was 13 m (43 ft) lower, and 28,000 years ago it was 41 m (134 ft) lower. Measurements of oxygen isotopes provide complementary information on glacial expansion and contraction. The New Guinea results have been found to be in substantial agreement with those from similar formations in Haiti and Barbados.

Rock Art and Shorelines. One interesting technique, useful not so much for accurate shoreline data as for clear indications of change in coastal environments, is the study of rock art devised by George Chaloupka for northern Australia. As the sea rose, it caused changes in the local plants and animals, which in turn produced modifications in technology, all of which seem to be reflected in the region's art. The deduced variations in sea level are themselves important in providing a date for the art.

Chaloupka's Pre-Estuarine period, broadly coinciding with the height of the last glaciation, depicts non-marine species including several that have been interpreted as animals now extinct. In the Estuarine period (starting 6000 or 7000 years ago, by which time the postglacial rise in sea level had ceased) one finds images of new species such as the barramundi (giant perch) and the saltwater crocodile, whose presence

Barramundi (giant perch) and saltwater crocodile depicted in northern Australian rock art.

can be explained by encroaching seawater that had partially filled the shallow valleys and creeks, creating a salt-marsh environment. Contemporaneously, other species, such as small marsupials, that had once occupied the pre-estuarine plains now moved further inland and disappeared from the coastal art, as did the boomerang, the human weapon used to hunt them. Finally, the Freshwater period (about 1000 years ago) brought another great environmental change when freshwater wetlands developed, supporting species of waterfowl and new food plants such as lilies and wild rice, all of which were depicted in the rock art.

All these sources of evidence – submerged land surfaces, raised beaches, coral reefs, rock art – give us an impressive amount of information about ancient coastlines. But it should be realized that most of this information applies to particular regions only: correlating the evidence over wider areas is difficult, because the dates lack consistency, and there are serious discrepancies in sea-level data worldwide.

This is a common problem in paleoclimatic studies: events do not always happen at the same moment in all areas. Nevertheless attempts have been made at producing paleoclimatic data for the world; one major example is the CLIMAP project, which has published maps showing sea-surface temperatures in different parts of the globe at various periods, based on results from many of the techniques mentioned here.

STUDYING THE LANDSCAPE

Having assessed roughly how much land was available for human occupation in different periods, we should now turn to methods for determining the effects of changing climate on the terrain itself.

Today it would be unthinkable to study any site without a thorough investigation of its sediments and the surrounding landscape. The aim is to achieve the fullest possible reconstruction of the local area (terrain, permanent or periodic availability of water, groundwater conditions, susceptibility to flooding, etc.) and set it in the context of the region, so that one can assess the environment faced by the site's inhabitants in different periods – and also gain some idea of the possible loss of sites through erosion, burial under sediment, or inundation.

Moreover, it is vital to know what happened to a landscape before one can begin to speculate about the possible reasons why it changed and how people adapted to the new conditions. Much of this work is best left to the earth scientist, but in the last few years a number of specialists have urged archaeologists to try to master some of these techniques themselves. Certain major changes in landscape are obvious even to the layman – for example, in cases where former irrigation channels can be seen in areas that are now desert; where well shafts are now exposed above ground through massive erosion of the surrounding sediment; or where volcanic eruptions have covered the land with layers of ash or lava.

Glaciated Landscapes

Some of the most dramatic and extensive effects of global climatic change on landscape were produced by the formation of glaciers. Study of the movements and extent of ancient glaciers rests on the traces they have left behind in areas such as the Great Lakes region in North America, and the Alps and the Pyrenees in Europe. Here one can see the characteristic U-shaped valleys, polished and striated rocks, and, at the limits of the glacier expansion, the so-called moraine deposits that often contain rocks foreign to the area but carried in by the ice (known as glacial erratics). In some areas the final glaciation obscured traces of its predecessors.

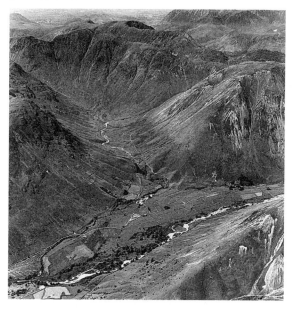

Glaciated landscape: formerly glaciated valleys at Wasdale Head, Cumbria, northern England. The U-shaped valley in the middle distance is a typical glacial feature.

Glaciers today: like great rivers of ice, two glaciers in Alaska are seen converging and joining into one stream, with so-called moraine deposits at their edges that carry forward rocks and other debris.

Examples of Ice Age glacial phenomena are readily observable in regions with glaciers today, such as Alaska and Switzerland, while the richness of modern periglacial areas (where part of the ground is permanently frozen in a permafrost layer) gives some idea of the potential resources in the regions at the edge of the ancient glaciers. The distribution of periglacial phenomena such as fossil ice wedges can be a guide to past conditions, since a mean annual temperature of –6°C to –9°C (21.2°F to 15.8°F) is required for ice wedges to form: they are caused when the ground freezes and contracts, opening up fissures in the permafrost that fill with the wedges of ice. The fossil wedges are proof of a past cooling of climate and of the depth of permafrost.

Varves

Among the most valuable periglacial phenomena for paleoclimatic information are varves, discussed as a method of dating in Chapter 4. Deep lakes around the edges of the Scandinavian glaciers received annual layers of sediment deposited after the spring thaw. Thick layers represent warm years with increased glacial melt, thin layers indicate cold conditions. As well as providing dating evidence, the varves often contain pollen which, as will be seen below, complements the climatic information inherent in the sediment. Unfortunately varves are of limited use outside Scandinavia, since most lakes are shallow, and their sediments can be disturbed, and new varves created by other factors such as violent storms.

Rivers

So much for frozen water and stationary water: but what are the effects of *flowing* water on the landscape? The reconstruction of past landscapes around major rivers – which tend to be areas of rapid change, through erosion or deposition of sediments along courses and at river mouths – is particularly valuable to archaeology because these environments were frequently the focus of human occupation. In certain cases, such as the Nile, Tigris-Euphrates, and Indus, the floodplains proved crucial to the rise of irrigation agriculture and urban civilization.

Many rivers actually changed their course at different periods, through complex processes of erosion, silting, and varying gradients. The channel of the Indus in modern Pakistan is not incised into the plain like those of most rivers, and therefore has a tendency to change its course from time to time. The lower Indus is shallow, with a gentle gradient, and thus deposits large quantities of alluvial material in its channel, actually raising its bed above the level of the surrounding plain, and frequently breaking out and inundating large areas with fertile silt, vital to early agriculture and, for example, the ancient city of Mohenjodaro.

Similarly, the lower Mississippi Valley is covered with the traces of meander changes over a long period. These abandoned channels have been detected and plotted, by topographic survey and aerial photography (Chapter 3), for the period AD 1765–1940. Using this information, a pattern of meander changes plotted at 100-year intervals has been constructed for the last 2000 years. Like the work on fossil beach lines in Alaska (see above), this sequence has formed the basis for a rough chronology for sites located along particular abandoned channels.

Aerial view of the deeply cut meander of the Colorado river, Utah. In some regions, abandoned meander channels have been used to build up a local chronology.

Cave Sites

A different type of abandoned water-channel is represented by the limestone cave, a category of site that has been of tremendous importance to archaeology through its conservation of a wide variety of evidence, not only about human activities but also about local climate and environment (see box overleaf).

Caves and rockshelters, although of enormous archaeological interest, are nevertheless special cases. Their importance as places of habitation has always been exaggerated in prehistoric studies at the expense of less well-preserved open sites. What can we learn from the great outdoors where people have spent most of their time?

Sediments and Soils

Investigation of sediments (the global term for material deposited on the earth's surface) and soils (the life-supporting, biologically weathered upper layers of those sediments) can reveal much about the conditions that prevailed when they were formed. The organic remains they may contain will be examined in subsequent sections on plants and animals, but the soil matrix itself yields a wealth of information on weathering, and hence on past climates. Geomorphology (the study of the form and development of the landscape) incorporates specializations such as sedimentology, which itself includes sedimentary petrography and granulometry. These combine to produce a detailed analysis of the composition and texture of sediments, ranging from freely-draining gravel and sand to water-retentive clay; the size of constituent particles in sediments, ranging from pebbles to sand or silt; and the degree of consolidation, ranging from loose to cemented. In some cases, the orientation of the pebbles gives some indication of the direction of stream-flow, of slope, or of glacial deposits. As we will see in Chapters 8 and 9, the X-ray diffraction technique can be used to identify specific clay minerals and thus the specific source from which a sediment is derived.

A growing number of archaeologists have gained sufficient field experience to undertake a basic assessment of sediments in the field – simply by rubbing a little of the dry sediment between their fingers, and then testing its plasticity by making it damp and rolling it in the palm. A primary classification can be made according to degree of friability or stickiness, and whether the sediment leaves a stain on the hand. Soil texture of this kind provides a basis for assessing landscape history and land-use potential. However, for a more accurate assessment the expertise of a specialist

is essential. Accurate and standardized descriptions of soil color are also vital, and are usually accomplished by means of the widely adopted Munsell Soil Color Charts (also used for describing archaeological layers).

Accurate analysis of the texture of a loose soil entails the use of a series of screens or sieves, with mesh sizes decreasing from *c.* 6 mm to 0.06 mm (0.2–0.002 in), in order to separate the different classes of particles. For really fine particles, wet sieving may also be necessary. However, where the sediment is cemented, it is necessary for the specialist to obtain thin-sections for microscopic analysis, as is mentioned for cave sediments (see box overleaf).

One technique for close study of sediments, developed before World War II, involved the application of a film of rubber or 'lacquer' to the stratigraphy, but modern materials have improved the method enormously. At the open-air Upper Paleolithic camp of Pincevent, near Paris, Michel Orliac has used a thin film of synthetic latex (about 1.5 kg per sq. m, 0.3 lb per sq. ft) painted onto a flat, carefully cleaned section. When dry, the latex preserves an image of the stratigraphy that is far easier than the original to

Studying sediments: at Pincevent, France, a film of latex was painted on to a stratigraphic section and peeled off when dry, with an image of the soil profile attached.

CAVE SEDIMENTS

The sediments that make up the floors of caves are composed of material brought in through entrances and holes in the roof by wind, water, animals, and people. A section through a cave or rockshelter floor usually shows a number of layers, often of differing textures and colors. The contents of these layers can indicate changing temperatures through time. For example, the percolation of water can loosen and break off rounded lumps from wall and roof, a type of weathering associated with a mild, humid climate. In cold conditions, water in rock fissures turns to ice, and this increase in volume puts pressure on the surface rock layer, which can disintegrate into angular, sharp-edged fragments, *c.* 4–10 cm (1½–4 in) long. Thus, after repeated phases of thawing and freezing, alternating layers of rounded and angular fragments ("rock spalls") will be produced near cave entrances and in rockshelters.

Although there are other potential causes of rubble layers, such as earthquakes, or attack by microbes, it is generally accepted that a study of changes in rubble size can provide information on environmental fluctuations. For example, in Cave Bay Cave, Tasmania, the Australian archaeologist Sandra Bowdler attributed the great accumulation of angular roof detritus between 18,000 and 15,000 years ago to the effects of frost wedging at the height of the last glacial. At the shallow cave of Colless Creek shelter, in tropical Queensland, on the other hand, the marked changes in sediments detectable through the 20 millennia of occupation seem to have been caused by fluctuations in rainfall. The Colless Creek sediments were studied in thin sections under the microscope for micromorphological differences; the lower layers (before

General and detailed sections of a hypothetical cave site.

18,000 years ago) were compacted, and had clearly been modified by the movement of water, which suggested a wetter climate.

Analysis in Practice
In general, analysis is carried out initially by visual examination. Samples need to be taken from several parts of the cave, in view of the microclimates and horizontal variation (e.g. the presence of a large hearth may have had considerable influence on a wall's

temperature in some periods). It is often hard to correlate sequences from within a single cave, let alone between caves and regions. Subsequent sieving and laboratory examination of grain size, and of color and texture of sediment, modifies or amplifies the initial assessment. Usually all blocks over 100 mm (4 in) are noted and removed; then the remainder is passed through a series of sieves and differentiated into blocks, granules, gravel, and sand/silt/clay. The more blocks and granules there are in a layer, the more severe the cold in that period.

Scholars such as the French archaeologist Yves Guillien have stressed that it is necessary to do experiments on a cave's limestone before attempting to interpret the fill. Laboratory simulation of the natural freeze/thaw successions gives one some idea of the rock's friability under the kind of climatic conditions that caused the real breakage.

Stalagmites and Stalactites

Caves often have layers of stalagmite, and of flowstone (travertine), laid down by water that picks up calcium carbonate in solution as it passes through limestone. Such layers are generally indicative of fairly temperate climatic phases, and sometimes also of humid conditions. Stalagmites and stalactites (collectively known as speleothems) can even be used for accurate assessment of past climate through the oxygen isotope technique. In cross-section, speleothems have a series of concentric growth rings, which can be dated by radiocarbon. Each ring preserves the oxygen isotope composition of the water that formed it, and hence of the average atmospheric precipitation and temperature at which it was deposited. Since the ultimate source of rainwater is the surface of the ocean, this method is a potentially valuable complement to ocean cores.

Scientists in New Zealand have drilled samples out of speleothems at Waitomo, North Island, and found that ocean temperature at the height of the last glaciation was 4° or 5°C lower than at present. They also found that there were more recent fluctuations, with warmer phases in the 14th and 16th centuries AD, and colder phases in the 15th and 17th centuries.

Since the rate of calcium carbonate deposition per square centimeter on speleothems can be much faster than the deposition of sediment on the ocean bed, this method may achieve more detailed temperature profiles than ocean cores: in fact, it is thought that temperature changes of only 0.2°C may be detectable.

examine in detail. Indeed, the imprint, composed of a very thin film of sediment that adheres to the latex, reveals much more than can be distinguished in the original section. Penetration of the latex into different layers according to their porosity brings out tiny contrasts in granulometry, and permeable layers appear darker than impermeable ones on the imprint. After it has been peeled off, the imprint can be stored flat or rolled up, and thus enables the archaeologist to keep or display a faithful record of a soil profile.

Analyses of sediments can provide data on processes of deposition and erosion in the past. For example, the way in which sediments have eroded from hillslopes down into valley bottoms has been widely studied in Mediterranean countries, where the process caused shifts in settlement. Hillside farms were abandoned in the face of soil loss, while settlement increased in valley bottoms. Sediment analyses suggest that misuse of the landscape in some Mediterranean areas dates back five millennia, to at least the Early Bronze Age. In Cyprus, for instance, a combination of deforestation, intensive agriculture, and pastoralism destabilized the fragile soil-cover on hillslopes in the Early Bronze Age

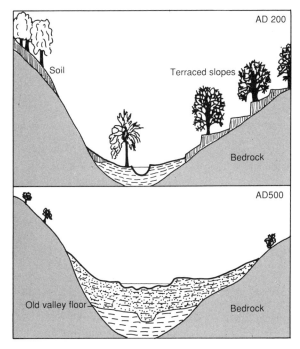

Sediments, erosion, and changing patterns of settlement. A typical Italian valley during the Roman period suffered erosion of hillslope soils under the combined effects of deforestation, intensive agriculture, and overgrazing. Human settlement eventually shifted from hillside to valley bottom.

and led to rapid infilling of sediment along coastal valleys. In the southern Argolid, Greece, a major project conducted by Tjeerd van Andel, Curtis Runnels, and their colleagues has revealed at least four phases of settlement, erosion, and abandonment between 2000 BC and the Middle Ages. At times here, careless land clearance seems to have been to blame, without suitable conservation measures; and on other occasions it was the partial abandonment or neglect of terracing, and hence of soil conservation, that led to soil erosion.

Loess Sediments. A pedologist (soil specialist) can examine a sediment profile, and from its composition and its changing textures and colors can tell whether it was laid down by water, wind, or human action, and can obtain some idea of the weathering it has undergone, and hence of the climatic conditions that existed locally throughout its history. One important wind-blown sediment often encountered in certain parts of the world is loess, a yellowish dust of silt-sized particles blown in by the wind and redeposited on land newly deglaciated or on sheltered areas. Loess has been found on about 10 percent of the world's land surface, in Alaska, the Mississippi and Ohio valleys, in northwest and central Europe, and particularly in China, where it covers over 440,000 sq. km (170,000 sq. miles) or about 40 percent of arable land there. It is important to the Paleolithic specialist as an indicator of ancient climate, while all students of Neolithic farming learn to associate it with the first agricultural settlements.

Loess works as a climatic indicator because it was only deposited during periods of relatively cold, dry climate when the fine silt particles were blown off a periglacial steppe-like landscape, with little vegetation or moisture to consolidate the sediment. The loess "rain" stopped in warmer and wetter conditions. Sediment sections taken in areas such as central Europe therefore show loess layers alternating with so-called "forest soils," themselves indicators of climatic improvement and the temporary return of vegetation.

Classic sequences of this kind are known at Paudorf and Göttweig in Austria, the former giving its name to the Paudorf Loess Formation (27,000–23,000 years ago) associated with the famous Upper Paleolithic open-air sites of Dolní Věstonice and Pavlov in Czechoslovakia. Similarly, in the Paris Basin, François Bordes established a Pleistocene sequence of alternating loess and warmer, more humid levels, associated with different Paleolithic industries, which could be correlated with the known glacial sequence. Recent studies of the climatic oscillations detectable in the extensive sequence available from China have shown a good correlation with the fluctuations of cold-water foraminifera and the oxygen isotope record from deep-sea sediments.

As well as being a good indicator of ancient climate (often containing land snails that provide confirmatory data), loess also played a crucial role in Neolithic farming. Rich in minerals, uniform in structure, and well drained, soils formed in loess provided fertile and easily worked land ideal for the simple technology of the first farming communities. The Linearbandkeramik (LBK, i.e. Early Neolithic) sites of central and western Europe have an extremely close association with soils formed in loess: at least 70 percent of LBK sites in a given area are found to be located on loess.

Buried Land Surfaces. Entire land surfaces can sometimes be preserved intact beneath certain kinds of sediment. For example, ancient soils and landscapes have been discovered beneath the peat of the English Fenlands, while at Behy in Ireland a Neolithic farming landscape with stone-built banks has emerged from the peat. We shall return to the subject of buried land surfaces below (evidence for plowing section).

By far the most spectacular occurrences of this type are those brought about by volcanic eruptions. The buried cities of Pompeii and Herculaneum in southern Italy, and Akrotiri on the Greek island of Thera, have been referred to in earlier chapters. But, from the point of view of environmental data, volcanically preserved natural landscapes are even more revealing. In 1984, the remains of a prehistoric forest were found at Miesenheim, western Germany. It was already known

Prehistoric trees and other plant material preserved in a waterlogged layer by a volcanic ash fall some 11,000 years ago at Miesenheim, western Germany. Rare finds such as this give important insights into the character of ancient landscapes.

that an eruption about 11,000 years ago had buried the nearby late Upper Paleolithic open-air sites of Gönnersdorf and Andernach under several meters of ash, but the discovery of a contemporaneous forest was a special bonus for the archaeologists. Trees (including willow), mosses, and fungi had been preserved by the ash in a waterlogged layer, 30 cm (11.8 in) thick; mollusc shells, large and small mammals, and even a bird's egg were also present. The forest seems to have been relatively dense, with a thick undergrowth, and this was confirmed by pollen analysis (see box below); study of the tree-rings will also add information on climatic fluctuations in this period.

Tree-Rings and Climate

Tree-rings, like varves (see above), have a growth that varies with the climate, being strong in the spring and then declining to nothing in the winter; the more moisture available, the wider the annual ring. As we saw in Chapter 4, these variations in ring width have formed the basis of a major dating technique. However, study of a particular set of rings can also reveal important environmental data, for example whether growth was slow (implying dense local forest cover) or fast (implying light forest). Tree growth is complex, and many other external and internal factors may affect it, but temperature and soil moisture do tend to be dominant.

The study of tree-rings and climate (dendroclimatology) has also progressed by using X-ray measurements of cell-size and density as an indication of environmental productivity. More recently, ancient temperatures have been derived from tree-rings by means of the stable carbon isotope ($^{13}C/^{12}C$) ratios preserved in their cellulose. A 1000-year-old kauri tree in New Zealand has been analyzed in this way, and the results correlated quite well with those spanning the same period obtained from New Zealand stalagmites and stalactites (see box on caves, above) – i.e., a series of fluctuations in mean annual temperature, with the warmest phase in the 14th century, followed by a decline and then a recovery to present conditions.

The importance of tree-rings makes it clear that it is organic remains above all that provide the richest source of evidence for environmental reconstruction. We must now take a detailed look at the surviving traces of plants and animals.

RECONSTRUCTING THE PLANT ENVIRONMENT

Our prime environmental interest in plant studies is to try to reconstruct the vegetation that people in the past will have encountered at a particular time and in a particular place. But we should not forget that plants lie at the base of the terrestrial food chain. The plant communities of a given area and period will therefore provide clues to local animal and human life, and will also reflect soil conditions and climate. Some types of vegetation react relatively quickly to changes in climate (though less quickly than insects, for instance), and the shifts of plant communities in both latitude and altitude are among the clearest indicators of climatic changes during the Ice Age.

Plant studies in archaeology have always been overshadowed by faunal analysis, simply because bones are more conspicuous than plant remains in excavation. Bones may sometimes survive better, but usually plant remains are present in greater numbers than bones. In the last few decades plants have at last come to the fore, thanks to the discovery that some of their constituent parts are much more resistant to decomposition than was believed, and that in fact a huge amount of varied data survives which can tell us something about long-dead vegetation. As with so many of the specializations on which archaeology can

call, these painstaking analyses require a great deal of time and funds.

Some of the most informative techniques for making an overall assessment of plant communities in a particular period involve analysis not of the biggest remains but of the tiniest, especially pollen.

Microbotanical Remains

Pollen Analysis. Palynology, or the study of pollen grains (see box overleaf), was developed by a Swedish botanist, Lennart von Post, at the beginning of the century. It has proved invaluable to archaeology, since it can be applied to a wide range of sites and provides information on chronology as well as environment – indeed, until the arrival of isotopic chronological methods, pollen analysis was used primarily for dating purposes (Chapter 4).

While palynology cannot produce an exact picture of past environments, it does give some idea of fluctuations in vegetation through time, whatever their causes may be, which can be compared with results from other methods. The best known application of pollen analysis is for the postglacial or Holocene epoch (after 12,000 years ago), for which palynologists have

POLLEN ANALYSIS

All hayfever sufferers will be aware of the pollen "rain" that can afflict them in the spring and summer. Pollen grains – the tiny male reproductive bodies of flowering plants – have an almost indestructible outer shell (exine) that can survive in certain sediments for tens of thousands of years. In pollen analysis the exines are extracted from the soil, studied under the microscope, and identified according to the distinctive exine shape and surface ornamentation of different families and genera of plants. Once quantified, these identifications are plotted as curves on a pollen diagram. Fluctuations in the curve for each plant category may then be studied for signs of climatic fluctuation, or forest clearance and crop-planting by humans.

Preservation

The most favorable sediments for preservation of pollen are acidic and poorly aerated peat bogs and lake beds, where bacterial activity is impeded and grains undergo rapid burial. Cave sediments are also usually suitable because of their humidity and constant temperature. Other contexts, such as sandy sediments or open sites exposed to weathering, preserve pollen poorly.

In wet sites, or unexcavated areas, samples are extracted in long cores, but in dry sites a series of separate samples can be removed from the sections. On an archaeological excavation, small samples are usually extracted at regular stratified intervals. Great care must be taken to avoid contamination from the tools used or from the atmosphere. Pollen can also be found in mud bricks, vessels, tombs, mummy wrappings, the guts of preserved bodies, coprolites (Chapter 7), and many other contexts.

Examination and Counting

The sealed tubes containing the samples are examined in the laboratory, where a small portion of each sample is studied under the microscope in an attempt to identify a few hundred grains in that sample. Each family and almost every genus of plant produce pollen grains distinctive in shape and surface ornamentation, but it is difficult to go further and pinpoint the species. This imposes certain limits on environmental reconstruction, since different species within the same genus can have markedly different requirements in terms of soil, climate, etc.

Alnus (alder) Betula (birch)

Corylus (hazel) Hedera helix (ivy)

Quercus (oak) Salix (willow)

Tilia (lime) Ulmus (elm)

Morphology of a selection of pollen grains, as seen under the microscope.

Slow and laborious manual counting and identification will probably be replaced in the next few years by an automated technique, in which pollen grains are identified through analysis in the scanning electron microscope of digitized images of the exine's shape and texture.

After identification, the quantity of pollen for each plant-type is calculated for each layer – usually as a percentage of the total number of grains in that layer – and then plotted as a curve. The curves are seen as a reflection of climatic fluctuations through the sequence, using the present-day tolerances of these plants as a guide.

However, adjustments need to be made. Different species produce differing amounts of pollen (pines, for example, produce many times more than oaks), and so may be over- or under-represented in the sample. The mode of pollination also needs to be taken into account. Pollen of lime, transported by insect, is probably from trees that grew nearby, whereas pine pollen, transported by the wind, could be from hundreds of kilometers away. The orientation of sites (and especially of cave-mouths) will also have a considerable effect on their pollen content, as will site location, and length/type of occupation.

It is necessary to ensure there has been no mixing of layers (intrusion is now known to be a common problem), and to assess human impact – samples should be taken from outside the archaeological site as well as within it. In urban archaeological deposits, for instance, pollen from well-fills or buried soils are mostly present through natural transport and deposition, and hence reflect the surrounding countryside. Pollen from urban living areas, on the other hand, derive primarily from food preparation and the many other human uses of plants.

In a study of pollen assemblages from a series of Roman and medieval towns in Britain, James Greig found that the Roman sites were rich in

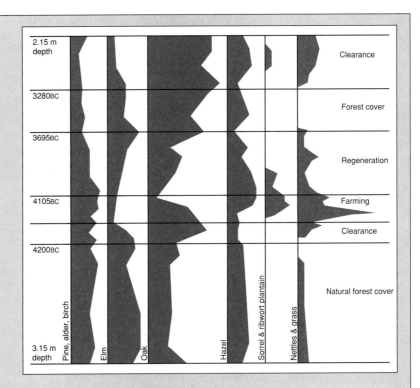

Postglacial pollen core from Fallahogy, Northern Ireland, reveals the impact of the first farmers in the region. Forest clearance is indicated c.4150 BC with a fall in tree pollen and a marked increase in open-country and field species such as grass, sorrel, and ribwort-plantain. The subsequent regeneration of forest cover, followed by a second period of clearance, shows the non-intensive nature of early farming in the area.

Long-term sequences for the Ice Age (below right) show the good correlation between a terrestrial pollen core from the Iberian peninsula (at right) and oxygen-isotope curves (at left) derived from deep-sea core SU 8132 extracted in the Bay of Biscay.

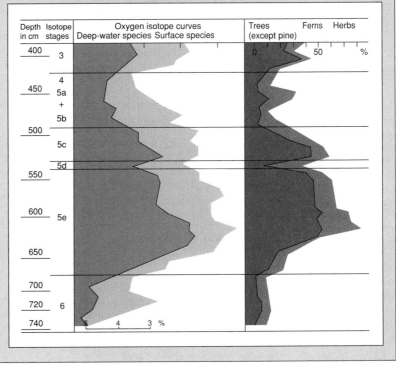

grasses but poor in cereals, whereas the medieval deposits produced the opposite result. The reason is not economic but hygienic – the Romans had a sewerage system for their towns, which were kept clean and, apparently, were surrounded by short grassland which dominates the pollen assemblages. In medieval times, however, garbage was allowed to accumulate in the towns, so that the food refuse remained for the archaeologist to find, and dominated the pollen samples.

As a rule, pollen in soils away from human settlement tends to reflect the local vegetation, while peat bogs preserve pollen from a much wider area. Results from pollen in deep peat-bog successions usefully confirm the long-term climatic fluctuations deduced from deep-sea and ice cores mentioned earlier in the main text.

delineated a series of *pollen zones* through time, each characterized by different plant communities (especially trees), although there is little agreement on the numbering system to be used or the total number of zones. But pollen studies can also supply much-needed information for environments as ancient as those of the Hadar sediments and the Omo valley in Ethiopia around 3 million years ago. It is usually assumed that these regions were always as dry as they are now, but pollen analysis by the French scientist Raymonde Bonnefille has shown that they were much wetter and greener between 3.5 and 2.5 million years ago, with even some tropical plants present. The Hadar, which is now semi-desert with scattered trees and shrubs, was rich, open grassland, with dense woodland by lakes and along rivers. The change to drier conditions, around 2.5 million years ago, can be seen in the reduction of tree pollen in favor of more grasses.

By and large, the fluctuations recorded for the postglacial and especially the historical periods are minor compared with what went before, and where regression of forest is concerned there is the ever present possibility that climate is not the only cause (see human impact section below). It is also worth noting that the British hydrologist Robert Raikes went much further than most scholars in playing down the significance of climatic changes during the postglacial period. He points out that in Europe variation in rainfall from one year or season to the next is almost certainly greater than rainfall differences generally deduced (though without quantification) from pollen diagrams. Any major climatic change that might have taken place would probably have been ecologically less significant than short-term variation of greater amplitude. Raikes concluded that ecological changes should more probably be ascribed to year-to-year variability of climate and rainfall. The archaeologist, he said, should therefore investigate minor, short-term local changes rather than try to squeeze all the sites in a region into a standardized succession of fixed pollen zones. Most specialists disagree with Raikes' line of argument, but his emphasis on the importance of local environmental reconstruction makes good sense for archaeologists working on individual sites.

Fossil Cuticles. Palynology is particularly useful for forested regions, but the reconstruction of past vegetation in grassy environments such as those of tropical Africa has been much hindered by the fact that grass pollen grains can be virtually indistinguishable from one another, even in the scanning electron microscope (SEM). Fortunately, help is at hand in the form of fossil cuticles. Cuticles are the outermost protective layer of the skin or epidermis of leaves or blades of grass, made of cutin, a very resistant material that retains the pattern of the underlying epidermal cells which have characteristic shapes. The cuticles thus have silica cells of different shapes and patterns, as well as hairs and other diagnostic features.

The scientist Patricia Palmer has found abundant charred cuticular fragments in core samples from lake sediments in East Africa. The fragments were deposited there as a result of the recurrent natural grass fires common during the dry season, and her samples date back at least 28,000 years. Many of the fragments are large enough to present well-preserved diagnostic features that, under the light microscope or in the SEM, have enabled her to identify them to the level of subfamily or even genus, and hence reconstruct changes in vegetation during this long period. Cuticular analysis is a useful complement to palynology wherever grass material, whole or fragmentary, is to be identified, and it is worth noting that cuticles can also be removed from stomachs or feces.

Phytoliths. A better known and fast-developing branch of microbotanical studies concerns phytoliths, which were first recognized as components in archaeological contexts as long ago as 1908, but have only been studied systematically in the last few decades. These are minute particles of silica (plant opal) derived from the cells of plants, and they survive after the rest of the organism has decomposed or been burned. They are common in hearths and ash layers, but are also to be found inside pottery, plaster, and even on stone tools and the teeth of herbivorous animals: grass phytoliths, for example, have been found adhering to ungulate teeth from Bronze Age, Iron Age, and medieval sites in Europe.

These crystals are useful because, like pollen grains, they are produced in large numbers, they survive well in ancient sediments, and they have myriad distinctive shapes and sizes that vary according to type, though it is usually difficult to identify their genus or species, even with a SEM. They inform us primarily about the use people made of particular plants, but their simple presence adds to the picture of the environment built up from other sources.

In particular, a combination of phytolith and pollen analysis can be a powerful tool for environmental reconstruction, since the two methods have complementary strengths and weaknesses. The American scholar Dolores Piperno has studied cores from the Gatun Basin, Panama, whose pollen content had already revealed a sequence of vegetation change from

11,300 years ago to the present – from mature tropical forest to mangrove, freshwater swamp, and finally to clearance through swidden (slash-and-burn) agriculture. She found that the phytoliths in the cores confirmed the pollen sequence, with the exception that evidence for agriculture and forest clearance (i.e. the appearance of maize, and an increase in grass at the expense of trees) appeared around 4850 years ago in the phytoliths, about 1000 years earlier than in the pollen. This early evidence is probably attributable to small clearings which do not show up in pollen diagrams because grains from the surrounding forest infiltrate the samples, as well as to the relatively poor production and dispersal of non-arboreal pollen.

Pollen analysis will nevertheless remain the more important technique, if only because of difficulties in phytolith identification.

Diatom Analysis. Another method of environmental reconstruction using plant microfossils is diatom analysis. Diatoms are unicellular algae that have cell walls of silica instead of cellulose, and these silica cell walls survive after the algae die. They accumulate in great numbers at the bottom of any body of water in which the algae live; a few are found in peat, but most come from lake and shore sediments.

Diatoms have been recorded, identified, and classified for over 200 years. The process of identifying and counting them is much like that used in palynology, as is the collection of samples in the field. Their well-defined shapes and ornamentations permit identifica-

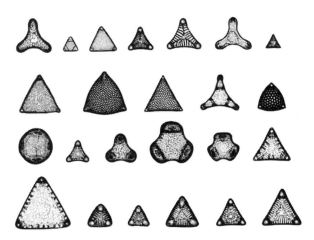

A variety of diatoms, the microscopic single-cell algae, whose silica cell walls survive in many sediments after death. Study of the changing species in a deposit can help scientists reconstruct fluctuations in past environments.

tion to a high level, and their assemblages directly reflect the floristic composition and the productivity of the water's diatom communities, and, indirectly, the water's salinity, alkalinity, and nutrient status. From the environmental requirements of different species (in terms of habitat, salinity, and nutrients), one can determine what their immediate environment was at different periods.

The botanist J. P. Bradbury looked at diatom assemblages from nine lakes in Minnesota and Dakota, and was able to show that the quality of their water had become "eutrophic" (more nutrient) since the onset of European settlement around the lakes in the last century, thanks to the influxes caused by deforestation and logging, soil erosion, permanent agriculture, and the increase in human and animal wastes.

Since diatom assemblages can also denote whether water was fresh, brackish, or salt, they have been used to identify the period when lakes became isolated from the sea in areas of tectonic uplift, to locate the positions of past shorelines, to indicate marine transgressions, and to reveal water pollution. For instance, the diatom sequence in sediments at the site of the former Lake Wevershoof, Medemblick (the Netherlands) suggests that a marine transgression occurred here around AD 800, taking over what had been a freshwater lake and causing a hiatus in human occupation of the immediate area.

Rock Varnishes. Even tinier fragments of plant material can provide environmental evidence. Rock varnishes, which have been formed on late Pleistocene desert landforms in many areas such as North America, the Middle East, and Australia, are natural accretions of manganese and iron oxides, together with clay minerals and organic matter. The organic matter comes from micrometer-sized airborne plant debris that accumulates on rock surfaces and is thus metabolized and cemented into the varnish by bacterial action. Less than 1 percent of the varnish is organic matter, however, so thousands of square centimeters are required for adequate analysis.

The reason for the analysis is that a strong correlation has been found between the ratio of stable carbon isotopes ($^{12}C/^{13}C$) in modern samples and their different local environments (desert, semi-arid, montane-humid, and so on). Therefore, the stable carbon isotope ratios of the organic matter preserved in the different layers of varnish on rocks can provide information about changing conditions, and especially about the abundance of different types of plant in the adjacent vegetation. The American scholars Ronald Dorn and Michael DeNiro have sampled surface and subsurface layers of varnish on late Pleistocene deposits in eastern California, and found that the basal layers were formed under more humid conditions than those on the surface, which supports the view that the Southwest of the United States was less arid in the last Ice Age than during the succeeding Holocene. Similarly, samples from the Timna Valley in Israel's Negev Desert have revealed a sequence of arid, humid, and arid periods.

The rock varnish technique, when combined with radiocarbon dating, can provide a minimum age for some landforms – and even for certain types of stone tool which also accumulate varnish – as well as for any rock art which underlies the accretions (see Chapter 4). However, there are difficulties with the technique, primarily because the layers are so thin that distinguishing stratification is not simple. Future work may resolve these problems.

All these microbotanical techniques – studies of pollen, cuticles, phytoliths, diatoms, and rock varnish – are clearly the realm of the specialist. For archaeologists, however, a far more direct contact with environ- mental evidence comes from the larger plant remains that they can actually see and conserve in the course of excavation.

Macrobotanical Remains

A variety of bigger types of plant remains are potentially retrievable, and provide important information about which plants grew near sites, which were used or consumed by people, and so on. We shall discuss human use in the next chapter; here we shall focus on the crucial contribution of macrobotanical remains to environmental reconstruction. As with microbotanical remains, they cannot assist us in quantifying the vegetation cover except in the most relative fashion, but some of them do provide valuable clues to local environmental conditions.

Retrieval in the Field. Retrieval of vegetation from sediments has been made simpler by the development of screening (sieving) and flotation techniques able to separate mineral grains from organic materials because of their different sizes (screening) and densities

COLLECTION OF PLANT REMAINS

Kind of remains	Sediment type	Information available from investigation	Method of extraction and examination	Volume to be collected
Soil	All	Detailed description of how the deposit formed and under what conditions	(Best examined *in situ* by environmental staff)	(Column sample)
Pollen	Buried soils, waterlogged deposits	Vegetation, land use	Laboratory extraction and high power (x400) microscopy	0.05 ltr or column sample
Phytoliths	All sediments	As above	As above	As above
Diatoms	Waterlain deposits	Salinity and levels of water pollution	Laboratory extraction and high power (x400) microscopy	0.10 ltr
Uncharred plant remains (seeds, mosses, leaves)	Wet to waterlogged	Vegetation, diet, plant materials used in building crafts, technology and fuel	Laboratory sieving to 300 microns	10–20 ltr
Charred plant remains (grain, chaff, charcoal)	All sediments	Vegetation, diet, plant materials used in building crafts, technology, fuel, processing of crops and behavior	Bulk sieving or flotation to 300 microns	75 ltr
Wood/(charcoal)	Wet to waterlogged, charred	Dendrochronology, climate, building materials and technology	Low power microscopy (x10)	Hand or lab. collection

Table summarizing collection methods for microbotanical and macrobotanical plant remains, with an indication of the range of information to be gained for each category.

(flotation). Archaeologists need to choose from a wide range of available devices in accordance with the excavation's location, budget, and objectives.

Sediments are by no means the only source of plant remains, which have also been found in the stomachs of frozen mammoths and preserved bog bodies; in the coprolites (fossilized feces) of humans, hyenas, giant sloths, etc.; on the teeth of mammoths, etc.; on stone tools; and in residues inside vessels. The remains themselves are varied:

Seeds and Fruits. In studying ancient seeds and fruits, often preserved by waterlogging or desiccation, one can usually identify them to species, despite the fact that many remains are carbonized, a process that causes distortion and shrinkage. In some cases, the remains have disintegrated but have left their imprint behind – grain impressions are fairly common on pottery, leaf impressions are also known, and imprints exist on materials ranging from plaster and tufa to leather and corroded bronze. Identification, of course, depends on type and quality of the traces. Not all such finds necessarily mean that a plant grew locally: grape

pips, for example, may come from imported fruit, while impressions on potsherds may mislead since pottery can travel far from its place of manufacture.

Plant Residues. Chemical analysis of plant residues in vessels – primarily by means of chromatograms – will be dealt with in the context of human diet in Chapter 7, but the results can give some idea of what species were available. Pottery vessels themselves may incorporate plant fibers (not to mention shell, feathers, or blood) as a tempering material, and microscopic analysis can sometimes identify these remains – for example, study of early pots from South Carolina and Georgia revealed the presence of shredded stems of Spanish Moss, a member of the pineapple family.

Remains of Wood. Study of *charcoal* (wood that has been burnt for some reason) is making a growing contribution to archaeological reconstruction of environments and of human use of timber. A very durable material, charcoal is usually found and extracted by the archaeologist. Once the fragments have been sieved, sorted, and dried, they can be examined

Water flotation for plant recovery: the flushing system, using recycled water, developed by Gordon Hillman from the method first devised at the British Institute of Archaeology, Ankara. Light material floats to the surface and is caught in flot sieves; heavier material sinks, to be caught in a nylon mesh.

FLOTATION TANK

CUTAWAY VIEW OF 1mm² NYLON MESH FOR RESIDUE

LIGHT FRACTION (FLOT)

HEAVY FRACTION

WATER INLET

FLOT SIEVES

FIRST SETTLING TANK

INTAKE SURROUNDED BY FINE MESH (1mm²)

SECOND SETTLING TANK

SLUDGE OUTLET

SLUDGE

DITCH

SLUDGE DRAIN

PUMP

Boomplaas Cave, Cape Province, South Africa. (Left) Scanning electron microscope photograph (x50) of charcoal from the thorn tree Acacia karroo. The appearance of this species at Boomplaas after 5000 years ago indicates a shift to hot, relatively moist summers. (Below) Excavations in progress at the cave in 1978. Compare the photograph on p.94 taken at an earlier stage of the work.

by the specialist under the microscope, and identified (thanks to the anatomy of the wood) normally at the genus level, and sometimes to species. Since no chemicals need to be used, charcoal has in addition proved the most reliable material from which to take samples for radiocarbon dating (Chapter 4).

Many charcoal samples derive from firewood, but others may come from wooden structures, furniture, and implements burnt at some point in a site's history. Samples therefore inevitably tend to reflect human selection of wood rather than the full range of species growing around the site. Nevertheless, the totals for each species provide some idea of one part of the vegetation at a given time. Quantification is tricky, since charcoal fragments do not come in standard sizes. Should one compare the number of fragments for each species, or the total mass of each?

Occasionally, charcoal analysis can be combined with other evidence to reveal something not only of local environment but also of human adaptation to it. At Boomplaas Cave, in southern Cape Province (South Africa), excavation of the deep deposits by Hilary Deacon and his team has uncovered traces of human occupation stretching back to about 70,000 years. There is a clear difference between all Ice Age charcoals and those postdating 12,000–14,000 years ago at the site. At times of extreme cold when conditions were also drier, as between 22,000 and *c.* 14,000 years ago, the species diversity both in the charcoals and the pollen was low, whereas at times of higher rainfall and/or temperature the species diversity increased. A similar pattern of species diversity is seen also in the small mammals.

The vegetation around Boomplaas Cave at the time of maximum cold and drought was composed mainly of shrubs and grass with few fruits and corms that could be used by people. The charcoal samples are dominated by the so-called rhinoceros bush, a small shrub that grows today in relatively dry areas. The larger mammal fauna during the Ice Age was dominated by grazers that included "giant" species of buffalo, horse, and hartebeest. These became extinct by about 10,000 years ago (the worldwide extinction of big-game is discussed in a later section).

The Boomplaas charcoal directly reflects the gradual change in climate and vegetation which led to the disappearance of the large grazers, and to a corresponding shift in subsistence practices by the cave's occupants. The charcoal analysis also highlights more subtle changes that reflect a shift in the season of maximum rainfall. The woody vegetation in the Cango Valley today is dominated by the thorn tree, *Acacia karroo*, characteristic of large areas in southern Africa where it is relatively dry and rain falls mostly in summer. Thorn-tree charcoal is absent in the Ice Age samples at Boomplaas but here and at the nearby site of Buffelskloof it appears from about 5000 years ago and by 2000 years ago is the dominant species. This shift to hot, relatively moist summers after about 5000 years ago in the Cango Valley is traceable also in the carbon isotope analysis of a stalagmite (see box on cave sediments, above) from the nearby Cango Caves. With encroachment of summer rainfall species the inhabitants of the cave were able to make more use of a new range of fruits; the seeds of some of these are preserved in deposits that postdate 2000 years ago.

By no means all wood subjected to this kind of analysis is charred. Increasing quantities of *water-*

logged wood are being recovered from wet sites in many parts of the world (see human environment section below, and Chapters 2, 8). And in some conditions, such as extreme cold or dryness, *desiccated wood* may survive without either burning or waterlogging; examination of a small slice (less than 1 mm (0.04 in) thick) under the microscope and in the SEM permits identification of wood in pristine condition.

Other Sources of Evidence. A great deal of information on vegetation in the less remote periods studied by archaeologists can be obtained from art, from texts (e.g. the writings of Pliny the Elder, Roman farming texts, accounts and illustrations by early explorers such as Captain Cook), and even from photographs.

No single category of evidence can provide us with a total picture of local or regional vegetation, of small-scale trends or long-term changes: each produces a partial version of past realities. Input is needed from every source available, and, as will be seen below, these must be combined with results from the other forms of data studied in this chapter in order to reconstruct the best approximation of a past environment.

RECONSTRUCTING THE ANIMAL ENVIRONMENT

Animal remains were the first evidence used by 19th-century archaeologists to characterize the climate of the prehistoric periods encountered in their excavations. Thus, concepts such as the Mammoth Age, the Aurochs Age, and the Reindeer Age were in common use until the classification of stone tools replaced them. Underlying these terms was the realization that different species were absent, present, or particularly abundant in certain layers and hence in certain periods, and the assumption that this reflected changing climatic conditions.

Today, in order to use faunal remains as a guide to environment, we need to look more critically at the evidence than did the 19th-century pioneers. We need to understand the complex relationship between modern animals and their environment. We also need to investigate how animal remains arrived at a site – either naturally, or through the activities of carnivores or people (see taphonomy box, Chapter 7) – and thus how representative they may be of the variety of animals in their period.

Microfauna

Just as tiny plant remains tend to be of greater importance to environmental studies than large ones, so small animals (microfauna) are better indicators of climate and environmental change than are large species, because they are sensitive to oscillations and adapt relatively quickly, whereas large animals have a relatively wide range of tolerance. In addition, since microfauna tend to accumulate naturally on a site, they reflect the immediate environment more accurately than the larger animals whose remains are often accumulated through human or animal predation. Like pollen, small animals, and especially insects, are also usually found in far greater numbers than larger ones, which improves the statistical significance of their analysis. It is essential to extract a good sample by means of dry and/or wet screening or sieving; huge quantities are otherwise missed in the course of excavation.

A wide variety of microfauna is found on archaeological sites.

Insectivores, Rodents, and Bats. These are the species most commonly encountered. A specialist can obtain a great deal of environmental information from the associations and fluctuations of these seemingly insignificant creatures, since most of them are present in archaeological sites naturally rather than through human exploitation.

It is necessary to ensure as far as possible that the bones are contemporaneous with the layer, and that burrowing has not occurred. One should also bear in mind that, even if the remains are not intrusive, they will not always indicate the *immediate* environment – if they come from owl pellets, for example, they may have been caught up to a few kilometers from the site (the contents of bird pellets can nevertheless be of great value in assessing local environments).

As with large mammals, certain small species can be indicative of fairly specific environmental conditions. Richard Klein of the University of Chicago has noted a strong correlation between rainfall and the size of the modern dune mole rat of South Africa – the rats seem to grow larger in response to a general increase in vegetation density brought about by higher rainfall. His analysis of the fauna from Elands Bay Cave, South Africa, revealed that the rats from layers dating to between 11,000 and 9000 years ago were distinctly bigger than those of the preceding seven millennia, and this has been taken as evidence of a rise in precipitation at the end of the Pleistocene.

Birds and Fish. Bones of birds and fish are particularly fragile, but are well worth studying. They can for example be used to determine the seasons in which particular sites were occupied (Chapter 7). Birds are sensitive to climatic change, and the alternation of "cold" and "warm" species in the last Ice Age has been of great help in assessing environment, though it is sometimes difficult to decide whether a bird is present naturally or has been brought in by a human or animal predator.

Land Molluscs. The calcium carbonate shells of land molluscs are preserved in many types of sediment, but especially in alkaline contexts where pollen grains cannot survive. They reflect local conditions, and can be responsive to changes in microclimate. But one needs to take into account that many species have a very broad tolerance, and their reaction to change is relatively slow, so that they "hang on" in adverse areas, and disperse slowly into newly acceptable areas.

As usual, it is necessary to establish whether the shells were deposited *in situ*, or washed or blown in from elsewhere. The sample of shells needs to be unbiased – sieving should ensure that not merely the large or colorful specimens that catch an excavator's eye are kept, but the whole assemblage. Quality of preservation is important since shell shape and ornamentation are key elements in identifying species. Once the assemblages have been determined, one can trace changes through time, and hence how the molluscan population has altered in response to environmental oscillations. Temperature and rainfall are the dominant factors; where a species is near the limit of its normal range, it can be a very sensitive indicator of change.

A great deal of work has been done on this topic by the British specialist John Evans and others at a number of prehistoric sites in Britain. For example, snails from sections at the Neolithic monuments of Woodhenge and Durrington Walls show that the area was wooded in that period. At Avebury nearby, the relative percentages of species found in successive layers of soil beneath the site's bank indicate a tundra environment about 10,000 years ago, open woodland 8000–6000 years ago, closed woodland 6000–3000 years ago, followed by a phase of clearance and plowing, and finally grassland.

Marine Molluscs. As we have already seen earlier in this chapter, middens of marine molluscs can sometimes help to delineate ancient shorelines, and their changing percentages of species through time can reveal something of the nature of the coastal micro-

environment – such as whether it was sandy or rocky – through study of the modern preferences of the species represented. The climatic change suggested by these alterations in the presence or abundance of different species can be matched with the results of oxygen isotope analysis of the shells – a strong correlation between the two methods has been found by Hiroko Koike in her work on Jomon middens in Tokyo Bay where, for example, the disappearance of tropical species implied a cold phase at 5000 or 6000 years ago, which was confirmed by an increase in oxygen 18 (and hence a decrease of water temperature) around 5000 years ago. In Chapter 7 we shall see how changes in mollusc shell growth can establish seasonality.

Worms and Insects. Besides molluscs, a narrow range of annelids (such as earthworms represented by egg-cases) may be found, especially in waterlogged deposits including cess-pits, as well as a wide range of arthropods such as mites and insects, the latter in the form of adults, larvae, and (in the case of flies) puparia. The study of *insects* (paleoentomology) was rather neglected in archaeology until about 30 years ago, since when a great deal of pioneering work has been done, particularly in Britain. Insect exoskeletons can be quite resistant to decomposition, and some assemblages comprise thousands of individuals.

Since we know the distribution and environmental requirements of their modern descendants, it is often possible to use insect remains as accurate indicators of the likely climatic conditions (and to some extent of the vegetation) prevailing in particular periods and

Land mollusc histogram based on excavations at Avebury, southern England. Fluctuating percentages of woodland species of snails reveal a change from open country (tundra) c.10,000 years ago to woodland and eventually to grassland.

local areas. Some species have very precise requirements in terms of where they like to breed and the kinds of food their larvae need. However, rather than use single "indicator species" to reconstruct a microenvironment, it is safer to consider associations of species, as with mammals or plant communities. Hence, the so-called mutual climatic range method is employed: this assumes that the present-day climatic tolerance of each species is the same as in the past, and therefore where several species are found together, the ancient climate must lie within the area of overlap of their tolerance ranges. It follows that the more species are present, the more precisely can this area of overlap be determined. Although insects reflect microclimates, it should be remembered that these are in turn largely governed by the overall climate.

In view of their rapid response to climatic changes, insects are useful indicators of the timing and scale of these events, and of seasonal and mean annual temperatures. A few depictions of insects even exist from the Ice Age, and reveal some of the types that managed to survive in periglacial areas.

Coleoptera (beetles and weevils) are particularly useful insects for microenvironmental studies. Their head and thorax are often found well preserved; almost all those known from the Pleistocene still exist; they are sensitive indicators of past climates, responding quickly to environmental change (especially temperature); and they form a varied group with well-defined tolerance ranges – some species are very selective in terms of vegetal environment, and live exclusively on particular plants, such as oak, or on certain fungi.

Grasshopper engraved on a bone fragment from the late Ice Age (Magdalenian) site of Enlène, Ariège, France. Insects respond rapidly to climatic change, and are sensitive indicators of the timing and scale of environmental variations.

In a recent study, the climatic tolerance ranges of 350 coleopteran species that occur as Pleistocene fossils were plotted; the mutual climatic range method was then applied to 57 coleopteran faunas from 26 sites in Britain. It was found that there had been very rapid major warmings at 13,000 and 10,000 years ago, and a prolonged cooling trend from 12,500 years ago (when conditions were the same as now, with average July temperatures around 17°C, 62.6°F) to 10,500 years ago, together with a number of minor oscillations.

Occasionally the discovery of insects in archaeological deposits can have important ramifications. To take a major example, the remains of the beetle *Scolytus scolytus*, found in Neolithic deposits in Hampstead, London, occur in a layer before the sharp decline in elm pollen known just before 5000 years ago in cores from the lake sediments and peats of northwest Europe. This archaeologically famous and abrupt decline was originally attributed to climatic change or degrading soils, and later to clearance by early farmers requiring fodder (see Chapter 12). However, *Scolytus scolytus* is the beetle that spreads the pathogenic fungus causing Dutch elm disease, and thus provides an alternative, natural explanation for the elm decline of 5000 years ago. The current outbreak of elm disease in Europe has allowed scientists to monitor the disease's effects on the modern pollen record. They have indeed found that the decline in elm pollen is of similar proportions to that in the Neolithic; not only that, but the accompanying increase in weed pollen caused by the opening of the woodland canopy is the same in both cases. This fact, together with the known presence of the beetle in Neolithic times, makes a strong case for the existence of elm disease in that period.

Insects have also come to the fore in excavations at York, where Viking timbers seem to have been riddled with woodworm and deathwatch beetle. A 3rd-century AD Roman sewer in the city was found filled with sludge, which had concentrations of sewer flies in two side channels leading to lavatories. The sewer was known from its position to have drained a military bath-house – and this was confirmed by the presence of a type of ant that today thrives in rotting wood in warm, humid conditions such as coal mines, a fact which implies that there was standing water in a building above the sewer, with a temperature of 19°C (66.2°F) under a closed roof of decaying wood! However, the remains of grain beetles and golden spider beetles in the mud showed that the sewer also drained a granary, confirmation of which came from bones of shrews, mice, and voles that foraged in there.

Clearly, insects are proving invaluable for the quantity and quality of information they can give archaeologists, not just about climate and vegetation, but about living conditions in and around archaeological sites as well.

Macrofauna

Remains of large animals found on archaeological sites mainly help us build up a picture of past human diet (Chapter 7). As environmental indicators they have proved less reliable than was once assumed, primarily because they are not so sensitive to environmental changes as small animals, but also because their remains will very likely have been deposited in an archaeological context through human or animal action. Bones from animals killed by people or by carnivores have been selected, and so cannot accurately reflect the full range of fauna present in the environment. The ideal is therefore to find accumulations of animal remains brought about by natural accident or catastrophe – animals caught in a flash flood perhaps, or buried by volcanic eruption, or mired (as in the case of the wide range of Pleistocene fauna found in the famous tarpits of Rancho La Brea, Los Angeles), or which became frozen in permafrost. But these are by any standards exceptional finds – very different from the usual accumulations of animal bones encountered by archaeologists.

Bone Collection and Identification in the Field. Bones are usually only preserved in situations where they have been buried quickly, thus avoiding the effects of weathering and the activities of scavenging animals. They can also survive, in a softened condition, in non-acidic waterlogged sites. In some cases, they may require treatment in the field before it is safe to remove them without damage. In sediments, they slowly become impregnated with minerals, and their weight and hardness increase, and thus their durability.

After collection, the first step is to identify as many fragments as possible, both as part of the body and as a species. This is the work of a zoologist or one of the growing number of zooarchaeologists, although every archaeologist should be able to recognize a basic range of bones and species. Identification is made through comparison with a reference collection. The resulting lists and associations of species can also sometimes help to date Paleolithic sites (see Chapter 4).

Once quantification of the bone assemblage has been completed (see box, Chapter 7), what can the results tell us about the contemporary environment?

COLLECTION OF ANIMAL REMAINS

Kind of remains	Sediment type	Information available from investigation	Method of extraction and examination	Volume to be collected
Small mammal bone	All but very acidic	Natural fauna, ecology	Sieving to 1 mm	75 ltr
Bird bone	As above	See large and small mammal bone	As above	As above
Fish bone, scales, and otoliths	As above	Diet, fishing technology, and seasonal activity	As above	As above
Land molluscs	Alkaline	Past vegetation, soil type, depositional history	Laboratory sieving to 500 microns	10 ltr
Marine molluscs (shellfish)	Alkaline and neutral	Diet, trade, season of collection, shellfish farming	Hand sorting, troweled sediment, and sieving	75 ltr
Insect remains (charred)	All sediments	Climate, vegetation, living conditions, trade, human diet	Laboratory sieving and paraffin flotation to 300 microns	10 – 20 ltr
Insect remains (uncharred)	Wet to waterlogged	As above	As above	As above
Large mammal bone	All but very acidic	Natural fauna, diet, husbandry, butchery, disease, social status, craft techniques	Hand sorting, troweled sediment, and sieving	Whole context troweled except when bulk samples are taken

Table summarizing collection methods for microfauna and macrofauna, with an indication of the variety of information to be gained for each category.

Assumptions and Limitations. The anatomy and especially the teeth of large animals tell us something about their diet and hence, in the case of herbivores, of the type of vegetation they prefer. However, most information about range and habitat comes from studies of modern species, on the assumption that behavior has not changed substantially since the period in question. These studies show that large animals will tolerate – i.e. have the potential to withstand or exploit – a much wider range of temperatures and environments than was once thought. Thus species characteristic today of arctic and temperate regions in fact show a marked overlap in their habitats, and share a very similar minimum-temperature tolerance. This means that we can no longer assume, as archaeologists once did, that Pleistocene species such as the woolly rhinoceros or cave bear necessarily indicate cold climate – the presence of these species should be regarded merely as proof of their ability to tolerate low temperatures.

If it is therefore difficult to link fluctuations in a site's macrofaunal assemblage with changes in *temperature*, we can at least say that changes in *precipitation* may sometimes be reflected quite directly in variations in faunal remains. For example, species differ as to the depth of snow they can tolerate, and this affects winter

faunal assemblages in those parts of the world that endure thick snow-cover for much of the winter.

Large mammals are not generally good indicators of *vegetation*, since herbivores can thrive in a wide range of environments and eat a variety of plants. Thus, individual species cannot usually be regarded as characteristic of one particular habitat. But there are exceptions. Some animals such as ibex, which today are restricted to the higher reaches of mountains, were forced by glaciations to live at lower altitudes, and there were similar latitudinal shifts by other animals and birds. For example, reindeer reached northern Spain in the last Ice Age, as shown not only by bones but also by cave art. Such major shifts clearly reflect environmental change.

In the rock art of the Sahara, too, one can see clear evidence for the presence of species that could not survive in the area today, and thus for dramatic environmental modification.

As will be seen in Chapter 7, fauna can also be used to determine in which seasons of the year a site was occupied. The techniques described there can go some way towards showing how the local environment changed from season to season.

It is possible as well to correlate macrofauna and other types of evidence. Many faunal sequences in

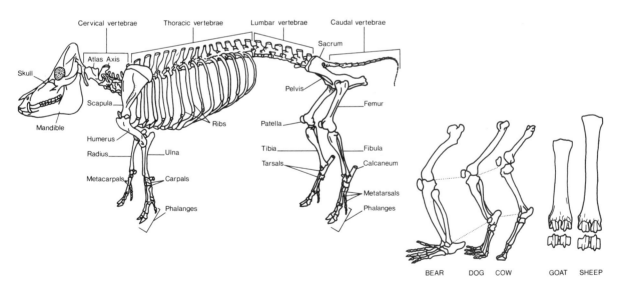

Identifying animal bones. (Left) Bones in the skeleton of a typical domesticated animal, the pig. (Center) Structural comparison of mammal limb bones. In bears (and humans), the whole foot touches the ground, whereas among carnivores such as the dog only the toes do so. Herbivores such as cattle walk on "tiptoe," with only the final digit on the ground. (Right) Sheep and goat bones are notoriously difficult to distinguish, although there are subtle differences as in these metacarpals.

ELANDS BAY CAVE

AFRICA

Elands Bay

The Verlorenvlei estuary today (above). Elands Bay Cave lies just around the tip of the peninsula seen in the distance.

Located near the mouth of the Verlorenvlei estuary on the southwest coast of Cape Province, South Africa, Elands Bay Cave was occupied for thousands of years and is particularly important for the documentation of changes in coastline and subsistence at the end of the Ice Age. Work at the cave by John Parkington and his associates has demonstrated clearly how, within 6000 or 7000 years, the rise in sea level transformed the site's territory from being inland riverine to estuarine and coastal.

During the period c.13,600–12,000 years ago, subsistence practices remained relatively stable, although the coastline must have approached to about 12 km (7½ miles) from the site according to present-day offshore sea-bed contours. The faunal remains left by the cave's occupants are dominated by an assemblage of large grazers such as rhinoceroses, equids, buffalo, and eland, suggesting that the local environment was one of fairly open grassland. The very low marine component in the remains reflects the considerable distance to the coast – still beyond the 2-hour distance considered normal for most hunter-gatherers (see Site Catchment Analysis box), and too far to make it economical to carry shellfish. The birds found are of riverine species, primarily ducks.

By about 11,000 years ago, the coast had approached to some 5–6 km (3.1–3.7 miles) west from the site, well within striking distance for hunter-gatherers. The first thin layers of shellfish now appear in the cave's sequence. In the following three millennia the sea encroached to 2 km (1¼ miles) or so from the site, and gradually drowned the lower reaches of the Verlorenvlei valley, turning them into estuary and then into coastline.

The disappearance of the habitats suited to the large grazers had radical effects on the faunal environment. At least two animals (the giant horse and giant buffalo) became extinct, and other large animals such as the rhinoceros and Cape buffalo are absent or extremely rare in the cave's deposits after 9000 years ago. They are replaced at this site and in other parts of the region by smaller herbivores such as grysbok – browsers rather than grazers, a fact that implies a different plant environment, probably linked to a change in precipitation.

At the same time, there is a clear rise to dominance of marine animals between 11,000 and 9000 years ago, and the cave's sequence changes from

Rising sea levels (below) at the end of the Ice Age drowned the coastal plain that once lay to the west of Elands Bay Cave.

c.13,000 yrs ago — Sea level -80m

c.11,000 yrs ago — Sea level -50m

c.8000 yrs ago — Sea level -15m

6000–5000 yrs ago — Sea level +0m

- - - Ancient shoreline ⌒ Modern shoreline ● Elands Bay Cave

6 miles
10 km

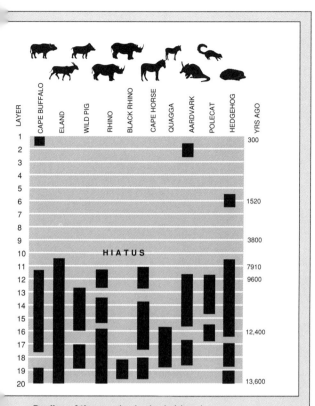

LAYER	CAPE BUFFALO	ELAND	WILD PIG	RHINO	BLACK RHINO	CAPE HORSE	QUAGGA	AARDVARK	POLECAT	HEDGEHOG	YRS AGO
1	■										300
2								■			
3											
4											
5											
6										■	1520
7											
8											
9											3800
10					H I A T U S						
11											7910
12											9600
13											
14											
15											
16											12,400
17											
18											
19											
20											13,600

Decline of the grassland animals (above) *as reflected in the faunal remains recovered from Elands Bay Cave. By 9000 years ago, when the sea had encroached to within 3 km (1.9 miles) of the site, these animals had virtually ceased to be exploited from the cave.*

a series of brown loams containing thin shell layers to a sequence of true shell middens. In addition there are very high frequencies (in relation to terrestrial species) of cormorants, marine fish, rock lobsters, and seals after 9500 years ago, by which period the coast was a little more than 3 km (1.9 miles) away. The drowning of the valley after 11,000 years ago is reflected in the abundance of hippopotamuses and shallow-water birds such as flamingos and pelicans. At this time the estuary was certainly within exploitable distance. Some 9000–8500 years ago the cave was roughly equidistant between coast and estuary, but after 8000 the coast was nearer, reaching its present position about 6000 years ago.

areas such as Europe or southern Africa display changes of species that are independent of culture change, span thousands of years, and can be correlated with sequences derived from sediment or plant studies. In coastal sites, including many caves in Cantabrian Spain, or around the shores of the Mediterranean (Franchthi Cave, see above), or on the Cape coast of South Africa (see box, Elands Bay Cave), marine resources and herbivore remains may come and go through the archaeological sequence as changes in sea level extended or drowned the coastal plain, thus changing the sites' proximity to the shore and the availability of grazing.

However, one always has to bear in mind that faunal fluctuations can have causes other than climate or people; additional factors may include competition, epidemics, or fluctuations in numbers of predators. Moreover, small-scale local variations in climate and weather can have enormous effects on the numbers and distribution of wild animals, so that despite its high powers of resistance a species may decline from extreme abundance to virtual extinction within a few years.

Big-game Extinctions. There is clear evidence from many Polynesian islands, as will be seen below, that the first human settlers devastated the indigenous fauna and flora. But in other parts of the world the question of animal extinctions, and whether and how people were involved, still forms a major topic of debate in archaeology. This is particularly true of the big-game extinctions in the New World and Australia at the end of the Ice Age, where losses were far heavier than in Asia and Africa, and included not just the mammoth and mastodon, but species such as the horse in the Americas.

There are two main sides in the big-game extinction debate. One group of scholars, led by the American scientist Paul Martin, believes that the arrival of people in the New World and Australia, followed by over-exploitation of prey, caused the extinctions. This view, however, does not account for the extinction at about the same time of mammal and bird species that were not obvious human prey, or that would not have been vulnerable to hunting. In any case, the precise date of each extinction is not yet known, while the dates of human entry into both continents are still uncertain (Chapter 11) and constantly being pushed back well beyond the extinctions.

The other view, presented by the geologist Ernest Lundelius and others, is that climatic change is the primary cause. But this does not explain why the many similar changes of earlier periods had no such effect,

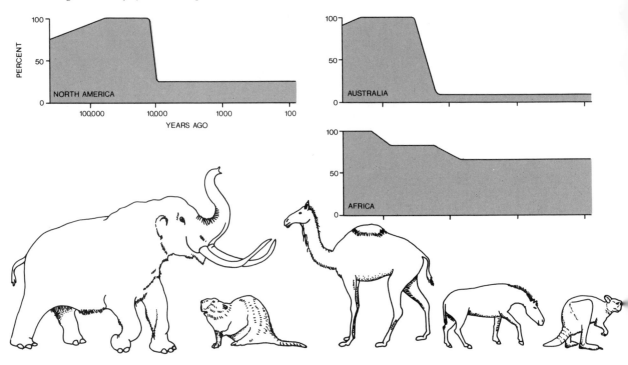

Big-game extinctions. (Top) Diagrams by Paul Martin illustrate the sudden decline of large animal species in North America and Australia around the time of human colonization, by comparison with Africa, where big game had longer to adapt to human predation. Other scholars emphasize the importance of environmental factors as well in the demise of megafauna such as (above, left to right) the mastodon, giant beaver, camel, and horse (all North American), and the Australian giant kangaroo, Sthenurus.

and in any case many of the species that disappeared had a broad geographic distribution and climatic tolerance. Extinctions caused by climatic change had occurred previously, but always tended to affect all size classes of mammal equally, and those that disappeared were replaced by migration or the development of new species – this did not happen in the Pleistocene extinctions. All big-game species weighing over 1000 kg (1 ton) as adults (the megaherbivores) disappeared from the New World, Europe, and Australia, as did about 75 percent of the herbivore genera weighing 100–1000 kg (0.1–1 ton), but only 41 percent of species weighing 5–100 kg (11–220 lb), and under 2 percent of the smaller creatures.

A compromise theory that takes these factors into account and links the two main hypotheses has been put forward by the South African scholar Norman Owen-Smith. He believes that human overexploitation led to the disappearance of the megaherbivores, which in turn caused a change in vegetation that led to the extinction of some medium-sized herbivores. In view of the tremendous effects that modern elephants in eastern and southern Africa have on vegetation – by felling or damaging trees, opening up clearings for smaller animals, and transforming wooded savanna into grassland – it is certain that the removal of megaherbivores must have radically affected the Pleistocene environment. In one game reserve in Natal Province, South Africa, which has had no elephants for the last 100 years, three species of antelope have also become locally extinct, and open-country grazers such as wildebeest and waterbuck are much reduced in numbers.

Owen-Smith's hypothesis has the merit that it can be tested through more detailed analysis of vegetation changes and the order in which extinctions took place.

Promising New Techniques. Eventually we may be able to extract more specific environmental data from bones using new techniques – for example, information on temperature and moisture histories from isotopic analysis of the type described in Chapter 4, or from analysis of the amino acids in bone collagen. Work by M.A. Zeder on trace elements in the bones of sheep and goat from Iran has established that calcium, magnesium, and zinc are found in significantly different concentrations in animals from different environments; it should therefore be possible to obtain information on past environments through similar analyses of ancient bones.

In the same way, Tim Heaton and his colleagues in South Africa have found that the ratio of nitrogen isotopes in bone may be a useful tool for studying past variations in climate. Samples from prehistoric and early historic skeletons of humans and wild herbivores from a variety of habitats and climatic zones in South Africa and Namibia were tested for their $^{15}N/^{14}N$ values. They discovered variations that could not be ascribed to diet: specimens from far inland, or that reflected consumption only of terrestrial plants, produced results similar to those from the coast. In short, the $^{15}N/^{14}N$ ratio seems to be linked to climatic variation, expecially in areas such as this where big changes in precipitation have occurred, with increasing aridity being reflected in a rise in ^{15}N.

Other Sources of Animal Evidence. Bones are not the only source of information about macrofauna. Frozen carcasses have already been mentioned, as has art. In some sites, *tracks* have been found. Examples range from the early hominid and animal prints – over 10,000 of them, including birds and insects – at Laetoli in Tanzania; tracks on Bronze Age soils (Chapter 7); and paw-prints on Roman tiles (Chapter 7). Caves are particularly rich in such traces, and the tracks of hyenas and cave bears are well known in Europe; one can also find the claw-marks and nest-hollows of the cave bear. Toothmarks of beaver have been found on Neolithic wood from the Somerset Levels, England.

Fossil dung (coprolites) has also survived in many dry caves, and can contain much information about fauna and flora. Bechan Cave in southeast Utah, for instance, has about 300 cu. m (392 cu. yd) of dehydrated mammoth dung, while many other species left their coprolites in other American caves. Quite apart from revealing which animals were present in different periods, the dung also shows what they ate, and even contributes to the debate on Pleistocene extinctions (see above). Paul Martin, a pioneer of fossil dung analysis, has shown that the contents of the coprolites of the extinct Shasta ground sloth do not change up to the time of its disappearance, and Jim Mead has reached the same conclusion with the dung of mammoths and the extinct mountain goat. These findings therefore suggest that these New World extinctions, at least, were not caused by a change in vegetation or diet. The decline in frequency and the eventual disappearance of the dung of certain species such as the ground sloth provide further (datable) evidence of extinctions even in the complete absence of skeletal material.

Other sources of evidence include horse and reindeer fat identified chemically from residues in sediment, and blood residues of various animals (Chapter 7) found on stone tools. Information can also be extracted from the writings and illustrations of early explorers, or the geographies of Roman writers. Even bone artifacts can sometimes be clear climatic indicators: large numbers of worn and polished bone skates, for instance, have been found in deposits of Anglo-Scandinavian date in York, England, suggesting that winters were harsh enough to freeze the Ouse river.

RECONSTRUCTING THE HUMAN ENVIRONMENT

All human groups have an impact on their environment, both locally and on a wider scale. One of the most important effects of human interference, the domestication of plants and animals, will be examined in Chapter 7. Here we shall concentrate on how people exploited and managed the landscape and natural resources.

The basic feature of the human environment is the site and the factors influencing the selection of a location. Many of these factors are readily detectable, either visually (proximity to water, strategic position, orientation) or by measurement. The climates of caves and rockshelters, for example, can be assessed through study of temperatures, shade and exposure to sunlight, and exposure to winds in different seasons, since these are the factors that determine their habitability. Site

exploitation territory analysis (see box overleaf) is one recognized procedure for assessing a site's location and the land around it.

Archaeologists should never forget that sometimes the choice of site will have been dictated by factors that we cannot assess: malevolent spirits, "good" or "bad" places – what Ernest Burch, in his study of the Alaskan Eskimo, has called the Nonempirical Environment.

The Immediate Environment: Human Modification of the Living Area

One of the first ways in which people modified their living places was by the controlled use of fire. Archaeologists have debated for decades just how early

People are geomorphic agents and bring a great deal of varied material into their sites – not just food but also tools, fuel, raw materials, etc. Indeed, the human contribution to a sediment can range from less than 1 percent to almost 100 percent. The catchment of a site is the total area from which the site's contents have been derived. At its simplest, therefore, **site catchment analysis** (SCA) is the attempt to work out the full inventory of a site's contents and their sources.

Site catchment analysis as more generally understood, however, is the technique devised by Eric Higgs and Claudio Vita-Finzi for studying the area immediately around a site that would have been exploited by the site's occupants – hence its more accurate name, analysis of **site exploitation territory** (SET). The objective is to calculate the proportions within the territory of such resources as arable or pastoral land, so that conclusions can be drawn

SITE CATCHMENT ANALYSIS

concerning the nature and function of the site.

The SET technique rests on the assumption that the further the resource area is from the site, the less likely will be its exploitation (the costs in terms of time and effort would simply be too great). Using ethnographic data, it was estimated that hunter-gatherers normally exploit an area of roughly 10 km radius around their base – or, since time rather than distance is the limiting factor, a radius of 2 hours' walk. Most farming communities, on the other hand, normally use an area of 5 km radius, or 1 hour's walk. Thus, modern investigators would walk for either 1 or 2 hours outwards from the site in

question, and study various aspects of the landscape and soils. The information gained was drawn up in map form, usually as a circle around the site, distorted by the effects of topography on the distances covered in the set time, and with different categories of land-use or soil-quality inserted.

Modifications and Assessment
Modifications have been made to the original method, primarily because it took a great deal of time. Some scholars simply draw circles around sites, or take shorter walks (on the assumption that the immediate surroundings of a site were the most crucial to its existence). Others assess the land from a high vantage point, or estimate the shape of the site's territory from detailed contour maps.

Assessment of the area around hunter-gatherer sites is relatively easy, involving a study of the landscape, and the location of water supply,

Hunter-gatherer *site exploitation territory: the Middle Paleolithic site of La Ferrassie, Périgord, France. The area within 2-hours' walking distance from the site is considerably smaller than the circle of 10 km radius, because of the distortions imposed by hills around the site.*

Land over 100 m   Land over 200 m

Farming *site exploitation territory: the Early Neolithic (Linear pottery) site of Boulanden, Upper Rhine Valley, Germany. The area within 1 hour's walk from the site has been subdivided into three categories of potential land use (an attempt having been made to reconstruct the likely Neolithic environment).*

Potential arable   Wet grazing   Rough grazing

fords, raw-material sources, natural passages for game, and natural corrals or traps for herds, etc. However, assessment of the area around farming sites is more complex, since it entails an attempt to reconstruct what land would have been exploitable in different periods with different farming technologies. The effects of erosion, irrigation, or terracing need to be taken into account.

Analysis of the soil (see main text) can provide a rough guide to its workability – how much energy is needed to disturb it. Heavy clays, for example, need stronger equipment than loose or sandy soil. Soil potential and fertility are harder to evaluate, and will have altered considerably through time as farming practices changed. Thus, assessments from SET analysis tend to be deliberately vague (good arable, potentially arable, good

grazing), and geomorphological expertise is required to obtain more detail. As much information as possible needs to be gathered about the area's history of land-use, both from documentation and from what the land and soils can reveal to an expert.

Flannery's Combined Method

A combination of catchment area and exploitation territory analysis has sometimes been employed, most notably by Kent Flannery and his colleagues in their work in Oaxaca (see Chapter 13). Here the starting point is not the potential productivity of the area but the resources actually found in the site. Investigation then focuses on where the resources probably came from, a task requiring an excellent knowledge of resource distribution. The result is a possible zonation of resource use around the site, together with the delineation of a catchment area which is usually far larger than the exploitation territory.

This approach avoids the artificiality of a predetermined area of study, but runs the risk of ignoring resources the area could have provided and that have not survived archaeologically. Both methods therefore have advantages and drawbacks. Ultimately it is always wise to combine detailed analyses of the area around particular sites with the more general techniques of regional survey (see Chapter 3), in order to assess how representative the conditions at individual sites really are.

Map legend:
- Alluvium
- Piedmont
- Mountains

2 miles / 3 km

Labels: Obsidian, 390 km; Magnetite, 27 km; Wild plants & small game; 5 km; Deer, peccary; pine, walnut, avocado; Maize, squash; Salt; San José Mogote; 1 km; Chert; 2.5 km; Salt; Pottery clay, Magnetite; Magnetite, 33 km; Shell, 200 km; Atoyac R.

Flannery's analysis of the catchment and exploitation territory around the village of San José Mogote, Oaxaca, Mexico. He concluded that most of the village's agricultural needs would have been satisfied within a 2.5-km radius of the site.

fire was introduced. Until recently the earliest contender was Zhoukoudian cave in China at some half a million years ago. In 1988, however, C. K. Brain and Andrew Sillen discovered pieces of apparently burnt animal bone at the Swartkrans Cave, South Africa, in layers dating to *c.* 1.5 million years ago. In order to confirm that the bones had indeed been altered by fire, Brain and Sillen carried out experiments with fresh bones, examining the cell structure and chemical changes that occurred when the bones were heated to various temperatures and cooled slowly. Microscopic analysis showed that these changes were very similar to those in the fossil bones, suggesting that the latter were probably cooled on a wood fire at temperatures of less than 300°C (572°F) up to 500°C (932°F). The bones came from antelope, warthog, zebra, and baboon. Remains of early hominids, including *Homo erectus*, found in the cave layers give a strong indication as to who tended those fires.

The presence of fire in a cave is important not only for cooking and human comfort, but also because it affects the cave's microclimates and can accelerate weathering of the walls, as was mentioned in the box on cave sediments in an earlier section.

Archaeologists can show that people adapted to cave life in the Upper Paleolithic in other ways too. Visual examination has found evidence for scaffolding in some decorated caves such as Lascaux in France. Excavations elsewhere have unearthed traces of pavements of slabs, and of shelters. Specialized analysis of cave sediments can even unearth proof of bedding and the use of animal skins as floor coverings. Arlette Leroi-Gourhan, for example, has used pollen analysis to show the presence of clusters of grasses in Lascaux, and armfuls of unburned grasses around a hearth at Fontanet, France, both of which probably indicate bedding. Cave sediments analyzed by Rolf Rottländer at the Upper Paleolithic cave of Geissenklösterle in western Germany showed such a huge proportion of fat that it suggests the floor was probably covered in the skins of large mammals.

Besides caves, archaeologists can investigate evidence from open sites for tents, wind-breaks, and other architectural remains as indicators of the way in which people modified their own immediate environment during the Paleolithic. For later periods, of course, this evidence multiplies enormously and we move into the realm of full-scale architecture and town planning discussed elsewhere (Chapters 5, 10).

Modification of the immediate environment is certainly fundamental to human culture. But how can we learn something about the varied ways in which people manipulated the world beyond?

Human Exploitation of the Wider Environment

Methods for Investigating Land Use. Examination of the soils around human habitations can be carried out where sections are exposed, or where an original land surface is laid bare beneath a monument. Specialists can go some way to reconstructing human use of the land by a combination of all the methods outlined in earlier sections. However, a different method is needed for cases where the area around the site has to be assessed on the surface.

This kind of off-site analysis was first developed systematically by Claudio Vita-Finzi and Eric Higgs in their work on sites in Israel, and has since been widely adopted, albeit with modifications and variations. Two distinct types of investigation are involved – site catchment analysis and site exploitation territory analysis – together with combinations and variations, and these methods are discussed in the box on the previous two pages.

Gardens. The archaeology of gardens, whether decorative or food-producing, is a subdiscipline that has only recently come to the fore, devoted to the accurate study, and in some cases the reconstruction, of ancient gardens. Examples include the complexes of mounds, terraces, and walls that constituted the Maori gardens of New Zealand; the formal garden of the 8th century AD imperial villa at Nara in Japan; and especially those of Roman villas like that at Fishbourne, southern England. The best known are probably those preserved by the volcanic debris at Pompeii and its adjacent settlements. In most cases, as at Nara, a combination of excavation and analysis of plant remains has led to an accurate reconstruction; but at Pompeii, identification of species comes not only from pollen, seeds, and charred wood, but also from the hollows left by tree-roots, casts of which can be taken in the same way as for corpses (see Chapter 11). Such casts can even provide details about gardening techniques: for instance, the base of a lemon tree in a garden of Poppaea's villa at Oplontis, near Pompeii, showed clearly that it had been grafted, a method still used in the region to obtain new lemon trees.

Human Impact on Water Resources. Human effects on water resources have not yet received much attention from archaeologists, but recent evidence shows clearly that pollution of rivers is by no means confined to our own epoch. Excavations in the city of York, northeast England, have revealed changes in the composition of freshwater fish over the past 1900 years, with a marked shift from clean-water species such as salmon and grayling to species more tolerant of polluted water (such as perch and roach). This change occurs around the 10th century AD, when the Viking town underwent rapid development, apparently intensifying pollution of the Ouse river in the process. The shift is mirrored in remains of freshwater molluscs, which change from species requiring well-oxygenated (i.e. clean) water to others that are less demanding.

Land Management Using Field Systems. Management of land is detectable in several ways. The clearest evidence comprises the various traces visible on the land surface, such as the 300 ha (741 acres) of Maya ridged fields at Pulltrouser Swamp, Belize, linked by a network of canals; the spectacular mountain terraces of the Incas; the *chinampas* (fertile reclaimed land, made of mud dredged from canals) of the Aztecs; or the similar but very much older drainage ditches and fertile garden lands of Kuk Swamp, New Guinea (see box overleaf). Similarly, in Britain archaeologists have discovered Bronze Age stone boundary walls, known as reaves, on Dartmoor, and field systems and lynchets (small banks that build up against field boundaries on slopes) in many areas.

Artifacts and art can also be a valuable source of information about ancient land management. Han dynasty sites in China, for example, have yielded pottery models of paddy fields, some of them with irrigation ponds with a movable gate at the center of a dam, used to regulate the flow of water into the field.

Evidence for Plowing. Investigation of mounds, including their mollusc and pollen content, and especially the original soils and land surfaces beneath them, can reveal whether there was any cultivation before they were erected. Occasionally, archaeologists are even fortunate enough to uncover buried land surfaces that preserve marks made by plows or ards (ards score a furrow but do not turn the soil). The marks found beneath the Neolithic burial mound at South Street, England, are a good example. Although evidence from prehistoric Danish burial mounds suggest that these marks are not in fact functional (that is, produced in the course of soil cultivation) but are a part of the mound-building ritual, they nevertheless provide some indication of the land management techniques available in different periods and on different soils.

Management of Woodland and Vegetation. Many of the techniques for analyzing plant remains, outlined

Buried land surface revealed beneath the Neolithic burial mound at South Street, southern England, showing criss-cross grooves in the soil made by an ard.

earlier in the chapter, can be used to demonstrate human manipulation of woodland and vegetation generally.

Waterlogged wood, found abundantly in archaeological deposits in the Somerset Levels, England, by John and Bryony Coles, has been used by them to demonstrate the earliest known examples of systematic pollarding and coppicing, dating from about 4000 BC. The evidence consists of remains of thin poles of regular size, produced by cutting trees down to stumps and thus stimulating rapid growth of spring shoots and rods that could be harvested repeatedly. In coppicing, the poles are grown near the ground, while in pollarding the trunks are left some meters high to avoid the effects of grazing animals.

Charcoal fragments have been discovered in turves used by Neolithic builders to construct a burial mound at Dalladies in Scotland. The presence of the charcoal indicated that the turves had been cut from grassland formed just after the burning of forest. It is also interesting to reflect on the fact that the farmers could sacrifice 7300 sq. m (8730 sq. yd) of this rich turf in order to build their monument.

Pollen analysis is another highly important method for demonstrating deliberate woodland clearance. The American scholar David Rue has analyzed pollen from cores taken near the Maya city of Copán, Honduras, and managed to trace the process of forest clearance and cultivation in the area. Since there is no evidence for any significant climatic change in the late postglacial of Central America, he could safely attribute the shifts in the pollen record to human activity. Clearings

ANCIENT GARDENS AT KUK SWAMP

Kuk Swamp is a 283-ha (700-acre) property in the Wahgi Valley, near Mount Hagen, at an altitude of 1550 m (5084 ft) in the highlands of New Guinea. It contains features that have been interpreted as evidence of some of the world's oldest gardening practices.

The area lay underwater until drainage was begun for a Tea Research Station, giving opportunity in 1972 for a study to begin led by Jack Golson and his colleagues. Air photographs had revealed that old ditch systems covered virtually the whole swamp. The widely- spaced ditches dug for the new plantation, then and in subsequent years, provided the researchers with many kilometers of cross-sections for stratigraphic study. Layers of ash found intermittently in the profiles from volcanic eruptions along the New Guinea north coast could be dated to provide the basis of a chronology. Swamp grasses were also cleared to reveal surface features such as 40 houses (some of which were excavated), and the filled outlines of old channels.

The results revealed a long history of agricultural use, with episodes of large-scale drainage for cultivation separated by periods of abandonment.

By about **9000 years ago**, when the climate had become similar to today's, a layer of grey clay began to be deposited in Kuk Swamp; geomorphological

UI, a native New Guinean, displays a paddle-shaped wooden spade excavated from a drainage ditch.

Intersecting drainage ditches of various prehistoric periods.

study indicated that this was inwashed soil eroding from the surrounding hills, where primary forest was being cleared, probably for gardens. Features such as ditches, pits, and stakeholes under the grey clay suggest that the swamp too was being gardened by this time, if only briefly. It is assumed that plants such as bananas, yams, and taro were being grown, although only banana phytoliths were recovered from a core through the Kuk deposits.

By **6000 years ago**, large-scale cultivation was underway. Several drainage channels, hundreds of meters long, were cut. A network of little channels enclosed circular island gardens, 1–2 m (3.3–6.6 ft) across.

By **5500 years ago**, the major drains were allowed to silt up, and there are no indications of human use of the area for the next 1500 years, for reasons as yet unknown. Thereafter, cycles of use and disuse, and the appearance of field systems with a grid pattern of trenches, have been explained in terms of deforestation; the introduction of pig husbandry; the advent of a new crop, the sweet potato, around 300 years ago; warfare; and malaria – which may account for the most recent abandonment in the 19th century.

The earliest houses date to about 250 years ago, some containing charred fragments of sweet potatoes. The contemporaneous grid patterns of ditches and beds are the same as those used in dry-land sweet-potato cultivation elsewhere in the region today. Another element of continuity is evident in the artifacts discovered: wooden tools ranging from 100 to 500 years old. These include digging sticks, and paddle-shaped spades up to 2 m (6.6 ft) long for scooping out the ditches – and having the same function in modern dry-land gardens.

It was the recent tea-plantation ditches that helped initiate the project, but swamp drainage undertaken for commercial projects of this kind is now threatening the survival – both at Kuk and at similar sites in the region – of some of the world's oldest agricultural remains.

Air view (above), looking north, showing large prehistoric drainage ditches together with smaller trenches defining a grid of gardens. All these features belong to the most recent systems at Kuk, ending in the 19th century. Two modern parallel drains of the Tea Research Station cut across the landscape from east to west.

Clearing swamp vegetation (below) to expose surface features, such as houses and the outlines of old ditches.

had been made in the forest using swidden (slash-and-burn) techniques and maize agriculture had begun apparently in the pre-ceramic phase at least 4500 years ago. Forest clearance was intensified 1500 years later, and then maintained on a large scale until Copán was abandoned in AD 1200. These findings support not only the early dates from phytolith work (see earlier section) but also the view that ecological stress and soil degradation were probably important in the downfall of cities such as this. (In Chapter 12 we consider more generally the possible reasons for the collapse of cities and civilizations.)

It is known that the vegetation of much of Australia has been changed by the controlled burning practices of the Aborigines, who have managed the landscape in ways that prevent out-of-control bushfires, and create new environments that attract grazing animals with new shoots. Indeed, these techniques – dubbed "fire-stick farming" by the archaeologist Rhys Jones – are being reintroduced in Australian National Parks to prevent uncontrolled fires. There is controversial evidence from pollen that such practices may perhaps be traced back 130,000 years, whereas the earliest archaeological evidence for people in Australia is only about 50,000 years old. Gurdip Singh's studies of sediment cores from Lake George, New South Wales, have revealed a period when there was a sudden increase in destructive bush fires, reflected in greatly increased quantities of charcoal, and coinciding with a sudden and dramatic change in vegetation, the first in 750,000 years, when fire-sensitive forests began to be replaced by the fire-tolerant eucalyptus, together with grasses. Singh has placed the event at around 130,000 years ago from pollen diagrams in conjunction with results from deep-sea cores. Many scholars find the date – though not the event – archaeologically unacceptable. The archaeologist Richard Wright, for instance, through a simple correlation of age with depth in the lake cores, has assigned the vegetation change to 60,000–54,000 years ago, a date far closer to the archaeologically agreed date for the earliest human presence in Australia.

Plant macroremains have also been used successfully together with other evidence to indicate woodland clearance. The Anasazi, one of the most advanced pre-Columbian societies in North America, erected buildings in Chaco Canyon, New Mexico, which were the largest and highest in that continent until the advent of the skyscraper. Construction began in the early 10th century AD, and it has been estimated that 100,000 ponderosa pine trees were needed for the timber. Recently, Julio Betancourt and his colleagues have examined plant macroremains at Chaco cemented into crystallized urine in ancient packrat middens that can be radiocarbon dated. Since packrats are known to gather plant materials from within 30 m (98 ft) of their dens, these fragments and their associated pollen have permitted the reconstruction of Chaco's vegetational history for the last 11,000 years.

It appears that during the first two centuries of human occupation in Chaco Canyon, the pinyon and juniper woodland of the surrounding clifftops was cleared for firewood for a radius of 20 km (12.5 miles). Only relentless woodcutting to meet the fuel demands of a growing population can explain this drastic reduction, because any climatic change in this period was within the range of climatic extremes of earlier millennia, when no such reduction occurred. Study of the timber in the buildings was also instructive: some of the ponderosa pine logs for construction had to be hauled from distances exceeding 40 km (25 miles); and, as the pines declined, the inhabitants began, in AD 1030, to fetch spruce and fir logs from over 75 km (46 miles) away. The environmental damage caused by all this activity was irreversible, and though tree-ring studies have suggested that a drought struck the final blow to the Chaco settlements, the inhabitants were clearly to blame to a large extent.

Human Impact on Island Environments

The most devastating human impact on environments can be seen on islands to which settlers introduced new animals and plants. While some of these "transported landscapes" became exactly what the colonists required, others went tragically wrong.

The most notable examples are to be found in Polynesia. The first European explorers who came to these islands assumed that the environments they saw there had remained unchanged, despite the earlier colonization by Polynesians. This view was due in large measure to their paternalistic view of the natives as noble savages, innocents living in harmony with their surroundings like other animals. However, archaeologists can never assume that "what is must always have been so," and work over the last few decades has proved that the Polynesian settlers were only too human in their environmental depredations.

A combination of palynology, analysis of plant and animal macro- and micro-remains, and many of the other techniques outlined above have produced a dramatic picture of change. The first arrivals exploited the indigenous resources very heavily during their settling-in phase: the faunal record generally shows an

Human impact on island environments is particularly evident in the Pacific region, where human colonization came relatively late (map pp. 144-45), but often with devastating effect on indigenous plants and animals. Botanical and faunal evidence shows that human predation, deforestation, and newly introduced competitor species caused widespread destruction. In New Zealand, 13 species of the great flightless moa became extinct (two are shown at right, with the much smaller kiwi that still survives).

immediate massive reduction in usable meat. For example, Patrick Kirch found that the remains of shellfish and turtle on Tikopia (Solomon Islands) quickly declined in both size and abundance. Most of these resources never recovered, and many were completely wiped out.

The chief cause of extinction was the range of new species introduced to the islands by the settlers. It was certainly necessary for them to bring some, since the islands generally had very few indigenous edible plants and animals. But in addition to the domestic pigs, dogs, and fowl, and the crop plants, they inadvertently brought stowaways such as the Polynesian rat, geckos, and all kinds of weeds and invertebrates (the rat may even have been brought intentionally). These new and highly competitive predators and weeds had drastic effects on the vulnerable island environments. Rats, for example, must have killed native birds and their eggs, which, combined with human predation for meat and plumage, led to large-scale extinction. In Hawaii, dozens of indigenous bird species were wiped out very rapidly, while in New Zealand about 13 species of the great flightless moa disappeared, together with 16 other kinds of birds.

However, predation was only part of the picture; destruction of habitat was probably the major killer. Pollen, phytoliths, charcoal, and landsnails in Hawaii, New Zealand, and elsewhere combine to reveal a rapid and massive deforestation in the lowlands, producing open grassland in a few centuries. Not only did this have a drastic effect on vegetation and birds, it also eliminated hundreds of molluscan species. In addition, the clearing of vegetation from hillsides to make gardens led to greater erosion: some early sites are covered with meters of alluvium and slopewash.

In other words, people brought their own "landscapes" to these islands, and rapidly altered them both dramatically and irrevocably, both intentionally and accidentally. Analysis of the environmental history of this part of the world makes it plain that (apart from volcanic eruptions) natural catastrophes such as hurricanes, earthquakes, and tidal waves have not affected vegetation to any extent. The changes in landscape and resources have occurred only since the arrival of humans – 1000 years ago in New Zealand, 2000 years ago in Hawaii, 3000 years ago in Western Polynesia.

Easter Island. The ultimate example of this process of devastation occurred on Easter Island, the most isolated piece of inhabited land in the world. Here, the settlers wrought environmental damage that is perhaps unique both in its extent and in its cultural and social consequences. Analysis by the British palynologist

Human impact on Easter Island. This remote Pacific island has long been famous for its giant statues (above), but palynologists have only recently discovered that this now treeless environment had forests of large palms before human arrival (top right: palm pollen; top left: palm endocarps).

John Flenley and his colleagues of pollen from cores taken from lakes in the volcanic craters of the island has revealed much of its vegetational history, and in particular the fact that until the arrival of humans in about AD 400 the island was covered with forest. The vegetation was probably dominated by a large palm tree, now extinct but closely related to the Chilean wine palm; not only has its pollen been identified, but a number of ancient endocarps (palm fruits, 820 years old) of this species have been recovered from caves on the island, and its root channels detected in the subsoil.

By the last century, every single tree on Easter Island had been cut down, and grassland prevailed. The pollen record shows the decline of forest over the course of a millennium, and since nothing similar had occurred in the pollen record before AD 400 it is clear that people were responsible. It is likely that much of the wood was used for transporting the hundreds of giant statues on the island. In addition, people probably ate the palm fruits; and since those found have all been gnawed by rodents, it is certain that the Polynesian rat, introduced here as elsewhere by the settlers, also ate them. This will have prevented regeneration and thus aided the decline of the tree.

The total loss of timber had several effects. It was probably one of the major reasons for the relatively abrupt termination of statue carving in about AD 1680, because they could no longer be moved. In addition, it was no longer possible to make good canoes, which must have caused a radical decline in exploitation of fish, the main protein source apart from chickens. Deforestation also led to soil erosion (detectable in chemical analysis of the lake-cores) and lower crop yields through the loss of fertile forest soils. The most clearcut case of deforestation in the archaeological record led to starvation and cultural collapse, culminating after AD 1500 in slavery and constant warfare.

SUMMARY

To sum up, humankind has developed from being an inconsequential species at the mercy of the environment to one with a huge influence over its surroundings. Environment is of crucial importance to archaeology. During every period of the past it has played a vital role in determining where and how people could live. Archaeologists now have a battery of techniques to help reconstruct such past environments.

Environmental analysis is no longer undertaken simply to set the scene for particular periods of past human activity, to give some indication of the climate or a site's surroundings. Archaeology now strives to understand former environments in order to assess the key variables that might have influenced the operation of cultural systems. With early farming communities in riverine or estuarine environments, for instance, we need to ascertain not only the basic climate and soil types but also potentially crucial factors such as the extent of the arable area, the frequency of droughts, the pattern of flooding, the rate of silting, and any problems of drainage. The emphasis is no longer on individual sites in isolation, but on site systems, and on changing patterns of land use through time.

Our present techniques may grant us only a partial and imperfect view of environmental change, but we are steadily developing improved methods, and already we know far more than the early archaeologists could ever have dreamed possible.

Further Reading

General introductions to environmental archaeology can be found in the following:

Butzer, K. W. 1971. *Environment and Archaeology*. (2nd ed.) Aldine; Chicago.

Butzer, K. W. 1982. *Archaeology as Human Ecology*. Cambridge University Press: Cambridge & New York.

Evans, J. G. 1978. *An Introduction to Environmental Archaeology*. Paul Elek: London; Cornell University Press: Ithaca, NY.

Shackley, M. 1981. *Environmental Archaeology*. Allen & Unwin: London & Boston.

Books on the broad environmental setting include:

Cornwall, I. W. 1958. *Soils for the Archaeologist*. Phoenix House: London.

Davidson, D. A. & Shackley, M. L. (eds.). 1976. *Geoarchaeology: Earth Science and the Past*. Duckworth: London

Limbrey, S. 1975. *Soil Science and Archaeology*. Academic Press: London & New York.

Vita-Finzi, C. 1978. *Archaeological Sites in their Setting*. Thames & Hudson: London & New York.

Books on the plant environment include:

Dimbleby, G. 1978 *Plants and Archaeology*. Paladin: London.

Pearsall, D.M. 1989. *Paleoethnobotany: A Handbook of Procedures*. Academic Press: New York & London.

Renfrew, J. 1973. *Paleoethnobotany*. Methuen: London

For the animal environment, good starting points are:

Klein, R. G. & Cruz-Uribe, K. 1984. *The Analysis of Animal Bones from Archaeological Sites*. University of Chicago Press: Chicago.

Davis, S. J. M. 1987. *The Archaeology of Animals*. Batsford: London. Yale University Press: New Haven.

7
What Did They Eat? Subsistence and Diet

Having discussed methods for reconstructing the environment, we now turn to how we find out about what people extracted from it. The study of subsistence is one of the most technically developed fields of archaeology. Subsistence is the most basic of all necessities. Although the term sometimes includes fuel and clothing – topics we will cover in Chapter 8 and elsewhere – it is usually taken to mean the quest for food, documented almost everywhere by the waste products of food preparation, both plant and animal. In addition, there have been significant recent developments in the study of human remains, mainly human bone, as a source of information about diet.

In discussing early subsistence, it is useful to make a distinction between *meals*, direct evidence of various kinds as to what people were eating at a particular time, and *diet*, which implies the pattern of consumption over a long period of time.

So far as meals are concerned, the sources of information are varied. Written records, when they survive, indicate some of the things people were eating, and so do representations in art. Even modern ethnoarchaeology helps indicate what they *might* have been eating by broadening our understanding of their range of options. And the actual remains of the foodstuffs eaten can be highly informative.

For the much more difficult question of diet, there are several helpful techniques of investigation. Some methods focus on human bones. As described in this chapter, isotopic analyses of the skeletal remains of a human population can indicate, for example, the balance of marine and terrestrial foods in the diet, and even show differences in nutrition between the more and less advantaged members of the same society.

Most of our information about early subsistence, however, comes directly from the remains of what was eaten. Zooarchaeology (or archaeozoology), the study of past human use of animals, is now big business in archaeology. There can be few excavations anywhere

that do not have a specialist to study the animal bones found. The Paleo-Indian rockshelter of Meadowcroft, Pennsylvania, for example, yielded about a million animal bones (and almost 1.5 million plant specimens). On medieval and recent sites, the quantities of material recovered can be even more formidable. Paleoethnobotany (or archaeobotany), the study of past human use of plants, is likewise a growing discipline, with a number of techniques for determining the plant species recovered. In both areas, a detailed understanding of the conditions of preservation on a site (Chapter 2) is a first prerequisite to ensure that the most efficient extraction technique is adopted. The excavator has to decide, for instance, whether a bone requires consolidation before it is removed, or whether plant material can best be recovered by flotation (Chapter 6). In both areas, too, the focus of interest has developed to include not just the species eaten, but the way these were managed. The process of domestication for both plants and animals is now a major research interest.

Interpretation of food remains requires quite sophisticated procedures. We can initially reconstruct the "menu" available in the surrounding environment (Chapter 6), but the only incontrovertible proof that a particular plant or animal species was actually consumed is the presence of its traces in stomach contents or in coprolites (fossilized feces), as will be seen in the section on human remains below. In all other cases, one has to make the inference from the context or condition of the finds: charred grain in an oven, cut or burned bones, or residues in a vessel. Plant remains need to be understood in terms of the particular stage reached in their processing at the time they were deposited. Bone remains have to be considered in terms of butchering practices. Plants that were staples in the diet may be underrepresented thanks to the generally poor preservation of vegetable remains. Fish bones likewise may not survive well.

In addition to these questions, the archaeologist has to consider how far a site's food remains are representative of total diet. Here one needs to assess a site's function, and whether it was inhabited once or frequently, for short or long periods, irregularly or seasonally (season of occupation can sometimes be deduced from plant and animal evidence as well). A long-term settlement is likely to provide more representative food remains than a specialized camp or kill site. Ideally, however, archaeologists should sample remains from a variety of contexts or sites before making judgments about diet.

WHAT CAN PLANT FOODS TELL US ABOUT DIET?

Macrobotanical Remains

The vast majority of plant evidence that reaches the archaeologist is in the form of macrobotanical remains, usually desiccated, waterlogged, or preserved by charring. Such remains can also survive by being partly or wholly replaced by minerals percolating through sediment, a process that tends to occur in places like latrine pits with high concentrations of salts. The remains are often retrieved by flotation (Chapter 6). It is the absence of moisture or fresh air that leads to good preservation by preventing the activity of putrefactive microbes. Plant remains preserved in several different ways can sometimes be encountered within the same site, but in most parts of the world charring is the principal or only cause of preservation on habitation sites.

Occasionally, a single sample on a site will yield very large amounts of material. Over 60 lb (27 kg) of charred barley, wheat, and other plants came from one storage pit on a Bronze Age farm at Black Patch, southern England, for example. This can give clues to the relative importance of different cereals and legumes and weed flora, but the sample nevertheless simply reflects a moment in time. What the archaeologist really needs is a larger number of samples (each of preferably more than 100 grains) from a single period on the site, and, if possible, from a range of types of deposit, in order to obtain reliable information about what species were exploited, their importance, and their uses during the period of time in question.

Having obtained sufficient samples, one needs to quantify the plant remains. This can be done by weight, by number of remains, or by some equivalent of the Minimum Number of Individuals technique used for bones (see below). Some scholars have suggested dispensing with percentages of plant remains in a site, and simply placing them in apparent order of abundance. But numerical frequency can be misleading, as was shown by the British archaeobotanist Jane Renfrew in her study of the material from the Neolithic settlement of Sitagroi, Greece. She pointed out that the most abundant plant in the sample may have been preserved by chance (such as an accident in the course of baking) and thus be overrepresented. Similarly, species that produce seeds or grains in abundance may appear to have an exaggerated importance in the archaeological record: at Sitagroi, 19,000 seeds of *Polygonum aviculare* or knotgrass barely filled a thimble; and it makes little sense to equate an acorn with a cereal grain or a vetch seed. Quite apart from size differences, they make very different contributions to a diet.

Interpreting the Context. It is crucial for the archaeologist or specialist to try to understand the archaeological context of a plant sample. In the past attention used to be focused primarily on the botanical history of the plants themselves, their morphology, place of origin, and evolution. Now, however, archaeologists also want to know more about the human use of plants in hunting and gathering economies, and in agriculture – which plants were important in the diet, and how they were gathered or grown, processed, stored, and cooked. This means understanding the different stages of plant processing; recognizing the effect different processes have on the remains; and identifying the different contexts in the archaeological record. In some cases it is the plant remains that reveal the function of the location where they are found, and thus the nature of the context, rather than vice versa.

In a farming economy, there are many different stages of plant processing. For example, cereals have to be threshed, winnowed, and cleaned before consumption, in order to separate the grain from the chaff, straw, and weeds; but seed corn also has to be stored for the next year's crop; and food grain might also be stored unthreshed in order to minimize damage from pests, and would then be threshed only when needed. Many of these activities are well documented in our recent agricultural past, before mechanization took over, and they are still observable ethnoarchaeologi-

BEHAVIOR IN THE PAST

1. THRESHING
straw flooring, etc.

2. RAKING to remove straw

3. WINNOWING

4. COARSE SIEVING

5. ROASTING (& MALTING)
accidental charring

6. POUNDING

7. WINNOWING

8. SIEVING

9. FINE SIEVING

10. OVEN DRYING

11. STORAGE
infested grain burnt, granary fire

12. HAND SORTING

13. MILLING

PRESERVATION OF
THE EVIDENCE

WELLS
AND PITS

HEARTHS

LATRINES

waterlogged sewage

Cereal crop processing: waste products from many of these stages may survive as charred or waterlogged remains.

cally in cultures with differing degrees of efficiency and technological capability. In addition, many experiments have been carried out in crop processing. From these observations it is known that certain activities leave characteristic residues with which archaeological samples can be compared, whether from ovens, living floors, latrines, or storage pits.

In his study of the plant material from the Bulgarian Neolithic site of Chevdar (6th millennium BC), the British archaeologist Robin Dennell noted that samples from the ovens had been processed, as one might expect, and were being either dried for storage or cooked when they were accidentally charred. Samples from floors on the other hand contained a higher percentage of weed seeds, but no spikelets (small, spike-shaped subdivisions of an ear of grain), which suggested that they were still in the process of being prepared, but had already been threshed and winnowed. The number and variety of weed species present can give clues to the effectiveness of the processing. Most samples show some mixing of different crops, and archaeologists need to bear this in mind when

interpreting the data – indeed, the crops may have been mixed at the sowing stage in a fail-safe strategy of growing everything together in the hope that at least something would ripen.

In short, it is desirable, as mentioned earlier, to take samples from as wide an area as possible in the site, and from a variety of contexts. A species that dominates in a number of samples and contexts may be reckoned to have been important in the economy. Change through time can be assessed accurately only by comparing samples from similar contexts and processing stages, because the plant remains recovered in a site are not random in composition, and may not necessarily reflect the full crop economy. This is particularly true of charred samples, for many important plant foods may never undergo charring. Hulled wheats such as emmer, for example, which require parching to free their grains, are far more likely to be charred than are free-threshing varieties such as bread wheat. Plants that are boiled, eaten raw, or used for juices and to make drinks may never undergo charring, and will therefore be underrepresented or totally

PALEOETHNOBOTANY: A CASE STUDY

The recovery and identification of plant remains from archaeological contexts are merely the first steps in a wide-ranging series of research issues that make up paleoethnobotany, also known as archaeobotany. Such issues encompass not only the reconstruction of past environments (Chapter 6) and economies, but also the origins and spread of agriculture (see box below, Farming Origins: A Case Study) and human use of – and

impact on – plant communities in the broadest sense. In addition to studying the plant remains themselves, archaeobotanists can learn a great deal from ethnoarchaeological observation among human groups still practicing traditional methods of plant use or farming, and from assessing the natural potential of the plants in the relevant ecological settings.

A good way to gain an insight into these methods is to look in detail at a recent successful case study.

Wadi Kubbaniya

Four sites dating to between 19,000 and 17,000 years ago were excavated by Fred Wendorf and his associates at this locality northwest of Aswan in Upper Egypt. The sites have produced the most diverse assemblage of food plant remains ever recovered from any Paleolithic excavation in the Old World. The material, which owes its good preservation to rapid burial by sand and the area's great aridity, is concentrated around hearths of wood charcoal, and is dominated by charred fragments of soft vegetable foods, a category of plant that normally has very low archaeological visibility. Flotation (Chapter 6) proved useless for this material, because the fragile, dry, remains disintegrated in water; instead, dry sieving had to be employed. Small roasted seeds were

also found in what appear to be the feces of human infants.

Analysis of the charred remains by Gordon Hillman and his colleagues at London's Institute of Archaeology has led to the identification of over 20 different types of food-plant brought into the sites, indicating that the occupants' menu was markedly diverse. By far the most abundant food-plants were tubers of wild nut-grass (*Cyperus rotundus*). Other species included different tubers, as well as club-rushes, dóm palm fruits, and various seeds. A study was carried out to ascertain what contribution the nutgrass tubers were likely to have made to the Paleolithic diet.

Investigation of the plant's modern locations, its yields, and its nutritional value suggested that literally tons of tubers could have been obtained easily each year by means of digging sticks. Annual harvesting stimulates the rapid production of abundant young tubers. Since prehistoric people would certainly have noticed this phenomenon, it is by no means impossible that they evolved a system of management, or proto-horticulture,

Wild nutgrass (Cyperus rotundus). Sketch of the living plant, with a few of its edible tubers. (Above left) One of the charred tubers found at Site E-78-3, during excavations at Wadi Kubbaniya.

Possible seasons of exploitation of major plant foods at Late Paleolithic Wadi Kubbaniya – assuming no storage of food. The varying widths of the bands indicate seasonal variations in the availability (and likely exploitation) of each plant, based on modern growth patterns and known preferences of modern hunter-gatherers. For two months floodwaters probably covered most of the plants, making them inaccessible during that time.

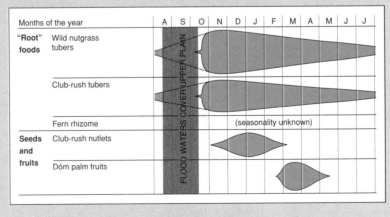

Months of the year		A	S	O	N	D	J	F	M	A	M	J	J
"Root" foods	Wild nutgrass tubers												
	Club-rush tubers												
	Fern rhizome				(seasonality unknown)								
Seeds and fruits	Club-rush nutlets												
	Dóm palm fruits												

FLOOD WATERS COVER UPPER PLAIN

to bring it about consciously.

Ethnographic evidence was available from further afield. Among farming populations in West Africa, Malaysia, and India nutgrass tubers have become a famine food, eaten when crops fail. In some desert areas of Australia, Aborigine hunter-gatherers exploit the tubers as a staple resource. As long as they are cooked to make them digestible and non-toxic, they can be the principal source of calories during months when they are available. Ethnographic evidence also shows that tubers are preferred over seeds because they involve less work in processing.

The next step at Wadi Kubbaniya was to use the plant evidence to study whether occupation at the site was seasonal or year-round. Nutgrass tubers were probably available for at least half the year; but they are at their most palatable during the period of active growth, from October to January. Wadi Kubbaniya has no evidence of storage which might have prolonged the tubers' availability, but their growth period together with that of the other species identified at the site would have ensured a food supply for the full year. This does not prove that occupation was not seasonal, but shows that year-round occupation was feasible on the basis of plant resources alone.

Finally, it should be noted that animal-product resources were also in evidence at the site (e.g. fish bones, molluscs), and that many plants prominent in the area today but unrepresented in the remains could have been of importance (e.g. additional palm fruits, rhizomes, leaves, and roots). What is clear, however, is that nutgrass tubers were the dominant resource – the only plant present in all levels at all four sites – and therefore were probably a dietary staple, if not *the* staple resource.

One of the *four Wadi Kubbaniya sites (designated E-78-3) under excavation.*

absent in an assemblage. If the charring is caused by some accident, the sample may not even be representative of that season's harvest, let alone the site's economy. This again emphasizes the importance of obtaining a variety of samples.

Reconstruction of the crop system that produced the samples is particularly challenging, since entirely different crop systems using the same resources can produce very similar pictures in the archaeological record. Furthermore, it is likely that a great deal of plant refuse was left in the field, used as fuel or fed to animals. Thus we may never know for certain, without literary evidence, precisely what system of fallow or crop rotation was employed at a particular site. But information about questions of this sort is being obtained from experimental work at Butser Farm in southern England (and similar establishments in Denmark, the Netherlands, Germany, and France), where different agricultural techniques are tried out – cultivation with and without manure, various alternations of crops and fallow, etc. This long-term work will take years to provide full results, but already short-term experiments have produced valuable data on crop yields, different types of storage pits, use of sickles, and so on (see box).

Microbotanical Remains

These can also be of help in the reconstruction of diet. Some of the minute particles of silica called *phytoliths* (Chapter 6) are specific to certain parts of a plant (to the root, stem, or flower), and thus their presence may provide clues to the particular harvesting or threshing technique employed on the species. As will be seen below, phytoliths can also help in differentiating wild from domestic species.

The Japanese scientist Hiroshi Fujiwara has found phytoliths of rice (*Oryza sativa*) incorporated in the walls of the latest Jomon pottery of Japan (*c.*500 BC), which shows that rice cultivation already existed at that time. The same scholar has also located ancient paddy fields through the recovery of rice phytoliths from soil samples, and used quantitative analysis of the phytoliths to estimate the depth and areal extent of the fields, and even their total yield of rice. Thus, for example, the Itazuke site in Kyushu district, the oldest paddy field in Japan (final Jomon period, mid–1st millennium BC), had a total yield of 1530 kg (1.5 tons), while the Hidaka site in Kanto district (late Yayoi, first centuries AD) yielded 1440 kg (1.4 tons) – the annual yield cannot yet be estimated since we do not know for how long the fields were in use, and it is not yet possible to compare these figures with modern yields.

BUTSER EXPERIMENTAL IRON AGE FARM

In 1972 Peter Reynolds established a long-term research project on Butser Hill, Hampshire, in southern England. His aim was to create a functioning version of an Iron Age farmstead dating to about 300 BC: a living, open-air research laboratory on a 6 ha (14 acre) area of land. Results were to be compared with evidence excavated from archaeological sites.

All aspects of an Iron Age farm are being explored – structures, craft activities, crops, and domestic animals. Only tools available in this prehistoric period are used. Likewise, prehistoric varieties of crops or their nearest equivalents have been sown, and appropriate livestock brought in.

Several round houses of different types have been constructed. The designs have to be inferred from the posthole patterns that are our only clues to the form of Iron Age houses.

Artist's impression of Butser Ancient Farm. Hurdle fences in the foreground enclose sheep pens. Beyond lie the two round houses of the farm itself.

Replica *Iron Age round house at Butser with its thatched roof.*

Much has been learned about the quantities of timber required (more than 200 trees in the case of a large house), and about the impressive strength of these structures, whose thatched roofs and walls of rods woven between upright stakes have withstood hurricane-force winds and torrential rain.

The farm is intended to be a long-term project, and results so far are only preliminary. But it has already been established that wheat yields are far beyond what was considered likely for the Iron Age, even in drought years, and this may cause a radical revision of population estimates. In addition, the primitive wheats used, such as einkorn (*Triticum monococcum)*, emmer (*Tr. dicoccum*), and spelt (*Tr. spelta*), were found to produce twice as much protein as modern wheats, and to thrive in weed-choked fields without modern fertilizers.

The farm's several fields have been tilled in different ways, such as by an ard (a copy of one found in a Danish peat bog) which stirs up the topsoil but does not invert it. Various systems of crop rotation and fallow are being tested, both with and without manure, and with spring and winter sowing. Also successfully tried out has been a replica of a "vallus," a kind of reaping machine dating to AD 200 that comprises a two-wheeled vehicle pulled by a draft animal and guided by one person.

Peter Reynolds' team have conducted experiments to assess the effects on grain of being stored in different types of pit. One conclusion, supported by ethnographic observations of storage pits in Africa and elsewhere, is that if the seal is impermeable, unparched grain can be stored for long periods without decaying and the germinability maintained.

As for animals, Soay sheep – a type that has remained virtually unaltered for 2000 years – were brought from some Scottish islands. They have proved difficult to keep because of their ability to leap fences. Long-legged Dexter cattle, similar in size and power to the extinct Celtic Shorthorn, have also been installed, and two of them trained for use in traction (pulling the ard).

The Butser Project gives us a fascinating glimpse of the Iron Age brought to life, a working interpretation of the past.

Dexter cattle *being trained as traction animals to pull the Iron Age ard or plow. After training, two men are sufficient, one to guide the cattle and another the ard.*

239

In addition, phytoliths found adhering to the edges of stone tools (see below) may provide information about the plants on which the tools were used, although such plants may not have figured in the diet.

Pollen grains often survive in coprolites, but most of them were probably inhaled rather than consumed, and thus they merely add to the picture of the contemporary environment, as shown in Chapter 6.

Plant Impressions

Impressions of plant remains are quite common in fired clay (Chapter 6), and do at least prove that the species in question was present at the spot where the clay was worked. Such impressions, however, should not be taken as representative of economy or diet, since they constitute a very skewed sample and only seeds or grains of medium size tend to leave imprints. One has to be particularly careful with impressions on potsherds, because pottery can be discarded far from its point of manufacture, and in any case many pots were deliberately decorated with grain impressions, thus perhaps overemphasizing the importance of a species. Imprints in other objects can be more helpful, such as those in clay bricks from the 3rd millennium BC in Abu Dhabi on the Persian Gulf which represent

An almost perfect grain impression: two-row barley (x4) from a brick used about AD 800 in the building of a weir in the Nahrwan Canal east of Baghdad, Iraq.

not only two-row barley but also one of the oldest known traces of the cereal crop sorghum.

Turning now from such "passive" evidence, what can be learned from objects that were actually applied to plant materials?

Tools and Other Equipment used in Plant Processing

Tools can prove or at least suggest that plants were processed at a site, and on rare occasions may indicate the species concerned, and the use that was made of it. In some parts of the world, the mere presence of pottery, sickles, or stone grinders in the archaeological record is taken to prove the existence of cereal farming and settled agricultural life. But in themselves they are inadequate indicators of such features, and require supporting evidence such as remains of domesticated plants. Sickles, for example, may have been used to cut reeds or wild grasses (and a polish or "sickle-sheen" on them is sometimes seen as proof of such a use), while grinders can be employed to process wild plants, meat, cartilage, salt, or pigments. Objects from more recent cultures often have clearer functions – for example, the bread ovens (containing round loaves) at the bakery of Modestus in Pompeii, the flour-grinding mills and wine-presses of the same city, or the great olive-crushers in a Hellenistic house at Praisos, Crete.

Analysis of Plant Residues

Since most tools are fairly mute evidence in themselves, it follows that we can learn far more about their function – or at least their final function before entering the archaeological record – from any residues left on them. Over 50 years ago the German scientist Johannes Grüss was analyzing such residues under the microscope, and identified substances such as wheat beer and mead in two North German drinking horns from a peat bog. Today this sort of analysis is taking on an increased importance.

As we shall see in Chapter 8, microwear analysis of a tool edge can identify broadly whether the tool was used to cut meat, wood, or some other material. Discovery of phytoliths, as mentioned above, can show what type of grasses were cut by a tool. Microscopic study can also reveal and identify plant fibers. A recent development is chemical analysis of residues on tool edges: certain chemical reagents can provide a means of proving whether plant residues are present on tools or in vessels – thus, potassium iodide turns blue if starch grains are present, and yellow-brown for other plant materials. Important work of this kind has been carried out at prehistoric sites by the American researcher Frederick Briuer. For example, under the light microscope he examined some unwashed stone tools from O'Haco Shelter in northeast Arizona, spanning the period 6700 BC-AD 1300, and revealed the presence of residues on their working edges. He then subjected scrapings from these residues to tests with chemical reagents, which led him to the conclusion that at least 25 percent of the tools had been used for some kind of plant processing or procurement.

Chemical investigation of fats preserved in vessels is also making progress, because it has been found that fatty acids, amino acids (the constituents of protein) and similar substances are very stable and preserve well. Samples are extracted from residues, purified, concentrated in a centrifuge, dried, and then analyzed by means of a spectrometer, and by a technique known as chromatography which separates the major constituent components of the fats. Interpretation of the results is made by comparison with a reference collection of "chromatograms" (read-outs) from different substances. By these means, not only the "menu" but even individual "recipes" from the past can sometimes be identified.

For example, the German chemist Rolf Rottländer has identified mustard, olive oil, seed oils, butter, and other substances on potsherds, including specimens from Neolithic lake dwellings. In work on sherds from the German Iron Age hillfort of the Heuneburg, he has been able to prove that some amphorae – storage vessels usually associated with liquids – did indeed contain olive oil and wine, whereas in the case of a Roman amphora the charcoal-like black residue proved to be not liquid but wheat flour. This important technique not only provides dietary evidence, but also helps to define the function of the vessels with which the fats are associated.

A further extension of chemical techniques involves isotopic analysis of organic residues, with particular reference to nitrogen and carbon isotope ratios. It is known that beans and other legumes obtain their nitrogen by means of bacterial fixation of atmospheric nitrogen, whereas all other plants obtain it from the soil. Since all legumes are terrestrial, and marine plants do not fix atmospheric nitrogen in this way (but have a distinctive ratio of carbon isotopes), it follows that isotopic analysis can divide plants into three groups: legumes, non-leguminous terrestrial plants, and marine plants.

Through this method, plant residues which were previously unidentifiable can now be characterized. The technique has been applied by Christine Hastorf and Michael DeNiro to prehistoric (200 BC-AD 1000)

material from the Upper Mantaro Valley in the central Peruvian Andes which was extracted by flotation but proved to be too burned for normal identification on the basis of morphology. Instead, encrusted organic matter was scraped from some potsherds for examination. Analysis in the scanning electron microscope indicated an absence of bone fragments, which suggested that it was plant material. Isotopic analysis (carbon and nitrogen) was compared with known values for plants from the region, and revealed that the residues came from tubers, including potatoes, which had been boiled and mashed before charring. This accounted for the even distribution of the encrustation on the pots, while the fact that it was limited to the plainest types of pot suggested that such food was probably typical of daily domestic cooking. This is a good instance where, thanks to a new technique, material that was useless to the archaeologist until recently now reveals information on diet and cooking processes. The analysis results corresponded well with modern practices in the same region.

It is not even necessary for actual residues to be visible in a vessel, since we now know that deposits such as oils and resins actually percolate into the clay's fabric and remain there indefinitely. A sherd can be pulverized, and treated with solvents to isolate any trapped organic residues; these are then analyzed by spectrometers and chromatography, which reveal minute amounts of the vessel's contents. Using these techniques, British chemist John Evans has even discovered traces of opium in a 3500-year-old vase from Cyprus, showing that our Neolithic ancestors were probably as interested in drugs as we are today, and suggesting the existence of a drug trade in the eastern Mediterranean at that time.

Strategies of Plant Use: Seasonality and Domestication

Many plants are only available at certain times of the year, and can therefore provide clues about when a site was occupied. For example, early Neolithic fish traps at Muldbjerg in Denmark were made from willow and hazel twigs less than two years old and cut in early June. Plant remains can also help indicate what was eaten in particular seasons – ripe seeds give an indication of harvest time, and many fruits are limited to certain seasons. Of course, such evidence of *seasonality* has to be extrapolated from modern representatives of the plants in question, and evidence of food storage may indicate that occupation of a site continued beyond the seasons when particular resources were available.

INVESTIGATING THE RISE OF FARMING IN THE NEAR EAST

The inception of farming (stock rearing and agriculture) was recognized as a decisive step many decades ago by Gordon Childe, who in 1941 coined the term Neolithic Revolution. Our interest here, like Childe's, focuses on the Near East, but we should not forget that comparable developments as we now know occurred independently in other parts of the world.

In the postwar years, a succession of multidisciplinary field expeditions have sought to find evidence for, and to extend, the ideas outlined by Childe. Robert J. Braidwood in Iraq, Frank Hole in Iran, Kathleen Kenyon in Palestine, and James Mellaart in Turkey led what one might call the first wave of research. Together their field projects embraced what Braidwood termed "the hilly flanks of the fertile crescent:" the slopes of the Zagros Mountains to the east, the Levant Plain to the west, and to the north the slopes of the Taurus Mountains and beyond. In recent decades, immense improvements in the recovery and analysis of plant and animal remains have transformed our understanding of the farming revolution.

From Jarmo to Jericho
In 1948 Braidwood, of the Oriental Institute in Chicago, led the first of many expeditions to Iraq which set new standards in problem-oriented field research. Braidwood realized that for farming origins the main issue was domestication. When and where had the principal domesticates (wheat and barley, sheep and goat) developed from their wild prototypes? He correctly reasoned that this could only have taken place in or near areas where the wild forms were available. At that time the best guide to the present-day distribution of such species came from rainfall and vegetation maps. But Braidwood knew that in order to establish the occurrence in prehistory of wild or domesticated varieties, he would need to excavate stratified deposits at a suitable archaeological site.

After survey and trial excavation, Braidwood selected the site of Jarmo, in northern Iraq. In his initial project, published in 1960, he enlisted the cooperation of several specialists. The first was Fred Matson, who undertook *technical ceramic studies* (pottery thin sections, see Chapters 8 and 9) and was also in charge of the collection of samples for the then new technique of *radiocarbon dating*. The geomorphologist Herbert E. Wright, Jr made a *paleoclimatic study*, which at that time was based largely on soil samples. Later the Dutch palynologist W. van Zeist obtained *pollen sequences* from Lake Zeribar which gave a more detailed and comprehensive picture of climatic change. This work allowed the nature of the environment to be established.

One of the most crucial contributions to the Jarmo project came from Hans Helbaek, a specialist in *paleoethnobotany*. He was able to recognize from the charred remains not only early domesticated cereal species, but their wild prototypes. Charles A. Reed surveyed the evidence on animal domestication in the early Near East, using in part the faunal evidence from Jarmo. *Archaeozoology* was thus added to help shape the emerging picture.

These results were significantly enhanced by work in the Levant – in Jordan, Israel, Syria, and Lebanon. A number of sites were excavated belonging to the immediately pre-farming period (the culture termed "Natufian"). It became clear that here there was already settled village life prior to the development of domesticated plants and animals. And at Jericho Kathleen Kenyon found a large, walled settlement already in early farming times and before pottery was used. Its size carried significant social implications, while the discovery there of buried skulls, with faces represented in modeled plaster, indicated religious beliefs of a kind beyond those suggested by baked clay figurines found at Jarmo.

Çatal Hüyük and Ali Kosh
This impression of a rather more complicated story was reinforced by James Mellaart's excavations in the 1960s at Çatal Hüyük on the Konya Plain of Turkey, a site 13 ha (32 acres) in extent, which could reasonably be called a town. It too was an early farming site, and it too suggested an intense spiritual life with its frescoes and plastered bulls heads. It was notable for fine objects (including pressure-flaked daggers and polished mirrors) in the volcanic glass obsidian, found locally in Turkey.

Again in the 1960s, the question of farming origins was set in a more coherently *ecological perspective* through the work of Frank Hole and Kent Flannery, who studied the regional pattern in the Deh Luran area of Iran, and excavated the site of Ali Kosh there. They laid stress on the evolution of sheep. The archaeozoologist Sandor Bökönyi deduced that the hornless variety found in early levels could be considered a domesticated form. Hans Helbaek also made significant progress here with recovery methods, introducing *flotation techniques* for the lighter components within the soil, notably charred plant remains.

New Perspectives
In the late 1960s the Cambridge archaeologist Eric Higgs argued that

too much emphasis was being given to the distinction between wild and domestic, and that what one was studying were long-term changes in the *exploitative relationship* between people and animals, and in the way humans used plants. He suggested that several of the important shifts in behavior went very much earlier than the Neolithic period. Gazelle, for example, might have been intensively exploited long before sheep and goat became important (cf. p.256). Higgs pioneered, with Claudio Vita-Finzi, the technique of *site catchment analysis* (box Chapter 6).

In a 1968 paper Lewis Binford likewise looked at longer-term trends. He laid stress on *demographic factors*, suggesting that it was the development of settled village life in the pre-farming phase which created population pressures that led to the intensive use and subsequent domestication of plant and animal species (see box, The Origins of Farming: A Processual Explanation, Chapter 12).

Much progress has been made in the last two decades with the investigation of certain key sites (see, for example, the work described on pp. 256–257). Some of the relevant factors leading to the emergence of farming have been identified: ecological, demographic, and social. But it is fair to say that, although we know much about what happened, we do not yet fully understand it.

Map showing the location of the principal excavated early farming villages in the Near East, and the domesticated crops found there (based on a 1988 summary by the paleobotanists Daniel Zohary and Maria Hopf). The longer the line extending from a site, the more common the relevant crop is among the plant remains from that site.

One of the major areas of debate in modern archaeology concerns the question of human management of plants. A prime factor is the status of the species in question, i.e. whether they were wild or *domesticated*. In terms of human behavior the dichotomy is artificial and often irrelevant since many types of cultivation do not change the morphology of the plant, and even in cases where such change occurs we do not know how long it took to appear. Thus any line drawn between wild and domestic plants does not necessarily correspond to a distinction between gathering and agriculture.

There are nevertheless cases where a clear distinction can be made between wild and fully domestic forms. Macrobotanical remains are of most use here. For example, the American archaeologist Bruce Smith recently found that 50,000 carbonized fruits of *Chenopodium* (goosefoot), nearly 2000 years old from Russell Cave, Alabama, exhibited a set of interrelated morphological characteristics reflecting domestication. He was thus able to add this starchy-seed species to the brief list of cultivated plants – including bottle gourd, squash, marsh elder, sunflower, and tobacco – available in the garden plots of the Eastern Woodlands before the introduction of maize in about AD 400.

There has been some debate in recent years about whether wild and domestic legumes can be differentiated on morphological criteria, but the latest archaeobotanical work by British scholars suggests that there is no foolproof way to do this, even in a scanning electron microscope. Cereals, on the other hand, where well preserved, are more straightforward, and domestication can be identified by clues such as the loss of anatomical features like the brittle rachis that facilitate the dispersal of seed by natural agents. In other words, once people began to cultivate cereals, they gradually developed varieties that retained their seeds until they could be harvested.

Phytoliths can be useful here, since they seem to be bigger in some modern domestic plants than in their wild ancestors. Deborah Pearsall used the appearance of a concentration of very big phytoliths as a criterion of the introduction of domestic maize in Real Alto, Ecuador, by 2450 BC. The large phytoliths were similar to those she had extracted from modern cultivated maize, but were absent from its wild ancestors. This criterion has been supported by macrobotanical remains from other regions, but it is possible that other factors such as climatic change are also involved which might affect the size of phytoliths.

Pollen grains are of little use in studies of domestication, since they cannot be used to differentiate wild and domestic categories except for some types of

Wild and domestic cereals. Left to right: wild and domestic einkorn, domestic maize, extinct wild maize. The wild einkorn is shedding its spikelets, which break off easily thanks to the brittle rachis at each spikelet's base. With a tougher rachis, the domestic form shatters only when threshed.

cereal. They can, however, provide indications of the rise of cultivation through time. Fossil buckwheat pollen and a sudden increase of charcoal fragments about 6600 years ago discovered in cores from Ubuka bog, Japan, suggest that agriculture began some 1600 years earlier in this part of the world than had previously been thought.

Meals and Cookery

It is now possible even to estimate at what temperature a plant was cooked. Samples of the material recovered from the stomach of Lindow man, the British bog body discovered in Cheshire in 1984 (see box, Chapter 11), were identified by the British archaeobotanist Gordon Hillman as charred bran and chaff, thanks to their characteristic cell patterns under the microscope. They were then subjected to electron spin resonance (Chapter 4), a technique that measures the highest temperature to which the material was subjected in the past. It was discovered some years ago that the burning of organic materials produces a so-called radical carbon which survives a long time, and which reveals not only the maximum temperature of previous heating (it can differentiate boiling at 100°C (212°F) from baking at 250°C (482 °F), but also the duration of that heating and its antiquity. In the case of Lindow man, the technique revealed that whatever he ate had been cooked on a flat, heated surface for about half an hour, and only at 200°C (392°F). This fact, together with the abundance of barley chaff, suggests that the remains are not derived from porridge, but come from unleavened bread or a griddle cake made using coarse wholemeal flour.

Plant Evidence from Literate Societies

Archaeologists studying the beginnings of plant cultivation, or plant use among hunter-gatherers, have to rely on the kind of scientific evidence outlined above, coupled with the judicious use of ethnoarchaeological research and modern experiments. For the student of diet among literate societies, however, particularly the great civilizations, there is a wealth of evidence for domestication of plants, as well as for farming practices, cookery, and many other aspects of diet to be found written in documents and in art. If we take the Classical period as an example, Strabo is a mine of information while the Jewish historian Josephus provides data on the food of the Roman army (bread was the mainstay of the diet). Virgil's *Georgics* and Varro's agricultural treatise allow an insight into Roman farming methods; we have the cookery book of Apicius; and there is a mass of documentary evidence about Greek and Roman cereal production, consumption, pricing, etc. Even the letters found on wooden writing tablets excavated at the fort of Vindolanda, on Hadrian's Wall, written by serving soldiers to their families, mention many kinds of food and drink such as Celtic beer, fish sauce, and pork fat.

Herodotus gives us plenty of information about eating habits in the 5th century BC, notably in Egypt, a civilization for which there is extensive evidence about food and diet. Much of the evidence for the pharaonic period comes from paintings and foodstuffs in tombs, so it has a certain upper class bias, but there is also information to be found about the diet of humbler folk from plant remains in workers' villages such as that at Tell el Amarna, and from hieroglyphic texts. In the later Ptolemaic period there are records of corn allowances for workers, such as the 3rd century BC accounts concerning grain allotted to workers on a Faiyum agricultural estate. Models are also instructive about food preparation: the tomb of Meketre, a nobleman of the 12th dynasty (2000–1790 BC) contained a set of wooden models, including women kneading flour into loaves, and others brewing beer.

On the other side of the Old World, in China, excavations at Luoyang, the eastern capital of the T'ang dynasty (7th–10th centuries AD), have encountered over 200 big subterranean granaries, some containing decomposed millet seeds, and on their walls inscriptions recording the location of the granary, the source of the stored grain, its variety and quantity, and the date of its storage – thus providing us with data on the economic situation in that period. As will be seen in a later section, the tombs of some Chinese nobles have been found to contain a range of prepared foods in different containers.

In the New World, we owe much of our knowledge of Aztec food crops, fishing practices, and natural history to the invaluable writings of the 16th-century Franciscan scholar Bernardino de Sahagún, based on his own observations and on the testimony of his Indian informants.

It should always be remembered, however, that written evidence and art tend to give a very short-term view of subsistence. Only archaeology can look at human diet, like many other aspects of the human past, with a long-term perspective.

Although plant foods may always have constituted the greater part of the diet – except in special circumstances or high latitudes like the Arctic – meat may well have been considered more important, either as food or as a reflection of the prowess of the hunter or the status of the herder. Animal remains are usually better preserved on archaeological sites too so that, unlike plant remains, they have been studied since the very beginnings of archaeology.

Harvesting and processing a cereal crop: scenes depicted on the walls of a New Kingdom tomb at Thebes in Egypt.

INFORMATION FROM ANIMAL RESOURCES

The study of animal bones from archaeological sites has evolved in the same way as that of plant remains. What little attention the first archaeologists paid to animal bones was directed primarily to the morphology of the different species, and what they could tell us about environment (Chapter 6) or chronology (Chapter 4). But on the question of the interactions between people and animals, few scholars went further than labeling animals as either wild or domestic, and the people as hunters or herders. At best, a quantified list of the species encountered in a site was provided.

Since World War II, however, animal remains have achieved such a high degree of importance through the influence of a number of scholars (e.g. Theodore White's analysis of butchering practices in North America, and the work of Grahame Clark and Eric Higgs in England) that archaeozoology or zooarchaeology has become a subdiscipline of its own. Emphasis is now placed not merely on the identification and quantification of animal species in a site, but on how the remains got there, and what they can tell us about a wide range of questions such as subsistence, domestication, butchering, and seasonality.

The first question the archaeologist must face when interpreting animal remains is to decide whether they are present through human agency rather than through natural causes or other predators (as in the case of carnivore refuse, owl pellets, burrowing animals, etc). Animals may also have been exploited at a site for non-dietary purposes (skins for clothing, bone and antler for tools). As with plant remains, therefore, one must be particularly careful to examine the context and content of faunal samples. This is usually straightforward in sites of recent periods, but in the Paleolithic, especially the Lower Paleolithic, the question is crucial; and in recent years the study of taphonomy – what happens to bones between the time they are deposited and dug up – has begun to provide some firm guidelines (see box).

Methods for Proving Human Exploitation of Animals in the Paleolithic

In the past, association of animal bones and stone tools was often taken as proof that humans were responsible for the presence of the faunal remains, or at least

TAPHONOMY

Taphonomy is the assessment of what has happened to a bone between its deposition and its discovery. Although bones have a better chance of preservation than plant material in most soils, they nevertheless survive only under special conditions – for example, if they are buried quickly, or deposited in caves. Those that escape destruction by carnivores, weathering, acid soils, etc., and survive long enough, become mineralized through slow percolation by ground water. Many are transported by streams and redeposited in secondary context. Much depends on the speed of the water-flow and the density, size, and shape of the bones. Any analysis has also to assume that taphonomic events in the past were the same as those observed today.

Much work is currently in progress concerning the accumulation and fragmentation of bones by carnivores, in the hope that criteria can be found to differentiate bone assemblages produced by humans from those produced by non-humans. This involves ethnoarchaeological observation of different human groups and carnivores, the excavation of animal dens (to study the bones that animals such as hyenas accumulate), and experimental breakage of bones with and without stone tools.

The pioneer of studies of this kind is C.K. Brain, whose work in South Africa has shown not only the effects of carnivores such as leopards, hyenas, and porcupines on animal carcasses, but also that bone fractures previously attributed to early "killer man-apes" were in fact caused by the pressure of overlying rocks and earth in limestone caves in the Transvaal. Indeed, Brain has demonstrated that the early hominids (australopithecines), far from being hunters, were probably themselves the victims of carnivores at cave sites such as Swartkrans.

Such studies are not confined to Africa. Lewis Binford, for example, has made observations in Alaska and the American Southwest involving the effects of wolves and dogs on bones. He seeks to differentiate human and carnivore interference by means of the relation between the number of bone splinters and the number of intact articular ends. Gnawing animals attack the articular ends first, leaving only bone cylinders and a number of splinters. A bone collection consisting of a high number of bone cylinders and a low number of bones with articular ends intact is therefore probably the result of activity by carnivores or scavengers. John Speth applied these criteria to the bones from the Garnsey site, a 15th-century AD bison-kill complex in New Mexico. The extreme rarity of bone cylinders indicated that there had been minimal destruction by scavengers, and that the bone assemblage could be assumed to be wholly the result of human activity.

One has to be cautious about comparisons of living carnivore behavior with prehistoric assemblages that may have been produced by a different carnivore perhaps now extinct. Since wide variations exist among living species, the behavior patterns of extinct species are far from easy to ascertain. Moreover, animals such as hyenas can produce faunal assemblages similar to those made by human beings, displaying consistent patterning in breakage, and forming similarly shaped fragments. This is not surprising, because the ways in which a bone can break are limited.

These factors may seem discouraging, but they are helping to establish a much sounder basis for the accurate interpretation of bone assemblages.

Early hominids as hunters or the hunted? Excavation of the underground cave complex at Swartkrans, South Africa (above), has yielded the remains of over 130 australopithecine individuals, together with those of carnivores and herbivores. Originally it was thought that the hominids had preyed on the other animals. But C.K. Brain matched the lower canines of a leopard jaw found in the cave to the holes in an incomplete australopithecine juvenile cranium (left). This hominid, at any rate, had been more prey than predator.
Brain discovered that modern leopards drag their victims up into trees, out of reach of hyenas. Perhaps the remains of the unlucky hominid, once its flesh had been consumed, fell from a tree into the cave.

exploited them. We now know, however, that this is not always a fair assumption (taphonomy box), and since in any case many used bones are not associated with tools, archaeologists have sought more definite proof from the marks of stone tools on the bones themselves. A great deal of work is currently aimed at proving the existence of such marks, and finding ways of differentiating them from other traces such as scratches and punctures made by animal teeth, etching by plant roots, abrasion by sedimentary particles or post-depositional weathering, and indeed damage by excavation tools. This is also part of the search for reliable evidence in the current major debate in Paleolithic studies as to whether early humans were genuine hunters, or merely scavenged meat from carcasses of animals killed by other predators, as Lewis Binford and others maintain.

Much attention has been directed to bones from the famous Lower Paleolithic sites of Olduvai Gorge and Koobi Fora, in East Africa, that are over 1.5 million years old. American archaeologist Henry Bunn claimed to be able to identify cutmarks and hammer fractures, made on some of the bones by stone tools, with nothing more than good light and the naked eye. Cutmarks are v-shaped with straight sides, while carnivore teeth tend to leave broader, u-shaped grooves; roots leave irregular marks; and abrasive particles leave faint, shallow grooves. Bunn supported his findings by comparisons with known butchery marks from more recent periods, and noted that the marks often occurred on bones at key points for butchery.

Pat Shipman and Richard Potts, on the other hand, found that it was necessary at the same sites to use light microscopes and even the scanning electron microscope in order to identify toolmarks, since to the naked eye there were too many similarities with other marks. They even claimed to be able to distinguish different types of tool-use, such as slicing, scraping, and chopping. Their method entails making a high-precision rubber impression of the bone surface, which is then used to produce an epoxy resin replica that can be examined under the microscope. This removes the necessity to handle fragile bones repeatedly, and resin imprints are far easier to transport, to store, and to examine under the microscope.

Like Bunn, Shipman and Potts compared their results with marks produced by known processes on modern bones. They found that many bones from Olduvai had both toolmarks and carnivore scratches, suggesting some competition for the carcass. In some cases, the carnivore marks were clearly superimposed on the toolmarks, but in most cases the carnivores

Carnivore marks or toolmarks? Bone surfaces analyzed in the scanning electron microscope by Shipman and Potts. (Top) Round-bottomed groove made on a modern bone by a hyena. (Center) V-shaped groove made on a modern bone by a sharp stone flake. (Below) Fossil bone from Olduvai Gorge that Shipman and Potts believe shows two slicing marks (S) made by a stone flake, and carnivore tooth marks (t) made later.

seem to have got there first! Carnivore marks occurred mostly on meat-bearing bones, whereas toolmarks occurred both on these and on non-meat-bearing bones, such as the bottom of horse limbs, indicating a possible use of tendons and skins.

For Shipman and Potts, the diagnostic feature of a cutmark produced by a slicing action is a v-shaped groove with a series of longitudinal parallel lines at the bottom. However, more recent work suggests that very similar marks can be produced by other causes. James Oliver's work in Shield Trap Cave, Montana, indicates that "cutmarks" can be scored on bones through trampling in the cave, which produces abrasions by particles, and Kay Behrensmeyer and her colleagues have come to similar conclusions from their analyses. Thus microscopic features alone are not sufficient evidence to prove human intervention. The context of the find, and the position of the marks on the bones need to be studied too.

Studies of this kind are not new – even the pioneer geologist Charles Lyell, in 1863, mentioned the problem of distinguishing cutmarks made by tools on bone from those made by porcupines – but the powerful microscopes now available, together with a greater understanding of taphonomic processes and carnivore behavior, have enabled us to make major advances in recent years. Nevertheless more work needs to be done before we can be sure of proving early human activity in this way, and of identifying episodes where our early ancestors were hunters rather than scavengers.

However, there are other types of evidence that can provide proof of human processing of bones. These include artificial concentrations of bones in particular places, such as the stacking of mammoth shoulder

Human exploitation of bones in the Paleolithic. Reconstruction from excavated remains of a mammoth-bone dwelling at Mezhirich in the Ukraine, dating from about 18,000 years ago. Over 95 mammoth mandibles were used in the structure.

blades in the Middle Paleolithic cave of La Cotte de St Brelade, Jersey, or the use of mammoth bones for the construction of huts in the Paleolithic of the Soviet Union. Burning of bones is another clear indication of human processing – for bird bones it may be the only proof of human use, because unburnt bone might have been brought to the site by non-human predators, or might be from birds that inhabited the site or its environs (although identification of the species will often answer this point).

Having demonstrated so far as possible that animal remains were produced by human action, the archaeologist can move on to try to answer questions such as what did people eat, in which seasons, how did they hunt and butcher the animals, and were the animals domesticated?

INVESTIGATING DIET, SEASONALITY, AND DOMESTICATION FROM ANIMAL REMAINS

The most abundant and informative residues of animals are the macroremains – bones, teeth, antlers, shells, etc. Numerous techniques are now available to help extract information from data of this type.

As with plant remains, the archaeologist needs to bear in mind that the bones encountered may represent only a fraction of what was originally present. Bones may have been cleared away out of the site, boiled for stock, used for tools, eaten by dogs or pigs, or even disposed of ritually (some California Indians avoided disrespect to the salmon by never discarding its bones; these were dried, pounded, ground in mortars, and consumed). Other foods such as grubs or the drinking of blood will leave no trace. In addition,

our interpretations are clouded by our own culture's tastes. Although herbivores, supplemented by fish and birds, have usually formed the staple animal foods for humans, other creatures such as insects, rodents, and carnivores may all have made a contribution to diet in some cultures.

And should human remains be included on the list of potential resources? In recent years, there has been a reappraisal (in particular by the anthropologist William Arens) of the archaeological and ethnographic evidence previously interpreted as proof of cannibalism, and all of it has been found open to other explanations. To take one example, the Neanderthal bones from Krapina, Yugoslavia, were found badly

QUANTIFYING ANIMAL BONES

Once as many bone fragments as possible in an assemblage have been identified, they need to be quantified. One problem to take into account is differential preservation. Bones of large mammals survive better than those of small creatures; some animals have more bones or teeth than others; and the degree of fragmentation may vary widely with the species. Thus it is unlikely to be sufficient simply to count the **number of identified specimens** (NISP), which by itself may produce a misleading assessment of the relative abundance of different species. Calculation of the **minimum number of individuals** (MNI) is also required – i.e. the smallest number of animals necessary to account for all of the identified bones. This may not be easy. There is little standardization in method, although calculations of MNI are usually made from the most abundant bone or tooth, and from either the left or right side of the animal. NISP and MNI should therefore be used together,

sometimes also taking into account the total weight of bone for each species.

It is then necessary to assess the relative importance of the bone sample to diet, which usually means deducing how much meat the bones represent. The species with the most individuals or fragments in a sample may not necessarily have been the staple resource: rabbits, for example, may far outnumber deer, but the deer will have provided far more meat. In small samples, on the other hand, a disproportionate emphasis may be given by the statistics to species represented by only a few fragments. The degree of fragmentation is a key factor, since differences in marrow fracturing techniques can produce different numbers of fragments for similar bones. This is a problem that can be overcome by measuring the weight of the bones in the sample.

The final step in any reconstruction of diet is to try to calculate for each species the actual weight of meat represented by the bones in the sample. The average modern meat-weight for each species is a good starting point. Logically one might expect to be able simply to multiply this figure by the relevant MNI, as was done in early analyses. But today it is recognized that one has to take

into account the fact that not all parts of the animal will have been used. One cannot assume that every carcass was treated alike, since in cases such as mass drives some will have been partly used, some fully, and others ignored (see box below, Bison Drive sites). Butchering techniques will have varied according to species, size, purpose, and distance from home. Bones thus represent not full animals but butchering units, or skeletal portions.

broken and scratched, and mixed with animal remains, the flesh assumed to have been cut off the human bones for food. But a reexamination by Mary Russell has shown that the marks on the human bones are quite different from those on defleshed meatbones, but very similar to those found on North American Indian skeletons that have been given secondary burial. In other words, the Krapina bodies were not eaten, but the bones were probably scraped clean for reburial. Recently, however, at the Neolithic cave of Fontbrégoua, southeast France (4000 BC), animal and human bones have been found in different pits, but with definite cutmarks in the same positions; six people were stripped of their flesh with stone tools shortly after death, and their limb bones cracked open. Although there is no direct evidence of consumption of flesh or marrow, Paola Villa and her colleagues have presented this as the most plausible case of prehistoric

cannibalism yet discovered. Ethnographic evidence from Australia, however, suggests that it could well be a mortuary practice.

Even if cannibalism existed occasionally, the contribution of human flesh to diet must have been minimal and sporadic, paling into insignificance beside that of other creatures, especially the big herbivores.

Analyzing a Macrofaunal Bone Assemblage

In analyzing an assemblage of bones, one has first to identify them (Chapter 6) but then also to quantify them, both in terms of numbers of animals and of meat weight (see box). The amount of meat represented by a bone will depend on the sex and age of the animal, the season of death, and geographical variation in body size and in nutrition.

THE STUDY OF ANIMAL TEETH

Teeth survive more successfully than bones, and quite accurate assessments of an animal's age are possible from them. Growth rings around a tooth can be counted (see below), but this involves destruction of the specimen, and mineralization can blur the rings. Most assessments therefore rely on eruption and wear.

Investigation of the presence or absence of milk teeth in a jawbone makes it possible to assign a rough age by reference to the eruption sequence in a modern population. Where permanent dentition is concerned, however, only the degree of wear can provide evidence, once again through comparison with a series of jaws from animals of known age.

One drawback to this method is that assessments of degree of wear tend to be subjective. Complete or nearly complete jaws are also required, and these may not exist in some sites. Moreover, tooth wear will depend on the diet, and does not occur at a constant rate. Young, rough teeth wear down more quickly than older, blunted teeth, so that there is no simple correlation between age and degree of wear.

The American paleontologist Richard Klein has devised a more objective method, relying on measurement of cumulative wear, and widely applicable since it can be used on single teeth. A measurement is taken of the tooth's "crown height," the distance between the occlusal (biting) surface and the "cervical line" that separates the enamel from the dentine of the root. Using data for each species concerning the age when a crown is unworn and when it is fully worn away, the age of the tooth's owner at death can be estimated. Klein and Kathryn Cruz-Uribe have developed a BASIC

computer program that uses these measurements to generate a mortality profile of the teeth in a site. In theory there are two fundamental patterns. The first is a **catastrophic age profile,** corresponding to what is thought to be a "natural" age distribution (the older the age group the fewer individuals it has). Such a pattern would be found in natural contexts – e.g. flash floods, epidemics, or volcanic eruptions – where a whole population has been destroyed. Where it is found in an archaeological context, it suggests the use of mass drives.

The second pattern, an **attritional age profile**, has an over-representation of young and old animals in relation to their numbers in live populations. In natural contexts it would suggest death by starvation, disease, accident, or predation. In an archaeological context it suggests scavenging, or hunting by humans of the most vulnerable individuals.

Klein has encountered both types of profile in the Middle Stone Age of Klasies River Mouth Cave, in Cape Province, South Africa, where the eland – easily driven – displayed a catastrophe profile, while the more dangerous Cape buffalo had an attrition profile.

Season of Death

Teeth can also provide clues to season of death through analysis of their growth rings. For example, the archaeozoologist Daniel Fisher studied the tusks and molars of mastodons (primitive, elephant-like animals) that had been killed or at least butchered by Paleo-Indians in southern Michigan in the 11th millennium BC. The layers of dentine formation enabled him to determine, to within a month or two, that the animals had been killed in mid-to-late fall.

In some mammals, annual rings of cementum, a mineralized deposit, form around the tooth roots below the gumline. When a thin-section is taken, stained, and placed under the microscope, the layers appear as

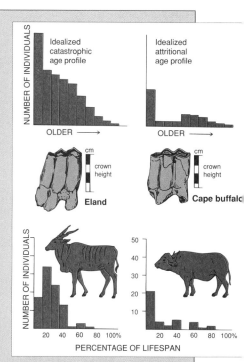

Ages at death *deduced from crown heights of lower third molars by Richard Klein. (Top row) Idealized catastrophic age profile and attritional age profile. (Bottom row) Evidence from the cave site of Klasies River Mouth, South Africa, showing a catastrophic profile for the eland and an attritional profile for the Cape buffalo. (Postdepositional leaching may have selectively destroyed teeth for the youngest age band, which would account for the lower than expected number of individuals estimated in that group.)*

series of translucent and opaque bands, representing alternating seasons of want and plenty which cause variation in the rate of deposition. The American scholar Arthur Spiess has applied this technique to reindeer teeth from the Upper Paleolithic site of Abri Pataud, France, and proved that the animals were killed between October and March. This excellent method's only drawback is that it entails destruction of the tooth.

A recent illustration of this fact is provided by the Garnsey site, a bison-kill site in New Mexico of the 15th century AD, where John Speth found more male skulls than female, but more female limbs than male. As the kill took place in the spring, when calving and lactating cows are under nutritional stress, the sexual imbalance in the remains suggested that the bones with the most meat and body fat at that time of year (male limbs) were taken away from the site, and the rest were ignored. Seasonal and sexual variation were involved in the nutritional decisions made at this kill site. It follows that where it is necessary to assess the original sex ratio in a collection of bones, the meat-bearing bones are likely to give a misleading picture; only bones with no nutritional value will be accurate.

But if factors of age, sex, and season of death need to be allowed for, how are they established?

Strategies of Use: Deducing Age, Sex and Seasonality from Large Fauna

Sexing is easy in cases where only the male has antlers (some deer), or large canines (pig) or where a penis bone is present (e.g. dog), or where the female has a different pelvic structure. Measurements of certain bones, such as bovid metapodials (feet), can provide two distinct clusters of results, interpreted as male (large) and female (small), although in many cases young or castrated males can blur the picture with an intermediate category.

The *age* of an animal can be assessed from features such as the degree of closure of sutures in the skull, or, to a certain extent, from the fusion between limb shafts and their epiphyses; the latter factor can be studied more closely by means of X-rays. Age is then estimated by comparison with information on these features in modern populations, though differences in geography or nutrition are hard to allow for. More accurate assessments can be obtained from analysis of the eruption and wear of teeth, and from study of their annual rings of cementum (see box, previous page).

Ageing gives some insights into dietary preferences and techniques of exploitation, but the *season of death* is also a crucial factor. There are many ways of studying seasonality from animal remains – for example, the identification of species only available at certain times of year, or which shed their antlers in specific seasons. If one knows at what time of year the young of a species were born, then remains of fetuses, or bones of the newly born, can pinpoint a season of occupation (see bison drive box) – though it should be stressed that, while one can sometimes prove a human presence in some seasons in this way, it is very rare

Mapping bones at the Boarding School site.

Excavation of a group of bison skulls at Gull Lake.

BISON DRIVE SITES

SASKATCH-
EWAN
Gull Lake
CANADA
Boarding School USA
MONTANA

The driving of bison over bluff or cliff edges was an important periodic hunting method for thousands of years in North America. Much was known from accounts by Indian informants recorded in the first decades of this century, but the picture needed filling out through archaeological investigation of actual drive sites.

The Boarding School Site

One of the first of such excavations was undertaken by Thomas Kehoe in the 1950s at the Boarding School site, Montana. The work was carried out with the help of the local Blackfoot Tribe. Boarding School was not a cliff, but one of the more common, lower but abrupt drops that led to a natural enclosure. In a deep stratigraphy, three main bone layers were found, with well-preserved bison remains that gave insights into the size and composition of the herd, and hence into the seasons of the drives. Bison numbers were assessed using the minimum number of individuals technique (box, p. 250). Ages of the animals came from the eruption sequence and degree of wear on the teeth (box, p. 251), and from bone-fusion, while sex was established on the basis of size and pelvic shape.

The site proved to have been used intermittently for a long period as a temporary camp. Then *c.*AD 1600 (according to radiocarbon dating of charred bone) a herd of about 100 bison was driven over the bluff. Their remains formed the "3rd bone layer," which included a fetal bone but no mature bulls, implying a late fall or winter drive of a herd composed of cows, calves, and young bulls. A season or two later, another herd of 150 were driven in, forming the "2nd bone layer." This had remains of mature bulls, and together with the lack of fetal or new-born calves it indicated a drive of a "cow-and-bull" herd in the rutting season, between July and September, when pemmican (dried meat) had to be prepared for the winter.

A much later drive (probably just before historic contact), produced the "1st bone layer." Here the remains of 30 bison were subjected to light butchering, probably for transport to a distant camp: much of what was left behind was in articulated units. In the earlier two layers, butchery techniques were similar but far more of each animal was utilized, and much was processed on the spot. Clearly, the distance to the home base was shorter than in the case of the later drive.

The lack of pottery at the site emphasized its role as strictly a kill and meat-processing station. The total of 440 projectile points found suggested an average of 4 or 5 arrows used on each animal.

The Gull Lake Site

In the early 1960s Kehoe carried out a similar excavation at the Gull Lake site, over the border in southwest Saskatchewan. Here too, bison had been driven over a bluff into a depression serving as a natural corral. Five bone layers were encountered, one of the latest (*c.* AD 1300) perhaps representing the remains of as many as 900 bison.

The drives began in the late 2nd century AD, and show little processing of bone: many limb bones and even spinal columns are intact. In the later drives, however, processing was far more thorough, with few articulated bones, and extensive scattering and burning of scrap, indicating a utilization for grease and pemmican.

Surveying *excavation trenches down the bluff slope at the Gull Lake site.*

Gull Lake *bison drive (right).*

that one can positively disprove a human presence at other times of year unless climatic conditions, such as at high altitude, would have made this suicidal.

By careful measurement and new analytical techniques one can therefore obtain quite precise data on age, sex, and season of death, which helps greatly in the evaluation of how and when people exploited their resources. Teeth alone can sometimes provide all this information. The Japanese scholar Noriyuki Ohtaishi has studied 1700 recent specimens of Sika deer (*Cervus nippon*) in order to obtain data on tooth eruption, replacement, and development. He has established an age sequence from the period of eruption and the wear patterns on the cheek teeth, and has determined the age and the season of death by examining the cementum and counting its annual layers. He then applied this information to archaeological specimens. With jaws of the same species from Torihama, an early Jomon site in Japan (3500 BC), he managed to determine their sex through measurements of jaw depth and of the area from the second premolar to the second molar – these were compared with measurements from specimens of known sex; his wear index provided the age at death; and thin-sections of the cementum layer established the season of death. Around 60 percent of the specimens were from old animals (over 5 years of age), a mortality pattern very similar to that from recent deer populations under protected conditions; whereas jaws from later Jomon sites such as Kidosaku (see box below), Yahagi (2000 BC), and Sambu-Ubayama (500 BC) came mainly from animals younger than 5 years, a pattern similar to a recent hunted population. He was therefore able to conclude that, with time, hunting pressure increased on this species.

The Question of Animal Domestication

The methods just described help to shed light on the relationship between human beings and their large animal resources, on the composition of herds, and on exploitation techniques. An entirely different set of methods, however, is required to assess the status of the animals – i.e. whether they were wild or domesticated. One criterion of animal domestication is human interference with the natural breeding habits of certain species, which has led to changes in the physical characteristics of those species from the wild state. But there are other definitions, and specialists disagree about which physical changes in animals are diagnostic of domestication. Too much emphasis on the wild/domestic dichotomy may also mask a whole spectrum of human-animal relationships, such as herd management without selective breeding. Nevertheless, domestication, by any definition, clearly occurred separately in many parts of the world, and archaeologists therefore need to differentiate fully wild from fully domestic animals, and to investigate the process of domestication. How is this done?

Bones and teeth are the most abundant kind of animal remains found on archaeological sites, and specialists have traditionally attempted to determine domestication through morphological changes such as a reduction in jaw size and the increased crowding of teeth. However, these have not proved wholly reliable criteria, because as yet we have no idea how long it took for such changes to take effect after humans began the process of domestication, and intermediate stages have not yet been recognized. Some species have certainly decreased in size through domestication, but environmental factors may have played a role here, as many wild species have also undergone a size decrease since the last Ice Age. Furthermore, we do not know the range of variation in wild populations, and there must have been a great deal of contact between early domestic and wild groups, with transmission of genes.

Decreasing tooth size as an indicator of pig domestication: a diagram based on the work of the British zooarchaeologist Simon Davis. Measurements (scale in millimeters) for (a) and (b) are from Late Pleistocene wild boars in the Levant; (c) represents modern Israeli wild boar. The size difference between (a/b) and (c) suggests an environmentally caused reduction in size at the end of the Ice Age. A further size reduction linked to domestication is suggested by the yet smaller size of domestic pig molars (d-i) from the eastern Mediterranean, as compared with the wild boar molars. (Individual measurements are given as circles, samples as mean averages with their ±95 percent confidence limits.)

A promising new technique looks at individual bones in another way. The zooarchaeologist Isabella Drew and her colleagues have attempted to differentiate wild from domestic animals by analysis of their bone microstructure. Examining thin-sections under the microscope of limb bones from sheep, goat, and cattle – which were *assumed* to be wild and domestic respectively – from two sites in Turkey dating to the 7th and 6th millennia BC, the team found that the sizes of the internal lacunae (the cavities forming the cellular structure) were entirely different, as was the thickness of bone between the lacunae. A similar observation was made using thin-sections of phalanges (foot bones) from wild and domestic llamas from prehispanic sites in the Atacama Desert, Chile (800 BC–AD 1535): the domesticated specimens had larger marrow cavities. Drew believes that the phenomenon is a response to stress. Whether through lack of exercise, poor nutrition, genetic deterioration, or a combination of factors, domestic animals do not develop bones as sturdy as those of their wild counterparts. If the results prove to be consistent, the technique will be very useful in identifying domestication.

Other changes brought about by domestication occur in features such as skin or fleece that very occasionally survive archaeologically. For example, the arrangement of wool and hair is quite different in the skins of wild and domestic sheep. The British scholar Michael Ryder has been able to identify breeds of sheep from the range and distribution of fibers from skins in Viking textiles and medieval costumes.

Another approach has been to study changes in animal populations rather than individuals. The introduction of domestic animals into areas where their wild ancestors were not indigenous is a criterion of human interference that is often applied, but our knowledge of the original distribution of wild species is inadequate, made more complex by the frequent development of feral (i.e. former domesticated animals which have run wild) populations. More telling would be a radical shift from one slaughter pattern to another in a short space of time; this would certainly make a strong case for domestication, especially if combined with evidence of incipient morphological change. Here again, however, the theory is not so easy to demonstrate in practice. In the past, it was assumed that a high number of immature or juvenile herd animals in a bone assemblage represented human interference, and differed radically from a supposed "normal" wild population. But now it is known that sex ratios or percentages of juveniles can vary enormously in a wild herd. Furthermore, all predators (not just human ones) hunt selectively, concentrating on the more vulnerable individuals. It follows that a high proportion of immature animals is insufficient evidence in itself for domestication.

A herd's age and sex structure can nevertheless be a guide as to whether the animals were kept primarily for meat or for dairying purposes. A meat herd will contain a high number of adolescent and young adult animals, whereas a dairy herd will consist mostly of adult females.

Certain tools may indicate the presence of domesticated animals – for example, plows, yokes, and horse trappings. An unusual context can also be informative – for instance, a 12,000-year-old human burial found at Ein Mallaha in Israel contains the remains of a puppy, indicating the close links that were forged early on between humans and dogs.

Artistic evidence suggests even earlier possible attempts to control animals. As shown by Paul Bahn, some images from the end of the last Ice Age hint at control of individual animals – most notably the Upper Paleolithic engraving of a horse's head from La Marche, France, with some form of bridle depicted.

In later times art is particularly informative about domestication, ranging from Greek, Roman, and Mesopotamian depictions of their domestic animals to the Egyptian murals featuring not only farming but also some sort of domestication of more exotic species.

Deformities and disease can provide convincing evidence for domestication. When used for traction, horses, cattle, and camels all sometimes suffer osteoarthritis or strain-deformities on their lower limbs – a splaying of the bone, or outgrowths. Many archaeological examples are known, such as cattle bones from medieval Norton Priory in England. In horses the condition known as spavin has the same cause, and involves a proliferation of new bone around the tarsal bones and the metatarsal, resulting in fusion. Some diseases can be an indication of mismanagement of herds: rickets, for example, indicates a deficient diet or poor pasture, while close-herding and overstocking predispose animals to parasitic gastroenteritis.

Certain diseases may be a direct proof of domestication. In a study of Telarmachay, a prehistoric site in the Peruvian Andes, Jane Wheeler found that at a certain point in the stratigraphy, around 3000 BC, there was a significant increase in remains of fetal and newborn camelids such as llamas and alpacas. From a normal figure of 35 percent there was a jump to 73 percent. It is highly unlikely that these were young wild animals hunted and brought to the site by humans. No hunter would have found it worthwhile to pursue such small creatures, which might in any case have grown into more productive game. It is far more likely that these

FARMING ORIGINS: A CASE STUDY

An outstanding example of how different types of evidence can be integrated into a rounded picture of a subsistence economy is to be found in the study of Tell Abu Hureyra, a site in Syria excavated by Andrew Moore in the early 1970s, and subsequently drowned beneath an artificial lake. The site's great interest lies in its remarkable assemblages of plant and animal remains from a region and a period crucial to the origins of farming in the Near East.

Abu Hureyra is a large mound, 11.5 ha (28 acres) in extent and with an 8-m (26-ft) stratigraphy. The site is located at the edge of the Euphrates valley, and was occupied by perhaps 200 or 300 people in the Epipaleolithic period (Mesolithic; 10th/9th millennia BC), and again in the Neolithic (after 7500 BC) by a population ten times larger. Flotation produced a diverse assemblage of charred plant remains, while dry sieving helped to retrieve over 60,000 identifiable bone fragments. In addition, the charred remains of what are probably the coprolites of infants were recovered.

Plant Remains

Analysis of the varied plant remains by Gordon Hillman and his colleagues at London's Institute of Archaeology involved the collection and study of modern seeds and fruits from the region in order to improve criteria of identification, and to learn about their present distribution and ecology. It was found that even the earliest (pre-pottery) Neolithic levels had fully domesticated cereals. By contrast, the Epipaleolithic layers had only morphologically "wild" forms (e.g. "wild" einkorn and rye). The absence in the Epipaleolithic period of all the common, toxic-seeded weeds

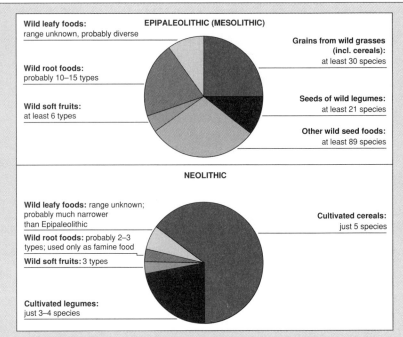

EPIPALEOLITHIC (MESOLITHIC)

Wild leafy foods: range unknown, probably diverse

Wild root foods: probably 10–15 types

Wild soft fruits: at least 6 types

Grains from wild grasses (incl. cereals): at least 30 species

Seeds of wild legumes: at least 21 species

Other wild seed foods: at least 89 species

NEOLITHIC

Wild leafy foods: range unknown; probably much narrower than Epipaleolithic

Wild root foods: probably 2–3 types; used only as famine food

Wild soft fruits: 3 types

Cultivated legumes: just 3–4 species

Cultivated cereals: just 5 species

Pie charts *comparing Epipaleolithic and Neolithic plant remains from Abu Hureyra. In the earlier period, 90 percent of the* plant-based diet came from 160 species. By the Neolithic, just 8 – 9 species supplied a similar proportion of the diet.

Likely gazelle *migration routes, reconstructed largely on the basis of the distribution of desert kites, where gazelle may have been slaughtered. In late spring* the animals moved north toward the area around Abu Hureyra, where the young were born. At the end of the summer they returned south.

(abundant in Neolithic levels) and the admixture of seeds of plants with which the wild-type cereals would have grown only in wild (natural) vegetation, indicates that the Epipaleolithic cereals were gathered from wild stands and were not under cultivation.

As for seasonality, the Epipaleolithic plant resources would have been available from late April till at least late October. And since seeds can be stored (although the site has no artifactual evidence of storage until the Neolithic), it is possible that there was year-round occupation here, based on a broad-spectrum plant economy, even before the emergence of agriculture. In whatever way the transition to cultivation came about, it seems to have taken only a few centuries. With the onset of farming, the spectrum of seed-based foods dropped from 150 species down to a mere 8, which may represent a marked deterioration in dietary quality.

Animal Remains

In the faunal assemblage, studied by Tony Legge and Peter Rowley-Conwy, 80 percent of the bones belonged to gazelle, not only in the Epipaleolithic but in the Early Neolithic as well. Although most were adults, there were also (on the

The site of Abu Hureyra in northern Syria: spoilheaps and an archaeological trench from the excavations are visible in the distance. (The buildings to the right are modern.)

basis of tooth analysis and bone fusion) many very young animals, including yearlings and newborn, which suggests that some annual killing took place around April or May when the young were born. Entire herds may have been driven to their deaths in specially built stone enclosures known as "desert kites" (from the shape of their ground-plan – see map).

If one relies on the evidence of bones alone, therefore, Abu Hureyra looks like a seasonal camp for gazelle hunting; but the size of the mound and, as shown above, the varied plant foods imply that permanent occupation was quite feasible.

The bones of sheep and goat (whether wild or domestic cannot be ascertained) constitute only 10 percent of the Epipaleolithic assemblage, and the same in the Early Neolithic, when cereal cultivation was underway. Analysis of the animals' teeth suggests that, unlike gazelle, they were killed throughout the year, as one might expect of domestic animals. But

they remained of little importance while gazelle were available. In the 7th millennium BC there was an abrupt change, with sheep/goats increasing to 80 percent and gazelles declining to only 20 percent of the bones. The cause may have been overkill of the gazelle, reflected in the proliferation of desert kites which perhaps disrupted the animals' migratory patterns.

Conclusions

An important conclusion is that for at least 1000 years after the first cultivation of morphologically domestic plants at Abu Hureyra, hunting still played a crucial part in the site's economy. In this region, as in many other parts of the world, farming did not suddenly appear as an all-in-one package, but as a series of steps, adapting to changing circumstances over an extended period.

This example underlines the importance of analyzing all available evidence about subsistence. Plants or bones alone may give a distorted view. An integrated approach incorporating paleoethnobotany, archaeology and, if possible, direct dietary clues from human remains, together with archaeological and geomorphological evidence about land-use, will provide the fullest possible picture of subsistence.

were domesticated animals, because mortality is very high among domestic llamas and alpacas, where the main cause of death is a kind of diarrhoea probably brought about by the spread of pathogens in dirty, muddy corrals, and not known to occur among wild species. If the massive mortality at Telarmachay was indeed caused in this way, evidence of this type may prove to be a useful indicator of domestication.

Great progress is therefore being made in studies of domestication. Some of the traditional criteria for demonstrating domestication – such as a reduction in size – may have proved to be less conclusive than was once thought. But these traditional approaches are being placed on a much sounder footing, and new scientific techniques, such as microscopic analysis of bone structure, as well as studies of deformity and disease, open up promising new ways of looking at the question of animal domestication.

Small Fauna: Birds, Fish, and Molluscs

Modern excavation techniques and screening or sieving have greatly improved retrieval of the fragile remains of small species. Identification requires the expertise of a specialist, since remains of the different species can be very similar.

Birds. Remains of birds consist not only of bones but also guano, feathers, mummified birds in Egypt, footprints, and eggshell that has even survived at several Upper Paleolithic sites in Europe such as Pincevent, France. In some cases, it is possible to examine the shell in the scanning electron microscope and identify the species from the distribution of its pores.

Birds were often exploited for their feathers rather than their meat, although the particular species involved may settle the point. The enormous flightless moa in New Zealand were clearly exploited for meat, as shown by the numerous sites yielding evidence for moa butchery and cookery, with rows of ovens and bone dumps. At Hawksburn, for instance, a site of about AD 1250, Athol Anderson found the remains of over 400 moa; most had been brought in as leg joints, with the less meaty parts of the carcass abandoned at the kill sites. Such mass exploitation and waste helps to explain the extinction of this and other species in the Pacific (see Chapter 6).

Where small birds are concerned, however, it is often likely that their bones were brought to the site by a non-human predator or, in some cases, that they inhabited the site or its environs themselves. Here again, identification of the species involved may help

one to solve the issue, but it is necessary to apply certain criteria in order to determine whether the birds were hunted by humans. A bone collection with a bias in favor of certain bones which differs from that in naturally occurring bone assemblages may suggest human intervention. Burning of the extremities of long bones is also a clue, though it will depend on the particular methods of cooking used. Identification of cutmarks under magnification gives evidence on butchery; while if the quantity of bird bones at a site fluctuates through time independently of the fluctuations in microfauna, this suggests that they were not brought in by birds of prey.

Fish. As with the bones of mammals, methods have been devised for calculating the weight of fish from their bones, and hence assessing their contribution to diet. Different types of fish can provide data on the fishing methods utilized – the bones of deep-sea species, for example, indicate open-sea fishing. Salted fish are often well preserved in Egyptian sites, and indeed certain fish were mummified in that civilization, like so many other animals. The Romans, for their part, had fish-ponds and cultivated oysters.

Microfauna and Insects. Remains of *microfauna* such as rodents, or frogs and toads, are poor indicators of diet, since so many of them came into sites through their own burrowing activities or through the attentions of other predators – owl pellets are even known in the Lower Paleolithic cave sediments at Swartkrans, South Africa.

Insects may or may not have been eaten, but in cases where their remains survive, they can provide important data on diet and seasonality. Wasp nests, for example, broken open to extract the larvae, have been found in some abundance in refuse layers at the Allen site in Wyoming, which not only points to consumption of larvae but also to summer occupation. At Pueblo Bonito, the well-known pueblo settlement in Chaco Canyon, New Mexico, some pots in graves contained fly pupae and fragments of a beetle whose larvae attack stored cereals; thus the insects revealed the vanished contents of the vessels. Similarly, a grave at Playa de los Gringos, Chile, contained a wooden vessel in which were found pupae cases of a type of fly that lives on meat. And, as mentioned in Chapter 6, the presence of the grain beetle and the golden spider beetle in a Roman sewer at York was sufficient to prove that it drained a granary; indeed the remains of a warehouse by the river at York proved to have a thick layer of carbonized grain beetles, millions of them to the square meter, while another warehouse had a few

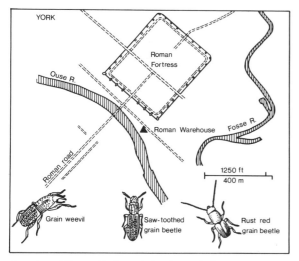

Insects and Roman York: grain beetles and other pests were found in huge numbers in the remains of a Roman grain store, which had evidently become infested.

grain beetles and some grain, which suggested to the excavators that the first building had become infested, was therefore burned, and then rebuilt.

Molluscs. Midden sites, almost by definition, provide far more direct clues to diet since humans were clearly responsible for most of the material deposited in them. Apart from occasional surviving remnants of crustaceans and echinoderms (the spines of sea-urchins, starfish, etc), the bulk of marine material in coastal middens usually consists of mollusc shells, together with the bones of whichever animals, birds, and fish were exploited. Similarly, in terrestrial middens, the shells of snails or freshwater molluscs generally vastly outnumber bones. Their predominance is made even greater by the fact that shells survive far more successfully than bones. For this reason, in the past, these ratios were taken to mean that molluscs had formed a staple resource for the occupants at such sites. However, in recent years, studies of the energy yield in calories of different species have revealed that the numerically inferior vertebrate resources were in fact the mainstay of the diet, and that molluscs were often only a crisis or supplementary resource, easy to gather when needed. One calculation showed that a single carcass of a red deer was the equivalent in calories of 52,267 oysters or 156,800 cockles!

In view of the vast amount of shells in most middens – a single cubic meter can contain a ton of material and 100,000 shells – only samples can be analyzed. These are screened (sieved), sorted, and identified, and the meat they represent then calculated from the ratio (which varies with species) of shell to flesh weight. The proportion by flesh weight of different species helps indicate their relative importance in the diet, but it is the calculation of their calorific value that provides the real evidence of their dietary contribution (see box overleaf). It has been found that one person would need to consume 700 oysters or 1400 cockles every day in order to "live by shellfish alone." Such figures, when seen against the timespan of a site's occupation, reveal that the numbers consumed per year could not have supported a large group of people. Calculations of this sort underline the dominant role of other resources in the diet.

Nevertheless, the molluscs present in a midden indicate what people were selecting from the range available. Changes in shell-size through time may reflect environmental fluctuations, but in many cases can reveal overexploitation by humans. The first occupants of the Polynesian island of Tikopia consumed giant shellfish, as well as turtles and wild flightless birds; within a few centuries the birds were extinct, and the turtles and shellfish were far smaller and fewer, and the diet had to be supplemented with other resources.

In sites other than middens, shells may be present in small quantities, and in many cases may not have been food at all. Snails, for example, may have lived in or around the site; and people often collected seashells to use as money, trinkets, or jewelry. Many of the seashells found in Upper Paleolithic sites in Europe are from small and inedible species.

Strategy of Use: Deducing Seasonality from Small Fauna

Some species of migratory birds, rodents, fish, and insects are available only at certain times of the year, and thus their simple presence at a site can provide useful information about the seasons in which humans occupied the site.

Although most fish are poor indicators of seasonality, since they can be treated and stored for consumption in lean times, techniques are emerging for extracting data of this type from their remains. Some species such as pike for example have year-rings in their vertebrae, by which one can calculate the season of death. One new method being developed is the use of fish otoliths (part of the hearing apparatus) as evidence of seasonality. In late Mesolithic (4th millennium BC) shell middens on the island of Oronsay, off the northwest coast of Scotland, 95 percent of the total fishbone material comes from the saithe or coalfish. A

SHELL MIDDEN ANALYSIS

Over 600 shell mounds of the Neolithic Jomon period are known in the area around Tokyo Bay, Japan, and contain many kinds of food remains. The mound of Kidosaku, on the east coast of the bay and dating from the early 2nd millennium BC, has been analyzed in depth by Hiroko Koike. Her results indicate the wealth of detail about diet, length and season of occupation, and population size that can be obtained from a small shell mound.

Size of population was assessed by studying the 10 circular dwelling pits on the site's terrace. From their overlapping it was established that an average of only 3 had been in use at any one time. The size of the dwellings (11-28 sq.m; 13-33 sq.yds) implies that between 3 and 9 people occupied each house (see Chapter 11), giving a maximum population for the site of 23, and more likely between 12 and 18.

The dwellings appear to have been rebuilt four times, and on that basis (together with pottery evidence for a brief occupation) the site's timespan has been estimated at 20 to 30 years.

On the fringe of the terrace and down a steep slope were 7 concentrations of shells, each up to a meter thick and yielding a total volume of about 450 cu. m (589 cu. yds). Samples proved to contain 22 species of mollusc, all typical of a tidal assemblage from a sandy bottom.

Although the most abundant shell type was a tiny gastropod, it was the dominant bivalve – the clam *Meretrix lusoria* – which was probably the most important mollusc. About 3 million clams were represented in the site. From their shell heights, Koike was able to calculate the wet weight of the living clams, and reached a figure of 30 to 45 tons of clams in the site.

Analysis of growth structures in shells, especially bivalves, can provide important information on the season of exploitation. Under the microscope, one can see that the shell's cross-section has fine striations – these are the daily growth lines. There is seasonal variation in growth, with the thickest lines in the summer and the thinnest in winter; the temperature of seawater seems to play a major role. The Kidosaku clams had an age composition and a seasonality very similar to those of modern clams collected in the nearby Midori river area, and their modest size indicates a collection pressure as high as that of today. Koike concluded that the Kidosaku clams had been harvested throughout the year as intensively as shellfish are today by modern commercial collectors.

The clams represent only one resource at the site. Apart from the other molluscan species, there were fish remains (retrieved through wet screening) and also mammal bones, dominated by wild boar (minimum no. of individuals 36) and sika deer (MNI 29), together with wild rabbit and raccoon dog. The age composition of the deer suggested that they were subject to high hunting pressure; and Koike has calculated that, with a probable density of 10 per square kilometer, deer could have accounted for 60 percent of the occupant's caloric needs.

Clams, therefore, were an important resource, but by no means the only staple food of the Kidosaku occupants.

Histograms *indicating how the seasonal pattern of clam collection at Kidosaku (top) – with a peak in the summer – is similar to that in the Midori river area today (second row). Collection seasons of the Kidosaku clams were estimated by studying growth lines.*

The Kidosaku *shell mound terrace (left) under excavation.*

Growth lines *in a clam record the time of the year it was harvested. In winter the clam hardly grows at all, whereas in spring and summer thicker growth lines mark a daily growth cycle. By sectioning the shell (A-B) and counting the lines in the last annual increment, the scientist can determine the season of death.*

The Kidosaku site *(below), showing (A) a plan of the shell deposits and 10 dwelling pits; (B) a section across one of the shell deposits; and (C) a plan of overlapping dwelling pits 1 to 4.*

Deducing seasonality from fish otoliths. On the island of Oronsay, Scotland, Mellars and Wilkinson used the varying sizes of coalfish otoliths (top left) from Mesolithic sites to deduce seasons of occupation at those sites (above).

statistical analysis by Paul Mellars and Michael Wilkinson of the sizes of sagittal otoliths (the largest and most distinctive of the three pairs found in the inner ear) has shown that the size distribution gives an accurate indication of the fishes' age at death, and therefore – assuming a standard date of spawning – of the season when they were caught. As usual in studies of this type, they had to assume that we can extrapolate modern rates of growth to the past. Their analysis showed that the coalfish were caught at 1 and 2 years of age. At each of the four sites studied around the island, the size of the fish varied, indicating that they were caught at different seasons of the year. At the site indicating winter occupation, when the fish had left the coast for deeper water, shellfish contributed a much higher percentage of the food than at the sites where coalfish were caught in greater numbers in the warmer seasons.

261

HOW WERE ANIMAL RESOURCES EXPLOITED?

Tools, Vessels, and Residues

Direct proof of human exploitation of animal resources is available in a variety of ways from tools, vessels, and residues.

Evidence for Fishing and Hunting Techniques. Stone Age fish traps are known from Denmark, while one of the earliest known European boats (4th millennium BC from Tybrind Vig in Denmark) was specially adapted for eel-fishing: the stern had a fireplace of sand and small stones, so that fire would attract them at night.

Working out the function of stone tools is less easy, but experiments on tool usage and microwear are at last providing us with a mass of detailed information (see also Chapter 8). Occasional examples of animal bones with points embedded in them, combined with studies of healed and unhealed wounds in bones and experiments on the efficacy of arrowheads and other projectiles against different materials are providing much evidence on hunting weapons and methods. For example, the Danish zooarchaeologist Nanna Noe-Nygaard has analyzed the skeletons of deer and boar from a number of Mesolithic sites, as well as isolated bog finds, in Denmark. She found that injuries inflicted by humans can usually be distinguished from damage caused naturally in, for example, rutting fights by comparison with marks on modern specimens. Her analysis of the size and outline of the fractures suggested that the bow and arrow, as well as the spear, were used in hunting. On shoulder blades, she noted that the unhealed (and therefore probably fatal) fractures were concentrated in the same part of the bone – the thin area covering vital internal organs – whereas the healed fractures from unsuccessful hunts were scattered all over the bone.

Analysis of microwear polishes is starting to reveal something of the uses of different stone tools. Lawrence Keeley, one of the pioneers in this field, found that tools from Koobi Fora, Kenya, dating to 1.5 million years ago, had a greasy wear similar to the traces produced experimentally by cutting meat and soft animal tissue, and two of the tools had been found near a bovid humerus bone with cutmarks.

Trails of Blood. Until recently it would have been difficult to prove on which species tools had actually been used, except in very rare cases where fragments of feathers or hair adhered to the tool and could be identified. But a new and still somewhat controversial technique, developed by the Canadian researcher Thomas Loy, apparently now allows us to identify the species in question from the bloodstains left on stone knives. After use of the tool, the blood dries and fixes quickly; and if the tool is not cleaned too well after excavation, this residue can be analyzed. The shape of the crystals of hemoglobin – the oxygen-carrying molecule that is found in red blood cells – varies between animal species, and thus provides a kind of molecular fingerprint. Tools are often buried under conditions that provide the right combination of temperature, moisture, and acidity to preserve the hemoglobin intact, although a certain amount of blood seeps into the surrounding soil.

Loy studied 104 tools of chert, basalt, and obsidian from open sites in coastal British Columbia, dating from 6000–1000 years ago, and identified hemoglobin of moose, caribou, grizzly bear, the Californian sea-lion, and other species. He also obtained radiocarbon dates from some blood residues, using accelerator mass spectrometry (Chapter 4). An artifact from Strawberry Bluff produced a corrected date of AD 940 from blood of the snowshoe hare, which matched a date from the charcoal of a nearby hearth.

Loy has recently extended and improved his technique. He has found that blood residues can survive on tools for at least 100,000 years. As will be seen in Chapter 11, he has also discovered traces of human blood on a number of artifacts, including one of that remote date.

The blood residue technique, if confirmed by further testing, will prove invaluable on sites where bones are not preserved, and may give more accurate identifications than feather or hair fragments.

Fat and Phosphate Residues. Other residues are identifiable to various degrees by methods already mentioned in the section on plant resources. Chemical investigation of fats, for instance, can reveal the presence of animal products: an example at Geissenklösterle in western Germany was cited in Chapter 6. Horse fat was identified in layers at the Lower Paleolithic cave of Tautavel, southern France, and reindeer bone-oil at the Upper Paleolithic open-air site of Lommersum, southern Germany. Fish fats have also survived in some sites.

Phosphate analysis of soils can point to animal rather than plant husbandry since phosphorus is very abundant in animal and human fats (phospholipids) and skeletons (phosphates). In some sites, phosphate concentrations can indicate areas of occupation, or places where livestock was concentrated (since phosphate also derives from decomposed dung). This technique is especially valuable for acid soils where the bones have not survived – it can, for example, reveal the former presence of bones in pits – and it underlines the importance of taking adequate soil samples from relevant areas of an excavation. In certain French caves occupied from the Neolithic onward, such as Fontbrégoua, it has been found that the presence of large quantities of so-called calcite spherulites, often associated with phosphate concretions in the floor sediments, is diagnostic evidence for cave-herding, since they represent the mineral residue of the dung of sheep and goats.

Residues in Vessels. Where vessels are concerned, residues can be examined in several ways, as for plants. Investigation under the microscope together with chemical analysis enabled Johannes Grüss to identify a black residue on Austrian potsherds of 800 BC as overcooked milk. Analysis by mass spectrometer provides a record of molecular fragments in a residue, and these fragments can be identified using a reference collection of chromatograms. Employing this technique, Rolf Rottländer has found milk fat and beef suet in Neolithic Michelsberg sherds from Germany, fish fat in sites at Lake Constance, and butter and pork fat in Roman pottery vessels.

Egyptian vessels of the 1st and 2nd dynasties (3rd millennium BC) have been found, through chemical analysis, to contain residues of substances as diverse as cheese, beer, wine, and yeast. In Japan, Masuo Nakano and his colleagues have identified dolphin fat in early Jomon potsherds (4000 BC) from the Mauraki site, while the edges of late Paleolithic stone scrapers from the Pirika site (9000 BC) had residues of fat which seemed to come from deer. It is worth noting that his technique, which extracts the fats by "ultrasonic cleaning," can also be used to identify from which species tiny fragments of bone have come, which hitherto would have been completely unidentifiable.

An extension of this technique, gas liquid chromatography, constitutes a very sensitive method of measuring components of complex volatile compounds. It has been applied at the prehistoric coastal midden of Kasteelberg in southwest Cape Province, South Africa, which is less than 2000 years old. Potsherds from the midden had a brown, flaky substance on the inside, resembling burnt food, and the nitrogen content of a sample was so high that it suggested the substance was animal. The chromatography technique was applied in order to determine its composition in terms of fatty acids, and the values obtained were then compared with those of modern species of plants and animals. The results pointed firmly to a marine animal, though not to a precise species. The presence of seal bones in the site makes it highly probable that the substance came from the boiling of seal meat in jars for food or for the extraction of blubber.

Animal Prints and Tracks. Another type of residue left by animals are pawprints and animal tracks, as we saw in Chapter 6. Many Ice Age tracks may not have been associated with human beings. More informative are the impressions of sheep or goat feet in mud brick from the Near East and Iran, such as those from the 6th millennium BC at Ganj Dareh Tepe. The English Bronze Age site of Shaugh Moor, Devon, revealed tracks of cattle, sheep or goat, and a badger, preserved at the bottom of a ditch by peat. At Duisburg, West Germany, the remains of the medieval city's market square have been found to comprise successive cobbled surfaces interleaved with thick layers of mud and rubbish in which the tracks of cattle hooves, wagon wheels, and human feet have been preserved by being infilled with gravel to support the next layer of cobbles.

However, the best known and most abundant prints are those on Roman roof tiles and bricks – dogs and cats are particularly abundant, as well as birds. Of all the tiles from the Romano-British town of Silchester, no fewer than 2 percent had impressions of this type.

Tools and Art: Evidence for the Secondary Products Revolution

The question of animal domestication, discussed earlier, is one of the key issues in archaeology. One scholar, the British archaeologist Andrew Sherratt, has looked beyond the initial stage of domestication to ask whether there was not in fact a second and later stage – what he calls the Secondary Products Revolution. Sherratt believes that in some parts of the Old World, during the middle and late 4th millennium BC, there was a marked change in the exploitation of domestic animals, no longer solely for the primary products of meat and hides but also for secondary products such as milk and cheese, wool, and animal traction. His evidence consists to some extent of tools, but largely of artistic depictions – in Sumerian pictograms from Uruk, Mesopotamian cylinder-seals, in murals and models – that show plowing, milking, and carts (assumed to have been drawn by animals such as oxen). Sherratt argues that the change was a response to population growth and territorial expansion initi-

Milking scene from a frieze at Ur, Mesopotamia, c.2900 BC. Use of secondary products may go back to early Neolithic times.

ated by the origins of agriculture. People found it necessary to penetrate more marginal environments and exploit livestock more intensively.

However, the American archaeologist Peter Bogucki has shown that in the early Neolithic *Linearbandkeramik* culture of temperate Europe the age and sex structure of the cattle, together with ceramic strainers (interpreted as cheese sieves), indicate the presence of dairying as early as 5400 BC. If this is so, then the "revolution" at the end of the Neolithic must be seen not as a beginning but merely as an intensification of an already existing phenomenon. Perhaps before long analysis of residues in early Neolithic vessels will determine whether they held milk, butter or cheese, and thus help solve the question of the timing and scale of human exploitation of secondary products.

Art and Literature

In addition to providing evidence for use of secondary products, art can be a rich source of other kinds of information. To take just one example, the American scholars Stephen Jett and Peter Moyle have been able to identify 20 species or families of fish depicted accurately on the inside of prehistoric Mimbres pottery from New Mexico (box, Chapter 14). As most of the fish are marine types, and the pottery has been found at least 500 km (311 miles) from the nearest sea, it is obvious that the artists had been to the coast and were very familiar with these resources.

Much information can also be obtained from writings, not only of the sort described in the section on plants, but texts dealing with veterinary medicine, which are known in Egypt from 1800 BC onward, and in Hittite and Mesopotamian sites of similar date, as well as from Greek and Roman times. As always, history, ethnography, and the experimental methods being applied to animal husbandry (see box above) help to flesh out the archaeological evidence.

The Romans liked to eat fish. Eleven species are shown in this 2nd-century AD mosaic from northern Italy.

Remains of Individual Meals

One of the most direct kinds of evidence of what people ate at a particular moment in the past comes from occasional finds of actual meals. At Pompeii, for example, meals of fish, eggs, bread, and nuts were found intact on tables, as well as food in shops. Food is often preserved in funerary contexts, as in the desiccated corncobs and other items in Peruvian graves, or at Saqqara, Egypt, where the 2nd-dynasty tomb of a noblewoman contained a huge variety of foodstuffs, constituting a rich and elaborate meal – cereals, fish, fowl, beef, fruit, cakes, honey, cheese, and wine – which, to judge by the tomb paintings, was not unusual. The Han period in China (206 BC–AD 220) has tombs stocked with food: that of the wife of the Marquis of Dai has a unique collection of provisions, herbal medicines, and prepared dishes in containers of lacquer, ceramic, and bamboo, with labels attached, and even slips giving the composition of the dishes!

We should not, however, let the very richness of these finds cloud an objective judgment that meals from funerary contexts are unlikely to be representative of everyday diet. Even the Pompeii meals are merely a tiny sample from a single day. The only way in which we can study what people ate habitually is to examine actual human remains.

A meal as a funerary offering: the rich and elaborate food remains found in the 2nd-dynasty tomb of a noblewoman at Saqqara, Egypt. (Right) The meal as discovered in the tomb. (Above) Some of the items set out in their dishes. Top row, left to right: triangular loaf of bread (made from emmer wheat); a form of porridge (made from ground barley); unidentified, perhaps a liquid; nabk berries (similar in appearance to cherries). Second row: cut ribs of beef; a cooked quail, cleaned and dressed; two cooked kidneys; stewed fruit, probably figs. Third row: small circular cakes (sweetened with honey); pigeon stew; a cooked fish, cleaned and dressed with the head removed; ribs and legs of beef. Impressive as such remains are, they are unlikely to be representative of the everyday diet of the ancient Egyptians.

ASSESSING DIET FROM HUMAN REMAINS

The only incontrovertible evidence that something was consumed by humans is its presence in either stomachs or feces. Both kinds of evidence give us invaluable information about individual meals and short-term diet. The study of human teeth also helps us reconstruct diet, but the real breakthrough in recent years in understanding long-term diet has come from the analysis of bone collagen. What human bones reveal about health and malnutrition will be examined in Chapter 11.

Individual Meals

Stomach Contents. Stomachs survive only rarely in archaeological contexts, except in bog bodies. It is sometimes possible to retrieve food residues from the alimentary tract of decomposed bodies – the physical anthropologist Don Brothwell achieved this, for example, by removing the grave earth from the lower abdominal area of some British Dark Age skeletons, and extracting the organic remains by means of flotation. Some mummies also provide dietary evidence: the overweight wife of the Marquis of Dai from 2nd-century BC China, mentioned above, seems to have died of a heart attack caused by acute pain from her gallstones an hour or so after enjoying a generous helping of watermelon (138 melon seeds were found in her stomach and intestines).

When stomachs survive in bog bodies, the dietary evidence they provide can be of the greatest interest. Paleobotanist Hans Helbaek's pioneering studies of the stomach contents of Danish Iron Age bogmen showed that Grauballe man, for instance, had consumed over 60 species of wild seeds, together with one or two cereals and a little meat (as shown by some small bone splinters), while Tollund man had eaten only plants. But it should be borne in mind that these results, while fascinating, are not necessarily linked to annual diet, since these victims were possibly executed or sacrificed, and thus their last meal – apparently consisting of dense chaff, larger plant fragments, and weed seeds, the residues from sieving in the latter stages of crop processing – may have been out of the ordinary. Such waste crop cleanings were often used as animal feed, as famine food, or were given to condemned criminals.

However, as noted in the section on plant remains, the British Lindow man (box, Chapter 11) had consumed a griddle cake before his death, and this rough bread, made of the primary product of crop processing, was nothing out of the ordinary for the period – certainly not a recognizably "ritual" dish.

Fecal Material. Experiments have been done to assess the survival properties of different foodstuffs relevant to the study of ancient diet, and it has been found that many organic remains can survive surprisingly well after their journey through the human digestive tract, to await the intrepid analyst of *coprolites*, or fossilized feces. Coprolites themselves survive only rarely, in very dry sites such as caves in the western United States and Mexico, or very wet sites. But, where they are preserved, they have proved to be a highly important source of information about what individuals ate in the past.

The first step in any analysis is to check that the coprolites are indeed human ones. Once this has been done, what can coprolite contents tell us about food intake? Macroremains can be extremely varied in a human coprolite, in fact this variety is an indication of human origin. Bone fragments, plant fibers, bits of charcoal, seeds, and the remains of fish, birds, and even insects are known. Shell fragments – from molluscs, eggs, and nuts – can also be identified. Hair can be assigned to certain classes of animals by means

of its scale pattern, visible under the microscope, and thus help us to know which animals were eaten. Eric Callen analyzed prehistoric coprolites from Tehuacán, Mexico (the valley studied and excavated intensively by Richard MacNeish in the 1960s), and identified hair from gophers, white-tailed deer, cottontail rabbit, and ring-tailed cats. He also managed to ascertain that some millet grains in the feces had been pounded, while others had been rolled on a metate (grinding stone).

Microremains such as pollen are of less help since, as we have already noted, most of the pollen present is inhaled rather than consumed. Pollen does, however, provide data on the surrounding vegetation, and on the season when the coprolite was produced. The fecal material from the recently discovered Greenland Eskimo mummies contained pollen of mountain sorrel, which is only available in July and August. Fungal spores, remains of the nematode worm plant parasites, algal remains, and other parasites have also been identified in coprolites.

Exceptional conditions in Lovelock Cave, Nevada, have preserved 5000 coprolites dating from 2500 to 150 years ago, and Robert Heizer's study of their contents yielded remarkable evidence about diet, which seems to have comprised seeds, fish, and birds. Feather fragments were identified from waterfowl such as the heron and grebe; fish and reptile scales, which pass through the alimentary canal unaltered, also led to identification of several species. Fish remains were abundant in some of the coprolites; one, for example, from 1000 years ago, contained 5.8 g (0.2 oz) of fish bone which, it was calculated, came from 101 small chubs, representing a total live weight of 208 g (7.3 oz) – the fish component of a meal for a single person.

Even where feces have not been preserved, we are now sometimes able to detect and analyze residues of digested food by studying sewers, cesspits, and latrines. Biochemical analysis of ditch deposits near latrines at the Roman fort of Bearsden, Scotland, revealed an abundance of coprosterol, a substance typically found in human sewage, as well as a bile acid characteristic of human feces. A low amount of cholesterol showed that there was little meat in the diet. Numerous fragments of wheat bran in the deposit probably formed part of the feces, and no doubt came from defecated bread or some other floury food.

Coprolites and fecal residues represent single meals, and therefore provide short-term data on diet, unless they are found in great quantities, as at Lovelock Cave, and even there the coprolites represent only a couple of meals a year. For human diet over whole lifetimes, we need to turn to the human skeleton itself.

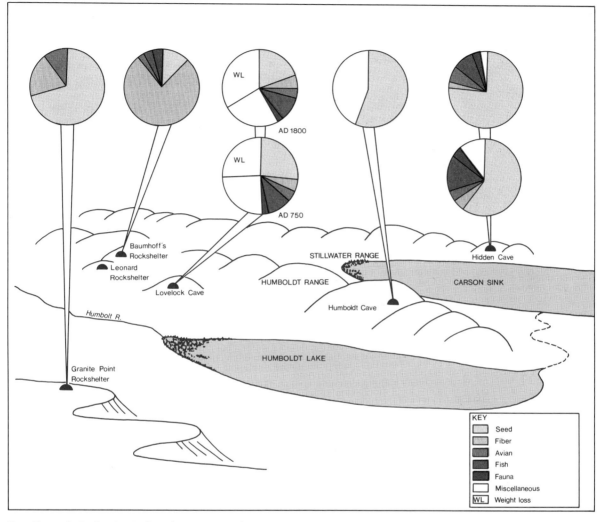

Coprolite analysis: dry sites in the Lahontan Basin of western Nevada have yielded remarkable numbers of human feces that preserve a record of prehistoric diet from before 1000 BC up to AD 1800. The pie diagrams attempt to indicated the proportions of different foods represented in each sample. However, studies of what happens to food as it is digested now suggest that the relationship between what people ate and what passed into their feces is more complex than was once thought.

Human Teeth as Evidence for Diet

Teeth survive in extremely good condition, made as they are of the two hardest tissues in the body. Pierre-François Puech is one of a number of scientists to have studied teeth from many periods in an attempt to find some evidence for the sort of food that their owners enjoyed. The method involves a microscopic examination of the abrasions on certain dental surfaces.

To study food intake, one should examine the lateral or side surfaces which best escape abrasion from inorganic particles in the food, and whose wear instead ought to reflect the movement of the organic food itself within the mouth. A replica is made by pouring a thin film of resin onto the tooth-face; when this is peeled off after solidification, it forms a faithful imprint which can be examined under the light microscope or in the scanning electron microscope. Puech began by studying recent teeth from individuals with known dietary habits. The principle involved was that abrasive particles in food leave striations on the enamel whose orientation and length are directly related to the meat or vegetation in the diet and its process of cooking. A modern meat-eating Peruvian was found to have almost exclusively vertical striations on his lateral surfaces, while a vegetarian had both vertical and horizontal striations, with a shorter average length.

When these results were compared with imprints from fossil teeth, it was found that from the late Lower Paleolithic onwards, there is an increase in horizontal and a decrease in vertical striations, and a decrease in average striation length. In other words, less and less effort was needed in the mastication of food, and meat may have decreased in importance as the diet became more mixed: early people crushed and broke down their food with their teeth, but less chewing was required as cooking techniques developed and improved. There are exceptions, such as a *Homo erectus* individual who seems to have been mainly vegetarian, eating thin, chewy vegetable foods, but on the whole the generalization seems sound.

The biting (occlusal) surfaces of human teeth are of limited help in Puech's technique, since much of the wear here is due to the method of food preparation – meat can be exposed to windborne dust, for example, or food may have been cooked on ashes, and the result is the incorporation of extraneous abrasive particles in the food. Furthermore, our ancestors often used teeth not simply for chewing but as a third hand, for cutting, tearing, and so on. All these factors add striations to the biting surfaces. The lower jawbone of the *Homo erectus* (or "archaic" *Homo sapiens*) individual from Mauer, near Heidelberg in western Germany, dating back some half a million years, has marks suggesting that meat was held in the front of the mouth and cut off with a flint tool that left its traces on six front teeth. Wear on Neanderthal teeth reveals that here too teeth were often used in the same way.

Tooth decay as well as wear will sometimes provide us with dietary information. Remains of the California Indians display very marked tooth decay, attributed to their habit of leaching the tannin out of acorns, their staple food, through a bed of sand which caused excessive tooth abrasion. Decay and loss of teeth can also set in thanks to starchy and sugary foods. Dental caries became abundant on the coast of Georgia (USA) in the 12th century AD, particularly among the female population. It was in this period that the transition occurred from hunting, fishing, and gathering to maize agriculture. The anthropologist Clark Larsen believes that the rise in tooth decay over this period, revealed by a study of hundreds of skeletons, was caused by the carbohydrates in maize. Since the women of the group were more subject to the caries than were the men, it is probable that they were growing, harvesting, preparing, and cooking the corn, while the men ate more protein and less carbohydrate. However, not all scientists accept these conclusions, pointing out that women may have suffered from more caries in a period of high population growth because of greater loss of calcium with the higher number of pregnancies.

Isotopic Methods: Diet over a Lifetime

Recently, a revolution has taken place in dietary studies through the realization that isotopic analysis of human bone collagen can reveal a great deal about long-term food intake. The method relies on reading the chemical signatures left in the body by different foods – we are what we eat.

Plants can be divided into three groups – two groups of land plants and one of marine plants – based on their differing ratios of the carbon isotopes ^{13}C and ^{12}C. Carbon occurs in the atmosphere as carbon dioxide with a constant ratio of ^{13}C:^{12}C of about 1:100; in ocean waters, the amount of ^{13}C is slightly higher. When atmospheric carbon dioxide is incorporated into plant tissues through photosynthesis, plants use relatively more ^{12}C than ^{13}C and the ratio is altered. Plants that fix carbon dioxide initially into a three-carbon molecule (called C3 plants) incorporate slightly less ^{13}C into their tissues than do those using a four-carbon molecule (C4 plants). Trees, most shrubs, and temperate grasses are C3 plants; tropical and savanna grasses, including maize, are C4 plants. Marine plants photosynthetically fix carbon differently from most land plants, and have a higher $^{13}C/^{12}C$ ratio.

As plants are eaten by animals, these three different ratios are passed along the food chain, and are eventually fixed in human and animal bone tissue. The ratio found in bone collagen by means of a mass spectrometer thus has a direct relation to that in the plants which constituted the main foods. The ratios can show whether diet was based on land or marine plants, and whether on C3 or C4 land plants. Only archaeological evidence, however, can provide more detail about precisely which species of plants or animals contributed to the diet.

Henrik Tauber applied this technique to collagen from prehistoric skeletons in Denmark, and found a marked contrast between Mesolithic people and those of the Neolithic and Bronze Age. In the Mesolithic, marine resources were predominant – even though fish bones were very scarce in the excavated material – whereas in the later period there was a change to reliance on land foods, even in coastal sites.

At coastal sites in other parts of the world, the technique has confirmed a heavy reliance on marine resources. In prehistoric sites on the coast of British Columbia, Brian Chisholm and his associates found that about 90 percent of protein had come from marine foods; little change was apparent over five millennia, and it was noted that adults seemed to eat more food from the sea than did children.

Bone Collagen Studies and the Rise of New World Agriculture. The carbon isotope bone collagen method is particularly useful for detecting changes in diet, and has revolutionized the study of the rise of food production in the New World. Anna Roosevelt employed the technique to assess the diet of the prehistoric inhabitants of the Orinoco floodplain in Venezuela. Analysis of samples from a number of skeletons by her colleagues Nikolaas van der Merwe and John Vogel revealed a dramatic shift from a diet rich in C3 plants such as manioc in 800 BC to one based on C4 plants such as maize by AD 400. Although the technique cannot specify the actual plants consumed, the abundant maize kernels and grinding equipment found in the area's sites from AD 400 onward confirm the insight provided by isotopic analysis.

The technique is even more crucial in North America, where the rise of agriculture was signaled by the introduction of maize, a C4 food native to Mesoamerica, into a predominantly C3 plant environment (in the Near East, where the first domesticated plants were themselves part of the C3 plant environment, the technique is of less use to studies of the origins of agriculture). In some cases, maize's contribution to a diet can be quantified. In skeletons from southern Ontario, Henry Schwarcz and his colleagues found that the proportion of C4 plants (i.e. maize) in the diet increased between AD 400 and 1650, reaching a maximum of 50 percent by about 1400.

Other Bone Collagen Techniques. Some scholars have attempted to extend the carbon isotope technique to apatite, the inorganic and major constituent of bone, in the hope that it could be applied even in cases where collagen has not survived (it often degrades after 10,000 years); others, however, have found this method unreliable, so that the collagen method is the only one whose validity is confirmed for the present. Nevertheless there are collagen techniques available involving isotopes of elements other than carbon. Ratios of *nitrogen isotopes* in collagen, for example, can reflect dietary preferences in the same way as carbon. The ^{15}N isotope increases as it passes up the food chain from plants to animals: a low ratio of ^{15}N to ^{14}N points to an agricultural subsistence, while a high ratio points to a marine diet.

One anomaly here is caused by coral reef resources such as shellfish, which, because of the way nitrogen is fixed by plants in reefs, give a low nitrogen value. Thus, in cases where a seafood diet seems likely, the carbon isotope method needs to be employed for confirmation. The two methods have also been applied together to historic and prehistoric material in East and South Africa by Stanley Ambrose and Michael DeNiro. They found it possible to distinguish marine foragers from people using land resources, pastoralists from farmers, camel pastoralists from goat/cattle pastoralists, and even grain farmers from non-grain farmers. Groups that depended on the meat, blood, and milk of domestic animals had the highest ^{15}N values, those dependent mainly on plant foods had the lowest. The results agreed well with ethnographic and archaeological evidence.

Scientists have also found that concentrations of *strontium*, a stable mineral component of bone, can provide data on diet. Most plants do not discriminate between strontium and calcium, but when animals eat plants, strontium is discriminated against in favour of calcium; most of the strontium is excreted, but a small constant percentage enters the blood stream and becomes incorporated into bone mineral. The contribution of plants to the diet can therefore be assessed through the proportions of strontium and calcium (Sr/Ca) in human bone – the bigger the contribution (e.g. in a vegetarian), the higher the Sr:Ca ratio, whereas a meat-eater's diet gives a low ratio.

Analysis by Margaret Schoeninger of strontium levels in bones from the eastern Mediterranean has shown that the proportions of plant and animal foods in the diet did not change radically from the Middle Paleolithic until the Mesolithic, when there was a shift toward a greater use of plant foods. Her results show that people in this part of the world had a plant-rich diet a considerable time before cereals were domesticated.

Schoeninger has used the same technique to study skeletal material at Chalcatzingo, an Olmec site in central Mexico at its peak around 700–500 BC, where a combination of strontium results and an assessment of grave-goods indicates a ranked society with a differential consumption of meat. She found that the highest-ranked people buried with jade had the lowest bone strontium (and therefore ate plenty of meat); those buried with a shallow dish had a higher strontium level (and thus ate less meat); while a third group lacking any grave-goods had the highest strontium level (and probably ate very little meat).

A different picture emerges where shellfish contributed to diet, because strontium concentrations are far higher in molluscs than in plants. Skeletons from an Archaic hunter-gatherer population of around 2500 BC at a northern Alabama site proved to have a higher strontium level, thanks to the molluscs in their diet, than those from an agricultural Mississippian population buried at the same site in about AD 1400.

Recent studies, however, suggest that because of contamination from sediments and ground water in which some bones are buried strontium values can be misleading. One should therefore keep an open mind about these analyses until the possible pitfalls are better understood. In any case, the technique is only a complement to – not a replacement for – the analysis of carbon isotopes. The Sr:Ca ratio reveals the proportionate amounts of meat and plants in the diet; but isotopic analysis is needed to learn what kinds of plants were being consumed; and it is archaeology that provides the tangible evidence that permits more precise identification of the plant and animal species involved.

SUMMARY

All the methods described in this chapter are providing archaeology with new tools, not to say with "food for thought." The evidence available varies from botanical and animal remains, both large and microscopic, to tools and vessels, plant and animal residues, and art and texts. We can discover what was eaten, in which seasons, and sometimes how it was prepared. We need to assess whether the evidence arrived in the archaeological record naturally or through human agency, and whether the resources were wild or under human control. Occasionally we encounter the remains of individual meals left as funerary offerings or as the contents of stomachs or feces. Finally, the human body itself contains a record of diet in its toothwear and in the chemical signatures left in bones by different foods.

Many of the techniques lie in the domain of the specialist, and particularly the biochemist, but archaeologists should know how to interpret the results, because the rewards are enormous for our knowledge of what people ate, how they exploited their resources, and in what proportions. Prospects for future research look good. Since we understand increasingly what a good or balanced diet entails, we can now begin to examine past diets in terms of nutritional value and assess the state of health of our ancestors.

Further Reading

Most of the sources given at the end of Chapter 6 are appropriate for this chapter as well. In addition, helpful volumes are:

Brothwell, D.&P. 1969. *Food in Antiquity: A Survey of the Diet of Early Peoples*. Thames and Hudson: London; Praeger: New York.

Chaplin, R.E. 1971. *The Study of Animal Bones from Archaeological Sites*. Seminar Press: London & New York.

Cornwall, I.W. 1974. *Bones for the Archaeologist*. Phoenix House: London.

Gilbert, R.I. and Mielke, J.H. (eds.). 1985. *The Analysis of Prehistoric Diets*. Academic Press: New York & London.

Olsen, S.J. 1970. *Osteology for the Archaeologist*. Peabody Museum: Cambridge, Mass.

8
How Did They Make and Use Tools? Technology

The human species has often been defined in terms of our special ability to make tools. And many archaeologists have seen human progress largely in technological terms. The 19th-century Danish scholar C.J. Thomsen divided the human past into "ages" of stone, bronze, and iron. His successors further divided the Stone Age into a Paleolithic period (with chipped or flaked stone tools), and a Neolithic period (with polished stone tools). The later addition of the term Mesolithic (Middle Stone Age) carried with it the implication that the very small flint tools, the "microliths," were somehow characteristic of this particular period of human existence.

Even if today we do not place so much emphasis on the particular form of artifacts as a reliable chronological indicator, it remains true that these were and are the basic means by which humans act upon the external world. Modern lasers and computers, guns and electrical appliances all have their origins in the simple tools created by our earliest ancestors. It is the physical remains of humanly made artifacts down the ages that form the bulk of the archaeological record. In other chapters we look at how archaeologists can use artifacts to establish typologies (Chapter 3), learn about diet (Chapter 7), discover past patterns of trade and exchange (Chapter 9), and even recreate systems of belief (Chapter 10). In this chapter, however, we address two questions of fundamental importance: how were artifacts made, and what were they used for?

As we shall see, there are several approaches to these two questions – the purely archaeological, the scientific analysis of objects, the ethnographic, and the experimental. Archaeologists should also seek the advice of modern experts in equivalent technologies. Contemporary craftspeople generally exploit the same materials as their forebears, and often use tools that are little changed. An ancient stone wall will be best understood by a stonemason, a brick building by a bricklayer, and a timber one by a carpenter, although in order to understand a medieval timber building, a modern carpenter will certainly need to know something of the period's materials, tools, and methods. For more recently developed technologies, such as those of the last 200 or 300 years, the growing field of *industrial archaeology* can also make use of eyewitness accounts by living craftspeople or verbal descriptions handed down from one generation to the next, as well as historical and photographic records.

The student of earlier periods has a narrower range of evidence to choose from. Questions of preservation arise, and indeed of how one decides whether an early "tool" is humanly made in the first place.

Survival of the Evidence

When assessing ancient technologies, the archaeologist always needs to bear in mind that the sample preserved may well be biased. During the long Paleolithic period implements of wood and bone must surely have rivaled those of stone in importance – as they do in hunting and gathering societies today – but stone tools dominate the archaeological record. As we saw in Chapter 2, fragile objects may sometimes survive on waterlogged, frozen, or dry sites, but these are exceptions. In view of the poor preservative qualities of many types of artifact, it is worth remembering that even those that have totally decayed can occasionally be detected by the hollows, soil-changes, or marks they have left. Examples include the imprint left in sand by the Sutton Hoo boat in eastern England; the imprint of a textile on a mummy; or, as will be seen below, the space within a mass of corroded metal. The vanished wheel of an Iron Age vehicle in a grave at Wetwang, Yorkshire, in northern England, has been successfully investigated by pumping polystyrene foam into the hollow, revealing that the wheel had 12 spokes.

Depictions of tools and weapons are common on rockshelter walls in Australia. This photograph shows the stencil of a V-shaped "killer" boomerang from the Central Queensland Sandstone Belt. Grahame Walsh and his colleagues estimate that there are 10,000 rock art sites in this area alone.

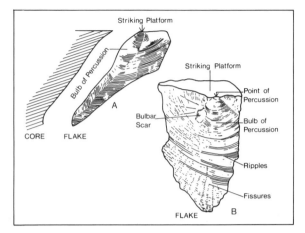

Features of a purposely made stone flake. Two views (A, B) of a flake struck from the edge of a core show the characteristic striking platform and, immediately beneath, the bulb of percussion and ripples produced by the shock waves after the blow has been struck.

Implements are also known from artistic depictions, such as boomerangs and axes stenciled on rockshelter walls by Aborigines in a number of regions of Australia. The former presence of some tools can also be detected by their effects – for example, a sword-cut on a skull, or a pick-mark on a quarry wall.

Are They Artifacts At All?

The archaeologist, when studying an object, must first decide whether it was made or used by people in the past. For most periods the answer will be obvious (although one has to beware of fakes and forgeries), but for the Paleolithic, and especially the Lower Paleolithic, judgment can be less straightforward. For many years a vehement debate raged concerning the problem of "eoliths" – pieces of stone found at the beginning of this century in Lower Pleistocene contexts in eastern England and elsewhere and believed by some scholars to have been shaped by early humans, but which other scholars thought were products of nature. The controversy led to early attempts to establish criteria by which human agency could be recognized, such as characteristic bulges or "bulbs of percussion" on pieces of flint purposely struck off (see diagram). Natural fractures caused by factors such as heat, frost, or a fall produce irregular scars and no bulb. On this basis the eoliths were pronounced to be of natural origin.

Where the very earliest tools are concerned, however – on which one would expect the traces of human work to be minimal – the question is less easy to resolve, since the crudest human working may be indistinguishable from the damage caused by nature. Here the examination of the context of a find may help. Perhaps the stone objects were discovered in association with fossil human remains and animal bones that can be studied for signs of human cutmarks made by stone tools (Chapter 7).

A complex case is that of the Calico Hills site, California, where thousands of pieces of fractured stone were found during the 1960s and 1970s in geological deposits dating to around 200,000 years ago. The discoverers claim that many of the stones are tools on the basis of their bulbs of percussion, regular shape, and comparison with tools knapped experimentally from local raw materials. If correct, this would suggest human occupation of the New World at least 160,000 years earlier than is indicated by other sites. It is this extraordinarily early date and lack of supporting evidence from other sites, as well as the crude nature of the "artifacts," that leads most archaeologists to reject the Calico finds as genuine tools.

Interpreting the Evidence: the Use of Ethnographic Analogy

If used with care, evidence from ethnography and ethnoarchaeology can shed light on both general and specific questions concerning technology. At the general level, ethnography and common sense together suggest that people tend to use whatever materials are easily and abundantly available for everyday, mundane tasks, but will invest time and effort into making implements they will use repeatedly (though perhaps rarely) and carry around with them. The abundance of a type of tool in the archaeological record is therefore not necessarily a guide to its intrinsic importance in the culture; the tool most frequently found may well have been quickly made, and discarded immediately after use, while the rarer implement was kept and re-used ("curated") several times, before eventually being thrown away.

At the specific level of perhaps identifying the function of a particular artifact, ethnography can often prove helpful. For example, large winged pendants of polished stone were found in sites of the Tairona Indians of northern Colombia, dating to the 16th century AD. Archaeologists could only assume that these were decorative, and had been hung on the chest. However, it was subsequently learnt that the modern Kogi Indians of the area, direct descendants of the Tairona, still use such objects in pairs, suspended from the elbows, as rattles or tinklers during dances!

There are innumerable examples of this sort. The important point is that the identification of tool forms by ethnographic analogy should be limited to cases where there is demonstrable continuity between archaeological culture and modern society, or at least to cultures with a similar subsistence level and roughly the same ecological background.

In recent years, the archaeological and ethnographic aspects of technological studies have been complemented by the ever increasing interest in bringing archaeology to life through experiment. As we shall see, experiments have contributed a great deal to our understanding of how artifacts were made and what they were used for.

For the purposes of the remainder of this chapter, it is convenient to draw a distinction between two classes of raw material used – between those that are largely unaltered, such as flint, and those that are synthetic, the product of human activities, such as pottery or metal. Of course even the supposedly unaltered materials have often been treated by heat or by chemical reactions in order to assist the manufacturing process. But synthetic materials have undergone an actual change in state, usually through heat treatment. The human use of fire – pyrotechnology – is a crucial factor here. We are becoming increasingly aware of just how precise human control of fire was at an early date.

UNALTERED MATERIALS: STONE

From the first recognizable tools, dating back about 2.5 million years, up to the adoption of pottery-making, no earlier than 12,000 years ago, the archaeological record is dominated by stone. How were stone artifacts of all kinds, from the smallest microlith to the greatest megalith, extracted, transported, manufactured, and used?

Extraction: Mines and Quarries

Much of the stone for early tools was probably picked up from streambeds or other parts of the landscape; but the sources most visible archaeologically are the mines and quarries.

The best-known *mines* are the Neolithic and later flint mines in various parts of northern Europe, such as at Spiennes in Belgium, Grimes Graves in England, and Krzemionki in Poland. The basic technology remained fundamentally the same for the later extraction of other materials, such as salt in the Iron Age mines at Hallstatt, Austria, copper at mines such as Rudna Glava and Ai Bunar in Yugoslavia, and silver and gold from mines of later periods.

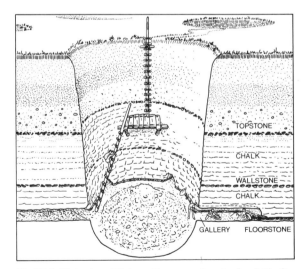

Neolithic flint mine at Grimes Graves, eastern England. Shafts some 15 m (50 ft) deep were sunk to reach the best-quality flint in the floorstone layer. Galleries, once exhausted, were back-filled with rubble from new galleries. Rough estimates suggest that the site could have produced 28 million flint axes.

Excavation has revealed a mixture of open-cast and shaft mining, depending on the terrain and the position of the desirable seams (a high degree of expertise is usually clear from the ignoring of mediocre seams and a concentration on the best material). For example, at Rijckholt in the Netherlands, archaeologists dug an exploratory tunnel for 150 m (490 ft), following the layer of chalk that Neolithic people of the 4th millennium BC had found to be especially rich in flint nodules. No less than 66 mine-shafts were encountered, 10–16 m (33–52 ft) deep, each with radiating galleries that had been backfilled with waste chalk. If the archaeologists' tunnel hit a representative sample of shafts, then the Rijckholt area must contain 5000 of them, which could have yielded enough flint for a staggering 153 million axeheads.

There were a variety of clues to the mining techniques at Rijckholt. Impressions in the walls of an excavated shaft indicated that cave-ins were prevented by a retaining wall of plaited branches. Deep grooves in the chalk at the points where the shafts end and the galleries begin imply that ropes were used to raise nodules to the surface. As for the tools used, over 15,000 blunted or broken axeheads were found,

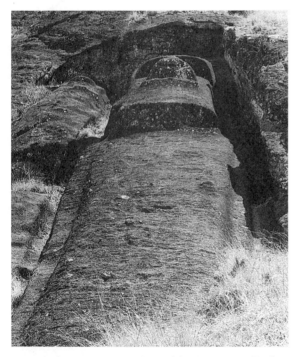

Stone quarry on Easter Island: one of the giant statues lies flat on its back, unfinished but at an advanced stage of manufacture—yielding important clues as to how it was made.

suggesting a figure of 2.5 million for the whole mine; in other words, less than 2 percent of the output was expended in extraction. Each shaft had about 350 axeheads – some next to the hollows in the waste chalk left by their vanished wooden handles – and it has been estimated that five would have been worn out in removing a single cubic meter of chalk. They were sharpened on the spot, as is shown by the hard hammerstones found with them (one for every 10 or 20 axeheads) and the abundant flakes of flint.

Few antler picks were found at Rijckholt as the chalk there is particularly hard, but they are known from other such mines. Experiments have shown how remarkably effective antler can be against hard rock. Traces of burning in other mines also indicate that rock faces were sometimes initially broken up by heating with a small fire, followed by cooling with water.

Finally, at copper mines in the Mitterberg area of the Austrian Alps some wooden tools have survived – a hammer and wedges, a shovel and torch, a wooden sled for hauling loads, and even a notched tree-trunk ladder. Such finds indicate the range of technological evidence missing from most sites and which we have to rediscover through analysis of clues such as those at Rijckholt.

Where *quarries* are concerned, the archaeologist is often aided in making technological reconstructions by unfinished objects or abandoned stones. The most impressive examples are the statue-quarry on the slopes of the volcano Rano Raraku, Easter Island, and the obelisk quarry at Aswan, Egypt. The Easter Island quarry contains scores of unfinished statues at various stages of manufacture, from a shape drawn on to a rock face to a completed figure attached to the rock only at the base. Discarded hammerstones by the thousand litter the area. Experiments have suggested that six carvers with such stone picks could have shaped a 5 m (16 ft) statue in about a year.

The granite obelisk at Aswan, had it been finished, would have been 42 m (138 ft) high and weighed an immense 1168 tons. The tools used in its initial shaping were heavy balls of dolerite, and experiments indicate that pounding the granite with them for one hour would reduce the level of the obelisk by 5 mm (0.2 in) over each person's work area. At that rate, the monument could have been shaped and undercut in 15 months by 400 workers, giving us some objective indication of the magnitude of Egyptian work of this kind. The pounding marks still visible in the Aswan quarries are very similar to marks on rocks at sites such as Rumiqolqa, Peru. This quarry, the most complete Inca quarry known, has 250 shaped blocks lying abandoned in an enormous pit 100 m (328 ft) long; the blocks had been pounded into shape with hardstone hammers which still bear the traces of the work.

Archaeology, combined with experiments, can therefore discover a great deal about stone extraction. The next stage is to ascertain how the material was moved to the place where it was used, erected, or fitted together.

How was Stone Transported?

In certain cases, simple archaeological observation can assist our inquiry. At the Inca quarry of Kachiqhata, near the unfinished site of Ollantaytambo, the Swiss architectural historian Jean-Pierre Protzen's investigations have revealed that slides and ramps were constructed to enable the workers to move the red granite blocks 1000 m (1094 yd) down the mountain. But discovering the route is one thing – the technique is another. For this, wear patterns need to be studied. At Ollantaytambo itself Protzen noted drag marks (polishing, and longitudinal striations) on some blocks; and since the marks are found only on the broadest face, it is clear that the blocks were dragged broad-face down.

It is not yet known how the dragging was accomplished, and commentaries by the 16th-century Spanish Conquistadors are of little help on this point. Perhaps the most challenging problem is how the ropes and men could have been arranged. At Ollantaytambo, for example, one block of 140 tons would have required 2400 men to move it, yet the ramp up which it was moved was only 8 m (26 ft) wide. Only experimentation will indicate the most feasible method employed.

The Egyptians faced similar and often greater problems in the transportation of huge blocks. Here, we have some information from an ancient representation showing a 7-m (23-ft) high alabaster statue of Prince Djehutihetep being moved; it must have weighed 60 tons. The statue is tied to a wooden sledge, and 90 men are pulling on ropes. This number was probably insufficient, and must be attributed to artistic licence; but at least depictions of this type serve to counter suggestions that huge statues and blocks could only be moved with the help of visiting astronauts. Calculations by engineers and actual experiments are prob-

Moving the stones: an experiment at Bougon, western France, in 1979. Three large wooden levers – each maneuvered by a team of 20 people – were used to erect a Neolithic block weighing 32 tons. Supporting wedges held the block as it rose.

ably the best way in which we can hope scientifically to solve the enigma of how great stone blocks – like the 300-ton Grand Menhir Brisé in Brittany – were transported and erected.

One such experiment, in 1955, tackled the great Olmec basalt columns or stelas at La Venta, Mexico, of the 1st millennium BC. Real-life trials proved a 2-ton column was the maximum load that could be lifted by 35 men, using rope slings, and poles on their shoulders. Since the largest La Venta stela weighs 50 tons, it must have required 500 men, at 100 kg (220 lb) per man. But 500 people could not all have got near enough to lift the stela, so it was deduced that the stone must have been dragged instead.

Inca stonework. (Above) The famous 12-angled stone in Cuzco, Peru, part of a wall of accurately fitted blocks built by the Incas. (Below) Diagrams illustrating Jean-Pierre Protzen's experiments to discover how Inca stonemasons may have dressed the blocks. Initially (left) Protzen pounded one face of the stone with a 4-kg (9-lb) hammer which he twisted at the last minute to deliver a glancing blow. Then (center) he used a smaller, 560-g (1.2-lb) hammer to prepare the edges of the next face. Having repeated the process for each face, he finally produced a finished block (right) with slightly convex corners, similar to the corners on actual Inca stonework.

How were Stones Worked and Fitted?

Here again, archaeology and experiment combine to provide valuable insights into construction techniques. For example, Inca stonework has always been considered a marvel, and the accuracy with which blocks of irregular shape were joined together once seemed almost fantastic. Jean-Pierre Protzen's work has revealed many of the techniques involved, which, though mundane, by no means detract from the Inca accomplishment. His experiments determined the most effective way to "bounce" hammerstones on the blocks to dress them, and found that one face could easily be shaped in 20 minutes. The bedding joint for each course of stones was cut into the upper face of the course already in place; then the new block was placed on the lower, the required edge outlined, and that shape pounded out of it with a hammerstone. Protzen found that a fit could be obtained in 90 minutes, especially as practice gave one a keen eye for matching surfaces. His experiments are supported by 16th-century accounts which state that many fits were tried until the stones were correctly adjusted. The Inca blocks also bear traces of the process – their surfaces are covered in scars from the hammerstones, while the finer scars on the edges indicate the use of smaller hammers. In addition, many blocks still have small protrusions which were clearly used when handling them. Similar protruding knobs can also be seen on certain Greek buildings such as the unfinished temple at Segesta, Sicily.

Until recently we had little knowledge of exactly how Greek architects achieved precision in both design and execution, since no written accounts or plans have survived. But the German archaeologist Lothar Haselberger has now found "blueprints" in the form of detailed drawings on the walls of the 4th-century BC temple of Apollo at Didyma, Turkey. Thin lines up to 20 m (65 ft) long, circles, polygons, and angles had been etched into the marble with a fine metal gouge.

Some drawings were full size, others were scaled down; different parts of the building could be recognized, and, since the walls bearing the drawings should logically have been built before the walls depicted in the drawings, the sequence of construction could be determined.

Other Greek temples have since been found to contain similar plans, but the Didyma drawings are the most detailed, and survived because the walls never received their customary final polish which would have obliterated the engravings. In Chapter 10 we consider the importance of plans in terms of the development of human intellectual skills.

So far we have examined the larger end of the lithic spectrum. But how were the smaller stone objects made? And what was their purpose?

Stone Tool Manufacture

For the most part, stone tools are made by removing material from a pebble or "core" until the desired shape of the core has been attained. The first flakes struck off (primary flakes) bear traces of the outer surface (cortex). Trimming flakes are then struck off to achieve the final shape, and certain edges may then be "retouched" by further removal of tiny secondary flakes. Although the core is the main implement thus produced, the flakes themselves may well be used as knives, scrapers etc. The toolmaker's work will have varied in accordance with the type and amount of raw material available.

The history of stone tool technology shows a sporadically increasing degree of refinement. The first recognizable tools are simple choppers and flakes made by knocking pieces off pebbles to obtain sharp edges. The best-known examples are the so-called Oldowan tools from Olduvai Gorge, Tanzania. After hundreds of thousands of years, people progressed to flaking both surfaces of the tool, eventually producing the symmetrical Acheulian hand-axe shape, with its finely worked sharp edges. The next improvement, around 100,000 years ago, came with the introduction of the "Levallois technique" – named after a site in a Paris suburb where it was first identified – where the core was knapped in such a way that large flakes of predetermined size and shape could be removed.

Around 35,000 years ago, with the Upper Paleolithic period, blade technology became dominant in some parts of the world. Long, parallel-sided blades were systematically removed with a punch and hammerstone from a cylindrical core. This was a great advance, not only because it produced large numbers of blanks that could be further trimmed and retouched into a wide range of specialized tools (scrapers, burins, borers), but also because it was far less wasteful of the raw material, obtaining a much greater total length of working edges than ever before from a given amount of stone. The stone itself was normally a homogeneous easily-worked type such as chert or obsidian. Loren Eiseley has worked out a helpful summary of this increasing efficiency, estimated assuming the use of 500 g (1 lb 1 oz) of high-quality chert:

Technology	Length of Cutting Edge Produced
OLDOWAN	5 cm
ACHEULIAN	20 cm
MOUSTERIAN (Middle Paleolithic)	100 cm
GRAVETTIAN (Upper Paleolithic)	300–1200 cm

This trend toward greater economy reached its peak in the Mesolithic (Middle Stone Age), around 10,000 years ago, with the rise to dominance of microliths, tiny stone tools many of which were probably used as barbs on composite weapons.

It is the archaeologist's task to reconstruct the sequence of manufacturing steps – a task made easier if the knapping was done in one place and all the waste material (called debitage) is still present. The discovery of a network of manufacturing sites also aids any analysis. In Japan, for example, the Taku site cluster of over 40 sites in Saga Prefecture, dating to between 15,000 and 10,000 years ago, is located at a stone source and yielded over 100,000 tools, with each site specializing in a different stage of manufacture, from raw material procurement to production of finished artifacts. More commonly, however, the archaeologist will find an industrial site with a full range of waste material and broken tools, but few finished tools since these were mostly removed. Finished tools often turn up in sites far from the source of stone. The types of tools found at a site can also provide clues to the site's function: a hunting kit with projectile points might be expected in a temporary camp, while a wide range of tools would be present in a base camp or a permanent settlement.

Some techniques of manufacture can be inferred from traces left on the tools, and many techniques can still be observed among the few living peoples, such as some Australian Aborigines or highland Maya, who continue to make stone tools. Much ethnoarchaeological work has been done in Australia and Mesoamerica in recent years, most notably by Richard Gould and

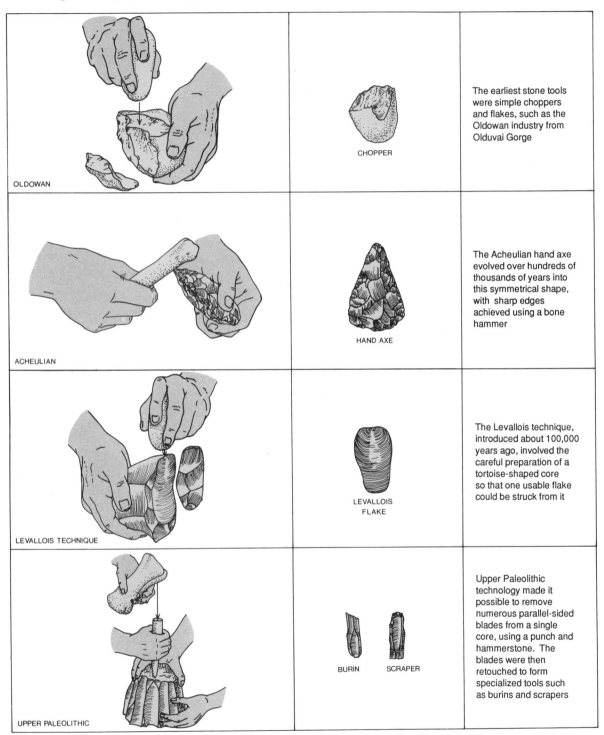

OLDOWAN	CHOPPER	The earliest stone tools were simple choppers and flakes, such as the Oldowan industry from Olduvai Gorge
ACHEULIAN	HAND AXE	The Acheulian hand axe evolved over hundreds of thousands of years into this symmetrical shape, with sharp edges achieved using a bone hammer
LEVALLOIS TECHNIQUE	LEVALLOIS FLAKE	The Levallois technique, introduced about 100,000 years ago, involved the careful preparation of a tortoise-shaped core so that one usable flake could be struck from it
UPPER PALEOLITHIC	BURIN SCRAPER	Upper Paleolithic technology made it possible to remove numerous parallel-sided blades from a single core, using a punch and hammerstone. The blades were then retouched to form specialized tools such as burins and scrapers

The evolution of stone tools, from the earliest, Oldowan technology to the refined methods of the Upper Paleolithic.

Brian Hayden. Artistic depictions can also be of some help, as in the paintings in the tomb of the 12th-dynasty Egyptian pharaoh Ameny at Beni Hassan, which show the mass production of flint knives under the supervision of foremen.

In most other cases, there are two principal approaches to assessing what decisions the knapper made: replication and refitting.

Stone Tool Replication. This is a type of experimental archaeology that involves making exact copies of different types of stone tool – using only the technology available to the original makers – in order to assess the processes entailed, and the amount of time and effort required. In the past only a handful of experimenters, notably François Bordes in the Old World and Donald Crabtree in the New, reached a high level of expertise, since many years of patient practice are required. Today, however, quite a few younger archaeologists have become proficient at tool replication, much to the benefit of our knowledge of ancient stone-knapping.

American archaeologist Nicholas Toth, for example, has made and used the entire range of early stone tools, as found at sites such as Koobi Fora, Kenya, and dating to about 1.5 to 2 million years ago – hammerstones, choppers, scrapers, and flakes. His work provides evidence to suggest that simple flakes may have been the primary tools, while the more impressive cores were an incidental by-product of flake manufacture. Previously, scholars tended to see the flakes as waste products, and the cores as the intentional end-product.

One specific problem that Donald Crabtree was able to solve through trial and error was how the Paleo-Indians of North America had made their fluted stone tools known as Folsom points, dating to some 11,000–10,000 years ago. In particular, how had they managed to remove the "flute" or channel flake? His experiments with a variety of techniques met with disappointing results, until the decisive clue was found in a 17th-century text by a Spanish priest who had seen Aztec Indians make long knife-blades from obsidian. The correct method, as new experiments proved, involves pressing the flake out, downwards, by means of a T-shaped crutch placed against the chest; the crutch's tip is forced down against a precise point on the core which is clamped firm.

One of the acknowledged masters of stone tool replication: the French Paleolithic specialist, François Bordes. He is seen here in 1975, knapping a piece of stone in order to assess the processes involved and the time and effort expended.

How were Paleo-Indian Folsom points made? Experiments by Donald Crabtree showed that the flakes were pressed from the core using a T-shaped crutch (left). Flintknappers have produced almost perfect replica points (right).

Archaeologists can also use replication and experiment to discover whether certain flint tools had been deliberately heated during manufacture, and if so, why. For example, in Florida many projectile points and much chipping debris have a pinkish color and a lustrous surface which suggests thermal alteration. Work by Barbara Purdy and H.K. Brooks has shown that when Florida cherts are slowly heated a color change occurs at 240°C (464°F), while after heating to 350–400°C (662–752°F) flaking leaves a lustrous appearance. Purdy and Brooks investigated the differences between unheated and heated chert. Petrographic thin-sections failed to detect any differences in structure, but in the scanning electron microscope it became clear that heated chert had a far smoother appearance. Furthermore, a study of rock mechanics showed that after heating the chert had an increase in compressive strength of 25–40 percent, but a decrease of 45 percent in the force needed to break it.

Confirmation – and more objective data than a flint's appearance – can be obtained from an entirely different method, electron spin resonance (ESR) spectroscopy, which can identify subatomic chemical structures in the molecular lattice of silica crystals. Heated material has a characteristic ESR signal which is absent from unheated flint, and which remains stable indefinitely. Tests with this method have proved that heat treatment was already present in the French Upper Paleolithic Solutrean culture, about 19,000 years ago. The heating was clearly performed after initial shaping but before final trimming. Experiments by Crabtree on chert indicate that one can obtain larger flakes by pressure flaking after heating. Thermoluminescence (Chapter 4) can also be used to detect heat alteration – and, in some cases, even estimate the temperature – as the amount of TL in a sample relates to the time since firing. A tool not subject to heat normally yields a high TL reading, while a heated specimen has a far lower reading due to the previous release of trapped electrons.

Replication cannot usually prove conclusively which techniques were used in the past, but it does narrow the possibilities and often points to the most likely method, as in the Folsom example above. *Refitting*, on the other hand, involves working with the original tools and demonstrates clearly the precise chain of actions of the knapper.

Refitting of Stone Tools. This type of work, which can be traced back to F.C.J. Spurrell at the Paleolithic site of Crayford, England, in 1880, has really come into its own in the last couple of decades thanks largely to the efforts of André Leroi-Gourhan at the Magdalenian

Excavation of the Meer site revealed four concentrations of artifacts – A, B, C, and D; the largest were A and D. Within area A were two "satellite' areas (A$_1$ and A$_2$) and 3 hearths. Area D also had two "satellites," but only one hearth.

Refitting studies have demonstrated links among the four Meer II concentration areas as shown in the diagram above. Each of these seven links traces one or more artifacts from one area to another.

Microwear analysis of Meer II artifacts has produced this plan, showing the breakdown and separation of activities at the site.

REFITTING AND MICROWEAR STUDIES AT THE MEER SITE

The Epipaleolithic (Mesolithic) site of Meer II, Belgium, dates from about 8900 years ago, and was excavated by the Belgian archaeologist Francis Van Noten in 1967–69 and 1975–76. Apart from a few fragments of eroded bone and scraps of charcoal and ocher, the site comprises a scatter of stone tools in a sand dune. There were hammerstones of quartzite and schist, and grinders of sandstone, but 98 percent of the 16,000 stone artifacts were of flint.

Van Noten plotted the horizontal distribution of the tools, which showed marked variation. Some meter squares had over 500 artifacts, others few or none, and there were four particular concentrations (labeled A to D on the site plan). Vertically, the tools were found scattered through a considerable depth of 45 cm (1ft 5³/₄ in). Did this mean that the site had been occupied several times, or had the abandoned tools from a single occupation been displaced vertically by natural processes, such as burrowing animals and plant roots?

In order to answer this question, a refitting project was carried out by Daniel Cahen, who succeeded in reconstituting many of the small flint nodules. He found that 18 percent of the artifacts were interrelated, and that there were definite links among the four areas of concentration. The work suggests strongly that occupation was shortlived and that the vertical displacement of tools is indeed due to natural post-depositional factors. When his results were combined with analysis of microwear traces by Lawrence Keeley, a remarkably detailed picture emerged of some activities at what had, at first, appeared an unpromising site.

For example, out of one group of 15 tools refitted from concentration

D, 12 showed microwear. The microwear indicated that one tool had been used to cut meat, while the others had all been used on bone – 8 as borers, 4 as groovers, and 2 as cutters. From this and other similar evidence, it was deduced that concentration D had been an area where flint tools were prepared for rough work on bone and antler. Furthermore, three of the boring tools in concentration D had done their work by being twisted

counter-clockwise, unlike the other borers which had been turned clockwise. It is therefore very likely that more than two people worked at concentration D, one of whom was left-handed.

At various stages right-handed knappers carried blanks and finished tools from concentration D to concentration A, where they were used for fine work on bone. Other small areas seem to have been used for hideworking and as a refuse dump.

Graph showing how a group of 17 flakes, from varying depths at the site, could be refitted – the arrows indicating refits among flakes struck successively from the same core. This demonstrates that the artifacts, although as much as 24 cm apart in depth, were from the same occupation period at the site. Disturbance of the soil by roots and other natural forces had displaced the flakes vertically through the deposit.

SURFACE OF SITE

DEPTH IN CENTIMETERS

● = Flake
⟶ = Refit

0 1 in
0 2 cm

Microwear and refitting studies combined. (Top row) Three views of a refitted block. (Bottom row) Microwear indicated a variety of uses for the flakes: **a,** borer for use on bone; **b,** tool for incising grooves in bone; **c,** another borer for bone; **d,** tool for graving a u-shaped groove. Borers **a** and **c** had been turned counter-clockwise, indicating their use by a left-handed person.

Stone flakes from the Upper Paleolithic site of Marsangy, France, refitted to show the original core from which they were struck. Such work allows the archaeologist to build up a picture of the different stages of the knapper's craft.

(late Upper Paleolithic) camp of Pincevent, near Paris, and that of his pupils at similar sites. Refitting, or conjoining as it is sometimes called, entails attempting to put tools and flakes back together again, like a 3-D jigsaw puzzle. The work is tedious and time-consuming, but can produce spectacular results. One refitted stone designated N103 from the Magdalenian site of Etiolles includes 124 pieces, some of which are blades over 30 cm (11.8 in) long.

Why exactly do archaeologists devote so many hours of hard work to refitting exercises? Very broadly because refitting allows us to follow the stages of the knapper's craft and – where pieces from one core have been found in different areas – even the knapper's (or the core's) movements around the site. Of course, displacement of flakes may have nothing to do with the changing location of the craftsperson: a burin spall, for example, can jump 7 m (23 ft) when struck off. And it should not be assumed automatically that each core was processed in one episode of work: we know from ethnography that a core can be re-used after a short or long period of absence. It is also now known from conjoined pieces that considerable vertical movement can occur through different layers of a site, even where there are no visible traces of disturbance. However, if these factors are allowed for, refitting provides a dynamic perspective on the spatial distribution of tools, and produces a vivid picture of actual movement and activity in an ancient site. Where these observations can be supplemented by information on the functions of the tools, the site really comes to life (see box, previous two pages, on the site of Meer).

But how can we discover the function of a stone tool? Ethnographic observation often gives valuable clues,

as we have already seen; and experimentation can determine which uses are feasible or most probable. However, a single tool can be used for many different purposes – an Acheulian hand-axe could be used for hacking wood from a tree, for butchering, smashing, scraping, and cutting – and conversely the same task can be done by many different tools. The only direct *proof* of function is to study the minute traces, or microwear patterns, that remain on the original tools.

Identifying the Function of Stone Tools: Microwear Studies

Like refitting, microwear studies can be traced back into the 19th century; but the real breakthrough came with the pioneering work, first published in 1957, by Sergei Semenov of the Soviet Union, who had experimented for decades with the microwear on ancient tools. Employing a binocular microscope, he found that even tools of the hardest stone retained traces of their use: primarily a variety of polishes and striations. Subsequent work by Ruth Tringham and others showed that Semenov's striations were not as universal as he had claimed, and attention was focused on microflaking (minute edge-chipping caused by use). Then the work entered a new phase with the introduction of the scanning electron microscope, which enabled Lawrence Keeley, now of the University of Chicago, and others to be far more precise about types of microwear and to record them on photomicrographs.

Describing the wear was all very well, but the different types needed to be identified with specific activities; experimental archaeology proved to be the answer. Different sorts of stone tools were copied, and each was used for a specific task. Study of the traces left by each task on different types of stone allowed Keeley to establish a reference collection with which wear on ancient tools could be compared. He found that different kinds of polish are readily distinguishable, and are very durable, since they constitute a real alteration in the tools' microtopography. Six broad categories of tool use were established: on wood, bone, hide, meat, antler, and non-woody plants. Other traces show the movement of the tool – e.g. in piercing, cutting, or scraping.

The effectiveness of this method was verified in a blind test, in which Keeley was supplied with 15 replicas that had been used for a series of secret tasks. He was able to identify correctly the working portions of the tool, reconstruct the way in which it was used, and even the type of material worked in almost every case. Turning to Lower Paleolithic artifacts from southern England, Keeley found that tools from Clacton (about 250,000 years old) had been used on meat, wood, hide, and bone, while some from Hoxne had also been used on non-woody plants. Sidescrapers seemed to have been used primarily for hide-working.

In a similar study, Johan Binneman and Janette Deacon tested the assumption that the stone adzes from Boomplaas Cave, South Africa, had been used primarily for woodworking (see Chapter 6 for the importance of charcoal at this site). Replicas of the Later Stone Age tools were made and then used to chisel and plane wood. When the resulting use-wear was compared with that on 51 tools from the site, dating back to 14,200 years ago, it was found that all the prehistoric specimens had the same polish, thus confirming the early importance of woodworking here.

The Japanese scholar Satomi Okazaki has focused on striations, since she feels that study of their density and direction is more objective than an assessment of degree of polish. In experiments she found that using obsidian produces striations, but no polish: striations parallel to the tool-edge are the results of a cutting motion, while perpendicular striations result from a scraping motion.

Establishing the function of a set of tools can produce unexpected results which transform our picture of activity at a site. For example, the Magdalenian site of Verberie, near Paris (12th millennium BC), yielded only one bone tool; yet studies of microwear on the site's flint tools show the great importance of bonework. Indeed an entire area of the site seems to have been devoted to the working of bone and antler. Certain traces left adhering to stone tools, such as blood and phytoliths, can also provide clues about function (Chapter 7).

As mentioned above, when microwear studies are combined with refitting, they help to produce a vivid picture of prehistoric life. At another French Magdalenian site, Pincevent, the tools and manufacturing waste generally cluster around the hearths; one particular stone core was found to have had a dozen blades removed from it beside one hearth, and eight of the blades had been retouched. The same core was later moved to a different hearth and work recommenced; some of the flakes struck off here were made into tools such as burins (graving implements), all of which were used to work reindeer antler.

A different category of manufacturing waste has recently been investigated, particularly by Knut Fladmark and other scholars in Canada: that of microdebitage, the "sawdust" of ancient knappers, comprising tiny flakes of rock, less than a millimeter in size, formed during the process of making stone tools. They are recovered by wet sieving or flotation (Chapter 6),

and then examined under the microscope to differentiate them from naturally formed dirt particles. Unlike larger waste products, microdebitage was never cleared away, and therefore serves to pinpoint the location of stoneworking at a site.

Identifying Function: Further Experiments with Stone Artifacts

Experimentation can be used in many other ways to help identify stone tool function. Replicas of almost every ancient stone artifact imaginable have been made and tested – from axes and sickles to grinders and arrowheads.

Sophie de Beaune recently undertook a study of the many varied objects in France claimed to be Upper Paleolithic stone lamps, using experiment, ethnographic observation of Eskimo lamps, and chemical analysis of the residues found in some of the alleged lamps. She found that only 302 objects were potential lamps, and of these only 85 were definite and 31 others probable. The combustion residues analyzed by spectrometry and chromatography (Chapters 6 and 7) proved to be fatty acids of animal origin, while remains of resinous wood clearly came from the wicks.

Sophie de Beaune tried out replica lamps of various types, with different fuels such as cattle lard and horse grease, and a variety of wicks. The tests left traces of use which corresponded with those in the ancient lamps; and the results were confirmed by study of the Eskimo lighting systems. Tests were also undertaken to determine the amount of light given out by the ancient lamps. They were found to be pretty dim, even in comparison with a modern candle. The power of the light depends on the quality and quantity of fuel; the flame is usually unstable and trembling. Experiments with a stone lamp using horse fat produced a flame of one-sixth the power of a candle, according to measurements with a photometer. But it was found that with only one lamp one can move around a cave, read, and even sew if one is close enough to the light – the eye cannot tell that the flame is weaker than a candle.

Other experiments with stone artifacts attempt to assess the time needed for different tasks. Emil Haury studied the minute beads from prehistoric pueblos in Arizona. One necklace, 10 m (33 ft) in length, had about 15,000 beads, which were an average of only 2 mm (0.08 in) in diameter. Replication, with the perforation done with a cactus spine, led to an estimate of 15 minutes per bead, or 480 working days for the whole necklace. Such exercises help to assess the inherent value of an object through the amount of work involved in its creation.

Assessing the Technology of Stone Age Art

In the field of prehistoric art, a number of analyses can be carried out to determine the pigments and binding medium used, and ancient methods of painting and engraving on stone. In the Upper Paleolithic cave art of southern France and northern Spain, for example, the most usual minerals found have proved to be manganese dioxide (black) and iron oxide (red), though recent analysis of black pigment in the Magdalenian cave of Niaux, France, proved that it was charcoal. Experiments suggest strongly that water – probably cave water – was the best binding medium available. In a few caves the height and inaccessibility of the art show that a ladder or scaffolding must have been used, and the sockets for a platform of beams still survive in the walls of a gallery in the French cave of Lascaux.

Analysis of pigments from prehistoric paintings in Monitor Basin, Nevada, by X-ray diffraction showed that gypsum had been the binding agent, and that reds and yellows had been made by adding various minerals. All the samples were different, suggesting that the paintings accumulated at different times.

It is not always apparent exactly how paint was applied in prehistoric times – whether by brush, pad, finger, or by blowing – but ethnographic observation together with experiments can be of great help in narrowing down the possibilities.

Moreover, infra-red film now makes it possible for us to distinguish between ocher pigments. Infra-red film sees through red ocher as though it were glass, so that other pigments beneath become visible. In addition, impurities in ocher can be detected since they are not transparent, so that different mixes of paint can be identified. Alexander Marshack used this technique to study the famous "spotted horse" frieze in the cave of Pech Merle, France, and to reconstruct the sequence in which the elements of the panel were painted. He found, for example, that the sets of red dots had been made by different types of ochers, and therefore possibly at different times.

A frieze of black paintings in the same cave led Michel Lorblanchet to an analysis by experiment, in an attempt to discover how long it might have taken to create the frieze. Having studied and memorized every stroke of the composition, he sought out a blank wall area of similar dimensions in a different cave, and drew an exact copy of the frieze on it. This exercise indicated that the entire composition could have been made in only one hour, a fact which underlines the view that much rock art was probably done in intensive bursts by talented artists.

Analysis of Stone Age art by experiment: Michel Lorblanchet draws from memory a copy of a frieze in the cave of Pech Merle, France. The exercise suggested that the entire frieze could have been sketched in only one hour.

The binocular microscope can be used to great effect in the study of engravings on stone, since it can determine the type of tool and stroke used, the differences in width and in transverse section of the lines, and sometimes the order in which the lines were made. Léon Pales, in his study of the Upper Paleolithic engraved plaquettes from the French cave of La Marche, also discovered that if one takes a plasticine or silicone relief-imprint of the engraved surface, the impression shows clearly which lines were engraved after which. The technique proved, for instance, that a supposed "harness" was a secondary feature added to a completed horse's head. Varnish replicas (see below) of engraved surfaces on stone can also be made, examined in the scanning electron microscope, and compared with surface features produced on experimental engravings. By this method one can study the micromorphology of the engraved lines, see exactly how they were created, in what order, and whether by one tool or several.

Many other methods of analysis used on stone artifacts have also been applied to other unaltered materials such as bone.

OTHER UNALTERED MATERIALS

Bone, Antler, Shell, and Leather

Since there is usually no difficulty in determining how these raw materials were obtained (except in cases such as when seashells or a sea mammal's bones are found far inland), the archaeologist's attention focuses on the method of manufacture and the function. First, however, one has to be sure that these are humanly made tools.

As with stone tools, it is not always easy to differentiate purposely made artifacts of organic material from accidents of nature. Debate still continues about the possible existence of shaped bone tools before the Upper Paleolithic. Common sense suggests that unshaped bones have been used as tools for as long as stones. After all, even in recent times, as in kill sites in North America (see bison drive box, Chapter 7) entire bones seem to have been used, unworked, as simple expediency tools during the dismemberment of carcasses.

Similarly, fragile objects such as shells may have perforations that are not necessarily artificial. The American scholar Peter Francis carried out experiments with shells in order to find criteria of human workmanship. Using shells beachcombed in western India, he perforated them in a variety of ways with stone tools: by scratching, sawing, grinding, gouging, and hammering. The resulting holes were examined under the microscope, and it was found that the first three techniques left recognizable traces, whereas gouging and hammering left irregular holes which were difficult to distinguish as artificial – in these cases, one would have to rely on the context of the find, and the position of the perforation (which depends on the shape of the shell), to help one decide whether people were responsible.

Deducing Techniques of Manufacture. On rare occasions the method of manufacture is clear archaeologically. For example, at the South African site of Kasteelberg, dating to about AD 950, a fabrication area has been discovered where every step in the process of making bone tools can be seen, revealing the complexity, the sequence, and the tools involved. The occupants of this stock-herding site worked in a sheltered spot, using primarily the metapodials (foot bones) of eland and hartebeest. The ends of the bones were removed using a hammerstone and a punch. Next, a groove was pounded along the bone's shaft, and then it was abraded and polished until the shaft was severed.

The resulting splinters were shaped with stones (many broken specimens were found discarded), and finally ground and polished into points which are very similar to ethnographic examples known from the San (Bushmen) of the Kalahari Desert.

Microwear studies using the scanning electron microscope combined with experimental archaeology are another successful means of determining methods of bone tool manufacture. Pierre-François Puech and his colleagues have overcome the problem that one cannot place the original tools in the SEM by making varnish replicas of the worked surfaces. A nitrocellulose compound is poured onto the bone, and later peeled off and turned into slide-mounts. They found that experimental marking of bone with various stone tools left characteristic traces which corresponded to marks on prehistoric bone artifacts. Each type of manufacture produced a different pattern of striations. Different methods of polishing bone also left recognizable traces. In this way it is becoming possible to reconstruct the history of manufacture of ancient bone artifacts.

Deducing Function. Experimental archaeology and study of wear patterns, either individually or in conjunction with each other, are highly effective in helping us deduce the function as well as the manufacturing techniques of organic artifacts.

One controversial and much-discussed issue is the original function of the perforated antler batons of the European Upper Paleolithic. The orthodox view, based on ethnographic analogy, is that they were arrowshaft-straighteners; but there are at least 40 other hypotheses, ranging from tent pegs to harness pieces. In order to obtain some objective evidence, the French archaeologist André Glory examined the wear patterns in and around the baton perforations. His conclusion

Antler baton from the Upper Paleolithic site of La Madeleine, France. Ethnography suggests that these objects were arrowshaft straighteners, but there are many other theories.

WOODWORKING IN THE SOMERSET LEVELS

As we saw in the box on Glastonbury Lake Village (Chapter 1), the wetlands in southwest England known as the Somerset Levels preserve a wide range of organic remains, including ancient wooden trackways. John and Bryony Coles, in their long-term Somerset Levels project, have been able to make a remarkably detailed analysis of the woodworking techniques used in track construction.

The chopped ends of pegs and stakes from the tracks often display facets or cutmarks left by the axes used to shape them. Experiments have shown that stone axes bruise the wood and leave dished facets, whereas bronze axes do not cause bruising, but leave characteristic stepped facets in the cuts. Imperfections in the axes – for example, nicks in their edges – can also be identified. Such faults have left their signature with each blow of the

axe, allowing archaeologists to pinpoint the use of particular axes on particular pieces of wood.

By this method, John and Bryony Coles have been able to prove that at least 10 different axes were used in the construction of one Bronze Age track in the Somerset Levels. Indeed, they have deduced the exact manner of working from these clues. One piece of wood has three facets – the top one's set of ridges is the reverse of the other two. It is therefore clear that the wood was first held vertically, and the axe came down "backhand;" it was then turned more obliquely to the ground, and the axe came down with a forehand stroke.

The large collections of preserved timber from waterlogged areas such

Experimental felling (below)of an ash tree by John Coles (right) and a colleague, using Neolithic and Bronze Age axes.

as the Somerset Levels, and Flag Fen in eastern England, are enabling archaeologists for the first time to gain insights into prehistoric techniques for splitting, cutting, joining, and piercing wood. It has become apparent that woodcraft changed little through time, even after the arrival of metal tools. For instance, it seems that wood was always split by the wedge-and-mallet method, just as in medieval times.

The Somerset Levels project has also demonstrated that woodlands were being carefully managed at least 5000 years ago. The thin wooden rods used for woven track panels laid flat on the marsh can only have come from the systematic cutting back or coppicing of tree stumps to produce regular crops of young rods.

Chopped ends *of pieces of wood reveal the dished facets produced by a Neolithic stone axe (left), and the angular, stepped facets from a bronze axe (right).*

Analysis *of the so-called Sweet Track, nearly 6000 years old, showed that Neolithic woodworkers had split large oaks radially into planks (right), but younger trees–too small to be cut radially – had been split tangentially (left).*

Bronze Age trackway, more than 3500 years old, called the Eclipse Track. The excavated length consisted of over 1000 hurdles, short track sections whose interwoven rods could only have been produced from a managed woodland, where tree stumps were deliberately cut back to encourage young, straight shoots.

was that the wear had definitely been made by the rubbing of a thong or rope of some sort. This result certainly narrows down the list of possible functions. Glory himself used it to bolster his own hypothesis that the batons had been used as handles for slings. On the other hand, analysis by the American archaeologist Douglas Campana of use-wear in the perforation of a deer shoulder-blade from Mugharet El Wad, Israel, dating to around the 9th millennium BC, suggests that here at any rate a similar if somewhat later perforated object had been employed in straightening wooden shafts. Experimental work supports this conclusion.

Experiments can likewise be used to help resolve all manner of questions about function and efficiency. Copies have been made, for example, of Upper Paleolithic barbed bone or antler points, and they have been hurled against animal carcasses and other objects. In this way M.W. Thompson was able to demonstrate that the small barbed points, with a central perforation, of the so-called Azilian culture at the end of the Ice Age in southwest Europe were probably toggle harpoons which swiveled and became firmly embedded in their prey.

In an experiment famous in British archaeological circles, John Coles investigated the efficiency of a leather shield from the Bronze Age of Ireland. It was the only one of its kind to have survived, all others of the period being of bronze. It was found that the shield could be hardened by means of hot water and beeswax, although it retained a degree of flexibility. Coles, armed with the leather replica, and a colleague using a copy of a metal shield, then attacked each other with slashing swords and spears of Bronze Age type. The metal shield was cut to ribbons, indicating that those specimens we have were not functional but for prestige or ritual. The leather shield, on the other hand, was barely perforated by the spear, and received only slight cuts on its outer surface from the sword. Its flexibility had absorbed and deflected the blows. This experiment reveals once again the importance to ancient people of the organic materials that so rarely come down to us intact.

Wood

Wood is one of the most important organic materials, and must have been used to make tools for as long as stone and bone. Indeed, as we have seen, many prehistoric stone tools were employed to obtain and work timber. If wood survives in good condition, it may preserve toolmarks to show how it was worked. As with other materials, one has to distinguish genuine toolmarks from those made by other means. John and

Bryony Coles have shown how important it is to differentiate toolmarks from the parallel facets left by beaver teeth. A combination of experiment and direct observation of beaver habits has helped them detect the distinction. As a result, a piece of wood from the famous Mesolithic site of Star Carr in northern England, thought to have been shaped by stone blades, is now known to have been cut in reality by beaver teeth.

A wide range of wooden tools can survive under special conditions, as we saw in Chapter 2. In the dry environment of ancient Egypt, for instance, numerous wooden implements for farming (rakes, hoes, grain-scoops, sickles), furniture, weapons and toys, and carpentry tools such as mallets and chisels have come down to us. Egyptian paintings such as those in the tomb of the nobleman Rekhmire at Thebes also sometimes depict carpenters using drills and saws. But it has been waterlogged wood that has yielded the richest information about woodworking skills (see box, p.286).

Larger wooden objects are not uncommon, such as the Bronze Age tree-trunk coffins of northern Europe, mortuary houses, bridges, waterfront timbers, remains of actual dwellings, and especially a wide range of wheeled vehicles: carts, wagons, carriages, and char-iots. Until the Industrial Revolution and the arrival of railways and motor vehicles, all wheeled transport was made of wood, with metal fittings in later periods. A surprising number of vehicles (e.g. entire ox-wagons in the Caucasus) or of recognizable parts (especially

wheels) have survived, as well as evidence in models, art, and literature. In the pre-Columbian New World, wheeled models are the only evidence: wheeled vehicles as such were not introduced until the Spanish Conquest, along with the beasts of burden needed to pull them. In the Old World, most finds are vehicles buried in graves. Wheeled vehicles first appeared in the 4th millennium BC in the area between the Rhine and the Tigris; the earliest wheels were solid discs, either single-piece (cut from planks, not transverse slices of tree-trunks) or composite. Spoked wheels were developed in the 2nd millennium for lighter, faster vehicles such as chariots, for instance the ones found in Tutankhamun's tomb (box, Chapter 2). Wheeled transportation clearly had a huge impact on social and economic development, but nevertheless had a very limited geographical spread when compared with the ubiquitous wooden technology displayed in watercraft.

Investigating Watercraft. Until the 19th century all boats and ships were made predominantly of wood, and in perhaps no other area of pre-industrial technology did the world's craftspeople achieve such mastery as in the building of wooden vessels of all kinds, from small riverboats to great oceangoing sailing ships. The study of the history of this technology is a specialized undertaking, far beyond the scope of the present book to summarize in any detail. But it would be wrong to imagine that the archaeologist has little to contribute to what is already known from historical records. For the prehistoric period such records are of course absent, and even in historic times there are great gaps in knowledge that archaeology is now helping to fill.

The richest source of archaeological evidence by far comes from the preserved remains of ships uncovered by underwater archaeology (box, Chapter 3). In the late 1960s, the excavation of a 4th-century BC Greek ship off Kyrenia, Cyprus, showed that vessels of that

Evidence for the wheel. (Left) In the Old World, the spoked-wheel chariot (Assyrian relief, 7th century BC) evolved from the original solid-wheel cart. (Right) In the pre-Columbian New World, the concept of the wheel was known (wheeled model from Veracruz), but full-size wheeled vehicles only arrived with the Spanish, together with the animals needed to pull them.

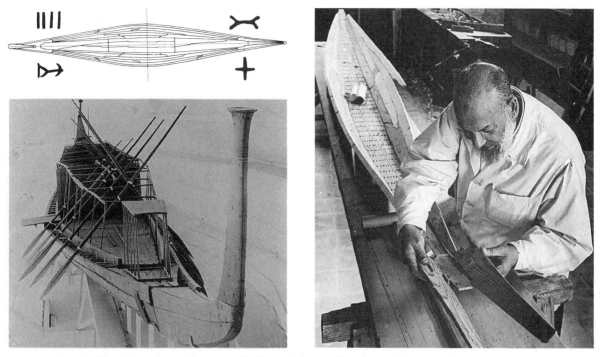

Reconstructing the oldest ship in the world. In 1954 the dismantled parts of a cedarwood boat were found buried in a pit on the south side of the Great Pyramid of King Cheops at Giza, Egypt. (Top left) One important clue to the reconstruction proved to be the four classifying signs, marked on most of the timbers, that indicated to which of the four quarters of the ship the timbers belonged. (Right) Hag Ahmed Youssef used a scale model to help in the task of reconstruction. (Left) After 14 years of work, the 1244 pieces of the ship were finally reassembled.

period were built with planks held together by mortise-and-tenon joints. The recent excavation by George Bass and his colleagues of a wreck at Ulu Burun, near Kaş, off the south coast of Turkey (box, Chapter 9), has now revealed a vessel 1000 years older that uses the same technique.

At the beginning of this chapter we stressed how important it is for archaeologists to obtain the advice of craftspeople in the technology concerned. This is particularly true for the accurate understanding of shipbuilding. J. Richard Steffy, of the Institute of Nautical Archaeology in Texas, has an unrivaled practical knowledge of the way ships are (or were) put together, a knowledge he has applied to excavated vessels in the Old World and the New. In his judgment the best way to learn how a ship was built and functioned is to refit the excavated timbers in the most likely original shape of the vessel, achieved through analysis of the excavation and painstaking trial and error, with the aid of exact copies at one-tenth scale of the remaining timbers. This was the procedure adopted by another craftsman, the Egyptian Hag

Ahmed Youssef, in his 14-year rebuilding of the dismantled ship of the pharaoh Cheops found at Giza, at 4500 years the oldest known ship in the world.

The next step in any assessment of a ship's construction techniques and handling capabilities is to build either a full-size or a scale replica, preferably one that can be tested on the water. Replicas based on excavated remains, such as the replica Viking *knarr* or cargo ship that sailed around the world in 1984–86, are more likely to produce scientifically accurate results than those built only from generalized artistic depictions, as in the case of replicas of the ships of Columbus. But the building of replicas based on depictions can still be immensely valuable. Until some British scholar-enthusiasts, led by J.F. Coates and J.S. Morrison, actually constructed and tested a replica of an ancient Greek trireme, or warship, in 1987, virtually nothing was known about the practical characteristics of this important seacraft of Classical antiquity.

Another contribution archaeology can make to seafaring studies is to demonstrate the presence of boats even where no ship remains or artistic depictions exist. The simple fact that people crossed into Australia some 50,000 years ago – when that continent was cut off from the mainland, even if not by so great a distance as it is today – suggests that they had craft capable of covering 80 km (50 miles) or more. Similarly, the presence of obsidian from the Aegean islands on the Greek mainland 10,000 years ago shows that people at that time had no difficulty in sailing to and from the islands.

Plant and Animal Fibers

The making of containers, fabrics, and cords from skins, bark and woven fibers probably dates back to the very earliest archaeological periods, but these fragile materials rarely survive. However, as we saw in Chapter 2, they do often survive in very dry or wet conditions. In arid regions, such as Egypt or parts of the New World, such perishables have come down to us in some quantity, and the study of *basketry and cordage* there reveals complex and sophisticated designs and techniques that display complete mastery of these organic materials.

Waterlogged conditions can also yield a great deal of fragile evidence. Well-preserved workshops such as those of Viking York have taught us much about a variety of crafts in England in the 10th century AD. In particular, a *tannery* was found with masses of animal hair in the soil from furs and skins, and a corner crawling with maggots because the skin scrapings had

been put there. Flotation (Chapter 6) was undertaken of some sediment, and recovered macrofossils of a number of plants: elderberry ferment for curing the skins; woodash for treating the leather before it was stretched; while dyestuffs included heather, madder root, and quantities of dyer's greenweed. These interpretations of the function of the plants were based on knowledge of the craft from historical sources, ethnography, and experiment; but they were confirmed by chemical analysis of samples of Viking textiles from the excavations. Chromatography (Chapters 6 and 7) identified a range of dyes in the textiles, including madder and woad.

Analyzing Textiles. Where textiles are concerned, the most crucial question is how they were made, and of what. In the New World, a certain amount of information on pre-Columbian weaving methods is available from ethnographic observation, as well as from Colonial accounts and illustrations, from depictions on Moche pottery, and from actual finds of ancient looms and objects (spindles and shuttles of wood, bone, or bamboo) found preserved in the Peruvian desert. There seem to have been three main types of loom: two were fixed (one vertical, the other horizontal), and used for really big pieces of weaving, while a small portable version was used for items such as clothing or bags.

The richest New World evidence, however, comes from Peruvian textiles themselves, which have survived in an excellent state of preservation thanks to the

New World textiles. Some of the finest woven designs ever made have come from Peru. This scene from the rim of a Moche vase depicts a Peruvian cloth factory. Eight women are shown weaving at their portable looms, supervised by the official top right. The meaning of the panel at lower right is not known.

aridity of much of the country. The Andean cultures mastered almost every method of textile weaving or decoration now known, and their products were often finer than those of today – indeed, were some of the best ever made. By about 3000 BC they had developed cotton textiles, which quickly took over from the previous techniques using fibers (such as reeds and rushes) that were far less supple and resistant. The Peruvians also came to use animal fibers from their domesticated camelids, particularly the vicuna and the alpaca. They had an extraordinary range of dyes: the huge textiles from the Nazca culture, dating to the 1st millennium AD, have up to 190 different color tones.

The precise weaving technique can often be deduced through careful observation by specialists. Sylvia Broadbent has studied some painted cotton fabrics of the pre-Hispanic Chibcha culture of Colombia, and has been able to ascertain that they are all woven of "one-ply S-twist cotton in a basic plainweave, single wefts over double warp threads." Counts of the number of threads range from 6 to 12 wefts (side to side) per centimeter, and from 11 to 14 warps (up/down) per centimeter. At the weft edge, the weft threads turn in groups rather than singly, a fact which implies the use of a weaving technique involving multiple shuttles. The end of the weaving was secured by a row of chainstitch.

It is also thanks to aridity that we have so many surviving textiles from ancient Egypt. Here, as in Peru, we can learn a great deal from surviving equipment and from models such as that found in the tomb of Meketre at Thebes (2000 BC) which shows a weaving workshop with a horizontal or ground loom. Flinders Petrie's excavation at Kahun, a town site for workers building a pyramid, dating to about 1890 BC, revealed weaver's waste on the floor of some houses: scraps of unspun, spun, and woven threads, colored red and blue. Analysis in the scanning electron microscope proved them to be from sheep's wool, while dye tests showed that madder had been used for red, and the blue probably came from the plant *Indigofera articulata*.

The wrappings of a male Egyptian mummy of 170 BC in Pennsylvania University Museum (designated PUM II) also underwent scanning electron microscopy, and proved to be a fabric of fine threads, whose straightness and markings were identical to modern flax fibers: in other words, the wrappings were a linen fabric.

But it is not only from Peru and Egypt that we have evidence for textiles. They can survive in waterlogged conditions, as we saw at Viking York, and even where preservation is less good, careful excavation may yield textile remains, as in the Celtic chieftain's tomb at Hochdorf, western Germany, dating to about 550 BC. Here analysis of the remains using a scanning electron microscope showed that the chieftain's death-bed had been covered with woven textiles of spun and twisted threads of hemp and flax. There were also coverings made of sheep's wool, horse hair, and badger wool, and furs of badger and weasel were present as well. In the SEM, the hair of different species can be identified if the diagnostic cuticle pattern is preserved, as in this case.

Microwear Analysis of Fibers. The analysis of microwear is chiefly associated with stone and bone tools, as shown above; but it has recently been applied with great success to textiles and fibers. Research at Manchester University's Department of Textiles using the SEM has shown that different kinds of fracture, damage, and wear leave diagnostic traces on different classes of fibers. Tearing or bursting leave a very different pattern from the prolonged flexing associated with fatigue and breakdown of the fibers – the latter produce longitudinal damage, resulting in the fibers having "brush ends." Cutting of fibers is easy to identify in the SEM, and razor-marks are readily distinguishable from those made by shears or scissors (see also Lindow Man box, Chapter 11).

In a recent application of their technique, the Manchester researchers examined two woollen items from the Roman fort of Vindolanda, northern England. For the first, a soldier's leg bandage, they had to determine whether it had been discarded because it was worn out, or whether it had been damaged by its prolonged burial. Analysis showed an abundance of "brush ends" indicating that the bandage had been much used, but there was also evidence of postdepositional damage (transverse fractures). The second item, an insole for a child's shoe, seemed to the naked eye to be in mint condition. However, in the SEM it became clear that there was considerable wear of the surface fibers, implying that the unused insole had been cut from a heavy fabric (perhaps a cloak) that was already quite worn.

This technique obviously holds enormous promise for future analyses of those fabrics that have come down to us. Even where textiles do not survive, they sometimes leave an impression behind, for example on mummies, from which the type of weave can be recognized. And similarly useful information can be derived from the study of imprints of fabrics, cordage, and basketry that are found on fired clay, by far the most abundant of the synthetic materials available to the archaeologist.

SYNTHETIC MATERIALS

Firing and Pyrotechnology

It is possible to consider the whole development of technology, as far as it relates to synthetic materials, in terms of the control of fire: pyrotechnology. Until very recent times, nearly all synthetic materials depended upon the control of heat; and the development of new technologies has often been largely dependent upon achieving higher and higher temperatures under controlled conditions.

Clearly the first step along this path was the mastery of fire, firm evidence for which already occurs in the Swartkrans Cave, South Africa, in layers dating to 1.5 million years ago (Chapter 6). Cooked food and preserved meat then became a possibility, as did the use of heat in working flint (see above), and in hardening wooden implements like the yew spear from the Middle Paleolithic site of Lehringen, Germany.

Terracotta (baked clay) figurines were produced sporadically in the Upper Paleolithic period at sites from the Pyrenees and North Africa to Siberia, but their most notable concentration occurs in Czechoslovakia at the open-air sites of Dolní Věstonice, Pavlov, and Předmosti, dating to about 26,000 years ago: they comprise small, well-modeled figurines of animals and humans. They were made of wetted loess soil, and fired at temperatures of 500-800° C (930-1470° F).

A significant development of the Early Neolithic period in the Near East, around 8000 BC, was the construction of special ovens used both to parch cereal grains (to facilitate the threshing process) and to bake bread. These ovens consisted of a single chamber in which the fuel was burnt. When the oven was hot the fuel was raked out and the grain or unbaked bread placed within. This represents the first construction of a deliberate facility to control the conditions under which the temperature was raised.

We may hypothesize that it was through these early experiences in pyrotechnology that the possibility of making pottery by firing clay was discovered. Initially pottery was made by firing in an open fire. "Reducing" conditions (the removal of oxygen) could be achieved by restricting the flow of air, and by adding unburnt wood.

These simple procedures may well have been sufficient in favorable cases to reach temperatures equivalent to the melting point of copper at 1083°C (1981°F). Given that copper was already being worked by cold hammering, and then by annealing (see below), and some copper ores such as azurite used as a pigment, it was to be expected that the smelting of copper from its ores and the casting of copper would be discovered. Potters' kilns, where there is a controlled flow of air, can produce temperatures in the range of 1000–1200°C (1832–2192°F), as has been documented for such early Near Eastern sites as Tepe Gawra and Susa, Iran, and the link between pottery production and the inception of copper metallurgy has long been noted.

Pyrotechnology: the control of fire. Initially pottery was made in an open fire. The introduction of the potter's kiln allowed higher temperatures to be achieved, which also spurred the development of metallurgy. (Left) Mesopotamian dome-shaped kiln of the early 4th millennium BC, built largely of clay, with an outer wall of stone or mud brick. (Center) Egyptian kiln of c.3000 BC reconstructed from tomb paintings. The potter may have stood on the small platform on the right to load the kiln. (Right) Greek kiln of c.500 BC, reconstructed from scenes on Corinthian plaques. The extended fire opening probably improved combustion.

Bronze technology subsequently developed with the alloying primarily of tin with copper.

Iron can be smelted from its ores at a temperature as low as 800°C (1472°F), but in order to be worked while hot, it requires a temperature of between 1000 and 1100°C (1832–2012 °F). In Europe and Asia, iron technology developed later than copper and bronze technology because of problems of temperature control and the need for stricter control of reducing conditions. In central and southern Africa, however, the technology of bronze does not appear to antedate that of iron. In the New World, iron was not worked in pre-Columbian times. For iron to be cast, as opposed to worked while hot, requires that its melting point be reached (1540°C, 2804°F), and this was not achieved until *c.* 500 BC in China.

There is thus a logical sequence in the development of new materials governed largely by the temperature attainable. In general the production of glass and faience – a kind of "pre-glass," see below – is first seen very much later in an area than that of pottery, since a higher temperature and better control are needed. They appear with the manufacture of bronze.

The study of the technology used to produce synthetic materials such as these naturally requires an understanding of the materials and techniques employed. Traditional crafts, for instance as observed today in many Near Eastern bazaars, can give valuable clues as to the way artifacts may have been made, and to the technical procedures carried out.

Pottery

We saw above that throughout the earlier periods of prehistory containers made of light, organic materials were probably used. This does not mean, as has often been assumed, that Paleolithic people did not know how to make pottery: every fire lit on a cave floor will have hardened the clay around it, and we have already noted that terracotta figurines were sometimes produced. The lack of pottery vessels before the Neolithic period is mainly a consequence of the mobile way of life of Paleolithic hunter-gatherers, for whom heavy containers of fired clay would have been of limited usefulness. The introduction of pottery generally coincides with the adoption of a more sedentary way of life, for which vessels and containers that are durable and strong are a necessity.

The almost indestructible potsherd is as ubiquitous in later periods as the stone tool is in earlier ones – and just as some sites yield thousands of stone tools, others contain literally tons of pottery fragments. For a long time, and particularly before the arrival of absolute dating methods, archaeologists used pottery primarily as a chronological indicator (Chapter 4) and to produce typologies based on changes in vessel shape and decoration. These aspects are still of great importance, for example in assessing sites from surface surveys (Chapter 3). More recently, however, as with stone tools, attention has shifted toward identifying the sources of the raw materials (Chapter 9); the residues in pots as a source of information about diet (Chapter 7); and above all to the methods of manufacture, and the uses to which vessels were put.

Where manufacture is concerned, the principal questions one needs to address can be summarized as: What are the constituents of the clay matrix? How was the pot made? And at what temperature was it fired?

Pot Tempers. Simple observation will sometimes identify the inclusions in the clay that are known as its temper – the filler incorporated to give the clay added strength and workability and to counteract any cracking or shrinkage during firing. The most common materials used as temper are crushed shell, crushed pottery, sand, grass, straw, or fragments of sponge. Experiments by the American scholars Gordon Bronitsky and Robert Hamer have demonstrated the qualities of different tempers. They found that crushed burnt shell makes clay more resistant to heat shock and impact than do coarse sand or unburnt shell; fine sand is the next best. The finer the temper, the stronger the pot; and the archaeological record in parts of the New World certainly shows a steady trend toward finer tempers.

How Were Pots Made? The making or "throwing" of pots on a wheel or turntable was only introduced after 3400 BC at the earliest (in Mesopotamia). The previous method, still used in some parts of the world, was to build the vessel up by hand in a series of coils or slabs of clay. A simple examination of the interior and exterior surfaces of a pot usually allows one to identify the method of manufacture. Wheelthrown pots generally have a telltale spiral of ridges and striations which is absent from handmade wares. These marks are left by the fingertips as the potter draws the vessel up on the turntable. Impressions can also be left on the outer surface of pots by the flat paddles – sometimes wrapped in cloth, which also leaves its mark – which were used to beat the paste to a strong, smooth finish.

How Were Pots Fired? The firing technique can be inferred from certain characteristics of the finished product. For example, if the surfaces are vitrified or glazed (i.e. have a glassy appearance), the pot was

Evidence for pot-making using a wheel. An Egyptian potter shapes a vessel on the turntable type of wheel in this limestone portrait of c.2400 BC.

fired at over 900°C (1652°F) and probably in an enclosed kiln. The extent of oxidization in a pot (the process by which organic substances in the clay are burned off) is also indicative of firing methods. Complete oxidization produces a uniform color throughout the paste. If the core of a sherd is dark (grey or black), the firing temperature was too low to fully oxidize the clay, or the duration of the firing was insufficient, factors which often point to the use of an open kiln. Open firing can also cause blotchy surface discolorations called "fire clouds." Experimental firing of different pastes at different temperatures and in various types of kiln provides a guide to the colors and effects that can be expected.

An exact approach to firing temperature was used by the American scholars W.D. Kingery and Jay Frierman on a sherd of graphite ware from the Copper Age site of Karanovo, Bulgaria. Their method entailed reheating the specimen until irreversible changes occurred in its microstructure, thus placing a ceiling on the temperature at which it could originally have been fired. Examination by scanning electron microscopy revealed a slight change in microstructure after firing at 700°C (1292°F) in a carbon-dioxide atmosphere; marked changes occurred after one hour at 800°C (1472°F), while the clay vitrified at 900°C (1652°F). They could thus conclude that the graphite ware was originally fired at a temperature below 800°C, and most probably at about 700°C. Such results contribute greatly to our assessment of the technological capabilities of different cultures, particularly as regards their possible mastery of metallurgy (see below).

The archaeology of kiln sites has contributed much to our knowledge of firing procedures. In Thailand, for example, high-fired or "stoneware" ceramics were in mass production from the 11th to the 16th centuries AD, and traded around Southeast Asia and to Japan and western Asia; yet contemporary texts say nothing about the industry. Australian and Thai archaeologists and scientists on this project found that two cities, Sisatchanalai and Sukhothai, were the most important production centers, and excavation of the villages around the former has revealed hundreds of large kilns, often built on earlier collapsed specimens, sometimes to a depth of 7 m (23 ft). This stratigraphy of kiln-types has shown the development of their design and construction – from the early, crude, clay forms to the technically advanced brick ones that could achieve the higher firing temperatures needed for the fine exported wares. The later kilns were built on mounds that kept them away from wet soil, ensuring production throughout the year, and reflecting the increasing demands being made on the industry.

Evidence from Ethnography. Unlike the making of stone tools, the production of pottery by traditional methods is still widespread in the world, so it is profitable to pursue ethnoarchaeological studies not only on the technological aspects but also from the social and commercial points of view. Among many successful projects, one could cite the long-term work of the American archaeologist Donald Lathrap among the Shipibo-Conibo Indians of the Upper Amazon (eastern Peru). Here the modern ceramic styles can be traced back to archaeological antecedents of the 1st millennium AD. Most of the women are potters, each producing vessels primarily for her own household, both for cooking and for other purposes such as storage. The pots are made of local clays, with a variety of tempers including ground-up old potsherds, but other minerals and pigments are imported from neighboring regions for slips and decorative work. The pots are built up with coils of clay. Though a year-round activity, potmaking tends to occur mostly in the dry season, from May to October. Studies such as these are useful for a wide range of questions: not only how pots are made, when, why, and by whom, but also how much time and effort are invested in different types of vessels; how often and in what circumstances they get broken; and what happens to the pieces – in other words, patterns of use, discard, and site-clearance.

Archaeologists can thus derive many valuable insights from ethnoarchaeological work. Historical sources and artistic depictions from a number of cultures provide supplementary data.

Faience and Glass

Glassy materials are relative latecomers in the history of technology. The earliest was *faience* (a French word derived from Faenza, an Italian town), and might be called a "pre-glass;" it was made by coating a core material of powdered quartz with a vitreous alkaline glaze. Originating in predynastic Egypt (before 3000 BC), it was much used in dynastic times for simple beads and pendants. Faience's main importance to archaeology has been in the evidence it can provide for the provenance or source of particular beads, through analysis of their composition, and hence in helping to assess how dependent prehistoric Europe's technology was on Egypt and the eastern Mediterranean.

Neutron activation analysis (box, Chapter 9), which can trace elements down to concentrations of a few parts per million, has been applied to Bronze Age faience beads, and proved that those from England had a relatively high tin content which made them clearly different from those from Czechoslovakia (which have high cobalt and antimony) and even from those from Scotland. All these groups were distinct from Egyptian beads, thus underlining the existence of local manufacture of this class of artifact.

By about 2500 BC Mesopotamia was making the first beads of real *glass*, which seem to have been highly prized. Once it had been discovered, glass was easy and cheap to make: it simply involves melting sand and cooling it again; the liquid cools without crystallizing, and therefore remains transparent. The problem to be overcome was the high melting point of silica (sand) – 1723°C (3133°F) – but if a "flux" such as soda or potash is added, the temperature is lowered. Soda lowers it to 850°C (1562°F), but the result is rather poor-quality glass. By trial and error, it must have been discovered that also adding lime produces a better result: the optimum mix is 75 percent silica, 15 percent soda, and 10 percent lime. As we have seen, glass can only have been made after the means of generating very high temperatures had been achieved; this occured in the Bronze Age with the development of charcoal furnaces for smelting metal (see below).

The first real glass vessels have been found in sites of the Egyptian 18th Dynasty, *c.* 1500 BC; the earliest known glass furnace is that at Tell el Amarna, Egypt, dating to 1350 BC. Vessels were made using a technique like the lost-wax method (see below): molten glass was fashioned around a clay core, which was scraped out once the glass had cooled. This leaves a characteristic rough, pitted interior. Statuettes and hollow vessels were also made in stone or clay molds.

Roman glass from northern Italy. The Romans introduced the technique of glass-blowing in about 50 BC, and created some of the finest pieces ever made. Their expertise was not matched until Venetian work of Renaissance times.

By 700 BC all the principal techniques of making glass had been developed (producing vessels, figurines, windows, and beads) except for one: glassblowing, which involves inflating a glob of molten glass with a metal tube, or sometimes blowing it into a mold. This quick and cheap method was finally achieved in about 50 BC by the Romans, whose expertise with glass was not equaled until the heyday of glasswork in Venice during the 15th and 16th centuries AD. Moreover, the Romans' output of glass was not matched until the Industrial Revolution. Why, then, is ancient glass so rare? The answer is not, as one might imagine, because it is fragile – it is often no more fragile than pottery – but because, like metals and unlike pottery, it is a reusable material, with fragments being melted down and incorporated into new glass.

Once again, *composition* and *production* are the keynotes of the archaeological approach to these materials. Until recent decades it was very hard to determine the exact raw materials used, since crystallographic observation provided no clues. In the last 30 years, however, new techniques have enabled specialists to analyze the constituents of a variety of ancient glasses.

E.V. Sayre and R.W. Smith, for example, undertook research to find systematic compositional differences in ancient glasses by analyzing them for 26 elements through a combination of three techniques: flame photometry, colorimetry, and above all optical emission spectrometry (Chapter 9). As a result, several categories of ancient glass were established, each with a different chemical composition. For instance, specimens of the 2nd millennium BC (primarily from Egypt, but also from throughout the Mediterranean area) were a typical soda-lime glass with a high content of magnesium. Specimens of the final centuries BC (from Greece, Asia Minor, and Persia) were rich in antimony, and had a lower content of magnesium and potassium. Roman glass proved to have less antimony and more manganese than the others.

Other methods which have been applied to ancient glass include the electron microbeam probe, which is a refinement of the non-destructive X-ray fluorescence technique (Chapter 9) and which can be used on tiny specimens. Neutron activation analysis can also be used in glass analysis.

Flaws in the glass such as bubbles can sometimes, by their size, shape, orientation, and distribution, inform the specialist how the specimen was handled from crucible to final shaping. By-products, too, can be informative. A "broken bead" from the Iron Age Meare lake village, southwest England, may actually be a mold for making glass beads.

ARCHAEOMETALLURGY

Non-Ferrous Metals

The most important non-ferrous metal – one not containing iron – used in early times was copper. In due course it was learnt that a harder, tougher product could be made by alloying the copper with tin to make bronze. Other elements, notably arsenic and antimony, were sometimes used in the alloying process; and in the later Bronze Age of Europe it was realized that a little lead would improve the casting qualities.

Gold and silver were also important, and lead should not be overlooked. Other metals such as tin and antimony were used only rarely in metallic form.

In most areas where copper and bronze were produced there was a natural progression, depending mainly on temperature, analogous to that for synthetic materials in general (see above). A basic understanding of these processes is fundamental to any study of early technology:

1   *Shaping native copper:* Native copper (metallic copper found in that form in nature, in nuggets) can be hammered, cut, polished, etc. It was much used in the "Old Copper" culture (4th–2nd millennium BC) of the Archaic period in the northern United States and Canada, and makes its appearance in the Old World at such early farming sites as Çatal Hüyük and Çayönü in Turkey and Ali Kosh in Iran by 7000 BC.

2   *Annealing native copper:* Annealing is simply the process of heating and hammering the metal. Hammering alone causes the metal to become brittle. This process was discovered as soon as native copper began to be worked.

3   *Smelting the oxide and carbonate ores of copper,* many of which are brightly colored.

4   *The melting and casting of copper,* first in a single (open) mold, and later in two-piece molds.

5   *Alloying with arsenic or tin* to make bronze.

6   *Smelting from sulphide ores,* a more complicated process than from carbonate ores.

7   *Casting by the lost-wax ("cire perdue") process* (see below) and use of the casting-on process, where most complicated shapes are produced by casting in several stages.

The origins of European copper metallurgy. Traditionally, the techniques of metalworking were seen to have spread to Europe from the more advanced lands of the Near East. But a somewhat different conclusion arises from studies of the early history of copper smelting in the Balkans and elsewhere. If one uses the calibrated radiocarbon chronology to draw a map where lines or "isochrons" indicate the earliest dates for metallurgy in each area, it becomes apparent that there were quite possibly three – not one – independent centers of origin: the Near East, the Balkans, and perhaps Spain and Portugal (Iberia).

Lead has a melting point of 327°C (620°F) and is the most easily worked of metals. It can be smelted from its ores around 800°C (1472°F). Silver melts at 960°C (1760°F), gold at 1063°C (1945°F), and copper at 1083°C (1981°F). So that in general, when craftspeople had mastered copper and bronze technology, they were also adept in working gold and silver and, of course, lead.

The techniques of manufacture of artifacts made from these materials can be investigated in several ways. The first point to establish is *composition*. Traditional laboratory methods readily allow the identification of major constituents. For instance, the alloys present in bronze may be identified in this way. However, in practice it is now more usual to utilize the techniques of trace element analysis which are also used in characterization studies (Chapter 9). For many years optical emission spectrometry (OES) was very widely used, but it has increasingly been superseded by atomic absorption spectrometry. X-ray fluorescence (XRF) is also often utilized, as on ceramic paste or glass. These methods are all reviewed in Chapter 9.

The other essential approach is that of *metallographic examination*, when the structure of the material is examined microscopically (see box overleaf). This will determine whether an artifact has been formed by cold-hammering, annealing, casting, or a combination of these methods.

Turning to the sequence of stages outlined above, the use of native copper may be suspected when the copper is very free of impurities. It can certainly be confirmed when the copper has not been melted and cast, for metallographic examination will then show that the artifact has been shaped only by cold-hammering or annealing. For example, when the American metallurgist Cyril Smith subjected a copper bead of the 7th millennium BC from Tepe Ali Kosh, Iran, to microscopic and metallographic examination, he found that a naturally occurring lump of copper had been cold-hammered into a sheet, then cut with a chisel, and rolled to form the bead. If the native copper has been melted and then cast, however, there is no way of distinguishing it with certainty from copper smelted from its ore.

METALLOGRAPHIC EXAMINATION

One of the most useful techniques for the study of early metallurgy is that of metallographic examination. It involves the examination under the light microscope of a polished section cut from the artifact, which has been chemically etched so as to reveal the metal structure. Since one cannot make translucent sections, it is necessary to direct reflected light to the object's surface (unlike petrographic study, for instance in the examination of pottery, where a thin section is usually examined in transmitted light).

The microscopic examination of metal structures can be highly informative, not only in distinguishing major phases in the manufacturing history of the artifact (such as casting on), but in the detection of more subtle processes.

In the case of copper, for instance, it is possible to recognize when the artifact has been worked from native copper. The structure will also clearly reveal whether or not the copper has been cold-worked, and whether or not it has been annealed (a process of heating and cooling to toughen and reduce brittleness). Indeed the whole history of the treatment of the material can be revealed, showing successive phases of annealing and cold-working.

Metallographic examination can be just as revealing in the cases of iron and steel. Wrought iron is easily recognizable: crystals of iron and streaks of slag can be clearly seen. The results of carburization – for instance, after part of an iron object has been heated in charcoal to give a hard cutting edge – are also very clear. The dark-etched harder edge is quite distinct from the softer white inner part.

Metallographic examination can thus furnish much information about the manufacturing process, and can reveal the very considerable mastery which many smiths exercised over their craft.

Copper – cast and fully annealed. Magnification x100.

The slip-bands (straight lines) indicate that the copper has been cold-worked (x100).

Copper that has been worked, fully-annealed, and cold-worked again (x150).

Silver that has been super-saturated with copper (x100).

Wrought iron at x200. The light grain is iron, the darker material slag.

Iron that has been partially hardened. The dark structure is harder than the lighter.

Alloying

The alloying of copper with arsenic or tin represents a great step forward in metallurgical practice. Alloying can have a number of beneficial effects. In the first place arsenical-bronze or tin-bronze is both harder and less brittle than copper. Mainly for this reason the metal blades of weapons – daggers and spears – are generally of bronze, and such weapons that were made of copper were probably of very little use in practice. Certainly the early swords of the Near East and of Europe are of bronze: copper swords would simply be too fragile to be of value.

The addition of arsenic or of tin can also facilitate manufacture in several ways. They can be useful in the casting process by avoiding the formation of bubbles or blow-holes in the copper, and they improve the workability of the object by allowing repeated hammering (with or without heating) without the object becoming brittle. The ideal proportion of tin to copper in tin-bronze is about 1 part in 10.

Naturally the presence of tin or arsenic is an indication that alloying may have taken place. But in the case of arsenic there is always the possibility that arsenic-rich copper ore was used in the first place, and that the arsenic is not a deliberate additive. There is no way of being certain for a single artifact in isolation. But analysis of a series of artifacts can reveal a consistent pattern indicating careful control and hence probably intentional alloying. For example, when applied to Bronze Age material from the Near East by E.R. Eaton and Hugh McKerrell, X-ray fluorescence showed an extensive use of arsenic minerals in the alloys, probably to provide a silver-colored coating on the copper. Indeed, they found that arsenical copper accounts for about one-quarter to one-third of all metal from Mesopotamia over the period 3000 BC to 1600 BC, making it two or three times more important than tin-bronze at that time.

The composition of gold and silver alloys can be deduced by determining their specific gravity. In this way, it has been found that Byzantine coins were debased to a lower silver value between AD 1118 and 1203. An examination of cross-sections of the coins also enabled M.F. Hendy and J.A. Charles to ascertain the method of manufacture, because the microstructure indicated that the coin blanks were cut from sheets (either cold or hot-worked), rather than stamped from cast droplets.

Casting

Information on the type of mold used can generally be obtained by the simple inspection of the artifact. If it shows evidence of casting on both upper and lower surfaces, a two-piece mold was presumably used. More elaborate shapes are likely to have required the lost-wax (*cire perdue*) technique which reached a high degree of perfection in the New World (see also Chapter 10). This ingenious and widespread technique

Casting. (Above) The lost-wax method. In this Egyptian example (c.1500 BC), a clay core is made and then a wax model built around it. The model is encased in a clay mold which is subsequently baked, allowing the melted wax to be poured off. Molten metal is poured into the now hollow mold (brown in the diagram), and finally the clay is broken away to reveal the metal casting. (Left) An Egyptian tomb painting of c.1500 BC shows foundrymen casting bronze doors. After heating using foot bellows (scene above), the molten metal is poured into a large clay mold (scene below).

COPPER PRODUCTION IN PERU

SOUTH
Batán Grande
AMERICA

At Batán Grande in the Central Andean foothills of northern coastal Peru, a team of archaeologists and allied specialists led by Izumi Shimada investigated various aspects of ancient copper production. From 1980 to 1983 they excavated over 50 furnaces at three sites near rich prehistoric copper mines; they estimate hundreds more furnaces at these sites. This was copper smelting on an industrial scale, from about AD 900 to 1532 when the

Spanish began their conquest of the Inca Empire. The sites provide ample field evidence that Central Andean metalworking was one of the major independent metallurgical traditions of the ancient world.

At one hillside site an entire smelting workshop was revealed, with furnaces, thick layers of crushed slag and charcoal, large grinding stones (*batanes*) up to a meter in diameter, and dozens of *tuyères* (ceramic blowtube

STEPWISE ANALYSIS OF METALLURGICAL REMAINS FROM BATAN GRANDE

Ores, slag, prills, ingots, and "finished objects"

Sample selection

Initial documentation: measurements, photography, etc

Metallography, petrography, scanning electron microscopy (SEM)

Compositional analysis: microhardness, XRF, AAS, PIXE, SEM

Experimental testing of models

Evaluation and reformulation of research questions and further sampling

Flowchart to indicate how specialists in various fields, using different techniques, worked together to help understand the smelting process. (XRF, AAS, and PIXE are explained in Chapter 9.)

Excavated furnaces (left), aligned east-west and north-south, dating to about AD 1000.

involves modeling the desired shape in wax, and then encasing the model in fine clay, but leaving a small channel to the exterior. When the clay is heated, the melted wax can be poured out; thus the clay becomes a hollow mold, and molten metal can be poured into it. After the clay casting is broken away, one is left with a metal copy of the original model. This is, of course, a "one-off" method.

There are several ways in which the technique can be detected in the archaeological record, quite apart from the scanty accounts and illustrations left, for the New World, by Spanish colonists, who mention gold (though not copper) being cast in this way. Apart from surviving molds (see below), evidence exists in the form of black fragments of clay casing which still

adhere to a few metal figures. Experiments, sometimes carried out with original unbroken molds, have shown the effectiveness of the lost-wax method.

The examination of sections by metallurgical microscopy (see box p.298) and electron probe microanalysis can also yield more detailed data on manufacture. The British metallurgist J.A. Charles studied some early copper axes from southeast Europe, and found a great increase in oxygen content towards the upper flat surface: the copper oxide content was 0.15 percent at the lower surface, but 0.4 percent at the upper. This was a clear indication that these Copper Age axes were cast in an open mold.

It should be noted, however, that hammering and annealing can produce results similar to casting. It tips), as well as food remains and some copper ore. The furnaces, typically about 1 m apart, were in rows of three or four, usually running north/south and aligned east/west since this was the prevailing wind direction – the wind helped disperse noxious fumes and heat. Replicative smelting experiments using a 600-year-old furnace have shown that it could attain temperatures of 1100 to 1250°C (the melting point of copper is 1083°C or 1981°F). Each furnace was lined with a specially prepared "mud" that gave a highly refractory, non-stick, smooth surface capable of withstanding numerous firings. Some furnaces had been relined up to three times.

It appears that copper ore was reduced to slag and metallic copper here, a process experiments suggest would have taken some three hours of

high temperatures sustained by continuous blowing. The furnaces could have held 5–8 kg (11–18 lb) of molten slag and copper. Once the furnace cooled, the slag was cracked and ground up nearby on *batanes* using a smaller rocking stone to release the copper prills (up to 1 cm droplets) from their unwanted slag residue. These prills were then picked out and remelted in crucibles into ingots. At another part of the site the resultant copper was annealed and forged using faceted stone hammers to produce sheet metal and implements. Prills and implements were all arsenical copper.

Prills extraction existed in the Near East from the 3rd millennium BC

onward. The Batán Grande evidence now suggests that it was later independently invented in the New World. New World metallurgists, however, apparently never had the benefit of bellows, and human lung-power limited the size of furnace and amount of ore smelted at one time.

3 people blowing

Sketch (above and left) to show how smelting might have taken place at Batán Grande.

Noxious fumes

Furnace wall

"Chimney"

Blowtubes

Smelting charge

Tuyères Air blast

Lining

Stone

Heat discolored

does not follow that a ribbed dagger was cast in a two-piece mold just because it has a rib on both sides, for this effect can be achieved by hot-working. Metallographic analysis is needed to be sure about the production method.

Detailed evidence of the method of manufacture can be obtained when the by-products of the process are examined, and deductions can also be made from surface traces on some objects. Lumps of excess metal at the ends of figurines were usually removed by the craftsperson, but occasionally they remain attached and thus show in what position it was cast (normally head downward). Similarly unfinished are objects on which the casting seams or "flashes" – where a little metal ran into the join between two halves of a mold –

have not been burnished away. On an incense burner from the Quimbaya region of central Colombia, made of a gold-rich alloy in the shape of a human face, one can see a vertical line on the forehead and chin, and a raised seam inside the hollow foot of the pedestal.

Molds can yield much useful information, and since they were often of stone they have frequently survived. Even the broken clay casings of the lost-wax method have occasionally been preserved. Two unbroken specimens have been found in an undated tomb at Pueblo Tapado, in the Quimbaya region of Colombia. Being unbroken, it is clear they were never used, but both were intended for the casting of small ornaments. According to a study done by Karen Bruhns, the molds themselves are shaped like a flattened flask; they have

In China, the casting of metal objects in ceramic piece-molds was perfected during the Shang dynasty, c.1500 BC. In contrast with the technique used in the western Old World, most care went into shaping the mold rather than the model. Large numbers of molds were produced in workshops to supply the foundries. Masterpieces such as these bronze ritual vessels were the result.

a small hole pierced in the bottom to permit air to escape when the metal was introduced, and thus avoid formation of a bubble.

The study of *slags* can also be informative. Analysis is often necessary to distinguish slags derived from copper smelting from those produced in iron production. It is relevant as well to test for sulphur which is an indicator of sulphide ores. Crucible slags (from the casting process) may be distinguished from smelting slags by their higher concentration of copper.

The microchemical analysis of *residues* in pottery vessels (Chapter 7) has also produced evidence of metalworking. Rolf Rottländer's analysis of several small pots from the Iron Age (Hallstatt) hillfort of the Heuneburg on the Upper Danube found that one had been used for melting down copper alloys, while another had traces of gold and two others traces of silver.

A fuller understanding of the technology must come from the thorough examination of the facilities at the *place of manufacture*. Ingots, slag, and other by-products such as molds, fragments of crucibles often with slag inside, broken tuyères (the nozzles of pipes for conducting air), failed castings, and scrap metal in general all provide clues to metallurgical methods. For example, ingots of copper often solidified at the bottom of smelting-furnaces, and their shape thus reveals the shape of the structure's base. One bronze-foundry site, at Hou-Ma, Shaanxi Province, China, dating to 500 BC, has yielded over 30,000 items including piece-molds, clay models, and cores. The Chinese perfected the system of piece-molding quite early on, already at the time of the Shang dynasty around 1500 BC. As with

most of the finest early bronze-working, the principle was that of lost-wax casting. Extraordinary works of craftsmanship were produced by the Chinese in this way.

The remains of furnaces can provide a whole range of information about the technology of the manufacturing process (see box on copper smelting, p. 300).

Silver, Lead, and Platinum

The low melting point of *lead* (327°C or 620°F) allows it to be worked easily, but it is very soft and so was not used for a wide range of purposes. However, figurines are found in this material, and in some areas small clamps of lead were used for mending broken pots.

Lead has a wider significance, however, since lead ores found in nature are often rich in *silver*. The extraction of silver from lead by the process known as cupellation involves the oxidization of lead to litharge (a lead oxide), and other base metals are likewise oxidized. The noble metals, silver and gold, are unaltered while the litharge is absorbed by the hearth or is skimmed off. A shallow hearth is needed so that a considerable surface area is exposed to the oxidizing blast of air that is provided by bellows. Charcoal or wood is used to maintain a temperature of about 1000–1100°C (1832–2072°F).

In Roman Britain, cupellation hearths have been found at the towns of Wroxeter and Silchester. The hearth at Silchester was lined with bone-ash, which is porous and absorbent. Analysis of this hearth suggested that it had been used for the cupellation of copper, since it contained globules which were 78

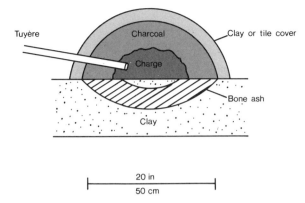

Reconstruction of a cupellation hearth found in the Romano-British town of Silchester. The hearth was probably used to extract silver from coins of debased silver and copper content.

percent copper. It is likely that it was used to extract silver from coins of very debased silver, with a large copper content.

Slag found in huge quantities (16–20 million tons) at the 8th/7th century BC site in Rio Tinto, Spain, proved to be primarily from silver metallurgy: the ore seems to have been very rich (600 g per metric ton), but very few metal objects have been found. The distribution of slag and drops of lead in many houses rather than in large piles suggested to the excavators, Antonio Blanco and J.M. Luzón, that the metalworking occurred as a domestic activity instead of in factories.

Platinum (melting point 1800° C or 3277° F) was being worked in Ecuador in the 2nd century BC, though it was unknown in Europe till the 16th century and Europeans only managed to melt it in the 1870s. In Ecuador they clearly liked it for its hardness and resistance to corrosion, and they often used it in combination with gold.

Fine Metalwork

There is no doubt that early craftspeople very soon discovered the full range of techniques which their control over pyrotechnology allowed. By the late Bronze Age of the Aegean, for example, around 1500 BC, as wide a range of techniques was available for working with non-ferrous metals as was used in the Classical or early medieval periods. For instance, the techniques of working sheet metal were well understood, as were those of stamping, engraving, and repoussé working (work in relief executed with hand-controlled punches from the back of sheet metal).

Filigree work (open work using wires and soldering) was developed by the 3rd millennium BC in the Near East, and granulation (the soldering of grains of metal to a background usually of the same metal) was used to establish remarkable effects, notably by the Etruscans.

In general, the method of manufacture can be established in such cases by careful examination, without more sophisticated analysis.

Most of these traditional techniques of manufacture may still be seen in use in towns of North Africa and in the bazaars of the Near East. There is usually much more to be learnt from careful study of the work of a skilled craftsperson operating with a traditional technology than there is from some less adept attempt at experimental archaeology undertaken by an experimenter who does not have the benefit of generations of experience.

Plating

Plating is a method of bonding metals together, for instance silver with copper, or gold with copper. The ancient Peruvians can be shown to have used methods of electrochemical plating of precious metals once thought to have been invented in late medieval or Renaissance Europe, where iron and steel armor was plated in gold.

Heather Lechtman and her colleagues undertook an analysis of some gold-plated objects of hammered sheet copper from a looted cemetery at Loma Negra, Peru. These dated to the first few centuries AD, the early Moche period, and included human figures, masks, and ear ornaments. Some had very thin gold surfaces that had not been attached mechanically to the copper. In fact the gold was so thin (0.5 to 2 micrometers) that it could not be seen in cross-section under a microscope at 500x magnification; but its thickness was very even, and it covered the edges of the metal sheets. This was clearly not a straightforward application of gold leaf or foil.

A zone of fusion between gold and copper indicated that heat had been applied to bind them together. It could not be modern electroplating, which uses an electric current, but its results were similar. Therefore the investigators looked at the possibility of electroplating by chemical replacement. In their experiments they used only chemicals available to the ancient Peruvians, and processes that did not require any external electrical current. They used aqueous solutions of corrosive salts and minerals (common in the deserts of the Peruvian coast and thus available to the Moche) to dissolve and then deposit the gold, and found that it spreads onto clean copper sheeting that is dipped into the solution, if boiling occurs for five minutes during immersion. To achieve a stable bonding, it is necessary to heat the plated sheet for a few seconds at 650–800°C (1202–1472°F). The results were so close to the Loma Negra artifacts that this method – or one very similar – was probably that used by the Moche.

Iron and Steel

Iron was not used in the New World during pre-Columbian times, and makes its appearance in quantity in the Old World with the inception in the Near East of the Iron Age around 1000 BC. There is evidence, however, that it was worked rather earlier, notably in Hittite Anatolia. Meteoric iron (iron deriving from meteorites, and found naturally in the metallic state) was widely known in the Near East, and cylinder seals and other ornaments are made from it. But there is no evidence that it was extensively worked.

Once the technique of *smelting iron* was well understood, it became very important, not least in Africa, since iron is more widely found in nature than is copper. But it is much more difficult to reduce – i.e. to separate from oxygen with which it is found combined in nature in the form of iron oxides. It requires much more strongly reducing conditions.

Iron may be reduced from pure iron oxide at about 800°C (1472°F) below its melting point of 1540°C (2804°F). But in practice the iron ores also contain other unwanted minerals, called gangue, in addition to the oxides. These must be removed in the smelting process by slagging, where a sufficiently high temperature is reached for the slag to become liquid and to drain away, leaving the iron in a solid state as a sponge or "raw bloom."

The simplest and easiest furnaces for iron smelting were bowl furnaces – hollows in the ground lined with baked clay or bricks. The ore and charcoal were placed in the bowl furnace and the temperature brought up to around 1100°C (2012°F) by the use of bellows.

The next stage is the hot working of the iron by forging, which takes place above ground in the smithy or forge. It is not always easy to distinguish between smelting sites and smithing sites, although if ore is found along with slag, that usually indicates smelting.

The production of *cast iron* requires a sophistication in the construction and operation of furnaces which did not become widespread in Europe until well into the Christian era, more than a thousand years after the production of wrought iron (although small statuettes of cast iron appear in Greece as early as the 6th century BC). In China, however, cast iron and wrought iron appear almost together in the 6th century BC, and cast iron was regularly used for making useful tools in China long before it was in the West. Cast iron is a brittle alloy of iron which has a carbon content between 1.5 percent and 5 percent. Its relatively low melting point (around 1150°C or 2102°F), which is lower than that of steel or of wrought iron, allows it to be cast in the molten state. The emphasis in early China is thus upon cast iron rather than wrought iron: in this respect metallurgy in the Far East and in Europe followed very different paths.

Steel is simply iron that contains between about 0.3 and 1.2 percent carbon, and it is both malleable and capable of hardening by cooling. True steel was not produced until Roman times, but a rather similar although less uniform product was made earlier by the process of carburizing (see ethnoarchaeology box): this was achieved by high temperature heating of the iron in contact with carbon. Initially it may have taken place by accident, while the iron was heated in contact with red-hot charcoal by the smith in the process of forging.

The extent to which iron has been carburized, and the processes used, are best assessed by metallographic examination of the artifact in question.

Some apparently featureless lumps of metal may be more than they seem. Corrosion products can "grow" out of an iron object to mineralize and even encase any associated wood. The resulting metal lump may contain a void in the exact shape of an object that has corroded out. X-rays can reveal the hidden shape inside, and, as with the bodies from Pompeii or endocasts of brains (Chapter 11), a cast can be made and extracted.

SUMMARY

In this chapter we have highlighted some basic questions about early technology, and considered how to find answers to them. The examples presented demonstrate the mass of varied technological information that the archaeologist can extract by a combination of excavation, laboratory analysis, ethnographic information, and insight from experimentation.

It could even be said that without experiments our knowledge of ancient technology would be minimal. Ethnography and archaeological context may suggest

EARLY STEELMAKING: AN ETHNOARCHAEOLOGICAL EXPERIMENT

Ethnoarchaeological projects that involve detailed observations about manufacturing processes are usually associated with the making of stone tools and ceramics, or with weaving; yet much has also been learned about metalworking by a number of investigators.

One such project, combining ethnography with archaeology and experiment, was carried out in northwest Tanzania by Peter Schmidt and Donald Avery who worked among the Haya, a Bantu-speaking agricultural people living in densely populated villages on the western shore of Lake Victoria. The Haya now use cheap European tools, but had oral traditions concerning their own ancient steelmaking process, which had been used as recently as 50 or 60 years ago. They still have an active blacksmithing tradition, in which scrap iron is employed. Some older men, a few of them smiths, remembered the traditional way in which iron had been smelted, and they were more than willing to recreate the experience.

The Haya were therefore easily persuaded to construct a traditional furnace, which was 1.4 m (4 ft 6½ in) high, cone-shaped, and made of slag and mud, built over a pit, 50 cm (20 in) deep, lined with mud and packed with partially burned swamp grass. These charred reeds provided carbon that combined with molten iron ore to produce steel. Eight ceramic blow tubes (*tuyères*) extended into the furnace chamber near its base, each one connected to a goatskin bellows outside. These tubes forced preheated air (up to 600° C or 1112° F) into the furnace, which was fueled by charcoal. With this apparatus the Haya could achieve temperatures between 1300° and 1400° C (2372–2552° F), high enough to produce carbon steel.

Archaeological verification of the Haya's claims came from excavations on the lakeshore which uncovered remains of 13 furnaces almost identical to the one built by the modern people. Radiocarbon dates obtained from charcoal showed that they were 1500 to 2000 years old. Iron slag was also found which had a flow temperature of 1350–1400° C (2462–2552° F.). Furnaces of similar date have since been found elsewhere in the same region of East Africa.

In short, the Haya had the technology to make medium-carbon steel in preneated forced-draft furnaces some 19 centuries before Europe developed the same capabilities.

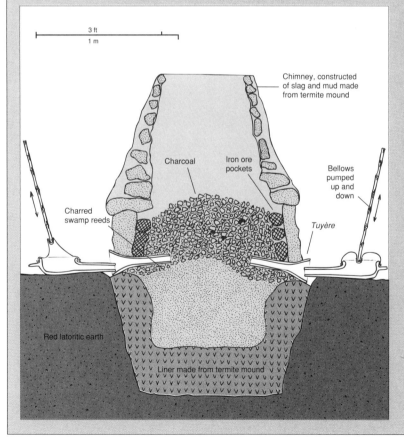

3 ft
1 m

Chimney, constructed of slag and mud made from termite mound

Charcoal

Iron ore pockets

Bellows pumped up and down

Charred swamp reeds

Tuyère

Red latoritic earth

Liner made from termite mound

Idealized profile *of a Haya iron smelting furnace, before the addition of the mixed iron ore and charcoal charge. Bellows that were pumped up and down with a stick forced air through* tuyères *(clay pipes) deep into the center of the furnace.*

the function of a stone tool; but only analysis of its microwear can demonstrate its most likely use. Microwear studies themselves depend on experiments for categories of wear and to give them meaning.

Nevertheless ethnoarchaeology is also proving extremely valuable. Observation of craftspeople in other living cultures by archaeologists who know what kind of information they require has probably arrived just in time, before the final vestiges of many of the ancient processes and traditions die away. No observation made in the present can definitively prove anything for certain about the past. But archaeology deals in degrees of probability, and a hypothesis which has been based on solid evidence from excavation, analysis, ethnography, and experiment is about as close to truth as we can come.

Further Reading

There are no up-to-date general accounts that cover all the methods discussed in this chapter. Broad surveys of ancient technology include:

Forbes, R. J. (series) *Studies in Ancient Technology*. E.J. Brill: Leiden.

Hodges, H. 1964. *Artifacts: an Introduction to Early Materials and Technology*. John Baker: London.

Hodges, H. 1971. *Technology in the Ancient World*. Penguin Books: Harmondsworth & Baltimore.

White, K.D. 1984. *Greek and Roman Technology*. Thames & Hudson: London; Cornell University Press: Ithaca, NY.

Other important sources are:

Anderson, A. 1984. *Interpreting Pottery*. Batsford: London; Universe: New York 1985.

Coles, J.M. 1979. *Experimental Archaeology*. Academic Press: London & New York.

Keeley, L.H. 1980. *Experimental Determination of Stone Tool Uses*. University of Chicago Press: Chicago.

MacGregor, A. 1985. *Bone, Antler, Ivory, and Horn Technology*. Croom Helm: London.

Rice, P.M. 1987. *Pottery Analysis: a Sourcebook*. Chicago University Press: Chicago.

Shepard, A.O. 1985. *Ceramics for the Archaeologist*. Carnegie Institute: Washington, D.C.

Tite, M.S. 1972. *Methods of Physical Examination in Archaeology*. Seminar Press: London & New York.

Tylecote, R.F. 1987. *The Early History of Metallurgy in Europe*. Longman: London & White Plains, NY.

9
What Contact
Did They Have?
Trade and Exchange

The study of exchange and trade in early societies has been one of the growth areas of archaeology in recent years. It was realized that the materials of which artifacts are made can be a far better guide than their style to the place of origin of such artifacts. Whole exchange systems can be reconstructed, or at least the movements of the goods can be investigated, if the materials in question are sufficiently distinctive for their source to be identified. Numerous chemical and other methods now exist for the precise characterization of these materials – that is, the determination of characteristics of specific sources that allow their products to be recognized.

These techniques allow us to tackle the whole question of the production and distribution of traded goods. It is a more ambitious task to try to reconstruct the organization of the trading system as a whole. It is a particularly difficult one if there are no written records to tell us what commodities were traded in exchange for the ones we find in the archaeological record.

Raw materials were not the only items traded, or offered as gifts. Manufactured goods were just as important. Certain prestige goods had symbolic values,

with precise meanings that are not always clear to us today, such as the jadeite axes of Neolithic Europe. But some prestige goods were highly significant, and this provides us with another line of investigation to be followed up.

Finds of the actual goods exchanged are the most concrete evidence that the archaeologist can hope to have for determining the contact between different areas, and different societies. But the communication of information, of ideas, may in many ways be more significant. Earlier generations of scholars were too willing to accept similarities between different cultures as a proof of contact, of the flow of ideas, or "diffusion" between the two. Partly in reaction against this tendency, the independent origins of things have been stressed, and the significance of interactions between neighbors somewhat understated. The time is now ripe for a reconsideration of such contacts.

All this relates closely to the social questions discussed in Chapter 5, and no clear separation is possible. Social structure itself may be defined as the pattern of repeated contacts between people, and social organization and exchange are simply different aspects of the same processes.

THE STUDY OF INTERACTION

Exchange is a central concept in archaeology. When referring to material goods, to commodities, it means much the same as trade. But exchange can have a wider meaning, being used by sociologists to describe all interpersonal contacts, so that all social behavior can be viewed as an exchange of goods, non-material as well as material. Exchange in this broader sense includes the exchange of information.

It is necessary, therefore, to consider the exchange transaction in rather more detail. In many exchanges

the relationship is more important than what is exchanged. Within a family, for instance, when presents are exchanged at Christmas, the giving of presents between relatives is generally more important than the actual objects that change hands: "it is the thought that counts." We shall see that there are different kinds of exchange relationship: some where generosity is the order of the day (as in the family Christmas); others where the aim is profit, and the personal relationship is not emphasized ("Would you buy a used car from this man?"). Moreover, there are different kinds of goods: there are everyday commodities that are bought and sold, and there are special goods, valuables, that are suitable for gifts. And in all of this we have to consider how exchange works in a non-monetary economy where not only coinage may be lacking, but any medium of exchange.

In the next section we shall consider the ways in which artifacts (traded objects) found by archaeologists can be made to yield information about early trade and exchange. But, first, we must consider further the nature of exchange.

Exchange and Information Flow

Let us imagine two societies, living on islands some tens of miles away from each other. If there was no contact between them they would lie in complete isolation, exploiting their island resources. They may, however, have had boats, and so been in contact with each other. In that case, the archaeologist of the future, in studying the settlements and the artifacts found in them, will recognize on island A objects made from materials that were only available on island B, and will thus be able to document the existence of such contact: there must have been travel between the islands. But what may have been of much more importance to the islanders was the possibility of social contacts, exchange of ideas, and marriage links. These, too, the archaeologist must consider, together with the material goods that were exchanged.

When there is exchange between island A and island B there is a flow of information. Ideas are exchanged,

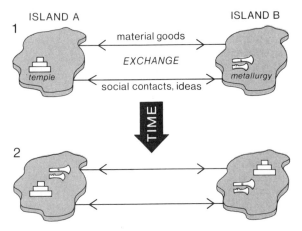

Contact between two islands has the effect that innovations on one (e.g. the building of a temple; metallurgy) may lead to similar developments on the other.

inventions are transmitted, and so are ambitions and aspirations. If the people of island A decide to build a temple of a new kind, those of island B may decide to follow suit. If those of island B develop the techniques of metallurgy, those of island A will not be far behind. There is thus a real equivalence between the interaction seen as a communications system, and the interaction as a system for the exchange of material goods.

For most of this chapter we shall be dealing with economic aspects of exchange, and with material things. But, at the end, we shall return to this theme of interaction as information exchange: in the long run, it is often more important.

Scale and "World System"

For some purposes it is convenient to distinguish between *internal exchange*, taking place within the specific society we are considering, and *external trade or exchange*, where goods are traded over much greater distances, moving from one social unit to another. In using the term "trade," we generally mean external trade – something that takes place with the outside world. But when we consider the interactions within a society, whether involving information or goods, we tend to use the terminology of social organization not of trade. The emphasis in this chapter is on external trade; relations internal to the social unit were dealt with in Chapter 5, where we considered questions of scale and organization of society. But the distinction between the two levels of exchange is not always clear.

Trading systems often have what is almost a life of their own. By definition, they extend widely, over the boundaries of many politically independent societies. But sometimes the different parts of a widespread trading system of this kind can become so dependent on each other commercially that one can no longer think of them as independent entities. This point has been stressed by the American historian Immanuel Wallerstein. He used the term "world system" or "world economy" to designate an economic unit, articulated by trade networks extending far beyond the boundaries of individual political units (e.g. nation states), and linking them together in a larger functioning unit. Wallerstein's initial example was the relationship that developed between the West Indies and Europe in the 16th century AD, when the economy of the West Indies was indissolubly linked with that of the European parent countries of which they were colonies. (It should be clearly understood that Wallerstein's rather odd term "world system" is not meant to refer to the entire world. He imagines a collection of several world systems, each of which might be conceived as a separate entity: one world system might involve Europe and the West Indies, another China and its Pacific neighbors.)

Wallerstein sees the emergence of the present world system, based on capitalism, as taking place during the Great Transformation of the 16th century AD. But archaeologists and ancient historians have applied the terminology to earlier periods. So that just as Wallerstein speaks of the "core" and the "periphery" of modern world systems, so these historians would like to use this terminology for earlier ages.

In the last section of this chapter we shall see that to adopt this terminology unthinkingly can lead to very dangerous archaeological assumptions. For the moment, it is enough to note that Wallerstein's approach helps us to pose a very important question: What was the scale of the effective functioning economic system in the past? In Chapter 5, we discussed the approaches that the archaeologist may take to define the scale of the effective social unit. Here, we need to discuss how we can define the scale of the economic system if it is larger than the social system, embracing several politically independent units.

Gift Exchange and Reciprocity

One of the most fundamental advances of anthropological theory was the revelation by the French sociologist, Marcel Mauss, of the nature of gift exchange. He saw that in a range of societies, especially in those lacking a monetary economy, the fabric of social relations was bound by a series of gift exchanges. Individual X would establish or reinforce a relationship with individual Y by means of a gift, a valuable object, which would pass from the hands of X to those of Y. This gift was not a payment: it transcended mere monetary considerations. It was a gesture and a bond, imposing obligations on both parties, especially, of course, on the recipient. For acceptance of the gift implied the obligation of repayment by another, equally munificent presentation.

The anthropologist Bronislaw Malinowski, in his celebrated work *Argonauts of the Western Pacific* (1922), described an exchange network, the *kula*, in which a series of exchange relationships between the inhabitants of some islands in Melanesia was cemented by the exchange of valuable gifts of objects, often of shell. The entire overseas contacts of these islanders centered on the ceremonial exchange with their exchange partners within the *kula*, although within this framework other exchanges of more everyday commodities, such as foodstuffs, took place.

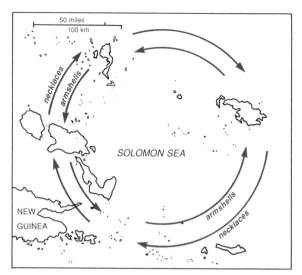

The kula network of Melanesia, in which necklaces were exchanged for armshells and armshells for necklaces in a cycle that cemented relations among the islanders.

Exchanges such as these, where the transfer of specific objects as gifts is only one part of a relationship with other obligations (including friendship) and with other activities (including feasting), are said to take place within a framework of reciprocity. The donor gains in status through the generosity of the scale of the gift. Gifts are often given with maximum publicity and ostentation. Indeed, in some New Guinea societies the position of "Big Man" is achieved by the munificent giving of gifts (often pigs) to exchange partners, and by the accumulation thereby not only of credit (i.e. the obligation of exchange partners to repay), but also what one may term kudos, the immense prestige that comes from being in the creditor position as donor.

The notion of reciprocal exchange of valuables, derived from anthropological studies including Malinowski's work on the *kula* exchange cycle of Melanesia, has been influential in shaping the thinking of many archaeologists about trade. For instance, in Britain during the Neolithic period, there was clearly an extensive network of trade in stone axes. The methods by which the exchange has been documented, including the petrographic study of thin sections, are discussed below. The long-distance exchange networks that such characterization studies document led the British archaeologist Grahame Clark to suggest that a system of gift exchange was in operation in the British Neolithic. He likened this to the system of exchanging stone axes that operated in Australia into the present century.

MODES OF EXCHANGE

Exchange, or trade, implies that goods change hands, and that this is a two-way transaction. The American anthropologist Karl Polanyi established that there are three different types or modes of exchange: reciprocity, redistribution, and market exchange.

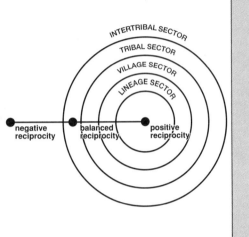

negative reciprocity   balanced reciprocity   positive reciprocity

= chief

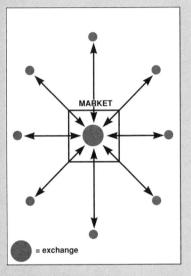

MARKET

= exchange

Reciprocity refers to exchanges that take place between individuals who are symmetrically placed: that is, they are exchanging more or less as equals. Neither is in a dominant position. In effect, it is the same as gift exchange. One gift does not have to be followed by another at once, but a personal obligation is created that a reciprocal gift will later take place. The American anthropologist Marshall Sahlins has suggested that the generosity or altruism associated with such exchange can be illustrated as positive reciprocity (i.e. generosity) and takes place among close kin. Balanced reciprocity takes place among those well known to each other in a definite social context. And negative reciprocity (i.e. exchange where you try to do better out of it than your exchange partner) operates between strangers or those socially distant from one another.

Redistribution implies the operation of some central organization. Goods are sent to this organizing center, or at least are appropriated by it, and are then redistributed. Sahlins suggested that many chiefdoms in Polynesia operate in this way: the chief redistributes produce, and geographical diversity can thus be overcome. The fisherman receives fruit, and the worker in the plantation gets fish. Such exchange can be much more highly ordered than a series of relatively unstructured reciprocal exchanges between individuals, and it is a feature of more centrally organized societies, such as chiefdoms or states (see Chapter 5). Since it implies the existence of a coherent political organization within which it works, redistribution is a form of internal exchange.

Market exchange implies both a specific central location for exchange transactions to occur (the market-place) and the sort of social relationship where bargaining can occur. It involves a system of price-making through negotiation. Polanyi argued that this kind of bargaining first became the basis of a true market system in ancient Greece, when coinage based on a well-defined monetary system also made its appearance. But other workers have argued that there were markets also in the ancient Near East, as there certainly were in Mesoamerica and China.

Markets are often internal in the socio-political unit – for example, the rural markets of China, or the Greek marketplace (agora). But they do not have to be. The port-of-trade is a place where traders of different nationalities (i.e. belonging to different political units) can freely meet, and where free bargaining and hence price-fixing can take place.

Another instance, perhaps even more comparable to the Melanesian *kula* system, is the exchange of bracelets and other ornaments made of the marine shell *Spondylus gaederopus*, which is a native of the Mediterranean. Such ornaments were distributed right across the Balkans and into central Europe around 4000 BC, and it is clear that a long-distance trade network was in operation then. Just as in the case of the *kula*, handsome marine shells were one of the most conspicuous features of the exchange. But in this case, the exchange was a land-based one. The archaeologist today sees the shell ornaments of that period as fulfilling the role of valuables. Once again, the extent of the trade has to be established through a careful characterization study (to determine the place of origin) before such explanations in terms of reciprocity between exchange partners can be proposed.

When exchange takes place outside close personal relationships, it takes on a different character: the positive reciprocity of the profit motive (see box). And when the symmetrical one-to-one relationship of gift exchange or direct barter gives way to the trader/buyer relationship of the marketplace or to the demands of the tax collector, a different kind of economic relationship is implied (see box, under redistribution and market exchange).

These ideas have become part of the mental toolkit of the student of early trade. In some cases, they can be extended by reference to early documents, such as the inscribed clay tablets from the Assyrian trading colony at Kültepe in Anatolia, dating from the 18th century BC. Here most of the trade was controlled by private merchants in the Assyrian capital of Assur, and the merchants at Kültepe were acting as agents: that may be regarded as redistribution. But in some cases they do seem to have been trading on their own account, for personal gain.

Ethnographic work offers a rich repertoire of examples of trading systems: the markets of West Africa, and those of pre-industrial China have been studied by anthropologists and geographers and provide valuable insights to the archaeologist as to the ways in which exchange can take place.

Valuables and Commodities

In gift exchanges, as observed by anthropologists, the high prestige gifts that are the focus of attention in any ceremonial exchange are of a special kind. They are valuables, and they are to be distinguished from the commonplace commodities – foodstuffs, pots, and other utilities – that may well be exchanged through a more mundane system of barter at the same time.

There are two important concepts here. The first is what the American anthropologist George Dalton has termed *primitive valuables*: the tokens of wealth and prestige, often of specially valued materials (see box), used in the ceremonial exchanges of non-state societies. Examples include the shell necklaces and bracelets of the *kula* system, and pigs and pearlshells, and, on the Northwest Coast of America in pre-European times, slaves and fur robes. Exotic animals were often thought appropriate for royal gifts. Thus, the Near Eastern potentate Haroun al-Rashid presented Charlemagne, the 8th–9th-century AD ruler of much of north-central Europe, with an elephant, while a 13th-century Icelandic tale relates how the Icelander Authin presented the King of Denmark with a polar bear from Greenland. Traces of such gifts are sometimes recoverable – for example, the remains of falcons from Greenland that have been recovered on several medieval sites in western Europe.

It should be noted, as Dalton remarks (1977), that "to acquire and disburse valuables in political or social transactions was usually the exclusive prerogative of leaders; or else the valuables were permissibly acquired by leaders in greater quantity or in superior quality than permissibly acquired by small men."

The second important concept is that of the *sphere of exchange*: valuables and ordinary commodities were exchanged quite separately. Valuables were exchanged against valuables in the prestige transactions already mentioned. Commodities were exchanged against commodities, with much less fuss, in mutually profitable barter transactions.

George Dalton has pointed out that ceremonial exchanges in non-state societies were of two different sorts. The first were ceremonial exchanges to establish and reinforce alliances, such as the *kula* system. The second were competitive exchanges, used to settle rivalries, in which the path to success was to outshine rivals in the richness of one's gifts and the conspicuous nature of public consumption. The potlatch, the ceremonial of the Northwest American Indians, was of this kind. These exchanges involved not only the making of conspicuous gifts of valuables, but also sometimes the actual destruction of valuables in a display of conspicuous wealth.

It is only through an awareness of the social roles that material goods can have, and of the way material exchange can either mask or represent a whole range of social relationships, that we can understand the significance of the exchange of goods. The study of early exchange thus offers many insights not only into the commerce but also into the structure of early societies.

Nearly all cultures have valuables. Although some of these are useful (e.g. pigs in Melanesia, which can be eaten) most of them have no use at all, other than display. They are simply prestige objects.

Valuables tend to be in a limited range of materials to which a particular society ascribes a high value. For instance, in our own society gold is so highly valued as to be a standard against which all other values are measured. We tend to forget that this valuation is an entirely

MATERIALS OF PRESTIGE VALUE

arbitrary one, and we speak of gold's *intrinsic* value, as if in some way it were inherent. But gold is not a very useful material (although it is bright, and does not tarnish), nor is it the product of any special skills of the craftsperson. Intrinsic value is a

misnomer: the Aztecs valued feathers more highly, unlike the Conquistadors who craved gold; both were following subjective systems of value.

When we survey the range of materials to which different societies have ascribed intrinsic value we can see that many of them had the qualities of rarity, of durability, and of being visually conspicuous:

• The bright **feathers** favored by the Aztecs and by tribes of New Guinea fulfill two of these qualities.

• **Ivory:** elephant and walrus tusks have been valued since Upper Paleolithic times.

• **Shell**, especially of large marine molluscs, has been highly prized in many cultures for millennia.

• That very special organic material **amber** was valued in Upper Paleolithic times in northern Europe.

• **Jade** is a favored material in many cultures, from China to Mesoamerica, and was valued as long ago as 4000 BC in Neolithic Europe.

• Other naturally hard and **colorful stones** (e.g. rock crystal, lapis lazuli, obsidian, quartz, and onyx) have always been valued.

• **Gemstones** have taken on a special value in recent centuries, when the technique of cutting them to a faceted, light-catching shape was developed.

• **Gold** has perhaps pride of place (certainly in European eyes) among "intrinsically" valuable commodities, followed by **silver**.

• **Copper** and other metals have taken a comparable role: in North America copper objects had a special value.

• With the development of pyrotechnology (Chapter 8) artificial materials such as **faience** (glazed terracotta) and **glass** came into full prominence.

• The finest **textiles** and other clothing materials (e.g. *tapa* in Polynesia) have also always been highly valued, for prestige often means personal display.

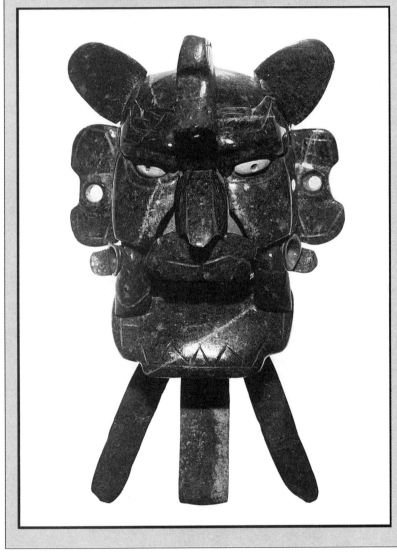

Zapotec mask from Monte Albán, Mexico, made of jade, the eyes of shell.

Feathered headdress (above) of the Aztec emperor Motecuhzoma II (Moctezuma). (Above center) The Portland vase, a superb example of 1st-century AD Roman glassworking.

Woven silk robe (above) from the reign of the Chinese emperor Yung Cheng (1723–35), bearing the Imperial dragon.

Upper Paleolithic ivory female figurine (above) from Lespugue, France (ht 14.7 cm). (Above center) Gold mask thought by Schliemann to represent King Agamemnon, from a shaft grave at Mycenae, late 16th century BC.

Prestige objects of North America's Mississippian culture (c. AD 900–1450). (Above) Embossed copper face, with typical forked eye motif. (Left) Shell pendant (c. 14 cm) from Texas, showing a panther and bird of prey.

DISCOVERING THE SOURCES OF TRADED GOODS: CHARACTERIZATION

Artifact forms can be imitated, or can resemble each other by chance. So it is not always safe to recognize an import in an archaeological context just because it resembles objects that are known to have been made elsewhere. Much more reliable evidence for trade can be provided if the raw material of which the object is made can be reliably shown to have originated elsewhere. Characterization refers to those techniques of examination by which characteristic properties of the constituent material may be identified, and so allow the source of that material to be determined. Some of the main methods for sourcing of materials by characterization (e.g. petrographic thin section) are described below.

For characterization to work, there must obviously be something about the source of the material that distinguishes its products from those of other sources. Of course, sometimes a material is so unusual and distinctive in itself that it can at once be recognized as deriving from a given source. That used to be thought to be the case with the attractive blue stone called lapis lazuli, for which, in the Old World, only one major source in Afghanistan was known. Now, however, other sources of lapis lazuli in the Indian subcontinent are known, so such claims must be treated with care.

In practice, there are very few materials for which the different sources can be distinguished by eye. Usually, it is necessary to use petrological, physical, or chemical techniques of analysis, which allow a much more precise description of the material. During the past 40 years there have been striking advances in the ability to analyze very small samples with accuracy. A successful characterization, however, does not just depend on analytical precision. The nature of the various sources for the material in question must also be considered carefully. If the sources are very different from each other in terms of the aspects being analyzed, that is fine. But if they are very similar, and so cannot be distinguished, then there is a real problem. For some materials (e.g. obsidian), the sources can be distinguished quite easily; for others (e.g. flint, or some metals), there are real difficulties in detecting consistent differences between sources.

Some materials are not well suited to characterization, because samples from different areas are difficult to distinguish. For example, organic remains, whether of plants or of animals, can present a problem. Of course, if a species is found far from its natural habitat – for instance, shells from the Red Sea in prehistoric Europe – then we have evidence for trade. But when the species has a widespread distribution, there can be genuine difficulties. However, as we shall see below, even here there may be techniques available, such as oxygen or strontium isotope analysis, to resolve the matter.

An important point to note is that the sourcing of materials by characterization studies depends crucially on our knowledge of the distribution of the raw materials in nature. This derives mainly from the fieldwork of such specialists as geologists. For example, one might have a good series of thin sections cut from a whole range of stone axes, and many of these might be distinctive in the eyes of a petrologist. But this would not help the archaeologist unless one could match those particular kinds of rock with their specific occurrences in nature (i.e. the quarries). Thus, good geological mapping is a necessary basis for a sound sourcing study.

There are two further important points. One is the extent to which the raw material of which the artifact is made may have changed during burial: for instance, some soluble and therefore mobile elements in a clay pot may have leached out into the surrounding soil; fortunately this problem is not normally too severe.

A more crucial factor is the extent to which the raw material was changed during the production of the artifact. For objects of stone, this is not a problem. For pottery, one needs to consider the effect of refining the clay, and of adding tempering material. For metals, however, the problem is serious because there are many significant changes in composition from the ore to the metal artifact. During smelting (Chapter 8), a proportion of the more volatile impurities (e.g. arsenic or bismuth) will be lost. And in the Old World, from the later part of the Bronze Age onward, there is the problem of the re-use of scrap copper and bronze that could have come from more than one source.

Analytical Methods

Visual Examination. Just looking at the material is often the best way to start, whether we are dealing with pottery or a stone object. But while appearance makes an excellent starting-point – it always pays to make a preliminary separation by appearance – it can never be a reliable or authoritative guide.

Microscopic Examination of Thin Section. Since the middle of the last century techniques have existed for cutting a *thin section* of a sample taken from a stone

Key

a altered and micrographic feldspars
b quartz
c plagioclase
d amphiole
e felsic volcanic
f biotite
g clinopyroxene
h void
i basalt
j slip
k glaze
m opaque oxide pigment
n chert

Examination of pottery thin section under the microscope: inclusions in the fabric have been used to characterize medieval ceramics from the Yemen, such as this example.

object or a potsherd to determine the source of the material. By means of petrological examination (studying the rock or mineral structure) with a light microscope, it is usually possible to recognize specific minerals that may be characteristic of a specific source. This part of the work has to be done by someone with petrological training.

This method has been applied to *stone* objects in different parts of the world – to building stones (e.g. the special colored stones used by the ancient Greeks and Romans), monuments (e.g. Olmec heads, Stonehenge), and portable artifacts, such as stone axes (e.g. in Australia, New Guinea, and in Britain). Indeed, the elucidation of the trade in stone axes in Neolithic times in Britain, which started before 3000 BC, is one of the success stories of characterization studies. It is further discussed in the section on the study of distribution below (box on trend surface analysis).

Difficulties are encountered when the stones are insufficiently distinctive: for instance, different kinds of flint are usually difficult to characterize by thin section, and the white marble used for building or statues is so pure and homogeneous that it also does not give good results with this method.

With *pottery*, the clay itself may be distinctive, but more often it is the inclusions – particles of minerals or rock fragments – that are characteristic. Sometimes the inclusions are naturally present in the clay. In other cases, the inclusions are deliberately added as temper to improve drying and firing qualities, and this can complicate characterization studies, since the pottery fabric may then consist of material from two or more separate sources. Fossil constituents, such as diatoms (Chapter 6), can also be an aid to identification of the source of the raw materials.

Studies of *grain sizes* in the clay have also proved useful. In much pottery, the only inclusions present are common minerals such as quartz sand, flint, and calcite/limestone/shell and these are of little help in identifying the sources. In such circumstances, study of the grain size of the quartz, etc. (but not the clay) has also proved useful. *Heavy-mineral analysis* is a closely related petrological technique. For this, the body of the pottery sample is broken down using a chemical reagent, and the heavy-mineral component (materials such as zircon and tourmaline) is separated from the lighter clay in a centrifuge. These constituent minerals can then be identified under the microscope. Those characteristic of a particular source area may help to identify the place of origin of the clay.

The picture of the prehistoric trade in pottery in Britain that such analyses have documented is quite surprising. Until the thin-section work of David Peacock and his associates it was simply not realized that pottery bowls and other vessels might be traded over quite long distances (of the order of 100 km (62 miles)) in Neolithic times, before 3000 BC. Now that we know the extent of the exchange of pottery in the British Neolithic, and that of stone axes already discussed, it is clear that many individuals and settlements were linked by quite far-flung exchange systems.

These characterization studies reveal clear evidence of widespread distribution of materials from their geological sources, but the interpretation of this evidence in human terms demands special techniques of spatial analysis and often the use of models based on ethnographic (or ethnoarchaeological) research.

Trace-Element Analysis. The basic composition of many materials is very consistent. Obsidian, a volcanic glass used in the manufacture of chipped stone tools in the same manner as flint, is a good example of this. The concentration of the main elements of which obsidian is formed (silicon, oxygen, calcium, etc.) is broadly similar whatever the source of the material. However, the *trace elements* (elements present only in very small quantities, measured in just a few parts per million) do vary according to the source, and there are several useful methods for measuring their concentration.

Optical emission spectrometry, or OES (see box), was the first of such methods to be applied to archaeological material. The Austrian archaeologist R. Pittioni and his scientific collaborators used it in the late 1930s in pioneering studies on early metallurgy in the Alpine region. In the 1950s and 1960s, it was used in further studies on early European metallurgy, in the study of faience beads in early Europe, and for the characterization of obsidian. It has now largely been replaced by inductively coupled plasma emission spectrometry (ICPS), as well as by atomic absorption spectrometry (see below).

Neutron activation analysis, or NAA (see box), was developed later and came into widespread use in the 1970s. It has been widely used for obsidian, pottery, metals and other materials. It is particularly useful for coins and other small objects, because it is entirely non-destructive.

Other methods for trace-element analysis include (see box) *atomic absorption spectrometry* (AAS), *X-ray fluorescence spectrometry* (XRF), and *PIXE and PIGME*. The PIXE and PIGME method has recently been automated, and applied to obsidian from the Admiralty Islands in the Pacific, indicating a trade from the Bismark Archipelago to Vanuatu (formerly the New Hebrides), a distance of 3000 km (1860 miles), over 3000 years ago.

These various methods simply produce a table giving the analyses, usually expressed in parts per million (ppm), for each artifact or sample, taking each element in turn. Some of the chemical elements are well-known ones, such as lead or tin, others are less common, such as vanadium or scandium. The problem then arises as to how to interpret them. Obviously, the aim is to match the compositions of the artifacts under examination with those of specific sources. But that can present problems. In the case of pottery, potters' clays are common, so there is little chance of matching specific pots with specific clay beds. Different sources can have similar compositions, thus giving misleading results. For this reason, the trace-element analysis of pottery, or indeed of metal, is not necessarily the best procedure for characterization. In the case of pottery,

ANALYSIS OF ARTIFACT COMPOSITION

A variety of scientific techniques can be used in artifact characterization studies, but these differ in cost, destructiveness, and sensitivity. Some are really only effective for certain ranges of element. So in choosing the method of analysis, the archaeologist must carefully match objectives and requirements against the cost and potential of the different techniques.

Optical emission spectrometry (OES) is based on the principle that the electrons of the atoms of every chemical element, when excited (e.g. heated to a high temperature) release light (and hence color) of a particular wavelength. A sample is burned in a carbon arc. The light given off is composed of different wavelengths, which can be separated into a spectrum when passed through a prism or diffraction grating. The presence or absence of the various elements can be established by looking for the appropriate spectral line of their characteristic wavelengths. The results, expressed as percentages for the commoner elements and in parts per million (ppm) for trace elements, are read off and expressed in tabular form. Generally the method gives an accuracy of only about 25 percent. OES has been more-or-less superseded by **inductively coupled plasma emission spectrometry** (ICPS). This is based on the same basic principles, but the sample in the solution is atomized and excited in a plasma rather than in a carbon arc. A very much higher temperature can be reached, which reduces problems of interference between elements. Also, ICPS has been largely automated so that a very high throughput of samples can be achieved. Only 10 mg of sample are needed, and accuracy of ±5 percent can be attained.

X-ray fluorescence spectrometry (XRF). In this method the sample is irradiated with a beam of X-rays which excite electrons in the surface. The electrons revert to their original positions when the X-ray beam is switched off, but as they do so they emit secondary or fluorescent X-rays. The energies and wavelengths of these secondary X-rays correspond to the concentrations of elements in the sample; each element emits X-rays of a characteristic energy. The secondary X-rays can be split into their different wavelengths by passing them through a diffraction grating. This indicates which elements are present, and by measuring the emitted X-rays is known as **wavelength dispersive XRF spectrometry.** An alternative method, known as **non-dispersive** or **energy dispersive XRF spectrometry,** simplifies the procedure by measuring the energy and intensity of the X-rays at the same time.

Although for certain elements there is theoretically no need to remove a sample from the object, in practice it is more usual to extract a sample, because the method can only measure the composition of the surface of an object. This is a particular problem with metal artifacts that have a corroded surface or where the object has been plated. In these cases, the surface layer must be removed from the area to be examined (which can be as small as 1 mm in diameter), so that the unaffected interior composition can be determined. But usually the problem is overcome by taking a sample from the interior of the object. XRF analysis is usually accurate to between ±2 and ±5 percent. It has been used to determine the composition of a wide range of archaeological materials, including metals, obsidian, and pottery. It has been particularly useful for examining glazes on pottery.

Electron probe microanalysis is in some respects similar to XRF. With this method, a fine beam of electrons is directed on a tiny spot on the surface of the artifact – one thousandth of a millimeter or a micrometer in diameter. As in XRF, the electron beam excites electrons which emit X-rays. The technique is more expensive than XRF. But it is useful for studying small changes in composition *within* the body of an artifact. The method is also suitable for the analysis of small inclusions in stone artifacts, in pottery (including glazes), and in metal objects.

Neutron activation analysis (NAA) depends on the excitation of the nuclei of the atoms of a sample's various elements when these are bombarded with slow neutrons. In order to do this the samples (about 50 mg) are placed in a metal can in a nuclear reactor and bombarded with a beam of neutrons. (Small objects, such as coins and faience beads, can be placed directly in the container without removal of a sample, but they will then often be radioactive for several years before it is safe to return them to the archaeologist or museum.)

The irradiation transforms the atomic nuclei of the elements in the sample into unstable radioactive isotopes (nuclides). These release gamma rays as they decay into stable isotopes. The energy levels of the gamma rays are characteristic of the particular element excited. Measuring the gamma ray energy emitted by a sample therefore indicates the elements present in it; the intensity of each spectral line shows the quantity of each element.

The method can be very convenient: it is accurate to about ±5 percent, it can measure concentrations ranging from 1 ppm to 100 percent, and it can be automated, so that numerous results become readily available. But there are some elements (e.g. lead) which form nuclides with very short or very long half-lives for which the method is not well suited. In addition, because it involves the use of a nuclear reactor, the method is available only at certain centers.

Atomic absorption spectrometry (AAS) is based on a principle similar to OES – the measurement of energy in the form of visible light. The sample to be analyzed (between 10 mg and 1 g) is dissolved in acid, diluted, and then heated by spraying it onto a flame. Light of a wavelength which is absorbed by the element of interest – and only that element – is directed through the solution. The intensity of the emergent light beam, after it has passed through the solution, is measured with a photomultiplier. The concentration of the particular element is directly related to the intensity of the beam.

By using different wavelengths of light over 40 elements can be measured, with an accuracy of ±1 percent for major elements and ±15 percent for trace elements. The method has the disadvantage of being slow and is also destructive. It does, however, have a particular advantage over other methods in detecting metals such as lithium and sodium which have low atomic numbers. AAS has been used archaeologically for analysis of non-ferrous metals (e.g. copper and bronze), flint artifacts, and other materials.

Proton-induced X-ray emission (PIXE) and **proton-induced gamma-ray emission** (PIGME) are similar in principle to XRF and NAA respectively, but, instead of X-rays or neutrons, the exciting agent is a beam of protons produced by a Van de Graaff accelerator. The secondary radiation given off by the sample is again either X-radiation (as with XRF) or gamma radiation (as in the case of NAA). PIXE and PIGME are used together, with the former being employed for the majority of elements, and the latter for those with low atomic weight (e.g. fluorine, sodium, and aluminium), which are less suitable or unsuitable for X-ray measurement (see XRF above).

petrological methods (see above) can be more satisfactory. However, trace-element analysis is more effective than petrology for distinguishing between clay sources near, and therefore similar petrologically, to one another, provided that as many trace elements as possible are considered. (Certainly, if sources are different petrologically it would be most unusual for them to be similar in terms of trace-element analysis.)

In general, rather than considering each sample in turn, with all its constituent elements, it is more satisfactory to group samples according to the concentration of just two or three elements in them. When samples are available from the sources, and the number of sources is limited (as with obsidian), clear results can emerge.

The trace-element analysis of obsidian from sources in Anatolia during the Neolithic period, undertaken by a British team, is a good example. It is described in more detail in the section on the Study of Distribution below. Several methods were employed including NAA, XRF, OES, and fission-track analysis. The resulting measurements allowed the grouping of samples from the various sources and of artifacts from different excavations.

For any chemical analysis, it is essential to have an interpretive strategy, and to understand the logic underlying the arguments. One of the least successful characterization projects of recent years involved the analysis (by OES) of thousands of copper and bronze objects from the Early Bronze Age of Europe. These were classed into groups on the basis of their composition, without recognizing clearly that very different source areas might produce copper with similar trace-element composition and, furthermore, that changes in the concentration of trace elements had occurred during smelting. From the standpoint of sourcing, the groups were more or less meaningless. The isotopic methods described below have proved much more effective for metal characterization.

Isotopic Analysis. A major breakthrough in recent years has been the application of isotopic chemistry to the question of metal sourcing, and subsequently to other materials also. (The importance of the different isotopes of carbon for dating procedures, and also of certain other elements, was reviewed in Chapter 4.)

Analysis of the isotopes of lead in raw materials (see box) has become the most important characterization technique for metal objects (and some other materials) because it successfully distinguishes lead from different sources in a way that trace-element analysis generally has failed to do. The method is of direct use not only for lead artifacts, but also for those of silver, in

which lead is usually present as an impurity. Copper sources always contain at least a trace of lead, and it has been shown by experimentation that a large proportion of that lead passes into the copper metal produced during smelting. Here, then, is a characterization method applicable to lead, silver, and copper artifacts.

Isotope ratios have also been used in the characterization of obsidian artifacts (strontium isotopes), and marble (oxygen isotopes). For a long time, the sourcing of marble has proved very difficult: it was well known that in the Mediterranean in the Classical period, good-quality white marbles were widely exported for sculpture or for building purposes. Many of the most important quarries (e.g. on Mount Pendeli and Mount Hymettos near Athens, and on the Aegean islands of Paros and Naxos) had been identified. But attempts at matching the quarry source to the building or sculpture using appearance or petrological methods (e.g. heavy-mineral and trace-element analyses) were disappointing. Analyses using two oxygen isotopes ($^{18}O/^{16}O$) and two carbon isotopes ($^{13}C/^{12}C$) are proving much more promising, although there are no definitive results as yet.

Oxygen isotope ratios have also proved useful for the characterization of marine shell. As mentioned above, the shell of *Spondylus gaederopus* was widely traded in the form of bracelets and decorations during the Neolithic in southeast Europe. The question at issue was whether it came from the Aegean, or possibly from the Black Sea. As discussed in the section on deep-sea cores in Chapter 4, the oxygen isotopic composition of marine shell is dependent on the temperature of the sea where the organism lives. The Black Sea is much colder than the Mediterranean, and analysis confirmed that the shells in question came from the Aegean.

Other Analytical Methods. Many other analytical methods have been employed for characterization purposes.

X-ray diffraction analysis, used in determining the crystalline structure of minerals, from the angle at which X-rays are reflected, has proved helpful in defining the composition of Neolithic jade and jadeite axes that have been found at several British sites: it seems that the stone may have come from as far away as the Alps. It has also been used extensively in the characterization of pottery.

Infra-red absorption spectroscopy has proved the most appropriate method for distinguishing between ambers from different sources: the organic compounds in the amber absorb different wavelengths of infra-red radiation passed through them.

LEAD ISOTOPE ANALYSIS

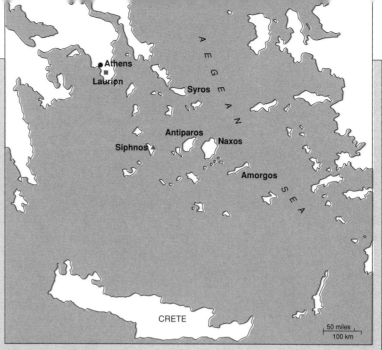

Places referred to in the Aegean area.

For most raw materials, the isotopic composition is of little interest, because different sources have much the same isotopic composition. In the case of lead, however, the isotopic composition depends on the geological age of formation of the ore deposit. Different sources, such as different lead mines, have different proportions of the three isotopes of lead – ^{206}Pb, ^{207}Pb, and ^{208}Pb – mainly because their ores were formed at different geological ages. Thus, in a given region, provided one has located the main lead sources and identified their distinctive lead isotope ratios, it is possible to demonstrate that, say, a particular lead artifact was made of lead from one specific source in that region. Since silver is extracted from lead ores, and retains measurable traces of lead, the technique applies to silver artifacts as well.

Lead isotope analysis has been applied to lead and silver sources and artifacts in the Aegean. Coins of the Classical period made with silver from the mines at Laurion can easily be distinguished from those made of silver from the island of Siphnos or other sources. The same approach has been applied by Oxford-based geologists Noel Gale and Zofia Stos-Gale to Bronze Age lead and silver artifacts from the area (see illustrations).

Smelting the lead or silver from the ore fortunately does not alter the isotopic composition of the metal. However, errors may arise if objects were made from scrap metal originating from several ore sources. Also, it should be noted that if an unknown source was of about the same geological age as one of the known sources, its lead isotope composition might be very similar to that of the known source.

Lead isotope ratios for the Siphnos ore samples (colored triangles), Laurion ore samples (colored squares), and 12 Early Bronze Age lead and silver artifacts (black) found on various Aegean islands. Ratios for 6 of the artifacts overlap with ratios for the Siphnos source, suggesting that the metal for these artifacts (all of lead) came from Siphnos. The other 6 artifacts (5 of silver and 1 of lead) are linked with the Laurion mines.

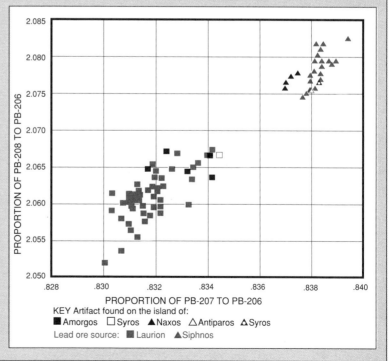

ARCHAEOLOGICAL MATERIAL	MOST SUITABLE METHODS FOR CHARACTERIZATION STUDIES
Pottery	Petrological thin-section, X-ray diffraction analysis, Mössbauer spectroscopy, XRF, NAA, AAS, ICPS, PIXE & PIGME
Flint	AAS, ICPS, NAA, XRF, PIXE & PIGME
Marble	Carbon & oxygen isotope analysis
Jade	X-ray diffraction analysis
Other stone	Petrological thin-section
Obsidian	AAS, ICPS, NAA, XRF, PIXE & PIGME, fission track
Marine shell	Carbon & oxygen isotope analysis
Amber	Infra-red absorption spectroscopy
Lead	Lead isotope analysis
Silver	Lead isotope analysis, NAA
Copper, bronze	Lead isotope analysis, NAA, AAS, ICPS
Coins	NAA (also lead isotope analysis if coins of copper or silver)
Iron ore (magnetite, ilmenite, hematite)	Mössbauer spectroscopy
Iron slag	Electron microprobe

Table summarizing the most appropriate characterization methods for various archaeological materials.

Fission-track analysis is mainly a dating method (Chapter 4), but has also been used to distinguish between obsidians from different sources, on the basis of their uranium content and the date of formation of the deposits.

Mössbauer spectroscopy is used in the study of iron compounds, notably in pottery. It involves the measurement of the gamma radiation absorbed by the iron nuclei, which gives information about the particular iron compounds in the pottery sample and on the conditions of firing when the pottery was being made.

This was the analytical technique used in the characterization of the mirrors made out of different kinds of iron ore (magnetite, ilmenite, and haematite) and widely traded in the Formative period in Oaxaca in Mesoamerica (see box on Oaxaca below).

These various methods enable archaeologists in many cases to identify the sources of the raw materials used to make particular artifacts. How the movements of these artifacts are to be interpreted in terms of exchange presents a series of interesting problems, which we shall discuss in the next section.

THE STUDY OF DISTRIBUTION

The study of the traded goods themselves, and the identification of their sources by means of characterization, are the most important procedures in the investigation of exchange. As we shall see below, the investigation of production methods in the source area can also be informative, and so can a consideration of consumption, which completes the story. But it is the study of distribution, or goods on the move, that allows us to get to the heart of the matter.

In the absence of written records it is not easy to determine what were the mechanisms of distribution, or what was the nature of the exchange relationship.

However, where such records exist, they can be most informative. The Minoan Linear B tablets from the palace at Knossos in Crete and from Pylos in Mycenaean Greece give a clear picture of the palace economy. They show inventories of material coming in to the palace, and they record outgoings, indicating the existence of a redistributive system. Comparable records of account from centrally administered societies have offered similar insights – for instance, in the Near East. This precise sort of information is, of course, rarely available. Most of what the tablets record relates to internal trade – the production and distribution of

A distribution study. Roman storage containers (amphorae) bearing the stamp of the potter Sestius have been found in northern Italy and widely throughout central and southern France. They and their contents (no doubt wine) were probably made on an estate near Cosa. The distribution map thus indicates the general pattern of the export from the Cosa area of this commodity.

goods within the society. But some Egyptian and Near Eastern records, notably in the archive dating to the 15th century BC found at Tell el Amarna in Egypt, talk of gifts between the pharaoh and other Near Eastern potentates: this was gift exchange between the rulers of early state societies. Examples of such princely gifts survive: one of the treasures of Vienna is the ceremonial headdress of feathers given by the Aztec ruler Moctezuma to Cortés as a gift for the King of Spain at the time of the Spanish Conquest of Mexico in the 16th century AD (see box above, Materials of Prestige Value).

Earlier evidence from preliterate societies – societies without written records – can, however, give some clear idea of ownership and of the managed distribution of goods. For example, clay sealings, used to stopper jars, to secure boxes, and to seal the doors of storehouses, and distinguished by the impression of a carved seal, are widely found in the preliterate phases in the Near East, and in the Aegean Bronze Age. In the past, these sealstones and their impressions have been studied more for their artistic content than for the light that they might throw on exchange mechanisms. However, if looked for, information about exchange is there, although once again, it relates mainly to internal exchange. The impressions are only occasionally found at any great distance from their place of origin.

In some cases, however, the traded goods themselves were marked by their owner or producer. For instance, the potters who produced storage containers for liquids (amphorae) in Roman times used to stamp their name on the rim. The map above shows the distribution of amphorae bearing the stamp of the potter Sestius, whose kilns, although not yet located,

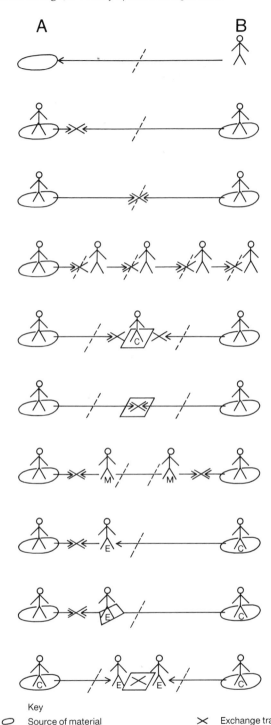

DIRECT ACCESS **B** has direct access to the source of the material without reference to **A**. If a territorial boundary exists, it can be crossed with impunity. There is no exchange transaction.

RECIPROCITY (HOME BASE) **B** visits **A** at **A**'s home base, and they exchange the special product each of them controls.

RECIPROCITY (BOUNDARY) **A** and **B** meet at their common boundary for exchange purposes.

DOWN-THE-LINE TRADE Reduplicated home-base or boundary reciprocity (shown here for clarity as one-way only), so that a commodity travels across successive territories through successive exchanges.

CENTRAL PLACE REDISTRIBUTON **A** takes produce to the central place as tribute for the central person (no doubt receiving something in exchange, then or subsequently). **B** likewise takes produce to the central place and receives some of **A**'s produce.

CENTRAL PLACE MARKET EXCHANGE **A** takes produce to the central place and there exchanges it directly with **B** for **B**'s produce. The central person is not immediately active in this transaction.

FREELANCE (MIDDLEMAN) TRADING The middleman exchanges with **A** and with **B**, but is not under the control of **A** or **B**.

EMISSARY TRADING **B** sends an emissary, who is under **B**'s control, to exchange goods with **A**.

COLONIAL ENCLAVE **B** sends emissaries to establish a colonial enclave near **A**, in order to exchange with **A**.

PORT OF TRADE Both **A** and **B** send their emissaries to a central place (port of trade) which is outside the jurisdiction of either.

Key

Source of material	✕	Exchange transaction	Controlling person
Central place	/	Territorial boundary	Middleman
Colonial enclave	𝘈	Person involved in transaction	Emissary

TREND SURFACE ANALYSIS

The aim of trend surface analysis is to highlight the main features of a distribution by smoothing over some of the local irregularities. In this way the important trends can be isolated from the background "noise" more clearly.

The first step is to divide the map into small, uniform areas or "cells." The number of finds within each cell is then noted. The patterning can be smoothed to reduce local irregularities by using not the actual figure of finds per cell but an average calculated from

Langdale axe

finds for each individual cell plus all its neighbors. In this way a moving average is produced from which a contour map may be drawn.

The example here shows the distribution density in Britain of so-called Group VI Neolithic stone axes, all of which came ultimately from the Langdale axe factories in northern England. This source was established for each axe by the petrological analysis of thin sections. But to display the distribution in this form may not reveal the mechanism underlying it. Grahame Clark suggested that gift exchange was involved for the British Neolithic axes, analogous to that among the Aborigines in Australia (see box on Production, below).

In a full trend surface analysis the principal trends would be defined by mathematics. This would allow the deviations from the trends (known as residuals) to be isolated and quantified.

Relative frequency distribution of findspots of Group VI Neolithic axes, deriving ultimately from the Langdale axe factories. Out of some 500 axes, well over 50 percent were found in East Lincolnshire.

---

were probably in the Cosa area of Italy. The general pattern of the export of oil or wine or whatever the amphorae contained (a question that can be decided by analysis of residues in the amphorae: see Chapter 7) can be made clear by the production of a distribution map. But a distribution map must be interpreted if we are to understand the processes that lay behind it, and at this point it is useful to distinguish again between reciprocity, redistribution, and market exchange, and to consider how the spatial distribution of finds may depend on the exchange mechanism.

"Direct access" refers to the situation where the user goes directly to the source of the material, without the intervention of any exchange mechanism. "Down-the-line" exchange refers to repeated exchanges of a reciprocal nature, and is further discussed below. "Freelance (middleman)" trading refers to the activities of traders who operate independently, and for gain: usually the traders work by bargaining (as in market exchange) but instead of a fixed marketplace they are travelers who take the goods to the consumer. "Emissary" trading refers to the situation where the "trader" is a representative of a central organization based in the home country.

Not all of these types of transaction can be expected to leave clear and unequivocal indications in the archaeological record, although, as we shall see, down-the-line trading apparently does. And a former port of trade ought to be recognizable if the materials found there come from a wide range of sources, and it is clear that the site was not pre-eminent as an administrative center, but specialized in trading activities.

Spatial Analysis of Distribution

Several formal techniques are available for the study of distribution. The first and most obvious technique is naturally that of plotting the distribution map for finds, as in the case of the stamped Roman amphorae mentioned above. Quantitative studies of distributions are also helpful; the size of the dot or some other feature can be used as a simple device to indicate the number of finds on the map. This kind of map can give a good indication of important centers of consumption and of redistribution. The distribution of finds on the map can be further investigated by the technique of trend surface analysis (see box) to obtain valuable insights into the structure of the data.

The quantity of a traded material usually declines as the distance from the source increases. This is not surprising, because one would expect abundance to decrease with distance. But in some cases there are regularities in the way in which the decrease occurs, and this pattern can inform us about the *mechanism* by which a material reached its destination.

The now-standard way to investigate this is to plot a fall-off curve, in which the quantities of material (on the Y axis) are plotted against distance from source (on the X axis). The first question is precisely what to measure. Simply plotting the number of finds at a site does not take into account the different conditions of preservation and recovery. Some kind of *proportional* method, measuring one class of find against another, can overcome this difficulty. For example, the percentage of obsidian in a total chipped stone industry is a convenient parameter to measure (although it is affected by the availability of other lithic materials).

In the study of Anatolian obsidian discussed in the main text, a plot of

FALL-OFF ANALYSIS

the quantity (i.e. percentage) on a *logarithmic scale* against distance (on an ordinary linear scale) produced a fall-off that followed an approximately straight line. That is the equivalent of a fall-off declining exponentially with distance, and it can be shown mathematically to be the equivalent of a "down-the-line" exchange mechanism, explained in the main text. A different exchange mechanism – for example involving central place redistribution – will produce a different fall-off curve (see main text).

Various interesting results come from fall-off analysis. For instance, when a plot was done of the decrease in quantity with distance of Roman pottery made at kilns in the Oxford region in Britain, and when sites that could be reached by water transport were distinguished from those that could not, a clear distinction was visible. Evidently, water transport was a much more efficient distribution method than

land transport for this commodity.

In principle, the fact that different models for the mechanism of distribution give different fall-off curves should allow an accurate plotting of the data to reveal which mechanism of distribution was operating. But there are two difficulties. The first is that the quality of the data does not always allow one to decide reliably which fall-off curve is the appropriate one. And the more serious difficulty is that, in some cases, different models for distribution produce the same curve.

Fall-off analysis can be very informative, but these two limitations restrict its usefulness.

The fall-off in Oxford pottery with increasing distance from the Oxford kilns during the Roman period. Sites with good access to the kilns by water (filled circles) show a much less steep fall-off gradient than those without such easy access, indicating the importance of water transport as a method of distribution at this time.

Distribution map showing the location of sites where Roman pottery from the Oxford kilns has been found.

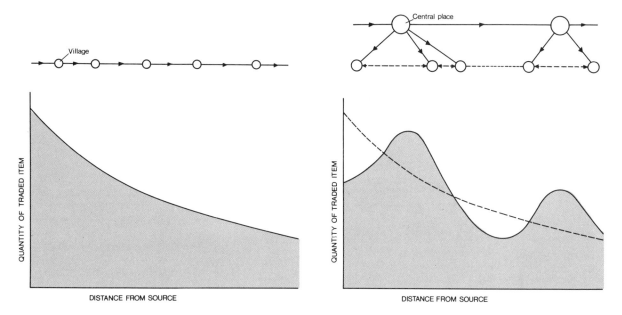

Relationship between settlement organization, type of exchange, and supply, for a commodity traded on land. (Left) Village settlement served by down-the-line exchange (on a basis of reciprocity) leads, in the archaeological record, to an exponential fall-off in abundance. (Right) Central place settlement with directional exchange between centers (and with either redistribution or central market exchange at local regional level) leads to a multi-modal fall-off curve. Note the tendency for lower-order settlements to exchange with the higher-order center, even if the latter lies further from the source than an accessible lower-order settlement.

Direct use of distribution maps, even when aided by quantitative plotting, may not, however, be the best way of studying the data, and more thorough analysis may be useful. Recently, there has been a considerable focus of interest on fall-off analysis (see box).

Although different mechanisms of distribution sometimes produce comparable end-results, the pattern of exponential fall-off is produced only by a down-the-line trading system. For instance, if one village receives its supplies of a raw material down a linear trading network from its neighbor up the line, retains a given proportion of the material (e.g. one-third) for its own use, and trades the remainder to its neighbor down the line, and if each village does the same, an exponential fall-off curve will result. When quantity is plotted on a logarithmic scale, the plot takes the form of a straight line. But a different distribution system, through major and minor centers, would produce a different fall-off pattern.

There are many examples where patterns of trade have been investigated using a reliable characterization technique together with a spatial analysis of the distribution of finds. It must be remembered, however, that such techniques rarely reveal the complete trading system, only one component of it.

Distribution Studies of Obsidian. A good example is the obsidian found at Early Neolithic sites in the Near East. Characterization studies by Colin Renfrew and his colleagues showed that two sources in central Anatolia and two in eastern Anatolia were in use. Samples were obtained from most of the known Early Neolithic sites in the Near East, dating from the 7th and 6th millennia BC. A rather clear picture emerged with the central Anatolian obsidians being traded in the Levant area (down to Palestine), while those of eastern Anatolia were mostly traded down the Zagros Mountain range to sites in Iran such as Ali Kosh.

A quantitative distributional study (see fall-off box) revealed a pattern of exponential fall-off, which as we have seen is an indicator of down-the-line trade. It could therefore be concluded that obsidian was being handed on down from village settlement to village settlement. Only in the area close to the sources (within 320 km (200 miles) of the sources) – termed the *supply zone* – was there evidence that people were going direct to the source to collect their own obsidian. Outside that area – within what has been termed the *contact zone* – the fall-off indicates a down-the-line system. There is no indication of specialist middleman traders at this time, nor does it seem that there were

325

central places which had a dominant role in the supply of obsidian.

In the early period, the position was as seen on the map. In the later period, from 5000 to 3000 BC, the situation changed somewhat, with a new obsidian source in eastern Anatolia coming into use. Obsidian was also then traded over rather larger distances. This is a case where it is possible to study the development of the obsidian trade over time.

Obsidian makes a very good material for a characterization and distribution study for several reasons.

First, there are relatively few sources of obsidian in the world, because the mineral is found only at volcanic outcrops of relatively recent geological age. Secondly, it transpires that the different sources are chemically different, so that they can be distinguished by such methods as neutron activation analysis. Thirdly, obsidian was greatly prized in prehistoric times and was used to make chipped stone tools in the same manner as flint, so that it is found at many prehistoric sites.

In the Aegean, obsidian was being collected from the Cycladic island of Melos as early as 10,000 years ago,

The obsidian trade in the Near East. Characterization studies revealed that Early Neolithic villages in Cyprus, Anatolia, and the Levant obtained their obsidian from two sources in central Anatolia, while villages such as Jarmo and Ali Kosh depended on two sources in Armenia (eastern Anatolia). At sites relatively close to the sources (e.g. Çatal Hüyük; Tell Shemsharah), obsidian formed 80 percent of the chipped stone tools, suggesting that within this "supply zone" (inner lines on the distribution map) people collected obsidian directly from the source. Beyond this zone there was an exponential fall-off in obsidian abundance (right), indicative of down-the-line trade.

as finds in the Franchthi Cave on the Greek mainland show. This is the earliest secure evidence for seafaring in the Mediterranean. The early trade of obsidian in the Pacific – for instance, within the early Lapita culture (Chapter 12) – has been documented by similar means. And in Central and North America, several investigations have been conducted of obsidian exchange systems – for example, in the Oaxaca region of Mexico in the Early Formative period (see pp.332–333).

Trade in Silver and Copper. In the Aegean again the technique of lead-isotope analysis (see above) has allowed the sources to be determined for the silver and copper artifacts in use in the 3rd millennium BC. The analyses have shown the operation of the silver mines at Laurion in Greece at a very early date, and have also unexpectedly revealed the importance during the 3rd millennium of a copper source on the island of Kythnos. Lead-isotope analyses also appear to indicate the surprising result that copper from Cyprus (in the eastern Mediterranean) was reaching the island of Sardinia (in the western Mediterranean) before 1200 BC. Sardinia has copper sources of its own, so the need for Cypriot imports is puzzling.

Shipwrecks and Hoards: Trade by Sea and Land. A different approach to distribution questions is afforded by the study of transport. Travel by water was often much safer, quicker, and less expensive than travel by land. The very best source of information, both for questions of transport and for the crucial question of what commodity was traded against what, and on which scale, is afforded by shipwrecks from prehistoric as well as later times. Probably the best known of these are the wrecks of the treasure ships of the Spanish Main; the artifacts in them give valuable insights into the organization of the trade. From earlier times, complete cargoes of the Roman amphorae referred to above have been recovered. Our knowledge of the marine trade several centuries before has been greatly extended by George Bass's investigations of two important Bronze Age shipwrecks off the south coast of Turkey, at Cape Gelidonya and Kaş (box overleaf).

The terrestrial equivalent of the shipwreck is the trader's cache or hoard. When substantial assemblages of goods are found in archaeological deposits, it is not easy to be clear about the intentions of those who left them there: some hoards evidently had a votive character, but those with materials for recycling, such as scrap metal, may well have been buried by itinerant smiths.

In such cases, particularly with a well-preserved shipwreck, we come as close as we shall ever do to understanding the nature of distribution. Just occasionally, we are lucky enough to see a depiction of traders, together with their exotic goods. Several Egyptian tomb paintings show the arrival of overseas traders: in a number of cases, for instance in the tomb of Senenmut at Thebes (c.1492 BC), they can be recognized as Minoans bringing characteristic Cretan goods.

THE STUDY OF PRODUCTION

One of the best ways of understanding what was going on in a system involving production, distribution (usually with exchange), and consumption, is to start at the place of production. Whether we are speaking of the place of origin of the raw material, the location where the material was turned into finished products, or the place of manufacture of an artificial material, such a location has much to teach us. We need to know how production was organized. Were craft specialists at work, or did people travel freely to the sources to collect what they wanted? If there were craft specialists, how were they organized, and what was the scale of production? In precisely what form was the product transported and exchanged?

The investigation of quarries and mines is now a well-developed field of archaeology. Detailed mapping of the source area, both in terms of the geological formation and of the distribution of discarded material, is a first step for quarries. The work of Robin Torrence at the obsidian quarries on the Aegean island of Melos offers a good example. The main question that she posed there was whether craft specialists resident on Melos were exploiting this resource, or whether it was utilized by travelers who came in their boats and collected the material when they wanted to do so. Her sophisticated analysis showed that the latter was the case, and that craft specialists had not worked there: this was a direct-access resource. (Torrence's research formed part of a wider project on Melos that is described in some detail in Chapter 13.)

One of the most interesting techniques for studying production is reconstituting the debris from the production of tool forms. C.A. Singer has done this at felsite quarries in the Colorado Desert of southern

DISTRIBUTION: THE KAŞ WRECK

It is difficult for the archaeologist to learn what commodity was traded against what other commodity, and to understand the mechanics of trade. The discovery of the shipwreck of a trading vessel, complete with cargo, is thus of particular value.

In 1982, just such a wreck, dating from the 14th century BC, was found at Ulu Burun, near Kaş, off the south Turkish coast in 46 m (151 ft) of water. It is being excavated by George F. Bass and Cemal Pulak of the Institute of Nautical Archaeology in Texas.

The ship's cargo contained 6 tons of copper in the form of over 20 of the so-called "oxhide" ingots (i.e. shaped like an oxhide) already known from wall paintings in Egypt and from finds in Crete and elsewhere. The copper for these ingots was almost certainly mined on the island of Cyprus (confirmation of this should come in due course from lead-isotope analysis, and perhaps also trace-element analysis). Also of particular importance are the ingots and other objects of tin found on the sea floor in the remains of the cargo. The

Three striking objects from the wreck: (clockwise, from top) impression of a hematite seal, cut in Mesopotamia c. 1750 BC, with a new scene carved over it some 400 years later; a gold scarab, the first ever found bearing the name of the famous Egyptian queen Nefertiti, who reigned with her consort Akhenaten during the 14th century BC; and gold pendant showing an unknown goddess with a gazelle in each upraised hand.

source of the tin used in the Mediterranean at this time is not yet clear. It seems evident that at the time of the shipwreck, the vessel was sailing westwards from the east Mediterranean coast, and taking with it tin, possibly from southern Anatolia or some eastern source, as well as copper from Cyprus.

The pottery included jars of the type known as the Canaanite amphora, because they were made in Palestine or Syria (the Land of Canaan). Most held turpentine-like resin from the terebinth tree, but one contained olives, another glass beads, and a third an arsenical compound called orpiment. Similar jars have been found in Greece, and especially along the Levantine coast.

The exotic goods in the wreck included lengths of a wood resembling ebony, which grew in Africa south of Egypt. Then there was amber, which came originally from the Baltic Sea in northern Europe (and which probably reached the Mediterranean overland). There was also ivory in the form of elephant and hippopotamus tusks, again from the eastern Mediterranean, and ostrich eggshells that probably came from North Africa or Syria. Bronze tools and weapons from the wreck show a mixture of types that include Egyptian, Levantine, and Mycenaean forms. Among other important finds were several cylinder seals of Mesopotamian type, ingots of glass (at that time a special and costly material), and a chalice of gold.

This staggering treasure from the sea bed gives a glimpse into Bronze Age trade in the Mediterranean. George Bass considers it likely that the trader started his final voyage on the Levantine coast. His usual circuit probably involved sailing north up the coast, then across to Cyprus, then along the Turkish coast, past Kaş, and west to Crete, and perhaps west again to the Mycenaean sites of Greece. Then, profiting from seasonal winds, he would head south across the open sea to the coast of North Africa, east to the mouth of the Nile and Egypt, and, finally, home again to Phoenicia. On this occasion, however, he lost his ship, his cargo, and probably his life at Kaş.

The map shows the probable route of the ill-fated ship found near Kaş. Also indicated are likely sources of materials for the various artifacts found on board the wreck.

The thousands of objects from the wreck were carefully drawn on the site plan before the painstaking work of recovery began. The photograph shows assistant director Cemal Pulak (left) removing sediment from copper ingots with an air lift. To the right another excavator clears sediment around stone anchors.

FINDS FROM THE WRECK

Gold 33 pieces: 9 pendants (Canaanite and Syrian?) • 4 medallions with star/ray design • Scarab of Nefertiti • Conical, collared chalice • Ring • Scrap *Silver* 5 bracelets (Canaanite?) • 3 bracelet fragments (scrap) • 3 rings (1 Egyptian) • Crumpled plate • Bowl fragment *Copper* Over 200 oxhide-shaped ingots (27kg/60 lb each) • Over 70 plano-convex or "bun" ingots • Other ingots *Bronze* Tools and weapons (Canaanite, Mycenaean, Cypriot, and Egyptian designs): daggers, swords, spearheads, arrowheads, axes, adzes, hoe, sickle blades, chisels, knives, razors, tongs, drill bits • 1 pair finger cymbals • Zoomorphic weights: 2 frogs, 2 bulls, sphinx, duck, waterfowl, calf, fly • Balance-pan weights • Figurines of man and 2 sheep on lead-filled disk • Bowl and caldron fragments • Rings • Pins • Fishhooks *Tin* Over 57 tin ingot fragments (round bun and oxhide shapes) • Mug, pilgrim flask, plate, whistle-like object *Lead* 100s of fish-net weights • Fish-line weights • Balance-pan weights *Faience* Over 5 rhyta (ram's head form) • Goblet in shape of woman's head • Tiny discoid beads • Biconical fluted beads • Other bead types *Glass* Over 50 cobalt-blue disk ingots (Canaanite?) • Beads (many stored in a Canaanite amphora) *Sealstones etc.* 2 quartz cylinder seals (1 with gold caps) Hematite seal (Mesopotamian) • Gold-framed bone or ivory scarab • Stone scarabs (Egyptian and ?Syrian) • Lentoid sealstone with Mycenaean design · Other cylinder seals • Amber beads from Baltic • Small stone plaque with hieroglyphs "Ptah, Lord of Truth" on obverse *Stone* 23 weight-anchors • Ballast stones • Balance-pan weights • Mace heads • 100s of agate beads • Mortar and trays • Whetstones *Pottery* 7 large pithoi (1 with 18 pieces Cypriot pottery inside) • Over 108 amphorae (Canaanite) · Mycenaean kylix (Rhodian?), stirrup jars, cup, jugs • Pilgrim flasks • Syrian jugs • Wide variety of Cypriot pottery *Ivory* 7 hippopotamus teeth • Segment of sawn elephant tusk *Wood* Ship's hull (fir planks fastened to fir keel by mortise-and-tenon joints pinned with hardwood pegs) • Logs of African blackwood (Egyptian ebony) • Wooden diptych (book): 2 wooden leaves joined by 3-piece ivory hinge *Other Organic Materials* Thorny burnet (shrub used as packing around cargo) • Olives stored in amphorae • Yellow terebinth resin (?ingredient of perfume or incense) stored in over 100 amphorae • Orpiment (yellow arsenic) stored in amphora • 100s of opercula (?ingredient of incense) • Bone astragals • Ostrich eggshells • Over 5 tortoise-shell fragments (?part of soundbox for lute)

Copper

Terracotta

Tin

Stone

Ship wood

N

6 ft
1 m

California, which have a long history of exploitation from the beginning of the Holocene. He was able to refit flakes and artifacts from one of the quarries (Riverton 1819) with those from an occupation site 63 km (39 miles) away, thus illustrating the movement of the raw material from its source.

This is an area where ethnographic studies, notably at quarries in Australia and Papua New Guinea, have proved very informative: insights are gained not only into the problems of working those and similar production systems, but also into the solutions available to overcome them (see box).

The excavation of mines offers special opportunities. For instance, at the Neolithic flint mines at Grimes Graves in Norfolk, eastern England (see p.273), it was possible for Roger Mercer to calculate the total flint obtained from each mine shaft, and to estimate the amount of work involved in digging the shaft, thus achieving a sort of time and motion study for the actual extraction process.

Studies of the specialist working of raw materials have been undertaken for several materials. One of these is Philip Kohl's study of the production and distribution of elaborately decorated stone bowls, made of green chlorite, in the Sumerian period (2900 – 2350 BC). He studied two sites in eastern Iran, at Tepe Yahya and Shahr-i-Sokhta, and compared the production methods used there with modern soft-stone workshops in Meshed. The rapid mass-production of vessels in Meshed, using modern tools such as lathes, contrasts markedly with the much slower production methods employed at Yahya. The distribution of the products also differs, with the ancient chlorite vessels restricted to the upper ruling strata of early urban centers, while the Meshed vessels were sold to a wider range of people. Such comparisons with modern situations can highlight important features of archaeological artifact distributions. The study of village craft specialization in present-day farming societies is another way of learning about techniques of production in the past.

The location of specialist workshops in urban sites is one of the main objectives of survey on such sites. But only the excavation of workshops and special facilities can give adequate insights into the scale of production and its organization. The workshops most commonly found are pottery kilns. The scale of the installation is sometimes sufficient to imply the nature of the production, and sometimes the products; for instance, bricks referring to the *Classis Britannica*, the fleet of Roman Britain, indicate production under official auspices, as part of the official organization.

THE STUDY OF CONSUMPTION

Consumption is the third component of the sequence that begins with production and is mediated by distribution or exchange. There have been only a few serious studies of the consumption of traded commodities. But such studies are necessary if the nature and scale of the exchange process are to be well understood. The issues soon return to a consideration of formation processes (Chapter 2), because there is no reason to suppose that the quantities of material recovered at a site represent accurately the quantities once traded.

It is necessary to ask first how the materials recovered came to be discarded or lost. Valued objects, carefully curated, are found in excavations less often than less-esteemed everyday ones. Secondly, it is necessary to consider how discarded or lost objects or debris found their way into the archaeological record. On a domestic site, questions of cleanliness and rubbish disposal are important. The study cannot proceed properly without a consideration of both these aspects of formation processes, and of the timespans involved.

The quantities of material will need estimating very carefully. This means explicit procedures for sampling the site, and standardized recovery procedures. On most excavations it is now standard practice to take samples of the excavated soil, and to sieve or screen it through a fine mesh, often with the aid of water (water sieving). The technique of flotation (Chapter 6) is also used for the recovery of plant residues. A mesh of 3 or 4 mm (0.1–0.15 in) is usually appropriate for the recovery of beads, flint chips, etc., but for pottery a mesh of a larger size is more suitable, so that only pieces above a given length (of say 1 or 2 cm (0.4–0.8 in)) are recovered. (It often makes sense to discard, or at least not to include in the counts, pieces less than about 1 or 2 cm (0.4–0.8 in) long.)

The American archaeologist Raymond Sidrys has attempted to study the pattern of consumption of a specific commodity: obsidian. He set out to see whether consumption of obsidian from source areas in Guatemala and El Salvador during ancient Maya times varied according to different types of site. In the Maya area as in the Near East (see illus. p.326), the

PRODUCTION: GREENSTONE ARTIFACTS IN AUSTRALIA

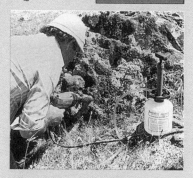

AUSTRALIA

One of the most thorough studies of the circumstances of production and distribution yet undertaken is that conducted by Isabel McBryde at the quarry outcrops on Mount William in the ranges north of Melbourne, in southeastern Australia. McBryde started with a large quarry site known from ethnographic accounts to have been an important source for the greenstone used in the manufacture of tomahawks, a basic and universal tool among the Australian Aborigines. She then followed up the quarry's products in museum collections, identifying them in collaboration with petrologist Alan Watchman. Similar-looking greenstone from other quarries could be distinguished by thin-section analysis, supplemented by major- and trace-element analyses.

McBryde mapped and sampled the worked outcrops at the quarry. On the top of the ridge at Mount William, where the outcrop of greenstone is buried, there are strings of quarry pits where the unweathered stone was mined. There are scree slopes of quarried waste around the worked outcrops, and isolated flaking floors indicate the location of the areas where cores and preforms were shaped.

The work also involved the study of the distribution of the artifacts derived from the quarry site. McBryde, drawing on the ethnographic evidence, discovered that access to the quarry was strictly limited, and its stone was available only through those with the kinship or ceremonial affiliations to the "owners" of the site.

In the words of McBryde: "The quarry was still in use when Melbourne was first settled in the 1830s, its operation controlled by strict

conventions. The outcrops were owned by a group of Woiwurrung speakers, and only members of a certain family were permitted to work them. The last man responsible for working the quarry, Billi-billeri, died in 1846."

Reed spears were brought from the Goulburn and Murray rivers in exchange. It is recorded that three pieces of Mount William stone would be exchanged for one possum skin cloak, "itself a considerable labor investment in hunting, skin preparation, sewing and decoration, when the skins of many animals might be needed for one garment." Thus the initial exchanges took the axes only to a fairly limited area around the quarry. The wider distribution – up to 500 km – was the result of successive further exchanges with neighboring groups.

Mount William, with its quarried outcrops along the ridge (right), and a map (above right) to show the distribution of artifacts made from the quarry's greenstone.

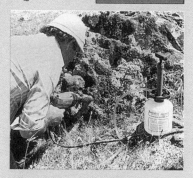

Petrologist Alan Watchman takes a rock sample from a greenstone outcrop at the Mount William quarry. Comparison of the rock's composition with that of greenstone axes found elsewhere made it possible to match the artifacts to their quarry source.

frequency of obsidian finds declines exponentially as the distance from source increases. But, allowing for this decay pattern, was there a marked difference in the amount of obsidian used at different types of site? Sidrys set out to answer this question with two measures of obsidian abundance. First he used a measure of obsidian density (OD), defined as:

OD = $\dfrac{\text{Mass of obsidian}}{\text{Excavated volume of earth}}$

for each site. This measure involved estimating the quantity of soil excavated and weighing the total quantity of obsidian recovered (finished artifacts and waste material) as the soil was passed through the sieve. The second measure was of obsidian scarcity (OS), defined as:

OS = $\dfrac{\text{Number of obsidian artifacts}}{\text{Number of potsherds}}$

Sidrys's calculations showed clearly that obsidian was less abundant at the minor centers than at the major ceremonial centers.

It is a matter for discussion as to whether this difference between the centers should be attributed to a difference in consumption patterns or to a difference in distribution, but with the major centers acting as the preferential recipients of supplies. The project is in any case a pioneering attempt to consider questions of consumption.

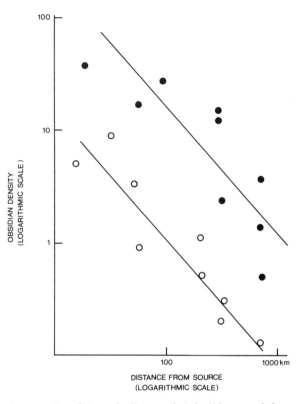

Consumption of Maya obsidian: analysis by Sidrys revealed two separate fall-off patterns, one for minor centers (open circles) and the other for major centers (filled circles).

EXCHANGE AND INTERACTION: THE COMPLETE SYSTEM

The archaeological evidence is rarely sufficient to permit the reconstruction of a complete exchange system. It is extremely difficult, for example, to establish without written records what was traded against what, and which values were ascribed to each commodity. Furthermore, exchange in perishable materials will have left little or no trace in the archaeological record. In most cases, all one can hope to do is to fit together the evidence about sources and distribution afforded archaeologically. A good example is the work of Jane Pires-Ferreira in Oaxaca, Mexico.

An Exchange System in Ancient Mexico. Jane Pires-Ferreira studied five materials used in Oaxaca during the Early and Middle Formative periods (1450–500 BC). The first was *obsidian*, of which some nine sources were relevant. These were characterized by means of neutron activation analysis, and relevant networks

were established. She then proceeded to consider exchange networks for *mother-of-pearl shell*, and concluded that two different networks were in operation, one bringing marine material from the Pacific Coast, the other material from freshwater sources in the rivers draining into the Atlantic.

For her next study she considered the *iron ore* (magnetite, ilmenite, and haematite) used to manufacture mirrors in the Formative period. Here the appropriate characterization technique was Mössbauer spectrometry. Finally, she was able to bring into consideration two classes of *pottery* whose area of manufacture (in Oaxaca and in Veracruz, respectively) could be determined stylistically.

These results were then fitted together onto a single map, showing some of the commodities that linked regions of Mesoamerica in the Early Formative period into several exchange networks. The picture is evi-

The complete system: Pires-Ferreira's map to show some of the commodities that linked regions of Early Formative Mesoamerica.

dently incomplete, nor does it offer any notion of relative values. But it does make excellent use of the available characterization data, and undertakes a preliminary synthesis that is securely based on the archaeological evidence.

Further Insights into the Exchange System. In a money economy, it may be possible to go further in our analysis, because some measure of the total turnover of the economy may be possible once there is a single, unified measure of value. In the case of coined money, various steps in the economic system can be reconstructed: the circumstances of minting may be examined, and something of the taxation system is sometimes known from other sources.

At a more specific level, coins can often give an accurate indication of the intensity of interactions in space and time because they can usually be dated and because the place of issue is frequently indicated. This is exemplified in the study by the American archaeologist J.R. Clark of the coinage of the Roman period from the site of Dura Europus in Syria. He examined a sample of 10,712 coins found there. These had been minted at 16 different Greek cities in the Near East, and by dividing the coins into four time periods he was able to show how Dura's commercial links with other cities had changed during the period 27 BC–AD 256, starting with an expansion of trade in the period up to AD 180, and a sharp decrease in the period AD 180–256.

In general, however, the exchange data in themselves are insufficient to document the functioning of the entire exchange system. It is necessary, then, to think of alternative models for describing the system, as advocated in Chapter 12. The use of such hypothetical models is entirely appropriate provided that the distinction between what has been documented and what is hypothesized is kept clearly in view. A good example is the Danish archaeologist Lotte Hedeager's study of the "buffer zone" in northern Europe between

333

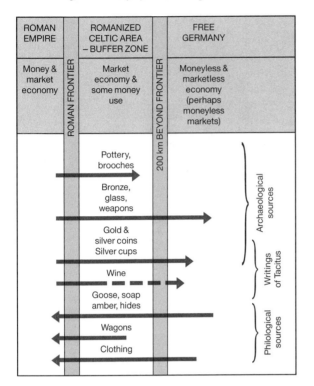

ROMAN EMPIRE	ROMAN FRONTIER	ROMANIZED CELTIC AREA – BUFFER ZONE	200 km BEYOND FRONTIER	FREE GERMANY
Money & market economy		Market economy & some money use		Moneyless & marketless economy (perhaps moneyless markets)

Lotte Hedeager studied the exchange system between the Roman empire and "Free Germany." Using archaeological, literary, and philological sources, she concluded that Roman-Germanic trade incorporated three economic systems: (1) the Roman empire, with money and market economy; (2) a "buffer zone," extending c.200 km (120 miles) beyond the frontier, which lacked independent coinage but maintained a limited money economy, perhaps including markets; and (3) Free Germany, with a moneyless and marketless economy, or perhaps with moneyless markets. Archaeological evidence indicated that the Germanic tribes mainly imported Roman luxury articles (bronze and glass; gold and silver in the form of coins) as prestige items (see Chapter 10). Philological and other evidence suggested that in exchange the Romans imported useful commodities such as soap, hides, wagons, and clothing.

the frontiers of the Roman Empire and the more remote lands of "Free Germany." She drew on literary and philological sources as well as archaeological ones to construct a hypothetical view of the whole system.

Trade as a Cause of Cultural Change

The possible role of trade in the development of a nation state or an empire from the trade interaction of smaller, initially independent units is seen in the illustration opposite. The city states or other indepen-

dent units (early state modules, ESMs) trade both at local level and through their capital centers. There are circumstances when these flows of goods can lay the basis for a larger economic unification.

This notion is related to that of the "world system" of Immanuel Wallerstein (see above), which some archaeologists have sought to apply to the pre-capitalist world in a manner that Wallerstein himself did not propose. But there are dangers here of definition being mistaken for explanation. To propose that certain areas were united in an economic "world system" does not of itself prove anything, and it may easily lead the analyst to exaggerate the effects of quite modest trading links. For it readily casts the discussion in terms of dominance (for the supposed core area) and dependency (for the supposed periphery). Indeed, it can easily lead to the rather unthinking explanation of changes by "dominance" (i.e. diffusion) that processual archaeology has worked hard to overcome.

If exchange systems are to have a central role in explanation, then the model needs to be framed explicitly, and it should show the role of exchange within the system as a whole, and the relationship between the flow of goods and the exercise of power within the system. One good example of such a model is the one offered by Susan Frankenstein and Michael Rowlands for the transition towards a highly ranked society in Early Iron Age France and Germany. They argued that it was the control of the supply of prestige goods from the Mediterranean world exercised by the local chiefs that allowed these individuals to enhance their status. They did so both by using and displaying the finest of these valuables themselves (the use including burial in princely graves, recovered by the archaeologist) and in allocating some of them to their followers. The transition to more prominent ranking was in large measure produced by control of the exchange network by the elite. William L. Rathje has presented a comparable model for the rise of a prominent elite in the Maya lowlands, and hence for the emergence of Classic Maya civilization.

These are models put forward to explain change in the cultural system, and a discussion of their implications belongs in Chapter 12, where the nature of explanation in archaeology is considered. It is appropriate to mention them here, however, as external trade and exchange play integral parts in many explanations proposed for cultural change.

Symbolic Exchange and Interaction

At the beginning of this chapter it was stressed that interaction involves the exchange not only of material

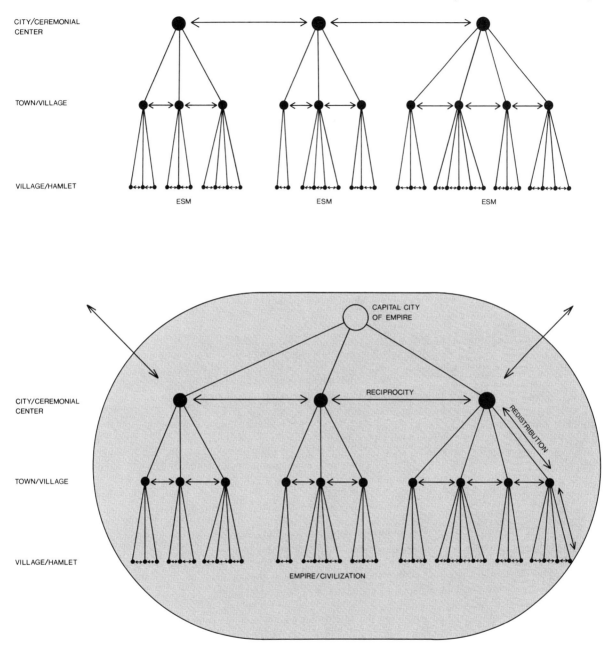

Trade and the development of an empire. (Top) Individual city states or other independent units (early state modules, ESMs) trade both at the local level, within each ESM, and at the higher level through their capital centers. (Above) In certain circumstances these higher-level interactions can lead to the integration of the ESMs within a larger-scale unit, the empire or civilization-state.

goods but of information, which includes ideas, symbols, inventions, aspirations, and values. Modern archaeology has learnt to cope tolerably well with material exchanges, using characterization studies and spatial analyses, but it has been less effective with symbolic aspects of interaction.

As noted above and as further reviewed in Chapter 12, there has been a tendency to label interactions between neighboring areas as simply "diffusion," with one area dominant over another. One response to such dominance models is to think in terms of autonomy: of complete independence of one area from another. But it seems unrealistic to exclude the possibility of significant interactions. The alternative solution is to seek ways of analyzing interactions, including their symbolic components, that do not assume dominance and subordination, core and periphery, but consider different areas as on a more or less equal footing. When discussing such interactions between polities (independent societies) of equal status – known as *peer polities* – it has been found useful to speak of *interaction spheres*, a term first applied to the interaction sphere of the Hopewell people of the eastern United States (see box) by the late Joseph Caldwell.

Peer-polity interaction takes many forms, some of which have been distinguished:

1   *Competition*. Neighboring areas compete with one another in various ways, judging their own success against that of their neighbors. This often takes a symbolic form in periodic meetings at some major ceremonial centers where representatives of the various areas meet, celebrate ritual, and sometimes compete in games and other enterprises. Such behavior is seen among hunter-gatherer bands, which meet periodically in larger units (at what in Australia are called *corroborees*). It is seen also in the pilgrimages and rituals of state societies, most conspicuously in ancient Greece at the Olympic Games and the other Panhellenic assemblies, when representatives of all the city states would meet.

2   *Competitive emulation*. Related to the foregoing is the tendency for one polity to try to outdo its neighbors in conspicuous consumption. The expensive public feasts of the Northwest Coast American Indians – the institution of the potlatch – was noted earlier. Very similar in some ways is the erection of magnificent monuments at regional ceremonial centers, each outdoing its neighbor in scale and grandeur. One can suspect something of this in the ceremonial centers of Maya cities, and the same phenomenon is seen in the magnificent cathedrals in the capital cities of medieval Europe. The same is also true for the temples of the Greek city states.

A more subtle effect of this kind of interaction is that, although these monuments seek to outdo each other, they end up doing so in much the same way. These different polities in a particular region, at a particular period, come to share the same mode of expression, without its being exactly clear where the precise form originates. Thus it is that in a certain sense all Maya ceremonial centers look the same, just as all Greek temples of the 6th century BC look the same. At a detailed level they are very different, of course, but they undeniably share a common form of expression. This is usually a product of peer-polity interaction: in most cases, one need not postulate a single innovatory core center, to which other areas are peripheral.

3   *Warfare*. Warfare is, of course, an obvious form of competition. But the object of the competition is not necessarily to gain territory. In Chapter 5 we saw that it might also be used to capture prisoners for sacrifice. It operated under well-understood rules, and was as much a form of interaction as the others listed here.

4   *Transmission of innovation*. Naturally a technical advance made in one area will soon spread to other areas. Most interaction spheres participate in a developing technology, to which all the local centers, the peer polities, make their own contributions.

5   *Symbolic entrainment*. Within a given interaction sphere, there is a tendency for the symbolic systems in use to converge. For instance, the iconography of the prevailing religion has much in common from center to center. Indeed, so does the form of the religion itself: each center may have its own patron deities, but the deities of the different centers somehow function together within a coherent religious system. Thus, in the early Near East, each city state had its own patron deity, and the different deities themselves were sometimes believed to go to war with each other. But the deities were conceived as together inhabiting the same divine world, just as mortals occupied different areas of the everyday world. The same comments may just as easily be made for the civilizations of Mesoamerica, or ancient Greece.

6   *Ceremonial exchange of valuables*. Although we have emphasized non-material (i.e. symbolic) interactions here, it is certainly the case that between the elites of the peer polities there was also a series of material exchanges, including the kinds already described earlier in this chapter – the transfer of marriage partners and of valuable gifts.

7   *Flow of commodities*. The large-scale exchanges between participating polities of everyday commodities should not, of course, be overlooked. The economies in some cases became linked together. This is

INTERACTION SPHERES: HOPEWELL

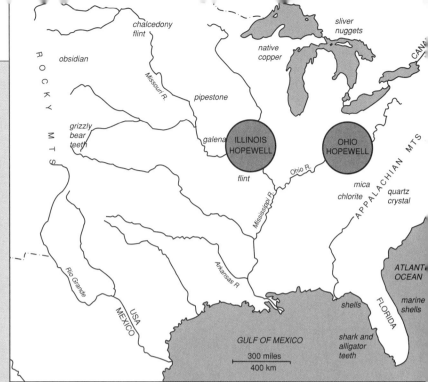

In many exchange systems, or interaction spheres, the exchange of valuables far outweighed in importance the exchange of ordinary commodities. Few commodities moved between regions because each region was relatively self-sufficient in these items. One interaction sphere, the Hopewell, operated on a very large scale in what is now the eastern United States during the first two centuries AD.

Eight regions participated in the exchange of valuables, two of which were more central in this exchange – the Scioto region of the Upper Ohio Valley and the Havana region of Illinois. The basic pattern of exchange was between the glaciated regions of the north and the lands to the south. Items of marine shell, shark teeth, mica, and other rocks and minerals came from the south; objects of native copper, silver, and pipestone came from the north. Several flints from different regions were commonly used in exchange, and obsidian was obtained far to the west in Oregon and Wyoming. These materials were made into highly distinctive objects for ritual and

Raven or crow cut from sheet copper, with a pearl eye. Length 38cm.

costumery. Native copper was hammered into various shapes, including axe and adze heads, large breastplates, headdresses, bicymbal earspools, and jackets for pan pipes. Sheets of mica were cut into geometric figures and naturalistic outlines. Flints,

obsidian, and quartz crystal were chipped into large bifaces. Marine shells were made into large cups and beads. Soft carvable stone was used to create distinctively styled pipes for smoking tobacco.

The widespread exchange of prestige goods was accompanied by a symbolic system that was adopted in each of the independent regions. Locally made items, including pottery and the decorative arts, conformed to the pan-regional style. Exchange goods were consumed in patterns of mortuary treatment and destruction by fire that are remarkably similar from one region to another. Thus, in a commonality of artifact form and consumptive pattern a veneer of cultural unity was created over the entire interaction area where none had existed before. Nevertheless, at the material level there were significant regional variations. The largest and richest burials are found at strategic locations where the most impressive earthworks were erected. Those in south-central Ohio are the largest and richest of all.

The American archaeologist David Braun has spoken of peer-polity

interaction within the Hopewell sphere (while emphasizing that these were relatively simple societies, not states), and has pointed out that competitive emulation and symbolic entrainment may be observed in Hopewell as in the case of other comparable interaction spheres.

Mica ornament of a human face, found in Ohio.

precisely what Wallerstein intended by his term "world system." However, it should be noted that in this case there need be no core and periphery, as there is in Wallerstein's colonial case of the 16th century AD, or indeed as there was in the ancient empires. Those, too, are valid cases, but although it is frequently appropriate both to the colonial world and to the ancient empires, these dominance relations should not be made a paradigm for the whole study of interactions in early societies.

8   *Language and ethnicity.* The most effective mode of interaction is a common language. This point is an obvious one, but it is often not explicitly stated by archaeologists. The development of a shared language, even when initially there was greater linguistic diversity, is one of the features that may be associated with peer-polity interaction. The development of a common ethnicity, and explicit awareness of being one people, is often related to linguistic factors. But archaeologists are only slowly coming to recognize that ethnicity is not something that always existed in the past: it is something that came about over time as a result of interactions, which ethnicity itself further influenced.

Such concepts, where as much stress is laid on symbolic aspects as on the exchange of material goods, can profitably be used to analyze interactions in most early societies and cultures. Systematic analysis of this kind has so far been rare in archaeology. In Chapter 12, where similar issues are raised in the discussion of explanation in archaeology, it is argued that a new synthesis in archaeological method is emerging, which one may term cognitive-processual archaeology. The analysis of interactions, including those of a symbolic nature, will have a significant role among the methods of that new synthesis.

SUMMARY

The study of exchange has been a growth area in modern archaeology. Scientific techniques of characterization – primarily microscopic examination of thin sections, trace-element analysis, and isotope analysis – now allow us to identify the distinctive characteristics of many materials, such as pottery, stone, and certain metals. Where the sources of raw materials in nature have likewise been identified – as for obsidian – one can then successfully plot on a map the distribution of such materials from source to archaeological findspot. Using techniques of spatial analysis (trend-surface analysis; fall-off analysis), the researcher goes on to investigate this exchange network further. Greater understanding of the network comes from studies of production (mines, quarries, craft workshops) and consumption, leading to as full a reconstruction of the complete exchange system as is possible without the benefit of written records.

Interpretation of exchange systems requires consideration of what the likely mechanism may have been: whether reciprocal exchange, redistribution, or market exchange. Nor should one forget that societies exchanged ideas and other information as well as material goods within a complete interaction sphere.

Further Reading

The following works provide a good introduction to the methods and approaches used by archaeologists in the study of trade and exchange:

Earle, T.K. & Ericson, J.E. (eds.). 1977. *Exchange Systems in Prehistory*. Academic Press: New York & London.

Ericson, J.E. & Earle, T.K. (eds.). 1982. *Contexts for Prehistoric Exchange*. Academic Press: New York & London.

Hodder, I. & Orton, C. 1976. *Spatial Analysis in Archaeology*. Cambridge University Press: Cambridge & New York.

Parkes, P.A. 1986. *Current Scientific Techniques in Archaeology*. Croom Helm: London & Sydney.

Polanyi, K., Arensberg, M. & Pearson, H. (eds.). 1957. *Trade and Market in the Early Empires*. Free Press: Glencoe, Illinois.

Renfrew, C. & Cherry, J.F. (eds.). 1986. *Peer Polity Interaction and Socio-political Change*. Cambridge University Press: Cambridge & New York.

Sabloff, J. & Lamberg-Karlovsky, C.C. (eds.). 1975. *Ancient Civilization and Trade*. University of New Mexico Press: Albuquerque.

10
What Did They Think?
Cognitive Archaeology, Art, and Religion

Cognitive archaeology – the study of past ways of thought from material remains – is in many respects one of the newer branches of modern archaeology. It is true that ancient art and ancient writing, both rich sources of cognitive information, have long been studied by scholars. But too often art has been perceived to be the province of the art historian, and texts that of the narrative historian, and the archaeological perspective has been missing. Moreover for the prehistoric period, where written sources are entirely absent, earlier generations of archaeologists tended in desperation to create a kind of counterfeit history, "imagining" what ancient people must have thought or believed. It was this undisciplined, speculative approach that helped to spark off the New Archaeology, with its pressure for more scientific methods, as described in Chapter 1. But it also led to a general neglect of cognitive studies among the first wave of New Archaeologists, deterred as they were by the seemingly untestable nature of so many ideas about the cognitive past.

In this chapter, we argue that the skepticism of the early New Archaeologists can be answered by the development of explicit procedures for analyzing the concepts of early societies and the way people thought. For example, we can investigate how people went about describing and measuring their world: as we shall see, the system of weights used in the Indus Valley civilization can be understood very well today. We can investigate how people planned their monuments and cities, since the layout of streets themselves reveals aspects of planning; and in some cases, maps and other specific indications of planning (e.g. models) have been found. We can investigate which material goods people valued most highly, and perhaps viewed as symbols of authority or power. And we can investigate the manner in which people conceived of the supernatural, and how they responded to these conceptions in their cult practice, for example, at the great ceremonial center of Chavín de Huantar in northern Peru.

In all these cases we can offer an outline methodology, even if it is as yet only a tentative one. As we shall see, some of the findings draw on other disciplines such as art history and epigraphy, for example in Maya studies, where the great advance in recent years in understanding Maya thought is very much an interdisciplinary achievement. But the interpretation and the overall perspective in this chapter are archaeological ones.

Theory and Method

It is generally agreed today that what most clearly distinguishes the human species from other life forms is our ability to use *symbols*. All intelligent thought and indeed all coherent speech is based on symbols, for words are themselves symbols, where the sound or the written letters stand for and thus represent (or symbolize) an aspect of the real world. Usually, however, meaning is ascribed to a particular symbol in an arbitrary way: there is often nothing to indicate that one specific word or one specific sign should represent a given object in the world rather than another. Take, for instance, the Stars and Stripes. We at once recognize this as the flag representing the United States of America. The design has a history that makes sense, if you know it. But there is nothing in the design itself to indicate which country is represented – or even that this is a flag representing a nation at all. Like many symbols, it is arbitrary.

Moreover, the meaning ascribed to a symbol is specific to a particular cultural tradition. When we look, for example, at a prehistoric Scandinavian rock carving of what appears to us to be a boat, we cannot without further research be certain that it *is* a boat. It might very well perhaps be a sledge in this cold region. But the people who made the carving would have had

Two people ride in a ship, or is it a sledge? The precise meaning for us of this Bronze Age rock carving from Scandinavia is obscure without additional evidence.

no difficulty in interpreting its meaning. Similarly, people speaking different languages use different words to describe the same thing – one object or idea may be expressed symbolically in many different ways. If we were all programmed at birth to ascribe the same meaning to particular symbols, and to speak the same language, the archaeologist's task would be very much easier – but the human experience would be singularly lacking in variety.

It is usually impossible to infer the meaning of a symbol within a given culture from the symbolic form of the image or object alone. At the very least we have to see how that form is used, and see it in the context of other symbols. Cognitive archaeology has therefore to be very careful about specific contexts of discovery: it is the assemblage, the ensemble, that matters, not the individual object in isolation.

Secondly, it is important to accept that depictions and material objects (artifacts) do not directly disclose their meanings to us – certainly not in the absence of written evidence. It is a fundamental of the scientific method that it is the observer, the researcher, who has to offer the interpretation. And the scientist knows that there can be several alternative interpretations, and that these must be evaluated, if necessary against one another, by explicit procedures of assessment or testing against fresh data. This is one of the tenets of processual archaeology, as discussed in Chapter 12.

Some processual archaeologists, notably Lewis Binford, argue that it is not useful to consider what people were thinking in the past. They argue that it is the actions not the thoughts of people that find their way primarily into the material record. That, however, is not the position taken here. We start from the assumption that the things we find are, in part, the products of human thoughts and intentions (which the critics of our approach would not deny), and that this offers potentialities as well as problems in their study. They belong, in short, to what the philosopher Karl Popper would term "world 3." As Popper indicates: "If we call the world of things – of physical objects – world 1, and the world of subjective experiences (such as thought processes) world 2, we may call the world of statements in themselves world 3 . . . I regard world 3 as being essentially the products of the human mind." "These . . . may also be applied to products of human activity, such as houses or tools, and also to works of art. Especially important for us, they apply to what we call 'language', and to what we call 'science'." This insight, however, although a helpful orientation, does not offer us a methodology.

As a first concrete step it is useful to assume that there exists in each human mind a perspective of the world, an interpretive framework, a cognitive map – an idea akin to the mental map that geographers discuss, but one not restricted to the representation of spatial relationships only. For human beings do not act in

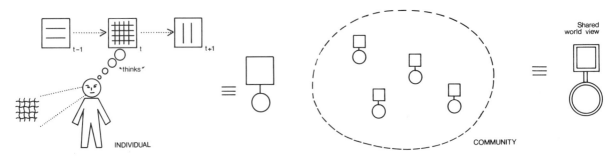

Cognitive maps. (Left) The human individual is accompanied by his or her personal cognitive map (represented by a square). The individual responds both to immediately perceived sense impressions and to this internalized map, which includes a memory of the world in the past (t − 1) and forecasts of the world in the future (t + 1). (Right) Individuals who live together in a community share in some sense the same world view. To this extent one can speak of a common cognitive map for the whole group.

relation to their sense impressions alone, but to their existing knowledge of the world, through which those impressions are interpreted and given meaning. In the diagram we see the human individual accompanied (in his or her mind) by this personal cognitive map, which allows the recollection of past states in the memory, and indeed the imagining of possible future states in the "mind's eye." Communities of people who live together and share the same culture, and speak the same language often share the same world view or "mind set." To the extent that this is so we can speak of a common cognitive map, although individuals differ, as do special interest groups.

This idea of a cognitive map is a useful one precisely because we can in practice use some of the relevant artifacts from Popper's world 3 to give us insights into the shared cognitive map of a given group. We can hope to gain insight into the way the group used symbols, and sometimes (e.g. in depictions of scenes) the relationships between the individuals making up the group. All of this may sound rather abstract. In the rest of this chapter, however, we discuss specific ways in which we can start putting together this shared cognitive map of a given place and time and social group.

INVESTIGATING HOW HUMAN SYMBOLIZING FACULTIES EVOLVED

We often tend to speak of the human species as if all humans are essentially alike in behavior and cognitive ability. This does in fact seem to be true for all living groups of *Homo sapiens sapiens*, if one allows for the fact that within every group there is inevitably some variation. In other words, there is no convincing evidence for systematic and significant ability differences between living human "races," however they may be defined. So when did these abilities of fully modern humans emerge?

Most physical anthropologists agree, as indicated in Chapter 11, that modern human abilities have been present since the emergence of *Homo sapiens sapiens* some 100,000–40,000 years ago. But as we look earlier, scholars are less united. As the neurophysiologist John Eccles puts it: "How far back in prehistory can we recognize the beginning, the origin, the most primitive world 3 existence? As I look at the prehistory of mankind, I would say that we have it in tool culture. The first primitive hominids who were shaping pebble tools for a purpose had some idea of design, some idea of technique." To which Karl Popper replies: "While I agree with what you say, I nevertheless prefer to regard the beginning of world 3 as having come with the development of *language*, rather than *tools*." Some archaeologists and physical anthropologists consider that an effective language may have been developed by *Homo habilis* around 2 million years ago, along with the first chopper tools, but others think that a full language capability developed very much more recently, with the emergence of *Homo sapiens sapiens*. This would imply that the tools made by hominids in the Lower and Middle Paleolithic periods were produced by beings without true linguistic capacities.

As yet there is no clear methodology for determining when language may have arisen. (The physical aspects, in terms of brain size, structure of throat, etc., are mentioned in Chapter 11.) But there are several lines of approach into other aspects of early human cognitive abilities.

Design in Tool Manufacture

Whereas the production of simple pebble tools – for instance by *Homo habilis* – may perhaps be considered a simple, habitual act, not unlike a chimpanzee breaking off a stick to poke at an ant hill, the fashioning by *Homo erectus* of so beautiful an object as an Acheulian hand-axe seems more advanced.

So far, however, that is just a subjective impression. How do we investigate it further? One way is to measure, by experiment, the amount of time taken in the manufacturing process. But a more rigorous quantitative approach, as developed by Glynn Isaac, is

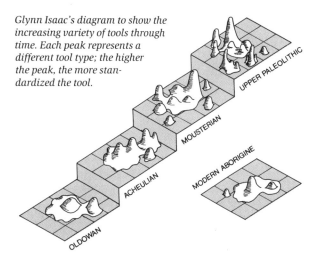

Glynn Isaac's diagram to show the increasing variety of tools through time. Each peak represents a different tool type; the higher the peak, the more standardized the tool.

to study the range of variation in an assemblage of artifacts. For if the toolmaker has, within his or her cognitive map, some enduring notion or image of what the end-product should be, one finished tool produced should be much like another. Isaac has distinguished a tendency through time to produce an increasingly well-defined variety or assemblage of tool types. This implies that each person making tools had in mind the notion of different tool forms, no doubt destined for different functions. Planning and design in tool manufacture thus become relevant to our consideration of the cognitive abilities of early hominids – abilities that moreover distinguish them from higher apes such as the chimpanzee.

Procurement of Materials and Planning Time

Another way of investigating the cognitive behavior of early hominids is to consider planning time, defined as the time between the planning of an act and its execution. For instance, if the raw material used to manufacture a stone tool comes from a specific rock outcrop, but the tool itself is produced some distance away (as documented by waste flakes produced in its manufacture), that would seem to indicate some enduring intention or foresight by the person who transported the raw material.

Similarly, the transport of natural or finished objects (so-called "manuports"), whether tools, sea shells, or attractive fossils, as has been documented (see Chapter 9), indicates at least a continuing interest in them, or the intention of using them, or a sense of "possession." The study of such manuports, by the techniques of characterization discussed in Chapter 9 and other methods, has now been undertaken in a systematic way.

Organized Behavior: the Living Floor and the Food-sharing Hypothesis

In recent years, as discussed in Chapter 2, a particular focus of research has been the nature of the formation processes by which particular archaeological sites were formed. For the Paleolithic period this is particularly crucial, not only because of the long timespan over which the deposits formed, but also in view of the interpretive care needed in respect of the human behavior. This has proved an area of special controversy at important early hominid sites in Africa and elsewhere – for instance, those at Olduvai Gorge in Tanzania, and Olorgesailie and Koobi Fora in Kenya. Scatters of animal bones, many in fragmentary form,

have been found with the stone artifacts at some sites. These sites, dating 2–1.5 million years ago, have been interpreted as activity areas, where the hominids who made the tools (supposedly *Homo habilis*) used them to work on animal carcasses (or parts of them) carried there and to extract marrow from the bones. These have been regarded as occupation sites, or temporary home bases, of small kin groups. Various workers including Glynn Isaac have argued that food-sharing among kin groups was taking place. These ideas have been criticized by Lewis Binford. In his view, these are not occupation sites of early hominids but places where hunting and scavenging animals killed their prey. The early humans were using their tools to extract marrow only after the animals who killed the game had taken their fill. He opposes the notion that early humans transported meat and marrow bones for processing and storing elsewhere.

Much work is going on at present to test these differing hypotheses. It involves the microscopic examination of the tooth-marks or cut marks on the broken bones (see discussion of taphonomy, Chapter 7), and the detailed analysis of the debris scatters on the supposed "living floors." Binford's argument would imply that no very intelligent behavior is involved, and no impressive social organization. The home-base/food-sharing view, on the other hand, implies a degree of stability in behavior, including social behavior, with more ambitious cognitive implications.

Lithic Assemblages as Functionally or Culturally Determined

When did human groups, inhabiting adjacent areas and exploiting similar resources, first develop behavior and material equipment that was culturally distinctive? This important question arises as a major issue when the various Middle Paleolithic stone tool assemblages associated generally with the Neanderthals (c. 100,000–40,000 years ago) are considered: the assemblages generally described as Mousterian. The French archaeologist François Bordes argued in the 1960s that the different artifact assemblages he had identified in southwest France were the material equipment of different groups of people co-existing at that time. These would then be an early equivalent of what archaeologists working with later time periods have traditionally termed archaeological "cultures," and equated by some with different ethnic groups. Lewis and Sally Binford, on the other hand, argued that the assemblages represent different toolkits, used for different functional purposes, by what were essentially the same or similar groups of people. They used factor analysis (see box, Chapter 5) of the lithic assemblages to document their view. Paul Mellars offered a third explanation, maintaining that there is a consistent chronological patterning among the different finds, so that one phase (with its characteristic toolkits) followed another.

The argument has not yet been resolved, but there are now many who believe that socially distinct groups, roughly equivalent to what one may term ethnic groups, only made their appearance with fully modern humans in the Upper Paleolithic period, and that the earlier Mousterian finds represent something simpler, perhaps along the lines suggested by Binford or Mellars.

Deliberate Burial of Human Remains

From the Upper Paleolithic period there are many well-established cases of human burial, where the body or bodies have been deliberately laid to rest within a dug grave, sometimes accompanied by ornaments of personal adornment. The act of burial itself implies some kind of respect or feeling for the deceased individual, and perhaps some notion of an afterlife (although that point is less easy to demonstrate). The adornment seems to imply the existence of the idea that objects of decoration can enhance the individual's appearance, whether in terms of beauty or prestige or whatever. A good Upper Paleolithic example is the discovery made at Sungir, some 200 km (125 miles) northeast of Moscow and dating from *c.* 23,000 years ago: burials of a man, boy, and girl, together with mammoth ivory spears, stone tools, ivory daggers, small animal carvings, and thousands of ivory beads.

Deliberate burial of the dead: an elderly man buried at Sungir, near Moscow, c.23,000 years ago, with thousands of ivory beads across his chest and a cap sewn with fox canines.

In assessing such finds, one must be sure to understand the formation processes – in particular what may have happened to the burial after it was made. For example, animal skeletons have been discovered alongside human remains in graves. Traditionally this would have been taken as proof that animals were deliberately buried with the humans as part of some ritual act. Now, however, it is thought possible that in certain cases animals scavenging for food found their way into these burials and died accidentally – thus leaving false clues to mislead archaeologists.

This problem becomes particularly acute when one moves back in time to consider the Neanderthals of the Middle Paleolithic period. On current evidence, the practice of deliberate burial – and therefore the idea of respect for the dead – began at this time. But what of adornment for the dead? Evidence for this once thought to be secure among Neanderthal burials has now in many cases been disputed. For instance, it has been suggested that the famous Neanderthal burial at Shanidar Cave in Iraq, supposedly with pollen indicating an offering of flowers, in fact represents a chance association of the pollen with the human remains. In general, the securest evidence for decorative items buried with the dead comes only from the Upper Paleolithic and later periods.

Representations

Any object, and any drawing or painting on a surface that can be unhesitatingly recognized as a depiction – that is, a representation of an object in the real world (and not simply a mechanical reproduction of one, as a fossil is) – is a symbol. General questions about representations and depictions for all time periods are discussed in a later section. For the Paleolithic period, there are two issues of prime importance: evaluating the date (and hence in some cases the authenticity), and confirming the status as a depiction. At present, it is generally accepted that the earliest depictions are of Upper Paleolithic date, and produced by *Homo sapiens sapiens* (see box). The examples given in the box indicate some of the important conclusions that are emerging from the application of new research methods to studies of Paleolithic art.

The analysis at the detailed level should not obscure the enormous cognitive significance of the act of depiction itself, in all the vividness seen in the art of Lascaux in France or Altamira in Spain. To admire this art is one thing; but to develop frameworks of inference that allow us to analyze carefully the cognitive processes involved is much more difficult.

PALEOLITHIC CAVE ART

Much has been written about the Ice Age caves of western Europe, decorated with images of animals and with abstract markings. Clustered in specific regions – most notably the Périgord and Pyrenees in southwest France and Cantabria in northern Spain – they span the whole of the Upper Paleolithic, from about 30,000 BC onward. The majority of the art, however, dates to the latter part of the Ice Age, to the Solutrean and especially the Magdalenian period, ending around 10,000 BC.

The cave artists used a great range of techniques, from simple finger tracings and modeling in clay to engravings and bas-relief sculpture, and from hand stencils to paintings using two or three colors. Much of the art is unintelligible – and therefore classified by scholars as "signs" or abstract marks – but of the figures that can be identified, most are

Principal locations of Paleolithic cave art in western Europe.

Position of the major figures (right) in Lascaux's Axial Gallery: mainly horses, aurochs (wild cattle), deer, ibex, and enigmatic dots and rectangles. About 17,000 years old.

Axial Gallery

animals. Very few humans and virtually no objects were drawn on cave walls. Figures vary greatly in size, from tiny to over 5 m (16½ ft) in length. Some are easily visible and accessible, while others are carefully hidden in recesses of the caves.

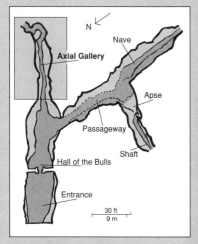

General plan of the cave of Lascaux.

The "jumping cow" in Lascaux's Axial Gallery, together with several horse figures. The mysterious rectangular sign is a particularly frequent motif in Lascaux. Some scholars see complex signs of this type as "ethnic markers," identifying a particular Paleolithic social group. Others interpret them more literally as fences or corrals – in this case the cow is skidding to a halt in front of the barrier. Most people prefer to classify them merely as "signs," since we do not know whether they were meant to represent objects or ideas.

The first systematic approach to the study of cave art ("parietal art") was that of the French archaeologist André Leroi-Gourhan, working in the 1960s. Following the lead of Annette Laming-Emperaire, Leroi-Gourhan argued that the pictures formed compositions. Previously they had been seen as random accumulations of individual images, representing simple "hunting magic" or "fertility magic." Leroi-Gourhan studied the positions and associations of the animal figures in each cave. He established that horse

and bison are by far the most commonly depicted animals, accounting for about 60 percent of the total, and that they are concentrated on what seem to be the central panels of caves. Other species (e.g. ibex, mammoth, and deer) are located in more peripheral positions, while less commonly drawn animals (e.g. rhinoceroses, felines, and bears) often cluster in the cave depths. Leroi-Gourhan therefore felt sure he had found the "blueprint" for the way each cave had been decorated.

We now know that this scheme is too generalized. Every cave is different, and some have only one figure whereas others (e.g. Lascaux in southwest France) have hundreds. Nevertheless, Leroi-Gourhan's work established that there is a basic thematic unity – profiles of a limited range of animals – and a clearly intentional layout of figures on the walls. Currently, research is exploring how each cave's decoration was adapted to the shape of its walls, and even to the areas in the cave where the human voice resonates most effectively.

345

PALEOLITHIC PORTABLE ART

Ice Age portable ("mobiliary") art comprises thousands of engravings and carvings on small objects of stone, bone, antler, and ivory. The great majority of identifiable figures are animals, but perhaps the most famous pieces are the so-called "Venus figurines," such as the limestone Venus of Willendorf, Austria. The frequent emphasis on the figurines' breasts and buttocks implies a possible connection with fecundity.

More systematic research methods have been devised by the American scholar Alexander Marshack. By microscopic examination of the engraved markings on some objects, he claims to have distinguished marks made by different tools, and by different hands on different occasions, producing what he terms "time-factored" compositions (made

Early Upper Paleolithic *bone from Abri Blanchard (Dordogne, France), with a serpentine series of 69 marks. Marshack found that some were gouged from left to right, others from right to left, and others as short arcs or simple jabs. Beginning in the center and following the curved line, he reads the marks as a complex notation of 2¼ lunar months.*

over a period of time rather than as a single operation). However, experiments using replica tools on stone slabs show that a single implement can produce a wide variety of traces. Only now, with the use of the scanning electron microscope, are scholars beginning to produce criteria by which one can reliably recognize marks made by the same tool (which leaves telltale tiny striations next to the purposely-made lines).

Some of the marks on Ice Age objects are incised in groups or lines. The Soviet scholar Boris Frolov and others claim that these marks represent repeated multiples of a variety of numbers, especially of 5 and 7, and see this numbering system as an incipient Paleolithic science. Marshack, however, argues that the marks, such as those on an early Upper Paleolithic object from Abri Blanchard, France, are more likely to be non-arithmetic "notations," used perhaps in observing the phases of the moon and also other astronomical events.

The phases of the moon would certainly have been the principal way Paleolithic people could measure the passage of time, and other scholars

have likewise sought evidence of lunar observation. For example, an Upper Paleolithic ivory plaque from Mal'ta in Siberia has hundreds of pits engraved on it in several spirals. According to Boris Frolov, the central spiral on this plaque has 243 pits in 7 turns, while the others form two sets of 122 each (122 + 243 = 365). By analogy with similar motifs found among modern Siberian tribes, he interprets it as calendrical ornamentation (243 days being the gestation period of the reindeer, the staple food of Mal'ta, as well as the length of the winter, while the summer lasts about 122 days). Other scholars interpret the spirals as representations of snakes, but the two views need not be mutually exclusive.

Ivory plaque *from Mal'ta, Siberia, showing the pits in a number of spirals.*

The limestone *Venus of Willendorf, Austria, c.11 cm tall.*

WORKING WITH SYMBOLS

In the previous section we looked at ways in which archaeologists can study the emergence of human cognitive abilities. In this and later sections we will be assessing the methods of cognitive archaeology for anatomically fully modern humans. Before going into details, it is worth outlining the scope of cognitive archaeology as it appears to us today, in the very early stage of the development of the discipline.

We are interested in studying *how symbols were used*. Perhaps to claim to understand their meaning is too ambitious, if that implies the full meaning they had for the original users. Without going into a profound analysis, we can define "meaning" as "the relationship between symbols." As researchers today we can hope to establish some, but by no means all, of the original relationships between the symbols observed.

In the pages that follow we shall consider cognitive archaeology in terms of five different uses to which symbols are put.

1 A fundamental cognitive step was the development of symbols of *measurement* – as in units of time, length, and weight – which help us organize our relationships with the natural world.
2 Symbols allow us to cope with the future world, as instruments of *planning*. They help us define our intentions more clearly, by making models for some future intended action, for example plans of towns or cities.
3 Symbols are used to regulate and organize *relations between human beings*. Money is a good example of this, and with it the whole notion that

some material objects carry a higher value than others. But beyond this is a broader category of symbols, such as the badges of rank in an army, that have to do with the exercise of power in a society.
4 Symbols are used to represent and to try to regulate *human relations with the Other World*, the world of the supernatural or the transcendental – which leads on to the entire question of the archaeology of religion and cult.
5 Above all, symbols may be used to describe the world through *depiction* – through the art of representation, as in sculpture or painting.

No doubt there are other kinds of uses for symbols, but this rather simplistic listing will serve to initiate the discussion of how we should set about analyzing them. Symbols of depiction provide us with perhaps our most direct insight into the cognitive map of an individual or a society for pre-literate periods. Among literate communities, however, written words – those deceptively direct symbols used to describe the world – inevitably dominate our sources of evidence. Ancient literature in all its variety, from poems and plays to political statements and early historical writings, provides rich insights into the cognitive world of the great civilizations. But, in order to use such evidence accurately and effectively, we need to understand something of the social context of the use of writing in different societies. That is the subject of the next section – after which we return to the five categories of symbol outlined above.

FROM WRITTEN SOURCE TO COGNITIVE MAP

The very existence of writing implies a major extension of the cognitive map. Written symbols have proved the most effective system ever devised by human beings not only to describe the world around them, but to communicate with and control people, to organize society as a whole, and to pass on to posterity the accumulated knowledge of a society.

Sometimes one can discern the beginnings of this evolved cognitive map in the form of sign systems that do not yet constitute a fully developed writing system – such as the signs found on pottery of the Vinča culture in southeast Europe before 4000 BC. The rongo-rongo tablets of Easter Island are another interesting exam-

ple. So far these are undeciphered, but they seem to employ a notation to help in the remembering of chants, although the signs were apparently not advanced enough to allow even a skilled "reader" to say the chant unless it had been previously memorized.

Societies with Restricted Literacy

Even where a proper writing system has developed, literacy is never shared by all members of a community, and it may be used for very restricted purposes. In Mesopotamia and Mesoamerica, literacy seems to have been restricted to the scribes and perhaps a few of the

Uruk IV c. 3100	Sumerian c. 2500	Old Babylonian c. 1800	Neo-Babylonian c. 600 BC	SUMERIAN *Babylonian*
				APIN *epinnu* plough
				ŠE *še'u* grain
				ŠAR *kirû* orchard
				KUR *šadû* mountain
				GUD *alpu* ox
				KU(A) *nunu* fish
				DUG *karpatu* jar

Writing and literacy. (Top) Map to show locations of the world's earliest writing systems. (Left) Evolution of the cuneiform script in Mesopotamia. (Above) Evolution of the Chinese script, using a sentence of classical Chinese composed of four characters "wan pang hsien ming" ("the multitudinous nations have laid down their arms"). First line, oracle bone script; second line, large seal of the Shang dynasty; third line, small seal of the Ch'in dynasty; fourth line, clerical writing of the Han dynasty.

elite minority. Mesopotamian writing was discussed in Chapter 5. In Mesoamerica inscriptions appear mainly on stone panels, lintels, stairways, and stelae, all largely intended as public commemorative monuments (see box below, Maya Symbols of Power). In addition, there is the store of Maya knowledge preserved in the codices, but only four of these survive. Inscriptions are found on other objects, such as pottery and jades, but these are all elite items and not evidence for any general spread of literacy among the Maya.

Widespread Literacy of Classical Greece

Against these examples of restricted literacy may be set those cases where literacy was widespread, as in Classical Greece. For extended texts, whether works of literature or accounts, the Greeks wrote on papyrus. Examples of such texts have been found at Pompeii (box, Chapter 1) and in the very dry conditions of the Fayum depression in Egypt. For public inscriptions, the Greeks used stone or bronze, although notices that were not of permanent interest were put on display on whitened boards (the simple alphabetic script of the Greeks favored such relatively casual use).

Among the functions of Greek inscriptions carved on stone or bronze were the following:

- Public decree by the ruling body (council or assembly)
- Award of honors by the ruling body to an individual or group
- Treaty between states
- Letters from a monarch to a city
- List of taxes imposed on tributary states
- Inventories of property and dedications belonging to a deity
- Rules for divination (understanding omens), e.g. from the flight of birds
- Building accounts, records of specifications, contracts, and payments
- Public notices: e.g. list for military service
- Boundary stones and mortgage stones
- Epitaph
- Curse on whoever disturbed a particular tomb.

It is clear from this list what an important role writing played within the democratic government of the Greek states.

In many ways, a better index both of literacy and of the role of writing in Greek daily life is given by the various objects bearing inscriptions, and by comments scrawled on walls (graffiti). One type of object, the *ostrakon*, was a voting ticket in the form of a fragment of pottery with the name of the individual – for (or

Greek literacy. (Top) In the Agora (marketplace) of Classical Athens, notices on whitened boards were displayed on this public monument. (Above) Potsherds (ostraka) inscribed with two famous Greek names: above, Themistokles; below, Perikles.

against) whom the vote was being cast – incised on it. Many have been found in Athens where (by the procedure of "ostracism") public men could, by a vote of the assembly, be driven into exile.

Other Greek uses of writing on objects were:

- On coins, to show the issuing authority (city)
- To label individuals shown in scenes on wall paintings and painted vases
- To label prizes awarded in competitions
- To label dedications made to a deity
- To indicate the price of goods
- To give the signature of the artist or craftsperson
- To indicate jury membership (on a jury ticket)

Many of these simple inscriptions are very evocative. The British Museum has a fine, black-figure drinking cup of about 530 BC, made in Athens and imported to Taranto in Italy, bearing the inscription: "I am Melousa's prize: she won the maiden's carding contest."

It can be seen from this brief summary that writing touched nearly all aspects of Classical Greek life, private as well as public. The cognitive archaeology of ancient Greece therefore inevitably draws to a great extent on the insights provided by such literary evidence – as will become apparent, for example, in our discussion of procedures for identifying supernatural beings in art and individual artists. But we should

not imagine that cognitive archaeology is thus *necessarily* dependent on literary sources to generate or test its theories. Textual evidence is indeed of paramount importance in helping us understand ways of thought among literate societies but, as we saw above for the Paleolithic period and shall shortly see below, there are in addition purely archaeological sources that may be used to create cognitive hypotheses, and purely archaeological criteria to judge their validity. Moreover, as we saw in Chapter 5, literary sources may themselves be biased in ways which need to be fully assessed before any attempt can be made to marry such sources with evidence from the archaeological record.

MEASURING THE WORLD

One aspect of the cognitive map we can readily reconstruct is the way in which it copes with measurement or quantitative description. The development of units was a fundamental cognitive step. In many cases, they can be recovered archaeologically, especially in the case of units of time, length, and weight.

Units of Time

The possibility that time-reckoning developed in the Upper Paleolithic was mentioned in the box on Paleolithic art above. To judge claims for time-reckoning at any period, it is necessary to show either a system of notation with a patterning closely related to that of the movements of heavenly bodies, or clear evidence of astronomical observation. The former is splendidly documented by the calendars of the Mesoamerican civilizations, in the inscriptions on their stelae, and in their codices (see box on the Maya calendar in Chapter 4).

Claims have been made that buildings and monuments in many places were aligned on significant astronomical events such as the rising of the midsummer sun. This was investigated quantitatively by Alexander Thom for the British megalithic circles. Although some of the details of Thom's claims for individual stone circles have been challenged, the cumulative picture argues plausibly for a preoccupation with such calendrical events. In the Americas, the work of the archaeoastronomer Anthony Aveni has done much to demonstrate that the Mesoamerican and Andean civilizations determined the orientation of many of their major buildings in accordance with astronomical alignments. He has shown, for example,

that the east-west alignment of the great Teotihuacan street plan is oriented on the heliacal rising of the Pleiades (the period when these stars first become visible before sunrise), important in Mesoamerican cosmology. The Maya site of Uaxactún provides another example, where the arrangement of a suite of three buildings on the east side of the plaza marks the positions of sunrise (as viewed from the west side of the plaza) at midsummer (north), midwinter (south), and the two equinoxes (center) (equinoxes being the midway points of spring and fall).

Measuring time: at the Maya site of Uaxactún, Mexico, buildings were positioned so that the rising sun at midsummer, midwinter, and the two equinoxes could be recorded.

THE MEGALITHIC YARD

DIAMETER IN UNITS OF 2 MEGALITHIC YARDS (UNITS OF 5.43 FEET)

0 2 4 6 8 10 12 14 16 18 20 22

0 10 20 30 40 50 60 70 80 90 100 110 120

DIAMETER IN FEET

Histogram (above) of the diameters of 46 megalithic rings (below, the Swinside Stone Circle, northern England), based on Alexander Thom's diagram of 1955. Each peak represents a diameter, measured in feet on the bottom scale. The higher and narrower the peak, the more accurate in Thom's view was the measurement for that diameter. Note how 8 diameters cluster around c.22 ft, 3 diameters around c.44 ft, 5 diameters around c.55 ft etc., suggesting that a standard unit of measure was being employed by the megalith builders. The top scale gives Thom's "best fit" for the unit for the diameters of 5.43 ft. Thom's megalithic yard was half this, i.e. 2.72 ft, since he thought that it would have been the radius of a circle, not its diameter, that was measured out.

The use of units of measure can be documented for several early literate civilizations. It is only since World War II, however, that formal statistical methods have been applied that allow us to look at the evidence from pre-literate societies (those without written sources). The first such application was to a supposed prehistoric unit of length, the "megalithic yard."

In 1955, the Scottish-born Professor of Engineering at the University of Oxford, Alexander Thom, published an article entitled "A statistical examination of megalithic sites in Britain." In this article, Thom measured the diameters of 46 circles of standing stones (megalithic rings), monuments which are first seen in Britain around 3000 BC and continued to be erected for about 1000 years (see box, Explaining the European Megaliths, in Chapter 12). Thom then recorded these diameters on a frequency plot. The results suggested to him that a unit of measure had been utilized, for the peaks of the frequency distribution seemed to fall at integral multiples of a unit for the diameters of about 5.435 ft (c.1.657 m). Thom argued that the radius rather than the diameter would have been used in laying out the circles (the circumference perhaps being marked out by a rope fixed to the center of each circle). He therefore proposed that the standard of length in use at the time, the "megalithic yard,"

was half the diameter, i.e. about 2.72 ft (c. 0.829 m). This is an example of the "quantum hypothesis:" that basic units of measure were employed.

Initially, there was no obvious way of assessing this interesting claim. But a paper published by the British statistician, S.R. Broadbent, offered several means of testing whether a given body of data involved the use of a quantum of measure, and these were followed up by another British statistician, D.G. Kendall. These tests show that Thom's 1955 data are significant at about the 1 percent level: that is if we had numerous samples of random data and tried to find the best-fitting unit, it would fit as well as Thom's unit in only 1 sample in about 100.

Thom's work has been criticized, but it is possible that a regular unit of length was used by the megalith

builders. If the accuracy of the layout of the circles was a little higher, it might support the view that measuring rods, 1 megalithic yard in length, were in use throughout Britain in the 3rd millennium BC. But the alternative suggestion has been put forward that the regularity is no more precise than would be expected from the use of a human dimension such as the pace in the layout of the circles.

The outcome of this discussion is not yet certain. What is clear is that statistical methods now exist to allow evaluation of such hypotheses. In cases where the result is shown to be significant at a very fine level, such as 0.1 percent, we may be confident that a regular unit of measure was used, provided always that the data have been fairly sampled, and that appropriate statistical tests have been applied.

Units of Length

There are statistical methods for assessing claims that a standard unit of length was used in a particular series of buildings or monuments. The statistical test based on what is known as "Broadbent's criterion" allows such a standard to be sought from the data without knowing or guessing in advance what the unit is. It also gives a measure of the probability that a unit of length discovered in this way is not just a product of chance, without any real existence. "Broadbent's criterion" has been used to assess the claim by Alexander Thom that a "megalithic yard" was used in the construction of the Neolithic stone circles of the British Isles (see box). Comparable claims have been made for units of measure in the construction of the Minoan palaces, for the Maya, and indeed in many early civilizations. In Egypt, measuring rods have actually been found.

Units of Weight

The existence of measurements of weight can be demonstrated by the discovery of objects of standard form that prove to be multiples of a recurrent quantity (by weight), which we can assume to be a standard unit. Such finds are made in many early civilizations. Sometimes the observations are reinforced by the discovery of markings on the objects themselves, that accurately record how many times the standard the piece in question weighs. Systems of coinage are

Units of weight: stone cubes from Mohenjodaro, Pakistan, were produced in multiples of 0.836 g (0.03 oz). Scale pans indicate the practical use to which the cubes were put.

invariably graded using measurement by weight, as well as by material (gold, silver, etc.), although their purpose is to measure differences in value, discussed in a later section. More directly pertinent here are discoveries of actual weights.

An excellent example comes from the site of Mohenjodaro, a major city of the Indus Valley civilization around 2000 BC. Attractive and carefully worked cubes of colored stone were found there. They proved to be multiples of what we may recognize as a constant unit of mass (namely 0.836 g, or 0.03 oz), multiplied by integers such as 1 or 4 or 8 up to 64, then 320 and 1,600. One can argue that this simple discovery indicates:

1   that the society in question had developed a concept equivalent to our own notion of weight or mass;
2   that the use of this concept involved the operation of units, and hence the concept of modular measure;
3   that there was a system of numeration, involving hierarchical numerical categories (e.g. tens and units), in this case apparently based on the fixed ratio of 16:1;
4   that the weight system was used for practical purposes (as the finding of scale pans indicates), constituting a measuring device for mapping the world quantitatively as well as qualitatively;
5   that there probably existed a notion of equivalence, on the basis of weight among different materials (unless we postulate the weighing of objects of one material against others of the same material), and hence, it may follow, a ratio of value between them;
6   that this inferred concept of value may have entailed some constant rate of exchange between commodities. (The notion of value is further explored in a later section.)

Items 5 and 6 of this list are more hypothetical than the others. But it seems a good example of the way that superficially simple discoveries can, when subjected to analysis, yield important information about the concepts and procedures of the communities in question.

PLANNING: MAPS FOR THE FUTURE

The cognitive map that each one of us carries in the "mind's eye" allows us to conceive of what we are trying to do, to formulate a plan, before we do it. Only rarely does the archaeologist find direct material evidence as to how the planning was carried out. But sometimes the product is so complex or so sophisticated that a plan prepared in advance, or a formalized procedure, can be postulated.

It is, of course, difficult to demonstrate purposive planning, if by that one means the prior formulation of a conscious plan in the construction of some work. At first sight, a village like Çatal Hüyük in Turkey (*c.* 6500 BC), or a sector of an early Sumerian town like Ur (*c.* 2300 BC), suggest prior planning. But when we look at the operation of various natural processes we can see that effects of very high regularity can occur simply by repetition within a well-defined scheme. There is no need to suggest that the polyps in a coral reef, or the worker bees in a beehive, are operating according to a conscious plan: they are simply getting on with the job, according to an innate procedure. The layouts of Çatal Hüyük and Ur may be no more sophisticated than that.

To demonstrate prior planning it is necessary to have some clear evidence that the scheme of construction was envisaged at the outset. However, such proof is rarely forthcoming. A few actual maps have come down to us from prehistoric or early historic times; but most of these probably represent depictions or representations of existing features, not the planning of future ones. Just occasionally, however, we find models of buildings that may have been constructed before the building itself. There are five or six models of Neolithic temples on the Mediterranean island of Malta that might represent planning in this way: they certainly show close attention to architectural detail.

Such direct projections in symbolic form of the cognitive map of the designer are rare. Sculptor's trial pieces and models, such as have been found in the ancient Egyptian city at Tell el Amarna, are likewise unusual discoveries.

An alternative strategy is to seek ways of showing that the regularities observed in the finished product are such that they could not have come about by accident. That seems to be the case for the passage grave of Newgrange in Ireland, which dates from *c.* 3200 BC. At sunrise on midwinter's day here the sun

The Çatal Hüyük village layout (above) may have been no more consciously planned than the cells in a beehive (top).

shines directly down the passage and into the chamber of the tomb. There is only a low probability that the alignment would be by chance in the approximate direction of the sun's rising or setting at one of its two major turning points, in terms of azimuth. But it is unlikely also that, in terms of altitude, the passage of such a tomb would be aligned on the horizon at all. In fact, there is a special "roof box" with a slit in it, built over the entrance, which seems to have been made to permit the midwinter sun to shine through.

Deliberate alignment: the rays of the midwinter sun illuminate the passage and chamber at Newgrange, Ireland.

ROOF BOX

LIGHT

END RECESS

ENTRANCE STONE

Often, careful planning can be deduced from the methods used in a particular craft process. Any metal objects produced by the lost-wax method (see Chapter 8) undoubtedly represent the result of a complex, controlled, premeditated sequence, where a version of the desired shape was carved in wax before the clay mold was constructed round it, which then allowed the shape in question to be cast in bronze or gold. Another example is the standardization in many early metal-using communities of the proportions of different metals in objects made of alloyed metal. The constant level of 10 percent tin in the bronze objects of the European Early Bronze Age is not fortuitous: it is evidently the result of carefully controlled procedures that must themselves have been the result of generations of trial and experiment.

The use of a unit of length will also document some measure of planning and was discussed in the box on the megalithic yard. Complete regularity in layout, where there is a grid of streets at right angles, evenly spaced, is also a convincing indication of town planning. Traditionally, it is claimed that the Greek architect Hippodamus of Miletus (in the 6th century BC) was the first town planner. But ancient Egypt furnishes much earlier examples – for instance, in the workmen's village at Tell el Amarna, which dates from the 15th century BC. And the cities of the Indus Valley civilization around 2000 BC show some very regular features. They are not laid out on an entirely rectilinear grid, but the main thoroughfares certainly intersect approximately at right angles. How much of this was deliberate prior planning, and how much was simply unplanned urban growth are questions that have not yet been systematically investigated.

A stronger case for deliberate town planning can be made when the major axis of a city is aligned on an astronomically significant feature, as discussed in the previous section on Measuring the World and the great Mesoamerican and Andean centers. The geographer Paul Wheatley, in his influential book *The Pivot of the Four Quarters* (1971), has emphasized how the desire to harmonize the urban order with the cosmic order influenced town planning. This seems to be true not just for the American civilizations but for Indian, Chinese, and southeast Asian ones as well. The argument is reinforced when the urban order is supplemented by a rich cosmic iconography, as in such cities as Angkor, capital of the Khmer empire, in modern Cambodia (Kampuchea).

So far, no archaeologist has sat down to work out in detail the minimum number of procedural steps that must have been planned in advance in undertaking major building works. Of course, like the master

The regularity in layout of the Indus Valley city of Mohenjodaro – with main streets approximately at right angles – hints at conscious town planning.

The Step Pyramid, Saqqara: (1–3) pre-pyramid building stages; (4) shafts to subsidiary tombs; (5) buttress walls; (6) pyramid with four steps; (7, 8) pyramid enlarged to six steps.

craftsmen responsible for many medieval cathedrals, the builders may have relied also on skill and judgment exercised simply as decisions arose, rather than on elaborate forward planning. Sometimes, too, there are examples of designs being altered during construction. The great Step Pyramid of King Djoser at Saqqara, the first of the major Egyptian pyramids, was clearly the product of several changes or developments of plan by its legendary creator, Imhotep. (His name comes to us from written texts, but our knowledge of the construction is from the study of the monument itself.)

SYMBOLS OF ORGANIZATION AND POWER

Symbols are used for regulating and organizing people as well as the material world. They may simply convey information from one person to another, as with language or, as in the case of archival records, from one point in time to another. But sometimes they are symbols of power, commanding obedience and conformity, for example the giant statues of rulers found in many civilizations.

Money: Symbols of Value and Organization in Complex Societies

In Chapter 5 we referred briefly to the existence of an accounting system as an important indicator of complex social structure. The symbols used in an accounting system – symbols of value such as standardized quantities of precious materials or coins – are both social and cognitive artifacts, reflecting the way in which the controlled elements of the economy are conceptualized within the society's shared cognitive map.

This is nowhere clearer than in the case of money. Money was briefly referred to as a measuring device in an earlier section, but it is something much more than this: it represents the recognition that we live in a world of commodities, which may be quantified and exchanged against one another, often in a marketplace. It represents also the realization that this is most effectively done using an artificial medium of exchange, in terms of gold or silver or bronze (if the money is in the form of coinage), by means of which the values of other commodities may be expressed. Money – and particularly coinage, where the form of the money is determined by an issuing authority – is a form of communication second in its power only to writing. In more recent times, token money, and now stocks and shares, are developments of comparable significance, indispensable to the workings of a capitalist economy.

Identifying Symbols of Value and Power in Prehistory

The existence of scales of value in non-monetary economies is more difficult to demonstrate, although several archaeological studies have sought to establish such scales. Robert Mainfort has used an ethnographic account from the 18th-century AD North American fur trade to aid such an investigation. The account, a list dated 1761 relating to trade at Miami, Ohio, itemized the values of certain goods in terms of beaver pelts (e.g. 1 musket=6 beaver pelts). On this basis Mainfort assigned values to grave-goods in burials at the Fletcher Site, a historic and roughly contemporary Indian cemetery in Michigan (see also discussion in Chapter 12). This analogy from the ethnographic record assumes, however, that the values operating at the Fletcher Site were the same as those recorded several hundred kilometers south in Miami, Ohio. This may be reasonable, but it does not help us establish a more general methodology for cases where ethnographic or written records are unavailable.

The Gold of Varna. Archaeological evidence on its own can in fact yield evidence of scales of value, as work by Colin Renfrew on the analysis of finds from the late Neolithic cemetery at Varna in Bulgaria, dating from *c.*

Deducing scales of value: the great worth of the gold from Varna, Bulgaria, is suggested by, among other things, its use to decorate significant parts of the body.

4000 BC, has shown. Numerous golden artifacts were discovered in the cemetery, constituting what is the earliest known major find of gold anywhere in the world. But it cannot simply be assumed that the gold is of high value (its relative abundance in the cemetery might imply the converse). Three arguments, however, can be used to support the conclusion that the gold here was indeed of great worth:

1   Its use for artifacts with evidently symbolic status: e.g. to decorate the haft of a perforated stone axe which, evidently, through its fine work and friability, was not intended for use.

2   Its use for ornaments at particularly significant parts of the body: e.g. for face decorations, for a penis sheath.

3   Its use in simulation: sheet gold was used to cover a stone axe to give the impression of solid gold; such a procedure normally indicates that the material hidden is less valuable than the covering material.

Indicators of this kind need to be developed if the formulation of such concepts of "intrinsic" value (which is a misnomer because the "value" of precious materials is ascribed rather than inherent) are to be better understood. In Chapter 9 we looked at materials other than gold that had prestige value in different societies.

The demonstration that gold objects were highly valued by society at this time in ancient Bulgaria also implies that the individuals with whom the gold finds were associated had a high social status. The importance of burials as sources of evidence for social status and ranking was discussed in Chapter 5. Here we are more interested in the use of grave-goods like the Varna gold-covered axes, and other discoveries, as *symbols of authority and power*. The display of such authority is not very pronounced in a society like the one at Varna, but it becomes more blatant the more hierarchical and stratified the society becomes.

Symbols of Power in Hierarchical Societies

The 6th-century BC chieftain's grave at Hochdorf, western Germany – mentioned in Chapter 5 – was accompanied by a rich array of accoutrements symbolizing his wealth and authority, but even this magnificent burial pales in comparison with some of the treasures buried with the rulers of state societies. It would be difficult, for example, to find a more potent example of royal wealth and power than the tomb of

MAYA SYMBOLS OF POWER

In the past 30 years our knowledge of the ancient Maya has increased significantly as a result of what has been called "the Last Great Decipherment" of an unknown script. Previously, we knew a good deal about the Maya, not least from their cities and from the stone stelae found there with complicated inscriptions on them.

However, the subject matter of the inscriptions (glyphs) had not been well understood. As recently as 1954, the great Maya scholar Sir Eric Thompson wrote: "so far as is known, the hieroglyphic texts of the Classic period deal entirely with the passage of time and astronomical matters... they do not appear to treat of individuals at all... Apparently no individual of that period is identified by his name glyph." In 1960, however, Tatiana Proskouriakoff of the Carnegie Institution, Washington, published a paper in which she identified rulers of specific Maya dynasties, and from that time, glyphs identifying persons (usually rulers) and places have been increasingly recognized. Indeed, it is possible to reverse Thompson's verdict. *Most* Maya stelae are now seen to commemorate events in the reigns of rulers who are almost invariably identified by name. Moreover, following the insights of the Soviet scholar Yuri Knorosov, we also know that the glyphs have phonetic values: they represent sounds, not concepts (as true ideograms do), and hence, language. Impressive progress is being made.

For the first time, Maya archaeology has become fully text-aided archaeology, like Egyptology, or the archaeology of other great civilizations. Previously we had the documentary evidence of the early Spanish historians in Mexico, such as Diego de Landa. Although writing six centuries after the end of the Classic Maya period, these scholars were able to draw on much knowledge that had survived into the post-Classic era. But now the decipherment of the stelae inscriptions has given us the benefit of a double literacy: that of the Spanish Conquistadors and that of the Classic Maya themselves.

A formidable amount can today be learned about Maya beliefs from the interpretation of a single stela. We may take as an example one of the masterpieces of Maya art, a lintel from the Classic Maya city of Yaxchilán, removed from there by Alfred Maudslay and given by him to the British Museum. This lintel has been analyzed by Proskouriakoff in some detail. It is also one of the works discussed by the American art historians Linda Schele and Mary Ellen Miller in their remarkable book *The Blood of Kings* (1986).

The standing figure is the ruler of Yaxchilán, named Shield Jaguar. He holds aloft a flaming torch, which suggests that the scene lay within a dark interior space. He has feathers at the rear of his head, and "the shrunken head of a past sacrificial victim is tied at the top of his head by a headband, marking Shield Jaguar's largesse in providing sustenance to the gods." In front of him kneels his wife, the Lady Xoc. She has begun the bloodletting rite in which he will shortly take part, and is pulling a thorn-lined rope through her mutilated tongue. Her cloak is a remarkable representation of Classic Maya weaving.

The inscription gives the names of the ruler and his wife, and indicates a date in the Maya Long Count calendar (see box,

Chapter 4) of 9.13.17.15.12 5 Eb 15 Mac, which is equivalent to 28 October AD 709.

This stela, and others like it, give us insights into a wide variety of fields: for example, they exemplify the use of Maya writing; they use the remarkably precise Maya calendar; they tell us something of the Maya view of the cosmos; and they provide a series of well-dated royal events as a framework to Maya history. In doing so they make major contributions to Maya political geography (see box on Maya

Territories, Chapter 5).

This and other similar depictions are an impressive instance of what the American archaeologist Joyce Marcus has appropriately termed "the iconography of power." They also indicate sacred rituals of the Maya, where the rulers had an obligation on specified occasions to shed their blood to give sustenance to the gods.

Now that we can interpret these monuments we can see more clearly than ever that this was one of the great art styles of the world.

5 Eb 15 Mac   he is letting blood   ?   ?   Shield Jaguar the captor of
9.13.17.15.12   4 Katun   Ah Ahaual
28 Oct.   Lord   Lord of Yaxchilán
A.D.709

she is letting blood

name or titles

Lady Xoc

Lady Batab

Lintel 24 from Yaxchilán showing Shield Jaguar and his wife, Lady Xoc, during a bloodletting ritual. The glyphs which frame their images give details of their names, the calendar date, and a description of the rite.

Philip II at Vergina in northern Greece (box, Reconstructing the Face, Chapter 11), or of Tutankhamun in the Valley of the Kings in Egypt (box, Chapter 2).

Indeed, among state societies and empires the symbolism of power goes far beyond merely the burial evidence to suffuse the whole of art and architecture – from the imposing stelae of the Maya (see box) and the giant statues of Egyptian pharaohs right up to their modern counterparts in Soviet Russia and elsewhere; from the Egyptian pyramids and Mesoamerican temples to the Capitol in Washington.

Symbols of power wherever they are found have in common the ability to evoke awe and thus acquiescence among humbler members of society. A very clear example from the present day are the badges of rank in modern armed forces (army, navy, airforce), which both express the status and authority of the bearers, and induce obedience among the lower ranks. But symbols of power can also be used to impress and intimidate members of *other* societies. A simple example would be the Great Wall of China, 2000 km (1250 miles) long and built with the defensive purpose of keeping out barbarians, but also acting as a gigantic symbol of the might of the Chinese empire.

A study of the art and architecture of the Assyrian palace at Khorsabad, in modern Iraq, provides a good example of symbols designed to impress both native subjects and foreign visitors. At Khorsabad the Assyrian King Sargon II (721–705 BC) built a heavily walled city, with a huge fortified citadel on its northwestern side. Dominating the citadel was Sargon's own palace, its walls decorated with friezes carved in low relief. The subject matter of the reliefs was specifically designed to suit the function of each room. Thus two outer reception rooms – used for visiting delegations – contained scenes of torture and execution of rebels, whereas inner rooms showed Assyrian military conquests to reinforce the status and prestige of Assyrian courtiers who used these rooms.

More general questions concerning symbols and art are considered in a later section. Inevitably there is a good deal of overlap between the different categories of symbol isolated for discussion in this chapter. The important point to remember is that these categories are for our convenience as researchers, and do not necessarily indicate any such similar symbolic divisions in the minds of members of the societies that are being studied.

SYMBOLS FOR THE OTHER WORLD: THE ARCHAEOLOGY OF RELIGION

One leading English dictionary defines religion as: "Action or conduct indicating a belief in, or reverence for, and desire to please, a divine ruling power." Religion thus entails a framework of beliefs, and these relate to supernatural or superhuman beings or forces that go beyond or transcend the everyday material world. In other words superhuman beings are conceptualized by humans, and have a place in the shared cognitive map of the world.

But religion is also a social institution, as the French anthropologist Emile Durkheim emphasized in his writings earlier this century. Durkheim pointed out the contribution of religion towards "upholding and reaffirming at regular intervals the collective sentiments and the collective ideas which make its [the social group's] unity and personality." More recently anthropologists such as Roy Rappaport have stressed the same idea, that religion helps regulate the social and economic processes of society. Indeed, more than a century ago Karl Marx argued that the leaders of society can manipulate such belief systems to their own ends.

One problem that archaeologists face is that these belief systems are not always given expression in

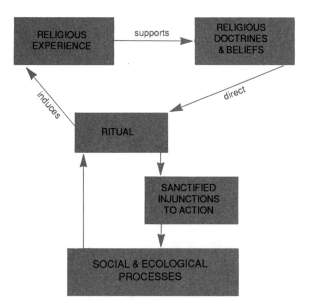

Religion as interpreted by Roy Rappaport: beliefs direct ritual which induces religious experience. Through ritual, religion helps regulate the social and economic processes of society.

material culture. And when they are – in what one might term the *archaeology of cult*, defined as the system of patterned actions in response to religious beliefs – there is the problem that such actions are not always clearly separated from the other actions of everyday life: cult can be embedded within everyday functional activity, and thus difficult to distinguish from it archaeologically. The first task of the archaeologist is to recognize the evidence of cult for what it is, and not make the old mistake of classifying as religious activity every action in the past that we do not understand.

Recognition of Cult

If we are to distinguish cult from other activities, such as the largely secular ceremonial that may attend a head of state (which can also have very elaborate symbolism), it is important not to lose sight of the transcendent or supernatural object of the cult activity. Religious ritual involves the performance of expressive acts of worship towards the deity or transcendent being. In this there are generally at least four main components (we will see below how these may then help us draw up a list of aspects that are identifiable archaeologically):

– *Focusing of attention* The act of worship both demands and induces a state of heightened awareness or religious excitement in the human celebrant. In communal acts of worship, this invariably requires a range of attention-focusing devices, including the use of a sacred location, architecture (e.g. temples), light, sounds, and smell to ensure that all eyes are directed to the crucial ritual acts.

– *Boundary zone between this world and the next* The focus of ritual activity is the boundary area between this world and the Other World. It is a special and mysterious region with hidden dangers. There are risks of pollution and of failing to comply with the appropriate procedures: ritual washing and cleanliness are therefore emphasized.

– *Presence of the deity* For effective ritual, the deity or transcendent force must in some sense be present, or be induced to be present. It is the divine as well as human attention that needs to be heightened. In most societies, the deity is symbolized by some material form or image: this need be no more than a very simple symbol – for instance, the outline of a sign or container whose contents are not seen – or it may be a three-dimensional cult image.

– *Participation and offering* Worship makes demands on the celebrant. These include not only words and gestures of prayer and respect, but often active partici-

pation involving movement, perhaps eating and drinking. Frequently, it involves also the offering of material things to the deity, both by sacrifice and gift.

From this analysis we can develop the more concrete archaeological indicators of ritual listed below, some of which will usually be found when religious rites have taken place, and by which the occurrence of ritual may therefore be recognized. Clearly, the more indicators that are found in a site or region, the stronger the inference that religion (rather than simple feasting, or dance, or sport) is involved.

Archaeological Indicators of Ritual

Focusing of attention:
1   Ritual may take place in a spot with special, natural associations (e.g. a cave, a grove of trees, a spring, or a mountaintop).
2   Alternatively, ritual may take place in a special building set apart for sacred functions (e.g. a temple or church).
3   The structure and equipment used for the ritual may employ attention-focusing devices, reflected in the architecture, special fixtures (e.g. altars, benches, hearths), and in the movable equipment (e.g. lamps, gongs and bells, ritual vessels, censers, altar cloths, and all the paraphernalia of ritual).
4   The sacred area is likely to be rich in repeated symbols (this is known as "redundancy").

Boundary zone between this world and the next:
5   Ritual may involve both conspicuous public display (and expenditure), and hidden exclusive mysteries, whose practice will be reflected in the architecture.
6   Concepts of cleanliness and pollution may be reflected in the facilities (e.g. pools or basins of water) and maintenance of the sacred area.

Presence of the deity:
7   The association with a deity or deities may be reflected in the use of a cult image, or a representation of the deity in abstract form (e.g. the Christian Chi-Rho symbol).
8   The ritualistic symbols will often relate iconographically to the deities worshipped and to their associated myth. Animal symbolism (of real or mythical animals) may often be used, with particular animals relating to specific deities or powers.
9   The ritualistic symbols may relate to those seen also in funerary ritual and in other rites of passage.

Participation and offering:

10 Worship will involve prayer and special movements – gestures of adoration – and these may be reflected in the art or iconography of decorations or images.

11 The ritual may employ various devices for inducing religious experience (e.g. dance, music, drugs, and the infliction of pain).

12 The sacrifice of animals or humans may be practiced.

13 Food and drink may be brought and possibly consumed as offerings or burned/poured away.

14 Other material objects may be brought and offered (votives). The act of offering may entail breakage and hiding or discard.

15 Great investment of wealth may be reflected both in the equipment used and in the offerings made.

16 Great investment of wealth and resources may be reflected in the structure itself and its facilities.

In practice, only a few of these criteria will be fulfilled in any single archaeological context. A good example is offered by the Sanctuary at Phylakopi on the Aegean island of Melos – discussed also in Chapter 13 – dating from about 1400 to about 1120 BC. Two adjacent rooms were found, with platforms that may have served as altars. Within the rooms was a rich symbolic assemblage including some human representations. Several of the criteria listed above were thus fulfilled (e.g. 2, 3, 7, and 14). However, although the assemblage was perfectly consonant with a cult usage, the arguments did not seem completely conclusive. It was necessary to compare Phylakopi with some sites in Crete that shared similar features. The Cretan sites could be recognized as shrines precisely because there were *several* of them. One such occurrence might have been attributable to special factors, but the discovery of several with closely comparable features suggested a repeated pattern for which the explanation of religious ritual seemed the only plausible one.

The case for religious ritual can, of course, be more easily proven when there is an explicit iconography in the symbols used. Representations of human, animal, or mythical or fabulous forms offer much more scope for investigation and analysis (see box on Chavín). The recognition of offerings can also be helpful. In general, offerings are material goods, often of high value, ritually donated or "abandoned" by their owners for the benefit and use of the deity. Naturally, the fact of abandonment is much easier to establish than its purpose. Yet collections of special objects, often symbolically rich, are sometimes found in association with buildings in such a way as to make clear that they

RECOGNIZING CULT ACTIVITY AT CHAVIN

SOUTH AMERICA
• Chavín de Huantar

Two views of the Lanzón or Great Image (top, complete image; above, rollout drawing), depicting a fanged anthropomorphic being.

The great site of Chavín de Huantar, high up in the Andes in north-central Peru, flourished in the years 850-200 BC and has given its name to one of the major art styles of ancient South America. Chavín-style art is dominated by animal motifs represented above all in sculpture, but also on pottery, bone, painted textiles, and worked sheets of gold found at this time in different parts of northern Peru.

First discovered in 1919 by the father of Peruvian archaeology, Julio Tello, Chavín de Huantar itself has long been recognized as a ceremonial center, the focus of a religious cult. But on what grounds? Excavations in recent years by Luis Lumbreras, Richard Burger, and others have indicated the presence of a substantial settled population, and also helped confirm the existence of cult activity. In the main text we listed 16 separate indicators of ritual that can be identified archaeologically, and at Chavín over half of these have now been established with at least some degree of certainty.

The most immediately obvious feature of the site is its imposing architecture, comprising a complex of stone-faced platforms built in the earliest phase on a U-shaped plan and set apart from living areas at the site–thus fulfilling many of the criteria of archaeological indicators **2** and **16** given in the main text. Ritual involving both conspicuous public display and hidden mysteries (**5**) is implied by the presence of an open circular sunken plaza that could hold 300 participants, and hidden underground passageways, the most important of which led to a narrow chamber dominated by a 4.5 m (14 ft 9 in) high granite shaft know as the *Lanzón* (Great Image). The carving on this

SECTION THROUGH CENTRAL PASSAGEWAY

E ←—

Lanzón

Lanzón chamber

CENTRAL PASSAGEWAY

Hidden passageways

SUNKEN PLAZA

OLD

TEMPLE

800 ft

250 m

N

Perspective and plan views of the early U-shaped platforms at the site, with a section through the central passageway showing the narrow chamber dominated by the Lanzón or Great Image.

Transformation of a masked shaman (far left) into a jaguar (left). These sculptures were displayed tenoned into the outer wall of the temple, and hint at drug-induced rituals.

shaft of a fanged anthropomorphic being, its location in a central chamber facing east along the temple's main axis, and its size and workmanship all suggest that this was the principal cult image of the site (**7**). Moreover, some 200 other finely carved stone sculptures were

Crested eagle motif from a Chavín ceramic bowl.

discovered in and around the temple, the iconography of which was dominated by images of caymans, jaguars, eagles, and snakes (**4**, **8**). A cache of over 500 broken high-quality pots containing food found in an underground gallery may have been offerings (**13**, **14**) (though the excavator, Lumbreras, believes they were used for storage). There is iconographic evidence for drug-induced rituals (**11**) and the possibility that canals beneath the site were used for ritual cleansing (**6**) and to create roaring sounds to heighten the impact of ceremonies.

The study of Chavín thus demonstrates that a careful archaeological and art historical analysis of different kinds of evidence can produce sound proof of cult activity – even for a site and society concerning which there are no written records whatsoever.

361

are not simply being stored there – for example, objects buried in the foundations, like the extraordinary caches of jaguar skeletons, jade balls, ceramics and stone masks deposited in discrete layers within the innermost structure of the Great Temple of Aztec Tenochtitlan (modern Mexico City – box, Chapter 14).

Notable assemblages of goods are also found in outdoor contexts – for example, the Iron Age weapons thrown into the river Thames in England, or the impressive hoards of metalwork deliberately deposited in the bogs of Scandinavia around 1000 BC. Individual objects found in this way may, of course, have been lost, or simply buried for safe-keeping, with the intention of later discovery. Sometimes, however, so many valuable objects are found – in some instances with rich symbolic significance, and in others damaged in a way that appears both deliberate and willful if further use were intended – that their ritual discard seems clear. A famous example is offered by the *cenote* or well at Chichén Itzá, the late Maya site in northern Yucatán, into which enormous quantities of symbolically rich goods had been thrown.

Identifying the Supernatural Powers

If the supernatural powers worshipped or served in the practice of cult are to be recognized and distinguished from each other by us, then there have to be distinctions within the archaeological record for us to recognize. The most obvious of these is a well-developed iconography (representations, often with a religious or ceremonial significance; from the Greek word *eikon* ("image")), in which individual deities are distinguished, each with a special characteristic, such as corn with the corn god, the sun with the sun goddess, etc.

The study of iconography is, for any well-developed system, a specialist undertaking in itself, and one in which the cognitive archaeologist needs to work hand in hand with epigraphers and art historians (see, for example, the box above on Maya Symbols of Power). Such work is well established for most of those religions that depicted their divine powers frequently. The iconography of Mesoamerica and Mesopotamia generally falls within this category, as does that of Classical Greece. On a painted Maya or Greek vase, for example, it is common to see scenes from their respective mythologies. In the Greek case particularly, we are dependent on literacy for our interpretation. In the first place, it is certainly convenient (although not always necessary if one knows the mythological repertoire) that one often finds the name of a mythic figure actually written on the vase. But the name itself

Identifying the Maya gods: this scene on a Late Classic Maya vase, probably from Naranjo, Guatemala, has been interpreted by Michael Coe as showing God L, a divine ruler of the Underworld identified by the cigar he smokes and his owl headdress.

usually has meaning only because it allows us to place the character within the rich corpus of Greek myths and legends known from Classical literature. Without that it is doubtful whether the scenes would in most cases divulge a great deal.

Where literacy and literary evidence are less widespread – for instance, in Mesoamerica – more emphasis has to be placed on a painstaking study of the different representations, in the hope of spotting recurrent attributes associated in a definable way with specific individuals. Michael Coe has successfully achieved this in his analysis of Classic Maya ceramics. The so-called Popol Vuh manuscript, discovered among the living Maya of the Guatemalan highlands during the 19th century, preserves a fragment of a great 2000-year-old epic concerning the Maya Underworld. Coe's careful research has demonstrated that there are highly explicit pictorial references to this epic on Classic Maya pottery. For example, one of the three divine rulers of the Underworld, God L, can be identified by the fact that he wears an owl headdress and smokes a cigar. His mythical opponents, the Hero Twins, often appear in ceramic scenes distinguished by, respectively, the black spots of death and patches of jaguar skin over face and body. Through this work Coe has not only enriched our understanding of Maya art and myth, but also in the process convincingly shown that Maya painted ceramics had a funerary function (from the Underworld imagery, backed up by the repeated discovery of such vessels in tombs).

The archaeology of death and burial is in fact an important aspect of the study of religion, as we shall now discuss.

The Archaeology of Death

Archaeologists have often used burial evidence as the basis for social interpretations, because material possessions buried with individuals offer information about differences in wealth and status within the community. These points were discussed in Chapter 5. But although the living use funerary rituals to make symbolic statements about the importance of themselves and their deceased relatives and associates, and thus to influence their relationships with others in the society, this is only a part of the symbolic activity. For they are guided also by their beliefs about death and what may follow it.

The deposition of objects with the dead is sometimes assumed in itself to indicate a belief in an afterlife, but this need not follow. In some societies, the deceased's possessions are so firmly associated with him or her that for another to own them would bring ill luck, and there is therefore a need to dispose of them with the dead, rather than for the future use of the dead. On the other hand, when food offerings accompany the deceased, this does more strongly imply the idea of continuing nourishment in the next world. In some burials – for instance, the pharaohs of Egypt or the princes of the Shang and Zhou dynasties in China (and indeed until more recent times) – a whole paraphernalia of equipment accompanied the dead person. As we saw in Chapter 5, in the Shang case, as in the Royal Graves at Ur in Mesopotamia, attendants were slaughtered in order to accompany the deceased in the burial – a practice found in Polynesia too, for example the 40 subjects discovered buried with the 13th-century AD ruler Roy Mata – and here it seems likely that some belief in an afterlife is to be inferred.

In many cultures, special artifacts were made to accompany the dead. The jade suits in which some early Chinese princes were buried, the gold masks in the Mycenaean shaft graves, and the masks of jade and other precious stones accompanying some Mesoamerican burials are artifacts of this kind. Naturally, they had a social significance, but they also carry implications for the way the communities that made them conceived their own mortality, which is an important piece of anybody's cognitive map.

Further inferences can perhaps be drawn from other aspects of the funerary rites: cremation as against inhumation or excarnation; collective as against individual burial; the use of major buildings for the purpose, and so on. Again, these are determined in part by the prevailing social system, and the uses to which the living put their own ideology. But they are also conditioned by the religious beliefs of the time and the culture involved.

DEPICTION: ART AND REPRESENTATION

We can obtain the greatest insight into the cognitive map of an individual or a community by representation in material form of that map, or at least a part of it. Models and plans, discussed above, represent special examples of this activity. But the more general case is that of depiction, where the world, or some aspect of it, is represented so that it appears to the seeing eye very much as it is conceived in the "mind's eye."

IDENTIFYING INDIVIDUAL ARTISTS IN ANCIENT GREECE

Artists were much valued in ancient Greek society for their skill. In the case of vase painting it was quite common for the painter (and sometimes the potter also) to sign the vessel in paint before it was fired. This means that numerous vessels are known from the hand of a single painter. For the Attic black-figure style (common in Athens in the 6th century BC, where human figures were shown in black on a red ground), twelve painters are known by name. It was the great work of the British scholar, Sir John Beazley, in the middle years of this century to assign three-quarters of the surviving black-figure vases either to individual artists (in many cases without a name known to us) or to other distinct groups.

When talking of "style" (see box), we must separate the style of a culture and period from the (usually) much more closely defined style of an individual worker within that period. We need to show, therefore, how the works that are recognizable in that larger group (e.g. the Attic black-figure style) divide on

Exekias, *the 6th-century BC Greek vase painter, signed many of the vessels he worked on. Above, part of a funerary plaque by Exekias, with two mourners. Below, Achilles and Ajax – Greek heroes of the Trojan War – depicted by Exekias playing a game.*

closer examination into smaller, well-defined groups. Moreover, we need to bear in mind that these smaller subgroupings might relate not to individual artists but to different time periods in the development of the style, or to different subregions (i.e. local substyles). Or they might relate to workshops rather than to single artists. In the Athenian case, Beazley was confident that in the main he was dealing with pots painted in Athens, and he was able to consider the chronological development separately. He was also greatly helped by the small number of signed vases, which confirmed the hypothesis that the grouping he arrived at did indeed represent individual painters.

Beazley used both an overall appraisal of the style and composition of the painted decoration on a pot in relation to other pots, and the comparative study of smaller but characteristic details, such as the rendering of drapery or aspects of anatomy. Where the name of the painter was unknown, he would assign an arbitrary name, often taken from a

Two Early Cycladic, female figurines of the folded-arm type, c. 2500 BC, both identified as being by the so-called Goulandris Master. The larger figurine is 63.4 cm (25 in) tall.

collection in which the most notable work was housed (e.g. the Berlin Painter, the Edinburgh Painter). All this sounds highly subjective, but it was also very systematic and the evidence was thoroughly published. Although scholars argue about the attribution of some pieces, there is general agreement that the main outlines of Beazley's system are correct.

But can one, using this procedure, identify individual artists for earlier periods in Greece? Many of the sculptures of the Early Cycladic period (c. 2500 BC) take the form of a standing woman with arms folded across the stomach. This well-defined series has been subdivided into groups, and the American scholar Patricia Getz-Preziosi has proposed that some of these may be assigned to the hands of individual sculptors or "masters," all of whom are inevitably anonymous in this pre-literate period. This proposal meets the criterion that there should be well-defined subgroups within the broader "cultural" style. There is no reason to suggest that these subgroups are chronologically or regionally distinguished. But in order to identify them with a specific "master" rather than, for example, with a larger workshop, it would certainly help to have the key evidence available to Beazley: a few signatures, or at least personal marks, or the discovery of a workshop. Nonetheless, Getz-Preziosi's assignments to individual sculptors are plausible.

The Work of the Sculptor

To re-create, in symbolic form and in three dimensions, an aspect of the world, represents an astonishing cognitive leap. It is a step that we see first taken in the early Upper Paleolithic period, with the portable or "mobiliary" art mentioned in the box on Paleolithic art. Bas reliefs of animals in stone and some clay models of animals are also known from this period. The clay models are smaller than natural size, but are much larger than miniatures. More common, however, are representations of the female figure. These are usually carved in stone or ivory, but a series of female figurines modeled in clay, and then baked (in itself quite a complicated process) have been found at the sites of Dolní Věstonice and Pavlov in Czechoslovakia.

Although the relevant abilities may have been latent within all members of our own subspecies *Homo sapiens sapiens*, it is nonetheless the case that such Upper Paleolithic sculptural work was mainly limited to Eurasia.

In the period of early farming, in many parts of the world, terracotta human figurines, using much the same technology as at Dolní Věstonice and Pavlov many thousands of years earlier, are found. They are certainly widespread in the Early Neolithic of the Near East and of southeast (but not central and western) Europe, and in Mesoamerica. The analysis of these small human figures has illuminated certain details of dress. Some scholars have also seen in them a representation of a near-universal Great Earth Mother or fertility goddess. But the rather weak arguments hitherto produced in support of that view have been effectively dismissed by Peter Ucko – for instance, by showing that most of them are not even clearly female in form. The figurines of southeast Europe have been subjected to iconographic study of the kind described in the previous section by Marija Gimbutas, who has claimed to see certain recurrent deities among them. As she points out, some of them do indeed appear to be masked figures. But the more detailed identifications have not yet won widespread acceptance.

Sculptures approaching life size were produced in prehistoric Malta and in the Cycladic Islands of Greece (see box opposite) – neither of which could be considered urban societies – and life size, or on a truly monumental, larger-than-life scale, in Early Dynastic Egypt and Sumer, and in most subsequent civilizations. Each society had its own sculptural conventions, and each requires specialist expertise to be properly understood and interpreted. The conventions of Egyptian sculpture and art generally are discussed in the box on the following two pages.

CONVENTIONS OF REPRESENTATION IN EGYPTIAN ART

All art styles employ conventions: indeed in a sense the conventions define the style. Where decorative motifs and abstract forms are concerned, the conventions may be entirely arbitrary. But when the aim of the artist is *depiction* – the representation of objects in the real world and of relationships between them – the conventions are more closely determined.

These conventions may be so different from our own that we may have real difficulty in "reading"

them. They therefore require careful study. It is useful also to define the range of subjects represented, and to consider those subjects *not* chosen. The conventions of the ancient Egyptians were investigated

The human body was drawn according to a strictly defined canon. Every body part (forehead, nose, navel, knees, feet, etc.) was at a set point on a standard grid, faces were normally in profile, the torso twisted so that it appeared to be facing forward.

in this way in 1919 by Heinrich Schäfer in his influential work, *Principles of Egyptian Art*, which can still serve as a model for studies of this kind.

The Egyptians did not organize their wall paintings and reliefs primarily by means of perspective. Rather, each object was shown as it was *known* to be. Thus a chest would be seen, usually, sideways on, and, if there were two, the second would be indicated a little out of line with the first. If it was necessary to show that a jar or a chest contained something, that would be shown protruding or on top of the container. The human body also had its standard conventions. As the Egyptologist Gay Robins puts it: "The human figure was represented by a composite diagram constructed from what was regarded as the typical aspect of each part of the body; yet the whole is immediately recognizable. The head was shown in profile, into which were set at the appropriate place a full-view eye

In Egyptian art a single chest was always shown from the long side. To indicate more than one, the chests would be represented slightly out of line with each other.

To show that jars (above) contained incense, the artist has depicted the contents as a ball standing proud of the actual jar. On the left it is entirely visible; on the right partially visible.

and eyebrow and a half mouth. The shoulders were shown full width from the front, but the boundary line on the forward side of the body from armpit to nipple or, on a woman, the breast, was in profile, as were the waist, elbows, legs and feet. It was traditional to show both feet from the inside with a single toe and an arch. ... It made perfect sense to have one form symbolizing 'foot' which was then used without differentiation for both near and far feet." (Robins 1986, 12-14.)

The major figure, whether pharaoh or tomb owner (in a tomb painting), was shown at a larger scale than his or her retainers. These minor figures were organized into horizontal registers placed vertically one above another. This was purely a method

In battle scenes, as in nature depictions, the artist could allow the sense of chaos to show in his work.

Two pictures of a colossal statue being dragged into position by teams of men – one Egyptian (above left), the other Assyrian (above right). The Egyptian rendering is exact in its detail, but the way of depicting the gangs of workers in horizontal registers creates a stilted, artificial effect. The more painterly Assyrian version appears "scenic" to modern eyes.

of ordering; it was not used to indicate spatial relationships or time sequence. But escape from the use of formal registers developed in desert and battle scenes, where forces associated with chaos rather than the ordered world were depicted.

In accordance with the same principles, scenes were shown as much as they were *known* to be as they were *seen* to be, and often a bird's-eye view principle was

The Egyptian artist had considerably more freedom when creating scenes of nature, as in this one of desert animal life.

followed. These principles are admirably brought out by Schäfer in comparing an Egyptian painting of a colossal statue being dragged with

The bird's-eye view principle: the artist has drawn the pool and its surrounding trees as he knew them to be rather than as he actually saw them.

an Assyrian relief of a similar subject (although the latter was carved a millennium later, around 700 BC). The Egyptian picture depicts with meticulous detail what is known. The Assyrian relief, while it follows its own conventions, appears to us as much more "scenic."

Analysis of this kind is indispensable for a proper understanding of such depictions. Indeed, comparable conventions may be seen in the reliefs, paintings, and codices of Mesoamerica (see, for instance, the box on Maya Symbols of Power above).

Pictorial Relationships

Painting, drawing, or carving on a flat surface in order to represent the world offers much more scope than the representation in three dimensions of a single figure. For it offers the possibility of showing relationships *between* symbols, between objects in the cognitive map. In the first place, this allows us to investigate how the artist conceived of space itself, as well as the way in which events at different times might be shown. It also allows analysis of the manner or *style* in which the artist depicted the animals, humans, and other aspects of the real world. The word "style" is a difficult one (see box). It may be concisely defined as the manner in which an act is carried out. Style cannot exist except as an aspect of an activity, often a functional activity. And no intentional activity, or more precisely no series of repeated activities, can be carried out without generating a style. Thus the 7000-year-old paintings in rockshelters in eastern Spain seem to share similarities that lead us to designate them collectively as the Spanish Levantine style. The style appears simplified and schematic in contrast to the more representational or naturalistic Upper Paleolithic cave paintings of southwest France and northern Spain dating to 5000 or 10,000 years earlier (see box above).

Even though the nature of what the act of depiction in itself entails from the cognitive viewpoint has yet to be analyzed in satisfactory detail, the probable purposes of this art are being profitably studied.

The depictions most successfully analyzed so far have been the more complex scenes, shown for instance in mural paintings. One example is the ship fresco from Akrotiri on Thera (box, Chapter 4), where the scene has been variously interpreted as the homecoming of a victorious fleet, or as a marine celebration or ritual – a sort of priestly regatta. Another excellent example is offered by some of the Mesoamerican frescoes and sculptural reliefs, where close study has allowed the elucidation of various pictorial conventions (see also box above on Maya Symbols of Power). For instance, Frances R. and Sylvanus G. Morley in 1938 identified a particular class of Maya human representations as captive figures, that is "subsidiary figures, generally though not always bound, in attitudes of degradation ... or of supplication." By a consideration of this convention, Michael Coe and Joyce Marcus have shown convincingly that the enigmatic *danzante* figures, the earliest sculptured reliefs from the site of Monte Albán in the valley of Oaxaca, some 400 km (250 miles) west of the Maya area, are not swimmers or dancers, as had been thought. The distorted limbs, open mouths, and closed eyes indicate that they are corpses, probably chiefs or kings slain by the rulers of Monte Albán (illus. p.453).

As we remarked for sculpture, the rules and conventions for depictions on a flat surface will vary from culture to culture, and require detailed study in each case. But similar approaches to those described above may be applied by the cognitive archaeologist to any past society – from the Bronze Age rock carvings of Sweden and Val Camonica in northern Italy, to the medieval wall paintings of Europe or India.

Decoration

Art is not, of course, restricted to the depiction of scenes or objects. The decoration of pottery and other artifacts (including weaving) with abstract patterns must not be overlooked. Various approaches are being developed, of which one of the most useful is *symmetry analysis*. Mathematicians have found that patterns can be divided into distinct groups or symmetry classes: 17 classes for those patterns that repeat motifs horizontally, and 46 classes that repeat them horizontally and vertically. Using such symmetry analysis, Dorothy Washburn and Donald Crowe have argued in their book *Symmetries of Culture* (1989) that the choice of motif arrangements within a culture is far from random. Ethnographic evidence suggests that specific cultural groups prefer designs that belong to specific symmetry classes – often as few as one or two classes. For example the modern-day Yurok, Korok, and Hupa tribes in California speak different languages, but share patterns in two symmetry classes on baskets and hats – a link confirmed by intermarriage between the tribes. When more work has been done, this may prove a fruitful method for analyzing patterns on artifacts, with a view to assessing objectively from material culture how closely connected different societies were in the past. But the interpretation of symmetry is undoubtedly more problematic than the formal analysis, and does not always tell us the meaning or purpose of a design, though it may reveal something of the cognitive structure which underlies it.

Art and Myth

At different times, anthropologists have tried to analyze what is special to the thinking, the logic of non-western, non-urban communities on a worldwide scale. This approach often has the unfortunate consequence of proceeding as if western, urbanized, "civilized" ways of thinking are the natural and right ones to help comprehend the world, whereas those others might be lumped together as "primitive" or

The concept of "style" has provoked much discussion among archaeologists and art historians. It is easy for a number of arguments to confuse the issue, and some clarifications are necessary.

Definition Style is *how you do something*. Most writers distinguish between the functional aspect (*what* you are doing) and the stylistic (*how* you are doing it). According to the art historian Ernst Gombrich: "Style is any distinctive and therefore recognizable way in which an act is performed or an artifact made."

Example If we look at any part of the world, we see artifacts made in a distinctive way. The pottery of Mimbres is different from that of the ancient Greeks. Decoration on early Chinese bronzes is different from that on Viking brooches, although both are highly elaborate.

Individual The word "style" derives from the Latin *stylus* (writing implement), referring initially to different styles of handwriting. This reminds us that the term originally referred to the style of the individual (see box above, Identifying Individual Artists in Ancient Greece). The paleographer, working with ancient manuscripts, readily recognizes the different "hands" of a number of scribes. Different hands have been identified in the archives of clay tablets at Knossos in Crete of 1300 BC and written in the Minoan Linear B script, and in comparable archives in the Near East.

A QUESTION OF STYLE

Stylistic Area At the beginning of this century, geographers and anthropologists were preoccupied with the definition of stylistic areas in different parts of the globe. Here one is obviously not talking of individual styles but of shared ways of producing and decorating artifacts. A correlation was established between stylistic area and the area occupied by a given ethnic group.

Several archaeologists in recent decades have taken different views:

James Sackett writes as an archaeologist viewing different assemblages of Paleolithic flint tools. He observes that there are longlasting traditions of style, what he terms "passive style," to be contrasted with active and intentional use.

Stephen Plog, in a study of pottery decoration in the American Southwest, has used a related view, where the degree of similarity in the pottery of neighboring areas is seen to be dependent on the degree of social interaction. Stylistic similarity is here dependent upon interaction.

Polly Wiessner undertook an ethnographic study of variation in projectile points among the San people of the Kalahari Desert. She distinguished between *assertive style*, which is personally based and carries information supporting individual identity, and *emblemic style*, which carries information about group affiliation.

Martin Wobst asserted that "much of what archaeologists label 'stylistic behavior' may be viewed as a strategy for information exchange." Using modern Yugoslavian peasant costume as his example, he showed how variations in dress can convey stylistic messages about status, age, and so forth. Wobst thus firmly links style with the process of information exchange.

There is the danger here, however, of confusing the question of style with the whole matter of non-verbal communication effected by visual means. When Wobst speaks in this way, or when Wiessner gives as an example of emblemic style the use of a flag to convey identity, they are losing sight of the original meaning of the word. It is not appropriate to subsume all visual communication under the rubric of "style."

The other distinctions remain valid. It is pertinent to ask whether we are talking of (1) the style of an individual or of the group; or (2) of a consciously adopted mode of decoration (which may well be shared by an ethnic group), or an involuntary similarity brought about by interaction (cf. Plog), or by shared tradition (cf. Sackett).

The analysis by archaeologists of the information contained in visual form in artifacts and on representations is still in its infancy. Prehistorians are much less practiced at this kind of study than are art historians and Classical archaeologists. There is much to learn.

"savage." In reality, there are many equally valid ways of viewing the world. Nevertheless, such broad researches have led to the basic realization of the significance of myth in many early societies. This was well brought out in an illuminating work, *Before Philosophy* (1946), by the archaeologist Henri Frankfort, one-time Director of the Oriental Institute, Chicago, and his colleagues. They stressed that much of the speculative thought, the philosophy, of many ancient societies took the form of myth. A myth may be described as a narrative of significant past events carrying such relevance for the present that it needs to be re-told and sometimes even re-enacted in dramatic or poetic form.

Mythic thought has its own logic. Most cultures and traditions have their own story of the creation of the world (and of human society), which succeeds in accounting for many features of the world in a single, simple narrative. The Old Testament story of the Creation is a very good example. The creation story of the Navajo American Indians is another.

Thus we should explore oral traditions and written records – where these survive – to help understand the myths and hence the art of such societies. To understand Aztec art, for example, we need to know something of Quetzalcoatl, the plumed serpent, father and creator who brought humans all knowledge of the arts and sciences and is represented by the morning and evening stars. Similarly, to understand the funerary art of ancient Egypt we have to comprehend Egyptian views of the underworld and creation myths (see also box above). We have already seen in the previous section how Michael Coe used his knowledge of Maya myths to interpret their pictorial ceramics.

It is easy for us to dismiss myths as improbable stories. Instead, we should see them as embodying the accumulated wisdom of their societies, in very much the same way that all of us, whatever our beliefs, can respect the Old Testament of the Bible as embodying the wisdom of Israel over many centuries down to the late 1st millennium BC.

Aesthetic Questions

The most difficult theme to treat in the study of early art is in a way the most obvious: why is some of it so beautiful? Or, more correctly: why is some of it so beautiful to us? We can be reasonably confident that many of the objects of display in imperishable and eye-catching materials, such as gold or jade, were attractive to their makers as they are attractive to us. But when it is not so much a matter of material as of the way the material is handled, the analysis is less easy.

One important criterion seems to be simplicity. Many of the works that we admire convey their impression with great economy of means. A near life-size head from the Cycladic Islands of Greece from around 2500 BC illustrates this point very well.

Another criterion seems to relate to the coherence of the stylistic convention used. The art of the American Northwest Coast is complex, but is susceptible of very coherent analysis, as Franz Boas, Bill Holm, Claude Lévi-Strauss, and others have shown.

Such questions have been extensively discussed, and will continue to be. They remind us in a useful way that in trying to understand the cognitive processes of these earlier craft workers and artists we are, at the same time, embarking on the necessary program of seeking to understand our own.

SUMMARY

In this chapter we have shown how archaeological evidence can be used systematically to provide insights into the way of thinking of cultures and civilizations long dead. Whether it be evidence for measurement, planning, means of organization and power, cult activity, or the whole field of artistic depiction – there are good archaeological procedures for analyzing and testing cognitive hypotheses about the past. An archaeological project may focus on one aspect of the way ancient people thought (for example, in the search for a possible unit of measurement, the megalithic yard), or it may be much broader (for example, the work at Chavín, which we looked at from the point of view of recognizing cult activity, but which in its way also touches on measurement, planning, symbols of power, and artistic depiction). The two fundamental points to remember are that methods of working need to be rigorous, and that while textual evidence may be of crucial importance in supporting or helping to assess cognitive claims – as in Mesoamerica or Mesopotamia – cognitive archaeology does not depend on literary sources for its validity.

Further Reading

The following provide an introduction to the study of the attitudes and beliefs of past societies:

Aveni, A.F. (ed.). 1988. *World Archaeoastronomy*. Cambridge University Press: Cambridge & New York.

Flannery, K.V. & Marcus, J. (eds.). 1983 *The Cloud People. Divergent Evolution of the Zapotec and Mixtec Civilizations*. Academic Press: New York & London.

Frankfort, H., Frankfort, H.A., Wilson, J.A. & Jacobson, T. 1946. *Before Philosophy*. Penguin: Harmondsworth.

Lévi-Strauss, C. 1966. *The Savage Mind*. Weidenfeld & Nicolson: London; University of Chicago Press: Chicago.

Marshack, A. 1972. *The Roots of Civilization*. McGraw-Hill: New York; Weidenfeld & Nicolson: London.

Renfrew, C. 1982. *Towards an Archaeology of Mind*. Cambridge University Press: Cambridge & New York.

Renfrew, C. 1985. *The Archaeology of Cult. The Sanctuary at Phylakopi*.British School of Archaeology at Athens: London.

Schele, L. & Miller, M.E. 1986. *The Blood of Kings*. Braziller: New York.

Wheatley, P. 1971. *The Pivot of the Four Quarters*. Edinburgh University Press: Edinburgh.

11
Who Were They?
What Were They Like?
The Archaeology of People

Introductory books on archaeology generally say little or nothing about the archaeology of people themselves – about their physical characteristics and evolution. This seems a strange omission, and one we hope to rectify in this chapter. One of archaeology's principal aims is to recreate the lives of the people who produced the archaeological record, and what more direct evidence can there be than the physical remains of past humanity? Certainly, it is the specialist physical anthropologist rather than the archaeologist who initially analyzes the relevant evidence. But archaeology draws on the skills of a great variety of scientists, from radiocarbon experts to botanists, and the role of the modern archaeologist is to learn how best to use and interpret all this information from the archaeological point of view. Physical anthropology yields a wealth of evidence to enrich the archaeologist's understanding of the past.

A major reason for the lack of integration between archaeology and physical anthropology in the decades immediately after World War II was the question of race. During the 19th and early 20th centuries some scholars (and many politicians) attempted to use physical anthropology to help prove their theories of white racial superiority. This stemmed from their belief that local, indigenous people were incapable of constructing impressive monuments, for instance the burial mounds of the eastern United States. As recently as the 1970s, the white government of Rhodesia maintained that the great monument that today gives the nation its name – Zimbabwe – could not have been the unaided work of the indigenous black population (box, Chapter 12).

Today, physical anthropologists are much less willing to recognize supposedly different human populations on the basis of a few skeletal measurements. That does not mean that racial distinctions cannot be looked for and studied, but a more robust methodology is needed, supported by well-conceived statistical methods to ensure that any variations observed are not simply of a random nature.

The main thrust of the work today is to use the human remains to show the age and sex of the deceased, to examine the state of health during life, and sometimes to establish family resemblances. In the future, developments in biochemistry and genetics may soon allow much more work to be done at the molecular level, instead of relying mainly on the osteology – the study of bones. There is real hope of approaching once again the whole question of racial distinctions, and how these may correlate with ethnic groups: social groups which regard themselves as separate and distinct.

Perhaps the most interesting field of study, however, is in the origins of the human species. When and how did the uniquely human abilities emerge? What were the processes that led to the development of the first hominids, and then of successive forms up to the emergence of our own species? And what changes have there been in the physical form and in the innate abilities of the human individual since that time?

The Variety of Human Remains

The initial step is to establish that human remains are present, and in what number. This is relatively easy where intact bodies, complete skeletons, or skulls are available. Individual bones and large fragments should be recognizable to competent archaeologists (except for ribs which resemble those of other animals and may therefore require identification by a specialist). Even small fragments may include diagnostic pieces by which human beings can be recognized. In cases such as fragmentary multiple burials or cremations, the minimum number of individuals (see box, Chapter 7) can be assessed from the particular part of the body that is most abundant.

The variety of human remains. (Left) At Sutton Hoo, eastern England, the early medieval burials could be recovered only as outlines in the acid sandy soil. (Right) The well-preserved body of a blindfolded girl, drowned in a bog pool at Windeby, north Germany, about 2000 years ago.

As we saw in Chapter 2, purposely made mummies are by no means the only bodies to have survived intact: others have become naturally desiccated, freeze-dried, or preserved in peat. Since so much of our appearance lies in the soft tissues, such corpses can reveal what mere skeletons cannot, namely features such as the length, style, and color of hair, skin color, and marks on the skin such as wrinkles and scars;

tattoos (sometimes very clear, as in the 5th-century BC frozen body of a Scythian chieftain); and details such as whether the penis is circumcised. In exceptional circumstances the lines on fingertips that produce fingerprints, and the corresponding lines on the soles of the feet, may survive – the most famous example being the Iron Age Grauballe man from Denmark. Sometimes chemical action will alter original hair color, but for mummies fluorescence analysis can often help to establish what that original color was.

Even where the body has disappeared, evidence may sometimes survive. The best-known examples are the hollows left by the bodies of the people of Pompeii as they disintegrated inside their hardened casing of volcanic ash (box, Chapter 1). Modern plaster casts of these bodies show not only the general physical appearance, hairstyles, clothing, and posture, but even such fine and moving detail as the facial expression at the moment of death. Foot- and hand-prints are a different kind of "hollow" in the archaeological record, and will be examined later.

Disappeared bodies can also be detected by other means. At Sutton Hoo, England (box, Chapter 3), the acid sandy soil has destroyed most remains, usually leaving only a shadowy stain in the soil – a kind of sand silhouette. If such traces are flooded with ultra-violet light, the "bone" in them fluoresces, and can be recorded photographically. Amino acids and other products of organic decay in the soil may help to identify the sex and blood groups of such "invisible" corpses.

Nevertheless the vast majority of human remains are in the form of actual skeletons and bone fragments, which yield a wide range of information, as we shall see. Indirect physical evidence about people also comes from ancient art, and assumes great importance when we try to reconstruct what people looked like.

IDENTIFYING PHYSICAL ATTRIBUTES

Once the presence and abundance of human remains have been established, how can we attempt to recon-struct physical characteristics – sex, age at death, build, appearance, and relationships?

Which Sex?

Where *intact bodies* and *artistic depictions* are con-cerned, sexing is usually straightforward from the genitalia. If these are not present, secondary character-istics such as breasts and beards and moustaches

provide fairly reliable indicators. Without such fea-tures, the task is more of a challenge – length of hair is no guide, but associated clothing or artifacts may be of help in making a decision. With depictions, one can go no further – for example, in the late Ice Age human figures of La Marche, France, the only definite females have vulvas or breasts, the definite males have male genitalia or beards/moustaches, and the rest of the figures have to be left unsexed.

Where *human skeletons and bone remains* without soft tissue are concerned, however, one can go a great

Skull larger
Brow ridge more prominent

Jaw larger

cranial bones

facial bones

mandible (jaw)

clavicle

scapula

sternum

rib

humerus

vertebra

Rib cage and
sternum shorter

Pelvis narrower and
arch higher

innominate bone

Pelvis wider and
cavity larger

sacrum

radius

ulna

carpals

metacarpals

phalanges

femur

patella

tibia

fibula

Difference in
circumference of tibia

tarsals

metatarsals

phalanges

MALE

FEMALE

Bones of the human skeleton, with salient differences between the sexes.

deal further. The best indicator of sex is the shape of the pelvis, since males and females have different biological requirements (see diagram, previous page). Not all populations display the same degree of difference between the sexes – for example, it is much less marked in pelvises of Bantu than in those of the San (Bushmen) or Europeans.

Other parts of the skeleton can also be used in sex differentiation. Male bones are generally bigger, longer, more robust, and have more developed muscle markings than those of females, which are slighter and more gracile. The proximal ends of male arm and thigh bones have bigger articular surfaces; females have a shorter chest bone (sternum); and males have bigger skulls, with more prominent brow-ridges and mastoid processes (the bump behind the ear), a sloping forehead, a more massive jaw and teeth, and in some populations a bigger cranial capacity (in Europeans, above 1450 cc tends to indicate a male, below 1300 cc a female). These criteria, used in blind tests on modern specimens, can achieve 85 percent accuracy – but females in certain parts of the world, such as some Polynesians and Australian Aborigines, often have very large skulls.

Anthropologists Yasar Iscan and Patricia Miller-Shaivitz have found that measurement of the circumference of the shin-bone (tibia), about a third of the way down from the knee, can accurately predict sex in 80 percent of samples. But the method is much more accurate for blacks than for whites; the length of bones seems more useful for sexing whites, and thus the method requires prior knowledge of the population involved and, to some extent, of its nutritional level. One should not therefore place too much faith in measurements of any one bone, but combine results from as many sources as possible.

But what if the fragments are too small or eroded for this type of analysis, as, for instance, in New Zealand where the soil often leaves bones in very poor condition? Here a chemical method can produce results: between puberty and menopause female bone has a higher level of citrate than male bone. Higher reserves of this salt of citric acid are needed because of the female hormonal cycle, and measurement of its level can give an accuracy of about 90 percent.

For *children* it is worth noting that, with the exception of preserved bodies and artistic depictions showing genitalia, they cannot be sexed with the same degree of reliability as adults, although dental measurements have had some success here. Faced with subadult skeletal remains one can often only guess – though the odds of being right are 50:50, far better than the odds of being right about age.

How Long Did They Live?

However confidently some scholars may indicate the exact age at death of particular deceased human beings, it should be stressed that what we can usually establish with any certainty is biological age at death – e.g. young, adult, old – rather than any accurate chronometric measurement in years and months. The best indicators of age, as with fauna, are the *teeth*. Here one studies the eruption and replacement of the milk teeth; the sequence of eruption of the permanent dentition; and finally the degree of wear, allowing as best one can for the effects of diet and method of food preparation.

A timescale for age at death derived from this kind of dental information in modern people works reasonably well for recent periods, despite much individual variation. But can it be applied to the dentition of our remote ancestors? New work on the microstructure of teeth suggests that old assumptions need to be tested afresh. Tooth enamel grows at a regular, measurable rate, and its microscopic growth lines form ridges that can be counted from epoxy resin replicas of the tooth placed in a scanning electron microscope. In modern populations a new ridge grows approximately each week, and a similar rate of growth has to be assumed in analyses of our hominid ancestors, though this is not yet proven.

By measuring tooth growth ridges in fossil specimens, Tim Bromage and Christopher Dean have concluded that previous investigators overestimated the age at death of many early hominids. The famous 1–2 million-year-old australopithecine skull from Taung, South Africa, for example, belonged to a child who probably died at just over 3 years of age, not at 5 or 6 as had been believed. These conclusions have been confirmed by analyses of root growth patterns and by independent studies of dental development patterns in early hominids by Holly Smith, and by a recent investigation of the Taung skull's dental development using computerized tomography (see below). All this suggests that our earliest ancestors grew up more quickly than we do, and that their development into maturity was more like that of the modern great apes. It should be noted, however, that other scholars argue that Bromage and Dean relied too heavily on data from American juveniles which are not universally applicable, and that the Taung child did in fact develop according to a human pattern. All concur, however, that Taung was less than 5 or 6 years old.

Bromage and Dean, together with Chris Stringer, have also studied the Neanderthal child from Devil's Tower Cave, Gibraltar, dating to perhaps 50,000 years ago, and changed its age at death from about 5 years to 3 years, a result confirmed by analysis of the temporal bone.

Other aspects of teeth can also provide clues to age. After a tooth's crown has erupted fully, its root is still immature and takes years to become fully grown – its stage of development can be assessed by X-ray – and thus, up to the age of about 20, results can be obtained with some accuracy by this means. The fully grown roots of a young adult's teeth have sharp tips, but from about 25 onward they become rounded and blunt because cement is deposited around them. Old people sometimes get dentine in their pulp cavities, and their roots gradually become translucent from the tip upwards.

Bones are also used in age assessment. The fixed sequence in which the articulating ends (epiphyses) appear and become fused to the shafts provides a timescale that can be applied to the remains of young people. The development of the wrist and hand bones is also useful. One of the last bones to fuse is the inner end of the clavicle (collar bone) at about 26; after that

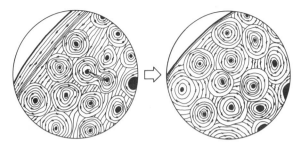

Assessing age: changes in bone structure are visible under the microscope as humans grow older. The circular osteons become more numerous and extend to the edge of the bone.

age, different criteria are needed. Synostosis, the joining of separate pieces of bone, can also indicate age: for instance, the sacrum (base of the spine) unifies between 16 and 23.

The degree of fusion of the sutures between the plates of the cranial vault (top of the skull) was once regarded as an important indicator of age, but recent work suggests that it is too inaccurate. It can, however, still be useful with small fragments in indicating a stage of development, or in differentiating between individuals. Skull thickness in immature individuals on the other hand does bear a rough relationship to age – the thicker the skull the older the specimen – and in old age all bones usually get thinner and lighter, although skull bones actually get thicker in about 10 percent of elderly people.

But what if the bone remains are small fragments? The answer lies under the microscope, in *bone microstructure*. As we get older, the architecture of our bones changes in a distinct and measurable way. A young longbone, at about 20, has rings around its circumference, and a relatively small number of circular structures called osteons. With age the rings disappear, and more and smaller osteons appear. By this method, even a fragment can provide an age. Putting a thin section of a femur (thigh bone) under the microscope and studying the stage of development is a technique which, in blind tests with modern specimens, has achieved accuracy to within 5 years.

Akira Shimoyama and Kaoru Harada have applied a new chemical method to a skeleton from a 7th-century AD burial mound in Narita, Japan. They measured the ratio of two sorts of aspartic acid in its dentine. This amino acid has two forms or isomers which are mirror images of each other. The L-isomer is used in building teeth, but converts slowly to the D-isomer during life through the process of racemization (Chapter 4). The D-L ratio increases steadily from the age of 8 to 83, and is therefore directly proportional to one's age. In this

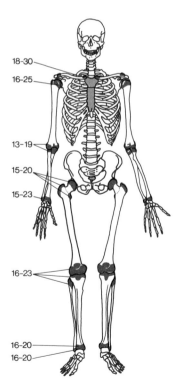

18-30
16-25
13-19
15-20
15-23
16-23
16-20
16-20

Assessing age: the years at which bone epiphyses fuse (dark brown). Areas in light brown indicate synostosis, the joining of a group of bones (e.g. the sacrum at 16–23 years).

case, it was shown that the skeleton was that of a 50-year-old. Since the L-isomer continues to convert to the D-isomer after death, depending on temperature, the burial conditions have to be taken into account in calculation.

Interpreting Age at Death. Once the ages of a sample of remains have been estimated, one can calculate the average and maximum lifespan within that sample. (It should be realized that calculating these lifespans will not indicate what percentages of people in a particular population lived to those average and maximum ages – if most deaths occur in childhood and old age, this would give an average age at death of around 30, even though few people actually die at that age.) It has been calculated, for instance, that the oldest Neanderthalers died before reaching 50, and most died before 40. By combining age information with sexing results, one can also see whether men or women lived longer. For

example, it seems that women in prehistory were more likely to die before the age of 40 than men, no doubt because of the stresses and dangers of childbirth. Among the prehistoric mummies of Arica, Chile, dating back 4000–7800 years, few individuals had lived beyond 50, and the birth-scarred women seem to have died on average two or three years before the men. In 450 skeletons from Roman Cirencester, studied by Calvin Wells, the average male age was 40.8, the female 37.8; both sexes did reach 65 occasionally. In a sample of 40 adults from Wairau Bar, New Zealand, dating from AD 1150–1450, however, women slightly outlived men on average, although members of both sexes tended to die in their early 20s, and the oldest only reached their 40s.

It must be stressed that one can only calculate average age at death for the bodies and skeletons that have survived and been discovered. Many scholars used erroneously to believe that to dig up a cemetery, and assess the age and sex of its occupants, provided an accurate guide to the life expectancy and mortality pattern of a particular culture. This entails the considerable assumption that the cemetery contains all members of the community who died during the period of its use – that everyone was buried there regardless of age, sex, or status; that nobody died elsewhere; and that the cemetery was not reused at another time. This assumption cannot realistically be made. A cemetery provides a sample of the population, but we do not know how representative that sample might be. Figures on life expectancy and average age in the literature should therefore be looked at critically before they are accepted and used by archaeologists.

But it is not sufficient to have a population broken down by age and sex. We also want to know something of their build and appearance.

What Was Their Height and Weight?

Height is easy to calculate if a body is preserved whole – as long as one allows for the shrinkage caused by mummification or desiccation. But it is also possible to assess stature from the lengths of some individual longbones, especially the leg bones. Tutankhamun's height, for example, was estimated from the mummy and from his intact longbones as 1.69 m (5 ft 6½ in), which corresponded to that of the two wooden guardian statues standing either side of the burial chamber door.

The formula for calculating stature from longbones is called a regression equation – the metrical relationship of bone length to full body length. However, different populations require different equations be-

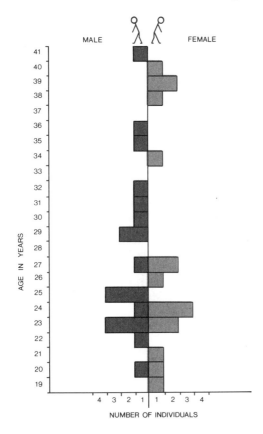

Ages at death of the people of Wairau Bar, New Zealand. Out of a sample of 40 adults dating from AD1150–1450, the majority died in their early 20s.

cause they have differing body proportions. Australian Aborigines and many Africans have very long legs that constitute 54 percent of their stature; but the legs of some Asian people may represent only 45 percent of their height. Consequently, people of the same height can have leg bones of very different lengths. The answer, in cases where the source population of the skeletal material is unknown, is to use a mean femoral stature (an average of the different equations), which will provide an adequate estimate of height, probably accurate to within 5 cm or a couple of inches, which is good enough for archaeological purposes. In Roman Cirencester, people seem to have been a little shorter than today: the average female height was 1.57 m (5 ft 2 in), and the tallest woman was equivalent in height to the average man (1.69 m or 5 ft 6½ in).

Arm bones can also be used where necessary to estimate stature, as in the legless Lindow man (see box below); hand stencils have occasionally been used.

Tutankhamun's mummy was unwrapped in 1923, revealing within the bandages a shrunken body. The young king's original height was estimated by measuring the longbones.

And footprints also give a good indication, since foot length in adult males is reckoned to be equivalent to 15.5 percent of total height; in children under 12 it is thought to be 16 or 17 percent. The Laetoli footprints in Tanzania, which date to 3.6–3.75 million years ago, are 18.5 and 21.5 cm (7.3 and 8.5 in) in length, and were therefore probably made by hominids of about 1.2 and 1.4 m (3 ft 11 in and 4 ft 7 in) in height, assuming that the same calculation is equally valid for pre-modern people.

Weight is also easy to calculate from intact bodies, since it is known that dry weight is about 25 to 30 percent of live weight. An Egyptian mummy of 835 BC at Pennsylvania University Museum (designated PUM III) was thus reckoned to have weighed between 37.8 and 45.4 kg (83–100 lb) when alive. Simply knowing the height can also be a guide, since from modern data we know the normal range of weight for people of either sex at given heights, who are neither obese nor unusually thin. Therefore, armed with the sex, stature and age at death of human remains, one can make a reasonable estimate of weight. A single leg bone could thus indicate not only the height but also the sex, age, and bulk of its owner. Where early hominids are concerned, body size is more a matter of conjecture. Nevertheless, because the skeleton of the australopithecine nicknamed "Lucy" (see section on walking, below) is 40 percent complete, it has been possible to reckon that this hominid was about 1.06 m (3 ft 6 in) tall, and weighed about 27 kg (60 lb).

So far, we have a sexed body of known age and size; but it is the human face that really serves to identify and differentiate individuals. How, therefore, can we pull faces out of the past?

What Did They Look Like?

Once again, it is preserved bodies that provide us with our clearest glimpses of faces. Tollund man, one of the remarkable Iron Age bog bodies from Denmark, is the best-known prehistoric example. Another finely preserved face belongs to the 50-year-old man from Tomb 168 near Jinzhou in China, who was buried in the 2nd century BC and perfectly preserved by a mysterious dark red liquid. Discoveries at Thebes in Egypt in 1881 and 1898 of two royal burial caches have given us a veritable gallery of mummified pharaohs, their faces still vivid, even if some shrinkage and distortion has taken place.

Thanks to artists from the Upper Paleolithic onward, we also have a huge array of portraits. Some of them, such as images painted on mummy cases, are directly associated with the remains of their subject. Others,

Faces from the past. (Far left) Bronze head of the Roman emperor Hadrian (reigned AD 117–138), from the Thames river. (Second left) Moche portrait vase, c. 6th century AD, from Peru. (Second right) Head of Tollund man, the Iron Age bog body from Denmark. (Far right) Mummified head of a man, perhaps the pharaoh Tuthmosis I (1504–1492 BC), from Deir el Bahri, Egypt.

such as Greek and Roman busts, are accurate likenesses of well-known figures whose remains may be lost for ever. The extraordinary life-size terracotta army found near Xi'an, China, is made up of thousands of different likenesses of soldiers of the 3rd century BC. Even though only the general features of each are represented, they constitute an unprecedented "library" of individuals, as well as providing invaluable information on hairstyles, armor, and weaponry. From later periods we have many life- or death-masks, sometimes used as the basis for life-size funerary effigies or tomb-figures, such as those of European royalty and other notables from medieval times onward.

Occasionally, one can identify historical individuals by juxtaposing bones and portraits. The Belgian scholar Paul Janssens developed a method of superimposing photographs of skulls and portraits. By this means one can confirm the identity of skeletons during the restoration of tombs. For instance, a photo of the skull thought to belong to Marie de Bourgogne, a French duchess of the 15th century AD, was superimposed on a picture of the head from her tomb's sculpture and the match proved to be perfect.

There are other ways of proving identity. X-ray investigations in the 1970s of the mummy of an important but unknown Egyptian lady, found in the 1898 royal burial cache at Thebes, showed that her skull resembled that of a woman called Thuya. Thuya was the mother of Queen Tiye who was the wife of Amenophis III and mother of Akhenaten, and probably also Tutankhamun's grandmother – a locket in his tomb was inscribed with Tiye's name and contained a lock of hair. A sample of this hair and a sample from that of the unidentified female mummy were subjected to scanning electron-microprobe analysis by James Harris and his colleagues at the University of Michigan. The almost identical X-ray scatters from these two samples suggested that the lady is indeed Tiye, although more recent work in Germany has cast some doubt on the validity of these results.

A different method has proved to some if not all scholars' satisfaction the identity of Philip of Macedon's remains (see accompanying box). It involved the reconstruction of the skull, and then the building up of facial tissue. The resulting head was compared with a portrait assumed to be of Philip and with written descriptions of his wounds.

Any jewelry or clothing found associated with bodies or skeletons are also invaluable in assessing how these people looked during life. And footprints provide clues about footwear. Nearly all Ice Age prints are barefoot, but one of those in the French late Upper Paleolithic cave of Fontanet seems to have worn a soft moccasin.

How Were They Related?

We have seen that in certain cases it is possible to assess the relationship between two individuals by comparing skull shape or analyzing the hair. There are other methods of achieving the same result, primarily by establishing blood groups from bone and other tissue. This technique has been developed particularly by Imre Lengyel in Hungary using a fluorescent dye coupled to an antibody which reacts with particular antigens, in this case with blood groups.

Blood groups can also be determined from soft tissue, bone, and even from tooth dentine up to more than 30,000 years old, since the polysaccharides responsible for blood groups are found in all tissues, not just in red blood cells, and survive well. Indeed,

HOW TO RECONSTRUCT THE FACE

Richard Neave reconstructs a face, perhaps of King Midas, from skull remains found at Gordion, Turkey, where Midas ruled (738-696 BC).

Attempts to reconstruct faces were already being carried out in the last century by German anatomists in order to produce likenesses from the skulls of celebrities such as Schiller, Kant, and Bach. But the best-known exponent of the technique this century was the Russian Mikhail Gerasimov, who worked on specimens ranging from fossil humans to Ivan the Terrible. It is now felt that much of his work represented "inspired interpretation," rather than factual reconstruction. Currently, the process has reached a higher degree of accuracy.

One of the most successful recent reconstructions has been of human remains from Tomb II at Vergina, northern Greece. These remains were suspected of belonging to Philip II of Macedon, assassinated in 336 BC, who was the father of Alexander the Great. Small family portrait figures in the tomb seemed to support the suspicion.

Richard Neave, John Prag and their colleagues in Manchester, England, first took casts of the cremated fragments of skull, and fitted them together – a difficult task owing to shrinkage of some of the parts, injury

and congenital deformity: the left side of the face proved to be markedly underdeveloped, with compensating overdevelopment of the right. An injury, to the right eye socket (a healed fracture, and a notch on the

Miniature ivory head thought to represent Philip II, from Tomb II at Vergina.

upper edge of the orbit) implied a blow by a missile from above, and tallied with hints from portrait heads as well as with an account by a 1st-century BC author who stated that Philip was hit in the right eye by an arrow at the siege of Methone.

The next step was to insert measuring pegs at 23 key points in the skull: the thickness of soft tissue at these points was known from

modern specimens. The size and distribution of facial features were largely determined by the skull's structure, and therefore the major muscles could be modeled on. Finally, the superficial layers of muscle and skin were added, though their degree of development was far less accurately determined.

Normally this is as far as the skull will allow one to go, though in the case of Philip a detailed scar was added to the right eye based on the study of an almost identical injury received by a present-day Canadian lumberjack! Only after the reconstruction was made was it discovered from reading Pliny's *Natural History* that Philip had received treatment that would have prevented or at least reduced scarring. Other details – hair type /color/style/length, skin color and condition, facial hair, eye color, and the shape and configuration of nose, lips, and ears – were not totally unknown, and were broadly determined by racial type. Facial hair depends on ethnic type (some lack it); configuration of nose, lips, and position of ears are determined within broad limits by the shape of the skull. In Philip's case, the confirmation of his identity meant that certain of these characteristics could be copied from family portraits (for example, the typical nose shape).

Reconstruction in progress (left to right): the frontal bone of the skull from the Vergina tomb; the skull after laboratory reconstruction; a plaster cast with marker pegs in position for the addition of soft tissue; a wax cast of the reconstructed head, with the eye wound rendered to give the impression of Philip's having received minimal medical treatment.

protein analysis by radioimmunoassay (the detection of reaction to antibodies) can now identify protein molecules surviving in fossils which are thousands or even millions of years old, and can decipher taxonomic relationships of fossil, extinct, and living organisms. In the near future we may obtain useful information on the genetic relationships of early hominids.

One potentially major advance in this direction has emerged from the Canadian Thomas Loy's still somewhat controversial analysis of blood residues on stone tools (see Chapter 7). In cases where identification points to human blood, he uses an immunological testing procedure that gives a positive reaction for the presence of human immunoglobulin. One tool, from the site of Barda Balka in Iraq, dates to 100,000 years ago, and the human blood on it is almost certainly Neanderthal.

Since blood groups are inherited in a simple fashion from parents, different systems – of which the best known is the A-B-O system in which people are divided into those with blood types A, B, O, AB etc. – can

Genes, the organizers of inheritance, are composed of DNA (deoxyribonucleic acid), which carries the hereditary instructions needed to build a body and make it work. Genes are copied or "replicated" with every new generation of living cells; DNA forms the blueprint for the cells, and is copied every time a new cell is produced. Thus, when cells are cultured in the laboratory, DNA is being grown. Sometimes a segment of DNA from humans or other animals can be inserted into bacteria and grown in the laboratory. This is called "cloning."

sometimes help clarify physical relationships between different bodies. For example, it was suspected that Tutankhamun was somehow related to the unidentified body discovered in Tomb 55 at Thebes in 1907. The shape and diameter of the skulls were very similar, and when X-rays of the two crania were superimposed there was almost complete conformity. Robert Connolly and his colleagues therefore analyzed tissue from the two mummies, which showed that both had blood of group A, subgroup 2 with antigens M and N, a type relatively rare in ancient Egypt. This fact, together with the skeletal similarities, makes it almost certain that the two were closely related. The exact identity of the mysterious Tomb 55 body is still unresolved, however, some scholars holding that it is Tutankhamun's possible father, Akhenaten, others that it is his possible brother, Smenkhkare.

New work in genetics means that it should soon be possible to work out family relationships through analysis of DNA (see diagram). The Swedish scientist Svante Pääbo has succeeded in extracting and cloning a sample of DNA from a 2400-year-old mummy of an Egyptian boy. Over such a time-period the DNA molecules were broken up by chemical action, so there is no question of reconstituting a functioning gene, far less a living body. But information on the DNA sequences of Egyptian mummies could perhaps indicate the relationships between members of royal families, and determine whether members of a dynasty did practice incest, as is commonly believed.

Genes have also been removed from 8000-year-old human brain cells in Florida by Glen Doran and his colleagues. An American Indian skull (age at death about 27 based on tooth wear), found in 1984 in Windover pond, a peat bog near Titusville, was placed in a brain scanner, and proved to contain a well-preserved and largely undamaged brain. If the genes extracted from the brain can be cloned, it may become possible to discover whether there are any survivors from this particular Indian group.

Pääbo has more recently retrieved some DNA molecules from the brain of an Archaic period American Indian (over 7000 years old) preserved in a skull found in 1988 in Little Salt Spring Bog, Florida. The molecules contained a previously unknown mitochondrial DNA sequence which suggests that an additional group of humans entered America (i.e. separate from the three lineages known to have migrated there – see below), but that they died out sometime after their arrival.

It is now possible also to extract the tiny amounts of DNA left in bones and teeth. Researchers at Oxford, using a technique recently invented in California known as "polymerase chain reaction," have been able to enlarge minute amounts of DNA for study. The team has already extracted and copied DNA from fossils over 5000 years old such as a human femur from Wadi Mamed in the Judaean desert, and from the 4000-year-old skull of a child from Maiden Castle, England.

The recent advances in genetic engineering thus open up fascinating possibilities for future work in human evolution and past human relationships.

So far in this chapter we have learned how one can deduce a great deal about our ancestor's physical characteristics; but the picture is still a static one. The next step is to learn how one reconstructs the way these bodies worked and what they could do.

ASSESSING HUMAN ABILITIES

The human body is a superb machine, but it has not always been able to perform the great variety of actions of which it is now capable. How then do we trace the development of human abilities?

Walking

One of the most basic uniquely human features is the ability to walk habitually on two legs – bipedalism. A number of methods provide insights into the evolution of this trait. Analysis of certain parts of the *skeleton*, and of body proportions, is the most straightforward method, but skulls are often the only parts of our early ancestors to have survived. One exception is the 40 percent complete australopithecine skeleton nicknamed "Lucy," dating from around 3.1 million years ago and found by Donald Johanson and his colleagues at Hadar in the Afar region of Ethiopia – hence its technical name, *Australopithecus afarensis*. Much attention has been focused on the lower half of Lucy's skeleton. The American paleoanthropologists Jack Stern and Randall Susman believe that it could walk, but still needed trees for food and protection – their evidence consists of the long, curved, and very muscular hands and feet, features that suggest grasping.

Another American researcher, Bruce Latimer, and his colleagues, on the other hand, think that Lucy was a fully adapted biped. They doubt that curved finger and toe bones are proof of a life in trees, and find that the lower limbs were "totally reorganized for upright walking:" the orientation of the ankle is similar to that in a modern human, which implies that the foot was less flexible in its sideways movements than an ape's. In short, Lucy's proportions are not incompatible with bipedalism, although it had not yet achieved the gait of modern humans, since the pelvis was still somewhat like that of a chimpanzee.

A different type of evidence for upright walking can be found in *skulls*. The position of the hole at their base, for example, where the spinal column enters, tells a great deal about the position of the body during locomotion. Even fossil skulls trapped inside a rock-hard matrix can now be examined through the technique of computerized axial tomography (CAT or CT), in which X-ray scans made at 5-mm intervals produce a series of cross-sections that the computer can reformat to create vertical or oblique images as required. A skull can therefore be seen from any angle. The technique is also useful for studying mummies without unwrapping them, and for revealing which organs still remain inside them.

Dutch scientists Frans Zonneveld and Jan Wind have used the CAT-scan technique on the very complete skull of *Australopithecus africanus*, 2–3 million years old, from Sterkfontein, South Africa, known as "Mrs Ples." The scans revealed the semicircular canals of the inner ear, entombed inside the solid fossil cranium. This feature is of special interest because it provides an indication of the carriage of the head: the horizontal canal has a relationship with the angle of the head in upright-walking humans. The angle in "Mrs Ples" suggested that she walked with her head at a greater forward-sloping angle than in modern humans. Thus a new technique opens up exciting possibilities for the better understanding of locomotion in early hominids.

Footprints in Time. A great deal can be learned from the actual traces of human locomotion: the footprints of early hominids. The best known specimens are the remarkable trails discovered at Laetoli, Tanzania, by Mary Leakey. These were left by small hominids around 3.6–3.75 million years ago, according to potassium-argon dates of the volcanic tuffs above and below this level. They walked across a stretch of moist volcanic ash, which was subsequently turned to mud by rain, and then set like concrete.

Observation of the prints' shape revealed to Mary Leakey and her colleagues that the feet had a raised arch, a rounded heel, a pronounced ball, and a big toe which pointed forward. These features, together with the weight-bearing pressure patterns, resembled the

The Laetoli footprints. (Top) One of the remarkable footprint trails left by early hominids 3.6–3.75 million years ago at this East African site. (Above) The contour pattern of one of the Laetoli footprints, left, is strikingly similar to that produced by a modern male foot impression in soft ground, right.

prints of upright-walking humans. The pressures exerted along the foot, together with the length of stride (average 87 cm, or 34 in), indicated that the hominids (probably early australopithecines) had been walking slowly. In short, all the detectable morphological features implied that the feet which did the walking were very little different from our own.

A detailed study has been made of the prints using photogrammetry (Chapter 3), which created a drawing showing all the curves and contours of the prints. The result emphasized that there were at least seven points of similarity with modern prints, such as the depth of the heel impression, and the deep imprint of the big toe. Michael Day and E. Wickens also took stereophotographs of the Laetoli prints, and compared them with modern prints made by men and women in similar soil conditions. Once again, the results furnished possible evidence of bipedalism. Footprints thus provide us not merely with rare traces of the soft tissue of our remote ancestors, but evidence of upright walking that in many ways is clearer than can be obtained from analysis of bones.

The study of fossil prints is by no means restricted to such remote periods. Hundreds of prints are known, for example, in French caves, dating from the end of the last Ice Age. Research by Léon Pales, using detailed silicon resin molds, has revealed details of behavior in these caves: we have already mentioned that most of these prints are barefoot. Many of the prints were made by children, who seem to have had no fear of exploring the dark depths of caves. In the cave of Fontanet one can follow the track of a child who was chasing a puppy or a fox. In the cave of Niaux, the prints show that children's feet were narrower and more arched than today.

Which Hand Did They Use?

We all know that many more people today are right-handed than left-handed. Can one trace this same pattern far back in prehistory? Much of the evidence comes from stencils and prints found in Australian rockshelters and elsewhere, and in many Ice Age caves in France, Spain, and Tasmania. Where a left hand has been stenciled, this implies that the artist was right-handed, and vice versa. Even though the paint was often sprayed on by mouth, one can assume that the dominant hand assisted in the operation. One also has to make the assumption that hands were stenciled palm-downward – a left hand stenciled palm-upward might of course look as if it were a *right* hand. Of 158 stencils in the French cave of Gargas, to which we shall return later, 136 have been identified as left, and only

22 as right: right-handedness was therefore heavily predominant.

Cave art furnishes other types of evidence of this phenomenon. Most engravings, for example, are best lit from the left, as befits the work of right-handed artists, who generally prefer to have the light source on the left so that the shadow of their hand does not fall on the tip of the engraving tool or brush. In the few cases where an Ice Age figure is depicted holding something, it is mostly, though not always, in the right hand.

Clues to right-handedness can also be found by other methods. Right-handers tend to have longer, stronger, and more muscular bones on the right side, and Marcellin Boule as long ago as 1911 noted that the La Chapelle aux Saints Neanderthal skeleton had a right upper arm bone that was noticeably stronger than the left. Similar observations have been made on other Neanderthal skeletons such as La Ferrassie I and Neanderthal itself.

Fractures and cutmarks are another source of evidence. Right-handed soldiers tend to be wounded on the left. The skeleton of a 40- or 50-year-old Nabataean warrior, buried 2000 years ago in the Negev Desert, Israel, had multiple healed fractures to the skull, the left arm, and ribs. Pierre-François Puech, in his study of scratches on the teeth of fossil humans (Chapter 7), noted that the Mauer (Heidelberg) jaw has marks on six front teeth; these were made by a stone tool, and their direction indicates that the jaw's owner was right-handed.

Tools themselves can be revealing. Long-handled Neolithic spoons of yew wood, preserved in Alpine lake villages dating to 3000 BC, have survived; the signs of rubbing on their left side indicate that their users were right-handed. The late Ice Age rope found in the French cave of Lascaux consisted of fibers spiraling to the right, and was therefore tressed by a right-hander.

Occasionally one can determine whether stone tools were used in the right hand or the left, and it is even possible to assess how far back this feature can be traced. In stone toolmaking experiments, Nick Toth, a right-hander, held the core in his left hand and the hammerstone in his right. As the tool was made, the core was rotated clockwise, and the flakes, removed in sequence, had a little crescent of cortex (the core's outer surface) on the side. Toth's knapping produced 56 percent flakes with the cortex on the right, and 44 percent left-orientated flakes. A left-handed toolmaker would produce the opposite pattern. Toth has applied these criteria to the similarly made pebble tools from a number of early sites (before 1.5 million years) at Koobi Fora, Kenya, probably made by *Homo habilis*. At

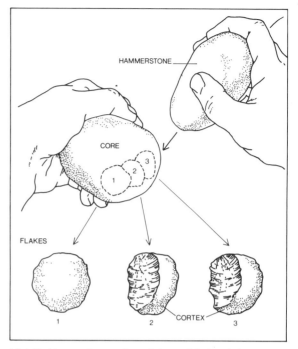

Nick Toth's experiments showed that a right-handed stone toolmaker will typically produce flakes 56 percent of which have the cortex on the right, as here. Tools over 1.5 million years old from Koobi Fora, Kenya, display an almost identical ratio.

seven sites, he found that 57 percent of the flakes were right-orientated, and 43 percent left, a pattern almost identical to that produced today.

About 90 percent of modern humans are right-handed: we are the only mammal with a preferential use of one hand. The part of the brain responsible for fine control and movement is located in the left cerebral hemisphere, and the above findings suggest that the hominid brain was already asymmetrical in its structure and function not long after 2 million years ago. Among Neanderthalers of 70,000–35,000 years ago, Marcellin Boule noted that the La Chapelle aux Saints individual had a left hemisphere slightly bigger than the right, and the same was found for brains of specimens from Neanderthal, Gibraltar, and La Quina.

When Did Speech Develop?

Like fine control and movement, speech is also controlled in the left part of the brain. Some scholars believe we can learn something about early language abilities from *brain endocasts*. These are made by pouring latex rubber into a skull; when set the latex forms an accurate image of the inner surface of the cranium, on which the outer shape of the brain leaves faint impressions. The method gives an estimate of cranial capacity – thus Ralph Holloway has examined two reconstructed skulls from Koobi Fora (KNM-ER 1470 and 1805), and calculated their brain volumes. Skull 1470, dating to about 1.89 million years and usually attributed to *Homo habilis*, had a capacity of either 752 cc or about 775 cc, while 1805, dating to about 1.65 million years and belonging to either *Homo* or *Australopithecus*, had a brain of australopithecine size (582 cc). According to American scholar Dean Falk, 1470's brain endocast shows clearly human features, while 1805 had a brain more like that of a gorilla or chimpanzee.

The speech center of the brain is a bump protruding on the surface of the left hemisphere, which an endocast should theoretically record. Certainly Dean Falk, following on from analyses done by Philip Tobias, argues that this area of 1470's brain is already specialized for language, and that this hominid was perhaps capable of articulate speech. But by no means all scholars are convinced that features of this type in fossil hominids are ever sufficiently clear for reliable interpretation.

Since fine control and movement are located in the same part of the brain as speech, some scholars go on to argue that the two may be interconnected. From this they develop the thesis that symmetry in tools could be a sign of the sort of intellectual skill needed to understand language. The increasing abundance and perfection of form of the Acheulian handaxe, or an increase in the number of tool categories, might imply an elevation in intellectual – and therefore language – capacity.

Others, however, deny any correlation between spatial (technological) abilities and linguistic behavior, arguing that toolmaking and language are not conceived or learned in the same way. Much of the apparent standardization of tools, they say, is probably the result of technological constraints in the material and manufacturing process, as well as in our archaeological classifications. Stone tools alone, these scholars conclude, cannot tell us much about language.

Reconstructing the Vocal Tract. Another approach to assessing speech ability is to try to reconstruct the vocal tract in the throat. Philip Lieberman and Edmund Crelin compared the vocal tract of Neanderthalers, chimpanzees, and modern newborn and adult humans, and claimed that the adult Neanderthal upper throat most closely resembles that of modern infants.

Neanderthalers, they argue, lacked a modern pharynx (the cavity above the larynx or voice box) and therefore could make only a narrow range of vowel sounds, not fully articulated speech. This claim rests on fragile evidence and has not been widely accepted.

However, the vocal tract work has received support from Jeffrey Laitman using a different method. He noted that the shape of the base of the skull, which forms a "ceiling" to the throat, is linked to the position of the larynx. In mammals and human infants, the base is flat, and the larynx high, below a small pharynx, but in adult humans the base is curved and the larynx low, with a large pharynx allowing greater modulation of vocal sounds.

Turning to fossil hominids, Laitman found that in australopithecines the base of the skull was flat, and

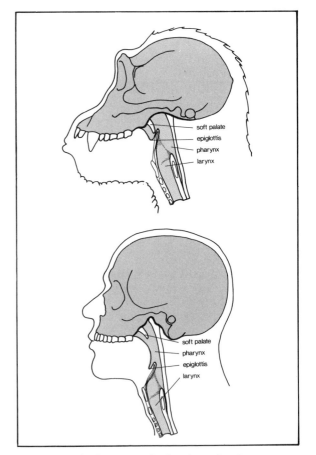

Vocal tracts of a chimpanzee (top) and a modern human (above) compared. The human larynx is lower, and the base of the skull is also more arched – a trait whose origins can be studied in the fossil record.

the pharynx therefore small – albeit slightly bigger than in apes. Australopithecines could vocalize more than apes, but probably could not manage vowels. Moreover, like apes and unlike humans, they could still breathe and swallow liquids at the same time. In skulls of *Homo erectus* (1.6 million to 300,000 years ago), the skull-base is becoming curved, indicating that the larynx was probably descending. According to Laitman, full curvature of modern type probably coincides with the appearance of *Homo sapiens*, though he agrees that Neanderthalers (*H. sapiens neanderthalensis*) probably had a more restricted vocal range than modern humans.

Debate about Neanderthaler speech abilities has been rekindled by the find, at Kebara Cave, Israel, of a 60,000-year-old human hyoid, a small U-shaped bone whose movement affects the position and movement of the larynx to which it is attached. The size, shape, and muscle-attachment marks put the find within the range of modern humans, thus casting more doubt on Lieberman's view and suggesting that Neanderthalers were indeed capable of speaking a language. However, several scholars have pointed out that language is a function of the brain and of mental capacity, and the simple presence of a hyoid is not involved so much as the level of the larynx in the neck.

Identifying Other Kinds of Behavior

Use of Teeth. As we saw in Chapter 7, marks on the teeth of our early ancestors can sometimes suggest that they often used their mouths as a sort of third hand to grip and cut things. In Neanderthalers this is indicated by the extreme wear on the teeth even of fairly young adults, and by the very high incidence of enamel chipping and microfractures, as well as by the jaw and nose that jut forward more than they do in modern people.

The history of dental hygiene may seem of remote interest to archaeologists, but it is certainly intriguing to know that science can now indicate use of toothpicks of some kind by our early ancestors. David Frayer and Mary Russell found grooves and striations on the cheek teeth of Neanderthalers from Krapina, Yugoslavia, consistent with regular probing by a small, sharp-pointed instrument. Such marks have been observed on the teeth of *Homo erectus* and *Homo habilis* as well. For a much more recent period, the 16th century AD, analysis in the scanning electron microscope of the front teeth of King Christian III of Denmark revealed striations whose form and direction indicated that the king had cleaned his teeth with a damp cloth impregnated with abrasive powder.

Use of Hands and Fingers. One can study surviving hands and fingers to assess manual dexterity and labor. Jonathan Musgrave analyzed the hand bones of Neanderthalers and concluded that they gave a somewhat less precise grip than we have between thumb and index finger. The manicured fingernails of Lindow man (see box below) suggested that he did not undertake any heavy or rough work.

Stresses on the Skeleton. Human beings repeat many actions and tasks endlessly through their lives, and these often have effects on the skeleton that physical anthropologists can analyze and try to interpret.

Squatting has been suggested by Erik Trinkaus as a habitual trait among Neanderthalers, on the basis of a high frequency of slight flattening of the ends of the thigh bone and other evidence. The deformed ankle joints of the female prehistoric mummies from Arica, on the Chilean coast, are also thought to have been caused by working crouched, perhaps while opening shellfish on the beach.

Load-carrying can lead to degenerative changes in the lower spine. In New Zealand such changes have been found in both sexes, but in other regions of the world they are predominantly associated with men. On the other hand, females seem to have done most of the carrying in Neolithic Orkney. In his analysis of the skeletons from the Orkney chambered tomb of Isbister, Judson Chesterman noted that several skulls had a visible depression running across the top of the cranium; it was associated with a markedly increased attachment of neck muscles to the back of the skull. These features are known from the Congo, where women get them from carrying loads on their back, held by a strap or rope over the head. In parts of Central and South America, northern Japan, and other regions, the strap goes across the forehead, and can leave a similar depression there. Numerous Aztec codices depict porters carrying goods in this way in pre-Columbian times.

In Mesoamerica, without beasts of burden, human porters like these Aztecs carried loads using straps around the forehead.

Theya Molleson's analysis of human remains from the early farming settlement of Tell Abu Hureyra, Syria (box, Chapter 7), reveals a common crushing of the 12th thoracic vertebra (halfway down the back), probably caused by carrying heavy baskets. Bones in the ankle and big toe bore polished facets attributable to kneeling and pushing with the toes while grinding cereals. The deformed bones are found in both sexes, and in adolescents as well as adults.

Hunting activities may also be detectable from human remains. Neolithic skeletons from a hunter-gatherer site in Niger, some 6000–7000 years old, displayed lesions (the technical term for injuries) representing hyperactivity of certain muscles – in this case, an inflammation of the arms and feet probably caused by the use of bows, throwing weapons, and long runs over hard ground. No such traces were found on females at the site.

Sexual Behavior and Childbirth. Art and literature provide evidence for innumerable human activities in the past and some, such as lovemaking, may not be detectable from any other source. The abundant pre-Columbian Moche pottery of Peru gives us a vivid and detailed display of sexual behavior in the period AD 200–700. If it can be taken as an accurate record, it appears that there was a strong predominance of anal and oral sex, with occasional homosexuality and bestiality – were these methods perhaps adopted as a means of contraception rather than out of preference? We also learn the position that Moche women adopted for childbirth.

Midwives assisting at the birth of a child: a scene from a Peruvian vase produced during the Moche period.

DISEASE, DEFORMITY, AND DEATH

So far, we have reconstructed human bodies and assessed human abilities. But it is necessary to look at the other, often more negative aspect of the picture: What was people's quality of life? What was their state of health? Did they have any inherited variations? We may know how long they lived, but how did they die?

Where we have intact bodies, the precise cause of death can sometimes be deduced – indeed, in some cases such as the asphyxiated people of Pompeii and Herculaneum it is obvious from the circumstances (the effect of the eruption of the volcano Vesuvius). For the more numerous skeletal remains that come down to us, however, cause of death can be ascertained only rarely, since most afflictions leading to death leave no trace on bone. Paleopathology (the study of ancient disease) tells us far more about life than about death, a fact of great benefit to the archaeologist.

Evidence in Soft Tissue

Since most infectious diseases rarely leave detectable traces in bones, a comprehensive analysis of ancient diseases can only be carried out on bodies with surviving soft tissue. The *surface tissue* can sometimes reveal evidence of illness, such as eczema or similar conditions. It can also reveal certain causes of violent death, such as the slit throats of several bog bodies.

Where *inner tissue* is involved, there are a number of methods at the analyst's disposal. X-rays can provide a great deal of information, and have been used on many Egyptian mummies, but newer, more powerful methods are now available (see box, pp. 388–389).

Occasionally, one can study soft tissue that is no longer there: the *footprints, handprints,* and *hand stencils* mentioned in an earlier section. *Fingerprints* have survived on pieces of fired loess from the Upper Paleolithic site of Dolní Věstonice, Czechoslovakia, and on artifacts from many other periods such as Babylonian clay disks and cuneiform tablets from Nineveh (3000 BC).

Some handprints and stencils may supply intriguing pathological evidence. The late Ice Age decorated cave of Maltravieso in Spain has about 30 hand stencils, a few of which have the thumb and joints of the little

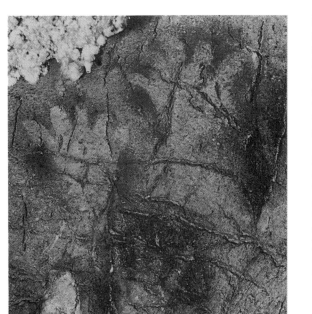

finger missing; this is usually interpreted as ritual mutilation. In three or four other caves, however, most notably that of Gargas, France, there are hundreds of late Ice Age hand stencils with far more severe damage. Some have all four fingers missing. Debate still continues as to whether the stencils were made with the fingers folded, as a kind of sign language, or whether the damage is real but caused by mutilation rather than disease.

Other forms of art from all periods yield evidence for illnesses. The small figures carved in medieval churches and cathedrals in western Europe illustrate various maladies and ills. The Mexican Monte Albán *danzante* figures carved on stone slabs have sometimes been interpreted as a kind of early medical dictionary, with symptoms and internal organs displayed, although the current view is that these figures represent slain or sacrificed captives (see Chapters 10 and 13).

Parasites and Viruses

Where soft tissue survives, one can usually find *parasites* of some sort. The first place to look is in the bodies themselves, and principally in the guts, although body and head lice can also be detected. Parasites can be identified from their morphology by a specialist. A huge diversity of such infestations has been found in Egyptian mummies – indeed, almost all have them, no doubt because of inadequate sanitation, and an ignorance of the causes and means of transmission of diseases. The Egyptians had parasites that caused amoebic dysentery, and bilharzia, and they had many intestinal occupants. Pre-Columbian mummies in the New World have eggs of the whipworm, and the roundworm. Grauballe man in Denmark must have had more or less continuous stomach ache through the activities of the whipworm *Trichuris*, since he had millions of its eggs inside him (see also the Lindow man box).

Another important source of information about parasites is human coprolites (Chapter 7). The parasite eggs pass out in the feces encased in hard shells, and thus survive very successfully. Parasites are known in prehistoric dung from Israel, Colorado, and coastal Peru – but it is worth noting that 50 coprolites from Lovelock Cave, Nevada, proved to have none at all. It is not uncommon for hunter-gatherers in temperate latitudes and open country to be parasite-free. On the other hand some 6000-year-old samples from Los Gavilanes, Peru, analyzed by Raul Patrucco and his colleagues, had eggs from the tapeworm *Diphyllobothrium*, with which one becomes infested from

Hand stencils from the late Ice Age cave of Gargas, France. (Top) Photograph of some of the stencils. (Above) Chart showing the numbers of hands found with particular types of "mutilation." Debate still continues as to whether the hands were indeed mutilated, or were shown with the fingers folded.

When examining human remains it is essential to extract the maximum information while causing minimum damage to the remains themselves. In some cases, such as the mummies of the Egyptian pharaohs, the authorities permit examination only under exceptional circumstances. But a considerable amount of knowledge can be gained by simply "seeing" into a body, and modern technology has placed several effective methods at scientists' disposal.

Non-destructive techniques
Archaeologists are often surprised by what **X-rays** of coffins and wrapped mummies reveal – animal bodies where human remains were anticipated, additional bodies in one coffin, or a mass of unexpected jewelry. **Xeroradiography** goes a step further. This technique is rather like a cross between X-rays and a photocopy, in that it produces electrostatic images through colored powder being blown onto a selenium plate. The result is a much sharper

LOOKING INSIDE BODIES

definition than that produced by normal X-rays; and the wide exposure latitude allows both soft and hard tissue to show clearly on the same image. With "edge enhancement," features are outlined like a pencil drawing. The technique can be used on mummies, either wrapped or in their coffins. When used on the head of the pharaoh Ramesses II, xeroradiography revealed a tiny animal bone inserted by the embalmer to support the nose; in cavities behind

When the mummy of Ramesses II was taken to Paris for specialized medical treatment in the 1970s, it was subjected to xeroradiography. Revealed for the first time was a tiny animal bone at the front of the king's nose; in the nasal cavities were clusters of tiny beads.

the nose a cluster of tiny beads became apparent.

Computed axial tomography using a scanner (hence the abbreviation CT or CAT scanner) is an important method that also allows wrapped mummies and other bodies to be examined in some detail non-destructively. The body is passed into the machine and images produced of cross-sectional "slices" through the body. CAT scanners are more effective at dealing with tissues of different density, enabling soft organs to be viewed as well.

In another technique for looking at internal organs, the body is placed in a **nuclear magnetic resonator**, a device which lines up the body's hydrogen atoms in a strong magnetic field, and causes them to resonate by radio waves. The resulting measurements are fed into a computer which produces a cross-sectional image of the body.

By using a **fiber-optic endoscope** – a narrow, flexible tube with a light source – analysts can look inside a

SUMATOM 2   BWH/HARVARD MED/BOSTON
30-JUN-84   14:34   TS/188   I:44   E53B
ANKH-PEF-HOR   900
                2*   FRONT

body, see what has survived, and in what condition (see box, Lindow Man, below). Endoscopy occasionally reveals details of the mummification process. When inserted into the head of Ramesses V, for example, the fibroscope showed an unexpected hole at the base of the skull through which the brain had been removed (the brain was often broken up and removed through the nose); a cloth had later been put inside the empty skull.

Destructive Techniques

In cases where it is acceptable for the body to have samples taken from it for analysis, there are several techniques at the disposal of the scientist. (It is worth noting that fiber optic endoscopy (above) is also used in some cases for removing tissue.)

When tissue samples are removed, they are rehydrated in a solution of bicarbonate of soda (becoming very fragile in the process). They are then dehydrated, placed in paraffin wax, and sliced into thin sections which are stained for greater clarity under a microscope. Using this technique on Egyptian mummies, analysts have detected both red and white corpuscles, and have even been able to diagnose arterial disease.

Finally, **analytical electron microscopy** (similar to scanning electron microscopy) permits elements in tissue to be analyzed and quantified. When Rosalie David's Manchester mummy team applied it to one Egyptian specimen, they found that particles in the lung contained a high proportion of silica and were probably sand – evidence of pneumoconiosis in ancient Egypt, where this lung disease was evidently quite a common hazard.

Computed axial tomography scanners allow scientists detailed views of mummies without the need to unwrap them. Top, scientists study the cross-sectional image (center, close-up of a similar image) produced by the scanner. The three-dimensional image of the Egyptian Tabes (left), mummified within her wrappings, was also generated by a CAT scanner.

389

eating raw or partially cooked sea-fish. Coprolites in other parts of the New World have yielded eggs of the tapeworm, pinworm, and thorny-headed worm, as well as traces of ticks, mites, and lice. Parasites can also be detected in medieval cesspits.

Certain parasites cause medical conditions that can be recognized if soft tissue survives. Some prehistoric mummies from the Chilean desert, dating from 475 BC to AD 600, had clinical traces of Chagas' disease – notably an inflamed and enlarged heart and gut. The muscles of these organs are invaded by parasites left on the skin in the feces of bloodsucking bugs.

Scabs and *viruses* can also survive in recognizable form in soft tissue, and may possibly even pose problems for the unwary archaeologist. We do not know for certain how long microbes can lie dormant in the ground. Most experts doubt that they pose any danger after a century or two, but there is a claim that anthrax spores survived in an Egyptian pyramid, and infectious microorganisms may also persist in bodies buried in the Arctic, preserved by the permafrost. The dangers in decaying bone and tissue may be very real – especially as our immunity to vanished or rare diseases has now declined.

A safer approach is provided by genetics, since some diseases leave traces in DNA. Smallpox and polio, for example, are caused by viruses, and a virus is simply DNA, or closely related RNA, in a "protective overcoat" of protein. A virus infects by releasing its DNA into the unfortunate host, and some of the host's cells are then converted to the production of viruses. In this way viral infections can leave traces of the DNA of the virus. Analysis of ancient genetic material may therefore help to trace the history of certain diseases.

Skeletal Evidence for Deformity and Disease

Skeletal material, as we have seen, is far more abundant than preserved soft tissue, and can reveal a great deal of paleopathological information. Effects on the outer surface of bone can be divided into those caused by violence or accident, and those caused by disease or congenital deformity.

Violent Damage. Where violence or accidents – known as traumas – are concerned, straightforward observation by an expert can often reveal how the damage was caused, and how serious its consequences were for the victim. For example, one of the Upper Paleolithic skeletons of children from Grimaldi, Italy, had an arrowhead buried in its backbone, a wound that was very probably mortal – as was the famous Roman

ballista bolt found by Mortimer Wheeler in the spine of an ancient Briton at the Iron Age hillfort of Maiden Castle, southern England. A study by Douglas Scott and Melissa Connor of the skeletal remains at the famous battle of the Little Big Horn, Montana – where General Custer and his entire force of 265 men were wiped out by the Sioux in 1876 – showed the extensive use of clubs and hatchets to deliver a *coup de grâce*. One poor soldier, about 25 years old, had been wounded in the chest by a .44 bullet, then shot in the head with a Colt revolver, and finally had his skull crushed with a war club.

In cases where the bones are masked by soft tissue, X-ray analysis is necessary (see Lindow Man box below).

Individual wounds and fractures, however compelling the personal stories they reveal, are nevertheless of limited interest to medical history. It is their frequency and type that are more useful. A community of hunter-gatherers will have encountered different dangers from those faced by a community of farmers, and their skeletal traumas should therefore be different. The aim should be to study the pathologies of entire groups and communities wherever possible.

As with other kinds of archaeological evidence, one has to be alert to the possibility that changes (in this case damage such as broken or deformed skulls) may have been caused by physical or chemical action after burial in the soil. Some human communities have even deformed skulls deliberately, by binding the brow of growing infants, with or without a board, or by applying pressure at regular intervals to produce a frontal flattening. Analysis of two of the Neanderthalers of Shanidar Cave, Iraq, has led Erik Trinkaus to claim that skull deformation was already being practiced at this early date. It also seems to have existed in Pleistocene or early Holocene Australia. Peter Brown compared deliberately deformed Melanesian skulls with normal specimens, in order to identify the

Skull deformation. (Right) Skull outlines of an artificially deformed Melanesian male–dashed line–and a normal male. (Left) A 13,000-year-old skull from Kow Swamp, Australia–dashed line–compared with that of a modern male Aborigine, which suggests that the Kow skull was deformed deliberately.

changes caused by deformation. He then applied his results to skulls from early Australian sites in Victoria, including Kow Swamp, and established beyond doubt that they had been artificially deformed. The oldest specimen, Kow Swamp 5, is 13,000 years old.

One of the Shanidar Neanderthalers, a man aged about 40, had suffered a blow to the left eye, making him partially blind. He also had a useless, withered right arm, caused by a childhood injury, a fracture in one foot bone, and arthritis in the knee and ankle. Individuals such as this could only have survived through the help of their fellows.

Other practices besides skull deformation are detectable. Tim White used the scanning electron microscope to analyze the skull of "Bodo," a large male *Homo erectus* or archaic *Homo sapiens* from Ethiopia, about 300,000 years old, and came to the conclusion that the skull had been scalped. The analysis revealed two series of cut marks, one on the left cheek under the eye socket, and the other across the forehead. These marks were made before the bone had hardened and fossilized, and therefore just before or just after death. Pre-Columbian Indian skulls that were scalped – for ritual reasons prior to burial – have similar marks in the same positions.

Identifying Disease from Human Bone. The small number of diseases that affect bone do so in three basic ways – they can bring about erosion, growths, or an altered structure. Each of these phenomena has many possible causes, but some afflictions leave quite clear signs. *Leprosy*, for example, erodes the bones of the face and the extremities in a distinctive manner, and there are clear specimens from medieval Denmark. Certain *cancers* also have a noticeable effect on bone (see box below, Life and Death Among the Eskimo).

In some diseases, the body produces hard structures distinct from bone – calcium compounds, which form stones in the gallbladder or kidney – and these often survive. Straightforward observation or X-ray analysis is sufficient for most studies of this kind.

Deformity in bone often reveals a congenital abnormality. The tiny mummified fetus of a female, one of two found in the tomb of Tutankhamun, was shown by X-ray analysis to have *Sprengel's deformity* – where the left shoulder blade is congenitally high, and spina bifida is present – which probably explains why the infant, perhaps Tutankhamun's own child, was stillborn. Egypt also provides skeletal evidence of *dwarfism*, a congenital birth abnormality, and the same has been found among Paleo-Indians in Alabama. However, the earliest known example of a dwarf is a male from the 10th millennium BC, no more than

Fetus from Tutankhamun's tomb with Sprengel's deformity.

1.1–1.2 m (3 ft 7 in–3 ft 11 in) tall, who died at the age of about 17 and was buried in the decorated cave of Riparo del Romito, Calabria, Italy.

Calvin Wells' analysis of the 450 skeletons from Roman Cirencester, England, revealed a number of congenital defects in the spine, and five skeletons with evidence of *Spina bifida occulta*. However, the most common ailment was *arthritis*, in most joints of the body, which was found in about half the males. At Mesa Verde, Colorado, in the period AD 550 to 1300, every known individual over 35 suffered from osteoarthritis.

Art may also provide evidence of congenital deformities. The most common motif in the Olmec art of Mexico is an anthropomorphic figure, a child with feline facial features known as the "were-jaguar motif." It often displays a cleft forehead, and a downturned, open mouth, with canine teeth protruding; the body is usually obese and sexless. Carson Murdy suggests that the motif represents congenital deformities, and Michael Coe has argued that the cleft forehead represents spina bifida, which is associated with a number of cranial deformities. Such afflictions usually occur only about once in every thousand live births and may therefore have been restricted to a certain social group, or even to a single extended family. Carson Murdy hypothesizes that a chief's family may have used the phenomenon in art and religion to reinforce their status, identifying their children's deformities with the characteristics of the supernatural jaguar. If "jaguar blood" ran in the family, it would be only natural to produce "were-jaguar" offspring.

X-ray analysis of bone may reveal lines of arrested growth known as *Harris lines* (see box overleaf for a study that detected these lines). These are opaque

LIFE AND DEATH AMONG THE ESKIMO

GREENLAND

Among the most interesting aspects of the study of human remains are the assessment of the state of health, the quality of life, and the cause of death of the individuals concerned.

In 1972, two collective burials were discovered under an overhanging rock at Qilakitsoq, a small Inuit settlement on the west coast of Greenland dating to about AD 1475. The eight bodies had all been mummified naturally by a combination of low temperature and lack of moisture. In one grave were 4 women and a six-month-old infant; in the other, 2 women and a four-year-old boy. The over- and under-clothing (a total of 78 items including trousers, anoraks, boots) had also survived in perfect condition.

The bodies were sexed by the genitalia of those that were unwrapped, and from X-ray examination of the pelvis and other bones of the mummies left intact; in addition, facial tattoos were usually restricted to adult women in this society.

Aging was done from dental development and other physical features. Three of the women died in their late teens/early 20s, but the other three had reached about 50 – a good age, since even at the turn of this century the average age of death for women in Greenland was only 29.

The young boy and one woman may have been in much pain. X-rays of the boy showed that he had a misshapen pelvis of a kind often associated with Down's Syndrome children. A disorder known as Calvé-Perthe's disease was also

Cold, dry conditions resulted in remarkable finds at Qilakitsoq. This six-month-old child (top right) was the best preserved of all the mummies. Leather clothing likewise survived, as in the boot and shorts above. The drawing is of a woman's garment made from feathers carefully chosen from different birds, and worn next to the skin for extra warmth.

Red-throated diver

Goose

Cormorant

Eider duck

Female mallard

Young cormorant

The eight bodies, layers of animal skins between them, lay protected by overhanging rock. Their frozen, moistureless grave resulted in natural mummification.

(Chapter 7) revealed that 75 percent of his diet came from marine products (seals, whales, fish) and only 25 percent from the land (reindeer, hare, plants).

Finally, analysis was carried out to ascertain the possible relationships among these individuals. Tissue typing established that some were not related at all, while others might have been. Either of two of the younger women could have been the mother of the four-year-old boy buried above them; while two of the women aged about 50 (including the one with cancer) may have been sisters. They also had identical facial tattoos, perhaps by the same artist, which were just like those on the earliest known portrait from this area (c. AD 1654). Another woman had a tattoo so different in style and workmanship that she probably came from a different region and had married into the group.

Infrared photography has made the tattoo design on this woman's face clearly visible.

destroying the head of a thigh bone, and he may have had to move around on all fours. The woman, one of those aged 50, had broken her left collarbone at some stage; it never knit, which perhaps impaired the function of her left arm. In addition, she had naso-pharyngeal cancer (cancer at the back of her nasal passage) which had spread to surrounding areas, causing blindness in the left eye, and some deafness.

Some of her features could be attributed to particular activities: her left thumbnail had fresh grooves on it, caused by cutting sinew against it with a knife (and, incidentally, showing that she was right-handed). She had also lost her lower front teeth, no doubt from chewing skins and using her teeth as a vice, like

the Barrow Eskimo in Alaska (box, Chapter 2).

Another similarity with the Alaskan case is that the youngest woman's lungs contained high levels of soot, probably from seal-blubber lamps. On the other hand, hair samples from the mummies showed low levels of mercury and lead, far lower than in the region today.

How these people met their deaths remains a mystery. At any rate, they did not die of starvation. The woman with cancer had Harris Lines showing arrested bone growth as a child caused by illness or malnutrition, but she was well nourished when she died. The youngest woman had a sizeable quantity of digested food in her lower intestine. Isotopic analysis of the young boy's skin collagen calcified formations, a few micromillimeters thick, that occur when growth is interrupted during childhood or adolescence because of illness or malnutrition. They are usually clearest in the lower tibia (shin-bone). The number of lines can provide a rough guide to the frequency of difficult periods during growth. If the lines are found in whole groups of skeletons of the same age group and period, they can indicate crises of subsistence, or, in other cases, some social inequality of the sexes.

Lead Poisoning. Analysis of bone can show that the danger of poisoning from toxic substances is by no means confined to our own times. Some of the Roman inhabitants of Poundbury, England, had a remarkably high concentration of lead in their bones, probably thanks to their diet. It is unlikely that they died of the condition, however.

Three British sailors, who died and were buried 140 years ago on Canada's Beechey Island, Northwest Territories, had been crew members of the 1845 Franklin expedition attempting to find a navigable Northwest Passage. Their bodies, well preserved in permafrost, were exhumed by the Canadian anthropologist Owen Beattie and his colleagues. Analysis of bone samples revealed an enormously high lead content, enough to cause poisoning if ingested during the expedition. The poisoning probably came from the lead-soldered tins of food, lead-glazed pottery, and containers lined with lead foil. Combined with other conditions such as scurvy, this could have been lethal.

Lead in skeletons has also provided insights into the lives of Colonial Americans. Arthur Aufderheide analyzed bones from burial grounds in Maryland, Virginia, and Georgia, dating from the 17th to 19th centuries. He found that the people there had been exposed to lead from the glaze in their ceramics, and also from pewter containers, which they used for storing, preparing, and serving food and drink. However, only the affluent could afford to poison themselves in this way, and this is the key to obtaining social data from the lead content. In two populations from plantations in Georgia and Virginia, white tenant farmers tended to have more lead than free blacks or slaves, but less than the wealthier plantation owners. On the other hand, white servants usually had low levels, especially those working for white tenant farmers. This suggests a sharp segregation from their employers.

Teeth

Food not only affects bones, it also has a direct impact on dentition, so that study of the condition of teeth can

Part of an adult female skull and jawbone from a Jomon-period site in Fujiidera City, Osaka, Japan, with teeth extracted and decorated—presumably for ceremonial or aesthetic reasons.

provide much varied information. Analysis of the teeth of ancient Egyptians such as Ramesses II, for example, shows that the frequently heavy wear and appalling decay was caused not just by sand entering the food, but by the consistency of the food and the presence of hard material in plants. X-ray analysis can in addition reveal dental caries and lesions. The skeletons from Roman Herculaneum had an average of only 3.1 dental lesions each, which indicates a low sugar intake compared with today, as in ancient Egypt.

When analyzing dentition one needs to remember that healthy teeth were sometimes extracted for ceremonial or aesthetic reasons. This practice was very common in the Jomon period in Japan (especially around 4000 years ago), and was applied to both sexes over the age of 14 or 15. Certain incisors, and occasionally premolars, were removed. Indeed, in the later Jomon (3000–2200 years ago), three different regional styles developed.

In Australia the Aboriginal custom of tooth avulsion – the knocking out of one or two upper incisors as part of a male initiation ceremony – has been found in a burial at Nitchie, New South Wales, dating to around 7000 years ago, while the skull from Cossack, Western Australia, some 6500 years old, also seems to have had a tooth removed long before death.

Finally, there is early evidence of dentistry. The world's oldest filling has been found in Israel, in the tooth of the Nabataean warrior buried 2000 years ago in the Negev Desert, mentioned in an earlier section. Investigation by Joe Zias found that one of his teeth was green because it had been filled with a wire that

Medical knowledge: an awe-inspiring set of Roman surgical instruments from Pompeii.

had oxidized. It is likely that the dentist had cheated him. Instead of inserting a gold wire, he had installed one in bronze, which is corrosive and poisonous.

The recent examination of the skull of Isabella d'Aragona (1470–1524), an Italian noblewoman and one of the possible inspirations for Leonardo da Vinci's Mona Lisa, revealed that her teeth were coated with a black layer which she had tried so desperately to remove that the enamel on her incisors was rubbed away. Analysis of the black layer showed that it was caused by mercury intoxication: inhalation of mercury fumes was common in that period as a treatment for syphilis. The result of protracted treatment was a serious inflammation of the teeth, and in fact it is probable that Isabella's death was caused by the mercury rather than the syphilis.

Medical Knowledge

Documentary sources are important to our understanding of early medicine. Egyptian literature mentions the use of wire to prevent loss of teeth by holding them together. Roman texts tell us something about dental treatment. Where general medicine is concerned, there are medical papyri from Egypt, and ample documentary and artistic evidence from Greece and Rome, as well as from later cultures.

The most common and impressive archaeological evidence for medical skill is the phenomenon of trepanation, or trephination, the cutting out of a piece of bone from the skull, probably to alleviate pressure on the brain caused by skull fracture, or to combat headaches or epilepsy. Over 1000 cases are known, and more than half of them had healed completely –

indeed, some skulls have up to seven pieces cut out of them.

Other evidence for early medical expertise includes bark splints found with broken forearms in 3rd-millennium BC Egypt; and actual examples of surgeons' equipment, such as instruments unearthed at Pompeii. A similar kit was discovered in the wreck of the *Mary Rose*, the 16th-century British ship, and comprised items such as flasks, jars, razors, a urethral syringe, and knives and saws.

A set of surgical instruments has also been found in Peru, dating to the Chimú period, AD 450–750. It consists of scalpels, forceps, bandages of wool and cotton, and, most interesting of all, some metal implements closely resembling modern instruments used to scrape a uterus in order to induce an abortion. It comes as no surprise that the ancient Peruvians had achieved this level of skill – we know from other evidence that they routinely did trepanation, and added artificial parts to support faulty limbs. Their pottery displays detailed medical knowledge, including the different stages of pregnancy and labor. It is also clear from Maya codices and Spanish records of the Aztecs that other peoples of the New World had quite sophisticated medical knowhow, including the use of hallucinogenic fungi.

Archaeologists and paleopathologists thus use a wide variety of methods and evidence to provide insights into the health of past peoples (see box overleaf). By combining these approaches with data on subsistence (Chapter 7), we can now go on to examine the quality of diet of our ancestors and the likely character and size of their populations.

LINDOW MAN: THE BODY IN THE BOG

In 1984, part of a human leg was found by workers at a peat-shredding mill in northwest England. Subsequent investigation of the site at Lindow Moss, Cheshire, where the peat had been cut revealed the top half of a human body still embedded in the ground. This complete section of peat was removed and later "excavated" in the laboratory by a multi-disciplinary team led by British Museum scientists. The various studies made of the body have yielded remarkable insights into the life and death of this ancient individual, now dated to the late Iron Age or Roman period – perhaps the 1st century AD – although results from radiocarbon have been conflicting.

Age and Sex

Despite the missing lower half, it was obvious from the beard, sideburns, and moustache that this was the body of a male. The age of Lindow Man (as he is now called) has been estimated at around the mid–20s.

Physique

Lindow Man appears to have been well-built, and probably weighed around 60 kg (132 lbs or nearly 10 stone). His height, calculated from the length of his humerus (upper arm bone), was estimated to be between 1.68 and 1.73 m (5 ft 6 in to 5 ft 8 in) – average today, but fairly tall for the period.

Appearance

Lindow Man wore no clothing apart from an armband of fox fur. His brown/ginger hair and whiskers were cut, and analysis by scanning electron microscopy indicated that their ends had a stepped surface, implying that they had probably been cut by scissors or shears. His manicured fingernails indicate that he did not do any heavy or rough work – he was clearly not a laborer.

Analysis of his skin has found a high copper content, suggesting that his body was painted.

The bog acid had removed the enamel from his teeth, but what survived seemed normal and healthy – there were no visible cavities.

State of Health

Lindow Man appears to have had very slight osteoarthritis; and computed axial tomography (see box, Looking Inside Bodies, above) revealed changes in some vertebrae caused by stresses and strains. Parasite eggs show that he had a relatively high infestation of whipworm and maw worm living inside him, but these would have caused little inconvenience. Overall, therefore, he was fairly healthy.

His blood group was found to be O, like the majority of modern Britons. Computed tomography scans showed that the brain was still present, but when an endoscope (box, Looking Inside Bodies) was inserted to explore

Cereal pollen grain (top) from the small intestine.

Egg of the intestinal worm Trichuris trichiura (above) from Lindow Man.

Cleaning the back of Lindow Man in the laboratory. Distilled water is being sprayed to keep the skin moist.

the interior of his skull it became clear that no brain structure remained, only a mass of putty-like tissue. As explained in Chapter 7, the food residues in the part of his upper alimentary tract that survived revealed that his last meal had consisted of a griddle cake.

How Did He Die?

Xeroradiography (box, Looking Inside Bodies) confirmed that his head had been fractured from behind – it revealed splinters of bone in the vault of the skull. A forensic scientist deduced from the two lacerated

Fully conserved remains of Lindow Man photographed in ultra-violet light to enhance the details.

wounds joined together that the skull had been driven in twice by a narrow-bladed weapon. There may also have been a blow (from a knee?) to his back, because xeroradiography showed a broken rib.

The blows to the head would have rendered him unconscious, if not killed him outright, so that he cannot have felt the subsequent garotting or the knife in his throat. A knotted thong of

sinew, 1.5 mm thick, around his throat had broken his neck and strangled him, and his throat had been slit with a short, deep cut at the side of the neck that severed the jugular. Once he had been bled in this way, he was dropped face-down into a pool in the bog.

We do not know why he died – perhaps as a sacrifice, or as an executed criminal – but we have been able to learn a great deal about the life and death of Lindow Man, who has been subjected to perhaps the most extensive battery of tests and analyses ever applied to an ancient human being.

ASSESSING NUTRITION

Nutrition can be described as the measure of a diet's ability to maintain the human body in its physical and social environment. We are of course interested to be able to learn that a particular group of people in the past enjoyed good nutrition. In his investigations in northeast Thailand, the archaeologist Charles Higham found that the prehistoric people of 1500–100 BC had abundant food at their disposal, and displayed no signs of ill health or malnutrition; some of them lived to over 50. But in many ways what is more informative is to discover that the diet was deficient in some respect, which may have affected bone thickness and skeletal growth. Furthermore, comparison of nutrition at different periods may significantly add to our understanding of fundamental changes to the pattern of life, as in the transition from hunting and gathering to farming.

Malnutrition

What are the skeletal signs of malnutrition? In the previous section, we mentioned the Harris lines that indicate periods of arrested growth during development, and that are sometimes caused by malnutrition. A similar phenomenon occurs in *teeth*, where patches of poorly mineralized dentine, which a specialist can detect in a tooth-section, reflect growth disturbance brought about by a diet deficient in milk, fish, oil, or animal fats. A lack of vitamin C produces scurvy, an affliction that causes changes in the palate and gums, and has been identified in an Anglo-Saxon individual from Norfolk, England. Scurvy was also common among sailors until the 19th century because of their poor diet.

The general size and condition of a skeleton's *bones* can provide an indication of aspects of diet. The adult skeletons of Roman Herculaneum, for example, had leg bones flatter than the modern average, an indication of diet poorer in protein than ours. As mentioned earlier, sand in food, or grit from grindstones, can have drastic effects on teeth. The excessive abrasion of teeth among certain California Indians can be linked to their habit of leaching the tannins out of acorns (their staple food) through a bed of sand.

Additional evidence for malnutrition can be obtained from *art and literature*. Vitamin B deficiency (beriberi) is mentioned in the *Su Wen*, a Chinese text of the 3rd millennium BC, and Strabo also refers to a case among Roman troops. Egyptian art provides scenes such as the well-known "famine" depicted at Saqqara, dating to 2350 BC.

Evidence for malnutrition: detail of a wall relief at Saqqara in Egypt depicting famine victims, c. 2350 BC.

Comparing Diets: the Rise of Agriculture

Chemical analysis of bone allows further insights. After bone has been burnt to ash, atomic absorption spectroscopy can reveal the proportions of various elements (strontium, zinc, calcium, sodium, etc.) present in it. Two burial populations from the eastern United States have been compared using this method. One was a group of hunter-gatherers of the Middle Woodland period (AD 400), while the other was a group of maize farmers of the Late Woodland (AD 1200). In the first group, males and females had statistically identical bone composition for every element. Among the maize farmers, on the other hand, there were significant differences between the sexes, in that males had less strontium and calcium, and more zinc, than females. All of these are diet-related elements, and it therefore appears that there existed dietary differences between the sexes by this period, with perhaps a greater differentiation of roles which may be linked to maize cultivation. The lower concentration of strontium in males indicates that they had more animal protein in their diet than the females, who presumably ate more maize than the men.

A maize diet can have other effects on the body. In a similar study of two eastern North American populations from a single site, Dickson Mounds in Illinois, John Lallo and Jerome Rose found that through time, from AD 1050 to 1300, there was a growing dependence on maize. This seems to have been accompanied by a rise in population density and hence in social contacts, associated with a marked increase in the frequency and severity of damage from disease in bones. They also found skeletal evidence for a deficiency of iron, and an increase in dental defects reflecting nutritional stress. In short, the skeletons showed how economic and social changes can be linked in this case to an increase in disease and nutritional problems.

These findings are supported by Clark Larsen's comparison of some 269 hunter-gatherer skeletons (2200 BC–AD 1150) and 342 agricultural community skeletons (AD 1150–1550) from 33 sites on the Georgia coast (see also Chapter 7). Larsen discovered that through time there was a decline in dental and skeletal health, but also a decrease in the sort of joint disease related to the mechanical stress of being a hunter (men of both periods suffered from this osteoarthritis much more than women). There was also a reduction in the size of the face and jaws – but only females had a decrease in tooth-size, and it was females who had the greater increase in dental decay and the most marked decrease in cranial and overall skeletal size (probably related to a reduction in protein intake and an increase in carbohydrates). These results

suggest that the shift to agriculture affected women more than men, who perhaps carried on hunting and fishing while the women did the field preparation, planting, harvesting, and cooking. Taken together, therefore, the eastern North American data are quite consistent in highlighting the differential effects of maize agriculture on males and females.

At a broader level of analysis, it is difficult to distinguish the effects of different aspects of the adoption of agriculture – not merely a changed diet, but a settled way of life, greater concentrations of population, differential access to resources, and so on. Nevertheless studies of skeletal pathology in many areas are beginning to form a pattern, suggesting that the adoption of agriculture (and its accompanying effects on group size and permanence) commonly led to increased rates of chronic stress, including infection and malnutrition. As in the case of Georgia, a decrease in mechanical stress was replaced by an increase in nutritional stress.

POPULATION STUDIES

In the preceding sections of this chapter we have looked at individuals or at small groups of people. The time has now come to extend the discussion to larger groups and to entire populations, a field of research known as paleodemography. All the techniques mentioned so far can be of assistance here, by helping us to investigate the lifespan of both sexes in different periods, or to assess fertility through the number of births. Study of disease or malnutrition can be combined with sex and age data to cast light on differential quality of life. But there remains one fundamental question: how can one estimate the size of population, and hence population densities, from archaeological evidence?

There are two basic approaches. The first is to derive figures from settlement data. The second is to try to assess the richness of a particular environment in terms of its animal and plant resources for each season, and therefore how many people that environment might have supported (the environment's "carrying capacity"). For our purposes the first approach is the most fruitful. In a single site, it is necessary to establish, as best one can, how many dwellings were occupied at a particular time, and then one can proceed to the calculation. (On waterlogged, or very dry sites as in the American Southwest, remains of timber dwellings can often be tree-ring dated to the exact years when they were built, occupied, and then

abandoned. Usually such results indicate that fewer buildings were lived in during a particular phase than archaeologists had previously imagined.) Assessments of occupied floor area are potentially the most accurate means of achieving population figures. The most famous equation is that proposed by the demographer Raoul Naroll. Using data derived from an examination of 18 modern cultures, he suggested that the population of a prehistoric site is equal to one tenth of the total floor area in square meters.

This claim has since been refined and modified by a number of archaeologists, who found that it was necessary to take into account the variation in dwelling environments. But just as Naroll's original formula was overgeneralized, some more recent equations have perhaps been too narrowly focused on a particular area – for example, "Pueblo population = one third of total floor area in square meters." One useful rule of thumb developed by S.F. Cook and R.F. Heizer, if one is starting with non-metric measurements, is to allow 25 sq. ft (2.325 sq. m) for each of the first 6 people, and then 100 sq. ft (9.3 sq. m) for every other person.

In the case of long houses of the Neolithic *Linear-bandkeramik* (LBK) culture in Poland, Sarunas Milisauskas first applied Naroll's formula and obtained a figure of 117 people for a total of 10 houses. He then tried using a colleague's ethnographic evidence, which assumes one family for every hearth in a long house, and thus one family for every 4 or 5 m (13–16 ft) of house length, and he obtained a figure of 200 people for the same houses. Samuel Casselberry has further refined the procedure for multi-family dwellings of this sort. Using data from ethnography he has established a formula for New World multi-family houses, claiming that "population = one sixth of the floor area in square meters." Applying this to the Polish LBK houses, he reached a figure of 192 people for the 10 dwellings, which is close enough to Milisauskas' second result to suggest that methods of this type are steadily achieving greater reliability, as long as the ethnographic data used are from types of dwelling similar to those under investigation in the archaeological record.

Other techniques are possible. For example, in her attempt to assess the population of a *pa* (hillfort) in Auckland, New Zealand, Aileen Fox used ethnographic data which showed that Maori nuclear families were relatively small in the late 18th and early 19th centuries AD. Archaeological evidence indicated an average of one household utilizing two storage pits on the *pa* terraces. A combination of both sets of data led to a formula of six adults to every two storage pits; thus the site's 36 pits indicated 18 households, and 108 people – a far smaller figure than had previously been believed.

It is also ethnography (primarily the !Kung San of the Kalahari Desert and the Australian Aborigines) that has given us the generalized totals of about 25 people in a hunter-gatherer local group or band, and about 500 people in a tribe. Since bands in Australia and elsewhere vary considerably in size through time and with the seasons, often numbering less than 25, it follows that such figures provide only a rough guide. Nevertheless, given that we can never establish exact population figures for prehistoric peoples, figures of this sort do provide useful estimates that are certainly of the right order of magnitude.

But what of the population of large areas? Where archaeological evidence is concerned, one can only count the number of sites for each region, assume how many in each cultural phase were occupied at the same time, estimate the population of each relevant site, and then arrive at a rough figure for population density. For historical periods, it is sometimes possible to use written evidence. On the basis of censuses and grain imports and other data, for example, it has been estimated that the population of Classical Attica, Greece, was 315,000 in 431 BC and 258,000 in 323 BC.

However, population estimates for wide areas during prehistory are no more than guesses. Estimates for world population in the Paleolithic and Mesolithic vary from 5 million to over 20 million. Perhaps in the future, with improved knowledge of the population densities of different economic groups and the carrying capacities of past environments, we may be able to achieve a more informed guess for the tantalizing question of world population.

Trends in world population: the rate of growth increased considerably after the farming revolution, and has accelerated dramatically in the last two centuries.

ETHNICITY AND EVOLUTION

Finally, we come to the question of identifying the origins and distribution of human populations from human remains. Modern techniques have ensured that such studies are on a sounder and more objective footing than they were before World War II.

Studying Genes: Our Past within Ourselves

Much the best information on early population movements is now being obtained from the "archaeology of the living body," the clues to be found in genetic material. For example, light has recently been cast on the old problem of when people first entered the Americas, and it has come not from archaeological or fossil evidence but from the distribution of genetic markers in modern native Americans (box overleaf).

It may also prove possible to compare ancient DNA, such as that extracted from the 8000-year-old Florida brain (see above), with that of modern native Americans. If the ancient DNA has patterns that no longer exist, this might indicate that the ancient group in question had disappeared or greatly changed. Adrian Hill has established that certain mutations in DNA have occurred in Polynesians, Melanesians, and Southeast Asians, but nowhere else, a fact which supports archaeological and linguistic evidence in casting considerable doubt on theories that Polynesians came from South America.

Other population movements in the distant past have been reassessed through genetic evidence, as a result of which it appears that Africans were the ancestors of modern humans. This has been deduced by James Wainscoat and his colleagues from mapping part of a human chromosome in eight different populations around the world. Members of the same population all tend to carry similar mutations, and populations that are geographically close have very similar patterns; but African samples differ markedly from non-Africans.

Africans have two unique patterns, and only 5 percent of African samples have the pattern most common among Eurasians. It seems, therefore, that the more "recent" Eurasians have lost, or never had, the predominant patterns of African people, a fact which suggests that the founder population of anatomically modern people was small and highly inbred; that there is a big genetic distance between African groups and the others, interpreted as a mark of great age; and that the strong genetic homogeneity among various non-African peoples points to a common center of origin. So does the origin of *Homo sapiens sapiens* lie in Africa? If so, the founder population could have been as small as 1000 people.

A very similar conclusion has been reached by Rebecca Cann, Mark Stoneking, and Allan Wilson by using different and rather unusual genes. Most of our genetic information in the form of DNA is stored in the nuclei of our cells, but other bodies in our cells (mitochondria) also contain such information. However, mitochondrial DNA (mtDNA) is passed on only by females, because the male sperm's mitochondria do not survive fertilization intact. Since mtDNA is thus inherited solely through the mother, unlike nuclear DNA which is a mixture of both parents' genes, it preserves a family record that is altered over the generations only by mutations.

Consequently mtDNA can be used to study the movements of women, and thus provide more information on the origins of modern people. Cann and her colleagues believe that mtDNA mutates at a known and steady rate (about 2–4 percent per million years), so that one can calculate the dates of these movements. These scholars have claimed that we are all descended from one woman who lived in Africa about 200,000 years ago: she has been nicknamed "Eve," although it must be stressed that she not only had a mother herself but lived at the same time as other people. Indeed, many other males and females must have contributed to her or her children's offspring in order to account for the genetic variability we possess in nuclear DNA.

The important point about "Eve" is that she was *not* the first woman, but the ancestor of everyone on earth today. Other females alive at the same time also have modern descendants, but "Eve" is the only one who appears in everyone's genealogy. Some of the other females' descendants will have included generations that produced no children or only males, thus halting the propagation of their mtDNA. This process can still be seen today – it is reckoned that of the French people alive in 1789, only 14 percent have descendants today.

Cann, Stoneking, and Wilson analyzed mtDNA from 147 present-day women from five different geographical populations (Africa, Asia, Europe, Australia, and New Guinea), and found (illus. p.403) that the people of sub-Saharan African descent showed the most differences among themselves, which implies that their mtDNA has had the most time to mutate – hence their ancestors must be the earliest.

However, analysis of mtDNA evidence by other biologists has led to the claim that "Eve" could have

GENETICS AND NEW WORLD COLONIZATION

Northeast Asia and Siberia have long been accepted as the launching ground for the first human colonizers of the New World. But was there one major wave of migration across the Bering Strait into the Americas, or several? And when did this event or events take place? In recent years new clues have come from research into genetics.

An important project led by the biological anthropologist Robert Williams focused on the variants (called Gm allotypes) of one particular protein – immunoglobulin G – found in the fluid portion of blood, the serum. All proteins "drift," or produce variants, over the generations and members of an interbreeding human population will share a set of such variants. Thus by comparing the Gm allotypes of two different populations (e.g. two Indian tribes) one can establish their genetic "distance," which itself can be calibrated to give an indication of the length of time since these populations last interbred.

Williams and his colleagues sampled the blood of over 5000 American Indians in western North America during a 20-year period. They found that their Gm allotypes could be divided into two groups, one of which corresponded to the genetic typing of Central and South American Indians as well. Other tests showed that the Eskimo (Inuit) and Aleut formed a third group. From this evidence it was deduced that there had been three major waves of migration. The first, Paleo-Indian wave before 15,000 years ago was ancestral to all Central and South American Indians, and most North American Indians. The second wave, about 14,000 – 12,000 years ago, brought Na-Dene hunters, ancestors of the Navajo and Apache (who only migrated south from Canada about 600 or 700 years ago). The third wave, perhaps 10,000 or 9,000 years ago, saw the migration from northeast Asia of groups ancestral to the modern Eskimo and Aleut.

How far does other research support these conclusions? Geneticist Douglas Wallace has studied mitochondrial DNA (see main text, p. 401) in blood samples from three widely separated native American groups: Pima-Papago Indians in Arizona, Maya in the Yucatán peninsula, Mexico, and Ticuna Indians in the Upper Amazon region of Brazil. As would have been predicted by Robert Williams' work, all three groups appear to be descended from the same ancestral (Paleo-Indian) population.

Evidence from Teeth and Linguistics

Studies of teeth and languages also tend to support the three waves of migration hypothesis. The biological anthropologist Christy Turner is an expert in the analysis of changing physical characteristics in human teeth. He argues that tooth crowns and roots have a high genetic component, minimally affected by environmental and other factors. Studies by him of many thousands of New and Old World specimens, both ancient and modern, suggest that the majority of prehistoric Americans are linked to northern Asian populations by crown and root traits such as incisor shoveling (a scooping out on one or both surfaces of the tooth), single-rooted upper first premolars, and triple-rooted lower first molars. According to Turner, this ties in with the idea of a single Paleo-Indian migration out of north Asia, which he sets at before 14,000 years ago by calibrating rates of dental microevolution. Tooth analyses also suggest that there were two later migrations of Na-Denes and Eskimo-Aleut.

The linguist Joseph Greenberg has since the 1950s argued that all native American languages belong to a single "Amerind" family, except for Na-Dene and Eskimo-Aleut – a view that gives credence to the idea of three main migrations. Greenberg is in a minority among fellow linguists, most of whom favor the notion of a great many waves of migration to account for the more than 1000 languages spoken at one time or another by American Indians. But there is no doubt that the new genetic and dental evidence provides strong backing for Greenberg's view. Dates given for the migrations should nevertheless be treated with caution, except where supported by hard archaeological evidence.

Evolutionary tree for modern humans, constructed by Rebecca Cann by measuring genetic divergence among living individuals whose ancestors came from Africa, Asia, Australia, New Guinea, and Europe. The tree has 134 different mitochondrial DNA types at the ends of its branches. There is a major split between African and non-African populations, with a common ancestor whom Cann and her colleagues believe was an African.

Two views of the origins of modern humans. (Left) According to this view, after the migration of Homo erectus *out of Africa around 1 million years ago, people evolved into modern humans independently in different parts of the world. (Right) Others believe the genetic evidence indicates that modern humans evolved first in Africa, migrating from there into other continents around 100,000 years ago and replacing earlier* Homo erectus *populations.*

lived either in Asia or Africa. Debate is currently raging over these new approaches to human evolution, not only among the biologists – who are uncertain about the mutation rate and whether it is constant – but among specialists in early hominids as well. The hominid experts either welcome the genetic evidence of a single origin or reject this position in favor of multiple origins and intermixing of different populations, according to their interpretation of the more traditional types of evidence (fossils and tools). With time, the disputes will no doubt be resolved, and the human relationships that modern DNA studies are only just beginning to reveal will be determined with much greater precision.

Genetic research techniques are thus revealing a good deal more about our past than we ever thought possible. This is proving of major assistance to archaeologists and anthropologists. Even the best fossil beds preserve only about one skeleton in every million, but we all carry a record of our history in some of the cells of our bodies. The archaeology of our cells has started to tell us much about ourselves.

SUMMARY

Since archaeology studies the relics of the human past, it follows that the archaeologist's ultimate interest must lie in the remains of the very people who produced the archaeological record. Much of the material in this chapter lies within the realm of physical anthropologists, but it is usually archaeologists who provide them with the specimens for study and who derive great benefit from their findings. A huge range of very varied information can now be extracted from even minor fragments of humanity. We can assess age, sex, height, weight, appearance, inter-relationships; abilities such as walking, talking, and left- or right-handedness; stresses, traumas, and disease; and whether nutritional level was good or inadequate. Finally, the newest field of inquiry – genetic history – is "archaeology within the human body," a kind of ethnoarchaeology where observations made in the present can have tremendous influence on our interpretation of the past. In modern archaeology, human remains have reached center stage, and rightly so since they were, so to speak, the actors in the play we are trying to reconstruct.

Further Reading

The following provide good general introductions to the study of human remains:

Brothwell, D. 1981. *Digging up Bones. The Excavation, Treatment and Study of Human Skeletal Remains.* (3rd ed.) British Museum (Natural History): London/Oxford University Press: Oxford.

Brothwell, D. 1986. *The Bog Man and the Archaeology of People.* British Museum Publications: London; Harvard University Press; Cambridge, Mass.

Ubelaker, D.H. 1984. *Human Skeletal Remains.* (Revised ed.) Taraxacum: Washington.

For the study of disease and deformity, one can begin with:

Brothwell, D.R. & Sandison, A.T. (eds.). 1967. *Diseases in Antiquity.* C.C. Thomas: Springfield, Illinois.

Manchester, K. 1983. *The Archaeology of Disease.* University of Bradford Press: Bradford.

Wells, C. 1964. *Bones, Bodies and Disease.* Thames and Hudson: London; Praeger: New York.

The standard work on population studies is:

Hassan, F.A. 1981. *Demographic Archaeology.* Academic Press: New York & London.

A useful summary by an archaeologist of the genetic evidence for the evolution of modern humans is:

Fagan, B.M. 1990. *The Journey from Eden.* Thames and Hudson: London and New York.

12
Why Did Things Change? Explanation in Archaeology

To answer the question "why?" is the most difficult task in archaeology. Indeed, it is the most challenging and interesting task in any science or field of knowledge. For with this question we go beyond the mere appearance of things, and on to a level of analysis that seeks in some way to *understand* the pattern of events. Yet this is the goal motivating many who take up the study of the human past, whether we are speaking of archaeology or of history more generally. There is a desire to learn something from a study of what is dead and gone that is relevant for the conduct of our own lives and those of our contemporaries today. Archaeology, which allows us to study early and remote prehistoric periods as well as the more recent historical ones, is unique among the human sciences in offering a considerable time depth. Thus, if there are patterns to be found among human affairs, the archaeological timescale may reveal them.

The eminent French historian Fernand Braudel distinguished three levels of historical events, and of historical analysis. At the surface, so to speak, are the specific occurrences of human history: *l'histoire événementielle*, as he termed it. Beneath these superficial happenings lie slower rhythms, including the cycles identified by economists with a periodicity measured perhaps in decades. Finally, beneath these rhythms are the basic, long-term trends, the *longue durée*, which usually prevail in the end.

That is only one man's view. Even so, it hints at the complexity of trying to explain history. Indeed, there is no agreed and accepted way of setting out to understand the human past. A chapter such as this is therefore bound to be inconclusive, and certain to be controversial. Yet it is a chapter worth writing and worth thinking about, for it is in this area of inquiry that archaeological research is now most active.

The past 25 years have seen the re-emergence of the use of archaeological theory. For several decades, the whole subject of explanation was in the doldrums.

However, with the development of the New Archaeology in the 1960s, and the accompanying "loss of innocence," came the realization that there was no well-established body of theory to underpin current methods of archaeological inquiry. To a large extent this is still true, although there have been many attempts sparked off by the processual approach of the New Archaeology to provide an underlying body of theory. Today there is a superabundance of approaches to explaining "why?." The archaeological literature is awash with polemical discussions between positivists, Marxists, structuralists, "post-processualists," etc., all claiming some special insight.

The early New Archaeology involved the explicit use of theory and of models, and above all of generalization. Subsequently, it was criticized as too "functionalist," too much concerned with ecological aspects of adaptation and with efficiency, and with the purely utilitarian and functional aspects of living. Meanwhile, an alternative perspective, inspired by Marxism, was laying more stress on social relations and the exercise of power. Nevertheless, the processual and Marxist approaches have much in common: they are compatible, as we show below, even though they use rather different terminologies (some would say jargons) to express their views.

In the 1970s, in reaction to the processual "functionalists," a structuralist archaeology was proclaimed, then a post-structuralist, and, finally, a "post-processual" one. These performed a useful service in stressing that the ideas and beliefs of past societies should no longer be overlooked in archaeological explanation.

In the 1980s, several of the practitioners of processual archaeology sought ways of dealing with the cognitive aspects of past societies in the framework of processual thinking. This "cognitive-processual" approach seeks to enlarge the scope of the now-traditional processual archaeology by stressing social and cognitive aspects, yet without rejecting the value of earlier work. We shall therefore discuss approaches to the explanation of the past in these terms, fully realizing that, when so many different schools of thought are in existence, no complete consensus is possible. "Why" questions are significant ones, but the answers given depend to a considerable extent on one's perceptions and preconceptions. In emphasizing the variety displayed in current approaches towards explanation in archaeology, we are perhaps revealing one of contemporary archaeology's greatest strengths – that it is as exciting at the intellectual level as it is rich in its subject material.

What Are We Trying to Explain?

Many of the current debates about archaeological explanation fail to notice that different workers are intent on explaining different things. Pronouncements about valid methods frequently appear contradictory, yet the contradiction often disappears when we realize the vast differences between the individual cases in question. For instance, an archaeologist seeking to explain the distribution of humankind during the last Ice Age, using timescales that are accurate only to within a few thousand years, will often lean more heavily on climatic and vegetational factors than on other aspects of community affairs. Such explanations at first sight lay themselves open to charges of "ecological determinism" – that changes in the environment automatically determine changes in human society. Certainly, a researchworker studying the designs on glazed tile floors of the Middle Ages would propose explanations far removed from the world of Paleolithic hunter-gatherers.

First, therefore, let us distinguish between some of the different things we may be trying to explain: they may, in fact, require different kinds of explanation.

Explaining Specific Conditions of Burial and Preservation. Our concern with a particular find or site may be with the essentially natural processes that have resulted in burial and preservation. These are the kind of processes that the American archaeologist Michael Schiffer has called "N-transforms" (i.e. the work of natural processes) to distinguish them from "C-transforms" (the work of culturally determined processes resulting from human actions) (see Chapter 2). The types of question one might be trying to answer are: How did these animal bones come to be buried with those tools? Why are these textiles so well preserved?

Explaining a Specific Event. Our concern may be to explain why a specific event took place. The philosopher of history R.G. Collingwood used to ask, "Why did Caesar cross the Rubicon?" Archaeology is less often concerned with events in the lives of named individuals, but it will still ask such specific questions as, "What caused the Classic Maya collapse?," or, "Why was the Second City at Troy destroyed when it was?"

Explaining a Specific Pattern of Events. Often, the archaeologist perceives some pattern in the archaeological record, and it is this pattern rather than a single, specific occurrence that seems to require explanation. A good example is offered by the "elm decline" in Neolithic Europe. Pollen sequences in much of northern Europe show that the percentage of elm pollen declined markedly, although the absolute date for the decline is not the same in each area. Why was this? Is the explanation climatic change? Did some pest attack the trees? Or was there a change in the pattern of exploitation by humans? The answer may not yet be clear: what is clear is that there is a pattern in need of explanation. (For a possible explanation of the elm decline, refer to Chapter 6.)

Explaining a Class of Events. Generalization, as we shall see, is still rare in archaeology. Yet some of the most interesting explanations of change concern not just one single event or pattern of events, but a whole, more general class of events. For instance, we might regard the development of food production in the Near East at the end of the last Ice Age as constituting a pattern of change over a wide area. We might say the same of the development of food production in Mesoamerica. When we compare the two, and then bring into consideration the inception of food production in China and in Southeast Asia, and then in sub-Saharan Africa, we are dealing with phenomena that may be unconnected. Yet it is remarkable that food production seems to have begun in all these areas within a relatively short timespan in the post-Pleistocene period. Why is this? Here, then, is a class of events that demands an explanation. (For one proposed explanation, see box below, p. 413.)

Another example is the emergence of state societies – of cities and "civilization" – in different parts of the world, some of these areas apparently not in significant contact with each other. How do we explain such a phenomenon? The issue of the rise of complex society is one of the most actively debated in contemporary archaeology and is discussed further below. Another example, the phenomenon of system collapse in early state societies, is likewise looked at in some detail later in the chapter.

Explaining a Process. In some cases, the problem is not to explain a given event or pattern or even a class of events. Instead, insight may be sought into processes at work in society of a continuous and long-enduring nature. The phenomenon of the intensification of agricultural production may be of this kind, or the development of ranked society. These processes may be seen as something common to large parts of humankind, at least under certain conditions. To explain such processes may by no means be an easy task, but their understanding must be one of the essential goals of archaeological and anthropological research.

As we shall see, there are many different kinds of explanation on offer. Some are more suitable for one of these types of problem than for others. This needs bearing in mind.

HOW TO CONSTRUCT A "TRADITIONAL" EXPLANATION

The term "traditional" is used here deliberately in a somewhat critical or pejorative sense. The New Archaeology made us much more aware of the shortcomings of traditional archaeological explanations. These shortcomings can be made clearer in an example of the traditional method – the appearance of a new kind of pottery in a given area and period, the pottery being distinguished by shapes not previously recognized and by new decorative motifs.

The traditional approach, in its own way a systematic one, will very properly require a closer definition of this pottery style in space and time. The archaeologist will be expected to draw a distribution map of its occurrence, and also to establish its place in the stratigraphic sequence at the sites where it occurs. The next step is to assign it to its place within an archaeological *culture*, defined (following Gordon Childe) as a "constantly recurring assemblage of artifacts." The pottery may itself be one of its most conspicuous features, but there will be others with which it is associated.

Using the traditional approach, it is argued that each archaeological culture is the manifestation in material terms of a specific *people* – that is, a well-defined ethnic group, detectable by the archaeologist by the method just outlined. This is an ethnic classification, but of course the "people," being prehistoric, will have to be given an arbitrary name. Usually, they will be named after the place where the pottery was first recognized (e.g. the Mimbres people in the American Southwest or the Windmill Hill people in Neolithic Britain), or sometimes after the pottery itself (e.g. the Beaker Folk).

Next it is usual to see if it is possible to think in terms of a folk *migration* to explain the changes observed. Can we locate a convenient homeland for this group of people? Careful study of the ceramic assemblages in adjoining lands may suggest such a homeland, and perhaps even a migration route.

Alternatively, if the migration argument does not seem to work, a fourth approach is to look for specific features of the cultural assemblage that have *parallels* in more distant lands. If the whole assemblage cannot be ascribed to an external source, there may be specific features of it that can. Links may be found with more civilized lands. If such "parallels" can be discovered, the traditionalist would argue that these were the points of origin, of departure as it were, for the features in our assemblage, and were transmitted to it by a process of cultural *diffusion*. Indeed, before the advent of radiocarbon dating, these parallels could also be used to date the pottery finds in our hypothetical example, because the features and traits lying closer to the heartlands of civilization would almost certainly already be dated through comparison with the historical chronology of that civilization itself. The occurrences of these traits may offer a *chronological horizon*, which will be of great use in dating the culture.

It would be easy to find many actual examples of such explanations. For instance, in the New World, the very striking developments in architecture and other crafts in Chaco Canyon in New Mexico, and with it Mesa Verde in Colorado, have been explained by comparisons of precisely this kind with the more "advanced" civilizations of Mexico to the south. Similarly, for a long time archaeologists in what is now Zimbabwe attempted misguidedly to explain the great stone monuments at the site of Great Zimbabwe in this way by saying it was built by foreigners, not by the indigenous Shona people (see box overleaf).

Traditional explanations rest, however, on assumptions that are easily challenged today.

First, there is the notion among traditionalists that archaeological "cultures" can somehow represent real entities rather than merely the classificatory terms devised for the convenience of the scholar. Second is the view that ethnic units or "peoples" can be recognized from the archaeological record by equation

DIFFUSIONIST EXPLANATION REJECTED: GREAT ZIMBABWE

AFRICA

Great Zimbabwe

The remarkable monument of Great Zimbabwe, near Fort Victoria in modern Zimbabwe, has been the object of intense speculation ever since this region of Africa was first explored by Europeans in the 19th century. For here was an impressive structure of great sophistication, with beautifully finished stonework.

Early scholars followed the traditional pattern of explanation in ascribing Great Zimbabwe to architects and builders from more civilized lands to the north. On a visit to the site by the British explorer Cecil Rhodes, the local Karange chiefs were told that "the Great Master" had come "to see the ancient temple which once upon a time belonged to white men." One writer in 1896 took the view that Great Zimbabwe was Phoenician in origin.

The first excavator, J.T. Bent, tried to establish parallels – points of similarity – between the finds and features found in more sophisticated contexts in the Near East. He concluded: "The ruins and the things in them are not in any way connected with any known African race," and he located the builders in the Arabian peninsula. This was thus a migrationist view.

Much more systematic excavations were undertaken by Gertrude Caton-Thompson, and she concluded her report in 1931: "Examination of all the existing evidence, gathered from every quarter, still can produce not one single item that is not in accordance with the claim of Bantu origin and medieval date." Despite her carefully documented conclusions, however, other archaeologists continued to follow the typical pattern of diffusionist explanation in speaking of "influences" from "higher centers of culture." Portuguese traders were one favored source of inspiration. But if the date of the monument was to be set earlier than European travelers, then Arab merchants in the Indian Ocean offered an alternative. As late as 1971, R. Summers could write, using a familiar diffusionist argument: "It is not unduly stretching probability to suggest some Portuguese stonemason may have reached Zimbabwe and entered the service of the great chief living there… Equally probably, although rather less plausible, is that some travelling Arab craftsman may have been responsible."

Subsequent research has backed up the conclusions of Caton-Thompson. Great Zimbabwe is now seen as the most notable of a larger class of monuments in this area.

Although the site has an earlier history, the construction of a monumental building probably began there in the 13th century AD, and the site reached its climax in the 15th century. Various archaeologists have now been able to give a coherent picture of the economic and social conditions in the area that made this great achievement possible. Significant influence – diffusion – from more "advanced" areas is no longer part of that picture. Today a processual framework of explanation has replaced the diffusionist one.

Carved soapstone *bird found in the Great Zimbabwe Eastern Enclosure in 1889, and later sold to Cecil Rhodes.*

An aerial view *(right) of the Elliptical Building.*

THE RIDDLE OF RHODESIA?

ZIMBABWE

Racism and archaeology: a subservient black slave presents his offering of gold to a ghostly Queen of Sheba in this Rhodesian government poster of 1938.

Site plan: the Elliptical Building, with its series of enclosed areas, platforms, and the conical tower displayed in the poster (shown above).

with these notional cultures. It is in fact clear that ethnic groups do not always stand out clearly in archaeological remains (the point is discussed further in the box on language and ethnicity in Chapter 5). Third, it is assumed that when resemblances are noted between the cultural assemblages of one area and another, this can be most readily explained as the result of a migration of people. Of course, migrations did indeed occur (see below), but they are not so easy to document archaeologically as has often been supposed. Finally, there is the principle of explanation through the diffusion of culture. Today, it is felt that this explanation has sometimes been overplayed, and nearly always oversimplified. For although contact between areas, not least through trade, can be of great significance for the developments in each area, the effects of this contact have to be considered in detail: explanation simply in terms of diffusion is not enough.

The traditional approach led to a kind of explanation which, in the words of Gordon Childe, "aimed at distilling from archaeological remains a preliterate substitute for the conventional politico-military history with cultures, instead of statesmen, as actors, and migrations in place of battles." Today, we need different approaches.

Nevertheless it is worth emphasizing that migrations did indeed take place in the past, and on rare occasions this can be documented archaeologically. The first colonization of the Polynesian islands in the Pacific Ocean offers a good example. A complex of finds – especially pottery with incised decoration – known as the Lapita culture provides a record of the rapid movement of islanders eastwards across a vast previously uninhabited area, from the northern New Guinea region to as far as Samoa, between 1600 and 1000 BC (see map overleaf).

It should also be remembered that innovations are frequently made in one place and adopted in neighboring areas, and it is still perfectly proper to speak of the mechanism as one of diffusion (see illustration of the origins of the Roman alphabet overleaf). Moreover, as archaeologists have recently argued afresh, interactions between societies are certainly an important element in cultural change (Chapter 9). The objection to the use of the term "diffusion" is, however, that it explains little in itself. A good explanation may indeed involve the notion of an innovation that reaches an area from outside its boundaries. But it will also lay much more emphasis on the local conditions – on social and economic factors that make the innovation effective – as well as on the precise nature of the interactions between areas, a question considered further in the last section of this chapter.

LAPITA POTTERY

Migration: a positive example. The question of first settlement of the Polynesian islands has apparently been resolved by the discovery of a finds complex known as the Lapita culture, characterized in particular by pottery with incised decoration. Lapita sites were small villages, often with evidence of permanent occupation. They provide a record of the rapid movement of islanders by boat, eastwards from the northern New Guinea region to as far as Samoa in western Polynesia, between 1600 and 1000 BC according to radiocarbon dating. It is generally accepted that the Lapita migrants were the ancestors of the Polynesians, while those (the majority) who remained in Melanesia formed a large part of the ancestry of the present island Melanesians.

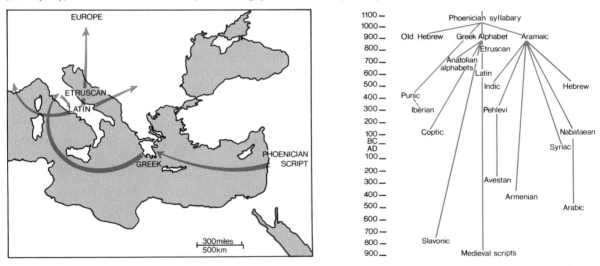

Diffusion: a positive example. One instance where an innovation in one place is known to have spread widely elsewhere through diffusion is that of the alphabet. Around the 12th century BC, on the Levantine coast, the Phoenicians developed a simplified phonetic script to write their Semitic language (a script now believed to derive ultimately from Egyptian hieroglyphic). By the early 1st millennium BC, the script had been adapted by the Greeks to write their language. This ultimately formed the basis for the Roman alphabet used today. (The Phoenician script also gave rise to the Hebrew, Arabic, and many other alphabets.) But of course the Greek alphabet had first to be modified and adopted in Italy, to write the Etruscan language and then Latin, the Roman language. It was through Latin that the Roman alphabet came to much of Europe, and later the rest of the world.

THE PROCESSUAL ALTERNATIVE

The processual approach attempts to isolate and study the different processes at work within a society, and between societies, placing emphasis on relations with the environment, on subsistence and the economy, on social relations within the society, on the impact which the prevailing ideology and belief system have on these things, and on the effects of the interactions taking place between the different social units.

In 1967, Kent Flannery summed up the processual approach to change as follows:

> Members of the process school view human behavior as a point of overlap (or "articulation") between a vast number of systems each of which encompasses both cultural and non-cultural phenomena – often much more of the latter. An Indian group, for example, may participate in a system in which maize is grown on a river floodplain that is slowly being eroded, causing the zone of the best farmland to move upstream. Simultaneously it may participate in a system involving a wild rabbit population whose density fluctuates in a 10-year cycle because of predators or disease. It may also participate in a system of exchange with an Indian group occupying a different kind of area from which it receives subsistence products at certain predetermined times of the year, and so on. All these systems compete for the time and energy of the individual Indian; the maintenance of his way of life depends on an equilibrium among systems. Culture change comes about through minor variations in one or more systems which grow, displace or reinforce others and reach equilibrium on a different plane.
>
> The strategy of the process school is therefore to isolate each system and study it as a separate variable. The ultimate goal of course is a reconstruction of the entire pattern of articulation, along with all related systems, but such complex analysis has so far proved beyond the powers of the process theorists. (Flannery 1967, 120.)

This statement moves at once into the language of systems thinking, discussed in a later section. But it is not always necessary to use systems language in this context. Moreover, Flannery places great emphasis here on the environment – on what he terms "non-cultural phenomena." Some critics of the New Archaeology in its early days felt that too much emphasis was placed on the economy, especially subsistence, and not enough on other aspects of

human experience, including the social and the cognitive. But that does not diminish the force of what processual archaeology at once achieved and has retained: the focus on the analysis of the working of different aspects of societies, and the study of how these fit together to help explain the development through time of the society as a whole.

Another important point was made already in 1958, before the New Archaeology had formally begun at all. Gordon Willey and Philip Phillips wrote then: "In the context of archaeology, processual interpretation is the study of the nature of what is vaguely referred to as the culture-historical process. Practically speaking it implies an attempt to discover regularities in the relationships given by the methods of culture-historical integration." (Willey and Phillips 1958, 5–6.) In other words, explanation involves some element of generalization, and the discovery of "regularities."

As we shall see in the next section, there is much discussion today about the role of generalization in explanation, and about how far the historical events we are analyzing were unique and, therefore, cannot be considered as general instances of any underlying process at all.

Applications

If all this seems rather abstract, it may be useful to give an example here of the way processual thinking has more to offer than the old school of thought. Our example comes from the ecological side of archaeology. This is appropriate because the ecological-economic approach was in many ways a precursor of the New Archaeology (see Chapter 1). In 1952, the British archaeologist Grahame Clark sought to explain the pattern of early farming settlements in Scandinavia, following his own studies of the Mesolithic (hunter-gatherer) period there. He plotted on a map the distribution of finds of the so-called "boat axe" culture – an indicator of the activities of the early farmers – and also the occurrence of megalithic tombs, taken again as an indicator of settled farming communities. On the same map he also plotted, using pollen information then becoming available, the distribution of deciduous (mainly oak) forests in the relevant climatic subdivision, termed in Scandinavia the Sub-boreal period (*c.*4000–1500 BC). After some discussion, and with careful reservations, he stated: "the coincidence of economic and ecological zones is sufficiently marked to justify the hypothesis that the

NEOLITHIC FARMERS
▨ "BOAT- AXE" CULTURE
▧ MEGALITHIC TOMBS

PERCENT MIXED OAK FOREST IN POLLEN ZONE VIII

| ○3% | ○5% | ○10% | ○15% | ○20% | ○25% |

Conjunction of Neolithic farming with deciduous forest in Scandinavia.

northern margins of the deciduous forest in fact determined the limits of the early spread of farming in the countries of northern Europe." (Clark 1952, 21.)

Clark thus explained the distribution of early farming cultures in terms of the extent of deciduous forest, making the inference from his data that there was some kind of necessary connection, and that these farming cultures were not adapted to live in the zone of coniferous forests beyond. Now, as we shall see below, it is a matter for discussion just how far the simple demonstration of a correlation between one thing and another actually takes us towards a truly satisfying explanation.

Grahame Clark's outlook in the 1950s, with its emphasis on the efficient adaptation of human society and culture to its environment, has much in common with the subsequent work of Lewis Binford. In 1968 Binford produced one of the first general explanations (where the New Archaeology set out to explain a class of events) of the farming revolution. In his paper, "Post-Pleistocene Adaptations," he gave the sort of generalizing explanation that the New Archaeology set as its goal (see box). Yet, as we shall see below, this general approach could be criticized as taking too "functionalist" a view of human affairs, laying more stress on the environment, demography, and subsistence than on social or cognitive factors.

It is interesting to contrast Binford's approach with that of Barbara Bender in 1978. Working from a broadly Marxist perspective, she argued that, before farming began, there was competition between local groups who tried to achieve dominance over their neighbors through feasting, and the expenditure of resources on conspicuous ritual and on exchange. It was these demands that led to the need to increase subsistence resources and so to a process of intensification in the use of land and the development of food production.

The early processual archaeology may reasonably be termed *functional-processual*. It is notable, and understandable, that many functional-processual explanations are applied to hunter-gatherer and early farming communities, where subsistence questions often seem to have had a dominant role. As we shall see later, however, for the study of more complex societies a development of this approach, which we may term the *cognitive-processual*, has recently seemed more promising.

Marxist Archaeology

Following the upsurge in theoretical discussion that followed the initial impact of the New Archaeology, there has been a re-awakening of interest in applying to archaeology some of the implications of the earlier work of Karl Marx, many of which had been re-examined by French anthropologists in the 1960s and 1970s. But it should be remembered that, already in the 1930s, such avowed Marxist archaeologists as Gordon Childe were producing analyses that were broadly in harmony with the principles of Marxist archaeology (described in the box overleaf). Childe's book *Man Makes Himself* (1936) is a splendid example, in which he introduced the concepts of the Neolithic (farming) and urban revolutions. Moreover, Soviet archaeologists today produce Marxist explana-

THE ORIGINS OF FARMING: A PROCESSUAL EXPLANATION

In 1968, Lewis Binford published an influential paper, "Post-Pleistocene adaptations," in which he set out to explain the origins of farming, or food production. Attempts to do this had been made by earlier scholars, notably Gordon Childe and Robert Braidwood (see box, Abu Hureyra, Chapter 7). But Binford's explanation had one important feature that distinguished it from earlier explanations and made it very much a product of the New Archaeology: its generality. For he was setting out to explain the origins of farming not just in the Near East or the Mediterranean – although he focused on these areas – but worldwide. He drew attention to global events at the end of the last Ice Age (i.e. at the end of the Pleistocene epoch, hence the title of his paper).

Binford centered his explanation on demography: he was concerned with population dynamics within small communities, stressing that once a formerly mobile group becomes sedentary – ceases to move around – its population size will increase markedly. For in a settled village the constraints no longer operate that, in a mobile group, severely limit the number of small children a mother can rear. There is no longer the difficulty, for instance, of carrying small children from place to place. Binford thus saw as the nub of the question the fact that in the Near East some communities (of the Natufian culture around 9000 BC) did indeed become sedentary before they were food-producing. He could see that, once settled, there would be considerable population pressure, in view of the greater number of surviving children. This would lead to increasing use of locally available plant foods such as wild cereals that had hitherto been considered marginal and of little value. From the intensive use of cereals, and the introduction of ways of processing them, would develop the regular cycle of sowing and harvesting, and thus

the course of plant-human involvement leading to domestication would be well under way.

But why did these pre-agricultural groups become sedentary in the first place? Binford's view was that rising sea levels at the end of the Pleistocene (caused by the melting of polar ice) had two significant effects. First, they reduced the extent of the coastal plains available to the hunter-gatherers. And second, the new habitats created by the rise in sea level offered to human groups much greater access to migratory fish ("anadromous" species, i.e. fish such as salmon that swim upriver from the sea to spawn) and to migrant fowl.

Using these rich resources, rather as the inhabitants of the Northwest Coast of North America have done in more recent times, the hunter-gatherer groups found it possible for the first time to lead a sedentary existence. They were no longer obliged to move.

That encapsulates all too concisely the outline of Binford's explanation. In some respects it is seen today as rather too simple. Nevertheless, it has many strengths. For although the focus was on the Near East, the same arguments can be applied to other parts of the world. Binford avoided migration or diffusion, and analyzed the position in processual terms.

MARXIST ARCHAEOLOGY: KEY FEATURES

Marxist archaeology, especially in its more traditional form, is based mainly on the writings of Karl Marx and Friedrich Engels, who were influenced by Charles Darwin and Lewis Henry Morgan (see Chapter 1). Several features may be stressed:

1 It is evolutionary: it seeks to understand the processes of change in human history through broad general principles.

2 It is materialist: it sets the starting point of the discussion in the concrete realities of human existence, with emphasis on the production of the necessities of life.

3 It is holistic: it has a clear view of the workings of society as a whole, and of the interrelation of the parts within that whole (see 8 below).

4 Marx constructed a typology of different forms of human societies or "social formations" to which correspond different "modes of production." These include, before the capitalist mode, primitive communism, the ancient (i.e. Greek and Roman), Asiatic, and feudal modes of production.

5 Change within a society comes about mainly from the *contradictions* that arise between the forces of production (including the technology) and the relations of production (mainly the social organization). Characteristically these contradictions emerge as a struggle between classes (if this is a society where distinct social classes have already developed). Emphasis on class struggle and internal differences is a feature of most Marxist explanations. This may be described as an *agonistic* view of the world where change comes about through the resolution of internal dissent. It may be contrasted with the *functionalist* view favored by the early New Archaeology where selective pressures towards greater efficiency are seen to operate, and changes are often viewed as mutually beneficial.

6 In traditional Marxism the ideological superstructure, the whole system of knowledge and belief of

the society, is seen as largely determined by the nature of the productive infrastructure, the economic base. This point is disputed by the neo-Marxists (see main text) who regard infrastructure and superstructure as interrelated and mutually influential, rather than one as dominant and the other subordinate. They can point to

passages in the writings of Marx which support this view.

7 Marx was a pioneer in the field of the sociology of knowledge where, as implied above, the belief system is influenced by, and indeed is the product of, the material conditions of existence, the economic base. This implies that as the economic base evolves, so too will the belief system of society, in a systematic way.

8 Marx's view of the internal structure of society may be set out as shown in the chart below. The analysis is applicable to the various different social formations into which human societies may be divided.

9 The systems approach within the mainstream of processual archaeology has a great deal in common with the above analysis. But to embrace the term "Marxist" often carries with it political overtones. Many Marxist archaeologists naturally apply the Marxian analysis of society to present-day societies also, which they see as being involved in a continuing class struggle in which their own alignment is with a proletariat in conflict with a putative capitalist elite. Most processual archaeologists would prefer to separate their own political views as far as possible from their professional work. Many Marxist archaeologists would argue that such a separation is impracticable, and would suspect the motives of those who make such a claim.

The internal structure of society according to Marx.

tions of change that owe more to traditional Marxism than to French neo-Marxism: a good example is the explanation by Igor Diakonoff for the emergence of state society in Mesopotamia, discussed below.

Even the explanations that have recently been developed by archaeologists influenced by French neo-Marxism ("structural Marxism"), such as by Antonio Gilman (1981), Michael Rowlands and Susan Frankenstein (1978), and Jonathan Friedman and Michael Rowlands (1978), can often be seen to fit well into the traditional Marxist mold. Examples that do not – where the neo-Marxist emphasis on the ideological and cognitive (on the so-called "superstructure") is particularly significant – are mentioned below.

Gilman's study sets out to explain the shift from egalitarian to ranked society in the Neolithic and Bronze Ages of Spain and Portugal. Some previous explanations had stressed that a society with a partly centralized administration (organized by a chieftain) could in certain ways work more efficiently than an egalitarian society without such a central figure. Gilman, on the other hand, questioned whether the institution of chieftainship was particularly beneficial to society as a whole. He argued rather that chiefs attained power through conflict and maintained themselves in power through force of arms, living a life of relative comfort through the exploitation of the common people. The notion of the clash of interests, the struggle between classes or sectors of society and the exploitation of the poor by the elite, is a typically Marxist one.

Frankenstein and Rowlands developed a model to explain the emergence of ranking in the central European Iron Age, emphasizing the significance of the importing of prestige goods from the Mediterranean by local chieftains. Once again, the chieftains do very well out of their privileged position. They effectively corner the market in imported goods, keeping the best for themselves and handing on other imports to their most trusted henchmen. According to the Marxist model, the chief is seen as perpetrating a "rip-off" rather than acting altruistically as a wise official for the greater good of the community as a whole.

Friedman and Rowlands in their 1978 paper developed what they call an "epigenetic" model for the evolution of "civilization" of much wider application. In the case of each civilization they locate the prime locus of change among social relations within the society in question, and in the tensions between differing social groups.

There is nothing here that is inappropriate to a processual analysis, and for that reason the two approaches cannot be clearly distinguished. The positive features that these Marxist analyses share with functional-processual archaeology include a willingness to consider long-term change in societies as a whole, and to discuss social relations within them. On the other hand, many such Marxist analyses seem, by comparison with the processual studies of the New Archaeologists, rather short on the handling of concrete archaeological data. The gap between theoretical archaeology and field archaeology is not always effectively bridged, and the critics of Marxist archaeology sometimes observe that since Karl Marx laid down the basic principles a century ago, all that remains for the Marxist archaeologists to do is to elaborate them: research in the field is superfluous.

Despite these differences, functional-processual archaeology and Marxist archaeology have much in common. The common ground is all the more clear when they are both contrasted with structuralist and "post-processual" approaches.

THE FORM OF EXPLANATION: GENERAL OR PARTICULAR

It is now time to ask rather more carefully what we mean by explanation. The different things we might try to explain were reviewed above. It was envisaged that different kinds of problem might require different kinds of explanation. An explanation relating to specific circumstances in the past, or to patterns of events, seeks to make us understand how they came to be that way, and not another. The key is understanding: if the "explanation" adds nothing to our understanding it is not (for us) an explanation.

As a first approximation we can distinguish two diametrically opposite approaches to the problem. The first approach is specific: it seeks to know more and more of the surrounding details. It operates with the belief that if one can establish enough of the antecedent circumstances, of the events leading up to the happening we hope to explain, then that happening itself will become much clearer for us. Such explanation has sometimes been called "historical," although it must be said that not all historians would be happy with that description.

Some historical explanations lay great stress on any insights we can gain into the ideas of the historical people in question, and for that reason are sometimes termed *idealist*. R.G. Collingwood used to say that if you wanted to know why Caesar crossed the Rubicon it was necessary to get inside the mind of Caesar, and thus to know as many of the surrounding details, and as much about his life, as possible.

The New Archaeology laid much more stress on generalization. Willey and Phillips, as we have seen, spoke in 1958 of "regularities," and the early New Archaeologists followed this lead, and turned to the philosophy of science of the time. Unluckily, perhaps, they turned to the American philosopher Carl Hempel, who argued that all explanations should be framed in terms of those most ambitious generalizations: *natural laws*. A lawlike statement is a universal statement, meaning that in certain circumstances (and other things being equal) X always implies Y, or that Y varies with X according to a certain definite relationship. For Hempel, the events or pattern we might be seeking to explain (the "explanandum") could be accounted for by bringing together two things: the detailed antecedent circumstances, and the law which, when applied, would by deductive reasoning allow the forecasting of what actually happened. The lawlike statement and the antecedent statement together form the "explanans." The form of explanation is seen as a *deductive* one, because the outcome is deduced from antecedent circumstances, plus the law. It is also *nomothetic* because it relies on lawlike statements (from the Greek *nomos*, "law"). This system of Hempel's is sometimes called the deductive-nomothetic or D-N form of explanation.

Just a few of the second and third generation New Archaeologists then set off to try to write archaeology in the form of universal laws: a notable example is the book by Patty Jo Watson, Steven LeBlanc, and Charles Redman, *Explanation in Archaeology* (1971). Most archaeologists, however, saw that it is very difficult to make universal laws about human behavior that are not either very trivial, or untrue. Traditionalists, such as the Canadian archaeologist Bruce Trigger, then argued for a return to the traditional explanations of history, for a form of explanation one might term *historiographic*. Certainly the initial foray into the philosophy of science by the New Archaeologists did not prove successful. The wilier archaeologists, such as Kent Flannery, saw that the "law and order" school was making a mistake, and producing only "Mickey Mouse laws" of little conceivable value. Flannery's favorite example was: "as the population of a site increases, the number of storage pits will go up." To which he replied, scathingly: "Leapin' lizards, Mr. Science!" Some critics of the New Archaeology have seized on this setback to suggest that this school is (or

was) in general "scientistic" (i.e. modeling itself unthinkingly on the hard sciences). But one of the positive contributions of the New Archaeology was in fact to follow the scientific convention of making specific and explicit, as far as is possible, the assumptions on which an argument rests.

Scholars writing since the mid-1970s, within the mainstream tradition of processual archaeology, still seek to learn from the philosophy of science, although it is no longer to Carl Hempel that they turn. The work of Karl Popper is much less rigid in its approach, with its insistence that every statement, so far as possible, should be open to testing, to setting up against the data: in this way, untrue statements, and generalizations that do not hold up, can be refuted. Moreover, these writers say, there is nothing wrong with deductive reasoning. It makes very good sense to formulate a hypothesis, establish by deduction what would follow from it if it were true, and then to see if these consequences are in fact found in the archaeological record by testing the hypothesis against fresh data: that is the *hypothetico-deductive* or H-D approach, and it does not carry with it the same reliance on lawlike statements as the D-N approach. It is this willingness to subject one's beliefs and assumptions to the confrontation with harsh reality that distinguishes scientific work from mere uncontrolled exercise of the imagination – or so philosophers of science, and with them processual archaeologists, would argue.

It does indeed seem that nearly all good explanations carry with them, and rely on, some form of generalization, as well as a sound analysis of the particulars of the case being explained. But precisely what the appropriate form of such generalization might be is a matter for further debate. As noted above, the form may change with the different kind of pattern or event that one is seeking to explain.

Recently, the Cambridge archaeologist Ian Hodder has argued that archaeologists should abandon the generalizing approach advocated by the New Archaeology, and seek to return to the idealist-historical outlook of R.G. Collingwood, laying much greater emphasis on the specific past social context (see below). Without claiming to resolve the debate, it is perhaps useful to see the two approaches not as polar opposites, but as the ends of a spectrum, which runs from Lewis Binford (with Carl Hempel or Karl Popper in the background) at one end, to Ian Hodder (with R.G. Collingwood in the background) at the other. Binford stresses generalization, and Hodder specific social context. But in reality it is difficult to conceive of any explanation that lacks at least some measure of both.

ATTEMPTS AT EXPLANATION: ONE CAUSE OR SEVERAL?

As soon as one starts to address the really big questions in archaeology, matters become complicated. For many of the big questions refer as we have seen not to a single event, but to a class of events. The enigma of the worldwide development of farming at the end of the last Ice Age has already been mentioned as one of these big questions in the main text above. Lewis Binford's attempted explanation was described in the box on the origins of farming. Kent Flannery's approach is discussed below.

Another of the big questions is the development of urbanization and the emergence of state societies. This process apparently happened in different parts of the world independently. Each case was, in a sense, no doubt unique. But each was also, it can be argued, a specific instance (with its own unique aspects) of a more general phenomenon or process. In just the same way, a biologist can discuss (as Darwin did) the process by which the different species emerged without denying the uniqueness of each species, or the uniqueness of each individual within a species.

If we focus now on the origins of urbanization and the state, we shall see that this is a field where many different explanations have been offered.

The Origins of the State

If we look at different explanations in turn, we shall find that some of them are in their way very plausible. Often, however, one explanation works more effectively than another when applied to a particular area — to the emergence of the state in Mesopotamia, for instance, or in Egypt, but not necessarily in Mexico or in the Indus Valley.

The Hydraulic Hypothesis. The historian Karl Wittfogel, writing in the 1950s, explained the origin of the great civilizations in terms of the large-scale irrigation of the alluvial plains of the great rivers. It was, he suggested, this alone that brought about the fertility and the high yields, which led to the considerable density of population in the early civilizations, and hence to the possibility of urbanism. At the same time, however, irrigation required effective management — a group of people in authority who would control and organize the labor needed to dig and maintain irrigation ditches, etc. So irrigation and "hydraulic organization" had to go together, and from these, Wittfogel concluded, emerged a system of differentiated leadership, greater productivity and wealth, and so on.

Wittfogel categorized the system of government characteristic of those civilizations founded on irrigation agriculture as one of "oriental despotism." Among the civilizations to which this line of thinking has been applied are:

- Mesopotamia: the Sumerian civilization from 3000 BC and its successors
- Ancient Egypt: the Valley of the Nile, from *c.*3000 BC
- India/Pakistan: the Indus Valley civilization from *c.*2500 BC
- China: the Shang civilization, *c.*1500 BC, and its successors

Comparable claims have been made for the agriculture (although the irrigation was not based on a major river) of the Valley of Mexico, and the Maya civilization.

Internal Conflict. In the late 1960s the Russian historian Igor Diakonoff developed a different explanation for state origins. In his model, the state is seen as an organization that imposes order on class conflict, itself arising from increased wealth. Internal differentiation within the society is here seen as a major causative element, from which other consequences follow.

Population Growth. An explanation much favored by many archaeologists focuses on the question of population growth. The 18th-century English scholar, Thomas Malthus, in his *An Essay on the Principle of Population* (1798), argued that human population tends to grow to the limit permitted by the food supply. When the limit or "carrying capacity" is reached, further population increase leads to food shortage, and this in turn leads to increased death rate and lower fertility (and in some cases to armed conflict). That sets a firm ceiling on population.

population growth ⟶ food shortage ⟶ increased death rate & lower fertility

Esther Boserup, in her influential book *The Conditions of Agricultural Growth* (1965), effectively reversed the position of Malthus. He had viewed food supply as essentially limited. She argued that agriculture will intensify — farmers will produce more food from the same area of land — if population increases. In other words, by shortening the periods during which

ORIGINS OF THE STATE I: PERU

In a 1970 paper, Robert Carneiro offered an explanation for the origins of the state in coastal Peru, laying stress on the factor of what he termed environmental circumscription (restrictions imposed by the environment). Population growth is also an important component of the explanation (and here his ideas relate to those of Esther Boserup discussed in the main text).

Early villages in coastal Peru were located in about 78 narrow valleys, flanked by desert. These villages grew, but as long as land was available for the settlement of splinter communities, they split from time to time so that they did not become too large. Eventually, a point was reached when all the land in a particular valley was being farmed. When this happened, the land already under cultivation was more intensively worked (with terracing and irrigation), and less suitable land, not previously worked, was brought into cultivation.

Carneiro argued that population growth outstripped the increase in production gained through intensification, and warfare became a major factor. In the past, armed conflict had occurred simply out of a desire for revenge – now it was in response to a need to acquire land.

A village defeated in war became subordinate to the victorious village, and its land was appropriated. Moreover, the defeated population had no means of escape from its valley environment, enclosed by mountains and sea. If it remained on its own land it was as a subordinate tribute payer. In this way, chiefdoms were formed, and the stratification of society into classes began.

As land shortages continued, Carneiro argued, so did warfare, which was now between larger political units – the chiefdoms. As chiefdom conquered chiefdom, the size of political units greatly increased and centralization developed. The result of this process was the formation of the state. Valley-wide kingdoms emerged, then multi-valley kingdoms, until finally all of Peru was unified in a single powerful empire by the Incas.

Carneiro has subsequently argued that the reduction in the number of political units and increase in their size is a process still continuing, one which will ultimately lead to a world state in the next millennium.

Like other so-called "monocausal" (single cause) explanations, this one does, in fact, draw on a series of factors working together. But it is highly selective in its choice of factors. And like all monocausal explanations, it has a "prime mover:" a basic process that sets the whole sequence of events going and continues to act as the driving force as they unfold. In this case, the prime mover is population growth. As is always the case with a prime mover explanation, we are not told what sets it in motion.

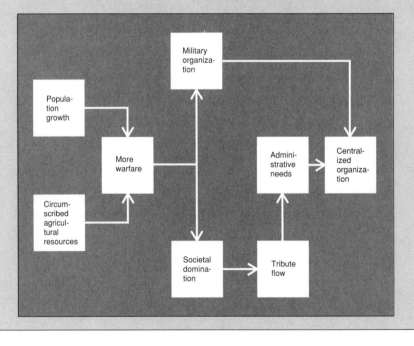

Flow diagram of Carneiro's explanation for the rise of complex societies.

Villages in two valleys, separated by mountains.

Population growth leads to more villages, with some now on marginal land.

Competition between villages leads to warfare.

Dominance of some villages over others, making them centers of chiefdoms.

One chiefdom dominates the others: creation of a state.

▨ Sea	• Village
☐ Valley	⊠ Chiefdom
▨ Mountain	⬤ Subordinate chiefdom
	— Conflict/Warfare

land is left to lie fallow, or by introducing the plow, or irrigation, farmers can increase their productivity. Population growth can then be sustained to new levels.

$$\text{population growth} \longrightarrow \text{introduction of new farming methods} \longrightarrow \text{increase in agricultural production}$$

So increase of population leads to intensification of agriculture, and to the need for greater administrative efficiencies and economies of scale, including the development of craft specialization. People work harder because they have to, and the society is more productive. There are larger units of population, and consequent changes in the settlement pattern. As numbers increase, any decision-making machinery will need to develop a hierarchy. Centralization ensues, and a centralized state is the logical outcome.

These ideas can be made to harmonize very well with the work of the American archaeologist Gregory Johnson, who has used them in the study of smaller-scale societies. From recent ethnographic accounts of !Kung San encampments in southwest Africa he showed that the level of organization rose with the increasing size of the encampment. Whereas in small camps the basic social unit was the individual or the nuclear family of 3–4 individuals, in large camps it was the extended family of around 11 people. In larger-scale societies, such as those of New Guinea, hierarchical social systems were needed in order to control disputes and maintain the efficient functioning of the society as a whole.

Environmental Circumscription. A different approach, although one that uses some of the variables already indicated, is offered by Robert Carneiro (see box). Taking as his example the formation of state society in Peru, he developed an explanation that laid stress on the constraints ("circumscription") imposed by the environment, and on the role of warfare. Population increase is again an important component of his model, but the model is put together in a different way, and the development of strong leadership in time of war is one of the key factors.

External Trade. The importance of trading links with communities outside the homeland area has been stressed by several archaeologists seeking explanations for the formation of the state. One of the most elaborate of these is the model put forward by the American archaeologist William Rathje for the emergence of state societies in the Maya lowlands. He argued that in lowland areas lacking basic raw materials there

ORIGINS OF THE STATE II: THE AEGEAN A MULTIVARIATE APPROACH

The palace civilization of Minoan Crete developed around 2100 BC, while that of Mycenaean Greece reached its climax in the centuries following 1600 BC. In *The Emergence of Civilization* (1972), Colin Renfrew outlined an explanation in systems terms for the development of these state societies. The subsystems considered were those listed in the table, which have a general application, together with the metallurgical subsystem. This subsystem was given special treatment in the book because of the considerable importance of early metallurgy in the Aegean.

Each subsystem can be considered in its own right. For instance, in the subsistence subsystem, wheat and barley were the principal crops in the Neolithic period (6500–3000 BC), and sheep and goats with some cattle and pigs, the principal animals. But, Renfrew argued, the new crops (olive and vine) took on a special significance during the Early Bronze Age and played a major part during the heyday of the palaces in the Late Bronze Age. They allowed diversification, and offered individual farmers the possibility of specializing. The exchange of products became necessary, and in this exchange the palaces could play a central redistributive role.

The mutual interactions of the subsystems were indicated by Renfrew in a simple diagram. He did not stress the dominance of any one subsystem: each interacted with all the others.

In the explanation of the rise of state societies in the Aegean, Renfrew emphasized the importance of what is known in systems theory as the multiplier effect: changes or innovations occurring in one field of human activity (in one subsystem of a culture) sometimes act so as to favor changes in other fields (in other subsystems). The multiplier effect is said to operate when these induced changes in one or more subsystems themselves act so as to enhance the original changes in the first subsystem.

For example, we might consider changes in some of the subsystems that favored growth in the metallurgical subsystem. In the craft technology subsystem, it was technical developments, notably the pyrotechnological discoveries of the potter, that made metallurgy possible (see Chapter 8). Several changes in the social subsystem affected metallurgy. First, there was an increasing need for metal weapons arising from an increase in military hostilities (documented by the construction of fortifications in the Early Bronze Age). Secondly, a market grew up for objects of display with the production of new objects in gold and silver. And thirdly, the growing custom of burying valuable metal objects with the dead helped to remove such objects from circulation and thus increase demand for them. The external trade subsystem also favored the development of metallurgy, because additional raw materials now became available.

Renfrew's explanation recognized that the essential drive towards growth and change came from the interaction of these various subsystems, through the working of the multiplier effect, and not primarily from any one prime mover. While it was possible to stress the importance of certain processes (e.g. increasing skill in metallurgy, and the development of the vine and olive), the explanatory emphasis was placed on the aggregate of the interactions.

The palace civilization of Mycenaean Greece, as exemplified at Pylos in this reconstruction drawing by Piet de Jong.

TABLE OF SUBSYSTEMS

Subsistence subsystem, *whose interactions and activities relate to the production and distribution of food resources;*

Technological subsystem, *defined by human activities that result in the production of material artifacts;*

Social subsystem, *where the defining activities are those that take place between the members of the society (other than those in the two preceding subsystems);*

Symbolic or projective subsystem, *embracing all those activities, notably religion, art, and science, by which humans express their knowledge, feelings, and beliefs about their relationships with the world;*

External trade and communications subsystem, *defined by all those activities by which information or material goods are transferred across the boundaries of the system;*

Population, *although not defined strictly by human activities, may be thought of as a further subsystem.*

Interactions between the subsystems of the culture system. Sustained positive feedback between them – the multiplier effect – resulted in cultural change and growth.

will be pressure for the development of more integrated and highly organized communities able to ensure the regular supply of those materials. He used this hypothesis to explain the rise of the Classic Maya civilization in the lowland rainforest.

Multivariate Explanations

All the preceding explanations for the origins of the state lay stress primarily on a chief variable, a principal strand in the explanation, even though there are several strands involved. Explanations, such as Karl Wittfogel's, which emphasize a single factor, are termed *monocausal*. In reality, however, when there are so many factors at work, there is something rather too simplified about monocausal explanations. It is necessary somehow to be able to deal with several factors at once. Such explanations are termed *multivariate*. Of course, none of the explanations summarized above is so naive as to be truly *monocausal*: each involves a number of factors. But these factors are not systematically integrated. Several scholars have thus sought for ways of coping with a large number of variables that simultaneously vary. Obviously, this is complicated and it is here that the systems terminology – already introduced in quite simple form in Kent Flannery's 1967 definition of processual archaeology cited in an earlier section – can prove very useful.

The Systems Approach. If the society or culture in question is regarded as a *system*, then it makes sense to consider the different things that are varying within that system, and to try and list these, and be explicit about them. Clearly, the size of population will be one of those *system parameters*. Measures of the settlement pattern, of production of different crops, materials, and so on, and measures of various aspects of social organization will all be parameters of the system. We can imagine the system proceeding over time through a series of successive *system states*, each defined by the values of the system variables at the time in question. The successive system states in sequence establish the *trajectory* of the system.

It is convenient to think of the overall system as broken down into several *subsystems*, reflecting the different activities of the system as a whole (see box, Origins of the State II). Each subsystem may be thought of as defined by the kind of activity that it represents: within it will be the humans involved in such activities, the artifacts and material culture involved, and those aspects of the environment that are relevant. Each subsystem will display, in common with all systems, the useful phenomenon of *feedback*. This concept was originally derived from the field of cybernetics (control theory).

The key notion is that of a system with *input* and *output*. If a portion of that input is channeled back to form a continuing part of the input, then that is known as "feedback." This is important because it means that what is happening to the system at one moment can have an effect on the system state at the next moment.

If the feedback is negative, then a change in the external input produces *negative feedback*, which goes back, as input, to counter the original change. That is very significant because the countering of change makes for stability. All living systems employ negative feedback in this way. For instance, the temperature of the human body acts so that when body temperature rises we sweat: the output is such as to reduce the input effect (i.e. the rise in external temperature). When a system is maintained in a constant state through the operation of negative feedback, this is known as *homeostasis* (from the Greek words, *homeo*, "the same", and *stasis*, "standing" or "remaining"). Similarly, all human societies have devices that ensure they carry on much as before: if they did not they would radically change their natures almost every moment of their existence.

However, *positive feedback* can occur. When it does, the change produced (in the output) has a positive effect on the input, thus favoring more of the same. Growth occurs, and with it sometimes change. Positive feedback is one of the key processess underlying progressive growth and change, and ultimately the emergence of totally new forms: this is termed morphogenesis.

It is thus possible to consider the influence of one subsystem on another, looking in turn at the interactions of each pair (see box, Origins of the State II).

In a 1968 paper, Kent Flannery applied the systems approach to the origins of food production in Mesoamerica during the period 8000–2000 BC. His cybernetic model involved an analysis of the various procurement systems used for the different plant and animal species that were exploited and of what he called "scheduling," namely the choice between the relative merits of two or more courses of action at a particular time. Flannery regarded the constraints imposed by the seasonal variations in the availability of the different species and the need for scheduling as

negative feedback in his systems model; that is to say, these two factors acted to hinder change and maintain the stability of the existing patterns of food procurement. Over the course of time, however, genetic changes in two minor species, beans and maize, made them both more productive and more easily harvested. The effects of these changes led to a greater and greater reliance on these two species, in a deviation amplifying or *positive feedback* manner. The ultimate consequence of the process thus set in motion – a consequence neither foreseen nor intended by the human population – was domestication. As Flannery concluded in his paper:

> The implications of this approach for the prehistorian are clear: it is vain to hope for the discovery of the first domestic corn cob, the first pottery vessel, the first hieroglyph, or the first site where some other major breakthrough occurred. Such deviations from the preexisting pattern almost certainly took place in such a minor and accidental way that their traces are not recoverable. More worthwhile would be an investigation of the mutual causal processes that amplify these tiny deviations into major changes in prehistoric culture. (Flannery 1968, 85.)

The systems approach is certainly convenient. It has, however, been criticized. The "post-processual" archaeologists (see below) apply to it most of the criticisms that they make of processual archaeology in general: that it is scientistic and mechanistic, that it leaves the individual out of account, and that systems thinking subscribes to the system of domination by which the elites of the world appropriate science to control the underprivileged. Criticisms from researchers who are not against scientific explanation in principle are particularly interesting. One of their most telling points is that the approach is ultimately descriptive rather than explanatory: that it imitates the world without really accounting for what happens within it. (But many would reply that to show how the world works is indeed one of the functions of explanation.) The critics also say that it is difficult in many cases to give real values to the various variables. They agree, however, that the approach does offer a practical framework for the analysis of the articulation of the various components of a society. And it does lend itself very readily to computer modeling and simulation (see next section). The models can become complicated, so that it is difficult to see the overall pattern. But that is the penalty when one is dealing with complicated systems like state societies, and difficult issues like the explanation of their emergence.

Simulation

Simulation involves the formulation of a dynamic model: that is, a model concerned with change through time. Simulation studies are of considerable help in the development of explanations. To produce a simulation one must have in mind, or develop, a specific model that leads to a set of rules. One can then feed in some initial data, or some starting conditions, and through the repeated application of the model (generally with the aid of a computer) reach a series of system states, which may or may not carry conviction in relation to the real world.

A simulation is thus an exemplification, a working out (and sometimes a test) of a model that has already taken shape. In reality, of course, no simulation ever works perfectly first time, but from the experience of simulation one can improve the model. That then, is the principal value of simulation: the actual explanation is the model rather than the simulation itself.

As an example, A.J. Chadwick decided to model the development of settlement in Bronze Age Messenia in Greece. He took some very simple rules for the growth and development of settlement, and then used the computer to apply these to the landscape of prehistoric Messenia. The outcome is a set of simulated settlement patterns through time. Moreover, they have interesting resemblances with the real settlement patterns as we know they developed. The simulation thus clearly

suggests that Chadwick's generative model was at least in part successful in seizing the essential of the settlement development process.

It is also possible to model the development of entire systems in this way, starting in essence from the systems approach outlined above. Here one analyzes the articulation or interplay of various subsystems. One then has to suggest precisely how these articulations might work in practice, how a change in the value of a parameter in one subsystem would alter the parameters in the other subsystems.

The simulation allows one to go through this in practice, starting from initial values for all the parameters, which one must oneself determine (or take from the real case). The System Dynamics modeling group at the Massachusetts Institute of Technology, led by Jay Forrester, has pioneered this technique in several fields, including the growth of towns and the future of the world economy. This simulation technique is generally in its infancy in archaeology, but there have been a few studies using it. For example, Jeremy Sabloff and his associates employed it to model the collapse of the Classic Maya civilization around AD 900, building in their own assumptions and constructing their own model. The results were instructive in showing that their model could achieve plausible results (see box overleaf).

The American archaeologist, Ezra Zubrow, modified the Forrester approach and applied it to model the

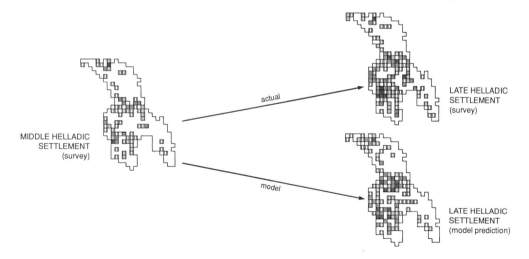

MIDDLE HELLADIC
SETTLEMENT
(survey)

actual

model

LATE HELLADIC
SETTLEMENT
(survey)

LATE HELLADIC
SETTLEMENT
(model prediction)

A. J. Chadwick's simulation of settlement growth in Bronze Age Messenia. The University of Minnesota Messenia Expedition had already mapped the distribution of settlement in Middle Helladic and Late Helladic times. The object of Chadwick's study was to see whether he could develop a simulation model which, if given the Middle Helladic pattern as the starting position, would then give rise to the Late Helladic pattern. The diagram shows the actual distribution of Middle and Late Helladic sites discovered by the survey, together with the best fit simulation result, using a combination of environmental (e.g. best soils) and human (e.g. density of existing occupation) factors. The intensity of shading indicates one, two, or three settlements, respectively, per 2×2-km cell.

THE CLASSIC MAYA COLLAPSE

Ever since the impressive remains of ancient states and cities were first discovered and studied by western scholars, the collapse of long-gone civilizations has been a focus of debate and inquiry. One of the earliest attempts to account for such a collapse was Gibbon's famous *Decline and Fall of the Roman Empire* (1776-88), in which he attributed the decline to the undermining effect of Christianity on Classical civilization. In the 1830s, the explorations of Stephens and Catherwood in Central America led to the discovery of a hitherto unknown civilization whose demise may have been as spectacular as that of Rome: the Maya.

The last 20 years has witnessed a number of theories seeking to account for the Classic Maya collapse in the 9th century AD, most of them based broadly on the concept of civilization as a system, and seeing collapse as the result of disequilibrium between different parts of the system. Two of the most influential simulations of the Maya collapse are those by Hosler, Sabloff, and Runge, and by Lowe.

Hosler, Sabloff, and Runge

This model sees the Classic Maya collapse as the result of imbalance between agricultural productivity and monument construction. There was a substantial increase in construction at Maya centers in the late 7th and 8th centuries AD. Dorothy Hosler, Jeremy Sabloff, and Dale Runge argue that this, coupled with population growth, will have put pressure on food supplies. The cause of the collapse, however, was a feedback loop: decline in food per person was countered by increased monument construction in order to placate the gods; but drawing off more of the agricultural labor force for monument building led to a still further decline in agricultural productivity, thus precipitating a rapid decline. Some scholars have found it difficult to believe that the Maya, faced with increasingly acute

Computer simulation of the Classic collapse by Hosler, Sabloff, and Runge. It shows how growing population, a resulting shortage of food, and increased monument construction could have caused the collapse.

food shortages, would have continued to divert labor from farming to monuments. However, the suggestion that over-investment in monuments contributed to the Maya collapse is persuasive, and features in a number of other Maya collapse models.

Lowe

One of the most recent simulations of the Classic Maya collapse is that by John Lowe. His work is based on the chronological patterning of the collapse, as determined from the latest dates of monument construction at different Maya centers. From this Lowe reconstructs a collapse which started in the peripheral areas and moved inwards, with sites in the northeast being the last to feel the effects. By correlating this pattern with site density and site hierarchy, Lowe is led to the conclusion that it was population pressure coupled with a top-heavy elite administration which precipitated the collapse.

The basic mechanism was pressure on land creating the need for more intensive agriculture, which in turn placed greater demands on the ruling elites for the regulation of food distribution and the allocation of manpower. Competition within and between the elites themselves placed still further strains on the system, requiring increasing labor inputs for the construction of ceremonial monuments.

The model owes much to earlier work, such as that of Willey and Shimkin, and Hosler, Sabloff, and Runge. It is, however, the most thorough attempt so far to account for the details of the Classic Maya collapse within a systems framework.

As the great Classic cities of the southern Yucatán declined, northern centers, such as Chichén Itzá (above, the Castillo or pyramid-temple), began to flourish. This suggests a shift northwards in the focus of Maya civilization, raising doubts as to whether there was in fact a general Classic Maya collapse in the 9th century AD.

Lowe's diagram, suggesting that increased population coupled with the demands of an overlarge elite helped trigger the Classic Maya collapse.

Was There a Collapse?

In recent years, many Maya scholars have come to realize that their studies of the collapse were too restricted. As they extended their research beyond the Southern Lowlands – the heartland of the Classic Maya – to the entire Maya Lowlands and initiated new work in the relatively neglected north, it became clear that at the same time as numerous cities in the south were declining, others such as Uxmal, Kabah, Sayil, and Chichén Itzá in the north were undergoing a florescence. Moreover, these northern centers continued many of the Classic cultural traditions and were in contact with several southern cities situated along trade routes. In view of this evidence, many archaeologists argue that instead of a collapse, there was a massive demographic, economic, and political shift in Maya civilization around AD 800 from south to north and towards locations along waterborne transportation routes. Certainly, many Southern Lowland cities were partially or completely abandoned – and the systems models just discussed may help to explain such declines – but Maya civilization as a whole, according to this line of argument, did not collapse.

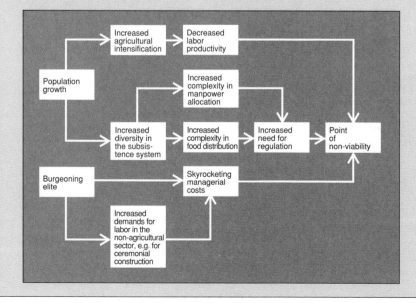

growth of ancient Rome from the period of the emperor Augustus. His aim was not to establish a complete simulated pattern of behavior for Rome, but to test which were the sensitive parameters that would have a crucial effect on growth and on stability. Some of Zubrow's results reveal a pattern of multiple cycles of sudden growth and decline, some three in 200 years. By undertaking different computer runs with different input variables (e.g. by doubling the size of the labor force), it is possible to see which changes would, according to the model, be highly significant. In fact,

doubling the labor force did not have a major effect: doubling it again did.

This is an example where simulation is being used as an exploratory tool with which to investigate the behavior of the system. So far, with such simulations, work has been of a preliminary nature, and more has been learnt about the procedures and potentialities of simulation than of the early culture under study. But the potential of the approach is considerable. (In Chapter 13 we see how simulation has been integrated into the major research project in Oaxaca, Mexico.)

"POST-PROCESSUAL" EXPLANATION

Since the mid-1970s, the early New Archaeology we have termed here functional-processual archaeology has come under criticism from several quarters. For example, early on it was criticized by Bruce Trigger in his book *Time and Tradition* (1978), who found the approach which sought to formulate explanatory laws (the nomothetic approach) too constraining. He preferred the historiographic approach, the broadly descriptive approach of the traditional historian. It was also criticized by Kent Flannery, who was scornful of the trivial nature of some of the so-called laws proposed and felt that more attention should be focused on the ideological and symbolic aspects of societies. Ian Hodder, likewise, felt that archaeology's closest links were with history, and wanted to see the role of the individual in history more fully recognized. Hodder also very validly stressed what he called "the active role of material culture," emphasizing that the artifacts and the material world we construct are not simply the reflections of our social reality that become embodied in the material record (by what Michael Schiffer would call a C-transform: see Chapter 2). On the contrary, material culture and actual objects are a large part of what makes society work: wealth, for instance, is what spurs many to work in a modern society. Hodder goes on to assert that material culture is "meaningfully constituted," the result of deliberate actions by individuals whose thoughts and actions should not be overlooked.

Out of these criticisms, some archaeologists in Britain (notably Ian Hodder, Michael Shanks, and Christopher Tilley) and in the United States (in particular Mark Leone) have tried to formulate new approaches, overcoming some of what they see as the limitations of functional-processual archaeology (and indeed much of traditional Marxist archaeology also). Among the influences on them have been structuralism, Critical Theory, and neo-Marxist thought.

Structuralist Approaches

Several archaeologists have been influenced by the structuralist ideas of the French anthropologist Claude Lévi-Strauss, and by the advances in linguistics of the American Noam Chomsky. Structuralist archaeologists stress that human actions are guided by beliefs and symbolic concepts, and that the proper object of study is the structures of thought – the ideas – in the minds of human actors who made the artifacts and created the archaeological record. These archaeologists argue that there are recurrent patterns in human thought in different cultures, many of which can be seen in such polar opposites as: cooked/raw; left/right; dirty/clean; man/woman, etc. Moreover, they argue that thought categories seen in one sphere of life will be seen also in other spheres, so that a preoccupation with "boundedness" or boundaries, for instance, in the field of social relations is likely to be detectable also in such different areas as the "boundedness" visible in pottery decoration.

The work of André Leroi-Gourhan in the interpretation of Paleolithic cave art (box, Chapter 10) was a pioneering project using structuralist principles. For this attempt at the interpretation of depictions of animals the approach seems particularly appropriate. In another example, the American archaeologist Dean Arnold has used the structuralist assumption that human thought categories in one field of experience are related to those in others in his study of the village of Quinua, near Ayacucho in Peru. Here he sought to relate the design elements on the pottery produced and used in the village to aspects of social patterning within the community, and to the community's perception of its own environment. Arnold studied 172 vessels of four different shapes with particular reference to the organization of design elements. He looked at the division of the surface of each pot into areas, and the use of the patterns of symmetry, and the variability of the motifs within the design zones. He then considered the organization of space within the landscape surrounding the village, and the social divisions governed by kinship categories. He was able to summarize the relationship of spatial organization and decorative space as shown in the accompanying table.

It should be noted that like most structuralist arguments the analysis is not concerned with change through time: it is synchronic. A more telling question

that the skeptic might pose, however, is whether there is any necessary relationship between the decorative principles detected for pottery, and the other superficially unrelated concepts involved in kinship and in describing the landscape. It is at this point that the processual archaeologist, perhaps to the irritation of the structuralist, would wish to investigate whether there are any hypotheses here that would be open to testing.

SPATIAL ORIENTATION	COMMUNITY PATTERN	DECORATIVE SPACE	VESSEL SHAPE	
Vertical	Vertical set of ecological zones	Set of vertically arranged decorative zones on vessels with vertically arranged space	*puyñu* *yukupuyñu*	*puyñu*
Horizontal	Division of savannah into two barrios based on the irrigation system	High frequency use of bilateral symmetry for motifs	All except the *tachu*	
		Bifurcation of space by a vertical plane created by two narrow bands	*tachu*	
		Mirroring of color and shape of framing lines on bands	*tachu*	
		High frequency use of vertical reflection to form band patterns	All except the *tachu*	
		Division of design space into two parts by one band	*plato*	*yukupuyñu*
Vertical	Division of savannah into upper and lower zones based on the complementary functions of the irrigation system	Use of horizontal reflection in conjunction with vertical reflection as the second most prominent band pattern	All except the *tachu*	*tachu*
Horizontal	Bilateral membership of individuals (the smallest unit of social space in the community) in each of two descent groups	Predominance of bilateral symmetry for production of motifs (the smallest unit of design space in the community)	All except the *tachu*	
	Social classes: higher class in the village, lower class in the rural area	Inner versus outer spatial organization	*plato*	*plato*

Dean Arnold's structuralist analysis of the relationship of spatial organization and decorative space in Quinua, Peru

EXPLAINING THE EUROPEAN MEGALITHS

A longstanding issue in European prehistory is that of the so-called megalithic monuments. These are impressive prehistoric structures built of large stones ("megalith" comes from the Greek *megas* [great] and *lithos* [stone]). In general, the stones are arranged to form a single chamber, buried under a mound of earth and entered from one side. The chambers may be large with a long entrance passage. Human remains and artifacts are usually found within these structures, and it is clear that most served as collective burial chambers, i.e. tombs for several people.

Megalithic monuments of various kinds occur widely along the Atlantic coasts of Europe. They are also found inland over most of Spain, Portugal, and France, but in other countries they do not occur more than about 100 km (65 miles) from the coast, and in general they are not present in central and eastern Europe. Most megaliths belong to the Neolithic period – the time of the first farmers. By the beginning of the Bronze Age they were going out of use in most areas.

Many questions arise. How were the Neolithic inhabitants of western Europe able to erect these great stone monuments? Why are they not found in other areas? Why were they built at this time and not earlier or later? What is the explanation for the range and variety of forms that they show?

Migrationist Explanation

In the 19th century megaliths were seen as the work of a single group of people, who had migrated to western Europe. Many of the explanations were offered in racial terms. But even when distinctions of race were not drawn, the explanations remained ethnic: a new population of immigrants was responsible.

Diffusionist Explanation

In the early 20th century alternative explanations were offered in terms of the influence of the higher civilizations of the eastern Mediterranean on those of the barbarian west. Trading links and other contacts between Crete and Greece on the one hand and Italy and perhaps Spain on the other were credited with the responsibility for a flow of ideas. Thus the custom of collective burial in built tombs seen in Crete around 3200 BC was thought to have been transmitted to Spain within a couple of centuries. From there it would have spread through the workings of diffusion. This view carried with it the idea that the megaliths of Spain and Portugal and then of the rest of Europe must be *later* than those of Crete.

Functional-processual Explanation

Radiocarbon dating made it clear that the megalithic tombs of western Europe were in many cases earlier than those of Crete. Now it was suggested that local communities had developed their own practices for the burial of the dead. A good processual explanation had to account for such a development in terms of the local social and economic processes at work.

Renfrew proposed (see box, Early Wessex, Chapter 5) that in the Neolithic period in many areas the settlement pattern was one of dispersed egalitarian groups. Each communal tomb would serve as a focal point for the dispersed community, and would help to define its territory. The megaliths were seen as the territorial markers of segmentary societies. A related idea was introduced by the British archaeologist Robert Chapman, drawing on the work of the American Arthur Saxe: that formal disposal areas for the dead (e.g. tombs) occur in societies where there is competition for land ownership. To be able to display the family tomb containing the bones of ancestors would legitimize one's claim to own and use the ancestral lands within the territory.

This explanation may appropriately be termed "functionalist" because it suggests how the tombs have served a useful function, in social and economic terms, within the society.

Neo-Marxist Explanation

In the early 1980s Christopher Tilley developed an account of the Middle Neolithic megaliths of Sweden, which (like the processual one) emphasized local factors. He saw such monuments as related to the exercise of power within these small societies by individuals who used the rituals associated with megaliths as a means of masking the arbitrary nature of control and of legitimizing inequalities within society. The mixing of body parts of different individuals within a tomb emphasized the organic wholeness of society, taking attention away from the inequalities in power and status which actually existed. The tombs and the rituals made the established order seem normal or natural.

The emphasis in Tilley's explanation on dominance within the group is typically Marxist, while that on ritual and ideology masking the underlying contradictions is typical of neo-Marxist thought.

Distribution of megalithic monuments in western Europe.

NORTH CHAMBERS

WEST CHAMBER

SOUTH CHAMBERS

FORECOURT & BLOCKING

FACADE

FACADE

BLOCKING STONES

Megalithic burial monument *known as the West Kennet Long Barrow in southern England, drawn by its excavator, Stuart Piggott.*

"Post-processual" Explanation

Ian Hodder, in criticizing both the processual and the neo-Marxist standpoints, has stressed symbolic aspects. He argues that earlier explanations have failed adequately to consider the particularity of the historical contexts in which the megaliths are found. And he argues that without consideration of the specific cultural context one cannot hope to understand the effects of past social actions.

Hodder maintains that many of the chamber tombs of western Europe referred symbolically to earlier and contemporary houses in central and western Europe: "the tombs signified houses." As he puts it: "the way megaliths were involved actively in social strategies in western Europe depended on an existing historical context. The existence of the tombs can only be adequately considered by assessing their value-laden meanings within European society" (Hodder, 1984, p. 53). Hodder brings into the argument a number of further issues, including the role of women in the societies in question. His aim is to arrive at some sort of insight for the meaning that the tomb in a specific context held for those who built it.

Comparison

No ready assessment of these various explanations can be attempted here. It is fair to say, however, that the first two forms of explanation, while perfectly appropriate in some cases, have been gravely overplayed in the past.

The functional-processual, neo-Marxist, and "post-processual" explanations all lay greater stress on internal factors. But are they in conflict with one another? We suggest that they are not, and that all three could be operating simultaneously. The processual idea that the monuments were useful to society in serving as territorial markers, and as the ritual focus of territorial belief and activity, does not necessarily contradict the Marxist view that they were used by the elders to manipulate the members of the society into the continued recognition of their social status. And neither of these need contradict the view that in particular contexts there were specific meanings for the tombs, and that the rich variety of the megalithic tombs needs to be considered further.

Another influential structuralist study is the work of the folklore specialist Henry Glassie on folk housing in Middle Virginia, USA. In it he uses such structuralist dichotomies as man/nature, public/private, internal/external, intellect/emotion, and applies them in a detailed way to the plans and other features of houses mainly of the 18th and 19th centuries AD. As he is working primarily from material culture with only limited reference to written records, his work is certainly relevant to archaeological interpretation. But whether his interpretations would seem so plausible if he were not able to claim that his subject matter belongs to the same cultural tradition as that within which he is working is another matter.

Critical Theory

Critical Theory is the term given to the approach developed by the so-called "Frankfurt School" of German social thinkers, which came to prominence in the 1970s. This stresses that all knowledge is historical, distorted communication, and that any claims to seek "objective" knowledge are illusory. By their interpretive ("hermeneutic") approach these scholars seek a more enlightened view, which will break out of the limitations of existing systems of thought. For they see research workers (including archaeologists) who claim to be dealing in a scientific way with social matters as tacitly supporting the "ideology of control" by which domination is exercised in modern society.

This overtly political critique has serious implications for archaeology. For the philosophers of this school stress that there is no such thing as an objective fact. Facts only have meaning in relation to a view of the world, and in relation to theory. Followers of this school are critical of the criterion of testing as used by processual archaeologists, seeing this procedure as merely the importing into archaeology and history of "positivistic" approaches from the sciences. These views have been advanced by Ian Hodder in his *Reading the Past* (1986) and by Michael Shanks and Christopher Tilley in their *Re-Constructing Archaeology* (1987). They call into question most of the procedures of reasoning by which archaeology has hitherto operated.

The processualists' response to these ideas is to point out that to follow them seems to imply that one person's view of the past is as good as another's (so-called "relativism"), without any hope of choosing systematically between them. This would open the way to the "fringe" or "alternative" archaeologies discussed in Chapter 14, where explanations can be offered in terms of flying saucers, or extra-terrestrial forces or any phantasms which the human mind may conjure up. It is not entirely clear how the Critical Theorists can answer this criticism.

Neo-Marxist Thought

One feature of neo-Marxist ("structuralist Marxist") thought, as noted earlier, is to stress that the ideological superstructure should not be assumed to be subordinate to the economic base of society. This opens the way to a much greater emphasis on the significance of ideology in shaping change in early societies.

One example is offered by the work of Mark Leone at Annapolis in Maryland, as part of a research project concerned with establishing a deeper historical identity for the area. His example is the 18th-century garden of William Paca, a wealthy landowner: the garden has been studied archaeologically and has now been reconstructed. Leone uses the neo-Marxist concept of ideology: "Ideology takes social relations and makes them appear to be resident in nature or history: which makes them apparently inevitable. ... Thus the class or interest group which controls the use of precedent does so to insure its own interests. It is in this sense that the classic Marxist writers have said that history tends to be written for class purposes." (Leone 1987, 26.) Leone examines the Annapolis garden in detail, and emphasizes the contradiction represented between a slave-owning society and one proclaiming independence in order to promote individual liberty, a contradiction seen in Paca's life. "To mask this contradiction," Leone writes, "his position of power was placed in law and in nature. This was done both in practicing law and in gardening."

This neo-Marxist outlook has its echo in the emerging local archaeologies of some Third World countries, where there is an understandable desire to construct a history (and an archaeology) that lays stress on the local population and its achievements before the colonial era. But some archaeologists, embracing also the relativist outlook encouraged by Critical Theory, have suggested that the archaeological *methods* used in those countries should also be different. They suggest that the whole framework of archaeological reasoning built up over the past century (and, let us admit, built up mainly in the western world) may have to be set aside. Certainly one must face the reality that different systems of values are at work, as is indicated by the controversy in North American archaeology over whether or not American Indians should have control over excavated remains of their ancestors (see Chapter 14).

TERRACE Nº1 | FALL Nº1 | TERRACE Nº2 | FALL Nº2 | TERRACE Nº3 | FALL Nº3 | BOTTOM LAND | FALL Nº4 | TERRACE Nº4

Reconstructed plan of the garden in Annapolis, Maryland, of the 18th-century landowner William Paca. Mark Leone and his colleagues were concerned to show how Paca's position of power "was placed in law and in nature . . . in practicing law and in gardening." The outlines of the garden are archaeologically derived, but the terraces and most of the plantings are conjectural.

COGNITIVE-PROCESSUAL ARCHAEOLOGY: THE NEW SYNTHESIS

During the past 5 to 10 years a new perspective has emerged, which transcends some of the limitations of functional-processual archaeology of the 1970s. This new synthesis, while willingly learning from any suitable developments in "post-processual" archaeology, remains in the mainstream of processual archaeology. It still wishes to explain rather than merely describe. It still emphasizes the role of generalization within its theoretical structure, and stresses the importance not only of formulating hypotheses but of testing them against the data. It rejects the total relativism that seems to be the end point of Critical Theory, and it is suspicious of structuralist (and other) archaeologists who claim privileged insight into "meaning" in ancient societies, or proclaim "universal principles of meaning." To this extent, it does not accept the revolutionary claims of "post-processual" archaeology in rejecting the positive achievements of

the New Archaeology. Instead, it sees itself (although its critics will naturally disagree) in the mainstream of archaeological thinking, the direct inheritor of the functional-processual archaeology of 20 years ago (and the beneficiary of Marxist archaeology and various other developments).

Cognitive-processual archaeology differs from its functional-processual predecessor in several ways:

1   It seeks actively to incorporate information about the cognitive and symbolic aspects of early societies into its formulations (see below).

2   It recognizes that ideology is an active force within societies and must be given a role in many explanations, as neo-Marxist archaeologists have argued.

3   Material culture is seen as an active factor in constituting the world in which we live. Indi-

431

viduals and societies construct their own social reality, and material culture has an integral place within that construction. This point has been effectively argued by Ian Hodder and his colleagues.

4   The role of internal conflict within societies is a matter to be more fully considered, as Marxist archaeologists have always emphasized.

5   The earlier, rather limited view of historical explanation being entirely related to the human individual, indeed of being often anecdotal, should be revised. This point is well exemplified in the work of the French historian Fernand Braudel, who considered cyclical change and underlying long-term trends.

6   An extreme "positivist" view of the philosophy of science can no longer be sustained: "facts" can no longer be viewed as having an objective existence independent of theory. Moreover, it is now recognized that the formulation of "laws of culture process" as universal laws like those of physics is not a fruitful path towards explanation in archaeology.

This last point deserves to be further expanded. Philosophers of science have for a long time contrasted two approaches to the evaluation of the truth of a statement. One approach evaluates the statement by comparing it with relevant facts, to which, if true, it should correspond (this is called the *correspondence* approach). The other approach evaluates the statement by judging whether or not it is consistent with (or coherent with, hence *coherence* approach) the other statements that we believe to be true within our framework of beliefs.

Now, although it might be expected that the scientist would follow the first of these two procedures, in practice any assessment is based on a combination of the two. For it is accepted that facts have to be based on observations, and observations themselves cannot be made without using some framework of inference, which itself depends on theories about the world. It is more appropriate to think of facts modifying theory, yet of theory being used in the determination of facts:

Fact   Theory

Cognitive-processual archaeologists, like their functional-processual predecessors, do believe that theories must be tested against facts. They reject the relativism of Critical Theory and "post-processual" archaeology, which seem to follow entirely a coherence view of truth. But they accept that the relation-

ship between fact and theory is a more complicated one than some philosophers of science 30 years ago may have recognized.

Cognitive-processual archaeology at present appears to be exploring two main directions: investigation of the role of symbols within processes of change, and exploration of the structure of transformations.

Symbol and Interaction

The point has already been made that the early New Archaeology aspired to investigate social structures, and the progress already made in that direction was reviewed in Chapter 5. But it was slow to explore symbolic aspects of culture, which is why cognitive-processual archaeology is a recent development.

The role of religious ritual within society has been investigated in a new way over the past 20 years by the cultural anthropologist Roy Rappaport. Instead of seeking to immerse himself in the agricultural society in New Guinea under study, becoming totally familiar with the meanings of its symbolic forms, he followed instead a strategy of distancing himself – of looking at the society from the outside, at what it actually does (not what it says it does) in its ritual behavior. This position is a convenient one for the archaeologist who is always outside the society under study, and unable to discuss issues of meaning with its participants. Rappaport has studied the way ritual is used within society and his focus is on the functioning of symbols rather than on their original meaning. His work influenced Kent Flannery, one of the few of the original generation of New Archaeologists to concern himself in detail with symbolic questions. Flannery's book, written with Joyce Marcus, *The Cloud People: Divergent Evolution of the Zapotec and Mixtec Civilizations* (1983), is one of those rare archaeological studies where symbolic and cognitive questions are integrated with subsistence, economic, and social ones to form an integrated view of society. This huge project is described in detail in Chapter 13.

Some of the other most promising studies in recent years, which give substance to the claim for a new synthesis, have also been concerned with early state societies of the Americas. Geoffrey Conrad and Arthur Demarest's *Religion and Empire, the Dynamics of Aztec Expansion* (1984) seeks to integrate ideological aspects within their analysis. They argue that the introduction by members of the Aztec elite of a new sun cult in the early 15th century AD fueled Aztec military expansion. The new ideology stressed the need for human sacrificial victims to feed the sun and ward off the forces of darkness. Such victims could be obtained only by military conquest. The Aztecs thus created an empire, and were fired in battle by the fanatical belief that they were the ones chosen to sustain the universe. Economic factors, such as tribute, and other forces undoubtedly played their part in this process, but ideology was a key motivating element in Aztec expansion.

Quite clearly religion and other ideologies such as modern Communism have brought about great changes, not just in the way societies think but in the way they act and behave – and this will leave its mark in the archaeological record. The whole field of official symbolism, and of religious symbolism within it, is now the focus of archaeological research in several parts of the world.

The Structure of Transformations

The role of symbols within processes of change is one current focus; another, of rather a different kind, is on the processes of change themselves. By what means do social forms change? How is growth sustained? What determines the new structures that emerge? Contemporary archaeology has sought inspiration from disciplines where questions of growth and form have been systematically considered for some time: from evolutionary biology, from the mathematics of non-linear systems, and from the general study of non-equilibrium systems. It is appropriate to say a brief word about each.

Positive Feedback. In the early days of systems analysis in archaeology it was argued by some that a functioning system maintained itself in relation to its environment in a position of stability or homeostasis through the operation of negative feedback. Essential changes within the system were thus seen as homeostatic changes (through negative feedback) in response to changes of external origin. As noted above, systems thinking is now very much at home with the notion of positive feedback as a cause of the growth of new forms (morphogenesis).

Punctuated Equilibria. One of the problems within archaeology, as within evolutionary thinking in general, has been to accommodate the notion of sudden change. Much of the thinking of Charles Darwin in *The Origin of Species* (1859) was towards the explanation of changes taking place over long periods of time. It is only recently, notably through the work of Stephen Jay Gould and Niles Eldredge (1977), that it has been accepted that sudden change is not in contradiction to Darwinian thought. It is now believed by many

evolutionary biologists that there were long time periods when plant and animal species changed very little, and much shorter periods ("punctuations") when evolution progressed at a very rapid rate. This general lesson is certainly applicable to archaeology, and the Cambridge archaeologist John Cherry has argued, in relation to the emergence of the palace society of Minoan Crete, that a gradualist approach does not seem appropriate. Inspired by the concept of "punctuated equilibria," he maintains that the sudden emergence of palace society may nonetheless be accommodated within an evolutionary perspective; the impact of gradual change over a period of more than a thousand years led to a rapid re-ordering of Minoan society at the end of the 3rd millennium BC.

Catastrophe Theory. Similar lessons are offered by catastrophe theory, a branch of mathematics which is employed to argue that when a number of variables are working together (in a non-linear way), gradual changes in the variables can produce sudden effects. Moreover, René Thom, in his *Structural Stability and Morphogenesis* (1975), was able to show that there are only a limited number of ways in which such changes can take place. These he describes as the elementary catastrophes, of which one has been applied to archaeological cases.

Self-Organization in Non-Equilibrium Systems. Using a related perspective, derived initially from thermodynamic studies in chemistry, the Belgian scientist Ilya Prigogine has stressed that many systems, and specifically those that are not at equilibrium and in which energy is dissipated, have a propensity towards self-organization. That means new and more complex forms emerge quite naturally within them. The paths or trajectories of growth arrive at bifurcation points at which sudden changes may occur.

These ideas, like those of Catastrophe Theory, have been of great interest to theoretical biologists. They have also been applied to the human sphere. For instance, Prigogine's colleague P.M. Allen has simulated the growth of urban centers using this approach, showing how the growth of new and more complex forms may be predicted. Taking into account such factors as industry, population, and retail trade, he modeled the development of a small town into a city, showing how the location of different activities within the city shifted as population grew and external demands of the industrial and financial sectors expanded.

These various approaches have not yet been comprehensively applied in the field of archaeology, although in each case the application has begun. At present, the models are in general too simple, and most of them fail to take into account the cognitive features to which the cognitive-processual archaeology aspires. "Post-processual" archaeologists will argue that such approaches are too mechanistic to account for the richness and complexity of human behavior. In the simple forms in which such models exist at present, that criticism is certainly justified. But already computer scientists such as J.E. Doran are devising simulations where individuals within a community, each with different perceptions of the world, will interact. Certainly, therefore, one of the aspirations of cognitive-processual archaeology is to develop more effective formal models within which human perceptions and the symbolic side of human society will have a significant role.

Modeling of this kind is, however, a specialized field. Most archaeologists will prefer to proceed in the first place from the archaeological material, and to frame their explanations initially in verbal rather than mathematical form. Cognitive-processual archaeology offers an appropriate framework for the development of such explanations. It is a framework in which the specifically human qualities of the human animal – the symbolic – will play a central role.

SUMMARY

A new emphasis on the importance of theory in archaeology was one of the cornerstones of the New Archaeology. For too long scholars had felt it sufficient to explain the past simply in terms of archaeological cultures interpreted as the remnants of distinct groups of people, who experienced change as a result of migrations and diffusion from other cultures. The New Archaeology seriously questioned the equation of cultures with peoples, and challenged the assumption that diffusion – even in the rare cases where it could be proved to have occurred – actually explained the underlying causes of change in societies. New Archaeologists sought to study societies as functioning cultural systems, and to find regularities in the culture-historical process. In this functional-processual approach, any new hypotheses derived from archaeological evidence were to be tested against fresh evidence – the hypothetico-deductive method. Marxist archaeologists likewise attempted to understand the processes of change in history, but tended to explain change in terms of the struggle between social classes.

In any explanation, it is important to be clear about what one is trying to explain – whether a specific event, a class of events, or a more general process. Two classes of events addressed by the New Archaeology have been the rise of agriculture and the origins of the state. Here the most successful explanations appear to be multicausal ones using the systems approach, which allows the use of computer simulation and modeling.

In the 1970s structuralists, post-structuralists, and then "post-processualists" reacted against the functionalism of the early New Archaeology, advocating greater emphasis on the ideas and beliefs of past societies, and criticizing the procedure of testing, since all knowledge is subjective. Processualists have responded by reaffirming the importance of testing – how else are we to choose between competing theories? – but have accepted the need to look afresh at ideas and beliefs, at the cognitive aspects of culture. A new cognitive-processual synthesis can thus be seen to have emerged in the 1980s.

Further Reading

Binford, L.R. 1983. *In Pursuit of the Past*. Thames & Hudson: London & New York.

Daniel, G. and Renfrew, C. 1988. *The Idea of Prehistory*. Edinburgh University Press: Edinburgh; Columbia University Press: New York.

Flannery, K.V. (ed.). 1976. *The Early Mesoamerican Village*. Academic Press: New York. (Book of well-argued case studies which reveals more about the structure of explanation than most works on archaeological theory.)

Hodder, I. 1986. *Reading the Past*. Cambridge University Press: Cambridge & New York. (The "contextual" and "post-processual" alternative.)

Renfrew, C. (ed.). 1973. *The Explanation of Culture Change*. Duckworth: London.

Renfrew, C. 1982. Explanation Revisited, in Renfrew, C., Rowlands, M., & Segraves, B.A. *Theory and Explanation in Archaeology*. Academic Press: New York, 5–24.

Shanks, M. & Tilley, C. 1987. *Social Theory and Archaeology*. Polity Press: Oxford; University of New Mexico Press: Albuquerque 1988.

PART III

The World of Archaeology

Part III: Introduction

The basic materials of archaeology, and the methods available for establishing a space-time framework, were reviewed in Part I of this book. The range of questions we can ask of the past, and the techniques available for answering them, were surveyed in Part II. Here, in Part III, our aim is to see how these various techniques are put into practice. In an actual field project one would like, of course, to answer all the questions at once (no archaeologist ever set out to answer just one of them without at the same time coming up with observations relevant to others).

In Chapter 13, three selected case studies show how several questions can be addressed at once. In a regional study we are concerned with the location of the relevant evidence, with establishing the time sequence of the remains discovered, with the investigation of the environment, with the nature of the society, and indeed with the whole range of issues raised in the various chapters of this book. Any director of a major project has, in a sense, to reach a compromise in order to be able to follow up several avenues of inquiry simultaneously. The aim here is to illustrate with a few informative examples how such compromises have indeed been reached in practice, with a fair degree of success. Thus we hope to give something of the flavor of archaeological research in practice.

An archaeological investigation, even on a regional scale, cannot, however, be considered in isolation. It is only one part of the world of archaeology, and hence of society as a whole. The last chapter in this book is therefore devoted to public archaeology – to the ethical, practical, and political relationships that relate the archaeologist to society at large. The aim of archaeology, after all, is to provide information, knowledge, and insight into the human past. This is not for the benefit of the archaeologist alone but for society at large. Society finances the archaeologist, and, in the final analysis, society is the consumer. The relationship merits examination.

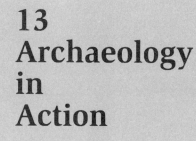

13
Archaeology
in
Action

In this volume we have sought to examine the various methods and ideas employed by archaeologists. We have tried to stress that the history of archaeology has been the story of an expanding quest, in which the finds made in the field can often be less important for progress than the new questions asked and the new insights gained. The success of an archaeological enterprise thus depends crucially on our learning to ask the right questions, and finding the most productive means of answering them.

It is for this reason that the chapters in this book have been organized around a series of key questions. Inevitably, that has meant focusing chapter by chapter on a number of different themes. But in reality the life of the archaeologist is not quite like that. For when you go out into the field with your research design, with the bundle of questions you would like to answer, you may in fact find something quite different from what you expected, yet obviously very important. The archaeologist excavating a multi-period site may be interested primarily in a single, perhaps early, phase of occupation. But that does not give him or her the right to bulldoze away the overlying levels without keeping any record. Excavation is destruction and (as we shall discuss in the final chapter) this brings to the archaeologist a series of responsibilities, some of them not always welcome, which cannot be avoided. The practice of archaeology, in the hard light of reality, is often very much more complicated – and therefore more challenging – than one might imagine.

This is particularly so at the organizational level. To undertake a project in the field takes money, and it is not the purpose of the present book to examine the funding or organization of such projects. Increasingly, as we review in the next chapter, archaeological sites are protected by law, and some sort of permit from the relevant authorities will be needed in order to undertake fieldwork and to excavate. Then there is the task of recruiting an efficient excavation team. What about transport, lodging, and food? After the excavation, who is to write what part of the excavation report? Are the photographs adequate, have the finds been suitably illustrated by drawings, who will finance the publication? These are the practical problems of the field archaeologist.

This book is primarily about how we know what we know, and how we find out – in philosophical terms, about the epistemology of archaeology. To complete the picture, it is important to see something of archaeology in action: to consider a few real field projects where the questions and methods have come together and produced, with the aid of the relevant specialisms, some genuine advance in our knowledge.

The questions we ask are themselves dependent on what, and how much, we already know. Sometimes the archaeologist starts work in archaeologically virgin territory – where little or no previous research has been undertaken – as for instance when the southeast Asian specialist Charles Higham began his fieldwork in Thailand in the late 1960s. By contrast, in the case of our first project below, on the Greek island of Melos, we are dealing with the prehistoric Aegean, where there has been almost a century of intensive research, and the problems, or at least some of them, are rather well understood.

In the Valley of Oaxaca in Mexico, on the other hand – our second case study – when Kent Flannery and his colleagues began work two decades ago, little was understood of the evolution in Mesoamerica of what we would call complex society, although the great achievements of the Olmec and the Maya were already well known. The work of the Flannery team has involved continual formulation of new models. It represents an excellent example of the truism that new facts (data) lead to new questions (and new theories), and these in turn to the discovery of new facts.

Our third and final case study follows the research project of Rhys Jones and his associates in Kakadu

National Park, northern Australia. Here the archaeologists worked closely with the legal owners of the region's sites, the Aborigines – an experience of growing relevance for all researchers in lands occupied by indigenous peoples (Chapter 14). The transformation in our knowledge of prehistoric Australia and Southeast Asia over the course of the last 30 years has been one of the most exciting developments to have taken place in modern archaeology. The Kakadu project, with its close integration of both environmental and archaeological studies, has played an important part in that transformation.

THE MELOS PROJECT

The outline of Aegean prehistory was already well known in 1974. This was no project *in terra incognita*, in unknown territory. The palaces of Crete, which many see as the indication of state society in the Aegean, emerged around 2000 BC, while on the Greek mainland comparable developments are heralded by the rich burials in the Shaft Graves at Mycenae c.1600 BC, which give their name to the civilization we call Mycenaean. The Cycladic Islands occupy a position between Crete and mainland Greece. The first major archaeological investigation there was from 1896 to 1899, when an excavation organized by the British School of Archaeology at Athens, led for most of the time by Duncan Mackenzie, took place on the island of Melos, at the important prehistoric settlement of Phylakopi.

From 1974 to 1977 a new series of excavations were undertaken at Phylakopi. This project, conducted (again on behalf of the British School) by Colin Renfrew, had as its general aim the better understanding of the Cycladic Islands during the formation of complex society in the Aegean. The general area of concern was the wider one: How do complex societies come about? How does civilization emerge? But all fieldwork operates in one place at a time, and such questions must be directed to the case in hand.

In the Cycladic Islands it was already well known that there was some settlement in the Neolithic period before 3000 BC, and that during the following millennium (3000–2000 BC, the Early Bronze Age) there was a remarkable upsurge of activity in the islands, with cemeteries which have produced special objects, including marble vessels and small sculptures of marble of remarkable sophistication. Occupation at Phylakopi was known to extend from this period through the whole of the Bronze Age, in a sequence of three successive settlements or "cities." During the Late Bronze Age (from c.1700 to c.1100 BC) the finds, notably the pottery, are so close in style to those of Minoan Crete, and later of Mycenaean Greece, that it seemed likely that the island had lost its political independence. Certainly, after 1000 BC came the "dark age" that engulfed so many Aegean sites, and one does not see activity on Melos again until about the 8th century BC when a new town begins to develop, in a different location from that of Phylakopi. This was the forerunner of Ancient Melos, the center on the island in Classical Greek times. The island entered the full glare of history for a brief instant with its siege and capture by the Athenians in the year 415 BC during the Peloponnesian War. This story was told by the world's first great historian, Thucydides, and his account, in the "Melian Dialogue," of the negotiations between the defending Melians and the besieging Athenians is a penetrating analysis of the totalitarian doctrine that "might means right."

Aims of the Project

There is no space to describe here all the archaeological questions that the project hoped to answer at the outset. The first aim, however, was to look at Phylakopi within its wider context on Melos, and to view the development of Melos through time for any insights into the processes of complex state formation already discussed. With these general aims came the more specific, secondary questions. What was the nature of the settlement at Phylakopi during the successive phases of the Bronze Age, and of its political organization? How did it relate to Melos as a whole in each phase? More specifically, could one define more closely its relationship with Crete during the period when Minoan styles dominated the pottery, and with the Mycenaean world subsequently? Were the effects of the great volcanic eruption of Thera during the early part of the Late Bronze Age (see box, Chapter 4) visible at all? (This last was an interesting question in view of the catastrophic effects on Minoan Crete itself that some workers had proposed for the eruption.) What was the Melian economy of the time? And how could an understanding of the Melian economy in later days, both during the heyday of its independence before the Athenian destruction, and then later during external domination, aid our view? The focus was therefore a diachronic one – looking at Melos over several thousand years – with the hope that an understanding of the system at one period would aid that at another.

The *research design* utilized the existing knowledge that for much of the Bronze Age there was a single, major center on Melos at Phylakopi, and that during the Classical period the center of settlement was at Ancient Melos. The strategy was to investigate these two centers further (although for practical reasons excavation was possible only at Phylakopi), and to consider both sites within the wider island environment by means of a systematic site survey on the island; a geomorphological survey to see how far the island's surface had changed during the Bronze Age and Classical periods; a study of modern traditional agricultural practices; and a geological survey of mineral resources. The largest single enterprise was the excavation undertaken at Phylakopi itself.

In a few paragraphs it is simply not feasible to summarize all the activities undertaken by the project. But what we can do is to attempt at least to indicate their scope and variety within the framework adopted in this book.

The Searchers

The first duty is to acknowledge the fundamental contributions of those earlier researchers who made the first discoveries and asked the right questions. For Melos, the pioneering role was carried out by Duncan Mackenzie (1861–1935) who was present during the excavations at Phylakopi, and who carried out what was not only the first survey of the islands (in which he located the obsidian sources) but what was at the same time a pioneering piece of site survey for the Aegean in general.

The searchers on Melos, then and now. (Top left) Duncan Mackenzie – center of back row – was the leader for much of the 1896–99 Phylakopi excavations. Here he is seen with other members of the team, including – front row – the expedition cook and his daughter. (Above left) Phylakopi excavations in progress in the late 1890s. (Top right) The 1974–77 field crew, Colin Renfrew at far left. (Above right) Measuring in a feature during the recent excavations.

What is Left?

In asking "what is left?" of the Aegean Bronze Age, one is dealing with what is in effect a semi-arid environment that is favorable to the formation of settlement mounds or tells. The deep stratigraphy at Phylakopi is an indication of this. Dry and wet sieving were routinely used, aiding in the recovery of small artifacts and abundant animal bones. However, no charred plant remains were recovered.

Where?

The problem of investigating the location of settlement on Melos was complicated by the fact that the land surface (the geomorphology) had changed significantly since prehistoric times: that issue is further discussed below when the environment is considered. Fortunately, the location of the two major early centers, Phylakopi (for the Bronze Age) and Ancient Melos (for Classical times) was already known. The sites were further studied by means of aerial photographs taken from a balloon, and (for the environs of Phylakopi) a survey using the proton magnetometer (see magnetism box, Chapter 3).

The knowledge that Phylakopi was a major site in the Bronze Age and that Ancient Melos was similarly important in Classical times did not guarantee, of course, that these were the only large-scale organizing centers. That was one reason for undertaking the systematic survey. Another was the desire for a clearer insight into the settlement structure. Given that these sites, each at its respective time, formed the principal organizing center for the island, what was the settlement hierarchy at the subsidiary level? Should one imagine most of the population as resident in the central town, or were there subsidiary villages and homesteads? And how did this settlement pattern change through time?

For the island as a whole it was decided to undertake an intensive field survey, a project organized by John Cherry. As time did not allow surface survey for the whole island, a sampling strategy was developed (a stratified random sampling strategy) where strips of land, about 20 percent of the total island area of 151 sq. km, were examined by the survey teams (a more detailed account is given in Chapter 3). The resulting picture allowed for the first time an insight into changing settlement patterns on Melos.

The survey confirmed that during the period of the ascendancy of Phylakopi and Ancient Melos, from about 2000 BC to 1100 BC and from about 700 BC into Roman times, respectively, these were indeed the dominant organizing centers. From around 2000 BC, Phylakopi was the only substantial settlement on the island, although in the preceding millennium there were several other settlements, and Phylakopi had not yet established its dominant role. The island seems to have been abandoned completely for two or three centuries after 1100 BC, following which several minor sites grew up with Ancient Melos soon taking on a dominant position.

When?

The question of dating in the Aegean, for the Late Bronze Age at any rate, is answered primarily on the basis of a close analysis of the local ceramic styles and (at least for Mycenaean times) of the Egyptian contexts within which these have been found – an excellent case of the cross-dating discussed in Chapter 4. For the Early Bronze Age, radiocarbon dating is also useful.

At Phylakopi, the first control had to be the stratigraphic one obtained by excavation, and the relative chronology for the site was re-investigated using Mackenzie's work as the starting point. The conclusion was that Mackenzie and the earlier excavators had made one significant mistake: they had divided the development of the town into three rather than four main phases – a perfectly understandable error when one remembers that they were working at a time before the ceramic sequences, upon which we now depend so heavily, had been established for the Aegean by analogy with the Egyptian chronology. The absolute chronology was established, in the main, from a close study of the imported pottery found at Phylakopi and its place within those established ceramic sequences.

There were other chronological possibilities to be considered. What effects, if any, did the volcanic eruption of Thera have on Melos (see box on Thera eruption, Chapter 4)? No obvious white layer, indicative of a deposit of ash (tephra), was observed at Phylakopi. But the potsherds in certain deposits at the site offered a preliminary indication that the settlement must have been occupied at around the time of the eruption. Small samples of soil were taken, in careful stratigraphic sequence, from layers containing pottery of the Late Minoan I period. These samples were examined in Bloomington, Indiana, by geologists Dorothy and Charles Vitaliano, who were able to recognize microscopic particles of tephra in a few layers, and to identify those with certainty as coming from the Thera eruption by virtue of their refractive index. The tephra thus established a chronological marker (see Chapter 4) for the layer in question. If the

Distribution of characteristic Cycladic pottery of the later Bronze Age, linking Phylakopi with other sites in the Aegean.

tree-ring data from Belfast (Irish oak) and Tucson, Arizona (California bristlecone pine), along with the data from the Greenland ice core, are to be interpreted as reflecting the eruption, as seems increasingly likely, then the layer in question at Phylakopi can be dated to within a year or two of 1628 BC. This new dating does not affect the *relative* chronology of pottery styles, but it does suggest that in terms of *absolute* chronology the Late Bronze Age at Phylakopi and other Aegean sites must have begun some 150 years earlier, and lasted 150 years longer, than had previously been thought (i.e. early 17th century BC to *c.*1100 BC).

Social Organization

The city plan (see overleaf), for the final period of Phylakopi's occupation, is based on the results of the project as well as those of the earlier work. The site was only some 200 m in length but it nonetheless has an urban character. The presence of a "palace," an imposing principal building with formal features (marked "Megaron" on the plan), suggests centralized control, and other features hint at a stratified society in Mycenaean times.

In the preceding period – the earlier part of the Late Bronze Age, around the 17th century BC (according to the new date for the Thera eruption) – the 1974–77 excavations gave unequivocal evidence of a predecessor to the Mycenaean "palace," which one may describe as a "mansion." In using this term one deliberately avoids any firm implication about the social organization of Phylakopi. But clear evidence of it comes from a small but significant find – a fragment of a clay tablet incised with signs in the script termed Minoan Linear A (illus. overleaf). It dates from the same time as the mansion, around 1650 BC. This at a stroke gives a clear indication of literacy in at least a segment of the population. If one assumes that the tablet was actually incised on Melos, which is likely, then this may indicate some centralized economic control of the kind exercised within their own territories by the Minoan palaces on Crete in the Late Bronze Age.

Environment

The best evidence for the environment of a specific site usually comes from pollen. Unfortunately, although

City plan for the final period of Phylakopi's occupation. Features suggesting an urban character include the fortifications, and the presence of a "palace," marked "Megaron" on the plan. The sanctuary was constructed c.1400 BC, and destroyed c.1120 BC.

Fragment of a clay tablet from Phylakopi incised with signs – so far undeciphered – in the Minoan Linear A script, and dating from c.1650 BC.

these microscopic grains have been sought on Melos none have been found preserved there. For climatic change, therefore, the project had to fall back on the pollen diagrams from other localities, such as Lake Copais in Boeotia in mainland Greece. However, on Melos there is evidence of changes in landform, and detailed geomorphological analysis was able to throw light on when some of the principal changes occurred. It is clear that a major phase of erosion on the higher land, with alluvial deposition in the river and stream valleys, has taken place over the past 3500 years. A trial section, which yielded a radiocarbon sample dated to around 1050 BC, documents that this process was underway before the end of the settlement at Phylakopi. Indeed, Phylakopi, previously on a peninsula with the sea in front and an inlet behind, soon lost the fine natural harbor that the inlet had offered. This may

well have been a factor contributing to the center's abandonment.

Diet and Technology

Attempts using flotation and water sieving to obtain samples of charred grain were unsuccessful, although the cultivation of barley and wheat can be assumed by comparison with what is known from other well-studied Aegean sites. The animal bones were much more forthcoming, showing that there were more cattle in the Late Bronze Age than earlier; they were probably used mainly for traction (i.e. for pulling the plow) and represent some intensification in agriculture. A decline in the number of cattle in the final phase of the settlement correlates with the first indications of the use of the donkey. Sheep and goat however were the dominant species in terms of numbers of bones, and conditions on Melos would have been very suitable for the production of wool. Large flocks of sheep may have been raised on the pastures in the less heavily settled western half of the island, and, though there is no definite evidence, some of the wool may have been for export.

It is clear that during the Bronze Age (c.3000–1000 BC) the practice of metallurgy developed markedly on Melos as it did on other islands. For the Early Bronze Age, Phylakopi offers little direct evidence of metallurgical practice, mainly because the areas excavated are small. But we know from other sites that during the 3rd millennium BC copper metallurgy developed, with the production of such useful artifacts as daggers and axes, and from around 2600 BC the copper was alloyed with tin to form bronze. During the 2nd millennium BC these techniques were further developed. There is proof of that at Phylakopi in the form of a stone mold for a bronze double axe, dating probably from around 1500 BC. The double axe was one of the forms accorded a symbolic significance in Minoan Crete at the same time, but it was also a very useful tool, and that was probably its primary role on Melos.

What Contact Did They Have?

Melos plays a central role in the story of Aegean trade, for the island contains the two major obsidian sources of the Aegean. One aim of the project was to survey these geologically (undertaken by Peter Shelford), another was to survey the chipping floors and other areas from the perspective of early use (undertaken by Robin Torrence). Trace-element analyses had previously been carried out by optical emission spectrometry and neutron activation analysis (Chapter 9) and by the fission track method (Chapter 4); further analyses were conducted using X-ray fluorescence. These amply confirmed the characteristics of the sources, and the conclusion that obsidian from Melos had been reaching the Greek mainland from before 8000 BC, where it is found in stratified contexts at the Franchthi Cave.

These methods allow one to show that finds of obsidian on various Aegean sites are indeed of Melian origin, but they do not determine the nature of the trade. For that purpose, Torrence's studies in the quarries and beyond were more illuminating. As mentioned in Chapter 9, she concluded from her study of the working areas near the quarries that they do not reflect craft specialist production. In the first place, no evidence was found at the quarries for a specialist toolkit used for extracting the obsidian or for preparing the large cores that were then transported overseas (because the production of the blades from the cores was not usually undertaken at the quarries). Second, no evidence was found near the quarries that might suggest that craftspeople had lived there on any long-term basis. Moreover, a wide variety of techniques was used in producing the macrocores, which suggested to Torrence "that the knappers working at the quarries had a very opportunistic approach to the task."

It seems likely, then, that those who wished to use Melian obsidian simply visited the quarries to collect it. This is a very different picture from that afforded by Isabel McBryde's study of the use of greenstone quarries at Mount William in southeastern Australia (see box, Chapter 9). There, the local residents exploited the quarries themselves and bartered their products for other goods with the visitors who came to obtain greenstone. In Melos, it seems, the local inhabitants did not claim that kind of "ownership" over the quarries.

The sources of metal objects were investigated by lead isotope analysis (Chapter 9) and the pottery was studied by various techniques, including microscopic examination of thin sections, heavy-mineral analysis and optical emission spectrometry. The analysis of the pottery allowed the amounts of imported material to be quantified for each period, and the results serve as an indicator of Phylakopi's changing relationship with the outside world. Imported pottery was particularly common in the later Early Bronze Age period (2700–2300 BC: 7 percent) and in the first part of the Late Bronze Age (1700–1400 BC: 7 percent), but it reached a peak of 18 percent in the following period 1400–1100 BC when Melos came under strong influence from mainland Greece.

What Did They Think?

Many aspects of the cognitive life of the early Aegean remain to be elucidated. But one area at least was in many ways amply documented on Melos: that of religion.

During the Early Bronze Age, Phylakopi seems to have participated in the religious beliefs then prevalent among the Cycladic islanders. This can be inferred from the finding of fragments at Phylakopi of several of the folded-arm figurines that are the most characteristic symbolic form of the Cycladic Early Bronze Age.

Religious beliefs during the 500 years or so of the Middle Bronze Age (c.2000–1700 BC) are not well documented, but from the Late Bronze Age, c.1700 BC, comes evidence that many symbolic decorative forms used on Melos were adopted from the murals and vase paintings of Minoan Crete. There are indications that the wall paintings at Phylakopi may have served to decorate rooms set aside for cult practices. Even if the paintings were not related to cult practice, but had a purely decorative function, it seems likely that the Melians and other Cycladic islanders were heavily influenced by Cretan beliefs and Cretan symbolism.

All this changed around 1400 BC with the construction of a sanctuary at Phylakopi – as discussed in Chapter 10 – which conforms much more closely to cult practices on the mainland of Mycenaean Greece. The sanctuary was not a large or impressive building,

The sanctuary at Phylakopi: a reconstruction by the expedition architect Alec Daykin of the West Shrine in use during phase 1b, soon after its construction c.1400 BC.

(Left) The "Lady of Phylakopi" from the sanctuary, c.1350 BC. (Center) Marble kouros statue from Melos, c.550 BC. (Right) The "Venus de Milo," late 2nd century BC. (Not to scale.)

but (happily for the archaeologist) it had been destroyed around 1120 BC, leaving many broken but abundant and restorable finds, including small terracotta cult figurines and various offerings. One important feature – new to Phylakopi and to the Aegean in general at this time – was the appearance of male figurines alongside the predominantly female ones.

Other Late Bronze Age sanctuaries have been discovered on Crete and the Greek mainland, but the Phylakopi example is particularly important because of the new light it throws on the development of religion in the Aegean and ultimately on the genesis of religion in Classical Greece in the 1st millennium BC. Several elements of Classical Greek religion may be recognized in the cult figurines of the Phylakopi shrine, and it is clear from this that the progression from the Bronze Age religion to that of Classical times was one of gradual transformation, not abrupt change. The discovery and excavation of the sanctuary resulted in a book by Colin Renfrew entitled *The Archaeology of Cult* (1985).

What Were They Like?

This is a question on which the Melos researches shed very little direct light, because few skeletal remains have been found on the island. Work from the prehistoric Aegean in general suggests that physically the population was not strikingly different from that of today. Representations of the human figure, both in the finds from the Bronze Age sanctuary and in marble sculptures from the island in the 6th century BC, certainly give a convincingly graphic impression. The famous "Venus de Milo" from the 2nd century BC does that even more.

Why Did Things Change?

The ultimate aim of the Melos enterprise was indeed to ask "why?" questions, as indicated earlier. Certainly, it is possible to examine the successive changes in the status of Melos from:

1   A society or group of societies not possessing a centralized state structure; *to*
2   An independent state polity (in the Middle Bronze Age and earlier Late Bronze Age, and again in the 6th and 5th centuries BC); *to*
3   A subordinate unit within a larger state or empire.

Out of the project came an increased awareness that it is inappropriate to think of Melos and the other Cycladic Islands either in complete isolation or simply as the recipients of cultural influences as a subordinate part of some larger cultural system. Instead, it is more plausible to suggest that the significant interactions in the Aegean were at an intermediate level; the relations were not between some notional center and an outer and less-significant periphery, but between political units (or polities) equivalent in status to each other and sometimes equivalent also in size (peer polities). The recognition and further analysis of such peer-polity interactions have provided a useful analytical tool to set between the extremes of diffusionism and the excessive emphasis on autonomous models of development.

The changes in the patterns of land utilization in Melos may be seen in terms of increasing intensification of production. During those periods when Melos was independent, the produce beyond that needed to feed the population (i.e. the production beyond subsistence, PBS) could be used for trade and exchange or to finance civic projects. The prosperity of the island as an independent city state during the 6th and 5th centuries BC (until it was conquered and subjugated by Athens in 415 BC) may be seen in that light. Once subordinated to an external power – whether Athens in the 5th century BC or perhaps also Minoan Crete in the 15th century BC – that PBS would be exacted in tax or tribute and removed from the island system.

When seeking to explain the intensification of production, it is appropriate to turn to the patterns of interaction between Melos and neighboring polities that in effect supplied the incentive for the island population to invest the additional labor required to increase production. During those periods when the island was subjugated by an outside power, it can be supposed that this additional labor was encouraged not through incentive but by the operation of duress.

The interdisciplinary work of the Melos project was published in *An Island Polity* (ed. C. Renfrew and M. Wagstaff, 1982). It showed that although islands are excellent laboratories for the study of prehistoric social change, they must never be considered in isolation, but as parts of regional political and economic systems.

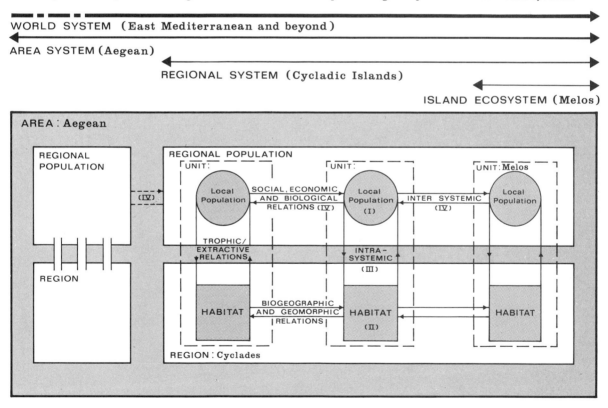

Interaction within the island, regional, area, and world systems. The project demonstrated that it is inappropriate to think of Melos and the other Cycladic islands either in complete isolation or simply as subordinate parts of a larger cultural system. Significant interactions were at an intermediate level, between political units (polities) equivalent in status to each other.

THE OAXACA PROJECTS: THE ORIGINS AND RISE OF THE ZAPOTEC STATE

The Valley of Oaxaca in the southern highlands of Mexico is best known for the great hilltop city of Monte Albán, one-time capital of the Zapotecs and famous for its magnificent architecture and carved stone slabs. Here, from 1930 onward, 18 seasons of fieldwork by the great Mexican archaeologist Alfonso Caso first laid the foundations of the region's time sequence. In recent decades, however, research has broadened to encompass the whole valley. There have been two major, long-term and complementary projects. The first, led by Kent Flannery from 1966 to 1973 and jointly directed by him and Joyce Marcus from 1974 to 1981, has concentrated on the earlier periods – before Monte Albán's heyday – with the aim of elucidating the origins of agriculture and evolution of complex society in the region. The second project, conducted by Richard E. Blanton, Stephen Kowalewski, and Gary Feinman, has focused on the later periods dominated by Monte Albán. In what follows we shall look at the work of both projects down to the end of the Formative period (*c.* AD 100), and how new light has been cast on the inception of agriculture, the process of state formation in the Valley of Oaxaca, and the emergence of the Zapotec state.

Background

The Valley of Oaxaca is the only broad riverine valley in the southern highlands of Mexico. Shaped like a wishbone, it is drained by two rivers. Surrounded by mountains, it lies at an altitude of between 1420 and 1740 m (4658–5708 ft) and has a semi-arid, semi-tropical environment where rainfall fluctuates markedly – both predictably, between wet and dry seasons, and unpredictably from year to year.

Building on work by Ignacio Bernal, who had already cataloged many sites in the valley through survey, the Flannery-Marcus project began by surveying and locating as many early sites as possible in selected areas, before deciding on those to be exca-

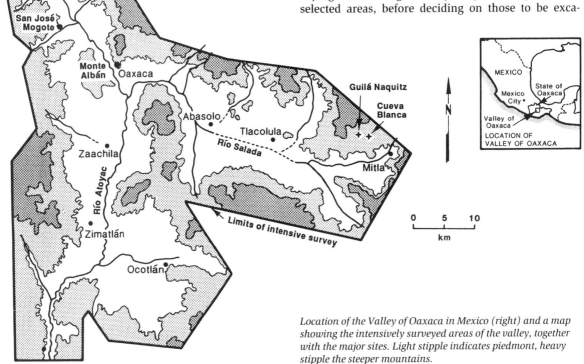

Location of the Valley of Oaxaca in Mexico (right) and a map showing the intensively surveyed areas of the valley, together with the major sites. Light stipple indicates piedmont, heavy stipple the steeper mountains.

vated. In fact, survey still continues to reveal sites in the area as land clearance and canal building expose buried horizons. Survey from the air has been particularly helpful, since one can see through the sparse vegetation and identify small details almost to the level of individual trees.

Guilá Naquitz and the Origins of Agriculture

One excavation, designed to clarify the transition from foraging to food production, was that of a small rockshelter, Guilá Naquitz (White Cliff).

Survey and Excavation. Surface collection of artifacts from more than 60 caves in the same area suggested that four, including Guilá Naquitz, had enough preceramic material (such as projectile points) and depth of deposit (up to 1.2 m or 3 ft 9 in) to warrant full excavation. After access for transport to the site had been improved, test excavations were carried out to determine the stratigraphic sequence, establish whether preceramic levels were present *in situ*, and assess how far back in the sequence plant remains might be preserved. The stratigraphy was complex, but very clear because of dramatic color changes.

It was to be expected that survival of food remains would be good, because the site is located in the driest

Work in progress inside Guilá Naquitz rockshelter, 1966. Zapotec Indian workmen from Mitla, Oaxaca, are excavating level D (the first level to include evidence of domestic plants).

part of the Valley of Oaxaca. The Flannery-Marcus team indeed found that preservation was outstanding, but the low densities of artifacts meant that all or most of the small cave would have to be dug in order to establish the nature of the tool assemblage. In the end, the entire area of preceramic occupation under the cave's overhang was removed through the excavation of 64 one-meter squares. Thorough screening and sieving techniques ensured that even the smallest items were recovered.

Dating. Radiocarbon dates obtained from charcoal found at Naquitz showed that its preceramic living floors extended from about 8750 to 6670 BC (there was also a little Formative and Postclassic occupation, not yet fully analyzed and published). The date of 8750 BC is close to the supposed transition from the Paleo-Indian period, characterized by extinct Pleistocene fauna, to the early Archaic, with Holocene fauna.

Environment. Analysis of pollen samples from the different levels provided a sequence of change for the area's vegetation with fluctuations in thorn, oak, and pine forest, and the probable utilization of cultivated plant resources from about 7000 BC onward, together with the collection of wild plant resources from the start of the sequence.

The microfauna recovered – rodents, birds, lizards, landsnails – were compared with their modern representatives in the region in order to cast further light on the preceramic environment, which was found to be not vastly different from that in existence today except for humanly induced changes. The present landscape is thus relevant to any interpretation of the ancient way of life.

Diet. Rodents had been very active in the cave, gnawing nuts and seeds, so that it was vital to establish from the start how many of the food resources had been introduced to the site by people. Burrows were very visible in the living floors, and their contents could be examined. None of the commonly gnawed items such as acorns or nuts were found inside them. In addition, the distribution of plant species on the floors showed a human pattern of large discard areas rather than the small pockets characteristic of rodent caches. Some plant remains also showed signs of food preparation. In short, the researchers could be confident that almost all the food resources in the site had been introduced by people.

Unfortunately, the six coprolites obtained from the preceramic levels all appeared to be from animals (probably coyote or fox). However, these creatures had

Plant	April	May	June	July	Aug	Sep	Oct	Nov	Dec	Jan	Feb	Mar	No. of grams consumed	No. of Kilocalories represented
acorns													629	1812
agave													140	176
nopales													97	12
guaje seeds													54	19
nanches													30	21
mesquite pods			pods				stored seeds						14	42
hackberries													13	4
opuntia fruits													12	9
susi nuts													5	30
beans			flowers		seeds								3	4
piñon nuts													1	6
wild onions			flowers						bulbs				1	0
cucurbit					flowers		seeds						1	4

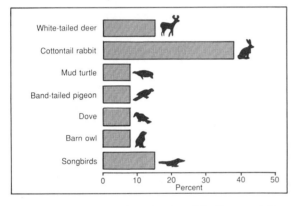

(Top) At Guilá Naquitz plants dominated the diet, especially acorns, agave, and mesquite pods and seeds. The site was occupied mainly from August (mesquite harvest) till early January (end of acorn harvest). (Above) Animals consumed.

probably scavenged food from the cave, and so the roasted plant remains (prickly pear and *agave*) in their feces provided clues to the human diet.

Clearer indications of diet were obtained through a combination of methods. These included data on plant and animal remains; modern plant censuses that provided information on the density, seasonality, and annual variations of various species in the area; and an analysis of the foods in the site from a nutritional point of view (calories, protein, fats, carbohydrates). The result was both a hypothetical diet for each living floor and an estimate of productivity of the Guilá Naquitz environment. Finally, all this information was pooled to reconstruct the "average diet" of the preceramic cave occupants and estimate the area needed to support them.

Over 21,000 identifiable plant remains were recovered, dominated by acorns, with *agave*, and mesquite pods and seeds. Dozens of other species were represented in small quantities. It thus became clear that, despite the wide variety of edible plants available, the occupants had adopted a selected few as staples. Acorns were probably stored after the autumn gathering for use throughout the year, because one of the major factors in life here is the great seasonal variation in the availability of different foods. It was found that the plant remains in each level reflected the harvest of an area from a few to a few hundred square meters.

At least 360 identifiable fragments came from animals hunted or trapped for food. They were counted both as numbers of fragments (with the parts of the body and the position in the cave noted) and as minimum numbers of individuals (in order to estimate the amount of meat consumed or the territory needed to account for the remains). All the species are still common in the area today, or would have been common until the arrival of firearms. The major source of meat seems to have been the white-tailed deer.

The site catchment of Guilá Naquitz was calculated as follows: plant food requirements probably came from no more than 5–15 ha (12–37 acres); the deer from at least 17 ha (42 acres); and raw materials from up to 50 km (31 miles) away.

Technology. Being a small camp, Guilá Naquitz did not contain the full range of stone tools known from the preceramic in the Valley of Oaxaca generally. Of the 1716 pieces of chipped stone recovered from the preceramic levels, no less than 1564 lacked any retouch, implying that most had been used "raw," without being worked further. Almost every living floor had evidence for flake production, in the form of cores. Only 7 projectile points were found, setting in perspective the evidence from the animal bones and suggesting that hunting was not a major activity during the season the cave was occupied. Sidescrapers and knives may have been used in butchering or hide preparation. A survey of stone sources showed that the coarse material from which most tools were made was available within a few kilometers, but higher quality chert had occasionally been obtained from sources 25 and 50 km (15 and 31 miles) distant.

It is assumed that most of the grinding stones had been used for plant processing, since remains of food plants were found in the same levels. Textile materials also survived – netting, basketry, and cordage, including the oldest radiocarbon-dated examples from Mesoamerica (before 7000 BC) – and there were a few artifacts of wood, reed, or cactus as well, including materials for firemaking and toolhafting. Fragments of charcoal occurred here and there, and were used by the research team for radiocarbon dating or to determine the woods preferred as fuels by the cave's occupants. It was found that the choice of timber in the preceramic period had been wide-ranging, unlike that of the Formative villagers of the Oaxaca Valley who later showed a marked preference for pine which continued into the Colonial and modern eras and which probably explains the disappearance of that tree from some areas.

Social Organization and the Division of Labor. The distribution of material on the living floors was subjected to three separate computer analyses in order to assess activity areas and the organization of labor. The activity areas – clusters in the distribution – were defined on the basis of association: i.e. showing that an increase in one variable (such as nut hulls or hackberry seeds) is a good predictor of an increase or decrease in other variables. Hence the raw data

consisted of the frequencies of different items per meter square of each floor, converted into density contour maps by computer.

When six living floors were analyzed, a number of repetitive patterns emerged that probably reflect regularities in the way tasks had been organized in the cave. These patterns are quite complex, and cannot be divided simplistically into men's and women's workspace. They include areas for light butchering, raw plant eating, toolmaking, meal preparation and cooking, and the discard of refuse. However, ethnographic research suggested some sexual division of work areas. Pathways into and within the cave were also isolated by the analyses.

Flannery and Marcus concluded that Guilá Naquitz was a small microband camp, used by no more than four or five people, perhaps a single family. It was occupied mainly in the fall, between late August/early September (the mesquite harvest season) and December/early January (the end of the acorn harvest season). Collecting wild plants was a major activity here, but hunting was less dominant than at other sites. Towards the end of preceramic occupation, there was a transition to food production. The very full picture of activities at this site now has to be compared with results from other sites in this area and with other regions in Mesoamerica in order to assess how representative or unusual they are for their period.

Why Did Things Change? In order to gain further insights into the process of adopting an agricultural way of life, Robert G. Reynolds designed an adaptive computer simulation model, in which a hypothetical microband of five foragers started from a position of

Reconstructed activity areas and pathways of Zone D at Guilá Naquitz. Area I is interpreted as a curving pathway with acorn, hackberry, and flint debris. Another path, Area II, runs between acorn storage and food preparation areas. Area III may have been where animal processing was carried out by one or two people (probably men). Area IV may have been used by one or two people (probably women) to process and cook both seasonally restricted and cactus/agave group plants.

449

ignorance and gradually learned how to schedule the gathering of the 11 major plant foods in the cave's environment by trial and error over a long period of time. At each step of the simulation the foragers were programmed to try to improve the efficiency of their recovery of calories and protein, in the face of an unpredictable sequence of wet, dry, and average years that changed the productivity of the plants. Information on their past performance was fed back into the memory of the system, and affected their decisions about modifying strategy with each change. When the system reached such a level of efficiency that it could scarcely be improved, agricultural plants were introduced into the simulation and the whole process began again. Priorities were changed, and a new set of strategies developed. Changes in the frequency of wet, dry, and average years were also tried out, as well as alterations in population level.

The results of this model based on artificial intelligence theory, with its built-in feedback relationships, were that the hypothetical foragers developed a stable set of resource collecting schedules (one for dry and average years, the other for wet) that closely mirrored those at Guilá Naquitz, as did the shifts in resource use that followed the introduction of incipient agriculture. No absolute time units were used in the simulation – we do not know how long a real-life group would take to achieve the same strategies. Nor was a "trigger" for agriculture, such as population pressure, introduced into the system. The resources were simply made available – as it were from a neighboring region – and adopted, first in wet years and later, when they proved reliable, in dry and average years. When the simulated climate changed significantly, or population growth was introduced, the rate at which cultivated plants were adopted into the system actually slowed down. This suggests that neither climatic change nor population growth are necessary to explain the rise of agriculture in the Valley of Oaxaca. Rather, the work implies that a major reason for the adoption of agriculture here was to help even out the effects of annual variation in food supplies, and was therefore merely an extension of the strategy already developed in pre-agricultural times.

The research project at Guilá Naquitz was fully published in 1986 in a volume edited by Kent Flannery after more than 15 years of analysis.

Village Life in the Early Formative (1500–850 BC)

Another part of the project's work that has been published in some depth concerns Early Formative villages in the Valley of Oaxaca, the period when true, permanent settlements of wattle-and-daub houses first became widespread in the region. The project's aim was to construct a model of how the early village operated, and to do that it studied them at every level, from features and activity areas within a single house to household units, groups of houses, whole villages, all villages in a valley, and, finally, interregional networks within Mesoamerica.

Settlement and Society. As seen in Chapter 3, the Flannery team took care to obtain as representative a sample as possible for each level, in order to gain a clear idea of the range of variation in artifacts, activities, site-types, etc. Before the Oaxaca project, not a single plan of an Early Formative house had been published. The project has recovered partial or nearly complete plans of 30 of them, together with others from later phases. Using Naroll's formula (see Chapter 11), it was estimated that these houses (15–35 sq. m or 161–376 sq. ft) were intended for nuclear families.

Activity areas were plotted for each house, and, through ethnographic analogy, tentatively divided into male and female work areas. After detailed analysis household activities could be divided into three types:

1 *Universal activities* such as food procurement, preparation, and storage – as revealed by grinding equipment, storage pits, and jars, and food remains recovered by excavation, screening, and flotation; some tool preparation was also classed in this group.
2 Possible *specialized activities* – activities found at only one or two houses, including manufacture of certain kinds of stone and bone tool.
3 Possible *regional specializations* – activities found in only one or two villages within a region; these include production of some shell ornaments, or featherworking; saltmaking, too, was limited to villages such as Fábrica San José near saline springs.

The project also produced the first maps showing the layout of a Formative village (principally that of Tierras Largas). Some evidence for differences in social status emerged, particularly at Santo Domingo Tomaltepec. Here one group of residences – deduced to be of relatively higher status – had not only a house platform built of higher-quality adobe and stone, but a greater quantity of animal bone, imported obsidian, and imported marine shell than the area of wattle-and-daub houses deduced to be of lower status. Significantly, locally available (and therefore less prestigious) chert formed a higher proportion of the tools in

Early Formative Oaxaca. (Left) Plan of a house at Tierras Largas, c.900 BC, with certain artifacts plotted in position. (Above) Zapotec workmen pour a solution of ash, water, and sodium silicate into a brass carburetor-mesh screen. By "floating" the charcoal fragments out of ash deposits at Early Formative sites such as Tierras Largas, the project was able to recover charred maize kernels, beans, squash seeds, chile pepper seeds, prickly pear seeds, and other food remains that were invisible to the eye while excavating.

the lower-status area. Other villages may have had a zone of public buildings, though their zonation was less formal than that of Classic and Postclassic sites.

The Early Formative settlements showed considerable variation in size on the basis of site surveys. About 90 percent were small hamlets, of between one and a dozen households, up to 12 ha (29 acres) in size, and with up to 60 people. Most remained stable at that size for centuries, but a few villages grew bigger. San José Mogote reached 70 ha (172 acres) by 850 BC, the largest settlement in the Valley of Oaxaca at that time and the central place for a network of about 20 villages. Flannery and Marcus postulated that the spacing of the villages about 5 km or 3 miles apart was probably determined socially, to avoid overcrowding, rather than by environmental or agricultural factors, because the available arable land could easily have supported a closer grouping of sites. On the other hand, factors of site catchment determined the precise location for each settlement.

Catchment Areas and Trade. The catchment areas for several sites were assessed. San José Mogote could have satisfied its basic agricultural requirements within a radius of 2.5 km (1.5 miles); its basic mineral resource needs and some important seasonal wild plants within 5 km (3 miles); deer meat, material for house construction, and preferred types of firewood had to be fetched from within 15 km (9.4 miles). Trade with other regions brought in exotic materials largely from a radius of 50 km (30 miles), but sometimes from as far as 200 km (125 miles; see box, p.225).

Trade in obsidian seems to have taken the egalitarian form of exchange in the Early Formative, with all villages participating. From its various sources, it traveled along chain-like networks of villages, to be distributed among households in each community. Unmodified shell was brought in from the coast, and apparently converted into ornaments in the larger villages by part-time specialists who were also farmers, as suggested by the range of materials on their floors.

What Did They Think? What Were They Like? The Oaxaca Early Formative project also examined the evidence for religion and burial. From a study of context, ritual paraphernalia could be distinguished at three levels: the individual, the household, and the community.

At the *community* level, only certain villages had structures that were evidently public buildings rather than residences, and it is assumed that some of the activities carried out in them were ceremonial in nature, and presumably served the neighboring hamlets as well. Conch shell trumpets and turtle shell drums also probably functioned in ritual at the community level (local ethnography supports this view), and were brought in from the coastal lowlands.

At the *household* level, features such as enigmatic painted circular areas within houses have tentatively been interpreted as ritual, or at least non-utilitarian, as have figurines of ancestors and dancers in costumes and masks. Ethnography and ethnohistory suggest that fish spines were used in personal rituals of self-mutilation and bloodletting; spines from marine fish were specially imported to the valley.

At the *individual* level, burials, like houses, suggest that ranking formed a continuum from simple to elaborate, rather than a rigid class system. The cemetery outside the village of Santo Domingo Tomaltepec had over 60 burials of 80 individuals, of whom 55 could be aged and sexed. There were no infants (these were usually buried near the house) and only one child. The oldest person was 50 years of age. Males and females were roughly equal in number, but most women had died between the ages of 20 and 29, while most men had survived into their 30s. All the burials were face-down, and almost all faced east, most in the fully extended position. But a few males were flexed and, although they constituted only 12.7 percent of the cemetery, they had 50 percent of the fine burial vessels, 88 percent of the jade beads, and a high proportion of the graves covered by stone slabs. Clearly, this group had some kind of special status.

Social Developments in the Later Formative (850 BC – AD 100)

The research designs for the two long-term projects initiated by Kent Flannery on the one hand and Richard Blanton on the other had as their ultimate joint goal the identification of the processes leading to the rise of societies with hereditary ranking and to the evolution of the Zapotec state.

Richard Blanton, Stephen Kowalewski, Gary Feinman, and their associates conducted intensive, valley-wide settlement surveys using the survey methods originally pioneered in the Valley of Mexico, and then drew up settlement maps for successive phases. They also carried out a very detailed survey of the major site of Monte Albán. This, it turned out, had been a new foundation sometime around 500 BC, and the site had at once become the principal center in the region. Meanwhile, the excavations by Flannery and his associates already mentioned, at no fewer than nine village sites, provided evidence of the development of houses, storage pits, activity areas, burials and other features throughout the Formative period. Subsistence was again a special focus of study through work with charred seeds, animal bones, pollen remains, and site catchment analysis.

Social organization was investigated by comparing residences from successive periods, by studying burials, and by considering public buildings in order to document the growth of various Zapotec state institutions out of the more generalized institutions of earlier times. Early Zapotec hieroglyphic writing was an important focus of study. And design element studies on pottery, undertaken by Stephen Plog, suggested that as complex regional networks of sites developed, certain groups of hamlets shared the services of a local civic-ceremonial center.

Already in the Early Formative period, as noted above, the site of San José Mogote had grown to pre-eminence in the valley. It was, however, in the succeeding Middle Formative period (850–500 BC) that a three-tier settlement hierarchy was observed through site survey. The site hierarchy at this time was identified by size, and there are no clear indications of administrative functions. But ceremonial functions are much clearer. San José Mogote reached its peak development as a chiefly center, a focus for some 20 villages, with a total population of perhaps 1400 persons. It boasted an acropolis of public buildings on a modified natural hill. An important find was a carved slab showing a sprawled human figure. (see illus. opposite).

The carved slab is one of those discoveries which carries wide implications. For it anticipates 300 or more stone slabs carved with human figures found at Monte Albán in the succeeding phase – the so-called *danzantes*, now interpreted as depicting slain captives. To find a precursor at San José Mogote before 500 BC is

The danzantes ("dancers"), now interpreted as slain captives. (Above left) The origins of danzante carving can be traced to this figure from Monument 3 at San José Mogote, dating to the Rosario phase (600–500 BC). (Above right) San José's largest Rosario phase public building. The workman stands beside structure 28. (Right and below) Photograph of one of the Monte Albán danzantes, and a drawing that reconstructs their probable arrangement on Structure L at that site, c.500–200 BC.

of particular interest. In addition it may be taken to imply the sacrifice of captives at this early time. Between the feet of the San José figure are signs that may be interpreted as giving the date or name-day "One Earthquake." This indicates that the 260-day calendar was already in operation.

Monte Albán. The major site of Monte Albán was founded around 500 BC on a mountain not previously occupied. Richard Blanton has suggested that the site was selected as an administrative center precisely because it was on unoccupied, politically neutral

ground in the "no man's land" between different arms of the valley. He suggests that its founding might be seen as the result of a confederacy among previously autonomous, and perhaps even competitive chiefdoms from various parts of the valley. This view is supported by the apparent cessation of monument construction at centers such as San José Mogote (the largest of them) and Huitzo at roughly the time that Monte Albán was founded. The deliberate fusing of different chiefdom territories in this way could be seen as the initial formation that later led to a state society, a society which continued without a break with Monte Albán as

View south across the central plaza at Monte Albán, with the restored ruins of several temples visible. Founded on a mountaintop in 500 BC, by phase II (200 BC–AD 100) Monte Albán had become a city.

its capital until the demise of the Classic Zapotec state sometime after AD 700.

By the time of Monte Albán phase II (200 BC – AD 100), the evidence for the Zapotec state is clear. Monte Albán had become a city with rulers living in palaces. Temples staffed with priests were to be found both here and at secondary and tertiary centers. Ceremonial inscriptions with multiple columns of texts appeared on buildings. These have been interpreted as listing the more than 40 places subjugated by Monte Albán.

This view of the emergence of the state throws the spotlight, as it were, on the earlier phase I at Monte Albán, from 500 to 200 BC. But unfortunately at Monte Albán itself the evidence is not altogether clear. It can however be established that the site was a large one, ultimately by the end of phase I the home of some 10,000–20,000 people. The 300 *danzante* slabs belong to this phase. Fortunately the evidence from Monte Albán can be supplemented by indications from contemporary secondary centers, such as San José Mogote.

Conclusion

The key to this analysis of the emergence of state society in the Valley of Oaxaca has been a sound chronology. This was based in the first instance on a study of the successive pottery styles. Later, radiocarbon dates provided an absolute chronology. The phases of settlement growth could then be studied.

The Oaxaca projects have been among the most successful in the entire history of archaeology for a number of reasons. One crucial component was the use of *intensive field survey* for settlements. And it should be noted that in the end a complete survey of the valley was preferred to any sampling strategy. The second component was the firm *ecological approach*, most crucial for the earlier periods when agriculture was developing, but important also in later phases when systems of intensification, such as irrigation, were introduced. The emphasis throughout on *social organization*, using evidence from settlement hierarchy, differences in residences within the settlements, and from burials, was a prominent feature of the projects. But so too was modern cognitive-processual archaeology: the emphasis on *religion and symbolic systems*. This is well brought out by Kent Flannery, Joyce Marcus, and their colleagues in their edited book, *The Cloud People* (1983), which also exemplifies their commitment to full publication of their research. The Oaxaca projects are thus of particular interest for their methods as well as their results.

RESEARCH IN CROCODILE DUNDEE COUNTRY: KAKADU NATIONAL PARK, AUSTRALIA

In 1981–82, a team led by Rhys Jones of the Australian National University carried out a multidisciplinary research program inside Kakadu National Park in the Northern Territory of Australia. This World Heritage area is a tropical region, close to the north coast, and has been made internationally famous as the main location for the *Crocodile Dundee* movies. Few people realize, however, that in terms of the number of its occupied rockshelters and the profusion and probable antiquity of its rock art, Kakadu can be compared with such classic archaeological regions as southwest France.

Preparatory Work, and Aims of the Project

The project involved site survey and excavation in a variety of environments, building on previous work in this and neighboring areas. The first stage was to review all earlier archaeological studies in the area, from 1926 until 1979. These had included some site surveys, and excavations of rockshelters, shell mounds, and open-air sites, and had resulted in a basic knowledge of the stone-tool industries and the regional chronology. It had been revealed – particularly through the work of Carmel Schrire – that the occupation of tropical Australia could be traced back more than 23,000 years. One of the most startling discoveries had been the existence of edge-ground axes 20,000 years ago: at first, doubts were expressed about them by the international archaeological community, because in Europe the grinding of stone was a phenomenon associated with the much later Neolithic period.

In addition, investigation of the region's rock art by George Chaloupka had led him to the conclusion that the earliest art there (the "dynamic figure style") was as old as the Upper Paleolithic art of Europe. As we saw in Chapter 6, Chaloupka's art sequence is linked to environmental change in the region, and particularly to the progression of the sea up the river estuaries.

The new research program was designed to test and improve the results of previous work. More basic information was required for the stratigraphic and typological sequences, as well as for the chronology, including the date of the earliest occupation. In addition, it was necessary to investigate the relationship of the archaeological sequences to paleoenvironmental conditions, including the impact of the first inhabitants and their fires. It was also hoped to obtain a large amount of ethnographic information from the Aboriginal inhabitants of the area.

Collaboration with the Aborigines. Before any new fieldwork could be planned or carried out, it was imperative to consult the local Aboriginal community (see Chapter 14), explain and discuss the plans, and alter or abandon them if necessary. The Aborigines had traditional ties with the areas and specific sites in question, and were the legal owners. They took a keen interest in the details of the project. It was stressed to them that everything would be done openly and could be scrutinized at all times by members of their community. The Aborigines felt that the work should indeed be "supervised" by one of their number, not out of distrust of the archaeologists but rather to protect the diggers from doing something that could bring practical or ritual danger: the totemic geography of a region contains some "dangerous places," into which archaeologists might stray through ignorance.

Kakadu National Park is rich in Aboriginal rock art. This figure comes from the Anbangbang site.

The location and boundaries of Kakadu National Park in Australia's Northern Territory, together with the sites studied.

The Aborigines therefore emphasized that permission to excavate would depend on their perception of the degree of responsibility and decorum with which the work was carried out. The team planned to limit the extent of its excavations (to extract a maximum of information with a minimum of digging), and, after completion, to refill the pits and return the sites to their original condition. The Aborigines also stipulated that work at one site must be finished before proceeding to another – an admirable dictum for all archaeology!

In order to streamline the work, the excavations were to be integrated not only with the sieving and processing of material but also with preliminary analysis in a field laboratory. Geomorphological work was carried out on the excavated deposits while they were still open. A portable computer was taken into the field, so that data from the worksheets could be entered quickly onto floppy disks. In this way, preliminary analyses could be carried out while still

excavating, enabling the team to use the results as a guide for formulating the questions about the next phase of excavation.

Senior Aborigine men representing relevant groups accompanied the team on field trips and monitored the excavations, while trainee Aboriginal rangers helped in the laboratory, and were instructed in archaeological procedures.

The Choice of Area and Sites

An area was selected about 60 km (37.5 miles) south of previous foci of investigation, so as to build up a regional pattern of site use. In order to take in a variety of environments, the team chose a transect running NW/SE, from huge open sites on the floodplains and freshwater swamplands of the South Alligator river to the large caves and rockshelters on the edge of a massif, and, finally, to the rockshelters in the inland valley of Deaf Adder Gorge, within the Arnhem Land escarpment. It was hoped that such a transect would provide information on seasonal differences of land use, and also help to contrast these freshwater systems with the estuarine areas previously studied to the north.

The project carried out excavations and/or surface collections of artifacts in seven rockshelters. Two of these proved to be of major importance: Anbangbang I for its wealth of preserved organic material, and the Lindner site for its stratified sequence of over 2.5 m (8.2 ft) of sands resting on artifact-bearing rubble that probably dates back at least 25,000 or 30,000 years. A total of 30 radiocarbon determinations have been obtained so far, two-thirds from archaeological sites and the other third from geomorphological locations designed to resolve archaeological problems: they span the period from 12,000 years ago to modern times.

Anbangbang I Rockshelter

Anbangbang I is a huge rockshelter that seemed suitable for investigation because the material on its ground surface suggested a rich and varied record. It was hoped that this might give a detailed picture of economic activities during the immediate precolonial period, which could in turn be linked with ethnographic information from written sources and from contemporary Aborigines of the area. Another factor was its ease of access from early in the dry season.

Dating and Preservation. It was found that humans started occupying the site considerably before 6000 years ago, and probably in the late Pleistocene (i.e.

before 10,000 years ago), judging by the depth and geomorphology of the artifact-bearing gravels. The intensity of occupation (the density of tools and organic remains) increased markedly about 6000 years ago, and then again about 1000 years ago.

The preservation of organic material is remarkable in the site's upper level. Usually, stone tools are the only things to survive in most sandstone rockshelters in tropical Australia – sandy soil conditions generally provide a poor environment for the preservation of anything else. The dry microenvironment at Anbangbang, however, has permitted good preservation, especially at the sheltered rear of the site.

Technology, Diet, and the Division of Labor. Thanks to the good preservation the team was able to assess the relative role of stone as opposed to wood and other organic implements within a "total" toolkit over the last millennium. Stone tools were clearly of less importance than they appear to be in most sites where

only inorganic tools survive. There were numerous bone implements (notably large awls), and some had traces of gum resin indicating that they had been barbs, probably hafted onto fishing spears. Almost 40 wooden tools were also recovered, including barbed spearpoints for hunting large game or for fighting.

Numerous slivers and shavings of wood indicated that the manufacture and maintenance of spears were carried out at the rockshelter (by the men, according to ethnography), while women were probably responsible for weaving the string (found in some quantity) from fibers and hair.

Fragments of reeds and bamboo represent the shafts of weapons, and most probably came from the wetlands, at least a day's walk away, perhaps through some system of seasonal trade. Remains of plant resources were so numerous (some of them were retrieved by flotation) that only a sample could be analyzed. Those present through human agency (deduced in part from ethnographic information) had

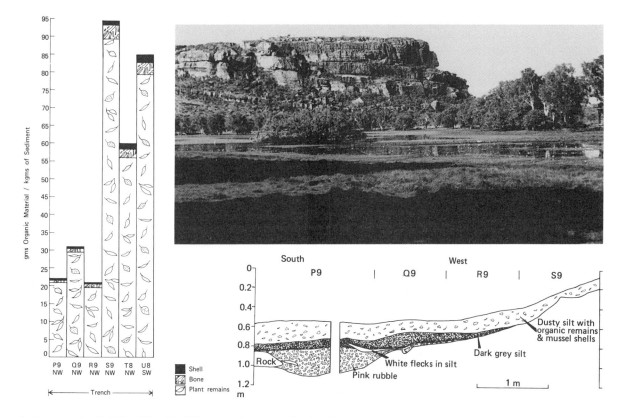

Anbangbang I rockshelter. (Top right) The general area near the site, showing the southwest face of Burrung-gui Cliff, with the Anbangbang lagoon in the foreground. (Left) The relative proportional weight of plant remains, bone, and shell from different trenches excavated at the site. (Above right) Cross-section across trenches P9–S9, showing the stratigraphy.

A sample of the numerous plant remains at Anbangbang I being washed after flotation (Rhys Jones center of picture).

been gathered from the nearby Anbangbang lagoon, no doubt by the women: water-lilies seem to have been exploited intensively, together with tubers and tree-fruits. Women probably also foraged the freshwater turtles, mussels, and crocodile eggs whose remains were recovered. The men, on the other hand, will have foraged the many large fish, as well as the larger animals: over 50 species were hunted. This was, therefore, a broad-spectrum economy.

Not all animals were represented by bones: for example, the echidna's presence was proven only by its quills and feces, a fact suggesting animal intrusion rather than human agency. Proof of human exploitation – as in the case of the large marsupials such as kangaroo and wallaby – lies in the broken and burnt bones, and in marks of butchering and percussion. The minimum numbers of each mammal species were calculated on the basis of jawbones: the little red flying fox and the short-nosed bandicoot were most abundant, but the large marsupials provided most meat.

Both plant and animal remains point to a human presence (during the site's final phase, over the last millennium) in the wet season and the early dry season. The site was probably a base camp for a community of men and women, such as a band of perhaps 25 people, who carried out a wide range of domestic activities here. Anbangbang is one of the richest sites in the whole continent.

Lindner Rockshelter

Technology and Art. The Lindner site (Nauwalabila I) is a rockshelter situated within a plateau valley. The meter square excavated to a depth of over 2.5 m (8.2 ft) yielded more than 30,000 stone artifacts – an average of 12,000 per cubic meter, though they were denser at the top of the stratigraphy than below. Only about 1 percent of the material was retouched, showing that quartz and chert tools were fashioned and trimmed on site. In the lower layers, quartzite tools seem to have been brought in ready-made, whereas in the upper layers the final manufacturing of stone spearpoints was carried out here, with most of the finished products being taken elsewhere. The introduction of these spearpoints occurred between 6200 and 5700 years ago, whereas that of adze/chisels has been dated here to around 3500 years ago. Before these tool types appeared, there were hand-held scrapers and edge-ground axes: flakes from the latter were found down to levels dating to at least 14,000 years ago, which confirm the earlier findings in the region by Carmel Schrire (see above).

No bone material survived in this site, apart from a few small burnt fragments from large mammals. However, one important find was the presence of coloring materials (pieces of red ocher with facets and traces of grinding) throughout the layers, down to a depth of 2.37 m (7 ft 9 in), estimated to be 30,000

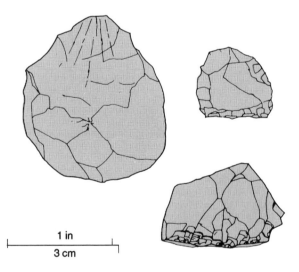

1 in
3 cm

Lindner rockshelter: steep edge scrapers from the lower layers of the site, which yielded more than 30,000 stone artifacts from a meter square excavated to a depth of over 2.5 m (8.2 ft). Clockwise from top left: quartz, red chert, and pink chert.

years old. Although they may have been used simply for body-painting, they do at least prove some artistic activity in the late Pleistocene, and it is quite probable that these "crayons" were used to prepare pigment for rock art, thus supporting the hypotheses of George Chaloupka about the antiquity of some of the region's depictions.

Thanks to flotation techniques, a sequence of about 200 charcoal samples was retrieved from the stratigraphy, and it is hoped that these will eventually provide a detailed basis for calculating the (apparently steady) rate of accumulation of the deposit, and hence obtain an accurate date for the lowest occupied layers. It is possible that the Lindner site is one of the oldest habitations in Australia.

The Wetland-Edge Sites

The wetland edges proved to have a series of large, open sites (up to 25,000 sq. m or 269,000 sq. ft in area) mostly on headlands of dry land strategically located close to the rich food resources of the swamps. They seemed to consist mostly of surface scatters of thousands of artifacts, though one site (Ki'na) was a shallow midden of freshwater mussel shells. The research team sampled each site's scatter by a line of 1 m squares, 10 m apart, along its major axis, thus providing some idea of variation in density of material, and within-site patterning of different elements. In addition, on each site at least one area, 5 m square, was laid out and subdivided into 25 x 1 m squares, from which separate, total collections of surface archaeological material were made, in order to obtain extra information on configurations of material. The 5-m squares were located arbitrarily, after initial survey, in areas of least disturbance or which seemed to provide as large and varied a sample as possible.

Among the millions of stone flakes and other artifacts – all carried into the sites by the occupants as there is no stone in the wetlands – there were many of quartz from nearby sources, whereas quartzite had been brought from a distance of 20–40 km (12–25 miles), and chert from over 50 km (31 miles). There were also grinding stones of sandstone and volcanic rock (brought from outcrops a few kilometers away, no doubt for the processing of plant foods), and adze/chisel slugs. Under strong magnification, it was found that some of the slugs had a narrow band of high polish, a few micrometers wide, together with striations at right angles to the edge, which fit the criteria for wear caused by working hardwoods.

In many wetland sites (but not the inland sites), flakes were found, often unretouched, with a thick silica polish on them, probably caused by plant opals (phytoliths) when cutting grasses or reeds. The Japanese researcher Hiroshi Fujiwara processed soil samples from the Ki'na freshwater swamp, and also from archaeological sites (both wetland open sites and from rockshelter excavations) and found phytoliths primarily from wild rice (*Oryza*), as well as from grasses and reeds. The fact that no rice phytoliths were found at Anbangbang suggests that this plant was unavailable at the nearby lagoon.

It is clear, therefore, that in the recent past the wetland edges were densely occupied, most probably in the dry season to take advantage of the wetland resources (especially plants and water birds). The base of the Ki'na midden was dated to 500 years ago, and it is reckoned that all of these sites are of similar age (between 1000 and 500 years). The reason for the increase in settlement around this time was established by paleoenvironmental work, to which we now turn.

The Broader Picture: Changes in Environment and Economy

A section of the team studied the past and present landscape around the archaeological sites, attempting to assess how and why it has changed, especially over the last 35,000 years. Soil samples were removed for sedimentary and pollen analysis as well as for radiocarbon dating of organic materials. One of the most crucial dates was that of about 1400 years ago for the base of the freshwater peats, showing that the creation of the freshwater swamps is a fairly recent event.

It was established that the most substantial change came when the postglacial rise in sea-level flooded the Alligator river valleys; these estuarine conditions existed by 6000 or 7000 years ago, a fact that fits well with the worldwide sea-level curve. Saltwater extended well up the valleys, and large areas of saline plains and mudflats evolved. Subsequently, there was a period of infilling of the river valleys, with silt and sand deposits building up into levees; freshwater was ponded up behind them, and eventually within the last 2000 years created the rich and productive freshwater wetlands that were seasonally flooded. It will be recalled (Chapter 6) that Chaloupka's theories link the styles of rock art in the region to these transformations of the landscape. No evidence was found by the project team for great change in the inland vegetation over this period.

The sparse early archaeological material suggests that, before the formation of the freshwater swamps,

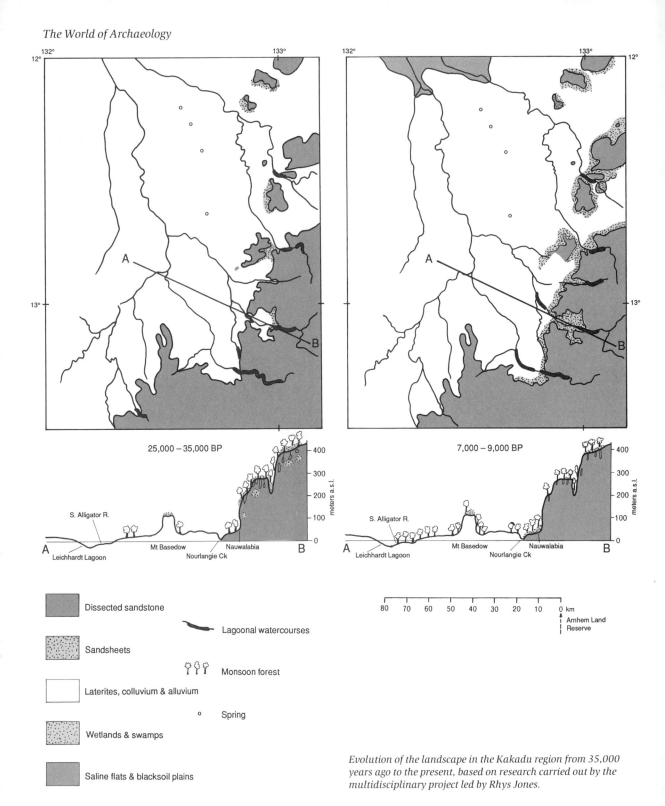

25,000 – 35,000 BP

7,000 – 9,000 BP

S. Alligator R.

Leichhardt Lagoon

Mt Basedow

Nourlangie Ck

Nauwalabia

A

B

meters a.s.l.

400

300

200

100

0

Dissected sandstone

Sandsheets

Laterites, colluvium & alluvium

Wetlands & swamps

Saline flats & blacksoil plains

Lagoonal watercourses

Monsoon forest

Spring

80 70 60 50 40 30 20 10 0 km

Arnhem Land Reserve

Evolution of the landscape in the Kakadu region from 35,000 years ago to the present, based on research carried out by the multidisciplinary project led by Rhys Jones.

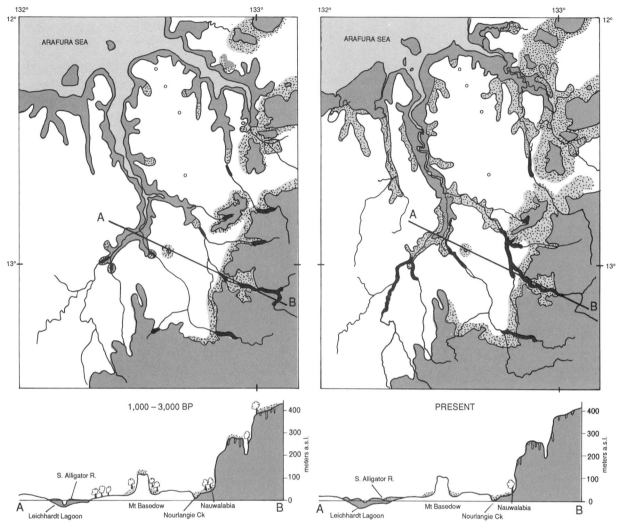

population density was low, with occupation perhaps sporadic or seasonal. The arrival of the sea around 6000 years ago seems (from the evidence at Anbangbang) to have led to denser occupation; but clearly it was the creation of freshwater swamps about 1000 years ago that transformed the landscape, dramatically increasing the population density and leading the local Aborigines to alter their economy so as to take full advantage of the newly available food resources. Large groups of people camped at the swamp edges, probably in the dry season, and carried out many maintenance and production activities there. The same groups may have occupied the inland shelters during the dry season; here the effects of the changed landscape are

less marked, but still detectable in the archaeological remains.

In addition, the sediments in the shelters provide some clues to the long-term human use of the landscape. Studies suggest that the sediments accumulate largely as a result of human activity in the vicinity. For example, the practice of regular burning caused soil erosion, which built up the sediments. The gradual erosion of the sandstone shelters themselves also contributed to the deposits. Changes in the rate of accumulation thus helped the team to judge how intensely people used the sites and the landscape, and corresponded well with the results from other types of evidence.

461

Conclusion

The Kakadu project therefore succeeded in producing a new and detailed picture of environment, subsistence, population, and technology in this important region for the past 30 millennia. In particular, it proved that there had been a significant increase in the number of sites, in population, and in the intensity of site-use that can be closely correlated with the transformation of the landscape and its productivity.

Publication of the work followed swiftly: an interim report was produced by March 1983, and a monograph appeared in 1985.

Further Reading

The fundamental sources for the three case studies are as follows:

Melos:

Renfrew, C. & Wagstaff, M. (eds.). 1982. *An Island Polity: The Archaeology of Exploitation in Melos*. Cambridge University Press: Cambridge & New York.

Renfrew, C. 1985. *The Archaeology of Cult: The Sanctuary of Phylakopi*. The British School at Athens Publication no. 18: London.

Oaxaca:

Blanton, R.E. 1978. *Monte Albán: Settlement Patterns at the Ancient Zapotec Capital*. Academic Press: New York.

Flannery, K.V. & Marcus, J. (eds.). 1983. *The Cloud People: Divergent Evolution of the Zapotec and Mixtec Civilizations*. Academic Press: New York.

Flannery, K.V. (ed.). 1986. *Guilá Naquitz: Archaic Foraging and Early Agriculture in Oaxaca, Mexico*. Academic Press: New York.

Kakadu:

Jones, R. (ed.). 1985. *Archaeological Research in Kakadu National Park*. Australian National Parks and Wildlife Service, Special Publication No. 13. Australian National University: Canberra.

14
Whose Past?
Archaeology and
the Public

This book is concerned with the way that archaeologists investigate the past, with the questions we can ask and our means of answering them. But the time has come to address two much wider questions: Why, beyond reasons of scientific curiosity, do we want to know about the past? And whose past is it anyway? These issues very soon lead us to questions of responsibility, public as well as private. For surely a national monument, such as Great Zimbabwe or the Athenian Acropolis, means something special to the modern descendants of its builders? Does it not also mean something to all humankind? If so, should it not be protected from destruction, in the same way as endangered plant and animal species? If the looting of ancient sites is to be deplored, should it not be stopped, even if the sites are on privately owned land? Who owns, or should own, the past?

These very soon become ethical questions – of right and wrong, of appropriate action and reprehensible action. The archaeologist has a special responsibility because, as we saw in Chapter 3, excavation itself entails destruction. Future workers' understanding of a site can never be much more than our own, because we will have destroyed the evidence and recorded only those parts of it we considered important and had the energy to publish properly.

Destruction on a much larger scale comes from another quarter, far exceeding anything suffered in earlier centuries. The earth's surface is now being exploited more exhaustively than ever before, for commercial, industrial, and agricultural purposes, and any fragile vestiges of earlier human activity are liable to be swept away if they hinder that exploitation. Moreover, the very interest that archaeology has generated in our past has created new destructive forces: not only looters and illicit excavators – whose plunder finds its way into private collections and public museums – but tourists, who by their numbers threaten the sites they seek to enjoy.

The past is big business – in tourism and in the auction rooms. The past is politically highly charged, ideologically powerful and significant. And the past, or what remains of it, is subject to increasing destruction. What can we do about these problems?

WHO OWNS THE PAST?

Until recent decades, archaeologists gave little thought to the question of the ownership of past sites and antiquities. Most archaeologists themselves came from western, industrialized societies whose economic and political domination seemed to impart an almost automatic right to acquire antiquities and excavate sites around the world. Since World War II, however, former colonies have grown into independent nation states eager to uncover their own past and assert control over their own heritage. Difficult questions have therefore arisen. Should antiquities acquired for western museums during the colonial era be returned to their lands of origin? And should archaeologists be free to excavate the burials of groups whose modern descendants may object on religious or other grounds?

Museums and the Return of Cultural Property

At the beginning of the last century Lord Elgin, a Scottish diplomat, removed some of the marble sculptures from the façade of the Parthenon, the great 5th-century BC temple that crowns the Acropolis in Athens. Elgin did so with the permission of the then Turkish

Part of the "Elgin Marbles:" a horseman from the façade of the Parthenon in Athens, c.440 BC.

overlords of Greece, and later sold the sculptures to the British Museum, where they still reside, finely displayed. The Greeks now want the "Elgin Marbles" back. That in essence is the story so far of perhaps the best-known case where an internationally famous museum is under pressure to return cultural property to the country of origin. But there are numerous other claims directed at European and North American museums. The Berlin Museum, for example, holds the famous bust of the Egyptian queen Nefertiti, which was shipped out of Egypt illegally. And London's Museum of Mankind possesses many treasures obtained in imperial days, such as the richly carved lintels taken by Alfred Maudslay from the Maya site of Yaxchilan in the 1880s, and which Mexico would like to retrieve.

The issues are complex. The British Museum's main argument against returning objects is that its trustees are expressly forbidden by British law to dispose of the objects in their charge. But there are ways round this – a fragment of the beard of the great Sphinx of Giza, for example, was recently returned by the museum to Egypt as a "permanent loan." Furthermore, modern materials and techniques make it feasible to produce virtually perfect casts and replicas. The question then is: should the original or the copy be presented to the country making the request? A crucial factor here is whether the original will be adequately protected and conserved once returned. Many fragile antiquities survive today only because they have been housed in western museums. The Elgin Marbles in the British Museum are in much better condition than those sections of the Parthenon frieze that were left in place on the Acropolis. On the other hand, the Greeks now plan to build a special museum to safeguard the sculptures if they are returned.

There is certainly a good case to be made for the restitution of objects of special religious or cultural significance, such as the kachinas (dolls representing spirits) of the North American Hopi Indians. Artifacts of this kind are not museum pieces but "living" and powerful things within their culture. It might also make sense to reassemble material from particular sites that is now scattered throughout the world's museums, and to repatriate at least a sample of objects that may be overrepresented in foreign collections but rare or absent in museums of the country of origin.

At the same time, one can set up the problem in a different way, and ask whether the interest of the great products of human endeavor does not in fact transcend the geographical boundaries of 20th-century nationalism. Does it make sense that all the Paleolithic hand-axes and other artifacts from Olduvai Gorge or Olorgesailie in East Africa should remain confined within the bounds of the modern nations where they have been found? Should we not all be able to benefit from the insights they offer? And is it not a profound and important experience to be able, in the course of one day in one of the world's great museums, to be able to walk from room to room, from civilization to civilization, and see unfolded a sample of the whole variety of human experience? Would it not be a greater service, in response to requests to repatriate one nation's antiquities, to offer instead great works belonging to a *different* cultural tradition?

Even if one is willing to work within a framework of 20th-century national chauvinism, it may be more appropriate for the works of one nation to be seen and appreciated overseas. Nearly all the important products of Minoan civilization remain in Crete, in the Herakleion Museum. In consequence, they are little known other than from glossy picture books and to Hellenic travelers. Are the nationalistic ends of Greek culture better served by the confining of Minoan works of art to Herakleion, or by the dispersal of Classical Greek art throughout the western world? There are difficult issues to unravel here, as much to do with national and international politics as with modern archaeology.

Excavating Burials: Should We Disturb the Dead?
The question of excavating burials can be equally complex. For prehistoric burials the problem is not so great, because we have no direct written knowledge of the relevant culture's beliefs and wishes. For burials dating from historic times, however, religious beliefs are known to us in detail. We know, for example, that the ancient Egyptians and Chinese, the Greeks, Etruscans, and Romans, and the early Christians all feared disturbance of the dead. Yet it has to be recognized that tombs were falling prey to the activities of robbers long before archaeology began. Egyptian pharaohs in the 12th century BC had to appoint a commission to inquire into the wholesale plundering of tombs at Thebes. Not a single Egyptian royal tomb, including that of Tutankhamun, escaped the robbers completely. Similarly, Roman carved gravestones became building material in cities and forts; and at Ostia, the port of ancient Rome, tomb inscriptions have even been found serving as seats in a public latrine!

However, disturbance and plunder by the ignorant and greedy cannot alone justify archaeological investigation, although the scholar certainly benefits more people than the robber. Can archaeology reconcile a respect for the people of the past with deliberate disturbance of their remains, destruction of their tombs, and removal of their bodies and grave-goods against the wishes of modern groups who for religious or other reasons see themselves as the living representatives of the deceased? Clearly archaeologists must show sensitivity on this issue. Where the modern descendants have a legitimate case, the only way forward lies in negotiation and compromise. In the longer term, archaeology should be made more relevant for, and open to, all sectors of the community.

Archaeology and Judaism. One religion which takes an intense and often hostile interest in archaeology is Judaism. In 1981 the issue erupted when thousands of militant, ultra-orthodox Jews held a demonstration in Jerusalem against the alleged desecration of graves at a major archaeological site in the city. The demonstration led to a heated debate over whether religious or secular law should apply in this case. Similarly, in August 1986, an important archaeological project at Tel Haror in the Negev Desert was vandalized, most probably by members of Atra Kadisha, an ultra-orthodox group dedicated to preserving the sanctity of Jewish cemeteries. So far there appears to be no meeting of minds, or satisfactory compromise, between the opposed camps.

The burial issue has also become a political and legal problem in several other countries, including Australia, New Zealand, and the United States.

The Australian Aborigines. In Australia, the present climate of Aboriginal emancipation and increased political power has focused attention on wrongdoings during the Colonial period, when anthropologists had little respect for Aboriginal feelings and beliefs. Sacred sites were investigated and published, burial sites desecrated, and cultural and skeletal material exhumed, to be stored or displayed in museums. The Aborigines were thus, by implication, seen as laboratory specimens. Inevitably, the fate of all this material, and particularly of the bones, has assumed great symbolic significance. Unfortunately, here as in other countries, archaeologists are being blamed for the misdemeanors of the non-archaeologists who obtained most of the human remains in question.

Broadly, the view of Aborigines in some parts of Australia is that all human skeletal material (and occasionally cultural material too) must be returned to them, and then its fate will be decided. Since the Aborigines have an unassailable moral case, the Australian Archaeological Association (AAA) is willing to return remains which are either quite modern or of "known individuals where specific descendants can be traced," and for these to be reburied. However, such remains are somewhat the exception. The University of Melbourne's Murray Black Collection consists of skeletal remains from over 800 Aborigines ranging in date from several hundred years to at least 14,000 years old. They were dug up in the 1940s without any consultation with local Aborigines. Owing to a lack of specialists the collection has still by no means been exhaustively studied – but nevertheless it has recently been returned to the relevant Aboriginal communities.

Archaeologists are understandably alarmed at the prospect of having to hand over material many thousands of years old. Some also point out that the Aborigines – like indigenous peoples elsewhere – tend to forget that not all of their recent forebears took pious care of the dead. But in view of Aboriginal sufferings at European hands, one must certainly look on their claims with sympathy.

This is particularly true of the Australian state of Tasmania, where the government recently ordered the Crowther Collection of skeletal material from known historical people to be returned to the Aboriginal community to dispose of as it saw fit. The way in which the material had been collected was so appalling that the AAA took the view that any potential scientific value was far outweighed by ethical considerations, and actually urged the Tasmanian government to hand over the material. The Crowther Collection underwent traditional cremation in 1985.

The future lies in negotiation, compromise, and involvement of Aborigines in archaeological work. Many Aborigines object to displays of skeletal material in museums, and these have now been replaced by casts, or removed altogether. They also demand to be consulted and are prepared to discuss each case on its merits. Already, for the Lake Mungo human remains (up to 30,000 years old), there is a special "keeping place" proposed at the site, an underground lockable store with Aboriginal custodians who will give access to scholars. In parts of Australia, the employment and training of Aborigines as museum curators is underway. Aborigines will thus develop an informed appreciation of their heritage, as the North American Indians have done. This is surely more worthwhile than destruction of material or reburial with no access.

Remarkable progress is being made. In 1982 an indigenous community at Robinvale, on the Murray river, requested that a prehistoric burial site endangered by erosion of the riverbank should undergo a rescue excavation. The dig was carried out with Aboriginal assistance and constant consultation with the local community who were most interested in the data from the site. When excavation revealed a major burial ground, the community halted the work, had the site saved and stabilized by soil conservation experts, and skeletal material reburied after being documented in the field.

New Zealand. In New Zealand, no display of skeletal material now occurs. As elsewhere, there is no single, standard indigenous viewpoint about these problems, but certainly many Maori (the indigenous New Zealanders) dislike the past being examined. The history they pass down among themselves is secret, sacred information, not for public discussion. Where burials are concerned, they often prefer to see them destroyed by nature or even by the impersonal bulldozer than to have them dug up and preserved. Currently, archaeologists in New Zealand (who now include a young Maori lecturer) maintain close consultation with local Maori, and as a result there is a great deal of cooperation between the two sides, though, as yet, there is little direct involvement on the part of the indigenous community.

The American Indians. The Indians of North America have expressed their grievances strongly in recent years, and in many respects they have greater political influence than the American archaeological community. Their campaigns have often proved successful, and archaeology has become a focal point for complaints about wrongdoings of the past. As a result, quite apart from the question of returning and reburying material, there have been vehement objections to new excavations. The Chumash Indians, for example, refused permission for scientists to remove what may be the oldest human remains in California, even though an offer was made to return and rebury the bones after a year's study. The bones, thought to be about 9000 years old, were eroding out of a cliff on Santa Rosa Island, 100 km (62 miles) west of Los Angeles. Under California's Antiquities Act the fate of the bones lay with their most likely descendants – and the Chumash were angry about past treatment of their ancestors' skeletons, with hundreds of remains scattered in various universities and museums. Like many Maori, they preferred to see the bones destroyed "in accordance with nature's law" than to have other people interfere with them.

Seminole Indian bones are reburied by archaeologists and American Indians at Wounded Knee, South Dakota, in 1989.

As in Australia and New Zealand, there is no single, unified indigenous tradition. American Indians have wide-ranging attitudes toward the dead and the soul. The solution to the problem has been found to lie in acquiescence, compromise, and collaboration. Quite often archaeologists have acquiesced in the return of very recent remains from known individuals or from fairly close ancestors of living objectors. Much material has also been returned that had no archaeological context and was thus of minimal value to science. Reburial of more important material is a difficult issue. Despite resolutions passed by the Society for American Archaeology and other anthropological associations in North America opposing such reburial except where lineal descendants can be traced, there is now a clear trend in favor of negotiated reburial on a large scale. Tribal representatives have worked out agreements to reinter extensive collections from several museums, including those at Stanford University and the American Museum of Natural History. The Smithsonian Institution has been likewise engaged in a major exercise to identify and possibly return thousands of skeletal remains and associated objects. And at Wounded Knee, South Dakota, Seminole Indian bones were reburied by archaeologists and American Indians in a joint ceremony in 1989 to mark the establishment of a national cemetery for American Indians.

Now that archaeologists have come to recognize American Indian rights, working relations have improved, and there are growing numbers of American Indian representatives who appreciate the contribution that archaeology is making to their history and, indeed, to their ethnic identity. But there are still tensions – some archaeologists have had their lives threatened as grave-robbers – so it is important for excavators to be sensitive to the wishes of the local community. One excellent example is the archaeological program at the Zuni Pueblo, New Mexico, begun in 1975, which involved consultation with the local community every step of the way. Although the Zuni abhor the exposure of human remains, let alone the handling of bones, they allowed the archaeologists to take photographs and record data. Influence was felt in both directions, in that the Zuni acknowledged the importance of new information about their mortuary customs, while some archaeologists experienced a qualitative change in their values and beliefs concerning excavation of such burials.

THE USES OF THE PAST

The uses of the past, and the problems surrounding them, go beyond the specific question of who owns what. They concern ideological and economic issues.

Ideology and Nationalism

China. Chairman Mao used to urge that the past should serve the present, and excavation of ancient sites in China certainly continued even at the height of the Cultural Revolution of the 1960s. Today there is widespread popular concern in that country for its ancient cultural relics. Great emphasis is placed on artistic treasures as products of skilled workers rather than as the property of rulers; they are seen as reflections of the class struggle, while the palaces and rich tombs of the aristocracy underline the ruthless exploitation of the laboring masses. The Communist message is also conveyed through humbler artifacts. The museum at the Lower Paleolithic site of Zhoukoudian, for example, proclaims that labor, as represented by the making and using of tools, was the decisive factor in our transition from apes to humans.

In addition, the relics and monuments of the past help to build up pride in Chinese art, technology, and traditions, and to affirm the national identity and cultural continuity. More prosaically, as in many other parts of the world, archaeological finds help attract much needed income from tourism.

Israel. Here too archaeology serves the twin masters of national ideology and tourism. The excavation by Yigael Yadin in the 1960s of the fortress of Masada resurrected the stirring story of the last stand of the Jewish Zealots against the besieging Romans in AD 73, and how they chose mass suicide instead of surrender. It has become a symbol of Israeli defiance and pride, as well as an important place of tourism. Israel employs prehistory as a means of underlining historical continuity and hence of justifying her existence.

Economic Lessons from the Past

The uses of archaeology are not, however, restricted to ideology. In some parts of the world they are proving to be of the utmost economic importance. Archaeology shows that in many areas where today the soil is barren agriculture once flourished. Are there lessons to be learnt here for modern farmers?

467

Nabataeans in the Negev Desert. Israel's Negev Desert is one of the world's most inhospitable places, with temperatures above 38°C (100°F) and less than 2 cm (0.79 in) rainfall each year. Yet about 2000 years ago the Nabataeans lived there in cities, growing grapes, wheat, and olives. How did they do it?

It used to be assumed that the climate was lusher and much wetter, but we now know that it has remained unaltered since well before these settlements. Aerial photographs reveal a complex pattern of ditches, terraces, and barriers crisscrossing the hills. Evidently the Nabataeans took advantage of the region's rare, violent cloudbursts and flash-floods to utilize the rainwater, which was collected in ditches and then channeled into terraced fields. The system also supplied drinking water, which was collected in large cisterns dug into limestone ridges. Thousands of such cisterns are known in the Middle East.

Scientists of the Ben-Gurion University of the Negev have used exactly the same methods, without irrigation or new technology, to reconstruct ancient farms such as that near the ruins of the Nabataean town of Avdat, which was an important stopping place for caravans between 300 BC and AD 600. Here they are able to grow a variety of cereals (with very high yields), fruits, vegetables, and nuts, even in years of drought. They have learned that the runoff technique requires hilly regions from which the water can flow down and where the soil is sufficiently firm to support the drainage channels. The rain-collection area needs to be 30 times larger than the growing area.

The ancients therefore show that by adapting intelligently to one's environment and natural resources, it should be possible to make fertile land once dismissed as worthless – perhaps 5 percent of all arid land. The techniques are being taught to agriculturists from developing nations.

Agriculture in the Andes. A similar lesson from the past has emerged in Peru, where the Cusichaca project, directed by Ann Kendall, is applying archaeology to the revival of agriculture. The ancient town of Patallacta, located between Cuzco and Machu Picchu on an Inca highway, stands on high slopes above the Cusichaca river. In its heyday it had 115 dwellings and a fortress, and may have supported 5000 people. Nowadays the land is barren, with a five-month dry season, and supports 15 families.

The Incas had built dozens of stone canals which carried water down from the glacier-fed streams above to the lower slopes by a winding route which prevented it overflowing or bursting the stonework. The canals were always kept free of rubble and silt – until

APPLIED ARCHAEOLOGY: FARMING IN PERU

In 1980, American archaeologist Clark Erickson, Peruvian agronomist Ignacio Garaycochea and their colleagues set up PACE (Proyecto Agricola de los Campos Elevados, or Raised Field Agricultural Project). The multidisciplinary team's aim was to reintroduce ancient agricultural practices around Lake Titicaca, in Peru and Bolivia.

As in many other parts of tropical Latin America, the ancient cultures constructed raised fields (known locally as *camellones* or *waru-waru*). These elevated planting surfaces are up to 1 m (3 ft) high, 4–10 m (13–32 ft 6 in) wide, and up to 100 m (325 ft) long, and made of the soil dug from the canals in between. They

The two stages of construction: drawings used in booklets produced by the Raised Fields project to teach the technique and its advantages to local communities.

combine good drainage and moisture control with excellent soil and growth conditions, and remarkable resistance to night frosts because the canal water stores heat during the day and releases it slowly at night. The canals can be manipulated either to drain excessive water during periods of heavy rainfall or to retain water during periods of drought.

Aerial photography and excavation have revealed that the high, flat pampas around Lake Titicaca had at least 82,000 hectares (33,000 acres) devoted to this system; it seems to have begun around 1000 BC, and was abandoned after the Inca Conquest about 500 years ago: the Spanish chroniclers make no mention of it at all.

On this altiplano (high plain), at an altitude of nearly 4000 m (13,000 ft), the soils are poor, rainfall is irregular, wet and dry seasons vary unpredictably, and frost and drought are constant threats. At the marshy lake edge fluctuating water levels

can cause widespread inundations. Modern agricultural methods have been introduced, involving heavy machinery, chemical fertilizers, irrigation, and imported crops, in the mistaken belief that the plain was being under-utilized. They have proved unsuccessful, falling prey to the adverse climatic conditions. Consequently, much of the area filled with relic raised fields is classed as of low agricultural potential and used as pasture.

The PACE team cleared and refurbished about 10 ha (4 acres) of abandoned but well-preserved raised fields at Huatta, near Puno (Peru), using only traditional tools, and planted them with potatoes and other traditional tuber crops. The yields have been excellent even in dry years. In the 1984/85 season alone potato production was increased by over two-and-a-half to four times.

In addition, the raised fields were unharmed by the severe drought of 1982/83 and by the massive flooding of the 1983/84 and 1985/86

growing seasons, which destroyed crops on land farmed with modern methods. Likewise, frosts severely damaged nearby fields, but had minimal effect on the raised fields.

It now seems clear that the prehistoric field technologies are an excellent solution to the development of agriculture in this kind of environment. They are perfectly adapted to its climatic factors; the rich organic muck that accumulates in the canals provides the fertilizer for the next growing season, and the only requirements are local labor, and traditional crops, tools, and skills. Initial high labor costs are soon offset by high production yields and low maintenance costs.

The local populace is taking a keen interest, as is the government, and the project has produced well-illustrated booklets, some of them in Quechua (the native language), aimed specifically at teaching the techniques to the local farmers. A videotape in Quechua is also used in the training program.

Peruvian villagers *(right) use footplows (chakitaqlla), hoes (rawkana), and carrying cloths (manta) for moving soil to create raised fields. The result of their endeavors are fields like those below, planted with potatoes.*

they were abandoned at the Spanish Conquest. Now the Cusichaca project is restoring the canals. An international team of volunteers has begun to repair and clear them, and has already succeeded in re-irrigating dozens of acres. As a result, the idea is being taken up by local farmers.

A similar project around Lake Titicaca has also proved a great success (see box, previous page).

From Building Lessons to the History of Disease. There are other lessons to be learned from archaeological remains. It is unwise, for example, to build modern settlements or dams in areas known to have been repeatedly damaged in the past by torrents, earthquakes, or volcanic eruptions. All over China, there are ancient stelae and documents that record past earthquakes, and "seismic archaeology" is considered of great importance here. Human remains can likewise,

as we saw in Chapter 11, yield important information on the history of specific diseases and pathologies, some of which are still a problem today. For example, medical specialists claim that the high incidence of ear-canal pathologies in the skeletons of ancient Australian Aborigines could help to pinpoint the causes of the high rate of chronic middle-ear infections among modern Aborigine children.

To sum up, the past can serve the present in a variety of ways – ideological, agricultural, constructional, and medical. Archaeologists could do worse than to lay more emphasis on the practical benefits of their discipline, thereby helping to justify their claim on public and private funds.

There will, however, be little archaeology for future generations to pursue unless the great tide of destruction of our heritage is stemmed and adequate conservation measures are introduced.

CONSERVATION AND DESTRUCTION

Most nations of the world now recognize that it is the public duty of a government to have some policy of conservation. That policy will apply to natural resources and wildlife, but it will also apply to archaeological remains. So most nations now have protective legislation – not all equally effective – for their ancient sites, minor as well as major, and government programs organized in the United States under the rubric of Cultural Resource Management (CRM), and often elsewhere of Archaeological Heritage Management.

There are two principal stages in archaeological conservation. The first is the gathering of information, so that relevant sites and areas may be recognized and properly recorded. The second is the conservation of those sites and areas that can be effectively protected. Sometimes damage or destruction cannot be prevented, in which case one adopts a policy of salvage or rescue archaeology, partially excavating or at least recording the site before it vanishes for good.

There are two main agencies of destruction, both of them human. One is construction of roads, quarries, dams, office blocks, etc. These are conspicuous and the threat is at least easily recognizable. A different kind of destruction – agricultural intensification – is slower but much wider in its extent, thus in the long term much more destructive. Ever increasing areas of the earth, once uncultivated or cultivated by traditional, non-intensive methods, are being opened up to mechanized farming. The tractor and the deep plow have replaced the digging stick and the ard. In other areas,

forest plantations now cover what was formerly open land, and tree roots are destroying settlement sites and field monuments. Elsewhere, reclamation schemes are transforming the nature of the environment, so that arid lands are being flooded, and the wetlands of say Florida or the Somerset levels are being reclaimed through drainage. In each case the result is destruction of remarkable archaeological evidence. More ancient remains have been lost in the last two decades than ever before in the history of the world.

There are two further human agencies of destruction, which should not be overlooked. The first is tourism, which makes the effective conservation of archaeological sites more difficult. The second is not new, but has grown dramatically in scale: the looting of archaeological sites by those who dig for monetary gain, seeking only saleable objects and destroying everything else in their search.

Legislative Basis of Conservation

The legislation for the ancient heritage varies considerably from nation to nation.

The Rise of CRM in the United States. Over the past two decades the whole pace and direction of American archaeology has been transformed by the development of public archaeology – archaeology funded primarily from federal or state resources and known, as we have seen, as Cultural Resource Management. The history of the legislation for public archaeology is very relevant to how CRM is practiced today.

The Antiquities Act of 1906 stated the responsibilities of the federal government for "antiquities" and extended these responsibilities to include lands controlled by, as well as owned by, the government. Then in 1935 the Historic Sites Act gave the National Park Service responsibility for identifying and protecting outstanding historic sites. The National Historic Preservation Act of 1966 (amended in 1976 and 1980) was an important milestone. It established a National Register of Historic Places, and provided for grants to state preservation programs. The National Environmental Policy Act of 1969 established the basis for CRM by laying down a firm policy for government land use, requiring federal agencies to consider environmental, historical, and cultural values whenever federally owned land is modified, or federal funds used on private land. The act required the preparation of an Environmental Impact Statement (EIS) for any federal works – thus bringing in archaeologists at an earlier stage – but it did not in itself provide funding for salvage archaeology to mitigate their effects.

In 1971, Executive Order 11593 was issued by President Nixon to unite existing legislation into a more coherent federal policy. This set the framework for the great upsurge of archaeological survey work funded by federal agencies such as the Forest Service, the National Parks Service, and the Army Corps of Engineers in the 1970s. It was, however, the Archaeological and Historic Preservation Act of 1974 that authorized federal agencies to provide funds for the preservation and recovery of archaeological or historic resources when endangered by federal projects. These funds were to be provided by contract – giving rise to the term *contract archaeology* – specifying that up to 1 percent of the cost of the project might be expended in this way. The legislation thus provided funds for excavation, analysis of finds, and publication of the results (but with no legal obligation to publish fully). Finally, the Archaeological Resources Protection Act of 1979 gave better protection to sites located on federal and Native American lands.

Unfortunately, the 1979 and earlier acts suffer from the great defect of all American heritage legislation: they offer no protection to sites located on privately owned land. Archaeologists Mark Michel and Steven LeBlanc have set up the independent Archaeological Conservancy precisely in order to purchase and protect such vulnerable sites, but the task is a huge one, at present beyond the means of a single private organization. Furthermore, current legislation is completely inadequate to protect the thousands of shipwrecks in American waters. Occasionally there are success stories, such as the World War II battleship USS *Arizona*, sunk in Pearl Harbor in 1941 and now preserved on the sea bed as a National Memorial. All too often, however, historic wrecks have been looted before archaeologists could reach them.

The scale of CRM funding is considerable. A major project may cost in the order of $1 million, whereas a research grant from the National Science Foundation will rarely exceed $100,000. The concern underlying this expenditure is with conservation rather than research. The result, however, has been to fund some very ambitious archaeological projects, where it has proved possible to formulate valid research aims and to advance our knowledge of the past. CRM archaeology is on such a large scale that, not surprisingly, some projects have been less well conducted, and especially less well published. This has led to tensions between academic and CRM archaeologists. Yet, although some academic criticisms may be justified, there is ample evidence that CRM archaeology can meet the highest scholarly standards (see box overleaf).

Britain and Denmark. Few other countries in the world have the comprehensive US-style legal provisions that bind the government to consider environmental and cultural factors in the course of government-funded work, and to pay for salvage archaeology where appropriate. On the other hand, many countries do have legislation that prevents the private developer from destroying important archaeological sites on private land.

In Britain, for instance, the official agency English Heritage advises the relevant government department on sites worthy of protection, whether or not these are on private land. If they are regarded as of national importance they are placed on a Schedule of Ancient Monuments. The Schedule includes not simply major sites – often in the care of English Heritage and open to the public – but minor ones as well. There are currently about 13,000 scheduled sites in England alone. When the private owner of a listed site wishes to develop it or the land around it, he or she has to apply for Scheduled Monument Consent. In cases where it is judged that the development should go ahead, English Heritage will usually pay the costs of excavation so that the site can be recorded.

In Denmark some 28,000 monuments are included in a "first category." Each of these is fully protected by law against destruction and is surrounded by a 100-m (328-ft) protection zone. All other fixed monuments fall within the "second category" of protection, which is only a legal one: there are over 100,000 of these.

THE PRACTICE OF CRM IN THE UNITED STATES

Federal construction projects in the United States – those on federal land, or on private land but federally funded – are legally required to consider environmental, cultural, and historical resources that may be adversely affected. Cultural Resource Management (CRM) has grown out of this requirement. Projects on state land, or funded by the states, are in general similarly protected.

Most projects develop in two phases: assessment, and mitigation. During assessment, the affected land is surveyed and an Environmental Impact Statement prepared. The decision is then made as to what steps need to be taken in "mitigation." Can project plans be altered? What salvage work should be carried out?

One good example is the vast Tennessee-Tombigbee Waterway project. Of the 682 sites revealed by survey, it was determined that 27 would be affected by waterway

construction. Of these, 17 had good research potential, and another 24 sites were selected for data recovery. Twelve sites could be preserved by altering the construction program.

Excavation was designed to investigate the evolution of cultures in the area, with emphasis on sampling a good range of sites. The largest site was Lubbub Creek, the only major settlement in the threatened area belonging to the Mississippian culture (AD 900–1450). It includes a major ceremonial mound surrounded by a fortified village. The work undertaken in mitigation of environmental impact gave an excellent opportunity for systematic excavation of both settlement and cemeteries.

Several institutions have established outstanding reputations for salvage archaeology. Among them are the Arizona State Museum, the Arkansas Survey, the University of South Carolina and the CRM Program of the University of Pittsburgh. These

reputations are based on the quality of their published reports – reflecting coherent project designs – and on efficient data recovery and clear-minded interpretation.

Not all contract archaeology is of this standard. "Cowboy" operators can be attracted by the large sums of money involved. But the Society of Professional Archaeologists (SOPA) and the American Society for Conservation Archaeology have considered standards of professional qualifications, training, and ethical guidelines. What has been termed "a crisis of quality" may in due course result in a more uniform and higher standard of work.

An aerial view *of the Lubbub Creek site on the Tombigbee River, Alabama. The smaller photograph shows two of the salvage archaeologists carefully cleaning a large urn.*

Australia and New Zealand. In both Australia and New Zealand considerable steps have been taken in recent years toward the recording and safeguarding of archaeological sites of all kinds. Only 20 years ago not one Australian state provided statutory protection for any Aboriginal relics or sites, but by 1981 all of them did so. Analogous legislation to protect the European cultural inheritance – material remains of 200 years of European settlement in Australia – lagged behind, but great progress has been made on this issue as well.

The Australian Heritage Commission was established in 1976 and has provided a national focus for the natural and cultural environment. Its first priority was a Register of the National Estate, published in 1981, which listed over 6600 places including many of archaeological importance. The register helps to protect sites from development projects. Preservation of the national heritage is one of the primary functions of the Commission, which also plays a vital role in the identification and documentation of sites, in serving as a planning tool for the government and developers, and in stimulating public consciousness of Australia's rich cultural background.

In New Zealand, the Historic Places Act of 1980 set out to preserve and protect places of historic significance, including archaeological sites associated with human activity over 100 years old, both Maori and European. The 100-year rule, however, does not preclude the Historic Places Trust being involved with much younger sites. Thanks to the 1980 act, no site can be modified or damaged in any way without the permission of the Trust, and this applies not only to known sites but also to places where there is reasonable cause to suspect the existence of a site.

Increasingly today archaeologists think in terms of entire landscapes rather than simply of single sites. In this respect, the legal systems of protection of many nations are proving inadequate, based as they are on the now rather old-fashioned notion of the single site. In some countries, however, it is proving possible to establish "conservation areas," where monuments are considered in relation to each other and to the landscape of which they form a part.

Recording of New Archaeological Sites

The first task in any program of Cultural Resource Management is that of locating sites and recording them systematically. The appropriate recording techniques are those of remote sensing and surface survey, discussed in Chapter 3. Here the issue is rather one of organization.

Although, as we have seen, most nations have registers of their more important known archaeological sites, few organize comprehensive survey programs in which new sites are methodically sought and recorded. Denmark is one of the most advanced in this field and Canada, too, has been a pioneer, with an early, computerized national archaeological survey.

In Britain, since the beginning of this century, the Royal Commissions on Historical Monuments have been carrying out surveys for each county – each administrative division of the country – publishing the principal sites in handsome inventories. In the early 1900s the national mapping agency, the Ordnance Survey, also set up its own archaeological section to provide information for the national survey of maps. This section produced a remarkable series of period maps that treated the archaeology of Britain on a period-by-period basis. Over the past 30 years, most counties have also set up their own County Sites and Monuments Record, to provide a full database for the County Planning Office, so that when some development is proposed, information on known sites within the development area is readily available. Gradually, these various enterprises are being brought together in a unified computerized database. However, the administrative problems involved in the cooperation of several national survey agencies (the Royal Commissions for England, Scotland, and Wales, now incorporating the Ordnance Survey Archaeological Section) with the local administrative records (the various County Sites and Monuments Records), and of all these with the national agencies responsible for actually implementing salvage or rescue work (English Heritage for England, and the relevant government departments for Scotland and Wales) have not yet been overcome.

In one sense a national archaeological record can never be complete, because new sites are being discovered all the time. For this reason, when any major development is proposed, it is necessary that the area in question be surveyed, or re-surveyed, intensively. In the terminology of CRM, it is necessary to produce an Environmental Impact Statement (EIS) – the impact being that of the development on the local archaeological remains. It is then possible to assess what damage will be done.

Threats to Archaeological Sites: Partial Solutions and Unresolved Problems

Damage by Developers. The ideal administrative arrangement, from an archaeological point of view, is that each developer should have to apply for planning

Threats to our heritage: concrete piles – foundations for a modern office block – have been driven into the ground around the archaeological remains of the Rose theater, where some of Shakespeare's plays were first performed in the 1590s.

and development permission. During the procedures leading to the granting of that permission, the drafting of an Environmental Impact Statement should be mandatory, paid for by the developer. If the EIS indicates that archaeological sites are likely to be damaged, alternative schemes should be devised. If there is no clear alternative, some judgment has to be taken as to whether the value of the threatened sites outweighs the importance of the proposed development. If the development has to go ahead, then archaeological survey including excavation should take place in advance of any unavoidable destruction. Such work, and its full publication, should be paid for by the developer.

In reality the situation and the specific threats vary from country to country. In *England*, it is the national agency (English Heritage) rather than the developer that normally meets most of the cost of rescue archaeology. Moreover, the discovery in London in 1989 of the Rose theater – where some of Shakespeare's plays were first performed in the 1590s – has highlighted certain weaknesses in current legislation and how it is applied. Archaeologists working in advance of property development unearthed remains of the wooden theater, which became the focus of huge public interest and concern. Unfortunately the site had not been scheduled (placed on the Schedule of Ancient Monuments), so there was no legal obligation on the part of the developer to alter his plans and thus protect the site for posterity. Under present legislation, retrospective scheduling would have made English Heritage liable for a bill for compensation from the developer estimated at $70 million, or 10 times the national annual budget for rescue archaeology. In the event, English Heritage came to a voluntary agreement with the developer who arranged and paid for the building plans to be altered, so that the office block's foundations generally avoid the known archaeological remains. Nevertheless existing legislation may need to be reconsidered. It is also worth noting that, before the issue of the Rose theater made headline news, English Heritage had launched a program aiming to schedule tens of thousands of unprotected sites.

In the *United States*, annual expenditure on salvage or contract archaeology is some 10 times greater than in England but, as we saw above, full protection is granted only to federally funded projects, or those on federal lands. There is, furthermore, no legislative provision for full publication of the work undertaken. The results can be notified to the State Historic Preservation Officer simply in the form of a "letter report," which is filed but often never published.

Problems of keeping up with the rate of development are particularly acute in *Japan*. In 1980 alone, more than 6200 sites were recorded as having been destroyed or exposed to destruction by developers. This is why the great majority of archaeological work in Japan has to be devoted to rapid salvage excavations. Processing of the voluminous data cannot keep pace with its extraction from the ground, so there is a mountainous backlog of material to be published.

In *Australia*, threats posed by development were made all too clear by the recent case of the proposed dam on the Franklin river, southwest Tasmania. This would have destroyed one of the last great natural temperate wilderness areas on earth, as well as some of the richest and most important early inhabited cave

Salvage excavations in Japan: work in progress at a site in Tama New Town, 1986. The conveyor belts are used to transport spoil from the site.

sites in Australia. Only an international outcry prevented the hydro-electric scheme from going ahead. The region has now been added to the UNESCO (United Nations) list of World Heritage Areas.

Nevertheless, given that development is an inevitable feature of the world economy, archaeologists have in most cases to learn to cooperate with developers. The fruits of such a policy can be seen in those towns and cities where archaeology is now accorded some importance in urban planning, often involving salvage work and subsequent preservation of important remains. A good example is Mexico City, where the discovery in 1978 of the *Templo Mayor* or Great Temple of the Aztecs led to the initiation of an impressive salvage and preservation project (see box overleaf). Other examples of successful preservation of archaeological remains in towns include the Roman mosaic in Cologne, Germany; Viking house foundations at York (see box below); the Roman and medieval foundations in front of Notre Dame in Paris; and the Lower Paleolithic camp of Terra Amata preserved in a museum under an apartment block in Nice, on the French Mediterranean coast.

Agricultural Damage. Although most countries keep some control over the activities of developers and builders, the damage to archaeological sites from farming is much more difficult to assess. The few

CONSERVATION: THE GREAT TEMPLE OF THE AZTECS IN MEXICO CITY

When the Spanish Conquistadors under Hernán Cortés occupied the Aztec capital, Tenochtitlan, in 1521, they destroyed its buildings and established their own capital, Mexico City, on the same site.

In 1790 the now-famous statue of the Aztec mother goddess Coatlicue was found, and also the great Calendar Stone, but it was not until this century that more systematic archaeological work took place.

Various relatively small-scale excavations have been carried out on remains within the city as they have come to light in the course of building work. But in 1975 a more coherent initiative was taken: the institution by the Department of Pre-Hispanic Monuments of the Basin of Mexico Project. Its aim is to halt the destruction of archaeological remains during the continuing growth of the city. In 1977, a Museum of Tenochtitlan Project was begun, with the aim of excavating the area where remains of what appeared to be the Great Temple of the Aztecs had been found in 1948. The project was radically transformed early in 1978 when electricity workers discovered a large stone carved with a series of

reliefs. The Department of Salvage Archaeology of the National Institute of Anthropology and History took charge. Within days, a huge monolith, 3.25 m (10 ft 7 in) in diameter, was revealed depicting the dismembered body of the Aztec goddess Coyolxauhqui who, according to myth, had been killed by her brother, the war god Huitzilopochtli. The Museum of Tenochtitlan Project, under the direction of Eduardo Matos Moctezuma, became the Great Temple Project, which over the next few years brought to light one of the most remarkable archaeological sites in Mexico.

No one had realized how much would be preserved of the Great Temple. Although the Spaniards had razed the standing structure to the ground in 1521, this pyramid was the

last of a series of re-buildings. Beneath the ruins of the last temple the excavations revealed those of earlier temples. In addition to these architectural remains was a wonderful series of offerings to the temple's two gods, Huitzilopochtli and the rain god Tlaloc – objects of obsidian and jade, terracotta and stone sculptures, and other special dedications, including rare coral and the remains of a jaguar buried with a ball of turquoise in its mouth.

A major area of Mexico City has now been turned into a permanent museum and national monument. Mexico has regained one of its greatest pre-Columbian buildings, and the Great Temple of the Aztecs is once again one of the marvels of Tenochtitlan.

The skeleton of a jaguar from a chamber in the fourth of seven building stages of the Great Temple. The jade ball in its mouth may have been placed there as a substitute for the spirit of the deceased.

The Great Temple excavation site, with stairways visible of successive phases of the monument. The building was originally pyramidal in form, surmounted by twin temples to the war god Huitzilopochtli and the rain god Tlaloc. Conservation work is in progress here on the Coyolxauhqui stone, visible under scaffolding (left of center).

The Great Stone, found in 1978, provided the catalyst for the Great Temple excavations. The goddess Coyolxauhqui is shown decapitated (left, a detail of her head) and dismembered – killed by her brother, the war god Huitzilopochtli.

published studies make sober reading. One of the best, *The Past Under the Plough* (ed. J. Hinchliffe and R.T. Schadla-Hall, 1980), shows that in Britain even those sites that are notionally protected – by being listed on the national Schedule of Ancient Monuments – are not, in reality, altogether safe. The position may be much better in Denmark and in certain other countries, but elsewhere only the most conspicuous sites are protected. The more modest field monuments and open settlements are not, and these are the sites that are suffering from mechanized agriculture.

Damage from Looting. The saddest kind of damage is that deliberately brought about by clandestine excavators, concerned only to find objects of high saleable value, and quite untroubled by the loss of information when the finds are divorced from their original context. Many of these looters use metal detectors, even on legally protected sites.

One such *clandestino*, Luigi Perticarari, a robber in Tarquinia, published his memoirs in 1986 (*I Segreti di un Tombarolo*) and makes no apology for his trade. He has more first-hand knowledge of Etruscan tombs than any archaeologist, but his activity destroys the chance of anyone sharing that knowledge. He claims to have emptied some 4000 tombs dating from the 8th to the 3rd centuries BC in the past 30 years. So it is that, while the world's store of Etruscan antiquities in museums and private collections grows larger, our knowledge of Etruscan burial customs and social organization does not.

The same is true for the remarkable marble sculptures of the Cycladic Islands of Greece, dating to around 2500 BC. We admire the breathtaking elegance of these works in the world's museums, but we have little idea of how they were produced or of the social and religious life of the Cycladic communities that made them. Again, the contexts have been lost.

In the American Southwest, 90 percent of the Classic Mimbres sites (*c.*AD 1000) have now been looted or destroyed (see box overleaf). In southwestern Colorado, 60 percent of prehistoric Anasazi sites have been vandalized. Pothunters work at night, equipped with two-way radios, scanners, and lookouts. They can be prosecuted under the present legislation only if caught red-handed, which is almost impossible.

The huaqueros of Central and South America, too, are interested only in the richest finds, in this case gold – whole cemeteries are turned into fields of craters, with bones, potsherds, mummy wrappings, and other objects smashed and scattered. The remarkable tomb excavated in 1987 at Sipán, northwest Peru, belonging to the Moche civilization, was partially rescued from

477

DESTRUCTION AND RESPONSE: MIMBRES

UNITED STATES

• Mimbres

One of the most melancholy stories in archaeology this century is that of Mimbres. The Mimbres potters of the American Southwest created a unique art tradition in the prehistoric period, painting the inside of hemispherical bowls with vigorous animalian and human forms. These bowls are now much prized by archaeologists and art lovers. But this fascination has led to the systematic looting of Mimbres sites on a scale unequaled in the United States, or indeed anywhere in the world.

The Mimbres people lived along a small river, the Rio Mimbres, in mud-built villages, similar in some respects to those of the later Pueblo Indians. Painted pottery began, as we now know, around AD 550, and reached its apogee in the Classic Mimbres period, from about AD 1000 to 1130.

Systematic archaeological work on Mimbres sites began in the 1920s, but it was not in general well published. Looters soon found,

however, that with pick and shovel they could unearth Mimbres pots to sell on the market for primitive art. Nor was this activity necessarily illegal. In United States law there is nothing to prevent excavation of any kind by the owner on private land, and nothing to prevent the owner permitting others to destroy

A masked coyote dancer is the subject of this fine Mimbres bowl, dating from AD 1100–1250.

archaeological sites in this way.

In the early 1960s, a method of bulldozing Mimbres sites was developed which did not destroy all the pottery. The operators found that by controlled bulldozing they could remove a relatively small depth of soil at a time and extract many of the pots unbroken. In the process sites were of course completely destroyed, and all hope of establishing an archaeological context for the material was lost.

Since 1973 there has at last been a concerted archaeological response. The Mimbres Foundation, under the direction of Steven LeBlanc, was able to secure funding from private sources to undertake excavations in the remains of some of the looted sites. They also made good progress

in explaining to the owners of those sites how destructive this looting process was to any hope of learning about the Mimbres past. From 1975 to 1978 a series of field seasons at several partially looted sites succeeded in establishing at least the outlines of Mimbres archaeology, and in putting the chronology upon a sure footing.

The Mimbres Foundation also reached the conclusion that archaeological excavation is an expensive form of conservation, and decided to purchase a number of surviving (or partially surviving) Mimbres sites in order to protect them. Moreover, this is a lesson that has been learned more widely. Members of the Mimbres Foundation have joined forces with other archaeologists and benefactors to form a national organization, the Archaeological Conservancy. Several sites in the United States have now been purchased and conserved in this way. The story thus has, in some sense, a happy ending. But nothing can bring back the possibility of really understanding Mimbres culture and Mimbres art, a possibility which did exist at the beginning of this century before the wholesale and devastating looting.

Unfortunately, in other parts of the world there are similar stories to tell.

Funerary bowl of the 10th century AD. The figures may be male and female, or life and death. The "kill" hole at the base allowed the object's spirit to be released.

Animalian forms were a popular Mimbres subject, as in this bowl with its depiction of geometric-patterned insects.

the plunderers only by the persistence and courage of the local Peruvian archaeologist.

England, too, has its well-organized gangs of professional treasure hunters. At least three gangs are said to exist in the region of East Anglia alone, feeding the demand from international collectors for antiquities. Nor are the depredations of looters restricted to unpublished sites and unknown finds. Famous Etruscan wall paintings from tombs excavated and published long ago are hacked off and sold in fragments, and the same is true of many Egyptian reliefs. The destruction to Maya stelae is notorious: they are cut into pieces using power saws so as to be more easily transportable. Reliefs in French megalithic tombs have been damaged in this way. Nor are the museums themselves free from such predation. In 1985, the National Museum of Anthropology in Mexico City was raided and some of its most precious smaller objects stolen – thankfully nearly all have been recovered.

The antiquities market in Europe and North America must ultimately take a good deal of the blame for this state of affairs, since antiquities bought without reliable provenance may well have been looted. In 1970, the University Museum in Philadelphia, shortly after acquiring artifacts in doubtful circumstances, pronounced the "Philadelphia Declaration:" that it would no longer acquire or accept antiquities without a reliable and honest provenance. In Britain, the British Museum and other members of the Museums' Association now refuse to buy goods without a reliable pedigree. But it has to be said that establishing such a pedigree for certain is no easy matter.

Developers, farmers, and looters are by no means the only threats to archaeological sites. Participants in wars have wrought untold damage over the centuries, and continue to do so. The great Roman site of Baalbek, Lebanon, is the base of one of the warring factions there. Angkor Wat in Cambodia deteriorated rapidly during the conflicts in that country, thanks to the prolonged interruption of maintenance. Even in peacetime, the military can do great damage, as in their exercises on Salisbury Plain in southern England or in parts of southern France which have irreparably damaged many prehistoric burial mounds.

Care of Protected Sites

Even though many archaeological sites now receive protection of one sort or another in many countries, the problems do not end there.

In Egypt, for example, many monuments are crumbling through a combination of salt in the building stone and moisture from the ground and air. At Thebes the tomb of Queen Nefertari – the wife of Ramesses II, who lived about 3000 years ago – has magnificent wall paintings that have been pushed off the walls by the build up of salt behind the plaster. A group of tourists in a tomb for an hour can significantly raise the humidity, and fluctuations in humidity encourage even more crystallization of salt. By 1950, Nefertari's tomb had deteriorated so much that only dignitaries were allowed in, and by 1983 it was fully closed.

Egypt's open-air sites are just as vulnerable. The Nile Valley's climatic extremes make dew condense on the stones on cold nights, which dissolves the salts near the surface. The dew evaporates during the day and the re-forming salt crystals result in crumbling and flaking. The Sphinx at Giza, 4600 years old, is crumbling for this reason and because sewage water from a Cairo slum is seeping into the monument's structure. A fragment recently fell from the Sphinx's right shoulder. The world's best restorers have been summoned, but not one of their 16 conservation reports claim the deterioration is reversible. At the very least the underground water will have to be drained, and it may even be necessary to rebury the Sphinx's body in sand.

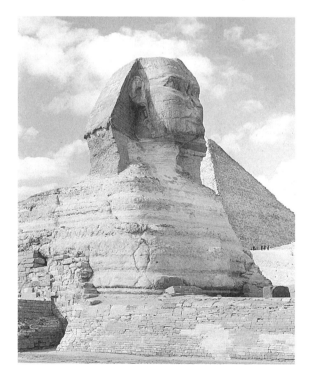

The Sphinx at Giza: one of the many monuments in Egypt under threat from encroaching moisture and corrosive salts.

479

The rescue and resiting of the temples of Abu Simbel and Philae, which would otherwise have been drowned thanks to the building of the Aswan Dam in 1970, was one of the great international triumphs of conservation two decades ago. The annual flooding of certain temples by the Nile was halted; but the permanent availability of water allowed increased irrigation, which has raised the water table in the area. There is thus a constant supply of moisture containing destructive impurities that can seep into the monuments.

There are several remedies for these problems in Egypt. Visitors to the tombs must be banned or strictly controlled, as in the tomb of Nefertari or the Paleolithic decorated caves in western Europe. Air-conditioning should be installed in the tombs to control the temperature and humidity, and a plastic barrier placed between the walls and the plaster. Open-air monuments require pumps to lower the underground water level, and trenches filled with gravel around the bases of walls to stop water seeping into the stone. Finally, silicon compounds can be applied to the stone – these penetrate deeply and bond its molecules together. But all of this will cost a great deal of money.

Egypt is not alone in experiencing difficulties in the care of its ancient monuments. Mohenjodaro, the great early city in Pakistan, is under threat from both a rising water table and corrosion by salts, as well as from erosion by the Indus river. Since 1922 the water table has risen from 8 m (26 ft) below the surface to 4–1.5 m (13–5 ft), depending on the season. Pumping and draining are needed to lower it again, and the walls need cleaning to leach out the accumulated salts. An

The walls of the great Indus Valley city of Mohenjodaro, Pakistan, are slowly being eaten away by salts. (A) Salt-impregnated water rises from the water table by capillary action. (B) Salt water infiltrates the brickwork through uncleared earth. (C) Dust-laden winds carry salts and deposit them on the bricks, which rainwater then helps penetrate the walls. (D) Accumulated salts within the bricks erode the walls.

international conservation campaign is being run by UNESCO, but again the task is a costly one.

The management of protected sites, therefore, in such a way that natural forces and tourism do not inflict damage, and yet that the public is allowed some sort of access, is now a complex and increasingly specialized field in its own right.

ARCHAEOLOGY AND PUBLIC UNDERSTANDING

Archaeologists have a duty, both to colleagues and to the general public, to explain what they are doing and why. Fundamentally this means publishing and disseminating discoveries so that the results are available to other scholars, and can be enjoyed and understood by that wider public which has usually paid the bill for the work, however indirectly. In some cases, such as the successful *Earthwatch* scheme, amateur enthusiasts directly provide the willing hands and financial support without which many projects could not survive.

Publish or Be Damned

We have already remarked several times in this volume that all excavation is to a certain extent

destruction – and we make no apology for repeating the point in our closing pages. All excavators have an obligation to record their findings fully and publish them quickly. In practice few do so, or at any rate did so in the past.

Estimates vary, but it has been claimed by the British archaeologist Peter Addyman that up to 60 percent of modern excavations remain unpublished after 10 years, and it is reckoned that only 27 percent of the digs funded by America's National Science Foundation since 1950 have ever reached print. There are many reasons for this appalling record. Archaeologists can be lazy or incompetent like people everywhere. They often prefer to dig new sites rather than devote time to laborious post-excavation analysis and publication.

They also often fail to allocate a large enough proportion of a project's budget for post-excavation work. Actual work in the field may sometimes represent only 10 percent of the project's total expenditure. Underwater teams, for example, need to be aware that for every month of diving there are about two years to be spent on conserving, recording, and publishing the finds.

Whatever the reason, deliberate non-publication is a form of theft – in fact a double theft, involving the misuse of other people's money and the withholding of unique information. Some archaeologists compound the felony by hoarding finds, which they consider to be their scientific property, deliberately preventing colleagues from gaining access to the material or from publishing research connected with the site.

One major scandal concerns the Dead Sea Scrolls, the oldest known Hebrew books, written on leather about 2000 years ago. The first scrolls were discovered in Qumran, Palestine, as long ago as 1947, but most of the thousands of fragments found in later excavations remain unpublished by the editorial team appointed in 1953 to decipher and edit the material. Only a fraction of the projected official volumes have appeared. Interested scholars have now called for all the available fragments to be published immediately in the form of photographs, without decipherment or interpretation, so that competent researchers all over the world can study them.

In a controversial comment after the death of the Romano-British specialist Ian Richmond, Mortimer Wheeler lamented that "not more than a quarter of his productive fieldwork can now ever see the light of day . . . in spite of the constant entreaties of his colleagues he obstinately declined to keep pace with his digging by the normal method of the interim report." A deceased scholar's disciples can certainly attempt to put something together from the notes and finds left behind – should either survive – but this is a poor substitute for a considered account by the original excavator while the details of the dig are fresh in the memory.

What can be done? It has been suggested that each country should issue a list of those sites whose publication is long overdue, together with the identity of the excavators. In Britain, English Heritage has taken action by devoting a high proportion of its archaeological budget in recent years to the analysis and publication of old as well as new excavations. However, measures are required to ensure better conduct in the future. Professional bodies such as the Society of Professional Archaeologists in the United States and the Institute of Field Archaeologists in Britain now require their members to abide by a Code of Conduct, which stipulates that continuing membership depends among other things on publication of excavations within a reasonable time.

In addition, the world archaeological community ought to establish a fixed period (perhaps from 5 to 20 years, depending on the scale of the project) when excavators might be allowed control over their finds and results, after which these would become available to all, even if unpublished. Many students around the world would find it more profitable as a research topic to retrieve and write up such material than to embark on unnecessary digs at sites not under threat.

Finally, all directors of excavations should act as if they expected to die before the project reaches completion. In Italy, for example, a copy of the excavation fieldnotes has to be left with the local authority to guard against such an eventuality. Excavators should ensure that their notes are fully comprehensible to others, that each season's finds are processed before starting the next, and that at least a manuscript report on each season's work is produced. Leaving all the analysis till the end is a recipe for disaster.

The Wider Audience

Although the immediate aim of most research is to answer specific questions, the fundamental purpose of archaeology must be to provide people in general with a better understanding of the human past. Skillful popularization – in on-site and museum exhibits, books and television – is therefore required, but not all archaeologists are prepared to devote time to it, and few are capable of doing it well.

Excavators often regard members of the public merely as a hindrance to work on-site. More enlightened archaeologists, however, realize the financial and other support to be gained from encouraging public interest, and they organize information sheets, open days, and on long-term projects even fee-paying daily tours, as at the Bronze Age site of Flag Fen in eastern England. In Japan, on-the-spot presentations of excavation results are given as soon as a dig is completed. Details are released to the press the previous day, so that the public can obtain information from the morning edition of the local paper before coming to the presentation.

Archaeologists at York, northern England, not only encouraged visits from the public during the Viking excavations there, but went on to preserve part of the remains and reconstruct streets and houses as the centerpiece for a hugely successful new museum that paid for itself within five years (see box overleaf). The high sales in the museum store of a cheap guide to the

DISPLAY AND FUNDING: VIKING YORK

The Jorvik Viking Centre in the city of York, northern England, is one of the most popular and financially successful museums to have been created on an archaeological site anywhere in the world.

In 1976, the York Archaeological Trust began a 5-year excavation beneath the foundations of a demolished Victorian factory in Coppergate, one of the main streets of old York. The excavators encountered 9 m (over 29 ft) of stratified debris, some of it waterlogged and much of it from the town's Viking period, dating to the 9th and 10th centuries AD. York was the capital of the northern kingdom of the Vikings in Britain, and known to the invaders as Jorvik.

The finds included complete walls of wooden buildings, and a wide range of objects linked to different crafts such as leatherworking, weaving, and woodwork. It became clear that coppergate – originally called Coopergate because of the coopers or cupmakers – and the narrow alleys leading off it had constituted a closely packed area of workshops, houses, and warehouses by the Foss river.

Since the dig had attracted about half a million visitors and aroused international interest, a decision was made to preserve part of the site, and to reconstruct some of the streets and houses. The result, opened in 1984, is the Jorvik Viking Centre, located underneath a new shopping complex. Visitors descend to Viking Street level, where a fleet of electronic cars take them "back in time" and along a predetermined route past thatched houses, workshops, and ships at the riverside wharf. In and around these structures are lifesize, fiber-glass figures of people in period costume. A soundtrack provides the noisy atmosphere of a busy street, with adults and children speaking authentic Old Norse. Even appropriate smells have been included, particularly around the pigsties and the latrine.

The cars then move on and pass through part of the excavation, left as if the archaeologists were still at work, with the original timbers conserved and replaced *in situ* in the humidity-controlled atmosphere. The visitors leave the cars, and enter a mock-up of a laboratory showing how artifacts and organic remains are studied. The visit concludes with a display area housing the principal finds, and a lucrative souvenir shop.

The Jorvik Centre is playing an important role, not only in presenting a particular excavation and period to the public, but in explaining the sequence of archaeological discovery and interpretation in an imaginative new medium. Financially the Centre will support new excavations in York. Its success has led to similar displays opening or being planned in other British towns as well as in other countries.

Excavations in progress, before construction of the shopping complex and Jorvik Viking Centre on the same site.

"Lothin's wood stall," part of the recreation of Viking York.

This magnificent iron and brass helmet from the Coppergate site, shown here under conservation, proved to be Anglo-Saxon not Viking. A dent and cut indicate that it had seen action, perhaps during the struggle for York between the Anglo-Saxons and Vikings in AD 866.

exhibit and a serious but popularly written book on the whole dig highlight the importance for archaeologists of reaching the public through a variety of media. The museum has certainly benefited from an association with a prominent presenter of archaeological television programs.

Clearly, there is an avid popular appetite for archaeology. In a sense, the past has been a form of entertainment ever since the early digging of burial mounds and the public unwrapping of mummies in the 19th century. The entertainment may now take a more scientific and educational form, but it still needs to compete with rival popular attractions if archaeology is to thrive.

SUMMARY

World Archaeology and the Human Past

Archaeology can be made to serve many masters. We have seen how it can be used for economic ends, to make arid lands fertile once again. Or it can be popularized and sold to a willing public, curious to know more of vanished cities and lost civilizations. Or again it can be used for national ends, to provide a sense of national identity by tracing back a link from an uncertain present to a past whose achievements are seen as significant and admirable.

But the ultimate value of archaeology goes beyond these specific and in a certain sense limited concerns. For world archaeology is something in which we can all share. The human origins revealed in Africa are the origins of us all. Archaeology can document the trajectory of growth of the population of every country on earth. Our concern need not be restricted to our own personal line of descent. The archaeology of every land has its own contribution to make to the understanding of human diversity and hence of the human condition. So it is that skeletal remains of the Australian Aborigines of earlier millennia, or of the North American Indians, ought to matter as much to Europeans or white Americans as skeletal remains found in Europe. Modern-day Aborigines and American Indians should also recognize that their contribution to the human story merits a significant place in the history of the world. Although earlier generations of scholars did indeed behave with flagrant disregard for the feelings and beliefs of native peoples, and some may continue to do so, the interest in these matters today is not some neocolonial attempt further to appropriate the native past. It is, rather, an assertion that this past has a

483

legitimate wider significance, in which others may properly be interested than those who inhabit the areas in question. That is not a negative message, nor a disparaging one.

If we are to have an adequate perception of our place as human beings in the modern world, the past matters. It is where we have come from, and it has determined what we are. For that reason, it is necessary for us to set our faces against the lunatics and the fringe archaeologists who seek (sometimes for their own gain, but sometimes simply from a misguided inability to think straight) to confuse or corrupt our view of the past. Writers such as Erich von Däniken, author of *Chariots of the Gods*, have written highly readable books purporting to give new insights into the past that differ markedly from those of modern archaeology. In von Däniken's case, the argument is that most of the developments of human civilization are due to the influence of alien beings arriving on earth in flying saucers. The matter would be comic if such views had not been so widely believed.

The objection to this kind of nonsense is not simply that it differs from the conventional archaeological wisdom. No one has a monopoly of the truth – not even the archaeologist. The objection is that such works gloss over the difficulties, and fail to submit their evidence to the kind of scientific scrutiny that we have been advocating in this volume. Anyone who has read this book, and who understands how archaeology proceeds, will already see why such writings, and others that propose ancient (and undocumented) catastrophes, or lost continents, or long-range migrations by the Lost Tribes of Israel, or the forces of "earth magic" at such sites as Stonehenge, are a snare and a delusion. These misconceptions have been well discussed by Jeremy Sabloff in his *Archaeology, Myth and Reality* (1982). The real antidote is a kind of healthy skepticism: to ask "where is the evidence?" Knowledge advances by asking questions – that is the central theme of the present book, and there is no better way to disperse the lunatic fringe than by asking difficult questions, and looking skeptically at the answers.

Further Reading

Cleere, H. (ed.). 1984. *Approaches to the Archaeological Heritage: A Comparative Study of World Cultural Resource Management Systems*. Cambridge University Press: Cambridge & New York.

Darvill, T. 1987. *Ancient Monuments in the Countryside: An Archaeological Management Review*. English Heritage: London. (A British perspective.)

Green, E.L. (ed.). 1984. *Ethics and Values in Archaeology*. Free Press: New York.

Greenfield, J. 1989. *The Return of Cultural Treasures*. Cambridge University Press: Cambridge & New York.

Gumerman, G. & Schiffer, M.B. (eds.). 1977. *Conservation Archaeology*. Academic Press: New York & London.

Layton, R. (ed.). 1989. *Conflict in the Archaeology of Living Traditions*. Unwin Hyman: London.

Mauch Messenger, P. (ed.) 1989. *The Ethics of Collecting Cultural Property: Whose culture? Whose property?* Univ. of New Mexico Press, Albuquerque.

McBryde, I. (ed.). 1985. *Who Owns the Past?* Oxford University Press: Melbourne, Oxford & New York.

McGimsey, C. 1972. *Public Archaeology*. Seminar Press: New York.

Glossary

(Terms in *italics* are defined elsewhere in the glossary)

absolute dating The determination of age with reference to a specific time scale, such as a fixed calendrical system; also referred to as chronometric dating. (Chapter 4)

achieved status Social standing and prestige reflecting the ability of an individual to acquire an established position in society as a result of individual accomplishments (*cf. ascribed status*). (Chapter 5)

aerial reconnaissance An important survey technique in the discovery and recording of archaeological sites (see also *reconnaissance survey*). (Chapter 3)

alloying A technique involving the mixing of two or more metals to create an entirely new material, e.g. the fusion of copper and tin to make bronze. (Chapter 8)

amino-acid racemization A method used in the dating of both human and animal bone. Its special significance is that with a small sample (10g) it can be applied to material up to 100,000 years old, i.e. beyond the time range of *radiocarbon dating*. (Chapter 4)

annealing In copper and bronze metallurgy, this refers to the repeated process of heating and hammering the material to produce the desired shape. (Chapter 8)

anthropology The study of humanity – our physical characteristics as animals, and our unique non-biological characteristics we call *culture*. The subject is generally broken down into three subdisciplines: *biological (physical) anthropology, cultural (social) anthropology*, and *archaeology*. (Introduction)

archaeobotany See *paleoethnobotany*.

archaeological culture A constantly recurring *assemblage* of artifacts assumed to be representative of a particular set of behavioral activities carried out at a particular time and place (*cf. culture*). (Chapter 1)

archaeology A subdiscipline of anthropology involving the study of the human past through its material remains. (Introduction)

archaeology of cult The study of the material indications of patterned actions undertaken in response to religious beliefs. (Chapter 10)

archaeomagnetic dating Sometimes referred to as paleomagnetic dating, it is based on the fact that changes in the earth's magnetic field over time can be recorded as remanent magnetism in materials such as baked clay structures (ovens, kilns, and hearths). (Chapter 4)

archaeozoology Sometimes referred to as zooarchaeology, this involves the identification and analysis of faunal species from archaeological sites, as an aid to the reconstruction of both human diets and to an understanding of the contemporary environment at the time of deposition. (Chapters 6 & 7)

artifact Any portable object used, modified, or made by humans; e.g. stone tools, pottery, and metal weapons. (Chapter 3)

ascribed status Social standing or prestige which is the result of inheritance or hereditary factors (*cf. achieved status*). (Chapter 5)

assemblage A group of artifacts recurring together at a particular time and place, and representing the sum of human activities. (Chapter 3)

association The co-occurrence of an artifact with other archaeological remains, usually in the same *matrix*. (Chapter 2)

atomic absorption spectrometry (AAS) A method of analyzing artifact composition similar to *optical emission spectrometry* (OES) in that it measures energy in the form of visible light waves. It is capable of measuring up to 40 different elements with an accuracy of *c.* 1 percent. (Chapters 8 & 9)

attribute A minimal characteristic of an artifact such that it cannot be further subdivided; attributes commonly studied include aspects of form, style, decoration, color, and raw material. (Chapter 3)

attritional age profile A mortality pattern based on bone or tooth wear which is characterized by an overrepresentation of young and old animals in relation to their numbers in live populations. It suggests either scavenging of attritional mortality victims (i.e. those dying from natural causes or from non-human predation) or the hunting by humans or other predators of the most vulnerable individuals. (Chapter 7)

augering A *subsurface detection* method using either a hand or machine-powered drill to determine the depth and character of archaeological deposits. (Chapter 3)

Australopithecus A collective name for the earliest known hominids emerging about 5 million years ago in East Africa. (Chapter 4)

band A term used to describe small-scale societies of hunters and gatherers, generally less than 100 people, who move seasonally to exploit wild (undomesticated) food resources.

Kinship ties play an important part in social organization. (Chapter 5)

bifurcation See *self-organization*.

biological anthropology See *physical anthropology*.

bosing (or bowsing) A *subsurface detection* method performed by striking the ground with a heavy wooden mallet or a lead-filled container on a long handle. (Chapter 3)

brain endocasts These are made by pouring latex rubber into a skull, so as to produce an accurate image of the inner surface of the cranium. This method gives an estimate of cranial capacity and has been used on early hominid skulls. (Chapter 11)

catastrophe theory A branch of mathematical topology developed by René Thom which is concerned with the way in which nonlinear interactions within systems can produce sudden and dramatic effects; it is argued that there are only a limited number of ways in which such changes can take place, and these are defined as elementary catastrophes. (Chapter 12)

catastrophic age profile A mortality pattern based on bone or tooth wear analysis, and corresponding to a "natural" age distribution in which the older the age group, the fewer the individuals it has. This pattern is often found in contexts such as flash floods, epidemics, or volcanic eruptions. (Chapter 7)

cation-ratio dating This method aspires to the direct dating of rock carvings and engravings, and is also potentially applicable to Paleolithic artifacts with a strong patina caused by exposure to desert dust. It depends on the principle that cations of certain elements are more soluble than others; they leach out of *rock varnish* more rapidly than the less soluble elements, and their concentration decreases with time. (Chapter 4)

cenote A ritual well, for example at the late Maya site of Chichén Itzá, into which enormous quantities of symbolically rich goods had been deposited. (Chapter 10)

central place theory Developed by the geographer Christaller to explain the spacing and function of the settlement landscape. Under idealized conditions, he argued, central places of the same size and nature would be equidistant from each other, surrounded by secondary centers with their own smaller satellites. In spite of its limitations, central place theory has found useful applications in archaeology as a preliminary heuristic device. (Chapter 5)

characterization The application of techniques of examination by which characteristic properties of the constituent material of traded goods can be identified, and thus their source of origin; e.g. petrographic *thin-section analysis*. (Chapter 9)

chiefdom A term used to describe a society that operates on the principle of ranking, i.e. differential social status. Different *lineages* are graded on a scale of prestige, calculated by how closely related one is to the chief. The chiefdom generally has a permanent ritual and ceremonial center, as well as being characterized by local specialization in crafts. (Chapter 5)

chinampas The areas of fertile reclaimed land, constructed by the Aztecs, and made of mud dredged from canals. (Chapter 6)

chronometric dating See *absolute dating*.

classification The ordering of phenomena into groups or other classificatory schemes on the basis of shared attributes (see also *type* and *typology*). (Chapters 1 & 4)

CLIMAP A project aimed at producing paleoclimatic maps showing sea-surface temperatures in different parts of the globe, at various periods. (Chapter 6)

cluster analysis A multivariate statistical technique which assesses the similarities between units or assemblages, based on the occurrence or non-occurrence of specific artifact *types* or other components within them. (Chapter 5)

cognitive archaeology The study of past ways of thought and symbolic structures from material remains. (Chapter 10)

cognitive map An interpretive framework of the world which, it is argued, exists in the human mind and affects actions and decisions as well as knowledge structures. (Chapter 10)

cognitive-processual approach An alternative to the materialist orientation of the functional-processual approach, it is concerned with (1) the integration of the cognitive and symbolic with other aspects of early societies; (2) the role of ideology as an active organizational force.

computed axial tomography (CAT scanner) The method by which scanners allow detailed internal views of bodies such as mummies. The body is passed into the machine and images of cross-sectional "slices" through the body are produced. (Chapter 11)

conjoining See *refitting*.

conjunctive approach A methodological alternative to traditional normative archaeology, argued by Walter Taylor (1948), in which the full range of a culture system was to be taken into consideration in explanatory models. (Chapter 1)

context An artifact's context usually consists of its immediate *matrix* (the material surrounding it e.g. gravel, clay, or sand), its provenience (horizontal and vertical position within the matrix), and its *association* with other artifacts (occurrence together with other archaeological remains, usually in the same matrix). (Chapter 2)

contextual seriation A method of *relative dating* pioneered by Flinders Petrie in the 19th century, in which artifacts are arranged according to the frequencies of their co-occurrence in specific contexts (usually burials). (Chapter 4)

contract archaeology Archaeological research conducted under the aegis of federal or state legislation, often in advance of highway construction or urban development, where the archaeologist is contracted to undertake the necessary research. (Chapter 14)

coprolites Fossilized feces; these contain food residues that can be used to reconstruct diet and subsistence activities. (Chapter 6)

core A lithic artifact used as a blank from which other tools or flakes are made. (Chapter 8)

Critical Theory A theoretical approach developed by the so-called "Frankfurt School" of German social thinkers, which stresses that all knowledge is historical, and in a sense biassed communication; thus, all claims to "objective" knowledge are illusory. (Chapter 12)

cultural anthropology A subdiscipline of anthropology concerned with the non-biological, behavioral aspects of society; i.e. the social, linguistic, and technological components underlying human behavior. Two important branches of cultural anthropology are *ethnography* (the study of living cultures) and *ethnology* (which attempts to compare cultures using ethnographic evidence). In Europe, it is referred to as *social anthropology*. (Introduction)

cultural ecology A term devised by Julian Steward to account for the dynamic relationship between human society and its environment, in which *culture* is viewed as the primary adaptive mechanism. (Chapter 1)

cultural evolution The theory that societal change can be understood by analogy with the processes underlying the biological evolution of species. (Chapter 1)

cultural group A complex of regularly occurring associated artifacts, features, burial types, and house forms comprising a distinct identity. (Chapter 5)

cultural resource management (CRM) The safeguarding of the archaeological heritage through the protection of sites and through salvage archaeology (rescue archaeology), generally within the framework of legislation designed to safeguard the past. (Chapter 14)

culture A term used by anthropologists when referring to the non-biological characteristics unique to a particular society (cf. *archaeological culture*). (Chapter 1)

culture-historical approach An approach to archaeological interpretation which uses the procedure of the traditional historian (including emphasis on specific circumstances elaborated with rich detail, and processes of *inductive* reasoning).

deduction A process of reasoning by which more specific consequences are inferred by rigorous argument from more general propositions (cf. *induction*). (Chapter 12)

deductive nomological (D–N) explanation A formal method of explanation based on the testing of hypotheses derived from general laws. (Chapter 12)

deep sea cores Cores drilled from the sea bed that provide the most coherent record of climatic changes on a worldwide scale. The cores contain shells of microscopic marine organisms (foraminifera) laid down on the ocean floor through the continuous process of sedimentation. Variations in the ratio of two oxygen isotopes in the calcium carbonate of these shells give a sensitive indicator of sea temperature at the time the organisms were alive. (Chapter 4)

demography The study of the processes which contribute to population structure and their temporal and spatial dynamics. (Chapter 11)

dendrochronology The study of tree-ring patterns; annual variations in climatic conditions which produce differential growth can be used both as a measure of environmental change, and as the basis for a chronology. (Chapter 4)

diachronic Referring to phenomena as they change over time; i.e. employing a chronological perspective (cf. *synchronic*). (Chapter 12)

diatom analysis A method of environmental reconstruction based on plant microfossils. Diatoms are unicellular algae, whose silica cell walls survive after the algae die, and they accumulate in large numbers at the bottom of rivers and lakes. Their assemblages directly reflect the floristic composition of the water's extinct communities, as well as the water's salinity, alkalinity, and nutrient status. (Chapter 6)

differential fluxgate magnetometer A type of magnetometer used in *subsurface detection* with the advantage of producing a continuous reading. (Chapter 3)

diffusionist approach The theory popularized by V.G. Childe that all the attributes of civilization from architecture to metalworking had diffused from the Near East to Europe. (Chapter 1)

DNA (Deoxyribonucleic acid) The material which carries the hereditary instructions (the "blueprint") which determine the formation of all living organisms. *Genes*, the organizers of inheritance, are composed of DNA. (Chapter 11)

dowsing The supposed location of subsurface features by employing a twig, copper rod, pendulum, or other instrument; discontinuous movements in these instruments are believed by some to record the existence of buried features. (Chapter 3)

echo-sounding An acoustic underwater survey technique, used to trace the topography of submerged coastal plains and other buried land surfaces (see also *seismic reflection profiler*). (Chapter 6)

ecofacts Non-artifactual organic and environmental remains which have cultural relevance, e.g. faunal and floral material as well as soils and sediments. (Chapters 2 & 6)

ecological determinism A form of explanation in which it is implicit that changes in the environment determine changes in human society. (Chapter 12)

electrical resistivity See *soil resistivity*.

electrolysis A standard cleaning process in archaeological conservation. Artifacts are placed in a chemical solution, and by passing a weak current between them and a surrounding metal grill, the corrosive salts move from the cathode (object) to the anode (grill), removing any accumulated deposit and leaving the artifact clean. (Chapter 2)

electron probe microanalysis Used in the analysis of artifact composition, this technique is similar to XRF (*X-ray fluorescence spectrometry*), and is useful for studying small changes in composition within the body of an artifact. (Chapter 9)

electron spin resonance (ESR) Enables trapped electrons within bone and shell to be measured without the heating that *thermoluminescence* requires. As with TL, the number of trapped electrons indicates the age of the specimen. (Chapter 4)

emulation One of the most frequent features accompanying competition, where customs, buildings, and artifacts in one society may be adopted by neighboring ones through a process of imitation which is often competitive in nature. (Chapters 5 & 9)

environmental archaeology A field in which inter-disciplinary research,

involving archaeologists and natural scientists, is directed at the reconstruction of human use of plants and animals, and how past societies adapted to changing environmental conditions. (Chapters 6 & 7)

environmental circumscription An explanation for the origins of the state propounded by Robert Carneiro that emphasizes the fundamental role exerted by environmental constraints and by territorial limitations. (Chapter 12)

eoliths Crude stone pebbles found in Lower Pleistocene contexts; once thought to be the work of human agency, but now generally regarded as natural products. (Chapter 8)

ethnicity The existence of ethnic groups, including tribal groups. Though these are difficult to recognize from the archaeological record, the study of language and linguistic boundaries shows that ethnic groups are often correlated with language areas (see *ethnos*). (Chapter 5)

ethnoarchaeology The study of contemporary cultures with a view to understanding the behavioral relationships which underlie the production of material culture. (Introduction & Chapter 8)

ethnography A subset of *cultural anthropology* concerned with the study of contemporary cultures through first-hand observation. (Introduction)

ethnology A subset of *cultural anthropology* concerned with the comparative study of contemporary cultures, with a view to deriving general principles about human society. (Introduction)

ethnos The ethnic group, defined as a firm aggregate of people, historically established on a given territory, possessing in common relatively stable peculiarities of language and culture, and also recognizing their unity and difference as expressed in a self-appointed name (ethnonym) (see *ethnicity*). (Chapter 5)

evolution The process of growth and development generally accompanied by increasing complexity. In biology, this change is tied to Darwin's concept of natural selection as the basis of species survival. Darwin's work laid the foundations for the study of artifact *typology*, pioneered by such scholars as Pitt-Rivers and Montelius. (Chapter 1)

excavation The principal method of data acquisition in archaeology, involving the systematic uncovering of archaeological remains through the removal of the deposits of soil and the other material covering them and accompanying them. (Chapter 3)

experimental archaeology The study of past behavioral processes through

experimental reconstructions under carefully controlled scientific conditions. (Chapters 2, 7, 8 & 14)

factor analysis A multivariate statistical technique which assesses the degree of variation between artifact types, and is based on a matrix of correlation coefficients which measure the relative association between any two variables. (Chapter 5)

faience Glass-like material first made in predynastic Egypt; it involves coating a core material of powdered quartz with a vitreous alkaline glaze. (Chapter 8)

fall-off analysis The study of regularities in the way in which quantities of traded items found in the archaeological record decline as the distance from the source increases. This may be plotted as a fall-off curve, with the quantities of material (Y-axis) plotted against distance from source (X-axis). (Chapter 9)

faunal dating A method of *relative dating* based on observing the evolutionary changes in particular species of mammals, so as to form a rough chronological sequence. (Chapter 4)

feature A non-portable *artifact*; e.g. hearths, architectural elements, or soil stains. (Chapter 3)

filigree Fine open metalwork using wires and soldering, first developed in the Near East. (Chapter 8)

fission-track dating A dating method based on the operation of a radioactive clock, the spontaneous fission of an isotope of uranium present in a wide range of rocks and minerals. As with potassium-argon dating, with whose time range it overlaps, the method gives useful dates from rocks adjacent to archaeological material. (Chapter 4)

flotation A method of screening (sieving) excavated *matrix* in water so as to separate and recover small *ecofacts* and *artifacts*. (Chapter 6)

formation processes Those processes affecting the way in which archaeological materials came to be buried, and their subsequent history afterwards. Cultural formation processes include the deliberate or accidental activities of humans; natural formation processes refer to natural or environmental events which govern the burial and survival of the archaeological record. (Chapter 2)

fossil cuticles The outermost protective layer of the skin of leaves or blades of grass, made of cutin, a very resistant material that survives in the archaeological record often in feces. Cuticular analysis is a useful adjunct to *palynology* in environmental reconstruction. (Chapter 6)

fossil ice wedges Soil features caused when the ground freezes and contracts, opening up fissures in the permafrost that fill with wedges of ice. The fossil wedges are proof of past cooling of climate and of the depth of permafrost. (Chapter 6)

frequency seriation A *relative dating* method which relies principally on measuring changes in the proportional abundance, or frequency, observed among finds (e.g. counts of tool types, or of ceramic fabrics). (Chapter 4)

functional-processual approach See *processual archaeology.*

genes The basic units of inheritance, now known to be governed by the specific sequence of the genetic markers within the DNA of the individual concerned. (Chapter 11)

geochemical analysis The investigatory technique which involves taking soil samples at regular intervals from the surface of a site, and measuring their phosphate content and other chemical properties. (Chapter 3)

geomagnetic reversals An aspect of archaeomagnetism relevant to the dating of the Lower Paleolithic, involving complete reversals in the earth's magnetic field. (Chapter 4)

geomorphology A subdiscipline of geography, concerned with the study of the form and development of the landscape, it includes such specializations as *sedimentology.* (Chapter 6)

georadar A technique used in ground reconnaissance, similar to *soil-sounding radar*, but with a much larger antenna and more extensive coverage. (Chapter 3)

gift exchange See *reciprocity.*

glottochronology A controversial method of assessing the temporal divergence of two languages based on changes of vocabulary (*lexicostatistics*), and expressed as an arithmetic formula. (Chapters 4 & 5)

granulation The soldering of grains of metal to a background, usually of the same metal, much used by the Etruscans. (Chapter 8)

ground reconnaissance A collective name for a wide variety of methods for identifying individual archaeological sites, including consultation of documentary sources, place-name evidence, local folklore and legend, but primarily actual fieldwork. (Chapter 3)

half-life The time taken for half the quantity of a radioactive isotope in a sample to decay (see also *radioactive decay*). (Chapter 4)

hand axe A Paleolithic stone tool usually made by modifying (chipping or flaking) a natural pebble. (Introduction & Chapter 8)

historical archaeology The archaeological study of historically documented cultures. In North America, research is directed at colonial and post-colonial settlement, analogous to the study of medieval and post-medieval archaeology in Europe. (Introduction & Chapter 3)

historical particularism A detailed descriptive approach to anthropology associated with Franz Boas and his students, and designed as an alternative to the broad generalizing approach favored by anthropologists such as Morgan and Tylor. (Chapter 1)

historiographic approach A form of explanation based primarily on traditional descriptive historical frameworks. (Chapter 12)

hoards Deliberately buried groups of valuables or prized possessions, often in times of conflict or war, and which, for one reason or another, have not been reclaimed. Metal hoards are a primary source of evidence for the European Bronze Age. (Chapters 2 & 10)

homeostasis A term used in *systems thinking* to describe the action of *negative feedback* processes in maintaining the system at a constant equilibrium state. (Chapter 12)

hunter-gatherers A collective term for the members of small-scale mobile or semi-sedentary societies, whose subsistence is mainly focused on hunting game and gathering wild plants and fruits; organizational structure is based on *bands* with strong kinship ties. (Introduction)

hypothetico-deductive explanation A form of explanation based on the formulation of hypotheses and the establishment from them by *deduction* of consequences which can then be tested against the archaeological data. (Chapter 12)

ice cores Borings taken from the Arctic and Antarctic polar ice caps, containing layers of compacted ice, useful for the reconstruction of paleoenvironments and as a method of *absolute dating.* (Chapter 4)

iconography An important component of *cognitive archaeology*, this involves the study of artistic representations which usually have an overt religious or ceremonial significance; e.g. individual deities may be distinguished, each with a special characteristic, such as corn with the corn god, or the sun with a sun goddess etc. (Chapter 10)

idealist explanation A form of explanation that lays great stress on the search for insights into the historical circumstances leading up to the event under study in terms primarily of the ideas and motives of the individuals involved. (Chapter 12)

induction A method of reasoning in which one proceeds by generalization from a series of specific observations so as to derive general conclusions (*cf. deduction*). (Chapter 12)

inductively coupled plasma emission spectrometry (**ICPS**) Based on the same basic principles as OES (*optical emission spectrometry*), but the generation of much higher temperatures reduces problems of interference and produces more accurate results. (Chapter 9)

infra-red absorption spectroscopy A technique used in the characterization of raw materials, it has been particularly useful in distinguishing ambers from different sources: the organic compounds in the amber absorb different wavelengths of infra-red radiation passed through them. (Chapter 9)

interaction sphere A regional or inter-regional exchange system, e.g. the Hopewell interaction sphere. (Chapter 9)

isostatic uplift Rise in the level of the land relative to the sea caused by the relaxation of ice age conditions. It occurs when the weight of ice is removed as temperatures rise, and the landscape is raised up to form *raised beaches.* (Chapter 6)

isotopic analysis An important source of information on the reconstruction of prehistoric diets, this technique analyzes the ratios of the principal isotopes preserved in human bone; in effect the method reads the chemical signatures left in the body by different foods. Isotopic analysis is also used in *characterization* studies. (Chapter 7)

kula ring A system of ceremonial, non-competitive, exchange practiced in Melanesia to establish and reinforce alliances. Malinowski's study of this system was influential in shaping the anthropological concept of *reciprocal exchange.* (Chapter 7)

LANDSAT See *remote sensing.*

landscape archaeology The study of individual features including settlements seen as single components within the broader perspective of the patterning of human activity over a wide area. (Chapter 1)

lexicostatistics The study of linguistic divergence between two languages, based on changes in a list of common vocabulary terms and the sharing of common root words (see also *glottochronology*). (Chapter 4)

lineage A group claiming descent from a common ancestor. (Chapter 5)

loess sediments Deposits formed of a yellowish dust of silt-sized particles blown by the wind and redeposited on land newly deglaciated, or on sheltered areas. (Chapter 6)

market exchange A mode of exchange which implies both a specific location for transactions and the sort of social relations where bargaining can occur. It usually involves a system of price-making through negotiation. (Chapter 9)

Marxist archaeology Based principally on the writings of Karl Marx and

Friedrich Engels, this posits a materialist model of societal change. Change within a society is seen as the result of contradictions arising between the forces of production (technology) and the relations of production (social organization). Such contradictions are seen to emerge as a struggle between distinct social classes. (Chapter 12)

material culture The buildings, tools and other artifacts that constitute the material remains of former societies. (Introduction)

matrix The physical material within which artifacts are embedded or supported. (Chapter 2)

Maya calendar A method employed by the Maya of measuring the passage of time, comprising two separate calendar systems: (1) the Calendar Round, used for everyday purposes; (2) the Long Count, used for the reckoning of historical dates. (Chapter 4)

megalithic yard A metrological unit (c.2.72 ft) proposed by Alexander Thom, and argued by him, on statistical grounds, as the standard unit of length used in the construction of megalithic monuments in Britain and France. (Chapter 10)

Mesolithic An Old World chronological period beginning around 10,000 years ago, situated between the *Paleolithic* and the *Neolithic*, and associated with the rise to dominance of *microliths*. (Chapter 8)

metallographic examination A technique used in the study of early metallurgy involving the microscopic examination of a polished section cut from an artifact, which has been etched so as to reveal the metal structure. (Chapter 8)

microlith A tiny stone tool, characteristic of the *Mesolithic* period, many of which were probably used as barbs. (Chapter 8)

microwear analysis The study of the patterns of wear or damage on the edge of stone tools, which provides valuable information on the way in which the tool was used. (Chapter 8)

midden The accumulation of debris and domestic waste products resulting from human use. The long-term disposal of refuse can result in stratified deposits, which are useful for *relative dating*. (Chapter 7)

Middle Range Theory A conceptual framework linking raw archaeological data with higher-level generalizations and conclusions about the past which can be derived from this evidence. (Introduction)

Midwestern taxonomic system A framework devised by McKern (1939) to systematize sequences in the Great Plains area of the United States, using the general principle of similarities between artifact *assemblages*. (Chapter 1)

MNI (minimum number of individuals) A method of assessing species abundance in faunal assemblages based on a calculation of the smallest number of animals necessary to account for all the identified bones. Usually calculated from the most abundant bone or tooth from either the left or right side of the animal. (Chapter 7)

mobiliary art A term used for the portable art of the Ice Age, comprising engravings and carvings on small objects of stone, antler, bone, and ivory. (Chapter 10)

monocausal explanation Explanation of culture change (e.g. for *state* origins) which lays stress on a single dominant explanatory factor or "prime mover." (Chapter 12)

Mössbauer spectroscopy A technique used in the analysis of artifact composition, particularly iron compounds in pottery. It involves the measurement of the gamma radiation absorbed by the iron nuclei, which provides information on the particular iron compounds in the sample, and hence on the conditions of firing when the pottery was being made. (Chapter 9)

multi-dimensional scaling (MDSCAL) A multivariate statistical technique which aims to develop spatial structure from numerical data by estimating the differences and similarities between analytical units. (Chapter 5)

multiplier effect A term used in *systems thinking* to describe the process by which changes in one field of human activity (subsystem) sometimes act to promote changes in other fields (subsystems) and in turn act on the original subsystem itself. An instance of *positive feedback*, it is thought by some to be one of the primary mechanisms of societal change. (Chapter 12)

multivariate explanation Explanation of culture change, e.g. the origin of the state, which, in contrast to monocausal approaches, stresses the interaction of several factors operating simultaneously. (Chapter 12)

native copper Metallic copper found naturally in nuggets, which can be worked by hammering, cutting, and *annealing*. (Chapter 12)

negative feedback In *systems thinking*, this is a process which acts to counter or "dampen" the potentially disruptive effects of external inputs; it acts as a stabilizing mechanism (see *homeostasis*). (Chapter 12)

Neolithic An Old World chronological period characterized by the development of agriculture and hence, an increasing emphasis on sedentism. (Chapter 4)

Neolithic Revolution A term coined by V.G. Childe in 1941 to describe the origin and consequences of farming (i.e. the development of stock raising and agriculture), allowing the widespread development of settled village life.

(Chapter 7)

neutron activation analysis (NAA) A method used in the analysis of artifact composition which depends on the excitation of the nuclei of the atoms of a sample's various elements, when these are bombarded with slow neutrons. The method is accurate to about plus or minus 5 percent. (Chapter 9)

neutron scattering A remote sensing technique involving the placing of a probe into the soil in order to measure the relative rates of neutron flows through the soil. Since stone produces a lower count rate than soil, buried features can often be detected. (Chapter 3)

New Archaeology A new approach advocated in the 1960s which argued for an explicitly scientific framework of archaeological method and theory, with hypotheses rigorously tested, as the proper basis for explanation rather than simply description (see also *processual archaeology*). (Introduction & Chapter 1)

NISP (number of identified specimens) A gross counting technique used in the quantification of animal bones. The method may produce misleading results in assessing the relative abundance of different species, since skeletal differences and differential rates of bone preservation mean that some species will be represented more than others. (Chapter 7)

non-equilibrium systems See *self-organization*.

non-probabilistic sampling A non-statistical sampling strategy (in contrast to *probabilistic sampling*) which concentrates on sampling areas on the basis of intuition, historical documentation, or long field experience in the area. (Chapter 3)

obsidian A volcanic glass whose ease of working and characteristically hard flint-like edges allowed it to be used for the making of tools. (Chapters 4, 9, etc.)

obsidian hydration dating This technique involves the absorption of water on exposed surfaces of obsidian; when the local hydration rate is known, the thickness of the hydration layer, if accurately measured, can be used to provide an absolute date. (Chapter 4)

off-site data Evidence from a range of information, including scatters of artifacts and features such as plowmarks and field boundaries, that provides important evidence about human exploitation of the environment. (Chapter 3)

Oldowan industry The earliest toolkits, comprising flake and pebble tools, used by hominids in the Olduvai Gorge, East Africa. (Chapters 4 & 8)

open-area excavation The opening up of large horizontal areas for *excavation*, used especially where single period deposits lie close to the surface as, for example, with the remains of American Indian or European Neolithic long houses. (Chapter 3)

optical emission spectrometry (OES) A technique used in the analysis of artifact composition, based on the principle that electrons, when excited (i.e. heated to a high temperature) release light of a particular wavelength. The presence or absence of various elements is established by examining the appropriate spectral line of their characteristic wavelengths. Generally, this method gives an accuracy of only 25 percent and has been superseded by ICPS (*inductively coupled plasma emission spectrometry*). (Chapter 9)

paleoentomology The study of insects from archaeological contexts. The survival of insect exoskeletons, which are quite resistant to decomposition, is an important source of evidence in the reconstruction of paleo-environments. (Chapter 6)

paleoethnobotany (archaeobotany) The recovery and identification of plant remains from archaeological *contexts*, important in the reconstruction of past environments and economies. (Chapter 7)

Paleolithic The archaeological period before *c*.10,000 BC, characterized by the earliest known stone tool manufacture. (Chapters 1, 4, 8, etc.)

paleomagnetism See *archaeomagnetic dating*.

palynology The analysis of fossil pollen as an aid to the reconstruction of past vegetation and climates. (Chapters 4 & 6)

parietal art A term used to designate art on the walls of caves and shelters, or on huge blocks. (Chapter 10)

peer-polity interaction The full range of exchanges taking place – including imitation, emulation, competition, warfare, and the exchange of material goods and information – between autonomous (self-governing) socio-political units, generally within the same geographic region. (Chapter 9)

physical anthropology A subdiscipline of anthropology dealing with the study of human biological or physical characteristics and their evolution. (Introduction)

phytoliths Minute particles of silica derived from the cells of plants, able to survive after the organism has decomposed or been burned. They are common in ash layers, pottery, and even on stone tools. (Chapter 6)

pinger (or boomer profiler) An underwater survey device, more powerful than *sidescan sonar*, capable of probing up to 60 m below the seabed. (Chapter 3)

piston corer A device for extracting columns of sediment from the ocean floor. Dates for the different layers are obtained by radiocarbon, paleomagnetism, or uranium series methods. (Chapter 6)

plating A method of bonding metals together, for instance silver with copper or copper with gold. (Chapter 8)

polity A politically independent or autonomous social unit, whether simple or complex, which may in the case of a complex society (such as a state) comprise many lesser dependent components. (Chapter 5)

pollen analysis See *palynology*.

positive feedback A term used in *systems thinking* to describe a response in which changing output conditions in the system stimulate further growth in the input; one of the principal factors in generating system change or morphogenesis (see also *multiplier effect*). (Chapter 12)

"Post-processual" explanation Explanation formulated in reaction to the perceived limitations of functional-processual archaeology. It eschews generalization in favor of an "individualizing" approach that is influenced by *structuralism, Critical Theory, and neo-Marxist* thought. (Chapter 12)

potassium-argon dating A method used to date rocks up to thousands of millions of years old, though it is restricted to volcanic material no more recent than *c*. 100,000 years old. One of the most widely used methods in the dating of early hominid sites in Africa. (Chapter 4)

prehistory The period of human history before the advent of writing. (Introduction)

prestige goods A term used to designate a limited range of exchange goods to which a society ascribes high status or value. (Chapter 9)

primitive valuables A term coined by Dalton to describe the tokens of wealth and prestige, often of specially valued items, that were used in the ceremonial exchange systems of non-state societies; examples include the shell necklaces and bracelets of the *kula* system (*cf. prestige goods*). (Chapter 9)

probabilistic sampling Sampling method, employing probability theory, designed to draw reliable general conclusions about a site or region, based on small sample areas. Four types of sampling strategies are recognized: (1) *simple random sampling;* (2) *stratified random sampling;* (3) *systematic sampling;* (4) *stratified systematic sampling.* (Chapter 3)

processual archaeology An approach that stresses the dynamic relationship between social and economic aspects of culture and the environment as the basis for understanding the processes of culture change. Uses the scientific methodology of problem statement, hypothesis formulation, and subsequent testing. The earlier functional-processual archaeology has been contrasted with *cognitive-processual archaeology*, where the emphasis is on integrating ideological and symbolic aspects. (Introduction & Chapter 12)

proton magnetometer A device used in *subsurface detection* which records variations in the earth's magnetic field. (Chapter 3)

pseudo-archaeology The use of selective archaeological evidence to promulgate nonscientific, fictional accounts of the past. (Chapter 14)

punctuated equilibria Principal feature of the evolutionary theory propounded by Niles Eldredge and Stephen J. Gould, in which species change is represented as a form of Darwinian gradualism, "punctuated" by periods of rapid evolutionary change. (Chapter 12)

pyrotechnology The intentional use and control of fire by humans. (Chapter 8)

radioactive decay The regular process by which radioactive isotopes break down into their decay products with a *half-life* which is specific to the isotope in question (see *half-life, radiocarbon dating*). (Chapter 4)

radiocarbon dating An absolute dating method that measures the decay of the radioactive isotope of carbon (^{14}C) in organic material (see *half-life*.). (Chapter 4)

radioimmunoassay A method of protein analysis whereby it is possible to identify protein molecules surviving in fossils which are thousands and even millions of years old. (Chapter 11)

raised beaches These are remnants of former coastlines, usually the result of processes such as *isostatic uplift* or *tectonic movements*. (Chapter 6)

ranked societies Societies in which there is unequal access to prestige and status e.g. *chiefdoms* and *states*. (Chapter 5)

reaves Bronze Age stone boundary walls, for instance on Dartmoor, England, which may designate the territorial extent of individual communities. (Chapter 6)

reciprocity A mode of exchange in which transactions take place between individuals who are symmetrically placed i.e. they are exchanging as equals, neither being in a dominant position. (Chapter 9)

reconnaissance survey A broad range of techniques involved in the location of archaeological sites, e.g. the recording of surface artifacts and features, and the sampling of natural and mineral resources. (Chapter 3)

redistribution A mode of exchange which implies the operation of some central organizing authority. Goods are received or appropriated by the central authority, and subsequently some of them are sent by that authority to other locations. (Chapter 9)

refitting Sometimes referred to as conjoining, this entails attempting to put stone tools and flakes back together again, and provides important information on the processes involved in the knapper's craft. (Chapter 8)

relative dating The determination of chronological sequence without recourse to a fixed time scale; e.g. the arrangement of artifacts in a typological sequence, or *seriation* (*cf. absolute dating*). (Chapter 4)

religion A framework of beliefs relating to supernatural or superhuman beings or forces that transcend the everyday material world. (Chapter 10)

remote sensing General term for *reconnaissance* and *surface survey* techniques that leave subsurface archaeological deposits undisturbed. (Chapter 3)

rescue archaeology See *salvage archaeology*.

research design Systematic planning of archaeological research, usually including (1) the formulation of a strategy to resolve a particular question; (2) the collection and recording of the evidence; (3) the processing and analysis of these data and its interpretation; and (4) the publication of results. (Chapter 3)

resistivity meter See *soil resistivity*.

rock varnishes Natural accretions of manganese and iron oxides, together with clay minerals and organic matter, which can provide valuable environmental evidence. Their study, when combined with radiocarbon methods, can provide a minimum age for some landforms, and even some types of stone tool which also accumulate varnish. (Chapters 4 & 6)

salvage archaeology The location and recording (usually through excavation) of archaeological sites in advance of highway construction, drainage projects, or urban development. (Chapters 3 & 14)

sedimentology A subset of *geomorphology* concerned with the investigation of the structure and texture of sediments i.e. the global term for material deposited on the earth's surface. (Chapter 6)

segmentary societies Relatively small and autonomous groups, usually of agriculturalists, who regulate their own affairs; in some cases, they may join together with other comparable segmentary societies to form a larger ethnic unit. (Chapter 5)

seismic reflection profiler An acoustic underwater survey device that uses the principle of *echo-sounding* to locate submerged landforms; in water depths of 100 m, this method can achieve penetration of more than 10 m into the sea floor. (Chapter 6)

self-organization The product of a theory derived from thermodynamics which demonstrates that order can arise spontaneously when systems are pushed far from an equilibrium state. The emergence of new structure arises at bifurcation points, or thresholds of instability (*cf. catastrophe theory*). (Chapter 12)

seriation A relative dating technique based on the chronological ordering of a group of artifacts or assemblages, where the most similar are placed adjacent to each other in the series. Two types of seriation can be recognized, *frequency seriation* and *contextual seriation*. (Chapters 4 & 5)

sidescan sonar A survey method used in underwater archaeology which provides the broadest view of the sea-floor. An acoustic emitter is towed behind a vessel and sends out sound waves in a fan-shaped beam. These pulses of sonic energy are reflected back to a transducer – return time depending on distance traveled – and recorded on a rotating drum. (Chapter 3)

simple random sampling A type of *probabilistic sampling* where the areas to be sampled are chosen using a table of random numbers. Drawbacks include (1) defining the site's boundaries beforehand; (2) the nature of random number tables results in some areas being allotted clusters of sample squares, while others remain untouched. (Chapter 3)

simulation The formulation and computer implementation of dynamic models i.e. models concerned with change through time. Simulation is a useful heuristic device, and can be of considerable help in the development of explanation. (Chapter 12)

site A distinct spatial clustering of *artifacts*, *features*, structures, and organic and environmental remains, as the residue of human activity. (Chapter 2).

site catchment analysis (SCA) A type of "off-site" analysis which concentrates on the total area from which a site's contents have been derived; at its simplest, a site's catchment can be thought of as a full inventory of artifactual and non-artifactual remains and their sources. (Chapter 6)

site exploitation territory (SET) Often confused with *site-catchment analysis*, this is a method of achieving a fairly standardized assessment of the area habitually used by a site's occupants. (Chapter 6)

slag The material residue of smelting processes from metalworking. Analysis is often necessary to distinguish slags derived from copper smelting from those produced in iron production. Crucible slags (from the casting process) may be distinguished from smelting slags by their high concentration of copper. (Chapter 8)

SLAR (sideways-looking airborne radar) A *remote sensing* technique that involves the recording in radar images of the return of pulses of electromagnetic radiation sent out from aircraft (*cf. thermography*). (Chapter 3)

social anthropology See *cultural anthropology*.

soil-sounding radar A method of *subsurface detection* in which short radio pulses are sent through the soil, such that the echoes reflect back significant changes in soil conditions. (Chapter 3)

soil resistivity A method of *subsurface detection* which measures changes in conductivity by passing electrical current through ground soils. This is generally a consequence of moisture content, and in this way, buried features can be detected by differential retention of groundwater. (Chapter 3)

sphere of exchange In non-market societies, prestige valuables and ordinary commodities were often exchanged quite separately i.e. valuables were exchanged against valuables in prestige transactions, while commodities were exchanged against commodities with much less ceremony, in mutually profitable barter transactions. These separate systems are termed spheres of exchange. (Chapter 9)

standing wave technique An acoustic method, similar to *bosing*, used in *subsurface detection*. (Chapter 3)

state A term used to describe a social formation defined by distinct territorial boundedness, and characterized by strong central government in which the operation of political power is sanctioned by legitimate force. In cultural evolutionist models, it ranks second only to the empire as the most complex societal developmental stage. (Chapter 12)

stela (pl. stelae) A freestanding carved stone monument. (Chapter 4)

step-trenching An *excavation* method employed on very deep sites, such as Near Eastern *tell* sites, in which the excavation proceeds downwards in a series of gradually narrowing steps. (Chapter 3)

stratification The laying down or depositing of strata or layers (also called deposits) one above the other. A succession of layers should provide a relative chronological sequence, with the earliest at the bottom and the latest at the top. (Chapters 3 & 4)

stratified random sampling A form of *probabilistic sampling* in which the region or site is divided into natural zones or strata such as cultivated land and forest; units are then chosen by a random number procedure so as to give each zone a number of squares proportional to its area, thus overcoming the inherent bias in *simple random sampling*. (Chapter 3)

stratified systematic sampling A form of

probabilistic sampling which combines elements of (1) *simple random sampling*, (2) *stratified random sampling*, and (3) *systematic sampling*, in an effort to reduce sampling bias. (Chapter 3)

stratigraphy The study and validation of *stratification*; the analysis in the vertical, time dimension, of a series of layers in the horizontal, space dimension. It is often used as a *relative dating* technique to assess the temporal sequence of artifact deposition. (Chapter 3)

structuralist approaches Interpretations which stress that human actions are guided by beliefs and symbolic concepts, and that underlying these are structures of thought which find expression in various forms. The proper object of study is therefore to uncover the structures of thought and to study their influence in shaping the ideas in the minds of the human actors who created the archaeological record. (Chapter 12)

style According to the art historian, Ernst Gombrich, style is "any distinctive and therefore recognizable way in which an act is performed and made." Archaeologists and anthropologists have defined "stylistic areas" as areal units representing shared ways of producing and decorating artifacts. (Chapter 10)

sub-bottom profiler See *underwater reconnaissance*.

subsurface detection A collective name for a variety of remote sensing techniques operating at ground level, and including *bosing* (or bowsing), *augering*, magnetometer, and radar techniques. (Chapter 3)

surface survey Two basic kinds can be identified: (1) unsystematic and (2) systematic. The former involves field-walking, i.e. scanning the ground along one's path and recording the location of artifacts and surface features. Systematic survey by comparison is less subjective and involves a grid system, such that the survey area is divided into sectors and these are walked systematically, thus making the recording of finds more accurate. (Chapter 3)

symmetry analysis A mathematical approach to the analysis of decorative style which claims that patterns can be divided into two distinct groups or symmetry classes: 17 classes for those patterns that repeat motifs horizontally, and 46 classes for those that repeat them horizontally and vertically. Such studies have suggested that the choice of motif arrangement within a particular culture is far from random. (Chapter 10)

synchronic Referring to phenomena considered at a single point in time; i.e. an approach which is not primarily concerned with change (*cf. diachronic*). (Chapter 12)

synostosis The joining of separate pieces of bone in human skeletons; the precise

timing of such processes is an important indicator of age. (Chapter 11)

systematic sampling A form of *probabilistic sampling* employing a grid of equally spaced locations; e.g. selecting every other square. This method of regular spacing runs the risk of missing (or hitting) every single example if the distribution itself is regularly spaced. (Chapter 3)

systematic survey See *surface survey*.

systems thinking A method of formal analysis in which the object of study is viewed as comprising distinct analytical sub-units. Thus in archaeology, it comprises a form of explanation in which a society or culture is seen through the interaction and interdependence of its component parts; these are referred to as system parameters, and may include such things as population size, settlement pattern, crop production, technology etc. (Chapter 12)

taphonomy The study of processes which have affected organic materials such as bone after death; it also involves the microscopic analysis of tooth-marks or cut marks to assess the effects of butchery or scavenging activities. (Chapter 7)

tectonic movements Displacements in the plates that make up the earth's crust, often responsible for the occurrence of *raised beaches*. (Chapter 6)

tell A Near Eastern term that refers to a mound site formed through successive human occupation over a very long timespan. (Chapter 2)

temper Inclusions in pottery clay which act as a filler to give the clay added strength and workability and to counteract any cracking or shrinkage during firing. (Chapter 8)

tephra Volcanic ash. In the Mediterranean, for example, *deep-sea coring* produced evidence for the ash fall from the eruption of Thera, and its *stratigraphic* position provided important information in the construction of a *relative chronology*. (Chapter 4)

thermal prospection A *remote sensing* method used in aerial reconnaissance. It is based on weak variations in temperature which can be found above buried structures whose thermal properties are different from those of their surroundings. (Chapter 3)

thermography A non-photographic technique which uses thermal or heat sensors in aircraft to record the temperature of the soil surface. Variations in soil temperature can be the result of the presence of buried structures. (Chapter 3)

thermoluminescence (TL) A dating technique that relies indirectly on radioactive decay, overlapping with radiocarbon in the time period for which it is useful, but also has the

potential for dating earlier periods. It has much in common with *electron spin resonance* (ESR). (Chapter 4)

Thiessen polygons A formal method of describing settlement patterns based on territorial divisions centered on a single site; the polygons are created by drawing straight lines between pairs of neighboring sites, then at the mid-point along each of these lines, a second series of lines are drawn at right angles to the first. Linking the second series of lines creates the Thiessen polygons. (Chapter 5)

thin-section analysis A technique whereby microscopic thin sections are cut from a stone object or potsherd and examined with a petrological microscope to determine the source of the material. (Chapter 9)

Three Age System A *classification* system devised by C.J. Thomsen for the sequence of technological periods (stone, bronze and iron) in Old World prehistory. It established the principle that by classifying artifacts, one could produce a chronological ordering. (Chapter 1)

trace element analysis The use of chemical techniques, such as *neutron activation analysis*, or *X-ray fluorescence spectrometry*, for determining the incidence of trace elements in rocks. These methods are widely used in the identification of raw material sources for the production of stone tools. (Chapters 7 & 9)

trajectory In *systems thinking*, this refers to the series of successive states through which the system proceeds over time. It may be said to represent the long-term behavior of the system. (Chapter 12)

tree-ring dating See *dendrochronology*.

trend surface analysis The aim of trend surface analysis is to highlight the main features of a geographic distribution by smoothing over some of the local irregularities. In this way, important trends can be isolated from the background "noise" more clearly. (Chapter 9)

tribes A term used to describe a social grouping generally larger than a *band*, but rarely numbering more than a few thousand; unlike bands tribes are usually settled farmers, though they also include nomadic pastoral groups whose economy is based on exploitation of livestock. Individual communities tend to be integrated into the larger society through kinship ties. (Chapter 5)

tuyère A ceramic blowtube used in the process of smelting. (Chapter 8)

type A class of artifacts defined by the consistent clustering of *attributes*. (Chapters 1 & 4)

typology The systematic organization of artifacts into types on the basis of shared *attributes*. (Chapters 1, 3 & 4)

underwater reconnaissance Geophysical methods of underwater survey include

(1) *a proton magnetometer* towed behind a survey vessel, so as to detect iron and steel objects which distort the earth's magnetic field; (2) *side-scan sonar* that transmits sound waves in a fan-shaped beam to produce a graphic image of surface features on the sea-bed; (3) a *sub-bottom profiler* that emits sound pulses which bounce back from features and objects buried beneath the sea floor. (Chapter 3)

Uniformitarianism The principle that the stratification of rocks is due to processes still going on in seas, rivers, and lakes; i.e. that geologically ancient conditions were in essence similar to or "uniform with" those of our own time. (Chapter 1)

uranium series dating A dating method based on the radioactive decay of isotopes of uranium. It has proved particularly useful for the period before 50,000 years ago, which lies outside the time range of radiocarbon dating. (Chapter 4)

varves Fine layers of alluvium sediment deposited in glacial lakes. Their annual deposition makes them a useful source of dating. (Chapter 4)

Wheeler box-grid An excavation technique developed by Mortimer Wheeler from the work of Pitt-Rivers, involving the retaining of intact balks of earth between excavation grid squares, so that different layers can be correlated across the site in the vertical profiles. (Chapter 3)

world system A term coined by the historian Wallerstein to designate an economic unit, articulated by trade networks extending far beyond the boundaries of individual political units (nation states), and linking them together in a larger functioning unit. (Chapter 9)

X-ray diffraction analysis A technique used in identifying minerals present in artifact raw materials; it can also be used in geomorphological contexts to identify particular clay minerals in sediments, and thus the specific source from which the sediment was derived. (Chapter 6)

X-ray fluorescence spectrometry (XRF) A method used in the analysis of artifact composition, in which the sample is irradiated with a beam of X-rays which excite electrons associated with atoms on the surface. (Chapter 9)

XTENT modeling A method of generating settlement hierarchy, that overcomes the limitations of both *central place theory* and *Thiessen polygons*; it assigns territories to centers based on their scale, assuming that the size of each center is directly proportional to its area of influence. Hypothetical political maps may thus be constructed from survey data. (Chapter 5)

zooarchaeology See *archaeozoology*.

Notes and Bibliography

Chapter 1: The Searchers (pp. 17–40)

General references Daniel 1967, 1975, 1980; Gräslund 1987; Grayson 1983; Heizer 1969; Trigger 1989. There is also an excellent brief introduction in Clarke, D.L. 1968 (pp. 4–11). Autobiographical retrospectives include Willey 1974; Daniel & Chippindale 1989. **Europe** Klindt-Jensen 1975 (Scandinavia); Sklenár 1983 (Central Europe); Laming-Emperaire 1964 (France). French pioneers are the subject of a series of articles entitled "Les Grands Archéologues" by Evelyne & Jean Gran-Aymerich in the journal *Archéologia* (since 1985). **New World** Willey & Sabloff 1974, 1980; Meltzer & others 1986; Fagan 1977; Bernal 1980 (Mexico). **Australia** Mulvaney 1969. **Africa** Clark 1970; Robertshaw 1990.

p. 28 **Layard** Lloyd 1980; Waterfield 1963 **Schliemann** Deuel 1977.
p. 32 **Childe** Trigger 1980.
p. 33 **Ecological approach** Steward 1955; Clark, J.G.D. 1952
pp. 33–34 **Archaeological science** Brothwell & Higgs 1969.
pp. 34–37 **The New Archaeology** Binford 1968; Clarke, D.L. 1968 & 1972.
pp. 37–39 **World archaeology** Braidwood & Howe 1960; MacNeish 1967–1972; Adams, R. McC. 1965; Leakey, M. 1979; Clark, J.D. 1970; Mulvaney 1969; Gould 1980; McBryde 1985.
Box Features
pp. 20–21 **Pompeii** Grant 1971; Corti 1951; Raper 1977; Maiuri 1970; Ling 1987.

pp. 24–25 **Evolutionary Thought** Harris 1968; Steward 1955; White 1959.
pp. 26–27 **19th-Century Pioneers** Willey & Sabloff 1980; Fagan 1977.
pp. 29–31 **Field Techniques** Thompson 1977 (Pitt-Rivers); Drower 1985 (Flinders Petrie); Hawkes 1982; Wheeler 1955 (Wheeler).
p.35 **The New Archaeology** Binford 1968; Clarke, D.L. 1968.
pp.36–37 **Glastonbury** Bulleid 1924; Clarke, D.L. 1972; Coles & Coles 1986.

Bibliography

ADAMS, R. McC. 1965. *The Land Behind Baghdad: A History of Settlement on the Diyala Plains.* Univ. of Chicago Press.

BERNAL, I. 1980. *A History of Mexican Archaeology.* Thames & Hudson: London & New York.

BINFORD, L.R. 1968. Post-Pleistocene adaptations, in *New Perspectives in Archaeology* (L.R. Binford & S.R. Binford eds.) 313–41. Aldine Press: Chicago.

BRAIDWOOD, R.J. & HOWE, B. 1960. *Investigations in Iraqi Kurdistan.* Studies in Ancient Oriental Civilization, No. 31. Oriental Institute of the Univ. of Chicago.

BROTHWELL, D.R. & HIGGS, E.S. 1969. *Science in Archaeology.* (Rev. ed.) Thames & Hudson: London; Praeger: New York.

BULLEID, A. 1924. *The Lake Villages of Somerset.* Glastonbury Archaeological Society: Yeovil.

CERAM, C.W. 1967. *Gods, Graves and Scholars.* (2nd ed.) Knopf: New York;

Gollancz: London 1971.

CLARK, J.D. 1970 *The Prehistory of Africa.* Thames & Hudson: London; Praeger: New York.

CLARK, J.G.D. 1952. *Prehistoric Europe: The Economic Basis.* Methuen: London.

CLARKE, D.L. 1968. *Analytical Archaeology.* Methuen: London.

———(ed.). 1972. *Models in Archaeology.* Methuen: London.

COLES, B. & COLES, J. 1986 *Sweet Track to Glastonbury. The Somerset Levels in Prehistory.* Thames & Hudson: London & New York.

CORTI, E.G. 1951. *The Destruction and Resurrection of Pompeii and Herculaneum.* Routledge & Kegan Paul: London.

DANIEL, G.E. 1967. *The Origins and Growth of Archaeology.* Pelican: Harmondsworth.

———1975. *150 Years of Archaeology.* Duckworth: London.

———1980. *A Short History of Archaeology.* Thames & Hudson: London & New York.

———(ed.). 1981. *Towards a History of Archaeology.* Thames & Hudson: London.

———& RENFREW, A.C. 1988. *The Idea of Prehistory.* (Rev. ed.) Edinburgh Univ. Press; Columbia Univ. Press: New York.

DANIEL, G.E. & CHIPPINDALE, C. (eds.). 1989. *The Pastmasters.* Thames & Hudson: London & New York.

DEUEL, L. 1977. *Memoirs of Heinrich Schliemann.* Harper & Row: New York.

DROWER, M. 1985. *Flinders Petrie.* Gollancz: London.

FAGAN, B. 1977. *Elusive Treasure. The Story of Early Archaeologists in the Americas.* Scribners: New York.

GOULD, R.A. 1980. *Living Archaeology.* Cambridge Univ. Press.

GRANT, M. 1971. *Cities of Vesuvius: Pompeii and Herculaneum.* Michael Grant Publications: London.

GRÄSLUND, B. 1987. *The Birth of Prehistoric Chronology.* Cambridge Univ. Press.

GRAYSON, D.K. 1983. *The Establishment of Human Antiquity.* Academic Press: New York & London.

HARRIS, M. 1968. *The Rise of Anthropological Theory.* Thomas Y. Crowell: New York.

HAWKES, J. 1982. *Mortimer Wheeler: Adventurer in Archaeology.* Weidenfeld: London.

HEIZER, R.F. 1969. *Man's Discovery of His Past – A sourcebook of original articles.* Peek: Palo Alto.

KLINDT-JENSEN, O. 1975. *A History of Scandinavian Archaeology.* Thames & Hudson: London.

LAMING-EMPERAIRE, A. 1964 *Origines de l'Archaéologie Préhistorique en France.* Picard: Paris.

LEAKEY, M. 1979. *Olduvai Gorge: My Search for Early Man.* Collins: London.

LING, R. 1987. A New Look at Pompeii, in *Origins* (B. Cunliffe ed.). BBC Books: London.

LLOYD, S. 1980. *Foundations in the Dust.* (2nd ed.) Thames & Hudson: London & New York.

MacNEISH, R.S. & others (eds.). 1967–1972. *The Prehistory of the Tehuacan Valley.* Univ. of Texas Press: Austin.

MAIURI, A. 1970. *Pompeii.* Institute Poligrafico dello Stato: Rome.

McBRYDE, I. (ed.). 1985. *Who Owns the Past?* Oxford Univ. Press: Melbourne.

MELTZER, D.J., FOWLER, D.D. & SABLOFF, J.A. (eds.). 1986. *American Archaeology Past and Future.* Smithsonian Institution Press: Washington D.C.

MULVANEY, D.J. 1969. *The Prehistory of Australia.* Thames & Hudson: London (Rev. ed. Penguin Books: Harmondsworth 1975).

RAPER, R.A. 1977. The analysis of the urban structure of Pompeii: a sociological examination of land use, in *Spatial Archaeology* (D.L. Clarke ed.), 189–222. Academic Press: London.

ROBERTSHAW, P. (ed.). 1990. *A History of African Archaeology.* Currey: London; Heinemann: Portsmouth, N.H.

SKLENÁR, K. 1983. *Archaeology in Central Europe: the first 500 years.* Leicester Univ. Press; St Martin's: New York.

STEWARD, J.H. 1955. *Theory of Culture Change, the Methodology of Multilinear Evolution.* Univ. of Illinois Press: Urbana.

TAYLOR, W.W. 1948. *A Study of*

Archaeology. American Anthropological Association Memoir 69.

THOMPSON, M.W. 1977. *General Pitt-Rivers.* Moonraker Press: Bradford-on-Avon.

TRIGGER, B.G. 1980. *Gordon Childe.* Thames & Hudson: London.

—— 1989. *A History of Archaeological Thought.* Cambridge Univ. Press.

TYLOR, E.B. 1871. *Primitive Culture.* Henry Holt: New York.

VASICEK, Z. & MALINA, J. (eds.). 1990. *Archaeology Yesterday and Today.* Cambridge Univ. Press.

WATERFIELD, G. 1963. *Layard of Nineveh.* John Murray: London.

WHEELER, R.E.M. 1955. *Still Digging.* Michael Joseph: London.

WHITE, L.A. 1959. *The Evolution of Culture.* McGraw-Hill: New York.

WILLEY, G.R. (ed.). 1974. *Archaeological Researches in Retrospect.* Winthrop: Cambridge, Mass.

—— & PHILLIPS, P. 1958. *Method and Theory in American Archaeology.* Univ. of Chicago Press.

—— & SABLOFF, J.A. 1974. *A History of American Archaeology.* Thames & Hudson: London (2nd ed. W.H. Freeman: San Francisco, 1980).

Chapter 2: What is Left? The Variety of the Evidence (pp. 41–60)

pp. 44–45 **Formation processes** Schiffer 1987; Nash & Petraglia 1987; Binford 1981; Brain 1981.

pp. 46–47 **Cultural formation processes** Schiffer 1976; Cockburn & Cockburn 1980 (mummies); Redford 1984 (destruction of Akhenaten's monuments).

p. 51 **Organic materials** Sutcliffe 1985 (La Brea tarpits); Bowman 1983 (Vindolanda writing tablets).

pp. 55–56 **Dry environments** Sheets 1984 (El Salvador); Jennings 1953 (Danger Cave); Lynch 1980; Zimmerman & others 1971 (Aleutian mummy); Cockburn & Cockburn 1980 (mummies in general).

pp. 56–58 **Cold environments** Sutcliffe 1985; Guthrie 1990 (frozen mammoths); Rudenko 1970 (Pazyryk): Hart Hansen & others 1985 (Qilakitsoq): Beattie & Geiger 1987 (the British sailors).

pp. 58–60 **Waterlogged environments** In general: Coles, B. & J. 1989; Coles, J. 1984, 1986; and the journal *Newswarp.* Coles & Lawson 1987 (European sites); Coles, B. & J. 1986 (Somerset Levels). Macdonald & Purdy 1982 (Florida); Glob 1969, 1973 (Danish bodies); Bocquet 1979; Bocquet & others 1982 (lake sites).

Box Features

p. 45 **Experimental Archaeology** Jewell & Dimbleby 1966; Fowler 1988/89; also

Evans & Limbrey 1974.

pp. 52–53 **Ozette** Gleeson & Grosso 1976; Kirk & Daugherty 1974.

pp. 54–55 **Tutankhamun** Carter 1972; Reeves 1990.

p. 57 **Barrow Site** Dekin 1987; Lobdell & others 1987.

Bibliography

ASCHER, R. 1970. Cues I: design and construction of an experimental archaeological structure. *American Antiquity* 35, 215–16.

BEATTIE, O. & GEIGER, J. 1987. *Frozen in Time.* Bloomsbury: London.

BINFORD, L.R. 1981. *Bones – Ancient Men and Modern Myths.* Academic Press: New York & London.

—— 1983. *In Pursuit of the Past.* Thames & Hudson: London & New York.

BOCQUET, A. 1979. Lake bottom archaeology. *Scientific American* 240 (2), 48–56.

—— & others. 1982. La vie au Néolithique. Charavines, un village au bord d'un lac il y a 5000 ans. *Dossiers de l'Archéologie* No. 64, June.

BODDINGTON, A., GARLAND, A.N. & JANAWAY, R.C. (eds.). 1987. *Death, Decay and Reconstruction. Approaches to Archaeology and Forensic Science.* Manchester Univ. Press.

BOWMAN, A.K. 1983. *Roman Writing Tablets from Vindolanda.* British Museum Publications: London.

BRAIN, C.K. 1981. *The Hunters or the Hunted? An Introduction to African Cave Taphonomy.* Univ. of Chicago Press.

CARTER, H. 1972. *The Tomb of Tutankhamen.* Sphere: London.

CLARK, G. 1960. *Archaeology and Society.* (3rd ed.) Methuen: London; Barnes & Noble: New York.

COCKBURN, A. & COCKBURN, E. (eds.). 1980. *Mummies, Disease and Ancient Cultures.* Cambridge Univ. Press.

COLES, B. & COLES, J. 1986. *Sweet Track to Glastonbury. The Somerset Levels in Prehistory.* Thames & Hudson: London & New York.

—— 1989. *People of the Wetlands.* Thames & Hudson: London & New York.

COLES, J. 1984. *The Archaeology of Wetlands.* Edinburgh Univ. Press.

—— 1986. Precision, purpose and priorities in Wetland Archaeology. *The Antiquaries Journal* 66, 227–47.

—— & LAWSON, A.J. (eds.). 1987. *European Wetlands in Prehistory.* Clarendon Press: Oxford.

DEKIN, A.A. 1987. Sealed in time: ice entombs an Eskimo family for five centuries. *National Geographic* 171 (6), 824–36.

DIMBLEBY, G. 1967. *Plants and Archaeology.* Baker: London (Paladin: London 1978).

EVANS, J.G. & LIMBREY, S. 1974. The

experimental earthwork at Morden Bog, Wareham, Dorset, England: 1963 to 1972. *Proc. Prehist. Soc.* 40, 170–202.

FOWLER, P.J. 1988/89. The experimental earthworks 1958–88. *Annual Report of the Council for British Archaeology* 39, 83–98.

GLEESON, P. & GROSSO, G. 1976. Ozette site, in *The Excavation of Water-saturated Archaeological Sites (wet sites) on the Northwest Coast of North America* (D.R. Croes ed.), 13–44. Mercury Series 50: Ottawa.

GLOB, P.V. 1969. *The Bog People. Iron-Age Man Preserved.* Faber: London.

—— 1973. *The Mound People. Danish Bronze Age Man Preserved.* Faber: London.

GUTHRIE, R.D. 1990. *Frozen Fauna of the Mammoth Steppe.* Univ. of Chicago Press.

HART HANSEN, J.P., MELDGAARD, J. & NORDQVIST, J. 1985. The mummies of Qilakitsoq. *National Geographic* 167 (2), 190–207.

JENNINGS, J.D. 1953. *Danger Cave.* Univ. of Utah Anth. Papers, No. 27: Salt Lake City.

JEWELL, P.A. & DIMBLEBY, G.W. 1966. The experimental earthwork on Overton Down, Wiltshire, England: the first four years. *Proc. Prehist. Soc.* 32, 313–42.

KIRK, R. & DAUGHERTY, R.D. 1974. *Hunters of the Whale.* Morrow: New York.

LOBDELL, J.E., DEKIN, A.A. and others. 1984. The Frozen Family from the Utqiagvik Site, Barrow, Alaska. *Arctic Anthropology* 21 (1), 1–154.

LYNCH, T.F. (ed.). 1980. *Guitarrero Cave. Early Man in the Andes.* Academic Press: New York & London.

MACDONALD, G.F. & PURDY, B.A. 1982. Florida's wet sites: where the fragile past survives. *Early Man* 4(4), 4–12.

MONTLUÇON, J. 1986. L'électricité pour mettre à nu les objets archéologiques. *La Recherche* 17, 252–55.

NASH, D.T. & PETRAGLIA, M.D. (eds.). 1987. *Natural Formation Processes and the Archaeological Record.* British Arch. Reports, Int. Series 352: Oxford.

REDFORD, D.B. 1984. *Akhenaten, the Heretic King.* Princeton Univ. Press.

REEVES, N. 1990. *The Complete Tutankhamun.* Thames & Hudson: London & New York.

REYNOLDS, P.J. 1974. Experimental Iron Age storage pits: an interim report. *Proc. Prehist. Soc.* 40, 118–31.

RUDENKO, S.I. 1970. *Frozen Tombs of Siberia: The Pazyryk burials of Iron Age horsemen.* Dent: London; Univ. of California Press: Berkeley.

SCHIFFER, M.B. 1972. Archaeological context and systemic context. *American Antiquity* 37, 156–65.

—— 1976. *Behavioral Archaeology.* Academic Press: New York & London.

—— 1987. *Formation Processes of the Archaeological Record.* Univ. of New Mexico Press: Albuquerque.

SHEETS, P.D. (ed.). 1984. *Archaeology and Volcanism in Central America.* Univ. of Texas Press: Austin.

SUTCLIFFE, A.J. 1985. *On the Track of Ice Age Animals.* British Museum (Natural History): London.

ZIMMERMAN, M.R. & others. 1971. Examination of an Aleutian mummy. *Bull. New York Acad. Medicine* 47, 80–103.

Chapter 3: Where? Survey and Excavation of Sites and Features (pp. 61–100)

p. 62 **Accidental discovery** Cotterell 1981 (China's first emperor).

pp. 63–69 **Ground reconnaissance: documentary sources** Much information, including an account of Schliemann's work, can be obtained from the books by Glyn Daniel on historical archaeology (Chapter 1 above). Ingstad 1977 (L'Anse aux Meadows); Pritchard 1987 (biblical archaeology); Matthiae 1980 (Tell Mardikh); Wainwright 1962, Carver 1987 (place-name evidence).

pp. 63, 64 **Reconnaissance survey** In general: Ammerman 1981; Heizer & Graham 1967; Nance 1983; Plog, Plog & Wait 1978; Redman & Watson 1970; Schiffer & others 1978. Dunnell & Dancey 1983, Lewarch & O'Brien 1981 (off-site studies); Isaac 1981, Foley 1981, Bower 1986 (Africa); Keller & Rupp 1983 (especially article by Cherry) (Mediterranean).

p. 68 **Extensive survey** Adams 1981, Redman 1982 (Mesopotamia); Flannery 1976, Blanton & others 1982 (Mesoamerica). **Intensive survey** Lehner 1985 (Giza); for Teotihuacan, see box feature references below.

pp. 69–73 **Aerial reconnaissance** General books include: Bradford 1957; Deuel 1973; Maxwell 1983; Riley 1987; Saint Joseph 1966; Vogt 1974; Wilson 1975. In French: Chevallier 1965, 1971; Dassie 1978; and *Dossiers de l'Archéologie* Nos. 1 (1973), 22 (1977) and 43 (1980). In German, Scollar 1965. Connah & Jones 1983 (Australia); Hampton & Palmer 1977 (recent developments); Wilson 1982 (air-photo interpretation). Palmer 1976, 1977 (computer methods for transcribing information from photographs). O'Brien & others 1982 (digital enhancement); Scollar 1978 (computer image processing); Gumerman & Neely 1972 (color infrared photography).

pp. 73–74 **Remote sensing from high altitude** Barisano & others 1986; Ebert 1984; Lyons & Mathien 1980; McManamon 1984. Maya archaeology: Adams, R.E.W. 1980, 1982; Adams,

R.E.W. & others 1981 (radar).

pp. 75–78 **Site surface survey** Flannery 1976, 51–52 (Oaxaca survey by Hole).

pp. 78–89 **Subsurface detection: probes** Thomas 1988 (St Catherine's Island); Lerici 1959 (Etruscan tombs); Holden 1987, El-Baz 1988 (second boat pit at Giza); Dormion & Goidin 1987, Kérisel 1988 (French and Japanese work inside the Great Pyramid).

pp. 80–89 **Remote sensing beneath the surface** In general: Clark, A. 1990. Also, specialized journals contain important articles, e.g. *Archaeometry* (since 1958), and *Prospezioni Archeologiche* (Fondazione Lerici, Rome since 1966). French work in this field can be consulted in *Dossiers de l'Archéologie* No. 39, 1979, as well as in Hesse 1966. An excellent German summary, particularly of geophysical and geochemical methods, can be found in Rottländer 1983.

p. 84 **Resistivity** Atkinson 1963; Clark, A. 1969, 1975a (the latter also focuses on fluxgate gradiometers), 1990; Weymouth 1986 (concerns radar and other methods too).

pp. 84–86 **Magnetic methods** Among the many general references are: Aitken 1969; Clark, A. 1975b, 1990; Scollar 1969; Steponaitis & Brain 1976; Tite & Mullins 1971; Colani 1966; Foster & Hackens 1969; Tite & Mullins 1970. Underwater applications: Clausen & Arnold 1976; Foster 1970; Hall 1966. Applications in Australia: Stanley 1983.

p. 87 **Neutron scattering** Alldred & Shepherd 1963. **Geochemical methods** Clark, A. 1977; Cook & Heizer 1965. The work in Virginia: Solecki 1951.

Phosphate analysis Craddock & others 1985; Eidt 1977, 1984; Proudfoot 1976; Sjöberg 1976; and at Cefn Graeanog, Conway 1983.

p. 87 **Dowsing** Graves 1980 (for believers; see review in *Antiquity* 58, 1984, 231–32); Bailey & others 1988 (medieval churches). Rigorous tests on dowsers are discussed by Aitken 1959; Randi 1982, 307–25.

pp. 90–100 **Excavation** In general: Barker 1983, 1986; Hester & others 1987; Joukowsky 1980; Spence 1990. It is still rewarding to look at Wheeler's best account of his approach and methods: Wheeler 1954. **Stratigraphy** Harris 1989.

p. 98 **Computer classification** Plog, F. & Carlson 1989.

Box Features

p. 65 **Melos Survey** Cherry, in Renfrew & Wagstaff 1981.

p. 66 **Sampling Strategies** Among the most important general books are: Mueller 1974, 1975; Cherry & others 1978. Articles include Binford 1964; Nance 1983; Plog 1976, 1978; Plog & others 1978; South & Widmer 1977. Sampling applications in Mesoamerica, including the work of Winter: Flannery 1976; for Turkey, Redman & Watson 1970. The special problems of sampling in forests are covered by Chartkoff 1978 and Lovis 1976 (North America).

pp. 70–71 **Aerial Photography** See main text references above.

pp. 76–77 **Teotihuacan** Cabrera Castro & others 1982; Millon 1967, 1972/73, 1981.

pp. 78–79 **Abu Salabikh** Postgate 1982; 1987.

p. 81 **Underwater Archaeology** Good general works include Bass 1972, 1988; Muckelroy 1978; Throckmorton 1987. Also of interest, though somewhat outdated, is Taylor 1965. Many useful articles can be found in the *International Journal of Nautical Archaeology, American Journal of Archaeology,* and *National Geographic.*

pp. 82–83 **Red Bay Wreck** Grenier 1988.

p. 85 **Measuring Magnetism** Clark, A. 1990; Rowley & Davies 1973; and see main text references.

pp. 88–89 **Sutton Hoo** Royle 1986 (methods of prospection); annual reports issued by Sutton Hoo Research Trust 1983-.

Bibliography

ADAMS, R.E.W. 1980. Swamps, canals, and the locations of ancient Maya cities. *Antiquity* 54, 206–14.

——— 1982. Ancient Maya canals. Grids and lattices in the Maya jungle. *Archaeology* 35 (6), 28–35.

——— BROWN, W.E. & CULBERT, T.P. 1981. Radar mapping, archeology, and ancient Maya land use. *Science* 213, 1457–63.

ADAMS, R.M. 1981. *Heartland of Cities: Surveys of Ancient Settlement and Land Use on the Central Floodplain of the Euphrates.* Univ. of Chicago Press.

AITKEN, M.J. 1959. Test for correlation between dowsing response and magnetic disturbance. *Archaeometry* 2, 58–59.

——— 1969. Magnetic location, in *Science in Archaeology* (D.R. Brothwell & E.S. Higgs eds.), 681–94. (Rev. ed.) Thames & Hudson: London.

——— 1974. *Physics and Archaeology.* (2nd ed.) Oxford Univ. Press.

ALLDRED, J.C. & SHEPHERD, A. 1963. Trial of neutron scattering for the detection of buried walls and cavities. *Archaeometry* 6, 89–92.

AMMERMAN, A.J. 1981. Surveys and archaeological research. *Annual Review of Anth.* 10, 63–88.

ATKINSON, R.J.C. 1963. Resistivity Surveying in Archaeology, in *The Scientist and Archaeology* (R. Pyddoke ed.), 1–30. Phoenix House: London.

BAILEY, R.N., CAMBRIDGE, E. & BRIGGS, H.D. 1988. *Dowsing and Church Archaeology.* Intercept: Wimborne, Dorset.

BARISANO, E., BARTHOLOME, E. & MARCOLONGO, B. 1986. *Télédétection et Archéologie.* CNRS: Paris.

BARKER, P. 1983. *Techniques of Archaeological Excavation.* (2nd ed.) Batsford: London; Humanities Press: New York.

——— 1986. *Understanding Archaeological Excavation.* Batsford: London.

BASS, G.F. 1968. New tools for undersea archaeology. *National Geographic* 134, 402–23.

——— 1972. *Archaeology Under Water.* (Rev. ed.) Penguin: Harmondsworth.

——— (ed.). 1988. *Ships and Shipwrecks of the Americas: A History based on Underwater Archaeology.* Thames & Hudson: London & New York.

BINFORD, L.R. 1964. A consideration of archaeological research design. *American Antiquity* 29, 425–41.

BLANTON, R.E. & others. 1982. *Ancient Mesoamerica: A Comparison of Change in Three Regions.* Cambridge Univ. Press.

BOWER, J. 1986. A survey of surveys: aspects of surface archaeology in sub-Saharan Africa. *The African Arch. Review* 4, 21–40.

BRADFORD, J.S.P. 1957. *Ancient Landscapes: Studies in Field Archaeology.* Bell & Sons: London.

CABRERA CASTRO, R. & others. 1982. *Téotihuacán 1980–82. Primeros Resultados.* Instituto Nac. de Antrop. e Historia: Mexico City.

CARVER, M. 1987. *Underneath English Towns. Interpreting Urban Archaeology.* Batsford: London.

CHARTKOFF, J.L. 1978. Transect interval sampling in forests. *American Antiquity* 43, 46–53.

CHERRY, J.F. 1983. Frogs round the pond: Perspectives on current archaeological survey projects in the Mediterranean region, in *Archaeological Survey in the Mediterranean Area* (D.R. Keller & D.W. Rupp eds.), 375–416. British Arch. Reports, Int. Series 155: Oxford.

——— and others. (eds.). 1978. *Sampling in Contemporary British Archaeology.* British Arch. Reports, Int. Series 50: Oxford.

CHEVALLIER, R. 1965. *L'Avion à la Découverte du Passé.* Fayard: Paris.

——— 1971. *L'Archéologie aérienne.* U2: Paris.

CLARK, A. 1969. Resistivity surveying, in *Science in Archaeology* (D.R. Brothwell & E.S. Higgs eds.), 695–707. (2nd ed.) Thames and Hudson: London.

——— 1975a. Archaeological prospecting: a progress report. *Journal of Arch. Science* 2, 297–314.

——— 1975b. Geophysical surveying in archaeology. *Antiquity* 49, 298–99.

——— 1977. Geophysical and chemical assessment of air photographic sites. *Arch. Journal* 134, 187–93.

——— 1990. *Seeing Beneath the Soil: Prospecting Methods in Archaeology.* Batsford: London.

CLARK, J.G.D. 1960. *Archaeology and Society.* (3rd ed.) Methuen: London.

CLAUSEN, C.J. & ARNOLD, J.B. 1976. The magnetometer and underwater archaeology. *Int. Journal of Nautical Arch.* 5, 159–69.

COLANI, C. 1966. A new type of locating device. 1: The instrument. *Archaeometry* 9, 3–8.

COLWELL, R.N. (ed.). 1983. *Manual of Remote Sensing.* (2nd ed.) Society of Photogrammetry: Falls Church, Virginia.

CONNAH, G. (ed.). 1983. *Australian Field Archaeology. A Guide to Techniques.* Australian Institute of Aboriginal Studies: Canberra.

——— & JONES, A. 1983. Photographing Australian prehistoric sites from the air, in *Australian Field Archaeology. A Guide to Techniques* (G. Connah ed.), 73–81. AIAS: Canberra.

CONWAY, J.S. 1983. An investigation of soil phosphorus distribution within occupation deposits from a Romano-British hut group. *Journal of Arch. Science* 10, 117–28.

COOK, S.F. & HEIZER, R.F. 1965. *Studies on the Chemical Analysis of Archaeological Sites.* Univ. of California Publications in Archaeology: Berkeley.

COTTERELL, A. 1981. *The First Emperor of China.* Macmillan: London; Holt, Rinehart & Winston: New York.

CRADDOCK, P.T. & others. 1985. The application of phosphate analysis to the location and interpretation of archaeological sites. *Arch. Journal* 142, 361–76.

DASSIE, J. 1978. *Manuel d'Archéologie Aérienne.* Technip: Paris.

DEUEL, L. 1973. *Flights into Yesterday.* Pelican: Harmondsworth.

DORMION, G. & GOIDIN, J-P. 1987. *Les Nouveaux Mystères de la Grande Pyramide.* Albin Michel: Paris.

DUNNELL, R.C. & DANCEY, W.S. 1983. The siteless survey: a regional data collection strategy, in *Advances in Archaeological Method and Theory* (M.B. Schiffer ed.) 6, 267–87. Academic Press: New York & London.

EBERT, J.I. 1984. Remote sensing applications in archaeology, in *Advances in Archaeological Method and Theory* (M.B. Schiffer ed.) 7, 293–362. Academic Press: New York & London.

EIDT, R.C. 1977. Detection and examination of anthrosols by phosphate analysis. *Science* 197, 1327–33.

——— 1984. *Advances in Abandoned Site Analysis.* Univ. of Wisconsin Press.

EL-BAZ, F. 1988. Finding a Pharaoh's funeral bark. *National Geographic* 173

(4), 512–33.

FLANNERY, K.V. (ed.). 1976. *The Early Mesoamerican Village*. Academic Press: New York & London.

FOLEY, R. 1981. *Off-site Archaeology and Human Adaptation in Eastern Africa*. British Arch. Reports, Int. Series 97: Oxford.

FOSTER, E.J. 1970. A diver-operated underwater metal detector. *Archaeometry* 12, 161–66.

FOSTER, E. & HACKENS, T. 1969. Decco metal detector survey on Delos. *Archaeometry* 11, 165–72.

GOODYEAR, F.H. 1971. *Archaeological Site Science*. Heinemann: London.

GRAVES, T. (ed.). 1980. *Dowsing and Archaeology*. Turnstone Books: Wellingborough.

GRENIER, R. 1988. Basque Whalers in the New World: The Red Bay Wreck, in *Ships and Shipwrecks of the Americas* (G. Bass ed.), 69–84. Thames & Hudson: London & New York.

GUMERMAN, G.J. & LYONS, T.R. 1971. Archeological methodology and remote sensing. *Science* 172, 126–32.

GUMERMAN, G.J. & NEELY, J.A. 1972. An archaeological survey of the Tehuacán Valley, Mexico: A test of color infrared photography. *American Antiquity* 37, 520–27.

HALL, E.T. 1966. The use of the proton magnetometer in underwater archaeology. *Archaeometry* 9, 32–44.

HAMPTON, J.N. & PALMER, R. 1977. Implications of aerial photography for archaeology. *The Archaeological Journal* 134, 157–86.

HARRIS, E. 1989. *Principles of Archaeological Stratigraphy*. (2nd ed.) Academic Press: New York & London.

HEIZER, R.F. & GRAHAM, J.A. 1967. *A Guide to Field Methods in Archaeology*. National Press: Palo Alto, Ca.

HESSE, A. 1966. *Prospections géographiques à faible profondeur. Applications à l'Archéologie*. Dunod: Paris.

HESTER, T.N., SHAFER, H.J. & HEIZER, R.F. 1987. *Field Methods in Archaeology*. (7th ed.) Mayfield: Palo Alto, Calif.

HOLDEN, C. 1987. A quest for ancient Egyptian air. *Science* 236, 1419–20.

INGSTAD, A.S. 1977. *The Discovery of a Norse Settlement in America. Excavations at L'Anse aux Meadows, Newfoundland, 1961–1968*. Oslo, Bergen, Tromsø.

ISAAC, G. 1981. Stone Age visiting cards: approaches to the study of early land use patterns, in *Pattern of the Past. Studies in Honour of David Clarke* (I. Hodder, G. Isaac & N. Hammond eds.), 131–55. Cambridge Univ. Press.

JOUKOWSKY, M. 1980. *A Complete Manual of Field Archaeology*. Prentice-Hall: Englewood Cliffs, N.J.

KELLER, D.R. & RUPP, D.W. (eds.). 1983.

Archaeological Survey in the Mediterranean Area. British Arch. Reports, Int. Series 155: Oxford.

KERISEL, J. 1988. Le dossier scientifique sur la pyramide de Khéops. *Archéologia* 232, Feb., 46–54.

LEHNER, M. 1985. The development of the Giza necropolis: The Khufu Project. *Mitteilungen dt. archäol. Inst. Abt. Kairo* 41, 109–43.

LERICI, C.M. 1959. Periscope on the Etruscan Past. *National Geographic* 116 (3), 336–50.

LEWARCH, D.E. & O'BRIEN, M.J. 1981. The expanding role of surface assemblages in archaeological research, in *Advances in Archaeological Method and Theory* (M.B. Schiffer ed.) 4, 297–342.

LOVIS, W.A. 1976. Quarter sections and forests: an example of probability sampling in the northeastern woodlands. *American Antiquity* 41, 364–72.

LYONS, T.R. & MATHIEN, F.J. (eds.). 1980. *Cultural Resources: Remote Sensing*. U.S. Govt. Printing Office: Washington.

MATTHIAE, P. 1980. *Ebla: An Empire Rediscovered*. Doubleday: New York.

MAXWELL, G.S. (ed.). 1983. *The Importance of Aerial Reconnaissance to Archaeology*. Council for British Arch. Research Report 49: London.

McINTOSH, J. 1986. *The Practical Archaeologist*. Facts on File: New York (published in Britain as *The Archaeologist's Handbook*, Bell & Hyman: London).

McMANAMON, F.P. 1984. Discovering sites unseen, in *Advances in Archaeological Method and Theory* (M.B. Schiffer ed.) 7, 223–92. Academic Press: New York & London.

MILLON, R. 1967. Teotihuacán. *Scientific American* 216 (6), 38–48.

——— (ed.). 1972/3. *Urbanization at Teotihuacán*. 2 vols. Univ. of Texas Press: Austin.

——— 1981. Teotihuacán: city, state and civilization, in *Archaeology (Supplement to the Handbook of Middle American Indians)* (J.A. Sabloff ed.), 198–243. Univ. of Texas Press: Austin.

MUCKELROY, K. 1978. *Maritime Archaeology*. Cambridge Univ. Press.

MUELLER, J.W. 1974. *The Use of Sampling in Archaeological Surveys*. Memoirs of the Soc. for American Arch. No. 28.

——— (ed.). 1975. *Sampling in Archaeology*. Univ. of Arizona Press: Tucson.

NANCE, J.D. 1983. Regional sampling in archaeological survey: the statistical perspective, in *Advances in Archaeological Method and Theory* (M.B. Schiffer ed.) 6, 289–356.

O'BRIEN, M.J. & others. 1982. Digital enhancement and grey-level slicing of

aerial photographs: techniques for archaeological analysis of intrasite variability. *World Arch.* 14, 173–90.

PALMER, R. 1976. A method of transcribing archaeological sites from oblique aerial photographs. *Journal of Arch. Science* 3, 391–94.

——— 1977. A computer method for transcribing information graphically from oblique aerial photographs to maps. *Journal of Arch. Science* 4, 283–90.

PLOG, F. & CARLSON, D.L. 1989. Computer applications for the All American Pipeline Project. *Antiquity* 63, 258–67.

PLOG, S. 1976. Relative efficiencies of sampling techniques for archaeological surveys, in *The Early Mesoamerican Village* (K.V. Flannery ed.), 136–58. Academic Press: New York & London.

——— 1978. Sampling in archaeological surveys: a critique. *American Antiquity* 43, 280–85.

———, PLOG, F. & WAIT, W. 1978. Decision making in modern surveys, in *Advances in Archaeological Method and Theory* (M.B. Schiffer ed.) 1, 383–421.

POSTGATE, N. 1982. Abu Salabikh, in *Fifty Years of Mesopotamian Discovery. The Work of the British School of Archaeology in Iraq, 1932–82* (J. Curtis ed.), 48–61. British School of Arch. in Iraq.

——— 1987. Excavations at Abu Salabikh 1985–86. *Iraq* XLIX, 91–119.

PRITCHARD, J.B. (ed.). l987. *The Times Atlas of the Bible*. Times Books: London.

PROUDFOOT, B. 1976. The analysis and interpretations of soil phosphorus in archaeology, in *Geo-archaeology* (D.A. Davidson & M.L. Shackley eds.), 93–113. Duckworth: London.

RANDI, J. 1982. *Flim-Flam! Psychics, ESP, Unicorns and other Delusions*. Prometheus: Buffalo.

REDMAN, C.L. 1982. Archaeological survey and the study of Mesopotamian urban systems. *Journal of Field Arch.* 9, 375–82.

——— & WATSON, P.J. 1970. Systematic intensive surface collection. *American Antiquity* 35, 279–91.

RENFREW, C. & WAGSTAFF, J.M. (eds.). 1981. *An Island Polity: The Archaeology of Exploitation on Melos*. Cambridge Univ. Press.

RILEY, D.N. 1987. *Air Photography and Archaeology*. Duckworth: London.

ROTTLÄNDER, R.C.A. 1983. *Einführung in die Naturwissenschaftlichen Methoden in der Archäologie*. Verlag Arch. Venatoria, Band 6. Institut für Vorgeschichte der Univ. Tübingen.

ROWLEY, T. & DAVIES, M. 1973. *Archaeology and the M40 Motorway*. Oxford Univ. Press.

ROYLE, C. 1986. Summary of prospection methods at Sutton Hoo. *Current Arch.* IX

(6), No. 101, 171.

SAINT JOSEPH, J.K. 1966. *The Uses of Air Photography*. A. & C. Black: London.

SCHIFFER, M.B. & others. 1978. The design of archaeological surveys. *World Arch.* 10, 1–28.

SCOLLAR, I. 1965. *Archäologie aus der Luft*. Landesmuseum: Bonn.

—— 1969. Some techniques for the evaluation of archaeological magnetometer surveys. *World Arch.* 1, 77–89.

—— 1978. Computer image processing for archaeological air photographs. *World Arch.* 10, 71–87.

SJÖBERG, A. 1976. Phosphate analysis of anthropic soils. *Journal of Field Arch.* 3, 447–54.

SOLECKI, R.S. 1951. Notes on soil analysis and archaeology. *American Antiquity* 16, 254–56.

SOUTH, S. & WIDMER, R. 1977. A subsurface sampling strategy for archaeological reconnaissance, in *Research Strategies in Historical Archaeology* (S. South ed.), 119–50. Academic Press: New York & London.

SPENCE, C. (ed.). 1990. *Archaeological Site Manual*. (2nd ed.) Museum of London: London.

STANLEY, J.M. 1983. Subsurface survey: the use of magnetics in Australian archaeology, in *Australian Field Archaeology. A Guide to Techniques* (G. Connah ed.), 82–86. AIAS: Canberra.

STEPONAITIS, V.P. & BRAIN, J.P. 1976. A portable Differential Proton Magnetometer. *Journal of Field Arch.* 3, 455–63.

TAYLOR, J. du P. (ed.). 1965. *Marine Archaeology*. Hutchinson: London.

THOMAS, D.H. 1988. *St. Catherine's Island: An Island in Time*. Georgia Endowment for the Humanities: Atlanta.

THROCKMORTON, P. (ed.). 1987. *The Sea Remembers: Shipwrecks and Archaeology*. Weidenfeld: New York (published in Britain as *History from the Sea: Shipwrecks and Archaeology*; Mitchell Beazley: London).

TITE, M.S. 1972. *Methods of Physical Examination in Archaeology*. Seminar Press: London & New York.

—— & MULLINS, C. 1970. Electromagnetic prospecting on archaeological sites using a soil conductivity meter. *Archaeometry* 12, 97–104.

—— 1971. Enhancement of the magnetic susceptibility of soils on archaeological sites. *Archaeometry* 13, 209–19.

VOGT, E.Z. (ed.). 1974. *Aerial Photography in Anthropological Field Research*. Harvard Univ. Press.

WAINWRIGHT, F. 1962. *Archaeology, Place-Names and History*. Routledge & Kegan Paul: London.

WEYMOUTH, J.W. 1986. Geophysical methods of archaeological site surveying, in *Advances in Archaeological Method and Theory* (M.B. Schiffer ed.) 9, 311–95. Academic Press: New York & London.

WHEELER, R.E.M. 1954. *Archaeology from the Earth*. Oxford Univ. Press (Penguin Books: Harmondsworth).

WILSON, D.R. (ed.). 1975. *Aerial Reconnaissance for Archaeology*. Council for British Arch. Research Report 12: London.

—— 1982. *Air Photo Interpretation for Archaeologists*. Batsford: London.

Chapter 4: When? Dating Methods and Chronology (pp. 101–148)

pp. 102–104 **Stratigraphy** See references for Chapter 3. **Bone age** Weiner 1955 (Piltdown hoax).

pp. 104–111 **Typological sequences** Montelius 1903 (classic example of artifact typologies constructed and used); Petrie 1899 (contextual seriation); Brainerd 1951; Robinson 1951; Kendall 1969; Dethlefsen & Deetz 1966 (frequency seriation).

p. 108 **Linguistic dating** Swadesh 1972.

p, 108 **Pleistocene chronology** Klein 1989; Sutcliffe 1985; also Brothwell & Higgs 1969; Oakley 1964; Zeuner 1958.

p. 110 **Deep-sea cores** See references for Chapter 6. **Ice cores** Lorius & others 1985; Jouzel & others 1987.

pp. 110–111 **Pollen dating** See references for Chapter 6. **Faunal dating** Klein 1989; Gowlett 1984.

p. 113 **Calendars etc.** In general: Tapsell 1984. Baines & Malek 1980 (Egypt); Coe & others 1986 (Maya).

pp. 117–118 **Varves** Zeuner 1958.

pp. 118–121 **Tree-ring dating** In general: Baillie 1982; Eckstein 1984. For the early work in the American Southwest: Douglass 1919–1936.

pp. 121–129 **Radiocarbon dating** In general: Bowman 1990; Mook & Waterbolk 1983; also Ralph 1971; Tite 1972; Fleming 1976. Specific: Libby 1952; Taylor 1987 (history of method); Renfrew 1973, 1979; Pearson 1987; Stuiver & Pearson 1986 (calibration); Bard & others 1990 (calibration via Barbados coral); Hedges 1991 (accelerator mass spectrometry).

pp. 129–131 **Thermoluminescence** Good recent accounts: Aitken 1985, 1990; Fleming 1979; Wagner 1983; McKeever 1985.

pp. 131–136 **Electron spin resonance** Aitken 1990; Schwarcz & others 1989; Grün 1989. **Potassium-argon** Aitken 1990; Schaeffer & Zähringer 1966. **Uranium-series** Schwarcz 1982. **Fission-track** Aitken 1990. Bishop & Miller 1982 provide examples of the results obtained by these methods.

pp. 136–39 **Calibrated relative methods** Aitken 1990; Brothwell & Higgs 1969; Weiner 1955. Specific methods: Michels & Bebrich 1971; Michels & Tsong 1980 (obsidian hydration); Bada 1985; Fleming 1976 (amino-acid racemization); Whitley & Dorn 1987 (cation-ratio); Bucha 1971 (archaeomagnetism).

pp. 139–142 **Chronological correlations** Kittleman 1979. Case studies: Harris & Hughes 1978 (New Guinea); Sheets 1979 (Central America).

pp. 142–148 **World chronology** Scarre 1988; Fagan 1989, 1990; Gowlett 1984.

Box Features

pp. 114–15 **Maya Calendar** Coe 1987; Coe & others 1986.

pp. 121–125 **Radioactive Decay/The Publication of Radiocarbon Dates/How to Calibrate** See main text references.

pp. 134–135 **Dating Our African Ancestors** Klein 1989; Lewin 1987, 1989; also Gowlett 1984; Leakey 1981.

p. 140 **Thera Eruption** Discussed by various specialists in Doumas 1978, and by Renfrew 1979; and the date by Hammer & others 1987; Baillie & Munro 1988; Hardy & Renfrew 1991.

Bibliography

AITKEN, M.J. 1985. *Thermoluminescence Dating*. Academic Press: London & New York.

—— 1990. *Science-Based Dating in Archaeology*. Longman: London & New York.

ANTIQUITY. 1987. Special Radiocarbon Section. Six articles. *Antiquity*. 61, 97–138.

BADA, J.L. 1985. Aspartic acid racemization ages of California Paleoindian skeletons. *American Antiquity* 50, 645–47.

BAILLIE, M.G.L. 1982. *Tree-ring dating and archaeology*. Croom Helm: London; Univ. of Chicago Press.

—— & MUNRO, M.A.R. 1988. Irish tree rings, Santorini and volcanic dust veils. *Nature* 332, 344–46.

BAINES, J. & MALEK, J. 1980. *Atlas of Ancient Egypt*. Phaidon: Oxford; Facts on File; New York.

BARD, E., HAMELIN. B., FAIRBANKS, R.G. & ZINDLER, A. 1990. Calibration of the ^{14}C timescale over the past 30,000 years using mass spectrometric U-Th ages from Barbados corals. *Nature* 345,405-10.

BISHOP, W.W. & MILLER, J.A. (eds.). 1982. *Calibration of Hominoid Evolution*. Scottish Academic Press: Edinburgh.

BOWMAN, S. 1990. *Radiocarbon Dating*. British Museum Publications: London.

BRAINERD, G.W. 1951. The Place of Chronological Ordering in Archaeological Analysis. *American*

Antiquity 16, 301–13.

BROTHWELL, D.R. & HIGGS, E.S. (eds.). 1969. *Science in Archaeology.* (2nd ed.) Thames & Hudson: London; Praeger: New York.

BUCHA, V. 1971. Archaeomagnetic Dating, in *Dating Techniques for the Archaeologist* (H.N. Michael & E.K. Ralph eds.), 57–117. Massachusetts Institute of Technology: Cambridge, Mass.

COE, M.D. 1987. *The Maya.* (4th ed.) Thames & Hudson: London & New York.

———— SNOW, D. & BENSON E. 1986. *Atlas of Ancient America.* Facts on File: New York & Oxford.

COOK, R.M. 1969. Archaeomagnetism, in *Science in Archaeology* (D. Brothwell & E.S. Higgs, eds.), 76–87. Thames & Hudson: London.

DALRYMPLE, G.B. & LANPHERE, M.A. 1969. *Potassium-Argon Dating. Principles, Techniques and Applications to Geochronology.* W.H. Freeman & Co: San Francisco.

DETHLEFSEN, E. & DEETZ, J. 1966. Death's Heads, Cherubs, and Willow Trees: Experimental Archaeology in Colonial Cemeteries. *American Antiquity* 31, 502–10.

DORN, R.I. & others. 1986. Cation-ratio and Accelerator Radiocarbon Dating of rock varnish on Mojave artifacts and landforms. *Science* 231, 830–33.

DOUGLASS, A.E. 1919, 1928 & 1936. *Climatic cycles and tree growth.* 3 vols. Carnegie Institution of Washington: Washington.

DOUMAS, C. (ed.). 1978. *Thera and the Aegean World.* London.

ECKSTEIN, D. 1984. *Dendrochronological dating.* European Science Foundation: Strasbourg.

EIGHMY, J.L. 1979. Logistic Trends in Southwest Population Growth, in *Transformations. Mathematical Approaches to Culture Change* (C. Renfrew & K.L. Cooke eds.), 205–20. Academic Press: New York & London.

EVANS, J. 1875. The Coinage of the Ancient Britons and Natural Selection. *Proceedings of the Royal Institution of Great Britain* 7, 476–87.

FAGAN, B.M. 1989. *People of the Earth: An Introduction to World Prehistory.* (6th ed.) Scott, Foresman: Glenview, Illinois & London.

———— 1990. *The Journey from Eden: The Peopling of Our World.* Thames & Hudson: London & New York.

FLEMING, S. 1976. *Dating in Archaeology. A Guide to Scientific Techniques.* J.M. Dent, London; St Martin's Press, New York.

———— 1979. *Thermoluminescence techniques in archaeology.* Oxford Univ. Press: Oxford & New York.

GOWLETT, J. 1984. *Ascent to Civilization: The Archaeology of Early Man.* Collins:

London; Knopf: New York.

GRÜN, R. 1989. *Die ESR – Alterbestimmungsmethode.* Springer: Heidelberg.

HAMMER, C.U., CLAUSEN, H.B., FRIEDRICH, W.L. & TAUBER, H. 1987. The Minoan eruption of Santorini in Greece dated to 1645 BC? *Nature* 328, 517–19.

HARDY, D. & RENFREW, C. (eds.). 1991. *Thera and The Aegean World III, Vol. 3. Chronology.* Thera Foundation: London.

HARRIS, E.C. & HUGHES, P.J. 1978. An early agricultural system at Mugumamp Ridge, Western Highlands Province, Papua New Guinea. *Mankind* 11, 437–44.

HEDGES, R.E.M. 1981. Radiocarbon dating with an accelerator: review and preview. *Archaeometry* 23, 3–18.

HOLE, F. & FLANNERY, K.V. 1968. The Prehistory of Southwestern Iran: A Preliminary Report. *Proc. Prehist. Soc.* 33, 147–206.

JOUZEL, J. & others. 1987. Vostok ice core: a continuous isotope temperature record over the last climate cycle (160,000 years). *Nature* 329, 403–8.

KENDALL, D.G. 1969. Some problems and methods in statistical archaeology. *World Arch.* 1, 68–76.

KITTLEMAN, L.R. 1979. Geologic methods in studies of Quaternary tephra, in *Volcanic Activity and Human Ecology* (P.D. Sheets & D.K. Grayson eds.), 49–82. Acdemic Press: New York & London.

KLEIN, R.G. 1989. *The Human Career.* Univ. of Chicago Press.

LEAKEY, R.E. 1981. *The Making of Mankind.* Michael Joseph: London.

LEWIN, R. 1987. *Bones of Contention: Controversies in the Search for Human Origins.* Simon & Schuster: New York; Penguin: Harmondsworth 1989.

———— 1989. *Human Evolution.* (2nd ed.) Blackwell Scientific Publications: Oxford & Cambridge, Mass.

LIBBY, W.F. 1952. *Radiocarbon Dating.* Univ. of Chicago Press.

LORIUS C. & others. 1985. A 150,000 year climatic record from Antarctic ice. *Nature* 316, 591–96.

LYELL, C. 1830–33. *Principles of geology, being an attempt to explain the former changes of the earth's surface by reference to causes now in operation.* 3 vols. John Murray: London.

McKEEVER, S.W.S. 1985. *Thermoluminescence of Solids.* Cambridge Univ. Press.

MICHAEL, H.N. & RALPH, E.K. (eds.). 1971. *Dating Techniques for the Archaeologist.* Massachusetts Institute of Technology: Cambridge, Mass.

MICHELS, J.W. 1973. *Dating Methods in Archaeology.* Seminar Press: New York.

———— 1979. *The Kaminaljuyu chiefdom.* Pennsylvania State Univ. Press:

University Park.

———— & BEBRICH, C.A. 1971. Obsidian Hydration Dating, in *Dating Techniques for the Archaeologist* (H.N. Michael & E.K. Ralph eds.), 164–221. Massachusetts Institute of Technology: Cambridge, Mass.

———— & TSONG, I.S.T. 1980. Obsidian Hydration Dating: A Coming of Age, in *Advances in Archaeological Method and Theory* 3 (M.B. Schiffer ed.), 405–44.

MONTELIUS, O. 1903. *Die Typologische Methode.* Stockholm.

MOOK, W.G. & WATERBOLK, H.T. 1983. *Radiocarbon Dating.* European Science Foundation: Strasbourg.

OAKLEY, K.P. 1964. *Frameworks for Dating Fossil Man.* Weidenfeld & Nicolson: London; Aldine Publishing Co: Chicago.

PEARSON, G.W. 1987. How to cope with calibration. *Antiquity* 60, 98–104.

PETRIE, W.M.F. 1899. Sequences in prehistoric remains. *Journal of the Anthropological Institute* 29, 295–301.

RALPH, E.K. 1971. Carbon–14 Dating, in *Dating Techniques for the Archaeologist* (H.N. Michael & E.K. Ralph eds.), 1–48. Massachusetts Institute of Technology: Cambridge, Mass.

RENFREW, C. 1973. *Before Civilisation.* Jonathan Cape: London; Knopf: New York (Pelican: Harmondsworth).

———— 1979. The Tree-ring Calibration of Radiocarbon: An Archaeological Evaluation, in *Problems in European Prehistory* (C. Renfrew), 338–66. Edinburgh Univ. Press: Edinburgh; Cambridge Univ. Press: New York.

ROBINSON, W.S. 1951. A method for chronologically ordering archaeological deposits. *American Antiquity* 16, 293–301.

SCARRE, C. (ed.). 1988. *Past Worlds: The Times Atlas of Archaeology.* Times Books: London; Hammond: Maplewood, N.J.

SCHAEFFER, O.A. & ZÄHRINGER, J. (eds.). 1966. *Potassium-Argon Dating.* Springer Verlag: Berlin & New York.

SCHWARCZ, H.P. 1982. Applications of U-series dating to archaeometry, in *Uranium Series Disequilibrium: Applications to Environmental Problems* (M. Ivanovich & R.S. Harmon eds.), 302–25. Clarendon Press: Oxford.

———— & others. 1989. ESR dating of the Neanderthal site, Kebara Cave, Israel. *J. Arch. Science* 16, 653–59.

SHEETS, P.D. 1979. Environmental and cultural effects of the Ilopango eruption in Central America, in *Volcanic Activity and Human Ecology* (P.D. Sheets & D.K. Grayson eds.), 525–64. Academic Press: New York & London.

STUIVER, M. & PEARSON, G.W. 1986. High-precision calibration of the radiocarbon time scale, AD 1950–500 BC, in *Radiocarbon* 28 (2B), calibration issue: proc. of the Twelfth International Radiocarbon Conference, 1985, Trondheim, Norway (M. Stuiver & R.S. Kra eds.).

SUTCLIFFE, A.J. 1985. *On the Track of Ice Age Mammals*. British Museum (Natural History): London.

SWADESH, M. 1972. *The Origin and Diversification of Language* (J. Scherzer ed.). Routledge & Kegan Paul: London; Aldine: Atherton, Chicago.

TAPSELL, R.F. 1984. *Monarchs, Rulers, Dynasties and Kingdoms of the World*. Thames & Hudson: London & New York.

TAYLOR, R.E. 1987. *Radiocarbon Dating: An Archaeological Perspective*. Academic Press: New York & London.

TITE, M.S. 1972. *Methods of Physical Examination in Archaeology*. Seminar Press: London & New York.

TRALING, D.H. 1983. *Palaeomagnetism*. Chapman & Hall: London.

VALLADAS, H, CHADELLE, J.-P., GENESTE, J.-M., JORON, J.-L., MEIGNEN, L. & TEXIER, P.-J. 1987. Datations par la thermoluminescence de gisements moustériens du Sud de la France. *L'Anthropologie* 91, 211–26.

WAGNER, G.A. 1983. *Thermoluminescence Dating*. European Science Foundation: Strasbourg.

WATKINS, T. (ed.). 1975. *Radiocarbon, Calibration and Prehistory*. Edinburgh Univ. Press.

WEAVER, K.T. 1967. Magnetic clues help date the past. *National Geographic* 131 (5), 696–701.

WEINER, J.S. 1955. *The Piltdown Forgery*. Oxford Univ. Press: London & New York.

WHITLEY, D.S. & DORN, R.I. 1987. Rock art chronology in eastern California. *World Archaeology* 19, 150–64.

ZEUNER, F.E. 1958. *Dating the Past*. (4th ed.) Methuen: London.

Chapter 5: How Were Societies Organized? Social Archaeology (pp. 153–194)

pp. 154–157 **Classification of societies** Service 1971; Sanders & Marino 1970; also Redman 1978.

p. 159 **Central Place Theory** Christaller 1933. **XTENT model** Renfrew & Level 1979.

pp. 162–166 **Middle Range Theory** Binford 1977, 1983. **Written records** *Archaeological Review from Cambridge* 1984, especially Postgate article. **Oral tradition** Wood 1985.

pp. 166–169 **Ethnoarchaeology** Yellen 1977; Hodder 1982; Binford 1983; Whitelaw 1983; Arnold 1985. Recent work is providing helpful insights into the Leroi-Gourhan/Binford debate: see Audouze 1987 and Valentin 1989.

pp. 170–171 **Investigation of activities** at an early hominid site is the subject of

Kroll & Isaac 1984.

pp. 171–174 **Territories in mobile societies** Foley 1981 discusses the problems and potential of off-site archaeology.

p.174 **Settlements in sedentary societies** Binford & others 1970 (Hatchery West); Hill 1970 (Broken K Pueblo); Longacre 1970 (Carter Ranch pueblo); Whitelaw 1981 (Myrtos).

pp. 175–179 **Ranking from burials** Shennan 1975 (Branč); Tainter 1980 (Middle Woodland burials).

pp. 179–181 **Collective works** Renfrew 1973, 1979 (Wessex and Orkney).

pp. 182–184 **Chiefdoms and states** see box feature references.

pp. 186–187 **Function of the center** Kemp 1984–87 (Amarna); Hammond 1982 (Tikal); Millon 1981, Millon & others 1973; Cowgill & others 1984 (Teotihuacan); Biddle 1975 (Winchester). Fieldwork techniques used at Abu Salabikh: Postgate 1983.

pp. 188–191 **Social ranking** Freidel & Sabloff 1984 (Cozumel); Kemp 1989; Lehner 1985 (pyramids); Sabloff 1989 (Pacal); Cotterell 1981 (China's first emperor); Biel 1985 (Hochdorf).

pp. 192–194 **Economic specialization** Morris & Thompson 1985 (Huánuco Pampa); Tosi 1984 (Shahr-i-Sokhta).

Box Features

pp. 160–161 **Settlement Patterns in Mesopotamia** Johnson 1972.

p. 169 **Language and Ethnicity** Renfrew 1987; Marcus 1983a; Dragadze 1980.

p. 173 **Space and Density** Yellen 1977; Whitelaw 1983.

p. 177 **Factor Analysis & Cluster Analysis** Binford & Binford 1966; Hill 1970; O'Shea 1984; Doran & Hodson 1975.

pp. 178–79 **Early Wessex** Renfrew 1973.

p. 183 **Maya Territories** Marcus 1983b; also Hammond 1982 (Maya political organization); Renfrew & Cherry 1986 (relations between polities); de Montmollin 1989.

pp. 184–85 **Multi-Dimensional Scaling** Cherry 1977; also Renfrew & Sterud 1969; Kruskal 1971.

pp. 190–91 **Moundville** Peebles 1987; Peebles & Kus 1977.

Bibliography

ALDEN, J.R. 1979. A reconstruction of Toltec period political units in the Valley of Mexico, in *Transformations. Mathematical Approaches to Culture Change* (C. Renfrew & K.L. Cooke eds.), 169–200. Academic Press: New York & London.

ARCHAEOLOGICAL REVIEW FROM CAMBRIDGE. 1984. Archaeology and Texts in *ARC* 3 (2).

ARNOLD, D.E. 1985. *Ceramic Theory and Cultural Process*. Cambridge Univ. Press.

AUDOUZE, F. 1987. Des modèles et des faits: les modèles de A. Leroi-Gourhan et de L. Binford confrontés aux résultats récents. *Bull. Soc. Préhist. française* 84, 343–52.

BIDDLE, M. 1975. Excavations at Winchester 1971. *Antiquaries Journal* 55, 295–337.

BIEL, J. 1985. *Der Keltenfürst von Hochdorf*. Konrad Theiss Verlag: Stuttgart.

BINFORD, L.R. (ed.). 1977. *For Theory Building in Archaeology*. Academic Press: New York.

——— 1983. *In Pursuit of the Past*. Thames & Hudson: London & New York.

——— BINFORD, S.R., WHALLON, R. & HARDIN, M.A. 1970. *Archaeology at Hatchery West*. Memoirs of the Society for American Archaeology No. 24: Washington, D.C.

BINFORD, S.R. & BINFORD, L.R., 1966. A preliminary analysis of functional variability in the Mousterian of Levallois facies. *American Anthropologist* 68, 238–95.

CHAPMAN, R., KINNES, I. & RANDSBORG, K. (eds.). 1981. *The Archaeology of Death*. Cambridge Univ. Press.

CHERRY, J.F. 1977. Investigating the Political Geography of an Early State by Multidimensional Scaling of Linear B Tablet Data, in *Mycenaean Geography* (J. Bintliff ed.), 76–82. British Assoc. for Mycenaean Studies: Cambridge.

CHRISTALLER, W. 1933. *Die Zentralen Orte in Süddeutschland*. Karl Zeiss: Jena.

CLARKE, D.L. 1972. A provisional model of an Iron Age society and its settlement system, in *Models in Archaeology* (D.L. Clarke ed.), 801–69. Methuen: London.

COTTERELL, A. 1981. *The First Emperor of China*. Macmillan: London; Holt, Rinehart & Winston: New York.

COWGILL, G.L., ALTSCHUL, J.H. & SLOAD, R.S. 1984. Spatial analysis of Teotihuacán: a Mesoamerican metropolis, in *Intrasite Spatial Analysis in Archaeology* (H.J. Hietala ed.), 154–95. Cambridge Univ. Press.

DAVIS, A.J. & LEWIS, H.B. 1985. Mechanisation of Pottery Production, in *Prehistoric Production and Exchange* (A.B. Knapp & T. Stech eds.), 79–92. Univ. of California at Los Angeles.

DORAN, J.E. & HODSON, F.R. 1975. *Mathematics and Computers in Archaeology*. Edinburgh Univ. Press.

DRAGADZE, T. 1980. The place of 'ethnos' theory in Soviet anthropology, in *Soviet and Western Anthropology* (E. Gellner ed.), 161–70. Duckworth: London.

FLANNERY, K.V. & MARCUS, J. (ed.). 1983. *The Cloud People: Divergent Evolution of the Zapotec and Mixtec Civilizations*. Academic Press: New York & London.

FOLEY, R. 1981. *Off-site archaeology and human adaptation in Eastern Africa*. British Arch. Reports: Oxford.

FREIDEL, D. & SABLOFF, J.A. 1984.

Cozumel: Late Maya Settlement Patterns. Academic Press: New York.

HAMMOND, N. 1982. *Ancient Maya Civilization.* Rutgers Univ. Press, N.J.; Cambridge Univ. Press.

HILL, J.N. 1970. *Broken K Pueblo: Prehistoric social organisation in the American Southwest.* Anthropological Papers of the Univ. of Arizona No. 18.

HODDER, I. 1982. *Symbols in Action.* Cambridge Univ. Press.

JOHNSON, G.A. 1972. A test of the utility of Central Place Theory in Archaeology, in *Man, Settlement and Urbanism* (P.J. Ucko, R. Tringham & G.W. Dimbleby eds.), 769–785. Duckworth: London.

KEMP, B.J. 1984–87. *Amarna Reports I-IV.* Egypt Exploration Society: London.

——— 1989. *Ancient Egypt: Anatomy of a Civilization.* Routledge: London & New York.

KROLL, E.M. & ISAAC, G.L. 1984. Configurations of artifacts and bones at early Pleistocene sites in East Africa, in *Intrasite Spatial Analysis in Archaeology* (H.J. Hietala ed.), 4–31. Cambridge Univ. Press.

KRUSKAL, J.B.. 1971. Multi-dimension scaling in archaeology: time is not the only dimension, in *Mathematics in the Archaeological and Historical Sciences* (F.R. Hodson, D.G. Kendall & P. Tautu eds.), 119–32. Edinburgh Univ. Press.

LEHNER, M. 1985. The development of the Giza necropolis: The Khufu Project. *Mitteilungen dt. archäol. Inst. Abt. Kairo* 41, 109–43.

LONGACRE, W.A. 1970. *Archaeology as anthropology: a case study.* Anthropological Papers of the Univ. of Arizona No. 17.

MANN, M. 1986. *The Sources of Social Power. I: A History of Power from the beginning to AD 1760.* Cambridge Univ. Press.

MARCUS, J. 1983a. The genetic model and the linguistic divergence of the Otomangueans, in *The Cloud People* (K. V. Flannery & J. Marcus eds.), 4–9 Academic Press: New York & London.

——— 1983b. Lowland Maya Archaeology at the Crossroads. *American Antiquity* 48 (3), 454–488.

MILLON, R. 1981. Teotihuacan: City, state and civilization, in *Archaeology (Supplement to the Handbook of Middle American Indians)* (J.A. Sabloff ed.), 198–243. Univ. of Texas Press: Austin.

———, DREWITT, R.B. & COWGILL, G.L. 1973. *Urbanization at Teotihuacan, Mexico. Vol. 1: The Teotihuacan Map.* Univ. of Texas Press: Austin.

DE MONTMOLLIN, O. 1989. *The Archaeology of Political Structure: Settlement Analysis in a Classic Maya Polity.* Cambridge Univ. Press.

MORRIS, C. & THOMPSON, D. 1985. *Huánuco Pampa: An Inca City and its Hinterland.* Thames & Hudson: London

& New York.

O'SHEA, J. 1984. *Mortuary Variability, An Archaeological Investigation.* Academic Press: New York & London.

PARSONS, J.R., BRUMFIEL, E., PARSONS, M.H. & WILSON, D.J. 1982. *Prehispanic Settlement Patterns in the Southern Valley of Mexico. The Chalco-Xochimilco Region.* Memoirs of the Museum of Anthropology, Univ. of Michigan, No. 14.

PEEBLES, C.S. 1987. Moundville from 1000–1500 AD in *Chiefdoms in the Americas* (R.D. Drennan & C.A. Uribe eds.), 21–41. Univ. Press of America: Lanham.

——— & KUS, S. 1977. Some archaeological correlates of ranked societies. *American Antiquity* 42, 421–48.

POSTGATE, J.N. 1977. *The First Empires.* Phaidon: Oxford.

——— (ed.). 1983. *The West Mound surface clearance (Abu Salabikh Excavations Vol. 1).* British School of Arch. in Iraq: London.

REDMAN, C. 1978. *The Rise of Civilization.* W.H. Freeman: San Francisco.

RENFREW, C. 1973. Monuments, mobilization and social organization in neolithic Wessex, in *The explanation of culture change: models in prehistory* (C. Renfrew ed.), 539–58. Duckworth: London.

——— 1979. *Investigations in Orkney.* Society of Antiquaries, London.

——— 1984. *Approaches to Social Archaeology.* Edinburgh Univ. Press.

——— 1987. *Archaeology and Language.* Jonathan Cape: London.

——— & CHERRY, J.F. (eds.). 1986. *Peer polity interaction and socio-political change.* Cambridge Univ. Press.

——— & LEVEL, E.V. 1979. Exploring Dominance: Predicting Polities from Centers, in *Transformations. Mathematical Approaches to Culture Change* (C. Renfrew & K.L. Cooke eds.), 145–67. Academic Press: New York & London.

——— & STERUD, G. 1969. Close proximity analysis: a rapid method for the ordering of archaeological materials. *American Antiquity* 34, 265–77.

SABLOFF, J.A. 1989. *The Cities of Ancient Mexico.* Thames & Hudson: London & New York.

SANDERS, W.T. 1981. Ecological adaptation in the Basin of Mexico: 23,000 B.C. to the present, in *Archaeology (Supplement to the Handbook of Middle American Indians)* (J.A. Sabloff ed.), 147–97. Univ. of Texas Press: Austin.

——— & MARINO, J. 1970. *New World Prehistory.* Prentice-Hall: Englewood Cliffs.

——— PARSONS, J.R. & SANTLEY, R.S. 1979. *The Basin of Mexico. Ecological*

Processes in the Evolution of a Civilization. Academic Press: New York & London.

SERVICE, E.R. 1971. *Primitive Social Organization. An Evolutionary Perspective.* (2nd ed.) Random House: New York.

SHENNAN, STEPHEN. 1988. *Quantifying Archaeology.* Edinburgh Univ. Press.

SHENNAN, SUSAN. 1975. The Social Organization at Branč. *Antiquity* 49, 279–88.

TAINTER, J.A. 1980. Behavior and status in a Middle Woodland mortuary population from the Illinois valley. *American Antiquity* 45, 308–13.

——— & CORDY, R.H., 1977. An archaeological analysis of social ranking and residence groups in prehistoric Hawaii. *World Arch.* 9, 95–112.

TORRENCE, R. 1986. *Production and exchange of stone tools: Prehistoric obsidian in the Aegean.* Cambridge Univ. Press.

TOSI, M. 1984. The notion of craft specialization and its representation in the archaeological record of early states in the Turanian Basin, in *Marxist Perspectives in Archaeology* (M. Spriggs ed.), 22–52. Cambridge Univ. Press.

VALENTIN, B. 1989. Nature et fonctions des foyers de l'habitation No 1 à Pincevent. *Nature et Fonction des Foyers Préhistoriques.* Actes du Colloque de Nemours 1987, Mémoires du Musée de Préhistoire de l'Ile de France 2, 209–19.

WHITELAW, T.M. 1981. The settlement at Fournou Korifi, Myrtos and aspects of Early Minoan social organisation, in *Minoan Society: Proceedings of the Cambridge Colloquium 1981* (O. Krzyszkowska & L. Nixon eds.), 323–46. Bristol Classical Press: Bristol.

——— 1983. People and space in hunter-gatherer camps: a generalising approach in ethnoarchaeology. *Archaeological Review from Cambridge* 2 (2), 48–66.

WOOD, M. 1985. *In Search of the Trojan War.* BBC Books: London.

YELLEN, J.E. 1977. *Archaeological Approaches to the Present.* Academic Press: New York & London.

Chapter 6: What Was the Environment? Environmental Archaeology (pp. 195–232)

p. 195 General studies in **environmental archaeology** include Fieller & others 1985. Pleistocene environments: Bradley 1985; Sutcliffe 1985. Holocene climates: Harding 1982. Climatic change in general is covered in special issues of the journals *World Archaeology* 8 (2), 1976; and *Dossiers de l'Archéologie* No. 93, 1985.

pp. 196–197 **Sea cores** Butzer 1983; Sancetta & others 1973; Shackleton, N.J.

1967; Shackleton, N.J. & Turner 1967; Chappell & Shackleton, N.J. 1986; Shackleton, N.J. 1987. Emiliani 1969 is still a useful, if outdated, introduction to core extraction. Also Thunell 1979 (east Mediterranean work); Brassell & others 1986 (fatty lipids). **Ice-cores** Dahl-Jensen & Johnsen 1986 **Ancient winds** Wilson & Hendy 1971; Parkin & Shackleton, N.J. 1973 (on W. Africa).

pp. 197–201 **Coastlines** In general: van Andel 1989; Masters & Flemming 1983; Thompson 1980. Work on Beringia: Hopkins & others 1982. **Submerged land surfaces** at Franchthi: van Andel & Lianos 1984; Shackleton, J.C. & van Andel 1980, 1986. **Raised beaches** Koike 1986 (Tokyo Bay.middens); Giddings 1966, 1967 (Alaskan beaches). **Coral reefs** Bloom & others 1974 (New Guinea); Dodge & others 1983. **Rock art** Chaloupka 1984 (Australia). The CLIMAP work is described in CLIMAP 1976.

pp. 201–207 **Studying the landscape** In general: Cornwall 1969; Gladfelter 1977; Hassan 1979; Pyddoke 1961; Rapp & Gifford 1982; Shackley 1975; Sutcliffe 1985; Vita-Finzi 1969, 1973; and *Geoarchaeology: an International Journal* (from 1986).

p. 202 **Rivers** Dales 1965 (Indus); Fisk 1944 (Mississippi); Adamson & others 1980 (Blue & White Niles); Sneh & Weissbrod 1973 (Nile Delta).

p. 203 **Cave sites** Collcutt 1979; Laville 1976; Laville & others 1980; Schmid 1969; Sutcliffe 1985.

pp. 203–207 **Sediments and soils** Clarke 1971; Courty & others 1990; Spence 1990 (assessment in the field). Orliac, M. 1975 (latex technique); van Andel & others 1986; Pope & van Andel 1984 (Argolid). **Loess** Bordes 1953 (Paris Basin); Kukla 1975 (Central Europe); 1987 (Central China). **Buried land surface** Street 1986 (Miesenheim forest).

p. 207 **Tree-rings and.climate** Fritts 1976; Grinsted & Wilson 1979 (isotopic analysis of tree-rings).

pp. 207–212 **Microbotanical remains** Good general works on **pollen analysis** are Traverse 1988; Faegri & others 1989; Dimbleby 1985, 1969; Moore & Webb 1978; Bryant & Holloway 1983; Edwards 1979; Wilkinson 1971. Also Bonnefille 1983 (Omo-Hadar pollen); Raikes 1984 (Raike's controversial opinions); Palmer 1976 (grass cuticles). Introductions to **phytoliths** include Piperno 1988; Pearsall 1982; Rovner 1971, 1983. Also Anderson 1980 (phytoliths on stone tools); Piperno 1985 (Panama work). **Diatom analysis** In general: Battarbee 1986; Mannion 1987. Also Bradbury 1975 (Minnesota work); Voorhips & Jansma 1974 (Netherlands). **Rock varnishes** Dorn & DeNiro 1985.

pp. 212–215 **Macrobotanical remains** General articles on **flotation** are Keeley 1978; Renfrew & others 1976; Struever 1968; also Pearsall 1989. Froth flotation: Jarman, H.N. & others 1972. Plant remains from frozen mammoths: Farrand 1961; from bog bodies: Helbaek 1958. **Wood and charcoal** Western 1969; Minnis 1987; also Deacon 1979 (Boomplaas Cave).

pp. 215–218 **Microfauna** Klein 1984 (dune mole rat); Evans 1972, 1969; Sparks 1969 (land molluscs); Koike 1986 (Tokyo Bay marine molluscs). General studies of **insects**: Buckland 1976; Osborne 1976. Also Coope 1977; Coope & others 1971 (beetles); Atkinson & others 1987 (British Pleistocene work); Girling & Greig 1985; Perry & Moore 1987 (Dutch elm disease); Addyman 1980; Buckland 1976, 388–91 (York Roman sewer).

pp. 218–222 **Macrofauna** Good introductions include Davis 1987; Chaplin 1971; Cornwall 1974. **Big-game extinctions** Martin & Klein 1984; Martin & Wright 1967. For the "combined explanation" of the extinctions: Owen-Smith 1987.

pp. 222–223 **New techniques: isotopes** Zeder 1978; Heaton & others 1986. **Other evidence** *Dossiers de l'Archéologie* 90, 1985 (tracks); Leakey 1987 (Laetoli tracks); Mead & others 1986 (fossil dung).

pp. 223–232 **Human environment** Burch 1971 (nonempirical); Brain & Sillen 1988 (Swartkrans fire); Legge 1972 (cave climates); Leroi-Gourhan 1981 (plant mattresses); Rottländer & Schlichtherle 1979, 264–66 (animal hides).

pp. 226–230 **Gardens** Leach 1984 (Maori); Cunliffe 1971 (Fishbourne); Jashemski 1979, 1986 (Pompeii). **Water resources** Addyman 1980 (York pollution). **Land management** In general: Aston 1985. Flannery 1982 (Maya ridged fields); Bradley, R. 1978 (British field systems). **Plow marks** under mounds: Fowler & Evans 1967; Rowley-Conwy 1987. **Woodland and vegetation** Coles & Coles 1986 (Somerset Levels); Piggott 1973 (Dalladies mound); Rue 1987 (Copán pollen analysis); Hallam 1975; Clark 1983 (Australian fire-stick farming: the Lake George controversy is argued in Singh & Geissler 1985 and Wright 1986);

Betancourt & van Devender 1981 (Chaco Canyon clearance).

pp. 230–232 **Island environments** Environmental destruction in general: Diamond 1986. Transformation and extinctions are discussed in Kirch 1982 (Hawaii), 1983 (Polynesia); Anderson 1983 (New Zealand). **Easter Island** Dransfield & others 1984; Flenley & King 1984.

Box Features

p. 197 **Sea and Ice Cores** See main text references above.

pp. 204–205 **Cave Sediments** Magee & Hughes 1982 (Colless Creek); Guillien 1970 (freeze thaw effects); Hendy & Wilson 1968 (speleothems).

pp. 208–209 **Pollen Analysis** Langford & others 1986 (automated pollen identification); Behre 1986 (human effects on pollen diagrams); Greig 1982 (pollen from urban sites).

pp. 220–221 **Elands Bay Cave** Parkington 1981; Buchanan 1988.

pp. 224–225 **Site Catchment Analysis** General: appendix in Higgs 1975 (223–224); Higgs & Vita-Finzi 1972. Applications: Bailey & Davidson 1983; Findlow & Ericson 1980; Jarman, M.R. 1972; Jarman & others 1982; Flannery 1976. Critiques can be found in Flannery 1976, especially 91–95; Roper 1979; Dennell 1980.

pp. 228–229 **Kuk Swamp** Golson 1976, 1977.

Bibliography

ADAMSON, D.A. & others. 1980. Late Quaternary history of the Nile. *Nature* 287, 50–55.

ADDYMAN, P.V. 1980. Eburacum, Jorvik, York. *Scientific American* 242, 56–66.

——— & others. 1976. Palaeoclimate in urban environmental archaeology at York, England. *World Arch.* 8 (2), 220–33.

van ANDEL, T.H. 1989. Late Quaternary sea level and archaeology. *Antiquity* 63 (241) 733–745.

van ANDEL, T.H. & LIANOS, N. 1984. High-resolution seismic reflection profiles for the reconstruction of post-glacial transgressive shorelines: an example from Greece. *Quaternary Research* 22, 31–45.

van ANDEL, T.H., RUNNELS, C.N. & POPE, K.O. 1986. Five thousand years of land use and abuse in the Southern Argolid, Greece. *Hesperia: Journal of the American School of Classical Studies at Athens* 55 (1), 103–28.

ANDERSON, A. 1983. *When all the moa-ovens grew cold.* Otago Heritage Books: Dunedin.

ANDERSON, P.C. 1980. A testimony of prehistoric tasks: diagnostic residues on stone tool working edges. World Arch. 12, 181–94.

ASTON, M. 1985. *Interpreting the Landscape.* Batsford: London.

ATKINSON, T.C., BRIFFA, K.R. & COOPE, G.R. 1987. Seasonal temperatures in Britain during the past 22,000 years, reconstructed using beetle remains. *Nature* 325, 587–92.

BAILEY, G.N. & DAVIDSON, I. 1983. Site exploitation territories and topography: Two case studies from Palaeolithic Spain. *Journal of Arch. Science* 10, 87–

115.

BATTARBEE, R.W. 1986. Diatom analysis, in *Handbook of Holocene Palaeoecology and Palaeohydrology* (B.E. Berglund ed.), 527–70. Wiley: London.

BEHRE, K-E. (ed.). 1986. *Anthropogenic Indicators in Pollen Diagrams.* Balkema: Rotterdam & Boston.

BETANCOURT, J.L. & van DEVENDER, T.R. 1981. Holocene vegetation in Chaco Canyon, New Mexico. *Science* 214, 656–58.

BLOOM, A.L. & others. 1974. Quaternary sea level fluctuations on a tectonic coast: New 230Th/234U dates from the Huon Peninsula, New Guinea. *Quaternary Research* 4, 185–205.

BONNEFILLE, R. 1983. Evidence for a cooler and drier climate in the Ethiopian uplands towards 2.5 Myr ago. *Nature* 303, 487–91.

BORDES, F. 1953. *Recherches sur les limons quaternaires du bassin de la Seine.* Archives de l'Institut de Paléontologie Humaine, No. 26: Paris.

BRADBURY, J.P. 1975. Diatom stratigraphy and human settlement in Minnesota. *Geol. Soc. of America, Special Paper* 171, 1–74.

BRADLEY, R. 1978. Prehistoric field systems in Britain and north-west Europe: a review of some recent work. *World Arch.* 9, 265–80.

BRADLEY, R.S. 1985. *Quaternary Paleoclimatology: Methods of Paleoclimatic Reconstruction.* Allen & Unwin: Boston & London.

BRAIN, C.K. & SILLEN, A. 1988. Evidence from the Swartkrans cave for the earliest use of fire. *Nature* 336, 464–66.

BRASSELL, S.C. & others. 1986. Molecular stratigraphy: a new tool for climatic assessment. *Nature* 320, 129–33.

BRYANT, V. M. & HOLLOWAY, R.G. 1983. The role of palynology in archaeology, in *Advances in Archaeological Method and Theory* 6 (M.B. Schiffer ed.), 191–224. Academic Press: London & New York.

BUCHANAN, W.F. 1988. *Shellfish in prehistoric diet. Elands Bay, S.W. Cape Coast, South Africa.* British Arch. Reports, Int. Series 455: Oxford.

BUCKLAND, P.C. 1976. The use of insect remains in the interpretation of archaeological environments, in *Geoarchaeology* (D.A. Davidson & M.L. Shackley eds.), 369–96. Duckworth: London.

BURCH, E.S. 1971. The nonempirical environment of the Arctic Alaskan Eskimos. *Southwestern Journal of Arch.* 27, 148–65.

BUTZER, K.W. 1971. *Environment and Archaeology* (2nd ed.) Aldine: Chicago.

——— 1982. *Archaeology as Human Ecology.* Cambridge Univ. Press.

——— 1983. Global sea-level stratigraphy: an appraisal. *Quaternary Science Reviews* 2, 1–15.

CHALOUPKA, G. 1984. *From Palaeoart to Casual Paintings.* Northern Territory Museum of Arts and Sciences, Darwin. Monograph 1.

CHAPLIN, R.E. 1971. *The Study of Animal Bones from Archaeological Sites.* Seminar Press: London & New York.

CHAPPELL, J. & SHACKLETON, N.J. 1986. Oxygen isotopes and sea level. *Nature* 324, 137–40.

CLARK, R. 1983. Pollen and charcoal evidence for the effects of aboriginal burning on the vegetation of Australia. *Archaeology in Oceania* 18, 32–37.

CLARKE, G.R. 1971. *The Study of Soil in the Field.* (5th ed.) Oxford Univ. Press.

CLIMAP Project Members. 1976. The Surface of the Ice-Age earth. *Science* 191, 1131–37.

COLES, B. & COLES, J. 1986. *Sweet Track to Glastonbury: The Somerset Levels in Prehistory.* Thames & Hudson: London & New York.

COLLCUTT, S.N. 1979. The analysis of Quaternary cave sediments. *World Arch.* 10, 290–301.

COOPE, G.R. 1977. Quaternary coleoptera as aids in the interpretation of environmental history, in *British Quaternary Studies: Recent advances.* (F.W. Shotton ed.), 55–68. Oxford Univ. Press.

——— & MORGAN, A. & OSBORNE, P.J. 1971. Fossil coleoptera as indicators of climatic fluctuations during the last glaciation in Britain. *Palaeogeography, Palaeoclimatology, Palaeoecology* 10, 87–101.

CORNWALL, I.W. 1958. *Soils for the Archaeologist.* Phoenix House: London.

——— 1969. Soil stratification and environment, in *Science in Archaeology* (D.R. Brothwell & E.S. Higgs eds.), 124–34. (Rev. ed.) Thames & Hudson: London.

——— 1974. *Bones for the Archaeologist.* Phoenix House: London.

COURTY, M-A., GOLDBERG, P. & MACPHAIL, R. 1990. *Soils and Micromorphology in Archaeology.* Cambridge Univ. Press.

CUNLIFFE, B. 1971. *Fishbourne.* Thames & Hudson: London.

DAHL-JENSEN, D. & JOHNSEN, S.J. 1986. Palaeotemperatures still exist in the Greenland ice sheet. *Nature* 320, 250–52.

DALES, G.F. 1965. Civilization and floods in the Indus valley. *Expedition* 7, 10–19.

DAVIDSON, D.A. & SHACKLEY, M.L. (eds.). 1976. *Geoarchaeology: Earth Science and the Past.* Duckworth: London.

DAVIS, S.J.M. 1987. *The Archaeology of Animals.* Batsford: London; Yale Univ. Press: New Haven.

DEACON, H.J. 1979. Excavations at Boomplaas Cave: a sequence through the Upper Pleistocene and Holocene in South

Africa. *World Arch.* 10 (3). 241–57.

DENNELL, R. 1980. The use, abuse and potential of Site Catchment Analysis, in *Catchment Analysis: Essays on prehistoric resource space* (F.J. Findlow & J.E. Ericson eds.), 1–20. Anthropology UCLA 10.

DIAMOND, J.M. 1986. The environmentalist myth. *Nature* 324, 19–20.

DIMBLEBY, G. 1969. Pollen analysis, in *Science in Archaeology* (D.R. Brothwell & E.S. Higgs eds.), 167–77. (Rev. ed.) Thames & Hudson: London.

——— 1978. *Plants and Archaeology.* Paladin: London.

——— 1985. *The Palynology of Archaeological Sites.* Academic Press: London & New York.

DODGE, R.E. & others. 1983. Pleistocene sea levels from raised coral reefs of Haiti. *Science* 219, 1423–25.

DORN, R.I. & DeNIRO, M.J. 1985. Stable carbon isotope ratios of rock varnish organic matter: a new palaeoenvironmental indicator. *Science* 227, 1472–74.

DRANSFIELD, J. & others. 1984. A recently extinct palm from Easter Island. *Nature* 312, 750–52.

EDWARDS, K.J. 1979. Palynological and temporal inference in the context of prehistory, with special reference to the evidence from lake and peaty deposits. *Journal of Arch. Science* 6, 255–70.

EMILIANI, C. 1969. The significance of deep-sea cores, in *Science in Archaeology* (D.R. Brothwell & E.S. Higgs ed.), 109–17. (Rev. eds.) Thames & Hudson London.

EVANS, J.G. 1969. Land and freshwater mollusca in archaeology: chronological aspects. *World Arch.* 1, 170–83.

——— 1972. *Land Snails in Archaeology.* Seminar Press: London.

——— 1978. *An Introduction to Environmental Archaeology.* Paul Elek: London.

FAEGRI, K., EKALAND, P. & KRZYWINSKI, K. (eds.) 1989. *Textbook of Pollen Analysis.* (4th ed.) Wiley: London.

FARRAND, W.R. 1961. Frozen mammoths and modern geology. *Science* 133, 729–35.

FIELLER, N.R.J., GILBERTSON, D.D. & RALPH, N.G.A. (eds.). l985. *Palaeoenvironmental Investigations: Research Design, Methods and Data Analysis.* British Arch. Reports, Int. Series 258: Oxford.

FINDLOW, F.J. & ERICSON, J.E. (eds.). 1980. *Catchment Analysis: Essays on prehistoric resource space.* Anthropology UCLA 10.

FISK, H.N. 1944. *Summary of the geology of the lower alluvial valley of the Mississippi River.* Mississippi River Commission: War Dept., US Army.

FLANNERY, K.V. (ed.). 1976. *The Early*

Mesoamerican Village. Academic Press: New York & London.

——— (ed.) 1982. *Maya Subsistence*. Academic Press: New York & London.

FLENLEY, J.R. & KING, S.M. 1984. Late quaternary pollen records from Easter Island. *Nature* 307, 47–50.

FOWLER, P.J. & EVANS, J.G. 1967. Plough marks, lynchets and early fields. *Antiquity* 41, 289–301.

FRITTS, H.C. 1976. *Tree Rings and Climate*. Academic Press: New York & London.

GIDDINGS, J.L. 1966. Cross-dating the archaeology of northwestern Alaska. *Science* 153, 127–35.

——— 1967. *Ancient Men of the Arctic*. Knopf: New York.

GIRLING, M.A. & GREIG, J. 1985. A first fossil record for *Scolytus scolytus* (F.) (elm bark beetle): Its occurrence in elm decline deposits from London and the implications for Neolithic elm disease. *Journal of Arch. Science* 12, 347–51.

GLADFELTER B.G. 1977. Geoarchaeology: the geomorphologist and archaeology. *American Antiquity* 42, 519–38.

GOLSON, J. 1976. Archaeology and agricultural history in the New Guinea Highlands, in *Problems in Economic and Social Archaeology* (G. Sieveking & others eds.), 201–20. Duckworth: London.

——— 1977. No room at the top: agricultural intensification in the New Guinea Highlands, in *Sunda and Sahul* (J. Allen, J. Golson & R Jones eds.), 601–38. Academic Press: New York & London.

GREIG, J. 1982. The interpretation of pollen spectra from urban archaeological deposits, in *Environmental Archaeology in the Urban Context* (A.R. Hall & H.K. Kenward eds.), 47–65. Council for British Arch., Research Report 43: London.

GRINSTED, M.J. & WILSON, A.T. 1979. Variations of 13C/12C ratio in cellulose of *Agathus australis* (kauri) and climatic change in New Zealand during the last millennium. *New Zealand Journal of Science* 22, 55–61.

GUILLIEN, Y. 1970. Cryoclase, calcaires et grottes habitées. *Bulletin de la Soc. Préh. française* 67, 231–6.

HALLAM, S.J. 1975. *Fire and Hearth*. Australian Inst. of Aboriginal Studies: Canberra.

HARDING, A. (ed.). 1982. *Climatic Change in Later Prehistory*. Edinburgh Univ. Press.

HASSAN, F. 1979. Geoarchaeology: the geologist and archaeology. *American Antiquity* 44, 267–70.

HEATON, T.H.E. & others. 1986. Climatic influence on the isotopic composition of bone nitrogen. *Nature* 322, 822–23.

HELBAEK, H. 1958. Grauballemandens sidste måltid (The last meal of Grauballe Man). *Kuml* 83–116.

HENDY, C.H. & WILSON, A.T. 1968. Palaeoclimatic data from speleothems. *Nature* 219, 48–51.

HIGGS, E.S. (ed.). 1975. *Palaeoeconomy*. Cambridge Univ. Press.

——— & VITA-FINZI, C. 1972. Prehistoric economies, a territorial approach, in *Papers in Economic Prehistory* (E.S. Higgs ed.), 27–36. Cambridge Univ. Press.

HOPKINS, D.M. & others. (eds.). 1982. *The Paleoecology of Beringia*. Academic Press: New York & London.

JARMAN, H.N., LEGGE, A.J. & CHARLES, J.A. 1972. Retrieval of plant remains from archaeological sites by froth flotation, in *Papers in Economic Prehistory* (E.S. Higgs ed.), 39–48. Cambridge Univ. Press.

JARMAN, M.R. 1972. A territorial model for archaeology, in *Models in Archaeology*. (D.L. Clarke ed.), 705–33. Methuen: London.

——— & BAILEY, G.N. & JARMAN, H.N. (eds.), 1982. *Early European Agriculture: its Foundations and Development*. Cambridge Univ. Press.

JASHEMSKI, W.F. 1979. *The Gardens of Pompeii, Herculaneum and the villas destroyed by Vesuvius*. Vol. 1. Caratzas Brothers: New Rochelle.

——— 1986. L'archéologie des jardins de Pompéi. *La Recherche* 17, 990–91.

KEELEY, H.C.M. 1978. The cost-effectiveness of certain methods of recovering macroscopic organic remains from archaeological deposits. *Journal of Arch. Science* 5, 179–83.

KIRCH, P.V. 1982. The impact of the prehistoric Polynesians on the Hawaiian ecosystem. *Pacific Science* 36, 1–14.

——— 1983. Man's role in modifying tropical and subtropical Polynesian ecosystems. *Archaeology in Oceania* 18, 26–31.

KLEIN, R.G. 1984. The large mammals of southern Africa: Late Pliocene to Recent, in *Southern Africa: Prehistory and Palaeoenvironments* (R.G. Klein ed.), 107–46. Balkema: Rotterdam & Boston.

——— & CRUZ-URIBE, K. 1984. *The Analysis of Animal Bones from Archaeological Sites*. Univ. of Chicago Press.

KOIKE, H. 1986. Jomon shell mounds and growth-line analysis of molluscan shells, in *Windows on the Japanese Past: Studies in Archaeology and Prehistory* (R.J. Pearson & others eds.), 267–78. Center for Japanese Studies, Univ. of Michigan.

KUKLA, G.J. 1975. Loess stratigraphy of Central Europe, in *After the Australopithecines* (K.W. Butzer & G.L. Isaac eds.), 99–188. Mouton: The Hague.

——— 1987. Loess stratigraphy in Central China. *Quaternary Science Reviews* 6, 191–219.

LANGFORD, M., TAYLOR, G. & FLENLEY, J.R. 1986. The application of texture analysis for automated pollen identification, in *Proc. Conference on Identification and Pattern Recognition*, Toulouse, June 1986, vol. 2, 729–39. Univ. Paul Sabatier: Toulouse.

LAVILLE, H. 1976. Deposits in calcareous rock shelters: analytical methods and climatic interpretation, in *Geoarchaeology* (D.A. Davidson & M.L. Shackley eds.), 137–57. Duckworth: London.

——— & RIGAUD, J-P. & SACKETT, J. 1980. *Rock shelters of the Périgord. Geological stratigraphy and archaeological succession*. Academic Press: London & New York.

LEACH, H. 1984. *1,000 Years of Gardening in New Zealand*. Reed: Wellington.

LEAKEY, M. 1987. Animal prints and trails, in *Laetoli, a Pliocene site in northern Tanzania* (M. Leakey & J.M. Harris eds.), 451–89. Clarendon Press: Oxford.

LEGGE, A.J. 1972. Cave climates, in *Papers in Economic Prehistory*, (E.S. Higgs ed.), 97–103. Cambridge Univ. Press.

LEROI-GOURHAN, A. 1981. Pollens et grottes ornées, in *Altamira Symposium* (1980), 295–97. Madrid.

LIMBREY, S. 1975. *Soil Science and Archaeology*. Academic Press: London & New York.

MAGEE, J.W. & HUGHES, P.J. 1982. Thin-section analysis and the geomorphic history of the Colless Creek archaeological site in Northwestern Queensland, in *Archaeometry: An Australian Perspective* (W. Ambrose & P. Duerden eds.), 120–28. Australian National Univ.: Canberra.

MANNION, A.M. 1987. Fossil diatoms and their significance in archaeological research. *Oxford Journal of Arch.* 6, 131–47.

MARTIN, P.S. & KLEIN, R.G. (eds.). 1984. *Quaternary Extinctions: A Prehistoric Revolution*. Univ. of Arizona Press.

MARTIN, P.S. & WRIGHT, H.E. (eds.). 1967. *Pleistocene Extinctions*. Yale Univ. Press.

MASTERS, P.M. & FLEMMING, N.C. (eds.). 1983. *Quaternary Coastlines and Marine Archaeology*. Academic Press: London & New York.

MEAD, J.I. & others. 1986. Dung of *Mammuthus* in the Arid Southwest, North America. *Quaternary Research* 25, 121–27.

MINNIS, P.E. 1987. Identification of wood from archaeological sites in the American Southwest. *Journal of Arch. Science* 14, 121–32.

MOORE, P.D. & WEBB, J.A. 1978. *An Illustrated Guide to Pollen Analysis*. Hodder and Stoughton: London.

ORLIAC, M. 1975. Empreintes au latex des coupes du gisement magdalénien de Pincevent: technique et premiers résultats. *Bulletin de la Soc. Préh. française* 72, 274–76.

OSBORNE, P.J. 1976. Evidence from the

insects of climatic variation during the Flandrian period: a preliminary note. *World Arch.* 8, 150–58.

OWEN-SMITH, N. 1987. Pleistocene extinctions: the pivotal role of megaherbivores. *Paleobiology* 13, 351–62.

PALMER, P. 1976. Grass cuticles: a new paleoecological tool for East African lake sediments. *Canadian Journal of Botany* 54, No. 15, 1725–34.

PARKIN, D.W. & SHACKLETON, N.J. 1973. Trade winds and temperature correlations down a deep-sea core off the Saharan coast. *Nature* 245, 455–57.

PARKINGTON, J. 1981. The effects of environmental change on the scheduling of visits to the Elands Bay Cave, Cape Province, South Africa, in *Pattern of the Past. Studies in Honour of David Clarke* (I. Hodder & others eds.), 341–59. Cambridge Univ. Press.

PEARSALL, D.M. 1982. Phytolith analysis: applications of a new paleoethnobotanical technique in archeology. *American Anthropologist* 84, 862–71.

———— 1989. *Paleoethnobotany.* Academic Press: New York & London.

PERRY, I. & MOORE, P.D. 1987. Dutch elm disease as an analogue of Neolithic elm decline. *Nature* 326, 72–73.

PIGGOTT, S. 1973. The Dalladies long barrow: NE Scotland. *Antiquity* 47, 32–36.

PIPERNO, D.R. 1985. Phytolithic analysis of geological sediments from Panama. *Antiquity* 59, 13–19.

———— 1988. *Phytolith Analysis: An Archaeological and Geological Perspective.* Academic Press: New York & London.

POPE, K.O. & van ANDEL, T.H. 1984. Late quaternary alluviation and soil formation in the Southern Argolid: its history, causes, and archaeological implications. *Journal of Arch. Science* 11, 281–306.

PYDDOKE, E. 1961. *Stratification for the Archaeologist.* Phoenix House: London.

RAIKES, R.L. 1984. *Water, Weather and Prehistory.* Raikes: Wales; Humanities Press: N.J.

RAPP. G. & GIFFORD, J.A. 1982. Archaeological geology. *American Scientist* 70, 45–53.

RENFREW, J. 1973. *Palaeoethnobotany.* Methuen: London.

RENFREW, J.M., MONK, M. & MURPHY, P. 1976. *First Aid for Seeds.* Hertford.

ROPER, D.C. 1979. The Method and theory of site catchment analysis: a review, in *Advances in Archaeological Method and Theory* 2 (M.B. Schiffer ed.), 119–40. Academic Press: New York & London.

ROTTLÄNDER, R.C.A. & SCHLICHTHERLE, H. 1979. Food identification of samples from archaeological sites. *Archaeo Physika* 10, 260–67.

ROVNER, I. 1971. Potential of opal phytoliths for use in paleoecological reconstruction. *Quaternary Research* 1, 343–59.

———— 1983. Plant opal phytolith analysis: major advances in archaeobotanical research, in *Advances in Archaeological Method and Theory* 6 (M.B. Schiffer ed.), 225–66. Academic Press: New York & London.

ROWLEY-CONWY, P. 1987. The interpretation of ard marks. *Antiquity* 61, 263–6.

RUE, D.J. 1987. Early agriculture and early Postclassic Maya occupation in western Honduras. *Nature* 326, 285–86.

SANCETTA, C., IMBRIE, J. & KIPP, N. 1973. Climatic record of the past 130,000 years in North Atlantic deep-sea core V23–82; correlation with the terrestrial record. *Quaternary Research* 3, 110–16.

SCHMID, E. 1969. Cave sediments and prehistory, in *Science in Archaeology.* (D.R. Brothwell & E.S. Higgs eds.), 151–66. (Rev. ed.) Thames & Hudson; London.

SHACKLETON, J.C. & van ANDEL, T.H. 1980. Prehistoric shell assemblages from Franchthi Cave and evolution of the adjacent coastal zone. *Nature* 288, 357–59.

———— 1986. Prehistoric shore environments, shellfish availability, and shellfish gathering at Franchthi, Greece. *Geoarchaeology: an International Journal* 1 (2), 127–43.

SHACKLETON, N.J. 1967. Oxygen isotope analyses and pleistocene temperatures re-assessed. *Nature* 215, 15–17.

———— 1987. Oxygen isotopes, ice volume and sea level. *Quaternary Science Reviews* 6, 183–90.

———— & TURNER, C. 1967. Correlation between marine and terrestrial pleistocene successions. *Nature* 216, 1079–82.

SHACKLEY, M. 1975. *Archaeological Sediments.* Butterworths: London.

———— 1982. *Environmental Archaeology.* Allen & Unwin: London.

SINGH, G. & GEISSLER, E.A. 1985. Late Cainozoic history of vegetation, fire, lake levels and climate at Lake George, New South Wales, Australia. *Phil. Trans. Royal Soc. London* B 311, 379–447.

SNEH, A. & WEISSBROD, T. 1973. Nile Delta: The defunct Pelusiac branch identified. *Science* 180, 59–61.

SPARKS, B.W. 1969. Non-marine mollusca and archaeology, in *Science in Archaeology* (D.R. Brothwell & E.S. Higgs eds.), 395–406. (Rev. ed.) Thames & Hudson: London.

SPENCE, C. (ed.). 1990. *Archaeological Site Manual.* (2nd ed.) Museum of London.

STREET, M. 1986. Un Pompéi de l'âge glaciaire. *La Recherche* 17, 534–35.

STRUEVER, S. 1968. Flotation techniques for the recovery of small archaeological

remains. *American Antiquity* 33, 353–62.

SUTCLIFFE, A.J. 1985. *On the Track of Ice Age Mammals.* British Museum (Natural History): London.

THOMPSON, F.H. (ed.). 1980. *Archaeology and Coastal Change.* Soc. of Antiquaries, Occasional Paper, New Series 1.

THUNELL, R.C. 1979. Eastern Mediterranean Sea during the last glacial maximum: an 18,000 years B.P. reconstruction. *Quaternary Research* 11, 353–72.

TRAVERSE, A. 1988. *Paleopalynology.* Unwin Hyman: Boston.

VITA-FINZI, C. 1969. Fluvial geology, in *Science in Archaeology* (D.R. Brothwell & E.S. Higgs eds.), 135–50. (Rev. ed.) Thames & Hudson: London.

———— 1973. *Recent Earth History.* Macmillan: London.

———— 1978. *Archaeological Sites in their Setting.* Thames & Hudson: London & New York.

VOORHIPS, A. & JANSMA, M.J. 1974. Pollen and diatom analysis of a shore section of the former Lake Wevershoof. *Geologie en Mijnbouw* 53, 429–35.

WESTERN, A.C. 1969. Wood and charcoal in archaeology, in *Science in Archaeology* (D.R. Brothwell & E.S. Higgs eds.), 178–87. (Rev. ed.) Thames & Hudson: London.

WILKINSON, P.F. 1971. Pollen, archaeology and man. *Arch. & Physical Anth. in Oceania* 6, 1–20.

WILSON, A.T. & HENDY, C.H. 1971. Past wind strength from isotope studies. *Nature* 234, 344–45.

WRIGHT, R. 1986. How old is zone F at Lake George? *Arch. in Oceania* 21, 138–39.

ZEDER, M.A. 1978. Differentiation between the bones of caprines from different ecosystems in Iran by the analysis of osteological microstructure and chemical composition, in *Approaches to Faunal Analysis in the Middle East* (R.M. Meadow & M.A. Zeder eds.), 69–84. Peabody Museum of Arch. & Ethnol., Bull. No. 2.

Chapter 7: What Did they Eat? Subsistence and Diet (pp. 233–270)

pp. 234–245 **Paleoethnobotany** In general: Renfrew 1973; van Zeist & Casparie 1984; Pearsall 1989; Hastorf & Popper 1989; for the New World, Ford 1979.

pp. 234–238 **Macrobotanical remains,** especially in an urban context: Hall, A. 1986; Greig 1983; Dennell 1974, 1976.

pp. 238–240 **Microbotanical remains** Fujiwara 1979, 1982 (rice phytoliths).

pp. 240–241 **Plant processing** Dennell 1974, 1976; Hubbard 1975, 1976. Also Hillman 1981 (charred remains); Jones

& others 1986 (crop storage). **Plant residues** In general: Hill & Evans 1987. In particular: Grüss 1932 (early work); Briuer 1976 (stone tools); Rottländer & Schlichtherle 1979 (Neolithic sherds); Rottländer & Hartke 1982 (Roman sherds); Rottländer 1986 (Heuneburg); Hastorf & DeNiro 1985 (isotopic analysis).

pp. 241–244 **Plant domestication** In general: Hillman & others 1990; Ucko & Dimbleby 1969. In particular: Jarman 1972 (cereals); Smith 1984 (*Chenopodium* work). Phytoliths and maize domestication: Piperno & others 1985; Pearsall 1978 (Ecuador). Ubuka Bog, Japan: Tsukuda & others 1986.

pp. 244–245 **Cookery and electron spin resonance** Hillman & others 1985. Lindow man work: Stead & others 1986.

p. 245 **Plant evidence from literate societies** Crawford 1979, Darby & others 1977, Saffirio 1972 (Egypt); Davies 1971 (Roman military diet); Garnsey 1988, Forbes & Foxhall 1978, Foxhall & Forbes 1982 (Graeco-Roman world); UNESCO 1984, 86 (T'ang granaries).

pp. 246–264 **Animal resources** In general: Davis 1987; Grayson 1984; Hesse & Wapnish 1985; Meadow 1980; Lyman 1982. A specialized journal began in 1987: *Archaeozoologia*.

pp. 246–249 **Human exploitation of animals** In general: Clutton-Brock & Grigson 1983; Blumenschine 1986. The Olduvai/Koobi Fora work is described in Bunn 1981; Bunn & Kroll 1986; Potts & Shipman 1981; Shipman & Rose 1983; Potts 1988. See also papers in Clutton-Brock & Grigson 1983, and in *Journal of Human Evolution* 15 (8), Dec. 1986. Trampling of bones: Behrensmeyer & others 1986.

pp. 249–250 **Cannibalism** Arens 1979; Russell 1987 (Krapina); for Fontbrégoua see Villa & others 1986 (and similar articles in *Gallia Préhistoire* 29, 1986, 143–71; *Archéologia* 223, April 1987, 40–52); against Fontbrégoua, Pickering 1989.

pp. 250–251 **Macrofaunal assemblage** Speth 1983 (Garnsey).

pp. 252–254 **Age, sex, and seasonality** Silver 1969; Wilson & others 1982. The Sika deer: Koike & Ohtaishi 1985, 1987.

pp. 254–258 **Animal domestication** In general: Bökönyi 1969; Clutton-Brock 1981; Collier & White 1976; Davis 1987; Higgs & Jarman 1969; Jarman & Wilkinson 1972; Olsen 1979. Bone microstructure analysis: Drew & others 1971 (Near East); Pollard & Drew 1975 (llamas). Ryder 1969 (work on skins); Bahn 1978 (control of Ice Age animals). Disease and deformity: Baker & Brothwell 1980. Telarmachay camelids: Wheeler 1984.

pp. 258–259 **Small fauna: Birds** Anderson, A. 1983 (moa sites,

Hawksburn in particular). **Fish** Casteel 1974a; Brinkhuizen & Clason 1986; Wheeler & Jones 1989; and on fish-meat weights, Casteel 1974b. **Microfauna and insects** Hall, R.A. & Kenward 1976 (York granaries). **Molluscs** Meighan 1969; Shackleton 1969; Bailey 1975; Kirch & Yen 1982 (Tikopia).

pp. 259–261 **Seasonality studies** Monks 1981. Oronsay fish otoliths: Mellars & Wilkinson 1980. Mollusc seasonality in general: Sheppard 1985.

pp. 262–263 **Exploitation of animal resources: Fishing and hunting** Andersen 1986, 1987 (Tybrind Vig boat); Noe-Nygaard 1974, 1975 (wounds on animal bones); Keeley & Toth 1981 (microwear analysis). **Blood residues** Loy 1983, 1987; Loy & Wood 1989. **Fat residues** Rottländer & Schlichtherle 1979 (Geissenklösterle & Lommersum); Brochier 1983 (cave-herding). **Residues in vessels** Grüss 1933 (milk); Rottländer & Hartke 1982 (Michelsberg); Rottländer & Schlichtherle 1979; Patrick & others 1985 (Kasteelberg). **Animal tracks** In general: Clottes & others 1981; Leakey 1987 (Laetoli).

pp. 263–264 **Secondary Products Revolution** Sherratt 1981; Bogucki 1986 (LBK dairying).

p. 264 **Art and literature** Jett & Moyle 1986 (Mimbres fish).

p. 264 **Individual meals** Hall 1974 (Chinese lady's tomb).

pp. 265–268 **Human remains: individual meals** Stomach contents of bogmen: Brothwell 1986; Helbaek 1958. Lindow man: Hillman 1986; Stead & Turner 1985; Stead & others 1986. **Fecal material** In general: Bryant & Williams-Dean 1975; Callen 1969. Tehuacán: Callen 1967; Callen & Cameron 1960. Nevada: Heizer 1969. Bearsden work: Knights & others 1983. Cesspits in general: Greig 1982; Worcester latrine: Greig 1981. The survival properties of organic residues through the human digestive system are listed in Calder 1977.

pp. 267–268 **Teeth** Puech 1978, 1979a, 1979b; Puech & others 1980; Fine & Craig 1981; Larsen 1983 (Georgia).

pp. 268–270 **Isotopic methods: bone collagen** Price 1989. **Carbon isotope analysis** Tauber 1981 (Denmark); Chisholm & others 1982, 1983 (British Columbia); van der Merwe & others 1981 (Venezuela); Schwarcz & others 1985 (Ontario); Sealy 1986; Sealy & van der Merwe 1986 (SW Cape); Ambrose & DeNiro 1986 (E. & S. Africa). **Nitrogen isotopes** Schoeninger & others 1983. **Strontium analysis** Schoeninger 1981 (Near East); Schoeninger 1979 (Chalcatzingo); Schoeninger & Peebles 1981 (molluscs).

Box Features

pp. 236–237 **Paleoethnobotany** Wendorf & others 1980; Hillman & others 1988

(Wadi Kubbaniya).

pp. 238–239 **Butser** Reynolds 1979.

pp. 242–243 **Rise of Farming in Near East** Braidwood & Howe 1960; Hole & others 1969; Mellaart 1967; Binford 1968; Flannery 1965; Higgs & Jarman 1969; Renfrew, J. 1973; Vita-Finzi & Higgs 1970.

pp. 246–247 **Taphonomy** In general: Weigelt 1989; Behrensmeyer & Hill 1980; Bahn 1983; Noe-Nygaard 1977, 1987; Gifford 1981. Also Brain 1981 (S. African work); Binford 1981; Binford & Bertram 1977 (N. American work); Speth 1983 (Garnsey site).

p. 250 **Quantifying Animal Bones** Problems: Grayson 1979, 1984. Estimation of meat weight: Lyman 1979; Smith 1975. Butchery studies: White 1953, 1953/4.

p. 251 **Teeth** In general: Hillson 1986. Klein & Cruz-Uribe 1984 (tooth-wear); Singer & Wymer 1982 (Klasies River Mouth Cave); Fisher 1984 (Michigan mastodons); Bourque & others 1978 (tooth sectioning technique); Spiess 1979 (Abri Pataud work).

pp. 252–253 **Bison Drive Sites** Kehoe 1967 (Boarding School). Kehoe 1973 (Gull Lake). Other drive sites: Speth 1983 (Garnsey) and Wheat 1972 (Olsen-Chubbock).

pp. 256–257 **Farming Origins** Abu Hureyra: Moore 1975, 1979; Hillman & others 1990; Legge & Rowley-Conwy 1987.

pp. 260–261 **Shell Midden Analysis** Growth lines: Koike 1986 (Kidosaku); Koike 1979, 1980 (Natsumidai). Mollusc seasonality from oxygen isotopes: Bailey & others 1983; Killingley 1981; Shackleton 1973.

Bibliography

AMBROSE, S.H. & DeNIRO, M.J. 1986. Reconstruction of African human diet using bone collagen carbon and nitrogen isotope ratios. *Nature* 319, 321–4.

ANDERSEN, S.H. 1986. Mesolithic dug-outs and paddles from Tybrind Vig, Denmark. *Acta Archaeologica* 57, 87–106.

————— 1987. Tybrind Vig: a submerged Ertebølle settlement in Denmark, in *European Wetlands in Prehistory* (J.M. Coles & A.J. Lawson eds.), 253–80. Clarendon Press: Oxford.

ANDERSON, A. (ed.) 1989. *Prodigious Birds: Moas and Moa-hunting in New Zealand.* Cambridge Univ. Press.

ARENS, W. 1979. *The Man-Eating Myth.* Oxford Univ. Press.

BAHN, P.G. 1978. The 'unacceptable face' of the West European Upper Palaeolithic. *Antiquity* 52, 183–92.

————— 1983. The case of the clumsy cave-bears. *Nature* 301, 565.

BAILEY, G.N. 1975. The role of molluscs in coastal economies: the results of midden analysis in Australia. *Journal of Arch. Science* 2, 45–62.

———, DEITH, M.R. & SHACKLETON, N.J. 1983. Oxygen isotope analysis and seasonality determinations: limits and potential of a new technique. *American Antiquity* 48, 390–8.

BAKER, J. & BROTHWELL, D. 1980. *Animal Diseases in Archaeology.* Academic Press: New York & London.

BEHRENSMEYER, A.K., GORDON, K.D. & YANAGI, G.T. 1986. Trampling as a cause of bone surface damage and pseudo-cutmarks. *Nature* 319, 768–71.

BEHRENSMEYER, A.K. & HILL, A.P. (eds.). 1980. *Fossils in the Making, Vertebrate Taphonomy and Paleoecology.* Univ. of Chicago Press.

BINFORD, L.R. 1968. Post-Pleistocene adaptations, in *New Perspectives in Archaeology* (L.R. & S.R. Binford eds.), 313–41. Aldine: Chicago.

——— 1981. *Bones: Ancient Men and Modern Myths.* Academic Press: New York & London.

——— & BERTRAM, J.B. 1977. Bone frequencies and attritional processes, in *For Theory Building in Archaeology* (L.R. Binford ed.), 77–153. Academic Press: New York & London.

BLUMENSCHINE, R.J. 1986. *Early Hominid Scavenging Opportunities.* British Arch. Reports, Int. Series 283: Oxford.

BOGUCKI, P. 1986. The antiquity of dairying in temperate Europe. *Expedition* 28 (2), 51–58.

BÖKÖNYI, S. 1969. Archaeological problems and methods of recognizing animal domestication, in *The Domestication and Exploitation of Plants and Animals* (P.J. Ucko & G.W. Dimbleby eds.), 219–29. Duckworth: London.

BOURQUE, B.J., MORRIS, K. & SPIESS, A. 1978. Determining the season of death of mammal teeth from archeological sites: a new sectioning technique. *Science* 199, 530–31.

BRAIDWOOD, R.J. & HOWE B. 1960. *Prehistoric Investigations in Iraqi Kurdistan.* Oriental Institute: Chicago.

BRAIN, C.K. 1981. *The Hunters or the Hunted? An Introduction to African Cave Taphonomy.* Univ. of Chicago Press.

BRINKHUIZEN, D.C. & CLASON, A.T. (eds.). 1986. *Fish and Archaeology. Studies in Osteometry, Taphonomy, Seasonality and Fishing.* British Arch. Reports, Int. Series No. 294: Oxford.

BRIUER, F.L. 1976. New clues to stone tool function: plant and animal residues. *American Antiquity* 41, 478–84.

BROCHIER, J-E. 1983. Combustion et parcage des herbivores domestiques. Le point de vue sédimentologique. *Bull. Soc. Préhist. française* 80, 143–45.

BROTHWELL, D. 1986. *The Bog Man and the Archaeology of People.* British Museum Publications: London.

——— & BROTHWELL, P. 1969. *Food in Antiquity: A Survey of the Diet of Early Peoples.* Thames & Hudson: London.

BRYANT, V.M. & WILLIAMS-DEAN, G. 1975. The coprolites of man. *Scientific American* 238, 100–9.

BUNN, H.T. 1981. Archaeological evidence for meat-eating by Plio-Pleistocene hominids from Koobi Fora and Olduvai Gorge. *Nature* 291, 574–77.

——— & KROLL, E.M. 1986. Systematic butchery by Plio/Pleistocene hominids at Olduvai Gorge, Tanzania. *Current Anth.* 27, 431–52.

CALDER, A.M. 1977. Survival properties of organic residues through the human digestive tract. *Journal of Arch. Science* 4, 141–51.

CALLEN, E.O. 1967. Analysis of the Tehuacán coprolites, in *The Prehistory of the Tehuacán Valley, 1: Environment and Subsistence* (D.S. Byers ed.), 261–89. Austin: London.

——— 1969. Diet as revealed by coprolites, in *Science in Archaeology* (D.R. Brothwell & E.S. Higgs eds.), 235–43. Thames & Hudson: London.

——— & CAMERON, T.W.M. 1960. A prehistoric diet revealed in coprolites. *New Scientist* 8, 35–40.

CASTEEL, R.W. 1974a. *Fish Remains in Archaeology and Paleo-environmental Studies.* Academic Press: New York & London.

———1974b. A method for estimation of live weight of fish from the size of skeletal elements. *American Antiquity* 39, 94–98.

CHAPLIN, R.E. 1971. *The Study of Animal Bones from Archaeological Sites.* Seminar Press: London & New York.

CHISHOLM, B.S., NELSON, D.E. & SCHWARCZ, H.P. 1982. Stable carbon isotope ratios as a measure of marine versus terrestrial protein of ancient diets. *Science* 216, 1131–32.

——— 1983. Marine and terrestrial protein in prehistoric diets on the British Columbia coast. *Current Anth.* 24, 396–98.

CLOTTES, J., DUDAY, H. & GARCIA, M.A. 1981. L'Ichnologie ou la longue traque des traces. *Spelunca* 23, 38–43.

CLUTTON-BROCK, J. 1981. *Domesticated Animals from Early Times.* Heinemann/British Museum (Natural History): London.

———& GRIGSON, C. (eds.). 1983. *Animals and Archaeology, Vol. 1.* British Arch. Reports, Int. Series 163: Oxford.

COLLIER, S. & WHITE, J.P. 1976. Getting them young? Age and sex inferences on animal domestication in archaeology. *American Antiquity* 41, 96–102.

CORNWALL, I.W. 1974. *Bones for the Archaeologist.* Phoenix House: London.

CRAWFORD, D.J. 1979. Food: Tradition and change in Hellenistic Egypt. *World Arch.* 11, 136–46.

DARBY, W.J., GHALIOUNGI, P. &

GRIVETTI, L. 1977. *Food: The Gift of Osiris.* 2 vols. Academic Press: New York & London.

DAVIES, R.W. 1971. The Roman military diet. *Britannia* 3, 122–42.

DAVIS, S. 1987. *The Archaeology of Animals.* Batsford: London; Yale Univ. Press: New Haven.

DENNELL, R.W. 1974. Botanical evidence for prehistoric crop processing activities. *Journal of Arch. Science* 1, 275–84.

——— 1976. The economic importance of plant resources represented on archaeological sites. *Journal of Arch. Science* 3, 229–47.

DIMBLEBY, G. 1978. *Plants and Archaeology.* Paladin: London.

DREW, I.A., PERKINS, D. & DALY, P. 1971. Prehistoric domestication of animals: effects on bone structure. *Science* 171, 280–82.

FINE, D. & CRAIG, G.T. 1981. Buccal surface wear of human premolar and molar teeth: a potential indicator of dietary and social differentiation. *Journal of Human Evolution* 10, 335–44.

FISHER, D.C. 1984. Mastodon butchery by North American Paleo-Indians. *Nature* 308, 271–72.

FLANNERY, K.V. 1965. The ecology of early food production in Mesopotamia. *Science* 147, 247–55.

FORBES, H.A. & FOXHALL, L. 1978. 'The Queen of all Trees'. Preliminary notes on the Archaeology of the Olive. *Expedition* 21, 37–47.

FORD, R.I. 1979. Paleoethnobotany in American Archaeology, in *Advances in Archaeological Method and Theory 2* (M.B. Schiffer ed.), 285–336. Academic Press: New York & London.

FOXHALL, L. & FORBES, H.A. 1982. *Sitometreia:* The role of grain as a staple food in classical antiquity. *Chiron* 12, 41–90.

FUJIWARA, H. 1979. Fundamental studies in plant opal analysis (3): estimation of the yield of rice in ancient paddy fields through quantitative analysis of plant opal. *Archaeology and Natural Sciences* 12, 29–42 (in Japanese, with English summary).

——— 1982. Fundamental studies in plant opal analysis. Detection of plant opals in pottery walls of the Jomon period in Kumamoto Prefecture. *Archaeology and Natural Sciences* 14, 55–65 (in Japanese, with English summary).

GARNSEY, P. 1988. *Famine and Food Supply in the Graeco-Roman World.* Cambridge Univ. Press.

GIFFORD, D.P. 1981. Taphonomy and Paleoecology: a critical review of Archaeology's sister disciplines, in *Advances in Archaeological Method and Theory 4* (M.B. Schiffer ed.), 365–438. Academic Press: New York & London.

GILBERT, R.I. & MIELKE, J.H. (eds.). 1985 *The Analysis of Prehistoric Diets.*

Academic Press: New York & London.

GRAYSON, D.K. 1979. On the quantification of vertebrate archaeofaunas, in *Advances in Archaeological Method and Theory* 2 (M.B. Schiffer ed.), 199–237. Academic Press: London & New York.

——— 1984. *Quantitative Zooarchaeology. Topics in the analysis of archaeological faunas.* Academic Press: New York & London.

GREIG, J. 1981. The investigation of a medieval barrel-latrine from Worcester. *Journal of Arch. Science* 8, 265–82.

——— 1982. Garderobes, sewers, cesspits and latrines. *Current Arch.* 8 (2), No. 85, 49–52.

——— 1983. Plant foods in the past: a review of the evidence from northern Europe. *Journal of Plant Foods* 5, 179–214.

GRÜSS, J. 1932. Die beiden ältesten Weine unserer Kulturwelt. *Forschungen und Fortschritte* 8, 23–24.

——— 1933. Über Milchreste aus der Hallstattzeit und andere Funde. *Forschungen und Fortschritte* 9, 105–6.

HALL, A. 1986. The fossil evidence for plants in mediaeval towns. *Biologist* 33 (5), 262–67.

HALL, A.J. 1974. A lady from China's past. *National Geographic* 145 (5), 660–81.

HALL, R.A. & KENWARD, H.K. 1976. Biological evidence for the usage of Roman riverside warehouses at York. *Britannia* 7, 274–76.

HASTORF, C.A. & DeNIRO, M.J. 1985. Reconstruction of prehistoric plant production and cooking practices by a new isotopic method. *Nature* 315, 489–91.

HASTORF, C.A. & POPPER, V.S. (eds.). 1989. *Current Palaeoethnobotany: Analytical Methods and Cultural Interpretations of Archaeological Plant Remains.* Univ. of Chicago Press.

HEIZER, R.F. 1969. The anthropology of prehistoric Great Basin human coprolites, in *Science in Archaeology* (D.R. Brothwell & E.S. Higgs eds.), 244–50. Thames & Hudson: London.

HELBAEK, H. 1958. Grauballemandens sidste måltid. *Kuml* 83–116.

HESSE, B. & WAPNISH, P. 1985. *Animal Bone Archaeology: From objectives to analysis.* Taraxacum: Washington.

HIGGS, E.S. & JARMAN, M.R. 1969. The origins of agriculture: a reconsideration. *Antiquity* 43, 31–41.

HILL, H.E. & EVANS, J. 1987. The identification of plants used in prehistory from organic residues, in *Archaeometry: Further Australasian Studies* (W.R. Ambrose & J.M.J. Mummery eds.), 90–96. Australian National Univ: Canberra.

HILLMAN, G. 1981. Reconstructing crop husbandry practices from charred remains of crops, in *Farming Practice in British Prehistory* (R. Mercer ed.), 123–

62. Edinburgh Univ. Press.

HILLMAN, G.C. 1986. Plant foods in ancient diet: the archaeological role of palaeofaeces in general and Lindow Man's gut contents in particular, in *Lindow Man. The Body in the Bog* (I.M. Stead and others eds.), 99–115. British Museum Publications: London.

———, COLLEDGE, S.M. & HARRIS, D.R. 1990. Plant-food economy during the Epi-Palaeolithic period at Tell Abu Hureyra, Syria: Dietary diversity, seasonality and modes of exploitation, in *Foraging and Farming: The Evolution of Plant Exploitation* (D.R. Harris & G.C. Hillman eds.). Unwin Hyman: London.

HILLMAN, G.C., MADEYSKA, E. & HATHER, J. 1988. Wild plant foods and diet at Late Palaeolithic Wadi Kubbaniya: Evidence from charred remains, in *The Prehistory of Wadi Kubbaniya. Vol. 2: Studies in Late Palaeolithic Subsistence* (F. Wendorf and others eds.). Southern Methodist Univ. Press: Dallas.

HILLMAN, G. & others. 1985. The use of Electron Spin Resonance Spectroscopy to determine the thermal histories of cereal grains. *Journal of Arch. Science* 12, 49–58.

HILLSON, S. 1986. *Teeth.* Cambridge Univ. Press.

HOLE, F., FLANNERY, K.V. & NEELY, J.A. 1969. *Prehistory and Human Ecology of the Deh Luran Plain.* Museum of Anthropology: Ann Arbor.

HUBBARD, R.N.L.B. 1975. Assessing the botanical component of human palaeoeconomies. *Bull. Inst. Arch. London* 12, 197–205.

——— 1976. On the strength of the evidence for prehistoric crop processing activities. *Journal of Arch. Science* 3, 257–65.

JARMAN, H.N. 1972. The origins of wheat and barley cultivation, in *Papers in Economic Prehistory* (E.S. Higgs ed.), Cambridge Univ. Press, 15–26.

JARMAN, M.R. & WILKINSON, P.F. 1972. Criteria of animal domestication, in *Papers in Economic Prehistory* (E.S. Higgs ed.), 83–96. Cambridge Univ. Press.

JETT, S.C. & MOYLE, P.B. 1986. The exotic origins of fishes depicted on prehistoric Mimbres pottery from New Mexico. *American Antiquity* 51, 688–720.

JONES, G. & others. 1986. Crop storage at Assiros. *Scientific American* 254, 84–91.

KEELEY, L.H. & TOTH, N. 1981. Microwear polishes on early stone tools from Koobi Fora, Kenya. *Nature* 293, 464–5.

KEHOE, T.F. 1967. *The Boarding School Bison Drive Site.* Plains Anthropologist, Memoir 4.

——— 1973. *The Gull Lake Site: a prehistoric bison drive site in southwestern Saskatchewan.* Publications in Anth. & History No. 1:

Milwaukee Public Museum.

KILLINGLEY, J.S. 1981. Seasonality of mollusk collecting determined from 0–18 profiles of midden shells. *American Antiquity* 46, 152–58.

KIRCH, P.V. & YEN, D.E. 1982. *Tikopia: the Prehistory and Ecology of a Polynesian Outlier.* Bishop Museum Bull. 238: Honolulu.

KLEIN, R.G. & CRUZ-URIBE, K. 1984. *The Analysis of Animal Bones from Archaeological Sites.* Univ. of Chicago Press.

KNIGHTS, B.A. and others. 1983. Evidence concerning Roman military diet at Bearsden, Scotland, in the 2nd century AD. *Journal of Arch. Science* 10, 139–52.

KOIKE, H. 1979. Seasonal dating and the valve-pairing technique. *Journal of Arch. Science* 6, 63–74.

——— 1980. *Seasonal dating by growth-line counting of the clam, Meretrix lusoria. Toward a reconstruction of prehistoric shell-collecting activities in Japan.* Univ. Museum Bull. 18, Univ. of Tokyo.

———1986. Prehistoric hunting pressure and paleobiomass: an environmental reconstruction and archaeozoological analysis of a Jomon shellmound area, in *Prehistoric Hunter-Gatherers in Japan – New Research Methods* (T. Akazawa & C.M. Aikens eds.), 27–53. Univ. Museum Bull. 27, Univ. of Tokyo.

——— & OHTAISHI, N. 1985. Prehistoric hunting pressure estimated by the age composition of excavated Sika Deer (*Cervus nippon*) using the annual layer of tooth cement. *Journal of Arch. Science* 12, 443–56.

——— & OHTAISHI, N. 1987. Estimation of prehistoric hunting rates based on the age composition of sika deer (*Cervus nippon*). *Journal of Arch. Science* 14, 251–69.

LARSEN, C.S. 1983. Behavioural implications of temporal change in cariogenesis. *Journal of Arch. Science* 10, 1–8.

LEAKEY, M. 1987. Animal prints and trails, in *Laetoli, a Pliocene site in northern Tanzania* (M. Leakey & J.M. Harris eds.), 451–89. Clarendon Press: Oxford.

LEGGE, A.J. & ROWLEY-CONWY, P.A. 1987. Gazelle killing in Stone Age Syria. *Scientific American* 257 (2), 76–83.

LOY, T.H. 1983. Prehistoric blood residues: detection on tool surfaces and identification of species of origin. *Science* 220, 1269–71.

——— 1987. Recent advances in blood residue analysis, in *Archaeometry: Further Australasian Studies* (W.R. Ambrose & J.M.J. Mummery eds.), 57–65. Australian National Univ.: Canberra.

———& WOOD, A.R. 1989. Blood residue analysis at Çayönü Tepesi, Turkey. *Journal of Field Arch.* 16, 451–460.

LYMAN, R.L. 1979. Available meat from

faunal remains: a consideration of techniques. *American Antiquity* 44, 536–46.

——— 1982. Archaeofaunas and subsistence studies, in *Advances in Archaeological Method and Theory* 5, (M.B. Schiffer ed.), 331–93. Academic Press: New York & London.

MEADOW, R.H. 1980. Animal bones: problems for the archaeologist together with some possible solutions. *Paléoorient* 6, 65–77.

MEIGHAN, C.W. 1969. Molluscs as food remains in archaeological sites, in *Science in Archaeology* (D.R. Brothwell & E.S. Higgs eds.), 415–22. Thames & Hudson: London.

MELLAART, J. 1967. *Çatal Hüyük*. Thames & Hudson: London.

MELLARS, P.A. & WILKINSON, M.R. 1980. Fish otoliths as evidence of seasonality in prehistoric shell middens: the evidence from Oronsay (Inner Hebrides). *Proc. Prehist. Soc.* 46, 19–44.

van der MERWE, N.J., ROOSEVELT, A.C. & VOGEL, J.C. 1981. Isotopic evidence for prehistoric subsistence change at Parmana, Venezuela. *Nature* 292, 536–38.

van der MERWE, N.J. & VOGEL, J.C. 1978. 13C content of human collagen as a measure of prehistoric diet in Woodland North America. *Nature* 276, 815–16.

MONKS, G.M. 1981. Seasonality studies, in *Advances in Archaeological Method and Theory* 4 (M.B. Schiffer ed.), 177–240. Academic Press: New York & London.

MOORE, A.M.T. 1975. The excavation of Tell Abu Hureyra in Syria: a preliminary report. *Proc. Prehist. Soc.* 41, 50–77.

——— 1979. A pre-Neolithic farmers' village on the Euphrates. *Scientific American* 241, 50–58.

NOE-NYGAARD, N. 1974. Mesolithic hunting in Denmark illustrated by bone injuries caused by human weapons. *Journal of Arch. Science* 1, 217–48.

——— 1975. Two shoulder blades with healed lesions from Star Carr. *Proc. Prehist. Soc.* 41, 10–16.

——— 1977. Butchering and marrow-fracturing as a taphonomic factor in archaeological deposits. *Paleobiology* 3, 218–37.

——— 1987. Taphonomy in Archaeology. *Journal of Danish Arch.* 6, 7–62.

OLSEN, S.J. 1979. Archaeologically, what constitutes an early domestic animal? in *Advances in Archaeological Method and Theory* 2 (M.B. Schiffer ed.), 175–97. Academic Press: New York & London.

PATRICK, M., DE KONING, A.J. & SMITH, A.B. 1985. Gas liquid chromatographic analysis of fatty acids in food residues from ceramics found in the Southwestern Cape, South Africa. *Archaeometry* 27, 231–36.

PEARSALL, D.M. 1978. Phytolith analysis of archaeological soils: evidence for maize cultivation in Formative Ecuador. *Science* 199, 177–78.

——— 1989. *Paleoethnobotany*. Academic Press: New York & London.

PICKERING, M.P. 1989. Food for thought: an alternative to Cannibalism in the Neolithic. *Australian Arch.* 28, 35–39.

PIPERNO, D.R. 1984. A comparison and differentiation of phytoliths from maize and wild grasses: use of morphological criteria. *American Antiquity* 49, 361–83.

——— & others. 1985. Preceramic maize in Central Panama: Phytolith and pollen evidence. *American Anthropologist* 87, 871–78.

POLLARD, G.C. & DREW, I.M. 1975. Llama herding and settlement in prehispanic Northern Chile: Application of an analysis for determining domestication. *American Antiquity* 40, 296–305.

POTTS, R. 1988. *Early hominid activities at Olduvai*. Aldine de Gruyter: New York.

——— & SHIPMAN, P. 1981. Cutmarks made by stone tools on bones from Olduvai Gorge, Tanzania. *Nature* 291, 577–80.

PRICE, T.D. (ed.). 1989. *The Chemistry of Prehistoric Human Bone*. Cambridge Univ. Press.

PUECH, P-F. 1978. L'alimentation de l'homme préhistorique. *La Recherche* 9, 1029–31.

——— 1979a. The diet of early man: evidence from abrasion of teeth and tools. *Current Anth.* 20, 590–92.

——— 1979b. L'alimentation de l'homme de Tautavel d'après l'usure des surfaces dentaires, in *L'Homme de Tautavel, Dossiers de l'Arch.* 36, 84–85.

——— & PRONE, A. & KRAATZ, R. 1980. Microscopie de l'usure dentaire chez l'homme fossile: bol alimentaire et environnement. *C.r. Acad. Sciences* 290, 1413–6.

RENFREW, J. 1973. *Palaeoethnobotany*. Methuen: London; Columbia: New York.

REYNOLDS, P.J. 1979. *Iron Age Farm. The Butser Experiment*. British Museum Publications: London.

ROTTLÄNDER, R.C.A. 1986. Chemical investigation of potsherds of the Heuneburg, Upper Danube, in *Proc. 24th Int. Archaeometry Symposium* (J.S. Olin & M.J. Blackman eds.), 403–5. Smithsonian Institution: Washington.

——— & HARTKE, I. 1982. New results of food identification by fat analysis, in *Proc. 22nd Symposium on Archaeometry* (A. Aspinall & S.E. Warren eds.), 218–23. Univ. of Bradford.

——— & SCHLICHTHERLE, H. 1979. Food identification from archaeological sites. *Archaeo-Physika* 10, 260–7.

RUSSELL, M. 1987. Mortuary practices at the Krapina Neandertal site. *American Journal of Phys. Anth.* 72, 381–97.

RYDER, M.L. 1969. Remains derived from skin, in *Science in Archaeology* (D.R. Brothwell & E.S. Higgs eds.), 539–54.

Thames & Hudson: London.

SAFFIRIO, L. 1972. Food and dietary habits in ancient Egypt. *Journal of Human Evolution* 1, 297–305.

SCHOENINGER, M.J. 1979. Diet and status at Chalcatzingo: some empirical and technical aspects of Strontium analysis. *American Journal of Phys. Anth.* 51, 295–310.

——— 1981. The agricultural 'revolution': its effect on human diet in prehistoric Iran and Israel. *Paléorient* 7, 73–92.

——— & PEEBLES, C.S. 1981. Effect of mollusc eating on human bone strontium levels. *Journal of Arch. Science* 8, 391–97.

——— DeNIRO, M.J. & TAUBER, H. 1983. Stable nitrogen isotope ratios of bone collagen reflect marine and terrestrial components of prehistoric human diet. *Science* 220, 1381–83.

SCHWARCZ, H.P. & others. 1985. Stable isotopes in human skeletons of Southern Ontario: reconstructing palaeodiet. *Journal of Arch. Science* 12, 187–206.

SEALY, J.C. 1986. *Stable Carbon Isotopes and Prehistoric Diets in the South-Western Cape Province, South Africa*. British Arch. Reports, Int. Series No. 293: Oxford.

——— & van der MERWE, N.J. 1986. Isotope assessment and the seasonal mobility hypothesis in the Southwestern Cape of South Africa. *Current Anth.* 27, 135–50.

SHACKLETON, N.J. 1969. Marine molluscs in Archaeology, in *Science in Archaeology* (D.R. Brothwell & E.S. Higgs eds.), 407–14. Thames & Hudson: London.

——— 1973. Oxygen isotope analysis as a means of determining season of occupation of prehistoric midden sites. *Archaeometry* 15, 133–43.

SHEPPARD, R.A. 1985. Using shells to determine season of occupation of prehistoric sites. *New Zealand Journal of Arch.* 7, 77–93.

SHERRATT, A. 1981. Plough and pastoralism: aspects of the secondary products revolution, in *Pattern of the Past, Studies in Honour of David Clarke* (I. Hodder & others eds.), 261–305. Cambridge Univ. Press.

SHIPMAN, P. & ROSE, J.J. 1983. Early hominid hunting, butchering and carcass-processing behaviours: approaches to the fossil record. *Journal of Anth. Arch.* 2, 57–98.

SILVER, I.A. 1969. The ageing of domestic animals, in *Science in Archaeology* (D.R. Brothwell & E.S. Higgs eds.), 283–302. Thames & Hudson: London.

SINGER, R. & WYMER, J. 1982. *The Middle Stone Age at Klasies River Mouth in South Africa*. Univ. of Chicago Press.

SMITH, B.D. 1975. Towards a more accurate estimation of the meat yield of animal species at archaeological sites, in *Archaeozoological Studies* (A.T. Clason ed.), 99–106. North-Holland: Amsterdam.

———— 1984. *Chenopodium* as a prehistoric domesticate in Eastern North America: Evidence from Russell Cave, Alabama. *Science* 226, 165–67.

SPENCE, C. (ed.). 1990. *Archaeological Site Manual.* (2nd ed.) Museum of London.

SPETH, J.D. 1983. *Bison Kills and Bone Counts: Decision Making by Ancient Hunters.* Univ. of Chicago Press.

SPIESS, A.E. 1979. *Reindeer and Caribou Hunters: An Archaeological Study.* Academic Press: New York & London.

STEAD, I.M., BOURKE, J.B. & BROTHWELL, D. (eds.). 1986. *Lindow Man. The Body in the Bog.* British Museum Publications: London.

STEAD, I.M. & TURNER, R.C. 1985. Lindow Man. *Antiquity* 59, 25–29.

TAUBER, H. 1981. 13C evidence for dietary habits of prehistoric man in Denmark. *Nature* 292, 332–33.

TSUKUDA, M., SUGITA, S. & TSUKUDA, Y. 1986. Oldest primitive agriculture and vegetational environments in Japan. *Nature* 322, 632–64.

UCKO, P.J. & DIMBLEBY, G.W. (eds.). 1969. *The Domestication and Exploitation of Plants and Animals.* Duckworth: London.

UNESCO. 1984. *Recent Archaeological Discoveries in the People's Republic of China.*

VILLA, P. & others. 1986. *Cannibalism in the Neolithic. Science* 233, 431–37.

VITA-FINZI, C. & HIGGS, E.S. 1970. Prehistoric economy in the Mount Carmel area of Palestine: site catchment analysis. *Proc. Prehist. Soc.* 36, 1–37.

WEIGELT, J. 1989. *Recent Vertebrate Carcasses and their Palaeobiological Implications.* Univ. of Chicago Press.

WENDORF, F., SCHILD, R. & CLOSE, A. (eds.). 1980. *Loaves and Fishes. The Prehistory of Wadi Kubbaniya.* Southern Methodist Univ. Press: Dallas.

WHEAT, J.B. 1972. *The Olsen-Chubbuck Site: a Paleo-Indian bison kill.* Soc. for American Arch., Memoir No. 26.

WHEELER, A. & JONES, A.K.G. 1989. *Fishes.* Cambridge Univ. Press.

WHEELER, J.C. 1984. On the origin and early development of camelid pastoralism in the Andes, in *Animals and Archaeology 3: Herders and their Flocks* (J. Clutton-Brock & C. Grigson eds.), 395–410. British Arch. Reports, Int. series 202: Oxford.

WHITE, T.E. 1953. A method of calculating the dietary percentage of various food animals utilized by aboriginal peoples. *American Antiquity* 18, 393–99.

———— 1953/4. Observations on the butchering techniques of some Aboriginal peoples. *American Antiquity* 19, 160–4, 254–64.

WILSON, B. GRIGSON, C. & PAYNE, S.

(eds.). 1982. *Ageing and Sexing Animal Bones from Archaeological Sites.* British Arch. Reports, Int. Series 109: Oxford.

van ZEIST, W. & CASPARIE, W.A. (eds.). 1984. *Plants and Ancient Man: Studies in Palaeoethnobotany.* Balkema: Rotterdam & Boston.

Chapter 8: How Did They Make and Use Tools? Technology (pp. 271–306)

p. 271 **Industrial archaeology** Hudson 1963, 1979, 1983; *World Archaeology* 15 (2) 1983; and the journals *Industrial Arch.* (since 1964) and *Industrial Arch. Review* (since 1976). **Experimental archaeology** Ascher 1961; Coles 1973, 1979; Ingersoll & others 1977. See also *Dossiers de l'Archéologie* 46 (1980) and 126 (1988).

p. 272 **Recognition of human agency** Barnes 1939; Patterson 1983. Calico Hills objects: Patterson & others 1987 ("for"); Haynes 1973 ("against").

p. 273 **Ethnographic analogy** Bray 1978, p. 177 (Tairona pendant).

pp. 273–275 **Mines and quarries** In general: Shepherd 1980; *World Archaeology* 16 (2), 1984. Sieveking & Newcomer 1987 (flint mines); Bosch 1979 (Rijckholt); Jovanovic 1979, 1980 (Rudna Glava); Protzen 1986 (Inca quarrying); Alexander 1982 (salt).

pp. 275–276 **Stone transportation** Protzen 1986 (Inca); Thom 1984 (Brittany menhirs). In general: Cotterell & Kamminga 1990.

p. 276 **Construction work** Coulton 1977 (Greece); Haselberger 1985 (Didyma temple).

pp. 277–282 **Stone tool manufacture** Ethnographic studies: Gould 1980; Gould & others 1971; Hayden 1979a (Australia); Hayden 1987 (Maya). Egyptian depictions of flint knife production: Barnes 1947. **Replication studies** Crabtree 1970; Sieveking & Newcomer 1987; Toth 1987. Folsom point: Crabtree 1966; Flenniken 1978. **Heat treatment** of stone tools: Gregg & Grybush 1976; Robins & others 1978; Rowlett & others 1974. Florida chert: Purdy & Brooks 1971. Solutrean: Bordes 1969; Collins 1973. Analysis by **thermoluminescence** Melcer & Zimmerman 1977. **Refitting** Cahen & Karlin 1980; Olive 1988. For a cautious view: Bordes 1980. Etiolles example: Pigeot 1988.

pp. 282–283 **Microwear** Hayden 1979b; Meeks & others 1982; Vaughan 1985. Soviet work: Semenov 1964; Phillips 1988. Tringham's work: Tringham & others 1974. Keeley's work: Keeley 1974, 1977, 1980; Keeley & Newcomer 1977. Boomplaas experiment: Binneman & Deacon 1986. Japanese work: Akoshima 1980; Kajiwara & Akoshima 1981. Vance 1987 covers **microdebitage**; Fischer &

others 1984 (Danish projectile point tests).

p. 283 **Identifying function** de Beaune 1987a, 1987b (Paleolithic lamps); Haury 1931 (Arizona beads).

p. 284 **Technology of Stone Age art** Bahn & Vertut 1988. Thomas 1983 (Monitor Basin); Marshack 1975 (Marshack's work); Lorblanchet 1980 (Pech Merle experiment); Pales & de St Péreuse 1966 (technique of making relief-imprints); d'Errico 1987 (varnish replicas).

pp. 285–287 **Technology of animal products** General introduction: Macgregor 1985. Johnson 1985 (natural or artificial bone tools); Francis 1982 (Indian shell experiments). **Manufacture** Smith & Poggenpoel 1988 (Kasteelberg). **Function** Thompson 1954 (bone point experiments); Bahn 1976 (perforated batons); Campana 1979 (Natufian shoulder-blade); d'Errico & others 1984a, 1984b (varnish replicas); Coles 1962 (leather shield experiment).

pp. 287–290 **Wood technology** General introduction: Noël & Bocquet 1987. Particular reference to Britain: Coles & others 1978. Beaver marks: Coles & Orme 1983; Coles & Coles 1986 pl. 25. Wheeled vehicles: Piggott 1983. **Watercraft** Bass 1972, 1988; Hale 1980; Jenkins 1980 (Cheops ship); Welsh 1988 (trireme).

pp. 290–291 **Plant and animal fibers** Basketry: Adovasio 1977. Cordage impressions: Hurley 1979. Dyeing at York: Hall & Tomlinson 1984; Tomlinson 1985. **Textiles** Anton 1987; Amano 1979 (Peru); Dwyer 1973 (Nazca); Broadbent 1985 (Chibcha). Egyptian: Lucas & Harris 1962; Cockburn & Cockburn 1980. Hochdorf: Körber-Grohne 1987, 1988.

p. 291 **Fiber microwear** Cooke & Lomas 1987.

pp. 292–296 **Synthetic materials** Singer & others 1954. General works on scientific analysis: Tite 1972; Rottländer 1983; and *Dossiers de l'Archéologie* 42, 1980 (L'analyse des objets archéologiques).

pp. 292–293 **Pyrotechnology** Good general introduction: Perlès 1977. Thermal shock: Vandiver & others 1989.

pp. 293–295 **Pottery** General works: Anderson 1984; Bronitsky 1986; Matson 1969; Millet 1979; Rice 1982, 1987; Rye 1981; Shepard 1985; Van der Leeuw & Pritchard 1984. See also *World Archaeology* vols. 15 (3), 1984 (Ceramics); 21 (1), 1989 (Ceramic Technology). **Pot tempers** Bronitsky & Hamer 1986. **Firing of pots** Tite 1969. Kingery & Frierman 1974 (Karanovo sherd); Burns 1987 (kilns in Thailand); DeBoer & Lathrap 1979 (Shipibo-Conibo).

pp. 295–296 **Faience** Aspinall & others 1972. **Glass** Frank 1982; also Biek & Bayley 1979; Smith 1969; Bimson & Freestone 1987. Green & Hart 1987 (Roman glass). Sayre & Smith 1961 (glass analyses); Henderson 1980; Hughes 1972 (British Iron Age).

pp. 296–304 **Archaeometallurgy** General works: Tylecote 1962, 1976; Lamberg-Karlovsky 1970. See also *World Archaeology* 20 (3), 1989. Coghlan 1951 (Old World); Tylecote 1987 (Europe); Tylecote 1986 (Britain); Benson 1979; Bray 1978 (S. America).

p. 299 **Alloying** Eaton & McKerrell 1976. Hendy & Charles 1970 (Byzantine coins).

pp. 299–302 **Casting** Long 1965; Bray 1978 (lost-wax method). Bruhns 1972 (preserved molds); Rottländer 1986 (residues). Barnard & Tamotsu 1965; Barnard 1961 (Chinese metallurgy).

pp. 303–304 **Silver** Blanco & Luzon 1969 (Rio Tinto). **Fine metalwork** Wulff 1966 (traditional methods). Grossman 1972 (goldwork). **Plating** Lechtman 1984; Lechtman and others 1982 (Loma Negra work). **Iron** Coghlan 1956.

Box Features

pp. 280–281 **Refitting and Microwear Studies** Meer site: Cahen & Keeley 1980; Cahen & others 1979; van Noten 1978; van Noten & others 1980.

pp. 286–287 **Woodworking in the Somerset Levels** Coles & Coles 1986.

p. 298 **Metallographic Examination** Brothwell & Higgs 1969.

pp. 300–301 **Copper Production in Peru** Shimada & others 1982; Merkel & Shimada 1988.

p. 305 **Early Steelmaking** Ethnoarchaeology in general: Kramer 1979. Haya of Tanzania: Schmidt & Avery 1978; van Noten & Raymaekers 1988.

Bibliography

ADOVASIO, J.M. 1977. *Basketry Technology. A Guide to Identification and Analysis.* Aldine: Chicago.

AKOSHIMA, K. 1980. An experimental study of microflaking. *Kokogaku Zasshi* (Journal of the Arch. Soc. of Nippon) 66, 357–83 (English summary).

ALEXANDER, J. 1982. The prehistoric salt trade in Europe. *Nature* 300, 577–78.

AMANO, Y. 1979. *Textiles of the Andes.* Heian/Dohosa: San Francisco.

ANDERSON, A. 1984. *Interpreting Pottery.* Batsford: London.

ANTON, F. 1987. *Ancient Peruvian Textiles.* Thames and Hudson: London.

ASCHER, R. 1961. Experimental archaeology. *American Anthropologist* 63, 793–816.

ASPINALL, A. and others. 1972. Neutron activation analysis of faience beads. *Archaeometry* 14, 27–40.

BAHN, P.G. 1976. Les bâtons percés....réveil d'une hypothèse abandonnée. *Bull. Soc. Préhist. Ariège* 31, 47–54.

———— & VERTUT, J. 1988. *Images of the Ice Age.* Windward: Leicester; Facts on File: New York.

BARNARD, N. 1961. *Bronze Casting and Bronze Alloys in Ancient China.* Australian National Univ. Canberra.

———— & TAMOTSU, S. 1965. *Metallurgical Remains of Ancient China.* Nichiosha: Tokyo.

BARNES, A.S. 1939. The differences between natural and human flaking on prehistoric flint implements. *American Anthropologist* 41, 99–112.

———— 1947. The technique of blade production in Mesolithic and Neolithic times. *Proc. Prehist. Soc.* 13, 101–13.

BASS, G. (ed.) 1972. *A History of Seafaring based on Underwater Archaeology.* Thames & Hudson: London.

———— (ed.) 1988. *Ships & Shipwrecks of the Americas.* Thames & Hudson: London & New York.

de BEAUNE, S. 1987a. *Lampes et godets au Paléolithique.* Supplément à Gallia Préhistoire.

———— 1987b. Palaeolithic lamps and their specialization: a hypothesis. *Current Anth.* 28, 569–77.

BENSON, E.P. (ed.) 1979. *Pre-Columbian Metallurgy of South America.* Dumbarton Oaks Research Library: Washington, DC.

BIEK, L. & BAYLEY, J. 1979. Glass and other vitreous materials. *World Arch.* 11, 1–25.

BIMSON, M & FREESTONE, J.C. (eds.). 1987. *Early Vitreous Materials.* British Museum Occasional Paper 56. British Museum: London.

BINNEMAN, J. & DEACON, J. 1986. Experimental determination of use wear on stone adzes from Boomplaas Cave, South Africa. *Journal of Arch. Science* 13, 219–28.

BLANCO, A. & LUZON, J.M. 1969. Pre-Roman silver miners at Riotinto. *Antiquity* 43, 124–31.

BORDES, F. 1969. Traitement thermique du silex au Solutréen. *Bull. Soc. Préhist. française* 66, 197.

———— 1980. Question de contemporanéité: l'illusion des remontages. *Bull. Soc. Préhist. française,* 77, 132–33; also see 230–34.

BOSCH, P.W. 1979. A Neolithic flint mine. *Scientific American* 240, 98–103.

BRAY, W. 1978. *The Gold of El Dorado.* Times Newspapers Ltd: London.

BROADBENT, S.M. 1985. Chibcha textiles in the British Museum. *Antiquity* 59, 202–5.

BRONITSKY, G. 1986. The use of materials science techniques in the study of pottery construction and use, in *Advances in Archaeological method and Theory* 9 (M.B. Schiffer ed.), 209–76. Academic Press: New York & London.

———— & HAMER, R. 1986. Experiments in ceramic technology. The effects of various tempering materials on impact and thermal-shock resistance. *American Antiquity* 51, 89–101.

BRUHNS, K.O. 1972. Two prehispanic *cire perdue* casting moulds from Colombia. *Man* 7, 308–11.

BURNS, P.L. 1987. Thai ceramics: the archaeology of the production centres, in *Archaeometry: Further Australasian Studies* (W.R. Ambrose & J.M.J. Mummery eds.), 203–12. Australian National Univ: Canberra.

CAHEN, D. & KARLIN, C. 1980. Les artisans de la préhistoire. *La Recherche* 116, 1258–68.

CAHEN, D. & KEELEY, L.H. 1980. Not less than two, not more than three. *World Arch.* 12, 166–80.

CAHEN, D., KEELEY, L.H. & Van NOTEN, F. 1979. Stone tools, tool-kits and human behaviour in prehistory. *Current Anth.* 20, 661–83.

CAMPANA, D.V. 1979. A Natufian shaft-straightener from Mugharet E1 Wad, Israel: an example of wear-pattern analysis. *Journal of Field Arch.* 6, 237–42.

COCKBURN, A. & E. (eds.). 1980. *Mummies, Disease and Ancient Cultures.* Cambridge Univ. Press.

COGHLAN, H.H. 1951. *Notes on the Prehistoric Metallurgy of Copper and Bronze in the Old World.* Pitt Rivers Museum: Oxford.

———— 1956. *Notes on Prehistoric and Early Iron in the Old World.* Pitt Rivers Museum: Oxford.

COLES, B. & J. 1986. *Sweet Track to Glastonbury. The Somerset Levels Project.* Thames and Hudson: London.

COLES, J.M. 1962. European bronze shields. *Proc. Prehist. Soc.* 28, 156–90.

———— 1973. *Archaeology by Experiment.* Hutchinson: London.

———— 1979. *Experimental Archaeology.* Academic Press: New York & London.

————, HEAL, S.V.E. & ORME, B.J. 1978. The use and character of wood in prehistoric Britain and Ireland. *Proc. Prehist. Soc.* 44, 1–46.

COLES, J.M. & ORME, B.J. 1983. *Homo sapiens* or *Castor fiber*? *Antiquity* 57, 95–102.

COLLINS, M.B. 1973. Observations on the thermal treatment of chert in the Solutrean of Laugerie-Haute, France. *Proc. Prehist. Soc.* 39, 461–66.

COOKE, W.D. & LOMAS, B. 1987. Ancient textiles – modern technology. *Archaeology Today* 8 (2), March, 21–25.

COTTERELL, B. & KAMMINGA, J. 1990. *Mechanics of Pre-Industrial Technology.* Cambridge Univ. Press.

COULTON, J.J. 1977. *Greek Architects at work: problems of structure and design.* Cornell Univ. Press.

CRABTREE, D.E. 1966. A stoneworker's approach to analyzing and replicating the Lindenmeier Folsom. *Tebiwa* 9, 3–139.

———— 1970. Flaking stone with wooden

implements. *Science* 169, 146–53.

DeBOER, W.R. & LATHRAP, D.W. 1979. The making and breaking of Shipibo-Conibo ceramics, in *Ethnoarchaeology: Implications of Ethnography for Archaeology* (C. Kramer ed.), 102–38. Columbia Univ. Press: New York.

DWYER, J.P. 1973 *Paracas and Nazca Textiles*. Museum of Fine Arts: Boston.

EATON, E.R. & McKERRELL, H. 1976. Near Eastern alloying and some textual evidence for the early use of arsenical copper. *World Arch.* 8, 169–91.

d'ERRICO, F. 1987. Nouveaux indices et nouvelles techniques microscopiques pour la lecture de l'art gravé mobilier. *Comptes rendus de l'Acad. Sciences Paris* 304, série II, 761–64.

———, GIACOBINI, G. & PUECH, P-F. 1984a. Varnish replicas: a new method for the study of worked bone surfaces. *Ossa. International Journal of Skeletal Research* 9/10, 29–51.

——— 1984b. Les répliques en vernis des surfaces osseuses façonnées: études expérimentales. *Bull. Soc. Préhist. française* 81, 169–70.

FISCHER, A. & others. 1984. Macro and micro wear traces on lithic projectile points. Experimental results and prehistoric examples. *Journal of Danish Arch.* 3, 19–46.

FLENNIKEN, J.J. 1978. Reevaluating the Lindenmeier Folsom: a replication experiment in lithic technology. *American Antiquity* 43, 473–80.

FORBES, R.J. (series) *Studies in Ancient Technology*. E.J. Brill: Leiden.

FRANCIS, P. Jr. 1982. Experiments with early techniques for making whole shells into beads. *Current Anth.* 23, 13–14.

FRANK, S. 1982. *Glass and Archaeology*. Academic Press: New York & London.

GOULD, R.A. 1980. *Living Archaeology*. Cambridge Univ. Press.

———, KOSTER, D.A. & SONTZ, D.A. 1971. The lithic assemblages of the Western Desert Aborigines of Australia. *American Antiquity* 36, 149–69.

GREEN, L.R. & HART, F.A. 1987. Colour and chemical composition in ancient glass: an examination of some Roman and Wealden glass by means of Ultraviolet-Visible-Infra-red Spectrometry and Electron Microprobe Analysis. *Journal of Arch. Science* 14, 271–82.

GREGG, M.L. & GRYBUSH, R.J. 1976. Thermally altered siliceous stone from prehistoric contexts: intentional vs unintentional. *American Antiquity* 41, 189–92.

GROSSMAN, J.W. 1972. An ancient gold worker's toolkit: the earliest metal technology in Peru. *Archaeology* 25, 270–75.

HALE, J.R. 1980. Plank-built in the Bronze Age. *Antiquity* 54, 118–27.

HALL, A.R. & TOMLINSON, P.R. 1984.

Dyeplants from Viking York. *Antiquity* 58, 58–60.

HASELBERGER, L. 1985. The construction plans for the temple of Apollo at Didyma. *Scientific American* 253, 114–22.

HAURY, E.W. 1931. Minute beads from prehistoric pueblos. *American Anthropologist* 33, 80–87.

HAYDEN, B. 1979a. *Palaeolithic Reflections. Lithic technology and ethnographic excavations among Australian Aborigines*. Australian Inst. of Aboriginal Studies: Canberra.

——— (ed.). 1979b. *Lithic use-wear analysis*. Academic Press: New York & London.

——— (ed.). 1987. *Lithic Studies among the Contemporary Highland Maya*. Univ. of Arizona Press: Tucson.

HAYNES, C.V. 1973. The Calico Site: Artifacts or Geofacts? *Science* 181, 305–10.

HENDERSON, J. 1980. Some new evidence for Iron Age glass-working in Britain. *Antiquity* 54, 60–61.

HENDY, M.F. & CHARLES, J.A. 1970. The production techniques, silver content and circulation history of the twelfth-century Byzantine Trachy. *Archaeometry* 12, 13–21.

HODGES, H. 1964. *Artifacts: an introduction to early materials and technology*. John Baker: London.

——— 1971. *Technology in the Ancient World*. Penguin Books: Harmondsworth & Baltimore.

HUDSON, K. 1963. *Industrial Archaeology*. John Baker: London.

——— 1979. *World Industrial Archaeology*. Cambridge Univ. Press.

——— 1983. *The Archaeology of the Consumer Society*. Heinemann: London.

HUGHES, M.J. 1972. A technical study of opaque red glass of the Iron Age in Britain. *Proc. Prehist. Soc.* 38, 98–107.

HURLEY, W.M. 1979. *Prehistoric Cordage. Identification of Impressions on Pottery*. Taraxacum: Washington.

INGERSOLL, D., YELLEN, J.E. & MACDONALD, W. (eds.). 1977. *Experimental Archaeology*. Columbia Univ. Press: New York.

JENKINS, N. 1980. *The Boat beneath the Pyramid*. Thames & Hudson: London; Holt, Rinehart & Winston: New York.

JOHNSON, E. 1985. Current developments in bone technology, in *Advances in Archaeological Method and Theory* 8 (M.B. Schiffer ed.), 157–235. Academic Press: New York & London.

JOVANOVIC, B. 1979. The technology of primary copper mining in South-East Europe. *Proc. Prehist. Soc.* 45, 103–10.

——— 1980. The origins of copper mining in Europe. *Scientific American* 242, 114–20.

KAJIWARA, H. & AKOSHIMA, K. 1981. An experimental study of microwear polish on shale artifacts. *Kokogaku Zasshi*

(Journal of the Arch. Soc. of Nippon) 67, 1–36. (English summary).

KEELEY, L.H. 1974. Technique and methodology in microwear studies: a critical review. *World Arch.* 5, 323–36.

——— 1977. The function of Palaeolithic stone tools. *Scientific American* 237, 108–26.

——— 1980. *Experimental determination of stone tool uses. A microwear analysis*. Univ. of Chicago Press.

——— & NEWCOMER, M.H. 1977. Microwear analysis of experimental flint tools: a test case. *Journal of Arch. Science* 4, 29–62.

KINGERY, W.D. & FRIERMAN, J.D. 1974. The firing temperature of a Karanovo sherd and inferences about South-East European Chalcolithic refractory technology. *Proc. Prehist. Soc.* 40, 204–5.

KÖRBER-GROHNE, V. 1987. Les restes de plantes et d'animaux de la tombe princière d'Hochdorf, in *Trésors des Princes Celtes*. Exhibition catalog, Min. de la Culture: Paris.

——— 1988. Microscopic methods for identification of plant fibres and animal hairs from the Prince's Tomb of Hochdorf, Southwest Germany. *Journal of Arch. Science* 15, 73–82.

KRAMER, C. 1979. *Ethnoarchaeology: Implications of Ethnography for Archaeology*. Columbia Univ. Press: New York.

LAMBERG-KARLOVSKY, C.C. 1970. Historical continuity, stage and process: the development of a metallurgical technology. *Zbornik Narodnog Muzeja u Beogradu* (Recueil du Musée National de Beograde) 6, 349–60.

LECHTMAN, H. 1984. Pre-Columbian surface metallurgy. *Scientific American* 250, 38–45.

———, ERLIJ, A. & BARRY, E.J. 1982. New perspectives on Moche metallurgy: Techniques of gilding copper at Loma Negra, Northern Peru. *American Antiquity* 47, 3–30.

LONG, S.V. 1965. Cire-perdue casting in pre-Columbian America: an experimental approach. *American Antiquity* 30, 189–92.

LORBLANCHET, M. 1980. Peindre sur les parois des grottes, in *Revivre la Préhistoire*, Dossiers de l'Archéologie 46, 33–39.

LUCAS, A. & HARRIS, J.R. 1962. *Ancient Egyptian Materials and Industries*. Arnold: London.

MACGREGOR, A. 1985. *Bone, Antler, Ivory and Horn Technology*. Croom Helm: London.

MARSHACK, A. 1975. Exploring the mind of Ice Age man. *National Geographic* 147, 62–89.

MATSON, F.R. 1969. Some aspects of ceramic technology, in *Science in Archaeology* (D.R. Brothwell & E.S. Higgs eds.), 592–602. Thames and

Hudson: London.

MEEKS, N.D. and others. 1982. Gloss and use-wear traces on flint sickles and similar phenomena. *Journal of Arch. Science* 9, 317–40.

MELCER, C.L. & ZIMMERMAN, D.W. 1977. Thermoluminescent determination of prehistoric heat treatment of chert artifacts. *Science* 197, 1359–62.

MERKEL, J. & SHIMADA, I. 1988. Arsenical copper smelting at Batán Grande, Peru. *IAMS* (Institute for ArchaeoMetallurgical Studies) No. 12, June, 4–7.

MILLET, M. (ed.). 1979. *Pottery and the Archaeologist*. Institute of Arch.: London.

NOEL, M. & BOCQUET, A. 1987. *Les Hommes et le Bois: Histoire et Technologie du Bois de la Préhistoire à Nos Jours*. Hachette: Paris.

Van NOTEN, F. 1978. *Les Chasseurs de Meer*. Dissertationes Archaeologicae Gandenses 18. De Tempel: Bruges.

——, CAHEN, D. & KEELEY, L.H. 1980. A Palaeolithic campsite in Belgium. *Scientific American* 242, 44–51.

Van NOTEN, F. & RAYMAEKERS, J. 1988. Early iron smelting in Central Africa. *Scientific American* 258 (6), 84–91.

ODELL, G.H. 1975. Micro-wear in perspective: a sympathetic response to Lawrence H. Keeley. *World Arch.* 7, 226–40.

OLIVE, M. 1988. *Une Habitation Magdalénienne d'Etiolles, l'Unité P15*. Mémoire 20 de la Soc. Préhist. française.

PALES, L. & de ST PÉREUSE, M.T. 1966. Un cheval-prétexte: retour au chevêtre. *Objets et Mondes* 6, 187–206.

PATTERSON, L.W. 1983. Criteria for determining the attributes of man-made lithics. *Journal of Field Arch.* 10, 297–307.

—— & others. 1987. Analysis of lithic flakes at the Calico Site, California. *Journal of Field Arch.* 14, 91–106.

PERLES, C. 1977. *Préhistoire du Feu*. Masson: Paris.

PHILLIPS, P. 1988. Traceology (microwear) studies in the USSR. *World Arch.* 19 (3), 349–56.

PIGEOT, N. 1988. *Magdaléniens d'Etiolles: Economie de Débitage et Organisation Sociale*. Centre National de la Recherche Scientifique: Paris.

PIGGOTT, S. 1983. *The Earliest Wheeled Transport*. Thames and Hudson: London.

PROTZEN, J-P. 1986. Inca Stonemasonry. *Scientific American* 254, 80–88.

PURDY, B.A. & BROOKS, H.K. 1971. Thermal alteration of silica materials: an archaeological approach. *Science* 173, 322–25.

RENFREW, C. 1979. *Problems in European Prehistory*. Edinburgh Univ. Press.

RICE, P.M. (ed.). 1982. *Pots and Potters: Current Approaches to Ceramic Archaeology*. State College: Pennsylvania State Univ. Press.

—— 1987. *Pottery Analysis: a Sourcebook*. Chicago Univ. Press.

ROBINS, G.V. & others. 1978. Identification of ancient heat treatment in flint artefacts by ESR spectroscopy. *Nature* 276, 703–4.

ROTTLÄNDER, R.C.A. 1983. *Einführung in die naturwissenschaftlichen Methoden der Archäologie*. Verlag Arch. Venatoria, Band 6: Tübingen.

—— 1986. Chemical investigation of potsherds of the Heuneburg, Upper Danube, in *Proc. 24th Int. Archaeometry Symposium* (J.S. Olin & M.J. Blackman eds.), 403–5. Smithsonian Inst. Press: Washington DC.

ROWLETT, R.M., MANDEVILLE, M.D. & ZELLER, E.J. 1974. The interpretation and dating of humanly worked siliceous materials by thermoluminescence analysis. *Proc. Prehist. Soc.* 40, 37–44.

RYE, O.S. 1981. *Pottery Technology*. Taraxacum: Washington.

SAYRE, E.V. & SMITH, R.W. 1961. Compositional categories of ancient glass. *Science* 133, 1824–26.

SCHMIDT, P. & AVERY, D.H. 1978. Complex iron smelting and prehistoric culture in Tanzania. *Science* 201, 1085–89.

SEMENOV, S.A. 1964. *Prehistoric Technology*. Cory, Adams & McKay: London.

SHEPARD, A.O. 1985. *Ceramics for the Archaeologist*. Carnegie Institute, 12th reprint.

SHEPHERD, R. 1980. *Prehistoric Mining and Allied Industries*. Academic Press: New York & London.

SHIMADA, I., EPSTEIN, S. & CRAIG, A.K. 1982. Batán Grande: a prehistoric metallurgical center in Peru. *Science* 216, 952–59.

SIEVEKING, G. & NEWCOMER, M.H. (eds.). 1987. *The Human Uses of Flint and Chert*. Cambridge Univ. Press.

SINGER, C., HOLMYARD, E.J. & HALL, A.R. 1954. *A History of Technology: I*. Clarendon Press: Oxford.

SMITH, A.B. & POGGENPOEL, C. 1988. The technology of bone tool fabrication in the South-western Cape, South Africa. *World Arch.* 20 (1), 103–15.

SMITH, R.W. 1969. The analytical study of glass in archaeology, in *Science in Archaeology* (D.R. Brothwell & E.S. Higgs eds.), 614–23. Thames and Hudson: London.

THOM, A. 1984. Moving and erecting the menhirs. *Proc. Prehist. Soc.* 50, 382–84.

THOMAS, D.H. 1983. *The Archaeology of Monitor Valley: Gatecliff Shelter*. Anth. Papers of the American Museum of Natural History, New York, vol. 59.

THOMPSON, M.W. 1954. Azilian harpoons. *Proc. Prehist. Soc.* 20, 193–211.

TITE, M.S. 1969. Determination of the firing temperature of ancient ceramics by measurement of thermal expansion.

Archaeometry 11, 131–44.

—— 1972. *Methods of Physical Examination in Archaeology*. Seminar Press: London & New York.

TOMLINSON, P. 1985. Use of vegetative remains in the identification of dye plants from waterlogged 9th–10th century AD deposits at York. *Journal of Arch. Science* 12, 269–83.

TOTH, N. 1987. The first technology. *Scientific American* 256 (4), 104–13.

TRINGHAM, R. & others. 1974. Experimentation in the formation of edge damage: a new approach to lithic analysis. *Journal of Field Arch.* 1, 171–96.

TYLECOTE, R.F. 1962. *Metallurgy in Antiquity*. Arnold: London.

—— 1976. *A History of Metallurgy*. Metals Soc.: London.

—— 1986. *The Prehistory of Metallurgy in the British Isles*. Institute of Metals.

—— 1987. *The Early History of Metallurgy in Europe*. Longman: London & New York.

VAN DER LEEUW, S.E. & PRITCHARD, A. (eds.). 1984. *The Many Dimensions of Pottery*. Univ. of Amsterdam.

VANCE, E.D. 1987. Microdebitage and archaeological activity analysis. *Archaeology* July/Aug., 58–59.

VANDIVER, P.B., SOFFER, O., KLIMA, B. & SVOBODA, J. 1989. The origins of ceramic technology at Dolni Vestonice, Czechoslovakia. *Science* 246, 1002–8.

VAUGHAN, P. 1985. *Use-wear Analysis of Flaked Stone Tools*. Univ. of Arizona Press: Tucson.

WELSH, F. 1988. *Building the Trireme*. Constable: London.

WHITE, K.D. 1984. *Greek and Roman Technology*. Thames & Hudson: London; Cornell Univ. Press: Ithaca, N.Y.

WULFF, H.E. 1966. *The Traditional Crafts of Persia*. MIT Press: Cambridge, Mass.

Chapter 9: What Contact Did They Have? Trade and Exchange (pp. 307–338)

pp. 307–313 **Study of interaction**
Exchange, economic and ethnographic background: Mauss 1925; Polanyi 1957; Sahlins 1972; Wallerstein 1974 & 1980; Gregory 1982; Appadurai 1986. Kula exchange network: Malinowski 1922; also Leach & Leach 1983. Primitive **valuables**: Dalton 1977; Renfrew 1978 & 1986; and especially Clark, J.G.D. 1986.

pp. 314–320 **Characterization** of traded materials: Tite 1972; Peacock 1982; Harbottle 1982; Brothwell & Higgs 1969; Catling & Millett 1965. Sourcing of marble: Craig 1972; Herz & Wenner 1981.

pp. 320–327 **Distribution** patterns of traded items: Hodder & Orton 1976. Stone axes: Cummins 1974; Clark 1965. Obsidian: Renfrew 1969; Renfrew &

Dixon 1976; Renfrew, Dixon & Cann 1968. Roman pottery: Peacock 1982. Prehistoric pottery: Peacock 1969. Wreck sites, with maritime trading patterns: Muckelroy 1980.

pp. 327–330 **Production** Torrence 1986; and Renfrew & Wagstaff 1982 (Melos); Singer 1984; Leach 1984 (Colorado Desert); Kohl 1975 (chlorite bowls); Peacock 1982 (Roman Britain).

pp. 330–332 **Consumption** Sidrys 1977 (Maya obsidian).

pp. 332–338 **Exchange: complete system** Renfrew 1975 and Pires-Ferreira 1976 (Mexico); Hedeager 1978 (buffer zone); Renfrew 1975 (trade and rise of the state); Wallerstein 1974 & 1980; Kohl 1987 ("world system"); Wells 1980; Frankenstein & Rowlands 1978 (Early Iron Age society); Rathje 1973 (Maya trade). See also Hodges 1982 (trade in early medieval Europe).

Box Features
p. 310 **Modes of Exchange** Polanyi 1957; Sahlins 1972.

pp. 312–313 **Materials of Prestige Value** Clark, J.G.D. 1986.

pp. 316–317 **Analysis of Artifact Composition** Tite 1972; Harbottle 1982.

p. 319 **Lead Isotope Analysis** Gale & Stos-Gale 1982.

p. 323 **Trend Surface Analysis** Cummins 1974, 1979.

p. 324 **Fall-off Analysis** Peacock 1982.

pp. 328–329 **Distribution: the Kaş Wreck** Bass 1987; Bass & others 1984, 1989.

p. 331 **Production: Greenstone Artifacts in Australia** McBryde 1979, 1984; McBryde & Harrison 1981.

p. 337 **Interaction Spheres: Hopewell** Brose & Greber 1979; Seeman 1979; Struever & Houart 1972; Braun 1986.

Bibliography

APPADURAI, A. (ed.). 1986. *The Social Life of Things*. Cambridge Univ. Press.

BASS, G.F. 1987. Splendors of the Bronze Age. *National Geographic*, 693–732.

———, FREY, D.A. & PULAK, C. 1984. A Late Bronze Age Shipwreck at Kaş, Turkey. *Internat. Journal of Nautical Arch.* 13 (4), 271–279.

———, PULAK, C., COLLON, D. & WEINSTEIN, J. 1989. The Bronze Age Shipwreck at Ulu Burun: 1986 Campaign. *American Journal of Arch.* 93, 1–29.

BRAUN, D.P. 1986. Midwestern Hopewellian exchange and supralocal interaction, in *Peer Polity Interaction and Socio-Political Change* (C. Renfrew and J.F. Cherry eds.), 117–126. Cambridge Univ. Press.

BROSE, D. & GREBER, N. (eds.). 1979. *Hopewell Archaeology: The Chillicothe Conference*. Kent State Univ. Press.

BROTHWELL, D. & HIGGS, E. (eds.). 1969. *Science in Archaeology*. (2nd ed.) Thames & Hudson: London.

CATLING, H.W. & MILLETT, A. 1965. A Study of the Inscribed Stirrup-jars from Thebes. *Archaeometry* 8, 3–85.

CLARK, J.G.D. 1965. Traffic in Stone Axe and Adze Blades. *Economic History Review* 18, 1–28.

——— 1986. *Symbols of excellence: precious materials as expressions of status*. Cambridge Univ. Press.

CRAIG, H. & V. 1972. Greek marbles: determination of provenance by isotopic analysis. *Science* 176, 401–3.

CUMMINS, W.A. 1974. The neolithic stone axe trade in Britain. *Antiquity* 68, 201–5.

——— 1979. Neolithic stone axes – distribution and trade in England and Wales, in *Stone axe studies* (T.H. Clough & W.A. Cummins eds.), 5–12. CBA Research Report No. 23: London.

DALTON, G. 1977. Aboriginal Economies in Stateless Societies, in *Exchange Systems in Prehistory* (T.K. Earle & J.E. Ericson eds.), 191–212. Academic Press: New York & London.

EARLE, T.K. & ERICSON, J.E. (eds.). 1977. *Exchange Systems in Prehistory*. Academic Press: New York & London.

FRANKENSTEIN, S. & ROWLANDS, M.J. 1978. The internal structure and regional context of Early Iron Age society in south-western Germany. *Bulletin of the Institute of Arch*. 15, 73–112.

GALE, N.H. & STOS-GALE, Z.A. 1982. Bronze copper sources in the Mediterranean: A new approach. *Science* 216, 11–20.

GREGORY, C.A. 1982. *Gifts and commodities*. Cambridge Univ. Press.

HARBOTTLE, G. 1982. Chemical Characterization in Archaeology, in *Contexts for Prehistoric Exchange* (J.E. Ericson & T.K. Earle eds.), 13–51. Academic Press: New York & London.

HEDEAGER, L. 1978. A Quantitative Analysis of Roman Imports in Europe North of the Limes (0–400 A.D.), and the Question of Roman-Germanic Exchange, in *New Directions in Scandinavian Archaeology* (K. Kristiansen & C. Paluden-Müller eds.), 191–216. National Museum of Denmark: Copenhagen.

HERZ, N. & WENNER, D.B. 1981. Tracing the origins of marble. *Archaeology* 34 (5), 14–21.

HODDER, I. & ORTON, C. 1976. *Spatial Analysis in Archaeology*. Cambridge Univ. Press.

HODGES, R.J. 1982. *Dark Age Economics. The origins of towns and trade AD 600–1000*. Duckworth: London.

KOHL, P.L. 1975. Carved chlorite vessels. *Expedition* 18, 18–31.

——— 1987. The use and abuse of World Systems theory. *Advances in Archaeological Method and Theory*. 11 (M.B. Schiffer ed.), 1–36. Academic Press: New York & London.

LEACH, H.M. 1984. Jigsaw: reconstructive lithic technology, in *Prehistoric Quarries and Lithic Production* (J.E. Ericson & B.A. Purdy eds.), 107–18. Cambridge Univ. Press.

LEACH, J.W. & LEACH, E. (eds.). 1983. *The Kula. New Perspectives on Massim Exchange*. Cambridge Univ. Press.

MALINOWSKI, B. 1922. *Argonauts of the Western Pacific*. Dutton: New York; Routledge: London.

MAUSS, M.G. 1925. *The Gift*. Routledge: London.

McBRYDE, I. 1979. Petrology and prehistory: lithic evidence for exploitation of stone resources and exchange systems in Australia, in *Stone Axe Studies* (T. Clough & W. Cummins eds.), 113–24. Council for British Arch.: London.

——— 1984. Kulin greenstone quarries: the social contexts of production and distribution for the Mount William site. *World Arch*. 16, 267–85.

——— & HARRISON, G. 1981. Valued good or valuable stone? Considerations of some aspects of the distribution of greenstone artefacts in south-eastern Australia, in *Archaeological Studies of Pacific Stone Resources* (F. Leach & J. Davidson eds.), 183–208. British Arch. Reports: Oxford.

MUCKELROY, K. (ed.). 1980. *Archaeology Under Water. An Atlas of the World's Submerged Sites*. McGraw-Hill: New York & London.

PEACOCK, D.P.S. 1969. Neolithic Pottery Production in Cornwall. *Antiquity* 63, 145–49.

——— 1982. *Pottery in the Roman World: an ethnoarchaeological approach*. Longman: London & New York.

PIRES-FERREIRA, J.W. 1976. Obsidian Exchange in Formative Mesoamerica, in *The Early Mesoamerican Village* (K.V. Flannery ed.), 292–306. Academic Press: New York & London.

POLANYI, K. 1957. The economy as instituted process, in *Trade and Market in the Early Empires* (K. Polanyi, M. Arensberg & H. Pearson eds.). Free Press: Glencoe, Illinois.

RATHJE, W.L. 1973. Models for mobile Maya: a variety of constraints, in *The Explanation of Culture Change* (C. Renfrew ed.), 731–57. Duckworth: London.

RENFREW, C. 1969. Trade and culture process in European prehistory. *Current Anthropology* 10, 151–69.

——— 1975. Trade as action at a distance, in *Ancient civilization and trade* (J. Sabloff & C.C. Lamberg-Karlovsky eds.), 1–59. Univ. of New Mexico Press: Albuquerque.

——— 1978. Varna and the Social context of Early Metallurgy. *Antiquity* 52, 199–203.

——— 1986. Varna and the emergence of wealth in prehistoric Europe, in *The Social Life of Things* (A. Appadurai ed.), 141–8. Cambridge Univ. Press.

———, & DIXON, J.E. 1976. Obsidian in western Asia: a review, in *Problems in Economic and Social Archaeology* (G. de G. Sieveking, I.H. Longworth & K.E. Wilson eds.), 137–50. Duckworth: London.

———, DIXON, J.E. & CANN, J.R. 1968. Further analysis of Near Eastern obsidians. *Proc. Prehist. Soc.* 34, 319–31.

——— & SHACKLETON, N. 1970. Neolithic trade routes realigned by oxygen isotope analyses. *Nature* 228, 1062–65.

——— & WAGSTAFF, J.M. (eds.). 1982. *An Island Polity: the archaeology of exploitation in Melos.* Cambridge Univ. Press.

SAHLINS, M.D. 1972. *Stone Age Economics.* Aldine: Chicago.

SEEMAN, M.L. 1979. *The Hopewell Interaction Sphere: the evidence for interregional trade and structural complexity.* Prehistory Research Series, Vol. 5 no. 2., Indiana Historical Society: Indianapolis.

SIDRYS, R. 1977. Mass-distance measures for the Maya obsidian trade, in *Exchange Systems in Prehistory* (T.K. Earle & J.E. Ericson eds.), 91–108. Academic Press: New York & London.

SINGER, C.A. 1984. The 63-kilometer fit, in *Prehistoric Quarries and Lithic Production* (J.E. Ericson & B.A. Purdy eds.), 35–48. Cambridge Univ. Press.

STRUEVER, S. & HOUART, G.L. 1972. An analysis of the Hopewell interaction sphere, in *Social Exchange and Interaction* (Univ. of Michigan Museum of Anthropology Anthropological Papers 46) (E.N. Wilmsen ed.), 47–79. Univ. of Michigan Museum of Anthrolopology: Ann Arbor.

TITE, M.S. 1972. *Methods of Physical examination in Archaeology.* Academic Press: London.

TORRENCE, R. 1986. *Production and exchange of stone tools: prehistoric obsidian in the Aegean.* Cambridge Univ. Press.

WALLERSTEIN, I. 1974 & 1980. *The Modern World System.* 2 vols. Academic Press: New York & London.

WELLS, P.S. 1980. *Culture contact and culture change: Early Iron Age central Europe and the mediterranean world.* Cambridge Univ. Press.

Chapter 10: What Did They Think? Cognitive Archaeology, Art, and Religion (pp. 339–370)

pp. 339–341 **Theory and method** Philosophy of science: Braithwaite 1953; Hempel 1966; Popper 1985.

pp. 341–346 **Evolution of human symbolizing faculties** Isaac 1976 (Paleolithic stone tools). **Organized behavior** of early hominids: Binford

1981. Opposing views on variability in Mousterian assemblages: Binford 1973; Binford & Binford 1966; Bordes & de Sonneville-Bordes 1970; Mellars 1969, 1970. Gamble 1986 provides a good general view of the European Paleolithic.

pp. 347–350 **Written sources** Diringer 1962. Early proto-writing of the Vinča culture: Renfrew 1973 (Ch. 9); Winn 1981. Oracle bones: Chou 1979. **Literacy in Classical Greece** Cook 1987; Camp 1986.

pp. 350–352 **Units of time** Heggie 1981 (Thom's work); Aveni 1980, 1982, 1988 (Americas). **Units of length** Heggie 1981. **Units of weight** Mohenjodaro: Wheeler 1968; Renfrew 1985a.

pp. 352–354 **Planning** O'Kelly 1982 (Newgrange); Wheatley 1971; Ward-Perkins 1974 (town planning); Lauer 1976 (Step Pyramid).

pp. 355–356 **Symbols of value** In general: Clark, J.G.D. 1986. Mainfort 1985 (Fletcher cemetery); Renfrew 1978 (Varna gold).

pp. 358–363 **Archaeology of religion** Durkheim 1912; Rappaport 1971; Renfrew 1985b (Phylakopi sanctuary); Parker Pearson 1984 (metal hoards in Scandinavian bogs); Tozzer 1957 (*cenote* at Chichén Itzá); Coe 1978 (Popol Vuh).

pp. 363–370 **Art and representation** Case for mother goddess cult argued by Gimbutas 1974; opposed by Ucko 1968. *Danzante* figures: see Chapter 13. Symmetry analysis: Washburn & Crowe 1989; Washburn 1983. Myth and philosophy in ancient societies: Frankfort & others 1946; Lévi-Strauss 1966.

Box Features

pp. 344–345 **Paleolithic Cave Art** Most up-to-date review: Bahn & Vertut 1988. Structuralist interpretation: Leroi-Gourhan 1968. Also: Leroi-Gourhan 1982; Couraud 1985.

p. 346 **Paleolithic Portable Art** Counting and notations in Paleolithic caves: Marshack 1972a. See also Marshack 1972b, 1975; Frolov 1977/79; d'Errico 1989.

p. 351 **Megalithic Yard** Thom 1967. Critical assessment: Heggie 1981.

pp. 356–357 **Maya Symbols of Power** Political symbolism of Maya art: Marcus 1974; Schele & Miller 1986. Hammond 1982 discusses "the Maya mind."

pp. 360–361 **Cult Activity at Chavin** Burger 1984; Saunders 1989.

pp. 364–365 **Individual Artists in Ancient Greece** Beazley 1965; Boardman 1974. Cycladic figurines: Getz-Preziosi 1987. General problems of attribution: Hill & Gunn 1977.

pp. 366–367 **Conventions in Egyptian Art** Schafer 1974; Robins 1986.

p. 369 **Style** Washburn 1983; Wiessner 1983; Wobst 1977; Plog 1980; Sackett 1973.

Bibliography

AVENI, A.F. 1980. *Skywatchers of Ancient Mexico.* Univ. of Texas Press: Austin.

——— (ed.). 1982. *Archaeoastronomy in the New World.* Cambridge Univ. Press.

——— (ed.). 1988. *World Archaeoastronomy.* Cambridge Univ. Press.

BAHN, P.G. & VERTUT, J. 1988. *Images of the Ice Age.* Windward: Leicester; Facts on File: New York.

BEAZLEY, J. 1965. *Attic Black Figure Vase Painters.* Oxford Univ. Press.

BINFORD, L.R. 1973. Interassemblage variability – the Mousterian and the 'functional' argument, in *The Explanation of Culture Change* (C. Renfrew ed.), 227–54. Duckworth: London.

——— 1981. *Bones, Ancient Men and Modern Myths.* Academic Press: New York & London.

BINFORD, S.R. & BINFORD, L.R. 1966. A preliminary analysis of functional variability in the Mousterian of Levallois facies. *American Anthropologist* 68, 238–95.

BOARDMAN, J. 1974. *Athenian Black Figure Vases.* Thames & Hudson: London & New York.

BORDES, F. & DE SONNEVILLE-BORDES, D. 1970. The significance of variability in Paleolithic assemblages. *World Arch.* 2, 61–73.

BRAITHWAITE, R.B. 1953. *Scientific Explanation.* Cambridge Univ. Press.

BURGER, R.L. 1984. *The Prehistoric Occupation of Chavín de Huantar, Peru.* Univ. of California Publications in Anthropology Vol. 14. Univ. of California Press: Berkeley.

CAMP, J.M. 1986. *The Athenian Agora.* Thames & Hudson: London & New York.

CHOU, H. 1979. Chinese oracle bones. *Scientific American* 240 (4), 100–9.

CLARK, J.G.D. 1986. *Symbols of Excellence: precious materials as expressions of status.* Cambridge Univ. Press.

COE, M.D. 1978. *Lords of the Underworld: Masterpieces of Classic Maya Ceramics.* Princeton Univ. Press.

COOK, B.F. 1987. *Greek Inscriptions.* British Museum Publications: London.

COURAUD, C. 1985. *L'Art Azilien. Origine – Survivance.* XXe Supplément à Gallia Préhistoire. CNRS: Paris.

DIRINGER, D. 1962. *Writing.* Thames & Hudson: London.

DURKHEIM, E. 1912. *The Elementary Forms of the Religious Life.* Transl. by J.W. Swain. Free Press: New York 1965.

d'ERRICO, F. 1989. Paleolithic lunar calendars: a case of wishful thinking? *Current Anth.* 30, 117–18, 491–500.

FLANNERY, K.V. & MARCUS, J. (eds.). 1983. *The Cloud People, Divergent Evolution of the Zapotec and Mixtec*

Civilizations. Academic Press: New York & London.

FRANKFORT, H., FRANKFORT, H.A., WILSON, J.A. & JACOBSEN, T. 1946. *Before Philosophy*. Penguin: Harmondsworth.

FROLOV, B.A. 1977/9. Numbers in paleolithic graphic art and the initial stages in the development of mathematics. *Soviet Anth. and Arch.* 16 (1977/8), 142–66; and 17 (1978/9), 41–74, 61–113.

GAMBLE, C. 1986. *The Palaeolithic Settlement of Europe*. Cambridge Univ. Press.

GETZ-PREZIOSI, P. 1987. *Early Sculptors of the Cyclades*. Univ. of Michigan. Ann Arbor.

GIMBUTAS, M. 1974. *The gods and goddesses of Old Europe 7000–3500 BC. Myths, legends and cult images*. Thames & Hudson: London.

HAMMOND, N. 1982. *Ancient Maya Civilization*. Rutgers Univ. Press, N.J.; Cambridge Univ. Press.

HEGGIE, D.C. 1981. *Megalithic Science. Ancient Mathematics and Astronomy in Northwest Europe*. Thames & Hudson: London & New York.

HEMPEL, C.G. 1966. *Philosophy of Natural Science*. Prentice-Hall: Englewood Cliffs, N.J.

HILL, J.N. & GUNN, J. (eds.). 1977. *The Individual in Prehistory*. Academic Press: New York & London.

ISAAC, G. 1976. Stages of cultural elaboration in the Pleistocene: possible archaeological indications of the development of language capabilities, in *Origins and evolution of language and speech* (S.R. Harnad, H.D. Steklis & J. Lancaster eds.), 275–88. Annals of the New York Academy of Sciences, Vol. 280.

LAUER, J.-P. 1976. *Saqqara*. Thames & Hudson: London.

LEROI-GOURHAN, A. 1968. *The Art of Prehistoric Man in Western Europe*. Thames & Hudson: London.

——— 1982. *The Dawn of European Art*. Cambridge Univ. Press.

LÉVI-STRAUSS, C. 1966. *The Savage Mind*. Weidenfeld & Nicolson: London; Univ. of Chicago Press.

MAINFORT, R.C. 1985. Wealth, Space and Status in a Historic Indian Cemetery. *American Antiquity* 50, 555–79.

MARCUS, J. 1974. The iconography of power among the Classic Maya. *World Arch.* 6, 83–94.

MARSHACK, A. 1972a. *The Roots of Civilization: the cognitive beginnings of man's first art, symbol and notation*. McGraw-Hill: New York; Weidenfeld & Nicolson: London.

——— 1972b. Cognitive aspects of Upper Paleolithic engraving. *Current Anth.* 13, 445–77. Also 15 (1974), 327–32; 16 (1975), 297–98.

——— 1975. Exploring the mind of Ice Age man. *National Geographic* 147 (1),

64–89.

MELLARS, P.A. 1969. The Chronology of Mousterian Industries in the Perigord region of South-West France. *Proc. Prehist. Soc.* 35, 134–71.

——— 1970. Some comments on the notion of 'functional variability' in stone tool assemblages. *World Arch.* 2, 74–89.

MILLER, D. and TILLEY, C. (eds.). 1984 *Ideology, Power and Prehistory*. Cambridge Univ. Press.

MITHEN, S. 1990. *Thoughtful Foragers: A Study of Prehistoric Decision Making*. Cambridge Univ. Press.

O'KELLY, M.J. 1982. *Newgrange*. Thames & Hudson: London and New York.

PARKER PEARSON, M. 1984. Economic and ideological change: cyclical growth in the pre-state societies of Jutland, in *Ideology, Power and Prehistory* (D. Miller & C. Tilley eds.), 69–92. Cambridge Univ. Press.

PLOG, S. 1980. *Stylistic Variation in Prehistoric Ceramics: Design Analysis in the American Southwest*. Cambridge Univ. Press.

POPPER, K.R. 1985. *Conjectures and refutations: the growth of scientific knowledge*. (4th ed.) Routledge & Kegan Paul: London.

RAPPAPORT, R.A. 1971. Ritual, Sanctity, and Cybernetics. *American Anthropologist* 73, 59–76.

RENFREW, C. 1973. *Before Civilization. The Radiocarbon Revolution and Prehistoric Europe*. Jonathan Cape: London.

——— 1978. Varna and the Social Context of Early Metallurgy. *Antiquity* 52, 199–203.

——— 1985a. *Towards an Archaeology of Mind*. Cambridge Univ. Press.

——— 1985b. *The Archaeology of Cult. The Sanctuary at Phylakopi*. British School of Archaeology at Athens Supplementary Vol. No. 18: London.

ROBINS, G. 1986. *Egyptian Painting and Relief*. Shire: Aylesbury.

SACKETT, J.R. 1973. Style, function and artifact variability in palaeolithic assemblages, in *The Explanation of Culture Change* (C. Renfrew ed.), 317–28. Duckworth: London.

SAUNDERS, N. 1989. *People of the Jaguar*. Souvenir Press: London.

SCHAFER, H. 1974. *Principles of Egyptian Art*. Clarendon Press: Oxford (first published 1919).

SCHELE, L. & MILLER, M.E. 1986. *The Blood of Kings, Dynasty and Ritual in Maya Art*. Kimbell Art Museum: Fort Worth; Sotheby's: London.

THOM, A. 1967. *Megalithic Sites in Britain*. Clarendon Press: Oxford.

TOZZER, A.M. 1957. *Chichen Itza and its Cenote of Sacrifice*. Peabody Museum Memoirs 11 & 12.

UCKO, P.J. 1968. *Anthropomorphic Figurines*. Royal Anthropological

Institute Occasional Paper No. 24: London.

WARD-PERKINS, J.B. 1974. *Cities of ancient Greece and Italy: planning in classical antiquity*. Sidgwick & Jackson: London.

WASHBURN, D.K. 1983. Symmetry analysis of ceramic design: two tests of the method on Neolithic material from Greece and the Aegean, in *Structure and Cognition in Art* (D.K. Washburn ed.), 138–63. Cambridge Univ. Press.

——— & CROWE, D. 1989. *Symmetries of Culture*.

WHEATLEY, P. 1971. *The Pivot of the Four Quarters: A preliminary enquiry into the origins and character of the ancient Chinese city*. Edinburgh Univ. Press.

WHEELER, R.E.M. 1968. *The Indus Civilization*. (3rd ed.) Cambridge Univ. Press.

WIESSNER, P. 1983. Style and social information in Kalahari San projectile points. *American Antiquity* 48, 253–76.

WINN, S.M.M. 1981. *Pre-Writing in Southeastern Europe: the Sign System of the Vinca Culture c. 4000 BC*. Western Publishers: Calgary.

WOBST, M. 1977. Stylistic behavior and information exchange, in *For the Director: Research Essays in Honor of James B. Griffin* (C.E. Cleland ed.), 317–42. Museum of Anthropology, Univ. of Michigan Papers 61.

Chapter 11: Who Were They? What Were They Like? The Archaeology of People (pp. 371–404)

pp. 371–372 Useful introductions to archaeological aspects of **human remains**: Brothwell 1972, 1986; Ubelaker 1984; Houghton 1980; Boddington & others 1987. Human evolution: Klein 1989; Durant 1989. Cremations: Gejvall 1969. Mummies and bogbodies: Cockburn & Cockburn 1980; Brothwell 1986. Egyptian mummies: David & Tapp 1984; David 1986; El Mahdy 1989. Scythian bodies: Rudenko 1970. Danish bodies: Glob 1973 (Bronze Age), 1969 (Iron Age). Pompeii & Herculaneum: Maiuri 1961; Gore 1984. Sutton Hoo inhumations: Bethell & Carver 1987.

pp. 372–374 **Which sex?** In general: Genoves 1969a. Pales & de St Péreuse 1976 (La Marche portraits); Iscan & Miller-Shaivitz 1984 (tibia method); Dennison 1979, Kiszely 1974 (citrate method).

pp. 374–376 **How long did they live?** In general: Genoves 1969b; Zimmerman & Angel 1986. Taung child: Bromage & Dean 1985; Dean 1985; Beynon & Dean 1988. Holly Smith's work: Smith 1986. **Computed tomography** application: Conroy & Vannier 1987. Gibraltar child: Dean & others 1986. Determining age from **bone microstructure**: Kerley 1965; Pfeiffer 1980. Chemical method of Shimoyama & Harada: *New Scientist* 2 May 1985, 22. **Interpreting age at death** Chilean mummies: Allison 1985. Problems in assessing age/sex data from cemeteries: Masset 1975.

pp. 376–377 **Height and weight** In general: Wells, L.H. 1969. Calculation from long bones: Trotter & Gleser 1958. **Facial characteristics** In general: Jordan 1983. Cotterell 1981 (terracotta army); Puech & Cianfarani 1985 p. 32 (Janssens and tomb of Marie de Bourgogne); Harris & others 1978 (Tiye and Thuya).

pp. 378–381 **How related?** Blood groups: Lengyel 1975 (Hungarian work). Radioimmunoassay of fossils: Lowenstein 1985. Human blood residues: Loy 1987. Blood group of Tutankhamun and Smenkhkare: Connolly & others 1969; Harrison & Abdalla 1972. DNA from Egyptian mummies: Pääbo 1985. Florida brains: Doran & others 1986; Benditt 1989; Pääbo 1989. A breakthrough in this field is reported by Hagelberg & others 1989.

pp. 381–382 **Walking** In general: Robinson 1972. Lucy in the trees: Stern & Susman 1983. Lucy as a biped: Latimer & others 1987. Computed axial tomography: Pahl 1980. **Footprints** Laetoli: Leakey 1979; Day & Wickens 1980; Leakey & Harris 1987, 490–523; Tuttle & others 1990. Fossil prints in general: Duday & Garcia 1986; Clottes & others 1986. Pales's work, and the Niaux prints: Pales 1976.

pp. 382–383 **Right-handedness** in Ice Age art: Bahn & Vertut 1988. See also Davidson 1986 (Nabataean); Puech 1978 (Mauer jaw); Bay 1982 (evidence from tools). Toth's work: Toth 1985.

pp. 383–385 **Speech** Endocasts: Holloway 1983; Falk 1983. Stone tools as evidence for speech: Isaac 1976; an opposite view: Dibble 1989. **Vocal tract** Neanderthal: Lieberman & Crelin 1971, 1974; an opposing view: Carlisle & Siegel 1974. Hyoid bone: Arensburg & others 1989. Skull-base analyses: Laitman 1986.

pp. 385–386 **Other behavior: Teeth** Smith 1983 (Neanderthal teeth as a third hand); Frayer & Russell 1987 (Neanderthal toothpicks). Puech & Cianfarani 1985, 32–33 (King Christian). **Hands** Musgrave 1971 (Neanderthal dexterity). **Skeletal stress** Trinkaus 1975 (Neanderthal squatting); Houghton 1980 (New Zealand); Hedges 1983 (Isbister); Molleson 1989 (Tell Abu Hureyra); Dutour 1986 (Niger/Mali). **Sexuality** Kauffmann-Doig 1979 (Peruvian pottery).

pp. 386–387 **Paleopathology** In general: Brothwell & Sandison 1967; Goldstein 1969; Hart 1983; Janssens 1970; Manchester 1983; Ortner & Putschar 1985; Wells, C. 1964. Also two journals:

Dossiers de l'Archéologie 97, Sept. 1985, "Les Maladies de nos Ancêtres;" and *World Archaeology* 21 (2) 1989, "The Archaeology of Public Health."

pp. 386–387 **Soft tissue** Vlcek 1952 (prehistoric fingerprints). Mutilated hand stencils: Groenen 1988; Bahn & Vertut 1988. Artistic representations of pathologies: e.g. *Dossiers de l'Archéologie* 97, Sept 1985, 34–41. Monte Albán figures: Marcus, in Flannery & Marcus 1983.

pp. 387–390 **Parasites and viruses** Patrucco & others 1983 (Peru); Rothhammer & others 1985 (Chagas' Disease).

pp. 390–394 **Skeletal evidence** Grimaldi skeleton: Dastugue & de Lumley 1976, 617 Little Big Horn: Scott & Connor 1986; Scott & others 1989. Cranial deformation: Trinkaus 1982 (Neanderthalers); Brown 1981 (Australian Aborigines). Shanidar man: Trinkaus 1983. Skull of Bodo: *New Scientist* 9 Sept. 1982, 688. **Disease from bone evidence** Harrison & others 1979 (Tutankhamun's tomb); Frayer & others 1987 (Paleolithic dwarf); Murdy 1981 (Olmec "were-jaguar"); Mays 1985 (Harris lines). **Toxic poisoning** In general: Ericson & Coughlin 1981. Molleson & others 1985 (Poundbury lead analysis); Beattie & Geiger 1987 (frozen sailors); Aufderheide and others 1985 (lead analysis of Colonial Americans).

pp. 394–395 **Teeth** Campbell 1981/2 (Aboriginal tooth avulsion); Davidson 1986 (Nabataeans); d'Errico & others 1988 (Isabella d'Aragona).

p. 395 **Medical knowledge** Urteaga-Ballon & Wells 1982 (Peruvian medical kit).

pp. 398–399 **Nutrition** In general: Brothwell 1969; Cohen & Armelagos 1984. Higham 1989 (Thailand). Evidence in teeth: Hillson 1979 & 1986; Smith, P. 1972. **Chemical analysis of bone** Lambert & others 1979 (Middle & Late Woodland sites); Lallo & Rose 1979 (Dickson Mounds); Larsen 1981 (Georgia).

pp. 399–400 **Population** In general: Hassan 1978, 1981; Masset 1975. Naroll 1962 (Naroll's equation); Milisauskas 1972 (LBK estimates); Casselberry 1974 (Casselberry's formula); Fox 1983 (Maori example). Other population estimates: Brothwell 1972 (Britain); Dobyns 1966 (America).

pp. 401–403 **Ethnicity and evolution: Genes** Chromosome mapping: Wainscoat & others 1986. Mitochondrial work and "Eve" theory: Cann & others 1987; Fagan 1990. Recent surveys of origins of modern humans: Fagan 1990; Stringer & Andrews 1988; Mellars & Stringer 1989/1990. For opposing views on human evolution: Leakey, R.E. 1981; Johanson & Edey 1981; Johanson & Shreeve 1989.

Box Features
p. 379 **How to Reconstruct the Face** Gerasimov 1971. Philip of Macedon: Prag 1984; Prag & others 1984.

pp. 388–389 **Looking Inside Bodies** Egyptian mummies: Cockburn & Cockburn 1980; David & Tapp 1984; David 1986; El Mahdy 1989; Goyon & Josset 1988; Harris & Weeks 1973.

pp. 392–393 **Life and Death Among the Eskimo** Hart Hansen & others 1985; Hart Hansen 1986.

pp. 396–397 **Lindow Man** Stead & others 1986; Brothwell 1986.

p. 402 **Genetics and New World Colonization** In general: Fagan 1987. Williams & others 1985 (Gm allotypes); Greenberg & others 1986 (review of linguistic, dental and genetic evidence).

Bibliography

ALLISON, M.J. 1985. Chile's ancient mummies. *Natural History*, Oct., 75–80. See also 'Les plus anciennes momies du monde' in *La Recherche* 16, No. 172, 1550–52.

ARENSBURG, B. & others. 1989. A middle palaeolithic human hyoid bone. *Nature* 338, 758–60.

AUFDERHEIDE, A.C. & others. 1985. Lead in bone III. Prediction of social correlates from skeletal lead content in four colonial American populations. *American Journal of Phys. Anth.* 66, 353–61.

BAHN, P.G. & VERTUT, J. 1988. *Images of the Ice Age*. Windward: Leicester; Facts on File: New York.

BARRIÈRE, C. 1976. *Palaeolithic art in the Grotte de Gargas*. British Archaeological Reports, Int. Series 14: Oxford.

BAY, R. 1982. La question du droitier dans l'evolution humaine. *Bull. Soc. d'Etudes et de Recherches Préhistoriques des Eyzies* 32, 7–15.

BEATTIE, O. & GEIGER, J. 1987. *Frozen in Time. The Fate of the Franklin Expedition*. Bloomsbury: London.

BENDITT, J. 1989. Molecular Archaeology. *Scientific American* 26, 12–13.

BETHELL, P.H. & CARVER, M.O.H. 1987. Detection and enhancement of decayed inhumations at Sutton Hoo, in *Death, Decay and Reconstruction* (A. Boddington & others eds.), 10–21. Manchester Univ. Press.

BEYNON, A.D. & DEAN, M.C. 1988. Distinct dental development patterns in early fossil hominids. *Nature* 335, 509–14.

BODDINGTON, A., GARLAND, A.N. & JANAWAY, R.C. (eds.). 1987. *Death, Decay and Reconstruction*. Manchester Univ. Press.

BROMAGE, T.G. & DEAN, M.C. 1985. Re-evaluation of the age at death of immature fossil hominids. *Nature* 317, 525–27.

BROTHWELL, D.R. 1969. Dietary variation and the biology of earlier human populations, in *The domestication and exploitation of plants and animals* (P.J. Ucko & G.W. Dimbleby eds.), 531–45. Duckworth: London.

—— 1972. Palaeodemography and earlier British populations. *World Arch.* 4, 75–87.

—— 1981. *Digging up bones. The excavation, treatment and study of human skeletal remains.* (3rd ed.) British Museum (Natural History): London/Oxford Univ. Press: Oxford.

—— 1986. *The Bog Man and the Archaeology of People.* British Museum Publications: London.

—— & SANDISON, A.T. (eds.). 1967. *Diseases in Antiquity.* C.C. Thomas: Springfield, Illinois.

BROWN, P. 1981. Artificial cranial deformation: a component in the variation in Pleistocene Australian Aboriginal crania. *Archaeology in Oceania* 16, 156–67.

CAMPBELL, A.H. 1981/82. Tooth avulsion in Victorian Aboriginal skulls. *Arch. in Oceania* 16/17, 116–18.

CANN, R.L., STONEKING, M. & WILSON, A.C. 1987. Mitochondrial DNA and human evolution. *Nature* 325, 31–36.

CARLISLE, R. & SIEGEL, H. 1974. Some problems in the interpretation of Neanderthal speech capabilities. *American Anthropologist* 76, 319–22.

CASSELBERRY, S.E. 1974. Further refinement of formulae for determining population from floor area. *World Arch.* 6, 116–22.

CLOTTES, J., DUDAY, H. & GARCIA, M.A. 1986. L'ichnologie ou la longue traque des traces. *Spelunca* No. 23, 38–43.

COCKBURN A. & COCKBURN, E. (eds.). 1980. *Mummies, disease and ancient cultures.* Cambridge Univ. Press.

COHEN, M.N. & ARMELAGOS, G.J. (eds.). 1984. *Palaeopathology at the origins of agriculture.* Academic Press: New York & London.

COLES, B. & J. 1989. *People of the Wetlands: Bogs, Bodies and Lake-Dwellers.* Thames & Hudson: London & New York.

CONNOLLY, R.C. and others. 1969. Kinship of Smenkhkare and Tutankhamen affirmed by serological micromethod. *Nature* 224, 325–26.

CONROY, G.C. & VANNIER, M.W. 1987. Dental development of the Taung skull from computerized tomography. *Nature* 329, 625–27.

COTTERELL, A. 1981. *The First Emperor of China.* Macmillan: London.

DASTUGUE, J. & de LUMLEY, M-A. 1976. Les maladies des hommes préhistoriques du Paléolithique et du Mésolithique, in *La Préhistoire française* Vol. 1:1 (H. de Lumley ed.), 612–22. CNRS: Paris.

DAVID, R. (ed.). 1986. *Science in Egyptology.* Manchester Univ. Press.

DAVID, R. & TAPP, E. (eds.). 1984.

Evidence Embalmed: Modern medicine and the mummies of Egypt. Manchester Univ. Press.

DAVIDSON, E. 1986. Earliest dental filling shows how ancients battled with 'tooth worms'. *Popular Archaeology* Feb, 46.

DAY, M.H. & WICKENS, E.H. 1980. Laetoli Pliocene hominid footprints and bipedalism. *Nature* 286, 385–87.

DEAN, M.C. 1985. Variation in the developing root cone angle of the permanent mandibular teeth of modern man and certain fossil hominids. *American Journal of Phys. Anth.* 68, 233–38.

——, STRINGER, C.B. & BROMAGE, T.G. 1986. Age at death of the Neanderthal child from Devil's Tower, Gibraltar, and the implication for studies of general growth and development in Neanderthals. *American Journal of Phys. Anth.* 70, 301–9.

DENNISON, K.J. 1979. Citrate estimation as a means of determining the sex of human skeletal material. *Archaeology & Phys. Anth. in Oceania* 14, 136–43.

DIBBLE, H.L. 1989. The implications of stone tools types for the presence of language during the Lower and Middle Palaeolithic, in *The Human Revolution* (P. Mellars & C. Stringer eds.), Edinburgh Univ. Press.

DOBYNS, H.F. 1966. Estimating Aboriginal American population. *Current Anthropology* 7, 395–449.

DORAN, G.H. & others. 1986. Anatomical, cellular and molecular analysis of 8,000-yr-old human brain tissue from the Windover archaeological site. *Nature* 323, 803–6.

DUDAY, H. & GARCIA, M.A. 1986. La paléo-ichnologie humaine (étude des empreintes fossiles). *Bull. Soc. Anth. Sud-Ouest* 21, 43–54.

DURANT, J.R. (ed.). 1989. *Human Origins.* Clarendon Press: Oxford.

DUTOUR, O. 1986. Enthesopathies (lesions of muscular insertions) as indicators of the activities of Neolithic Saharan populations. *American Journal of Phys. Anth.* 71, 221–24.

EL MAHDY, C. 1989. *Mummies, Myth and Magic in Ancient Egypt.* Thames & Hudson: London & New York.

ERICSON, J.E. & COUGHLIN, E.A. 1981. Archaeological toxicology. *Annals of the New York Academy of Sciences* 376, 393–403.

d'ERRICO, F., VILLA, G. & FORNACIARI, G. 1988. Dental esthetics of an Italian Renaissance noblewoman, Isabella d'Aragona. A case of chronic mercury intoxication. *Ossa* 13, 207–28.

FAGAN, B.M. 1987. *The Great Journey: The Peopling of Ancient America.* Thames & Hudson: London & New York.

—— 1990. *The Journey from Eden.* Thames & Hudson: London & New York.

FALK, D. 1983. Cerebral cortices of East

African early hominids. *Science* 221, 1072–74.

FLANNERY, K.V. & MARCUS, J. 1983. *The Cloud People: Divergent Evolution of the Zapotec and Mixtec Civilizations.* Academic Press: New York & London.

FOX, A. 1983. Pa and people in New Zealand: an archaeological estimate of population. *New Zealand Journal of Archaeology* 5, 5–18.

FRAYER, D.W. & RUSSELL, M.D. 1987. Artificial grooves in the Krapina Neanderthal teeth. *American Journal of Phys. Anth.* 74, 393–405.

—— and others. 1987. Dwarfism in an adolescent from the Italian late Upper Palaeolithic. *Nature* 330, 60–62.

GEJVALL, N-G. 1969. Cremations, in *Science in Archaeology* (D. Brothwell & E.S. Higgs eds.), 468–79. (2nd ed.) Thames & Hudson: London.

GENOVES, S. 1969a. Sex determination in earlier man, in *Science in Archaeology* (D. Brothwell & E.S. Higgs eds.), 429–39. (2nd ed.) Thames & Hudson: London.

—— 1969b. Estimation of age and mortality, in *Science in Archaeology* (D. Brothwell & E.S. Higgs eds.), 440–52. (2nd ed.) Thames & Hudson: London.

GERASIMOV, M.M. 1971. *The Face Finder.* Hutchinson: London.

GLOB, P.V. 1969. *The Bog People.* Faber: London.

—— 1973. *The Mound People. Danish Bronze Age man preserved.* Faber: London.

GOLDSTEIN, M.S. 1969. The palaeopathology of human skeletal remains, in *Science in Archaeology* (D. Brothwell & E.S. Higgs eds.), 480–89. (2nd ed.) Thames & Hudson: London.

GORE, R. 1984. The dead do tell tales at Vesuvius. *National Geographic* 165 (5), 556–613.

GOYON, J-C. & JOSSET, P. 1988. *Un Corps pour l'Eternité. Autopsie d'une Momie.* Le Léopard d'Or: Paris.

GREENBERG, J.H., TURNER, C.G. & ZEGURA, S.L. 1986. The settlement of the Americas: a comparison of the linguistic, dental and genetic evidence. *Current Anth.* 27, 477–97.

GROENEN, M. 1988. Les Répresentations de mains négatives dans les grottes de Gargas et de Tibiran. *Bull. Soc. Royale Belge d'Anth. et de Préhist.* 99, 81–113.

HAGELBERG, E., SYKES, B. & HEDGES, R. 1989. Ancient bone DNA amplified. *Nature* 342, 485.

HARRIS, J.E. & WEEKS K.R. 1973. *X-Raying the Pharaohs.* Macdonald: London.

—— and others. 1978. Mummy of the 'Elder Lady' in the tomb of Amenhotep II. *Science* 200, 1149–51.

HARRISON, R.G. & ABDALLA, A.B. 1972. The remains of Tutankhamun. *Antiquity* 46, 8–14.

————— and others. 1979. A mummified foetus from the tomb of Tutankhamen. *Antiquity* 53, 19–21.

HART, G.D. (ed.), 1983. *Disease in ancient man*. Clarke Irwin: Toronto.

HART HANSEN, J.P. 1986. Les momies du Groenland. *La Recherche* 17, 1490–8.

—————, MELDGAARD, J. & NORDQVIST, J. 1985. The mummies of Qilakitsoq. *National Geographic* 167 (2), 190–207.

HASSAN, F.A. 1978. Demographic archaeology, in *Advances in Archaeological Method and Theory* 1 (M.B. Schiffer ed.), 49–103. Academic Press: New York & London.

————— 1981. *Demographic Archaeology*. Academic Press: New York & London.

HEDGES, J.W. 1983. *Isbister: A chambered tomb in Orkney*. British Arch. Reports, Int. Series 115: Oxford.

HIGHAM, C. 1989. *The Archaeology of Mainland Southeast Asia*. Cambridge Univ. Press.

HILLSON, S.W. 1979. Diet and dental disease. *World Arch.* 11, 147–61.

————— 1986. *Teeth*. Cambridge Univ. Press.

HOLLOWAY, R.L. 1983. Cerebral brain endocast pattern of *Australopithecus afarensis* hominid. *Nature* 303, 420–22.

HOUGHTON, P. 1980. *The First New Zealanders*. Hodder & Stoughton: Auckland.

ISAAC, G.L. 1976. Stages of cultural elaboration in the Pleistocene: possible archaeological indicators of the development of language capabilities, in *Origins and Evolution of Language and Speech* (S.R. Harnad & others eds.), 276–88. Annals of the New York Acad. of Sciences 280.

ISCAN, M.Y. & MILLER-SHAIVITZ, P. 1984. Determination of sex from the tibia. *American Journal of Phys. Anth.* 64, 53–57.

JANSSENS, P. 1970. *Palaeopathology*. Humanities: New Jersey.

JOHANSON, D.C. & EDEY, M.A. 1981. *Lucy: The Beginnings of Humankind*. Granada: London.

JOHANSON, D.C. & SHREEVE, J. 1989. *Lucy's Child. The Discovery of a Human Ancestor*. Morrow: New York; Viking: London 1990.

JORDAN, P. 1983. *The Face of the Past*. Batsford: London.

KAUFFMANN-DOIG, F. 1979. *Sexual Behaviour in Ancient Peru*. Lima.

KERLEY, E.R. 1965. The microscopic determination of age in human bone. *American Journal of Phys. Anth.* 23, 149–64.

KISZELY, I. 1974. On the possibilities and methods of the chemical determination of sex from bones. *Ossa* 1, 51–62.

KLEIN, R.G. 1989. *The Human Career*. Univ. of Chicago Press.

LAITMAN, J.T. 1986. L'origine du langage articulé. *La Recherche* 17, No. 181, 1164–73.

LALLO, J.W. & ROSE, J.C. 1979. Patterns of stress, disease and mortality in two prehistoric populations from North America. *Journal of Human Evolution* 8, 323–35.

LAMBERT, B., SZPUNAR, C.B. & BUIKSTRA, J.E. 1979. Chemical analysis of excavated human bone from Middle and Late Woodland sites. *Archaeometry* 21, 115–29.

LARSEN, C.S. 1981. Skeletal and dental adaptations to the shift to agriculture on the Georgia coast. *Current Anthropology* 22, 422–23; see also 24 (1983) 225–26.

LATIMER, B., OHMAN, J.C. & LOVEJOY, C.O. 1987. Talocrural joint in African hominoids: implications for *Australopithecus afarensis*. *American Journal of Phys. Anth.* 74, 155–75.

LEAKEY, M.D. 1979. Footprints in the ashes of time. *National Geographic* 155 (4), 446–57.

————— & HARRIS, J.M. (eds.). 1987. *Laetoli, a Pliocene Site in Northern Tanzania*. Clarendon Press: Oxford.

LEAKEY, R.E. 1981. *The Making of Mankind*. Michael Joseph: London.

LENGYEL, I.A. 1975. *Palaeoserology. Blood typing with the fluorescence antibody method*. Akademiai Kiado: Budapest (Hungarian Academy of Sciences).

LIEBERMAN, P. & CRELIN, E.S. 1971. On the speech of Neanderthal Man. *Linguistic Inquiry* 11, 203–22.

————— 1974. Speech and Neanderthal Man. *American Anthropologist* 76, 323–25.

LOWENSTEIN, J.M. 1985. Molecular approaches to the identification of species. *American Scientist* 73, 541–47.

LOY, T.H. 1987. Recent advances in blood residue analysis, in *Archaeometry, further Australasian studies* (W.R. Ambrose & J.M.C. Mummery eds.), Dept of Prehistory, Australian National Univ.: Canberra.

MAIURI, A. 1961. Last moments of the Pompeians. *National Geographic* 120 (5), 650–69.

MANCHESTER, K. 1983. *The archaeology of disease*. Univ. of Bradford Press.

MASSET, C. 1975. La mortalité préhistorique. *Cahiers du Centre de Recherches Préhistoriques* 4 (Paris), 63–90.

MAYS, S.A. 1985. The relationship between Harris Line formation and bone growth and development. *Journal of Arch. Science* 12, 207–20.

MELLARS, P. & STRINGER, C.B. (eds.). 1989/1990. *The Human Revolution*, 2 vols. Edinburgh Univ. Press.

MILISAUSKAS, S. 1972. An analysis of Linear culture longhouses at Olszanica BI, Poland. *World Arch.* 4, 57–74.

MOLLESON, T.I. 1989. Seed preparation in the Mesolithic: the osteological evidence. *Antiquity* 63, 356–62.

—————, ELDRIDGE, D. & GALE, N. 1985. Identification of lead sources by stable isotope ratios in bones and lead from Poundbury Camp, Dorset. *Oxford Journal of Arch.* 5, 249–53.

MURDY, C.N. 1981. Congenital deformities and the Olmec were-jaguar motif. *American Antiquity* 46, 861–71.

MUSGRAVE, J.H. 1971. How dextrous was Neanderthal Man? *Nature* 233, 538–41.

NAROLL, R. 1962. Floor area and settlement population. *American Antiquity* 27, 587–89.

ORTNER, D.J. & PUTSCHAR, W.G.J. 1985. *Identification of Pathological Conditions in Human Skeletal Remains*. (2nd ed.) Smithsonian Contribs. to Anth. No. 28: Washington DC.

PÄÄBO, S. 1985. Preservation of DNA in ancient Egyptian mummies. *Journal of Arch. Science* 12, 411–17.

————— 1989. Ancient DNA: Extraction, characterization, molecular cloning and enzymatic amplification. *Proc. Nat. Acad. of Science USA* 86, 1939–43.

PAHL, W.M. 1980. Computed tomography – a new radiodiagnostical technique applied to medico-archaeological investigation of Egyptian mummies. *Ossa* 7, 189–98.

PALES, L. 1976. *Les empreintes de pieds humains dans les cavernes*. Archives de l'Institut de Paléontologie Humaine No. 36, Masson: Paris.

————— & DE ST PÉREUSE, M.T. 1976. *Les Gravures de La Marche. II: Les Humains*. Ophrys: Paris.

PATRUCCO, R. and others. 1983. Parasitological studies of coprolites of pre-Hispanic Peruvian populations. *Current Anth.* 24, 393–94.

PFEIFFER, S. 1980. Bone-remodelling age estimates compared with estimates by other techniques. *Current Anth.* 21, 793–4; and 22, 437–38.

PRAG, J. 1984. Philip of Macedon – the flesh on the bones. *Popular Arch.* 5 (9), 8–11.

PRAG, A.J.N., MUSGRAVE, J.H. & NEAVE, R.A.H. 1984. The skull from tomb II at Vergina: King Philip of Macedon. *Journal of Hellenic Studies* 104, 65–68.

PUECH, P-F. 1978. L'alimentation de l'homme préhistorique. *La Recherche* 9, 1029–31.

————— & CIANFARANI, F. 1985. La Paléodontologie: étude des maladies des dents, in *Les Maladies de nos Ancêtres*. *Dossiers de l'Archéologie* 97, Sept., 28–33.

ROBINSON, J.T. 1972. *Early Hominid Posture and Locomotion*. Univ. of Chicago Press.

ROTHHAMMER, F. and others. 1985. Chagas' Disease in Pre-Columbian South America. *American Journal of Phys.*

Anth. 68, 495–98.

RUDENKO, S.I. 1970. *The Frozen Tombs of Siberia.* Dent: London.

SCOTT, D.D. & CONNOR, M.A. 1986. Postmortem at the Little Bighorn. *Natural History* June, 46–55.

SCOTT, D.D., FOX, R.A., CONNOR, M.A. & HARMON, D. 1989. *Archaeological Perspectives on the Battle of the Little Bighorn.* Univ. of Oklahoma Press: Norman.

SMITH, B.H. 1986. Dental development in *Australopithecus* and early *Homo. Nature* 323, 327–30.

SMITH, F.H. 1983. Behavioral interpretation of change in craniofacial morphology across the archaic/modern *Homo sapiens* transition, in *The Mousterian Legacy* (E. Trinkaus ed.), 141–63. British Arch. Reports, Int. Series 164: Oxford.

SMITH, P. 1972. Diet and attrition in the Natufians. *American Journal of Phys. Anth.* 37, 233–38.

STEAD, I.M., BOURKE, J.B. & BROTHWELL, D. (eds.). 1986. *Lindow Man.* British Museum Publications: London.

STERN, J.T. & SUSMAN, R.L. 1983. The locomotor anatomy of *Australopithecus afarensis. American Journal of Phys. Anth.* 60, 279–317.

STRINGER, C.B. & ANDREWS, P. 1988. Genetic and fossil evidence for the origin of modern humans. *Science* 239, 1263–68.

TOBIAS, P. 1987. The brain of *Homo habilis*: A new level of organization in cerebral evolution. *Journal of Human Evolution* 16, 741–65.

TOTH, N. 1985. Archaeological evidence for preferential right-handedness in the lower and middle Pleistocene, and its possible implications. *Journal of Human Evolution* 14, 607–14.

TRINKAUS, E. 1975. Squatting among the Neanderthals: a problem in the behavioural interpretation of skeletal morphology. *Journal of Arch. Science* 2, 327–51.

——— 1982. Artificial cranial deformation in the Shanidar 1 and 5 Neanderthals. *Current Anth.* 23, 198–99.

——— 1983. *The Shanidar Neandertals.* Academic Press: New York & London.

TROTTER, M. & GLESER, G.C. 1958. A re-evaluation of estimation of stature based on measurements of stature taken during life and of long bones after death. *American Journal of Phys. Anth.* 16, 79–123.

TUTTLE, R., WEBB, D. & WEIDL, E. 1990. Further progress on the Laetoli trails. *Journal of Arch. Science* 17, 347–362.

UBELAKER, D.H. 1984. *Human Skeletal Remains.* (Rev. ed.) Taraxacum: Washington.

URTEAGA-BALLON, O. & WELLS, C. 1968. Gynaecology in Ancient Peru. *Antiquity* 42, 233–34.

VLCEK, E. 1952. Empreintes papillaires d'un homme paléolithique. *L'Anthropologie* 56, 557–58.

WAINSCOAT, J.S. and others. 1986. Evolutionary relationships of human populations from an analysis of nuclear DNA polymorphisms. *Nature* 319, 491–93; see also p. 449.

WELLS, C. 1964. *Bones, bodies and disease.* Thames & Hudson: London.

WELLS, L.H. 1969. Stature in earlier races of mankind, in *Science in Archaeology* (D. Brothwell & E.S. Higgs eds.), 453–67. (2nd ed.) Thames & Hudson: London.

WILLIAMS, R.C. and others. 1985. Gm allotypes in native Americans: evidence for three distinct migrations across the Bering land bridge. *American Journal of Phys. Anth.* 66, 1–19.

ZIMMERMAN, M.R. & ANGEL, J.L. (eds.). 1986. *Dating and age determination of biological materials.* Croom Helm: London.

Chapter 12: Why Did Things Change? Explanation in Archaeology (pp. 405–434)

p. 405 **Historical analysis** Braudel's three levels: Braudel 1972.

pp. 407–409 **"Traditional" explanation** Culture=people hypothesis first set out in English: Childe 1929; its history traced: Trigger 1978; Trigger 1989. Renfrew 1969 & 1973a, (Ch.5) discusses Childe's Vinča/Troy diffusionist link. Lapita: Green 1979; Bellwood 1987. Spread of alphabet: Gelb 1952. Issue of local innovation versus diffusion: Renfrew 1978a.

pp. 411–412 **Processual archaeology** Flannery 1967; Binford 1972, 1983. **Applications** Clark, J.G.D. 1952 (Swedish megaliths). Binford 1968 (origins of agriculture); Bender 1978 (alternative model).

pp. 412–415 **Marxism** and human society: Childe 1936. **Marxist archaeology**: Gilman 1976, 1981; Friedman & Rowlands 1978; Frankenstein & Rowlands 1978; Spriggs 1984. Structural Marxism: Friedman 1974.

pp. 415–416 **Universal laws** in the natural sciences: Hempel 1966. Other accounts of scientific reasoning: Braithwaite 1960; Popper 1985. Application of universal laws to archaeology: Watson, LeBlanc & Redman 1971, criticized by Flannery 1973 and Trigger 1978. Collingwood 1946 and Hodder 1986 cover the contrasting idealist-historical standpoint. pp. 417–426 **Origins of the state** Alternative theories: Wittfogel 1957; Diakonoff 1969; Carneiro 1970,

1978; Renfrew 1972. Agricultural intensification: Boserup 1965. Greg Johnson's work: Johnson 1982. Rathje's Maya work: Rathje 1971. Systems approach to origins of Mesoamerican agriculture: Flannery 1968. **Simulation** Chadwick's work: Chadwick 1979. Systems Dynamic Modeling: Zubrow 1981 (ancient Rome).

pp. 426–430 **"Post-processual" explanation** Structuralist approaches: Glassie 1975; Arnold 1983 examines a recent case study.

p. 430 **Critical Theory** Hodder 1986 and Shanks & Tilley 1987a, 1987b. **Neo-Marxist thought** Leone 1984 (Paca). Miller 1980 (Third World).

pp. 431–434 **Cognitive-processual archaeology** Good examples are found in Flannery & Marcus 1983; Schele & Miller 1986; Conrad & Demarest 1984; Freidel 1981. **Punctuated equilibria** and Darwinian evolution: Gould & Eldredge 1977. Rise of Minoan palaces: Cherry 1984, 1986. **Catastrophe theory** is analyzed by Thom 1975; Zeeman 1977; Renfrew 1978a, 1978b. **Self-organization in non-equilibrium systems** Prigogine 1979, 1987; Prigogine & Stengers 1984; Allen 1982.

Box Features

pp. 408–409 **Great Zimbabwe** Garlake 1973.

p. 413 **Origins of Farming** Binford 1968.

p. 414 **Marxist Archaeology** See main text references above.

pp. 418–419 **Origins of the State I: Peru** Carneiro 1970.

pp. 420–421 **Origins of the State II: The Aegean** Renfrew 1972. Utility of systems theory in archaeology: Salmon 1978.

pp. 424–425 **Classic Maya Collapse** Culbert 1973; Hosler & others 1977; Renfrew 1979; Doran 1981; Lowe 1985. Recent studies of state collapse: Tainter 1988; Yoffee & Cowgill 1988.

pp. 428–429 **European Megaliths** Different interpretations: Renfrew 1976 and Chapman 1981 (functional-processual); Tilley 1984 (neo-Marxist); Hodder 1984 ("post-processualist").

Bibliography

ALLEN, P.M. 1982. The genesis of structure in social systems: the paradigm of self-organization, in *Theory and Explanation in Archaeology* (C. Renfrew, M.J. Rowlands & B.A. Segraves eds.), 347–74. Academic Press: New York & London.

ARNOLD, D.E. 1983. Design structure and community organization in Quinua, Peru, in *Structure and Cognition in Art* (D.K. Washburn ed.), 40–55. Cambridge Univ. Press.

BELLWOOD, P. 1987. *The Polynesians* (Rev. ed.) Thames & Hudson: London & New York.

BENDER, B. 1978. Gatherer-hunter to farmer: a social perspective. *World Arch* 10, 204–22.

BINFORD, L.R. 1968. Post-Pleistocene adaptations, in *New Perspectives in Archaeology* (L.R. Binford & S.R. Binford eds.), 313–41. Aldine: Chicago.

―――― 1972. *An Archaeological Perspective*. Seminar Press: New York & London.

―――― 1983. *In Pursuit of the Past*. Thames & Hudson: London & New York.

BOSERUP, E. 1965. *The Conditions of Agricultural Growth*. Aldine: Chicago.

BRAITHWAITE, R.B. 1960. *Scientific Explanation*. Cambridge Univ. Press.

BRAUDEL, F. 1972. *The Mediterranean and the Mediterranean World in the Reign of Philip II*. Collins: London.

CARNEIRO, R.L. 1970. A theory of the origin of the state. *Science* 169, 733–38.

―――― 1978. Political expansion as an expression of the principle of competitive exclusion, in *Origins of the state: the anthropology of political evolution* (R. Cohen & E.R. Service eds.), 205–23. Institute for the Study of Human Issues: Philadelphia.

CHADWICK, A.J. 1979. Settlement simulation, in *Transformations. Mathematical Approaches to Culture Change* (C. Renfrew & K.L. Cooke eds.), 237–255. Academic Press: New York & London.

CHAPMAN, R. 1981. The emergence of formal disposal areas and the 'problem' of megalithic tombs in prehistoric Europe, in *The Archaeology of Death* (R. Chapman, I. Kinnes & K. Randsborg eds.), 71–81. Cambridge Univ. Press.

CHERRY, J.F. 1983. Evolution, revolution, and the origins of complex society in Minoan Crete, in *Minoan Society. Proceedings of the Cambridge Colloquium 1981* (O. Krzyszkowska & L. Nixon eds.). Bristol Classical Press: Bristol.

―――― 1984. The emergence of the state in the prehistoric Aegean, *Proceedings of the Cambridge Philological Society* 30, 18 –48.

―――― 1986. Polities and palaces: some problems in Minoan state formation, in *Peer polity interaction and socio-political change* (C. Renfrew & J.F. Cherry eds.), 19–45. Cambridge Univ. Press.

CHILDE, V.G. 1929. *The Danube in Prehistory*. Clarendon Press: Oxford.

―――― 1936. *Man Makes Himself*. Watts: London.

CLARK, J.G.D. 1952. *Prehistoric Europe: the Economic Basis*. Methuen: London.

COLLINGWOOD, R.G. 1946. *The Idea of History*. Oxford Univ. Press.

CONRAD, G.W. & DEMAREST, A.A. 1984. *Religion and Empire. The Dynamics of Aztec and Inca Expansion*. Cambridge Univ. Press.

CULBERT, T.P. (ed.). 1973. *The Classic Maya Collapse*. Univ. of New Mexico Press: Albuquerque.

DANIEL, G.E. & RENFREW, C. 1988. *The Idea of Prehistory*. Edinburgh Univ. Press.

DIAKONOFF, I.M. 1969. The rise of the despotic state in Ancient Mesopotamia, in *Ancient Mesopotamia: socio-economic history* (I.M. Diakonoff ed.). Moscow.

DORAN, J. 1981. Multi-actor systems and the Maya collapse, in *Coloquio: Manejo de Datos y Metodos Matematicos de Arqueologia* (G.L. Cowgill, R. Whallon & B.S. Ottaway eds.), 191–200. UISPP: Mexico City.

FLANNERY, K.V. 1967. Culture history vs. cultural process: a debate in American archaeology. *Scientific American* 217, 119–22.

―――― 1968. Archaeological Systems Theory and Early Mesoamerica, in *Anthropological Archaeology in the Americas* (B.J. Meggers ed.), 67–87. Anthropological Society of Washington.

―――― 1973. Archaeology with a capital 'S', in *Research and Theory in Current Archaeology* (C.L. Redman ed.), 47–53. Wiley: New York.

―――― (ed.). 1976. *The Early Mesoamerican Village*. Academic Press: New York & London.

―――― & MARCUS, J. (eds.). 1983. *The Cloud People: Divergent Evolution of the Zapotec and Mixtec Civilizations*. Academic Press: New York & London.

FRANKENSTEIN, S. & ROWLANDS, M.J. 1978. The internal structure and regional context of Early Iron Age society in south-western Germany. *Bulletin of the Institute of Archaeology* 15, 73–112.

FREIDEL, D. 1981. Civilization as a state of mind: the cultural evolution of the Lowland Maya, in *The Transition to Statehood in the New World* (G.D. Jones & R.R. Kautz eds.), 188–227. Cambridge Univ. Press.

FRIEDMAN, J. 1974. Marxism, structuralism and vulgar materialism. *Man* 9, 444–69.

―――― & ROWLANDS, M.J. 1978. Notes towards an epigenetic model of the evolution of 'civilisation,' in *The Evolution of Social Systems* (J. Friedman & M.J. Rowlands eds.), 201–78. Duckworth: London.

GARLAKE, P.S. 1973. *Great Zimbabwe*. Thames & Hudson: London; McGraw-Hill: New York.

GELB, I.J. 1952. *A Study of Writing*. Univ. of Chicago Press.

GIBBON, G. 1989. *Explanation in Archaeology* Blackwell: Oxford & New York.

GILMAN, A. 1976. Bronze Age dynamics in south-east Spain. *Dialectical Anthropology* 1, 307–19.

―――― 1981. The development of social stratification in Bronze Age Europe. *Current Anth.* 22, 1–23.

GLASSIE, H. 1975. *Folk Housing in Middle Virginia*. Univ. of Tennessee Press: Knoxville.

GOULD, S.J. & ELDREDGE, N. 1977. Punctuated equilibria: the tempo and mode of evolution reconsidered. *Palaeobiology* 3, 115–51.

GREEN, R.C. 1979. Lapita, in *The Prehistory of Polynesia* (J.D. Jennings ed.), 27–60. Harvard Univ. Press: Cambridge, Mass.

HEMPEL, C.G. 1966. *Philosophy of Natural Science*. Prentice-Hall: Englewood Cliffs, N.J.

HODDER, I. 1984. Burials, houses, women and men in the European Neolithic, in *Ideology, Power and Prehistory* (D. Miller & C. Tilley eds.), 51–68. Cambridge Univ. Press.

―――― 1986. *Reading the Past*. Cambridge Univ. Press.

HOSLER, D.H., SABLOFF, J.A. & RUNGE, D. 1977. Simulation model development: a case study of the Classic Maya collapse, in *Social Processes in Maya Prehistory* (N. Hammond ed.), 553–90. Academic Press: New York & London.

JOHNSON, G.A. 1982. Organizational Structure and Scalar Stress, in *Theory and Explanation in Archaeology* (C. Renfrew, M.J. Rowlands, & B.A. Segraves (eds.). Academic Press: New York & London.

KELLEY, J.H. & HANEN, M.P. 1988. *Archaeology and the Methodology of Science*. Univ. of New Mexico Press: Albuquerque.

LEONE, M. 1984. Interpreting ideology in historical archaeology: using the rules of perspective in the William Paca Garden in Annapolis, Maryland, in *Ideology, Power and Prehistory* (D. Miller & C. Tilley eds.), 25–35. Cambridge Univ. Press.

LOWE, J.W.G. 1985. *The dynamics of apocalypse: a systems simulation of the Classic Maya collapse*. Univ. of New Mexico Press: Albuquerque.

MILLER, D. 1980. Archaeology and development. *Current Anth.* 21, 726.

MORRIS, I. 1987. *Burial and Ancient Society: The Rise of the Greek City State*. Cambridge Univ. Press.

PINSKY, V. & WYLIE, A. (eds.). 1989. *Critical Traditions in Contemporary Archaeology*. Cambridge Univ. Press.

POPPER, K.R. 1985. *Conjectures and Refutations: the growth of scientific knowledge*. (4th ed.) Routledge & Kegan Paul: London.

PRIGOGINE, I. 1979. *From Being to Becoming*. Freeman: San Francisco.

―――― 1987. Exploring complexity. *European Journal of Operational Research* 30, 97–103.

―――― & STENGERS, I. 1984. *Order out of chaos: man's new dialogue with nature*. Heinemann: London.

RATHJE, W.L. 1971. The Origin and Development of Lowland Classic Maya

Civilization. *American Antiquity* 36, 275–85.

RENFREW, C. 1969. The Autonomy of the South-East European Copper Age. *Proc. Prehist. Soc.* 35, 12–47.

—— 1972. *The Emergence of Civilisation. The Cyclades and the Aegean in the Third Millennium B.C.* Methuen: London.

—— 1973a. *Before Civilisation.* Jonathan Cape: London; Pelican: Harmondsworth.

—— (ed.). 1973b. *The Explanation of Culture Change: Models in Prehistory.* Duckworth: London.

—— 1976. Megaliths, Territories and Populations, in *Acculturation and Continuity in Atlantic Europe (Dissertationes Archaeologicae Gandenses XVI)* (S.J. de Laet ed.), 298–320.

—— 1978a. The anatomy of innovation, in *Social Organisation and Settlement* (D. Green, C. Haselgrove & M. Spriggs eds.), 89–117. British Arch. Reports: Oxford.

—— 1978b. Trajectory discontinuity and morphogenesis, the implications of catastrophe theory for archaeology. *American Antiquity* 43, 203–44.

—— 1979. System collapse as social transformation, in *Transformations. Mathematical Approaches to Culture Change* (C. Renfrew & K.L. Cooke eds.), 481–506. Academic Press: New York & London.

—— 1980. The great tradition versus the great divide. *American Journal of Arch.* 84, 287–98.

—— 1982. Explanation revisited, in *Theory and Explanation in Archaeology* (C. Renfrew, M.J. Rowlands & B.A. Segraves, eds.), 5–24. Academic Press: New York & London.

ROWLANDS, M., LARSEN, M. & KRISTIANSEN, K. (eds.). 1987. *Centre and Periphery in the Ancient World.* Cambridge Univ. Press.

SALMON, M. 1978. What can systems theory do for archaeology? *American Antiquity* 43, 174–83.

—— 1982. *Philosophy and Archaeology.* Academic Press: New York & London.

SCHELE, L. & MILLER, M.E. 1986. *The Blood of Kings. Dynasty and ritual in Maya art.* Kimbell Art Museum: Fort Worth; Sotheby's: London.

SHANKS, M. & TILLEY, C. 1987a. Re-constructing Archaeology. Cambridge Univ. Press.

—— 1987b. *Social Theory and Archaeology.* Polity Press: Oxford.

SPRIGGS, M. (ed.). 1984. *Marxist Perspectives in Archaeology.* Cambridge Univ. Press.

TAINTER, J.A. 1988. *The Collapse of Complex Societies.* Cambridge Univ. Press.

THOM, R. 1975. *Structural Stability and Morphogenesis.* Benjamin: Reading, Mass.

TILLEY, C. 1984. Ideology and the legitimation of power in the Middle Neolithic of Sweden, in *Ideology, Power and Prehistory* (D. Miller & C. Tilley eds.), 111–46. Cambridge Univ. Press.

TRIGGER, B. 1978. *Time and Tradition.* Edinburgh Univ. Press.

—— 1989. *A History of Archaeological Thought.* Cambridge Univ. Press.

WALLERSTEIN, I. 1974. *The Modern World System.* Academic Press: New York & London.

WATSON, P.J., LEBLANC, S.A. & REDMAN, C.L. 1971. *Explanation in Archaeology. An Explicitly Scientific Approach.* Columbia Univ. Press: New York & London.

WITTFOGEL, K. 1957. *Oriental Despotism, a Comparative Study of Total Power.* Yale Univ. Press: New Haven.

YOFFEE, N. & COWGILL, G.L. (eds.). 1988. *The Collapse of Ancient States and Civilizations.* Univ. of Arizona Press.

ZEEMAN, E.C. 1977. *Catastrophe Theory, Selected Papers 1972–77.* Addison-Wesley: Reading, Mass.

ZUBROW, E.B.W. 1981. Simulation as a heuristic device in archaeology, in *Simulations in Archaeology* (J.A. Sabloff ed.), 143–88. Univ. of New Mexico Press: Albuquerque.

Chapter 13: Archaeology in Action (pp. 437–462)

Bibliography

BLANTON, R.E. 1978. Monte Albán: *Settlement Patterns at the Ancient Zapotec Capital.* Academic Press: New York.

—— & KOWALEWSKI, S.A. 1981. Monte Albán and after in the Valley of Oaxaca, in *Archaeology. Supplement to the Handbook of Middle American Indians I* (J.A. Sabloff ed.), 94–116. Univ. of Texas Press: Austin.

FLANNERY, K.V. (ed.). 1976. *The Early Mesoamerican Village.* Academic Press: New York & London.

—— (ed.). 1986. *Guilá Naquitz: Archaic Foraging and Early Agriculture in Oaxaca, Mexico.* Academic Press: New York.

—— & MARCUS, J. (eds.). 1983. *The Cloud People: Divergent Evolution of the Zapotec and Mixtec Civilizations.* Academic Press: New York.

——, MARCUS, J. & KOWALEWSKI, S.A. 1981. The Preceramic and Formative of the Valley of Oaxaca, in *Archaeology. Supplement to the Handbook of Middle American Indians I* (J.A. Sabloff ed.), 48–93. Univ. of Texas Press: Austin.

JONES, R. (ed.). 1985. *Archaeological Research in Kakadu National Park.* Australian National Parks and Wildlife Service, Special Publication No. 13. Australian National Univ.: Canberra.

RENFREW, C. 1985. *The Archaeology of Cult: The Sanctuary at Phylakopi.* British School of Archaeology at Athens Supplementary Vol. No. 18: London.

—— & CHERRY, J.F. (ed.). 1986. *Peer Polity Interaction and Socio-Political Change.* Cambridge Univ. Press.

—— & WAGSTAFF, M. (eds.). 1982. *An Island Polity. The Archaeology of Exploitation in Melos.* Cambridge Univ. Press: Cambridge & New York.

SCHRIRE, C. 1982. *The Alligator Rivers: Prehistory and Ecology in Western Arnhem Land.* Terra Australis 7, Australian National Univ.: Canberra.

WHITE, J.P. & O'CONNELL, J.F. 1982. *A Prehistory of Australia, New Guinea and Sahul.* Academic Press: New York & London.

Chapter 14: Whose Past? Archaeology and the Public (pp. 463–484)

General introductions to the topic of **archaeological ethics** and public relations: Clark 1960 (Ch. 8); Green 1984; King 1983; McGimsey 1972; Smith 1974. Archaeology and politics: Ucko 1987. Garlake 1973 discusses Great Zimbabwe in particular. Regional approaches: *World Archaeology* 1981/2, 13 (2 & 3).

pp. 463–467 **Who owns the past? Return of cultural property** Greenfield 1989; McBryde 1985; Mturi 1983. Particular reference to the Elgin Marbles: Hitchens 1987. **Should we disturb the dead?** Bahn 1984; Bahn & Paterson 1986; Layton 1989. **Australian aborigines** Ucko 1983. **American Indians** Rosen 1980; Talmage 1982; Ferguson 1984 (Zuni Pueblo).

p. 467 **Ideology and nationalism** China: Pearson 1976; Olsen 1987. Israel: Yadin 1966; Shay 1989; Silberman 1989.

pp. 467–470 **Economic lessons from the past** In general: Ford 1973. Desert agriculture: Evenari & Koller 1956; Evenari & others 1971; Agarwal 1977. Andes, Cusichaca project: Kendall 1984. Seismic archaeology in China: Guo Zhan 1985.

pp. 470–473 **Conservation and destruction** Salvage (rescue) archaeology: Chamberlin 1979; Gumerman & Schiffer 1977; Rahtz 1974. Approaches to the archaeological heritage: Cleere 1984. Conservation and legislation in Australia & New Zealand: Mulvaney 1981; McKinlay & Jones 1979.

pp. 473–477 **Damage by developers** Rose theater, England: Fagan 1990; Wainwright 1989. Japanese rescue: Tanaka 1984. Franklin dam affair: Kiernan & others 1983; Lewin 1982.

Mexico City: Matos Moctezuma 1980, 1988.

pp. 477–479 **Damage from looting** Chamberlin 1983; Hamblin 1970; Hess 1974; Meyer 1973. Egypt: Fagan 1975. American Southwest: Basset 1986.

pp. 479–480 **Care of protected sites** Egypt: Toufexis 1985; *New Scientist* 21 April 1988, 65. Mohenjodaro: Naqvi 1985.

pp. 480–481 **Publish or be damned** Callow 1985; editorials in *Antiquity* 31, 1957 (121–22); & 47, 1973 (261–262). Wheeler's comment: Wheeler 1968.

pp. 481–483 **The wider audience** Evans & others 1981 (especially 191–229); Fagan 1984. Japanese site presentation: Kiyotari 1987, 100.

pp. 483–484 **World archaeology** Cult- and pseudo-archaeology in general: Adam 1975; Cole 1980; Sabloff 1982; Stiebing 1984; Story 1976, 1980; White 1974; Wilson 1972, 1975. See also special issue Vol. 29 (2), 1987, of *Expedition* on "Archaeological Facts and Fantasies." For von Däniken himself: Ferris 1974 as well as the above works. Many excellent articles on this topic can be found in the journal *The Skeptical Inquirer*.

Box Features

pp. 468–469 **Applied Archaeology** Raised field project: Erickson 1985, 1988; Garaycochea 1987.

p. 472 **The Practice of CRM** Gumerman & Schiffer 1977. Tombigbee: Jenkins & Krause 1986; Peebles 1981.

pp. 476–477 **The Great Temple of the Aztecs** Matos Moctezuma 1988.

p. 478 **Mimbres** LeBlanc 1983.

pp. 482–483 **Viking York** Hall, R. 1984.

Bibliography

ADAM, J-P. 1975. *L'Archéologie devant l'Imposture*. Laffont: Paris.

AGARWAL, A. 1977. Coaxing the barren deserts back to life. *New Scientist* 15, Sept., 674–75.

BAHN, P.G. 1984. Do not disturb? Archaeology and the rights of the dead. *Oxford Journal of Arch*. 3, 127–39.

——— & PATERSON, R.W.K. 1986. The last rights: more on archaeology and the dead. *Oxford Journal of Arch*. 5, 255–71.

BASSET, C.A. 1986. The culture thieves. *Science 86*, July/Aug., 22–29.

CALLOW, P. 1985. An unlovely child: the problem of unpublished archaeological research. *Archaeological Review from Cambridge* 4, 95–106.

CHAMBERLIN, E.R. 1979. *Preserving the Past*. Dent: London.

——— 1983. *Loot! the Heritage of Plunder*. Thames & Hudson: London.

CHAPELOT, J. & SCHNAPP, A. (eds.). 1984. *La Politique de l'Archéologie en Europe*. CNRS: Paris.

CLARK, J.G.D. 1960. *Archaeology and Society*. (3rd ed.) Methuen: London.

CLEERE, H. (ed.). 1984. *Approaches to the Archaeological Heritage*. Cambridge Univ. Press.

COLE, J.R. 1980. Cult archaeology and unscientific method and theory, in *Advances in Archaeological Method and Theory* 3 (M.B. Schiffer ed.), 1–33. Academic Press: New York & London.

DARVILL, T. 1987. *Ancient Monuments in the Countryside, an Archaeological Management Review*, English Heritage: London.

———, PARKER PEARSON, M., SMITH, R.W. & THOMAS, R.M. (eds.). 1978. *New Approaches to Our Past, an Archaeological Forum*. Dept. of Archaeology: Southampton.

ERICKSON, C.L. 1985. Applications of prehistoric Andean technology: experiments in raised field agriculture, Huatta, Lake Titicaca: 1981–2, in *Prehistoric Intensive Agriculture in the Tropics* (I.S. Farrington, ed.), 209–32. British Arch. Reports, Int. Series. No. 232: Oxford.

——— 1988. Raised field agriculture in the Lake Titicaca Basin: Putting ancient agriculture back to work. *Expedition* 30 (3), 8–16.

EVANS, J.D., CUNLIFFE, B. & RENFREW, C. (eds.). 1981. *Antiquity and Man. Essays in Honour of Glyn Daniel*. Thames & Hudson: London.

EVENARI, M. & KOLLER, D. 1956. Ancient masters of the desert. *Scientific American* 194 (4), 39–45.

EVENARI, M. & others. 1971. *The Negev: The Challenge of a Desert*. Harvard Univ. Press.

FAGAN, B.M. 1975. *The Rape of the Nile*. Scribners: New York.

——— 1984. Archaeology and the wider audience, in *Ethics and Values in Archaeology* (E.L. Green, ed.), 175–83. Free Press: New York.

——— 1990. The Rose Affair. *Archaeology* 43 (2), 12–14, 76.

FERGUSON, T.J. 1984. Archaeological ethics and values in a Tribal Cultural Resource Management Program at the Pueblo of Zuni, in *Ethics and Values in Archaeology* (E.L. Green, ed.), 224–35. Free Press: New York.

FERRIS, T. 1974. *Playboy* Interview: Erich von Däniken. *Playboy* 21 (8), Aug., 51–52, 56–58, 60, 64, 151.

FORD, R.I. 1973. Archaeology serving humanity, in *Research and Theory in Current Archaeology* (C.L. Redman ed.), 83–93. Wiley: New York.

GARAYCOCHEA, I. 1987. Agricultural experiments in raised fields in the Lake Titicaca Basin, Peru. Some preliminary considerations, in *Pre-Hispanic Agricultural Fields in the Andean Region* (W. Denevan & others eds.), 385–98. British Arch. Reports, Int. Series No. 359: Oxford.

GARLAKE, P. 1973. *Great Zimbabwe*.

Thames & Hudson: London; McGraw-Hill: New York.

GREEN, E.L. (ed.). 1984. *Ethics and Values in Archaeology*. Free Press: New York.

GREENFIELD, J. 1989. *The Return of Cultural Treasures*. Cambridge Univ. Press.

GUMERMAN, G. & SCHIFFER, M.B. (eds.). 1977. *Conservation Archaeology*. Academic Press: New York & London.

GUO ZHAN 1985. My Life as an Archaeologist. *Unesco Courier* July, 36–37.

HALL, R. 1984. *The Viking Dig*. Bodley Head: London.

HAMBLIN, D.J. 1970. *Pots and Robbers*. Simon and Schuster: New York.

HASELGROVE, C., MILLET M. & SMITH, I. (eds.). 1985. *Archaeology from the Ploughsoil*. Dept. of Archaeology: Sheffield.

HESS, J.L. 1974. *The Grand Acquisitors*. Houghton Mifflin: Boston.

HITCHENS, C. 1987. *The Elgin Marbles: Should they be returned to Greece?* Chatto & Windus: London.

JENKINS, N.J. & KRAUSE, R.A. 1986. *The Tombigbee Watershed in Southeastern Prehistory*. Univ. of Alabama Press.

KENDALL, A. (ed.). 1984. *Current Archaeological Projects in the Central Andes*. British Arch. Reports, Int. Series. No. 210: Oxford.

KIERNAN, K., JONES, R. & RANSOM, D. 1983. New evidence from Fraser Cave for glacial age man in SW Tasmania. *Nature* 301, 13, 28–32; see also Vol. 300 (1982), 679; Vol. 305 (1983), 354; & Vol. 306 (1983), 636, 726.

KING, T.F. 1983. Professional responsibility in public archaeology. *Annual Review of Anth*. 12, 143–64.

KIYOTARI, T. (ed.). 1987. *Recent Archaeological Discoveries in Japan*. Centre for E. Asian Cultural Studies/ UNESCO.

LAYTON, R. (ed.). 1989. *Conflict in the Archaeology of Living Traditions*. Unwin Hyman: London.

LeBLANC, S.A. 1983. *The Mimbres People*. Thames & Hudson: London & New York.

LEWIN, R. 1982. Tasmanian Ice Age sites threatened by dam. *Science* 218, 988.

LOWENTHAL, D. 1985. *The Past is a Foreign Country*. Cambridge Univ. Press.

MACDONALD, W.K. (ed.). 1976. *Digging for Gold: Papers on Archaeology for Profit*. Univ. of Michigan: Ann Arbor.

McBRYDE, I. (ed.). 1985. *Who Owns the Past?* Oxford Univ. Press. Melbourne.

McGIMSEY, C. 1972. *Public Archaeology*. Seminar Press: New York.

——— & DAVIS, H.A. (eds.). 1977. *The Management of Archaeological Resources: the Airlie House Report*. Society for American Archaeology: Washington.

McKINLAY, J.R. & JONES, K.L. (eds.). 1979. *Archaeological Resource Management in Australia and Oceania.* New Zealand Historic Places Trust: Wellington.

MATOS MOCTEZUMA, E. 1980. Tenochtitlán: New finds in the Great Temple. *National Geographic* 158 (6), 766–75.

—— 1988. *The Great Temple of the Aztecs.* Thames & Hudson: London & New York.

MESSENGER, P. MAUCH (ed.). 1989. *The Ethics of Collecting Cultural Property: Whose Culture? Whose Property?* Univ. of New Mexico Press: Albuquerque.

MEYER, K.E. 1973. *The Plundered Past.* Atheneum Press: New York.

MTURI, A.A. 1983. The return of cultural property. *Antiquity* 57, 137–39.

MULVANEY, D.J. 1981. What future for our past? Archaeology and society in the eighties. *Australian Arch.* 13, 16–27.

NAQVI, W.Q. 1985. Mohenjodaro, threatened centre of an ancient civilization. *Unesco Courier*, July, 32–35.

OLSEN, J.W. 1987. The practice of archaeology in China today. *Antiquity* 61, 282–90.

PEARSON, R.J. 1976. The social aims of Chinese archaeology. *Antiquity* 50, 8–10.

PEEBLES, C. (ed.) 1981. Excavations in the Lubbub Creek Archaeological Locality. Vol. 1. Report on file. Museum

of Anthropology, Univ. of Michigan: Ann Arbor.

RAHTZ, P. (ed.). 1974. *Rescue Archaeology.* Pelican: Harmondsworth.

RENFREW, C. 1983. Divided we stand: aspects of archaeology and information. *American Antiquity* 48, 3–16.

ROSEN, L. 1980. The excavation of American Indian burial sites: a problem in professional responsibility. *American Anthropologist* 82, 5–27.

SABLOFF, J.A. 1982. Introduction, in *Archaeology: Myth and Reality. Readings from Scientific American*, 1–26. Freeman: San Francisco.

SHAY, T. 1989. Israeli archaeology – ideology and practice. *Antiquity* 63, 768–72.

SILBERMAN, N.A. 1989. *Between Past and Present. Archaeology, Ideology and Nationalism in the Modern Middle East.* Anchor/Doubleday: New York.

SMITH, R.H. 1974. Ethics in field archaeology. *Journal of Field Arch.* 1, 375–83.

STIEBING, W.H. 1984. *Ancient Astronauts, Cosmic Collisions and other Popular Theories about Man's Past.* Prometheus: Buffalo.

STORY, R.D. 1976. *The Space-Gods Revealed.* New English Library: London.

—— 1980. *Guardians of the Universe?* New English Library: London.

TALMAGE, V.A. 1982. The violation of sepulture: is it legal to excavate human

burials? *Archaeology* 35 (6), 44–49.

TANAKA, M. 1984. Japan, in *Archaeological Approaches to the Present* (H. Cleere, ed.), 82–88. Cambridge Univ. Press.

TOUFEXIS, A. 1985. Egypt battles a sleeping devil. *Time*, 27 May, 42–43.

UCKO, P.J. 1983. Australian academic archaeology: Aboriginal transformations of its aims and practices. *Australian Arch.* 16, 11–26.

—— 1987. *Academic Freedom and Apartheid: The story of the World Archaeological Congress.* Duckworth: London.

U.S. DEPARTMENT OF THE INTERIOR. 1979. *Archaeological and Historical Data Recovery Program.* National Park Service: Washington.

WAINWRIGHT, G.J. 1989. Saving the Rose. *Antiquity* 63 (240), 430–35.

WHEELER, R.E.M. 1968. *Review of Hod Hill* by Ian Richmond & others. *Antiquity* 42, 149–50, 292–96.

WHITE, J.P. 1974. *The Past is Human.* Angus & Robertson: Sydney.

WILSON, C. 1972. *Crash Go the Chariots.* Lancer Books: New York. (Rev. ed. Master Books: San Diego, 1976).

—— 1975. *The Chariots Still Crash.* Signet/New American Library: New York.

YADIN, Y. 1966. *Masada. Herod's Fortress and the Zealots' Last Stand.* Weidenfeld & Nicolson: London.

Acknowledgments

The authors and publishers are indebted to the many scholars who read parts of the text and/or provided advice and illustrations. They include Peter Addyman, Cyril Aldred, Wal Ambrose, Tjeerd van Andel, Manolis Andronicos, Gina Barnes, George Bass, Sophie de Beaune, Peter Bellwood, Martin Biddle, Morris Bierbrier, Lewis Binford, John Boardman, Gerhard Bosinski, Sheridan Bowman, Warwick Bray, Don Brothwell, James Brown, Susan Bulmer, Sarah Bunney, Richard Burger, John Camp, Martin Carver, George Chaloupka, John Cherry, Henry Cleere, Michael Coe, John Coles, Malcolm Cooper, Ruth Daniel, Janette Deacon, Albert Dekin, Richard Diehl, Philip Duke, Christiane Eluère, Clark Erickson, Francisco d'Errico, Kent Flannery, John Flenley, Robert Foley, Yuriko Fukasawa, Clive Gamble, Ignacio Garaycochea, Michel Garcia, Jack Golson, Mrs D.N. Goulandris, Stephen Green, James Greig, Robert Grenier, Sylvia Hallam, Fekri Hassan, Douglas Heggie,

Gordon Hillman, Simon James, Martin Jones, Rhys Jones, Thomas F. Kehoe, Patrick Kirch, Vernon James Knight, Hiroko Koike, Roy Larick, Arlette Leroi-Gourhan, Michel Lorblanchet, Jim Mallory, Joyce Marcus, Paolo Matthiae, Isabel McBryde, Alan Millard, Mary Ellen Miller, Jean-Pierre Mohen, Gerda Møller, Theya Molleson, John Mulvaney, Yasushi Nishimura, J.P. Northover, F. van Noten, Michel & Catherine Orliac, John Parkington, Christopher Peebles, Dolores Piperno, Nicholas Postgate, John Prag, Cemal Pulak, Paul Reilly, Jane Renfrew, Peter Reynolds, Peter Rowley-Conwy, Andrée Rosenfeld, Rolf Rottländer, Makoto Sahara, Nicholas Saunders, Béatrice Schmider, Brian Sheppard, Izumi Shimada, Pat Shipman, Chris Stringer, Migaku Tanaka, Michael J. Tooley, Robin Torrence, Grahame Walsh, Fred Wendorf, Todd Whitelaw, Gordon R. Willey, Roger Wilson, and Pat Winker.

Special thanks are due to Jeremy Sabloff, Chris Scarre, and Michael Tite for their

contributions to many parts of the book.

The glossary was compiled by James McGlade and the index by Sasha Roberts.

Illustration Credits

Abbreviations: a-above; b-below; c-center; l-left; r-right; t-top

Africana Museum, Johannesburg (photo L. Fourie) 173b

R. Agache, Service des Fouilles 71ar

Agora Excavations, American School of Classical Studies at Athens 349

Manolis Andronicos 379c

American Museum of Natural History, Dept of Library Services, photographer J. Bird 69r

Archaeological Survey of India 30bl

Archives Photographiques 345a

Associated Press Ltd 38, 104

ATA Stockholm 164br

Paul Bahn 276a, 279l, 394 (courtesy Hideji Harunari), 466, 475

M.G.L. Baillie 118a
George Bass 13bl, 328a, 329b
Peter Bellwood 231b, 274
Martin Biddle 187l, 187r
Lewis Binford 12br, 44l, 44r, 167a, 167bl,
167br (photo H. Steyn), 173b (photo L.
Fourie), 247a, 247c
Boston Museum of Fine Arts 389c, 389b
(© Myron Marx)
G. Bosinski 206
British Library 165bl
British Museum (Natural History) 211
Trustees of the British Museum 124l, 128,
165ar, 313ac, 357, 366l, 378l, 396l, 397
The British Society for the Turin Shroud 128
Richard Burger 360b, 361bl
Cambridge University Collection of Air
Photos 71l, 201
Canadian Parks Service 82t (photo Denis
Pagé), 82c (photo Rock Chan, Denis Pagé),
82b (drawn by P. Waddell & J. Farley)
D.A. Casey, courtesy D.J. Mulvaney 39
Michael D. Coe 164cl, 362 (drawn by Diane
Griffiths Peck), 453c, 477b (drawn by David
Kiphuth)
John Coles 236 (drawn by R. Walker), 286l
(photo G. Owen), 286a, 286b, 287, 340a
Colorado Springs Fine Art Center – Taylor
Museum Collection 478c
E. de Croisset 282
Danebury Trust 72r (from B. Cunliffe,
Danebury 1983, fig. 64)
Danish National Museum 378cr
Richard D. Daugherty 52–53
H.J. Deacon 94b, 214l, 214r
C. Desroches-Noblecourt 13ar
Albert A. Dekin, State University of New York
at Binghamton 57
Richard A. Diehl 288r
Egypt Exploration Society 164
Clark Erickson 469
Brian Fagan 279r
Kent V. Flannery 446, 447, 451r
John Flenley 231a
Irving Friedman, U.S. Geological Survey,
Denver 136
Robert Foley 172
Andrew Fulgoni Photography & the Museum
of London 474
Werner Forman 313b, 313br, 337l, 478l, 478r
Giraudon 313bl
John Glover 351b
G. Goakimedes 140
Jack Golson 228, 229
Mrs D.N. Goulandris 365a
Stephen Green 132, 133
Herb Greer 13bl
Griffith Institute, Oxford 55a, 55c
Salvador Guilliem Arroyo, courtesy the Great
Temple Project 63, 476l, 476r, 477a
Norman Hammond 75 (from Hammond,
Ancient Maya Civilization 1982, figs. 5.14,
5.15, drawn by Richard Bryant)
R.D.K. Hadden 408l
Gordon Hillman 244l, 257
Hirmer Verlag München 165al, 364a, 364b,
464, 479
Historic Annapolis Foundation 431 (drawn
by Barbara Paca)
Ian Hodder 168r
Institute of Archaeology, University College
London 13br
Simon James 237a, 237b
Rhys Jones 455, 456, 457, 458

Thomas F. Kehoe 252–253
Vernon James Knight, Jnr 94al
Hiroko Koike 260l
André Leroi-Gourhan 387a
Wilfredo Loayza L. 361br
Michel Lorblanchet 284
Peter Lindman 389a
Luis Lumbreras 361r (drawn by Felix
Caycho)
Joyce Marcus 453al, 453ar
Paolo Matthiae 164bl
Isabel McBryde 331a, 331b
Department of Medical Illustration,
University of Manchester 379bcl, 379bcr,
379br
Mary Ellen Miller 425, 454
René Millon 76–77
J.-P. Mohen 275
Musée des Antiquités Nationales, St-
Germain-en-Laye 355
Musée du Louvre 444r
Museo Archeologico del Castello Visconteo
di Pavia 295
Museum of London 12bl, 96 (from C. Spence
(ed.) *Archaeological Site Manual* 1990), 97,
474 (photo Andrew Fulgoni)
Museo Nacional de Antropología 312
Museum National d'Histoire Naturelle 388r
Museum of New Mexico 31c
Museum für Völkerkunde, Berlin 386
Museum für Völkerkunde, Vienna 313al
J.H. Musgrave, courtesy M. Andronicos
379bl
Naples Museum, Soprintendenza alle
antichita della campania, 395
Naples National Museum 21br
National Monuments Record 36
Nationalmuseet, Copenhagen 392l, 392a
(photos John Lee), 393r (photo E. Løytved
Rosenløv)
National Museum of Denmark 378cr
National Archives of Zimbabwe, Harare 409a
Netherlands Institute for the Near East,
Leiden 265
National Archaeological Museum, Athens
313c
Novosti Press Agency 343
Oriental Institute, University of Chicago 49,
294
Michel Orliac 203
John Parkington 220a
Peabody Museum, Harvard University
26a2ndl, 26a2ndr, 337r
Christopher Peebles 93, 190b, 472
Petrie Museum of Egyptian Archaeology,
University College London 30a, 30c
Stuart Piggott 429
Pitt-Rivers Museum, University of Oxford
29ar
Nicholas Postgate 79
John Prag 379t
Princeton University Press & the University
of Cincinnati 420l (painting by Piet de
Jong)
Robert Rausch 12br
Colin Renfrew 180 (drawn by Alec Daykin),
352, 439, 441, 442, 444l (drawn by Alec
Daykin), 444 (3rd and 2nd from r) 445
Joan Root 328a
John G. Ross 289bl, 289r
Jeremy A. Sabloff 68, 95b
Salisbury & South Wiltshire Museum 70r
The St. Louis Art Museum, Eliza McMillan
Fund 27a

Schloss-Gothorp, Schleswig-Holsteinisches
Landesmuseum 372
Béatrice Schmider 282
Izumi Shimada 13ac, 300
Pat Shipman & Richard Potts 248
Edwin Smith 21bl
Smithsonian Institution, National
Anthropological Archives, Bureau of
American Ethnology Collection 26a3rdl,
26a4thl, 26ar
Staatliches Museum für Völkerkunde,
Munich 378cl
Sutton Hoo Research Trust, photos Nigel
Macbeth 12al, 89a, 92, 372l
Sutton Hoo Research Trust/IBM UK Ltd 13al
Texas Antiquities Committee 50
Thamesdown Archaeological Unit 85 (from
A. Clark, *Seeing Beneath the Soil* 1990, fig.
105)
David Hurst Thomas & the American
Museum of Natural History 127
UCLA Institute of Geophysics & Planetary
Physics 33
U.S. Geological Survey 202r
University Museum, Philadelphia 115
Victoria & Albert Museum 165br, 264r, 313ar
Virginia Division of Historic Landmarks,
photo R. Adams 95a
P. Vouga 69l
Grahame L. Walsh 272l
Bradford Washburn 202l
West Air Photography, Weston-super-Mare
70l
Wiltshire Archaeological & Natural History
Society 19
Yorkshire Archaeological Trust 482, 483

The publishers would also like to
acknowledge the work of the following
illustrators:

Annick Boothe 10, 11 (after Rathje), 46
(adapted from W. Rathje & M. Schiffer,
Archaeology 1982, fig. 4.11), 57br (after
Dekin 1984), 58 (after Coles & Lawson
1987, fig. 10), 66 (after Winter in Flannery
(ed.) 1976, fig. 3.5), 67 (after Flannery
(ed.) 1976, figs. 3.2, 5.2), 71br (after
Oxford Archaeological Unit), 72l (after
Connah & Jones, in Connah 1983, p.77),
81l (after *The Courier*, Unesco Nov. 1987,
p.16, drawing by M. Redknap), 81r (after
National Geographic, supplement Jan.
1990), 84 (after Joukowsky 1980, fig. 4.11),
88a, 89b (after Sutton Hoo Research
Project), 91 (after M. Carver, *Underneath
English Towns* 1987, fig. 2), 94ar (after J.
Coles, *Field Archaeology in Britain* 1972,
fig. 61), 99 (after J. Deetz, *Invitation to
Archaeology*, Natural History
Press/Doubleday & Co, New York 1967),
105, 106 (after Rathje & Schiffer,
Archaeology 1982, fig. 4.17), 114, 117 (after
Zeuner 1958), 121, 122 (122l after Hedges
& Gowlett in *Scientific American* 254 (1),
Jan. 1986, p.84), 126 (after Hedges &
Gowlett 1986, p.88), 129l (after Scarre (ed.)
1988, p.25), 129r, 129b (after Aitken 1990,
figs. 6.1, 6.7), 141a, 143 (adapted from R.
Foley & R. Dunbar, *New Scientist* 14 Oct.
1989, p.40), 146 (adapted from K. Feder &
M. Park, *Human Antiquity* 1989, figs. 12.1,
13.1), 151, 154 (after Scarre (ed.) 1988,
p.78), 159, 161 (after Johnson 1972), 164al

(after Bowen), 168l (after Hodder), 175 (after Scarre (ed.) 1988, p.30), 176 (after Shennan 1975), 177 (after Peebles), 183l (after Page, and Renfrew), 183r (after Marcus), 188, 189a (after Lehner), 191a (after Peebles), 198 (after van Andel 1989), 199ar (after Sutcliffe 1985, fig, 5.4), 199b (after Shackleton & van Andel 1980, fig. 1), 204 (after K. Butzer, *Archaeology as Human Ecology* 1982, fig. 4.3), 208 (after Shackley 1981, fig. 4.3), 209a (after Scarre (ed.) 1988, p.107), 209b (after Sutcliffe 1985, fig. 6.4), 213 (after Hillman, and Pearsall 1989), 219 (after Davis 1987, figs. 2.10, 2.12, 1.8), 221 (after Parkington), 222 (after Davis 1987, figs. 5.5, 5.11), 230r (after Anderson), 235 (after J. Greig, Plant Foods in the Past, *Jnl. of Plant Foods* 5 1983, 179–214), 247b (after Brain), 251 (after Klein 1989, fig. 6.29), 254 (after Davis 1987, fig. 6.13a), 259 (after M. Jones, *England Before Domesday* 1986, fig. 30), 261l (after Koike), 261r (after Davis 1987, fig. 4.5), 267 (after F. Hole & R. Heizer, *Prehistoric Archeology* 1977, fig. 11.4), 272r (after K. Oakley, *Man the Toolmaker* (6th ed.) 1972, fig. 4), 273 (after I. Longworth & J. Cherry (eds.), *Arch. in Britain since 1945* 1986, fig. 22), 276b (after J.P. Protzen, Inca Stonemasonry, *Scientific American* 254, Feb. 1986, 84), 278, 280 (after F. van Noten & others, A Paleolithic Campsite in Belgium, *Scientific American*, 242 (4), April 1980, 52, 55), 292 (after Hodges 1970, figs. 51, 52, 172), 299 (after Hodges 1970, fig. 139), 301 (after Shimada), 303 (after R. Tylecote, *Metallurgy in Archaeology*, fig. 15), 305 (after P. Schmidt & D.H. Avery in *Science* 201 (4361), Sept. 1978, 1087), 322 (after Renfrew), 323 (after Cummins 1979), 325 (after Renfrew), 332 (after Sidrys), 333 (after Pires-Ferreira in Flannery (ed.) 1976, fig. 10.16), 335 (after Renfrew), 340b (after Renfrew), 341 (after Isaac 1976), 350 (after Morley), 351a (after Thom), 353b (after O'Kelly), 360a, 361al (after Burger), 366r (after Schäfer), 367al (after Schäfer), 367bl,c,r (after Robins 1986), 373, 375b (after Brothwell 1981, fig. 3.4), 376, 380, 383 (after Toth), 384 (after R. Lewin, *In the Age of Mankind* 1988, p.181), 392br, 398, 400 (after R. Lewin, *Human Evolution* 1984, p.95), 403 (after Lewin 1984), 410a (after Kirch), 410b (after Gelb), 412 (after Clark), 421 (after Renfrew), 427 (after Arnold), 468 (after Jesus Raymundo).

Ian Bott 54.

Sue Cawood 20br, 45, 393a (after *National Geographic*, Feb. 1985, 194).

Simon S.S. Driver 118b (information from Bannister & Smiley in *Geochronology*, Tucson 1955), 144–145, 155, 178 (after Renfrew), 279c.

John Fuller 346l.

ML Design 20bl, 37 (after Bulleid, and Clarke), 42–43 (after A. Sherratt (ed.) *Cambridge Encyc. of Arch.*, 1980, fig. 20.5), 48, 65 (after Renfrew & Wagstaff (eds.)

1982, fig. 2.1), 88 br (after Sutton Hoo Research Project), 107 (after K.L. Feder & M.A. Park, *Human Antiquity* 1989, fig. 4.11), 111 (after Brothwell & Higgs 1969, fig. 28), 116 (after Renfrew), 141b (after Renfrew), 205 (after Butzer 1982, fig. 8.8), 220b (after Parkington), 224l (after Vita-Finzi 1978, ill. 12), 224r (after M. Jarman & others (eds.), *Early European Agriculture* 1982, fig. 87), 225 (after Flannery 1976, fig. 4.6), 243 (after Zohary & Hopf 1988), 256b (after Legge & Rowley-Conwy), 309, 310, 319, 321 (after Peacock 1982, fig. 80), 326 (after Renfrew), 328b (after Bass), 331c (after McBryde), 337, 344l, 348a, 409b (after Garlake), 419, 420a, 424 (after J. Sabloff, *The New Archaeology and the Ancient Maya* 1990, p.121), 428, 448 (after Scarre (ed.) 1988, p.208), 449 (after Flannery).

Lucy Maw 130, 190a, 197l, 249, 331t, 345b, 356a (after Marshack), 353a (after Mellaart), 396r, 480 (after *The Courier* Unesco July 1985).

Iva Ellen Morris 44l, 44r (courtesy Lewis R. Binford).

P.P. Pratt, after Ruz 189r.

Schelay Richardson 288l.

Maggi Smith 460–461 (after Rhys Jones).

Tracey Wellman 171 (after Isaac), 200 (after Chaloupka 1984), 308, 375a (after Houghton 1980), 382 (after M.H. Day & E.H. Wickens in *Nature* 286, July 1980, 386–387), 453b (after Marcus).

Other Sources
page

18   W. Stukeley, *Stonehenge* 1740.
21   *Voyages Pittoresques de Naples et de Sicile* vol. II.
23l   Drawing by Magnus Petersen 1846.
25   *The Hornet* 1871.
28a   A.M. Layard, *Nineveh and its Remains* vol. I, London 1849.
28b   H. Schliemann, *Ilios: City and Country of the Trojans*, 1880.
29   A. Pitt-Rivers, *Excavations in Cranborne Chase*, 1893–1898.
56   After Rudenko.
59   From B. Coles & J. Coles, *People of the Wetlands* 1989, ill. 11 (after M. Egloff, *Helvetia Archaeologica* 1980, 43–44).
60   G.F. Macdonald & B.A. Purdy, Florida's wet sites, *Early Man* 4(4) 1982, 4–12.
62l   Piranesi, *Vedute di Roma*, 1757.
73   From R.E.W. Adams, W.E. Brown, Jr & T. Patrick Culbert, in *Science* 213, 25 Sept. 1981, p.1460.
86   After Stanley, in Connah 1983, p.86.
103   Wheeler in *Ancient India* 3 Jan. 1947.
108   After F. Hole, K.V. Flannery & J. Neely, *Prehistory and Human Ecology of the Deh Luran Plain*, Univ. of Michigan Memoirs of the Museum of Anthropology, No.1, fig. 64.

120   After B. Arnold, *Cortaillod-Est* Editions du Ruau: Saint-Blaise (redrawn by M. Rouillard in B. & J. Coles, *People of the Wetlands* 1989, ill. 85).
124r, After Gordon Pearson.
125
135   After R. Klein, *The Human Career* 1989, fig. 3.9.
160   After C. Renfrew & E.V. Level in C. Renfrew & K.L. Cooke (eds.), *Transformations* 1979, figs. 6.11, 6.12.
192   After Craig Morris.
199al After W.M. Davis 1933.
212   Adapted from C. Spence (ed.), *Archaeological Site Manual*, Museum of London 1990.
216   After J.G. Evans & others, in *Proc. of Preh. Soc.* 51, 1985, p.306.
217   After A. Marshack, *The Roots of Civilization* 1972, fig. 78b.
218   Adapted from C. Spence (ed.) 1990.
227   After Fowler 1971, fig. 10.
230l   From P. Bellwood, *The Polynesians* (Rev. ed.) 1987, ill. 1.
244r   After Mangelsdorf.
281r   After D. Cahen & L. Keeley in *World Arch.* 12(2), 1980, fig. 5.
285   After Zervos 1959.
297   After Renfrew 1979.
298   From D. Brothwell & E. Higgs, *Science in Archaeology* 1969, pls. XXV, XXVI.
302   After J. Rawson, *Ancient China* 1980, ill. 43.
315   After R.B. Mason & E.J. Keall, Provenance and Petrography of Pottery from Medieval Yemen, *Antiquity* 62(236), Sept. 1988, 452–463.
324   After Fulford & Hodder 1975, in Peacock 1982, figs. 86, 87.
344r   After M. Ruspoli, *The Cave of Lascaux* 1987, p.200.
348bl From J. Oates, *Babylon* 1979, ill. 6.
348br From A. Toynbee (ed.), *Half the World* 1973, p.27.
354b   After K. Mendelssohn, *The Riddle of the Pyramids* 1974, fig. 9.
367ar From Layard 1853.
385   From E. Matos Moctezuma, *The Great Temple of the Aztecs* 1988, ill. 23.
387b   From E. Hadingham, *Secrets of the Ice Age* 1979, P.147, after C. Barrière 1975, fig. 17.
390   After J. Flood, *Archaeology of the Dreamtime* 1983, fig. 4.3 (after Brown 1981).
391   From R.G. Harrison & others in *Antiquity* 53 (207), March 1979, pl. VII.
403l   After R. Lewin, *Human Evolution* (2nd ed.), 1989.
423   After A.J. Chadwick 1979.
451l   From B. Fagan, *In the Beginning* (6th ed.) 1988, fig. 16.4 (after Winter in Flannery (ed.) 1976, fig. 2.17).

Index